JOHN DUKE OF MARLBOROUGH.

G. Kneller pinxt.   In the Collection of the Honble John Spencer.   Impensis J.&P. Knapton, London.   G. Vertue sculp. Ao 1745.

Marlborough: *A Survey*

Marlborough: *A Survey*

Panegyrics, Satires, and Biographical Writings, 1688-1788

Robert D. Horn, Ph.D.

*Emeritus Professor of English
the University of Oregon*

Garland Publishing, Inc., New York & London

1975

Library of Congress Cataloging in Publication Data

Horn, Robert Dewey.
   Marlborough: a survey.

    1. Marlborough, John Churchill, 1st Duke of, 1650-
1722--Bibliography.
Z8550.38.H67   016.94206'9'0924   74-14647
ISBN 0-8240-1054-X

To my beloved wife, Eve,
Our daughter Elena,
And the memory of our son, Peter.

Contents

Introduction

The brilliant and strenuous life of John Churchill, the first Duke of Marlborough (1650-1722), provides a richer and more graphic impression of the political and military activities of the early Eighteenth Century than does that of any other personage. His motto, *Fidelis sed infortunatus* (on his official coat of arms as *Fiel pero desdichado),* attests to his fidelity to Queen Anne and the Protestant cause, even though he cannot be seen as entirely unfortunate. The coincidence which brought the vogue of monumental, adulatory verse at the precise time of his career, led to an outpouring of panegyrics which probably surpasses that devoted to any other person in history. Added to this are the political oppositions of the two-party system of government, with all the train of envy, spite, and detraction, which evoked a corresponding flood of satire. The total writing related to Marlborough and his Duchess Sarah (1660-1744) is formidable indeed. The earliest modern biographer of the latter, Mrs. A. T. Thomson, writing in 1839, remarks: "It appears an endless task to enumerate and to portray the numerous literary characters who poured forth their tribute to the greatness of the Duke, or who shared the favour of the Duchess of Marlborough." *(Memoirs of Sarah, Duchess of Marlborough,* II, 427)

While most of the productions are occasional verse, at times descending to the lowest levels of squibs, doggerel, and scatalogical diatribe, or rising to the highest levels of absurd adulation, all are given importance by the eminence and cool detachment of their subject, the invincible Captain-General. It has been too common for writers to toss them off, when they knew them at all, as unworthy of notice. In a massive, cumulative way they attain to an impressive expression quite comparable to the vast palace of Blenheim itself. Their authorship probably far surpasses even Mrs. Thomson's estimate. Among the contributors are Addison, Swift, Pope, Defoe, Steele, Dennis, Prior, Congreve, Fielding, even Dr. Johnson, most of them with several entries. A host of lesser names follows: Thomas Tickell, John Philips, Laurence Eusden, Nahum Tate, John Oldmixon, Elijah Fenton, Sir Richard Blackmore, Samuel Cobb, Catherine Trotter Cockburn, Edmund Smith, Tom Brown, Ned Ward. Aside from their literary pretensions all of these are associated with the development of critical theories and methods. The list diminishes to a mere mass of names and anonymous contributors. While many of the nearly 600 works listed might go unnoticed for any literary importance, from the broad historical point of view, of biographical, social, economic, bibliographical and other considerations, the shabbiest often have distinct value. Most of them deserve considerably more attention.

The purpose of this volume is to supply identifications for the large body of literary pamphleteering relative to Marlborough. It does not pretend to be biography, military or social history, nor formal bibliography, even though it is hoped that it will contribute to all of these. It attempts to describe documents, to date them, provide locations in libraries, and to offer other factual data of use to biographers, literary historians, and critics. The Duke's career, devoid of any military defeat, offered repeated challenges to the poets. His character and conduct in war, and in diplomatic maneuver as well, were no less stimulating. The normal subjects of panegyric and satire, public events, births, marriages, deaths of nobility, accessions, coronations, jubilees for victories, admittedly often produce what Gilbert Highet has called "bombastic failures." When the poet's feeling fails to rise to the level of the event this result is inevitable. But, as

INTRODUCTION

T.S. Eliot has remarked, how little truly great poetry there is anyway.

There has been no need to pad this book with extraneous items to achieve bulk. However, two types of entries might seem superfluous. One of these includes figures associated with Marlborough – Queen Anne, Sydney, First Earl of Godolphin, Prince Eugene, co-commander at Blenheim, the Duke of Ormond, and a few of his staff. Works dealing with these are introduced only as they complete the background of panegyric in which Marlborough is the central figure. The second group consists of entries which, though known by title, have no known location. Most of these are taken from Morgan's great bibliography. Some may be in private hands or even may have ceased to exist. Not to mention these would provoke inquiries concerning their omission. Two or three are included simply because their titles suggest that Marlborough might be involved in them, even though upon examination they proved otherwise. *The Patriots of Great Britain*, No. 216, has only a bare reference to the Duke, and *The British Heroes*, No. 220, from its title and date of 1707, could hardly seem to avoid Marlborough. That it does so might be interpreted as a slight on him, but such is not the case. Still, to exclude such titles would be to invite the charge of oversight. Even when poems do not have direct pertinence, they contribute toward an understanding of political pamphleteering in the period.

To be sure, the body of writing under consideration is in no sense superior; but it did exist, even though a considerable proportion has barely escaped extinction. In many instances it was printed in handsome format, often in folio. Typographically it often corresponded to the spires of Wren and Gibbs, to the oratorios and sonatas of Handel and Haydn, and to the achievements in landscape architecture that were to convert England into a land of extraordinary beauty and cool, satisfying composure. It reflects an age which admired

ix

orderly thought as well as controlled and measured expression in all the arts. In such an atmosphere panegyric was a moral obligation for poets, far from contemptible. Still Marlborough felt a strong distaste for even favorable pamphlets, and hostile ones goaded him into fury even amidst the most strenuous campaigning. Hence his Duchess's stipulation in her will to Richard Glover and David Mallet, who were commissioned to write the history of Marlborough's life, "that no part of the said History may be in Verse." Yet, late in life, she confessed to having perused for the first time a portion of Addison's *The Campaign,* in Lediard's *Life* of 1726, and found it a "very pretty thing." The Marlboroughs belong to the life of action, of great actions, not to literary efforts, even though both did write prodigiously, though largely in routine correspondence.

DISTRIBUTION OF ENTRIES AND THEMES

While the major portion of writing relative to Marlborough falls in the reign of Queen Anne (1702-1714), documents appear throughout his long life, particularly in the previous reigns of her father James II and William III and Mary. These may largely be grouped as reflecting the following moments and events.

1. Military service under James II and William III, 1688-1702
2. Battle of Blenheim, *August 13, 1704

---

*Most users of this book will be familiar with the use of the Julian Calendar, Old Style, in England, and the Georgian, New Style, eleven days ahead, on the Continent. Thus Blenheim was dated as August 13th, but in England, August 2nd. Usually, also, the year in England was dated as beginning on Lady Day, March 25, rather than January 1. See Trevelyan's Introductions to *The Age of Queen Anne.*

INTRODUCTION

3. Battle of Ramillies, May 23, 1706
4. Battle of Oudenarde, July 11, 1708
5. The Scottish Union, 1706-8
6. Battle of Malplaquet (Blaregnies), September 11, 1709
7. Marlborough's banishment, 1710-12
8. Return from exile, 1714-16
9. Death of Marlborough, June 12, 1722
10. Biographical accounts, 1705-7; 1713-15; 1722-45
11. Incidental and related subjects: the building of Blenheim Palance, the Sacheverell Trial, the political careers of Robert Harley, Abigail Hill Masham, Generals Cadogan, Webb, Orkney, the Duke of Ormond, *et al.*

GENRES AND LOCATIONS

While completeness in covering literary works related to Marlborough has been sought, certain limits have been inevitable. The three types indicated in the title are primary, panegyrics and satires notably, and early biographical accounts, since they have affinities with the other two. Sermons have been included only when they were preached in the field, by authors of other pieces mainly. Some attention has been given to plays, again where they are written by authors of other Marlborough interest. Fiction has been excluded, even to the exclusion of Sterne's Uncle Toby. Mrs. Manley's works, though labeled novels, were primarily produced as part of the satiric war carried on by Swift against the Duke. Newpapers and gazettes have been cited for dating of works, and are quoted for the excitement of early victories.

FORMULATION OF ENTRIES

1. The serial number. These are arranged chronologically

within the groups indicated above, or in successive years.

*2. Date, by year, and usually by month and day. Works undatable by month are listed alphabetically at the end of the section for the year.

3. Author, by name, initials, or pseudonym, Anonymous works are nòt so specified, but doubtful names are set in square brackets.

4. Title, as on title page. While capital letters have been retained, no effort has been made to distinguish between sizes of type, or for 'rules' and other variations, where only photographic reproduction could convey a true impression of the title page. Half- and drop-titles are specified.

5. Latin mottoes are indicated by source and number of lines. Only brief examples are quoted entire.

6. Printers' ornaments, allegorical designs, and the like are noted as suggestive of more pretentious printing.

7. Publishers are given as on title page or in colophon for broadsides.

8. Description by format, as half-sheet, folio, quarto, etc., as 1/2° (most broadsides), 2°, 4°, etc. The analysis does not include subtleties, such as canceled leaves and other bibliographical complexities.

---

*Newspaper dates are largely taken from the BM copies. Most other dates are based on those recorded by the industrious Tory antiquarian Narcissus Luttrell (1670-1732). Luttrell normally recorded the day of purchase, usually the first day of publication, and also the purchase price. A very few have some critical comment reflecting his party bias, and some filling in of names where only initials had been printed. Happily the antiquarian Joseph Haslewood (1769-1813) recorded some 90 Luttrell datings in his copy of Giles Jacob's *Register of Poets and Dramatists*. Where he supplies a Luttrell date for a copy for which no location is verifiable, the Haslewood date is cited. Thus we can be certain that Luttrell purchased Addison's *Campaign* although no certain copy survives. (The notations on the Clark copy do not seem to be his.)

All Luttrell copies are indicated by present owner, thus: MH-Luttr. For the Harvard copies, etc. Of Luttrell copies listed in this volume, 76 are identifiable. Of these the distribution is as follows: Horn, 23; Harvard, 16; Clark, 13; Texas, 6; British Museum, Folger, 3; Bodley, Huntington, Indiana, 2; Yale, Chicago, Newberry, 1. A few advertised in sales catalogs are also listed.

9. For verse, the number of lines and the metrical form are stated. Since most of the panegyrics are in heroic couplets, these poems are labeled simply as 'couplets.' Hudibrastics, odes, songs, and other varieties of verse are so listed.

10. Locations. For American libraries the Library of Congress symbols are normally used. However, the principle of immediate clarity is followed. BM seems preferable to L for the British Museum; Bod (Bodleian) rather than O. For infrequent examples the full name, i.e. Clark, Newberry, or a university, is used.

11. For verse, the first two lines are quoted. This supplies some indication of the style and quality of the poem, and since most are couplets, an appropriate suggestion of content.

12. Summary of content. In general the summaries are weighted in terms of the historical and critical importance of the poem and its author. Sufficient quotation is introduced for stylistic sampling, political flavor, relation to Marlborough, and the like. The general 'argument' of the poem is intended to convey to the reader some conception of the usefulness of the particular piece, for biographical, historical, or other purposes.

13. The year for entries. This is stated at the top right of each page, not only for convenience, but because some of the references, as with Addison's *Campaign,* are dated ahead. Though actually published December 14, 1704, the work is dated 1705.

INTRODUCTIONS

Separate introductions have been inserted for periods of particular importance. These are designed to supply basic information on political and literary developments. It is assumed that most readers will have at least a general familiarity with Marlborough and his career. Sir Winston Churchill's *Marlborough: His Life and Times,* 1933-38, will always stand as the great authority. His sources, particularly Archdeacon Coxe, Stuart Reid, and Frank Taylor call for notice. Of more recent studies, A. L. Rowse, *The Early Churchills,* 1956, and Ivor F. Burton, *The Captain-General,* 1968, are of particular interest. David Green, author of the beautiful volume, *Blenheim Palace,* 1951, has published a series of books, *Gardener to Queen Anne,* on *Grinling Gibbons,* and on *Queen Anne* herself. More particularly, Mr. Green's book *Sarah, Duchess of Marlborough,* 1967, is one of several works on Marlborough's consort of recent years.

For a general impression of the period Professor George Macaulay Trevelyan's three-volume series, *England Under Queen Anne,* 1930-34, stands supreme for its rich exploiting of literary materials as well as for its splendid feeling for the period. Trevelyan is the only historian to make such abundant use of poetic extracts. Still most of this is from tavern songs and ballads, although he is familiar with the plays and longer poems of the period. His mellow, well-informed pages seem to make the more recent controversies over party divisions rather petty. Nevertheless, for detailed probing into the pressures and mentality of Stuart politics, the various volumes of Geoffrey Holmes of the University of Glasgow are eminently useful. His *British Politics in the Age of Anne,* 1967, concluded with the recognition that the "vast majority of politicians" had become "reconciled to something like a two-party *system* as well as a two-party legislature . . . to the two irreconcileable forces of Whig and Tory" (p. 418). Still, Holmes, aside from some use of newspapers, shows no awareness of works of literary, or quasi-literary, character. Even in his excellent study of the *Trial of Dr. Sacheverell,* 1973, he cites only two short squibs. These exploit the monstrous prank played on the corpse of the man who turned the country over to the Tories in 1710. In an age of intense party-writing it cannot be denied that history and literature often touch hands in their reporting on persons and affairs.

While Marlborough's four greatest victories dominate as subjects in the literary response, other themes appear. The marriage of the Marlboroughs was too early and obscure for comment; but the premature death of their son, the Marquess of Blandford, and the favorable marriages of their four beautiful daughters; political associations with Godolphin, Harley, and other ministers in the government, and their final banishment from the court; and their happy and triumphant return to London and Blenheim Palace are all amply treated. For most of these both panegyrics and satires were published, according to the political bias of their authors. That the poets read each other's productions is evidenced by extensive allusions within the poems, as in poems of retort. A notable lack of duplication in titles also suggests familiarity with competing productions. Many are maiden efforts, often by undergraduates at the universities. Except for the names of battles, and such labels as *An Excellent Song,* titles are remarkably devoid of duplication.

Early biographical works are included since they often border on panegyric. Also, as with the poems, most of them are rare or little known. The earliest, unknown to Churchill and the other biographers, seems to survive in only one copy, in the possession of the writer, although a unique copy of the second edition has survived. (See No. 112.) This work, by Dr. Francis Hare, is the source for most later accounts, at least until memoirs by Sergeant Millner, Captain Robert Parker, and Colonel Richard Kane appear.

While quantitative estimates might seem to have slight critical value, they do have the merit of being positive. Historically, they show the number of contributors to political, if not always to poetic, expression. The ablest pens of the day were dipped in ink to celebrate Marlborough, or to defame him; innumerable obscure and anonymous figures add their efforts. This tells us something specific about the activities of Grub Street and also in the more aristocratic circles and the Universities. That a total of over 67,000 lines of verse were produced supplies evidence of the quantity of that outpouring, if not its quality. Writing usually in prose, the satirists added a corresponding volume. These are no less interesting as reflective of party sentiment, Whig, Tory, or otherwise.

ABBREVIATIONS, PUNCTUATION, and SPELLING

It should be noted that many apparent misspellings are actually Eighteenth Century usages; thus: battel, ecchoing, pil, wellcome, etc. Variants for proper names abound: Briton, Brittain; Marlbrough, Marlboro, Marlbro'. The Danubian village of Blindheim, normalized into Blenheim, could also be Bleinheim, or even Pleintheim; Ramillies, Ramellies, Ramilly; Oudenard, Audenarde, Odenarde, appear. It is usual for Spenser to be spelled Spencer, and Johnson for Jonson is common. While purists insist on the spelling marquess, Congreve has marquis in a title, and both forms are common. French influence is apparent in pindarique for pindaric. Lyrick, musick, and similar spellings probably show the same influence. It has been the practice of this book to avoid the overuse of *sic* for such variants. It is eschewed for titles entirely. The same policy is followed for peculiarities of punctuation. Thus the omission of the apostrophe in possessives, such as majesties.

The following abbreviations are rather freely used:

bl . . . . blank
bot . . . . bottom
CBEL . . Cambridge Bibliography of English Literature

col .... column
ded .... dedication
ed .... edition
half sheet .... indicated by 1/2°
fol 2°......................... folio, indicated by 2°
4 to .... quarto, indicated by 4°
8 vo .... octavo, indicated by 8°
n. d .... no date recorded or known
n. p .... no publisher
t. p .... title page
hft .... half-title
drop-t .... drop-title
p .... page
pr .... printed
rptd .... reprinted
s. sh .... single sheet, usually a half sheet
bds .... broadside, broadsheet, same as s. sh.
sgnd .... signed
Luttr .... Narcissus Luttrell
Morgan . *Bibliography of British History,* 1700-15, 5 vols.
LAS .... London Society of Antiquaries

LIBRARIES

As noted above, American libraries are indicated by library of Congress symbols. Exceptions are infrequently listed libraries or ones for which a short name is more convenient, as Clark, Folger. The same applies to English libraries, as Lambeth Palace, Dr. Williams, London, and Christ Church, Oxford. The main purpose has been to make the locations readily recognizable. An apology is in order for the frequency of appearance of the author's name in connection with locations. In order to develop this volume it seemed necessary to own as many of the pamphlets and books as possible.

One of the chief satisfactions in producing this book has been the correspondence with English booksellers. Any user of rare books will understand that their names have a noble, heart-warming resonance for the writer. McLeish, Dobell, Blackwell, Pickering & Chatto, Traylen, Peter Murray Hill, Maggs, Thorpe, Webster — these are a few of the many who made it possible to pursue the personalities of Queen Anne society in the very works which they read with approval or contempt. All during World War II these booksellers' well-wrapped packages penetrated the blockade, bringing that peculiar happiness which ignorant persons describe as bibliomania. That most of these are not listed in the section on acknowledgements is simply because they are above such recognition. They are a part of literature itself.

EIGHTEENTH CENTURY ENGLISH NEWSPAPERS

Bap	*British Apollo*
DCour	*Daily Courant*
DivP	*Diverting Post*
Ex	*Examiner*
FlyP	*Flying Post*
HReg	*Historical Register*
LGaz	*London Gazette*
Med	*The Medley*
Obs	*Observator*
PBoy	*Post Boy*
Rev	*Weekly Review of the Affairs of France*
Spec	*Spectator*
Tat	*Tatler*
WEx	*Whig Examiner*
WL	*History of the Works of the Learned*

INTRODUCTION

ACKNOWLEDGMENTS

Preceding the endless list of persons meriting gratitude for assistance in a work of so many and so widely scattered items, first place must still be reserved for a building, for Blenheim Palace, and its former owner, the late 10th Duke of Marlborough, who shares the name John with the subject of this volume. The inspiration of that vast structure, with its massive towers and great courtyards, was immense. Through the generosity and courtesy of the Duke the writer was privileged to work in the Muniment room, with its vast store of manuscripts, and in the Long Library. Particular gratitude must go to the late Mr. Primrose Jenkins, Estate Manager, and to his lovely wife, Hyacinth Hazel, and subsequently to Mr. W. L. Murdock, and to Mr. A. M. Illingworth and other members of the staff.

It would be impossible to express the full extent of the indebtedness of this book to Mr. David Foxon, who has been mentioned. Mr. Foxon will soon publish, on the Cambridge Press, his 5-volume bibliography of all separately printed poems, 1700-1750. He made his enormous files available to me, and in a correspondence extending over some ten years has been constantly generous and helpful. Happily the writer has been able to reciprocate as both of us have combed the libraries on both sides of the Atlantic. Mr. Foxon's descriptions show a bibliographical expertness to which this book does not aspire. As a trial run he has published his material on Defoe with the *London Bibliographical Society,* 1965.

The British Museum staff, and similar personnel at the Bodleian, Cambridge University, Lambeth Palace, the Rylands Library, Manchester, and the Dr. Williams Library, London, have all made the long search immensely satisfying. On the American side the university libraries and their staffs at Harvard, Yale, Princeton, Columbia, Chicago, Lehigh, Indiana, Kansas, Michigan, Texas, Oregon, Illinois, and

INTRODUCTION

California have all been notably helpful. The library of Congress, the Public Libraries of New York and Boston, the Folger, Newberry, Huntington and Clark Libraries have been enormously important contributors. Since it is impossible to thank all of the many staffs individually, perhaps profound thanks to Miss Fannie Ratchford, formerly curator of Rare Books at the University of Texas, may serve for all. Her patience and scholarly thoroughness were noble, generous, and unflagging.

Personal encouragement and assistance have come from many individuals. Professor Louis I. Bredvold first attracted me to the field and to Marlborough. Professors Fredson Bowers, Henry L. Snyder, Henry Pettit, Carl G. Anthon, and Franklin Dickey have all assisted at various stages of the work. Among those who have left the world, and left it better for their presence, are several. I owe a lifelong debt to the late Professor Oscar James Campbell. In the early years of work Professor W. T. Morgan and his wife were both most helpful, as was Professor John R. Moore. I owe much to the inspiration of G. M. Trevelyan, Master of Trinity College, Cambridge. All these are deceased, but returning to the living, I must acknowledge assistance from Mr. Peter Smithers, M.P., and Sir Tresham-Lever, authors of books on Addison and Godolphin respectively.

Finally grateful acknowledgment should be made to the University of Oregon Graduate School for a grant which aided in the purchase of Xerox copies, and to Miss Barbara Rice for typing assistance. Most of all for the patient, indefatigable work of Mrs. Ivan L. Collins in typing and re-typing of the manuscript, whose aid has reached far beyond any possible acknowledgment, I wish to express special gratitude.

INTRODUCTION

CHRONOLOGY OF MARLBOROUGH'S CAREER

1650　Baptized May 26

1667　Admitted as page to the Duke of York; also to King's Regiment of Foot Guards

1668-9　As a volunteer to Tangier

1672　Naval action off Suffolk Coast; promoted to captaincy in Lord High Admiral's regiment

1673　Distinguishes self at Siege of Maestricht, under the eye of Louis XIV

1674　Appointed Colonel of "Royal English Regiment" by Louis XIV, on request of Charles II; service under Marshal Turenne for five years

1677　Gazetted as colonel of a regiment of English foot in the British Army

1677-8　Secret marriage to Sarah Jennings

1683　Created Baron Churchill of Aymouth, Kingdom of Scotland, on request of King James II, thus entering the peerage

1685　Aids in the defeat of Monmouth at Sedgemoor; made Major General as reward; elevated to Baron Churchill of Sandridge

1689　Created Earl of Marlborough at coronation of William III

1701　Made General of Infantry and Commander of all the Forces

1702　In December made Duke of Marlborough by Queen Anne as reward for services in taking of Kaiserswerth, on the Rhine, and of Venlo, on the Meuse

1703　Death of son, the Marquess of Blandford, March 10 O.S.

INTRODUCTION

1704   Battle of Blenheim, August 13 N. S.

1704   Battle of Blenheim, August 13 N. S.

1706   Battle of Ramillies, May-23 N. S.

1708   Battle of Oudenarde, July 11 N. S.; the Siege of Lille

1709   Battle of Malplaquet (Blaregnies), September 11 N. S.

1711   Last campaign and the forcing of the *Ne plus ultra* lines, August 2-4. The capture of Bouchain, September 13, N.S.

1712   Dismissed from all employments, January 11

1713   The Peace of Utrecht, April 11

1714   The death of Queen Anne, August 1, and Marlborough's return to London

1715   Restored to command of all the forces as Captain-General by King George I; serves against the Jacobites in the Scottish Rebellion

1722   Dies at Windsor Lodge, June 16

The full outpouring of works related to Marlborough
did not begin until the news of Blenheim came in the high
summer of 1704. From then on till his death poems of
"fame and elegy" strained the presses to turn them out.
Praise and blame, panegyric and satire, increasingly reflected the polarization of English life in the two-party
system. It is fitting that the first example should be
from John Churchill himself. It is his explanation for
his defection from James II, a drastic action that reflects
both the religious and political tensions of the year of
the Glorious Revolution. Much had occurred in the life of
the future duke, his early adventures in Restoration court
society, his happy marriage, and his induction into a military career of unprecedented brilliance. At Sedgemoor,
1685, in putting down Monmouth's rebellion, he won a position in the peerage as Baron Churchill. Thus, on his native soil, he affirms his support of the crown.

In 1688 he shows the beginning of his diplomatic
career, so essential to his military success. He affirms
his allegiance to the Protestant religion, and to William
IIId and the Revolution as well. Since William did not
come over till October-November, the document in which
Churchill addresses his former master could not have been
printed till late in the year. Sir Winston Churchill
quotes it entire, I, 263-4, but seems unaware of the
printed version which is entry No. 1 below. On April 9,
1689, John Churchill was elevated to the earldom of Marlborough. In December of 1702 he was granted the ducal
title by Queen Anne and is first hailed in panegyric. The
poetic form and printer's folio format for such poems had
been developed by Dryden. Several poems on Queen Anne's
accession, and Prince Eugene and the Duke of Ormond are
noted as closely related to Marlborough's career; but it
is with the poem of November 23d, 1704, that Marlborough's
services first received full tribute. This poem, dated by
Luttrell, is in the collection of the writer.

The poem is called *The Retrievement*. The author asserts that the praise of Marlborough should be expressed
"in Pindars high unimitable Verse" (1. 74) although he
writes in couplets. Here at the beginning is an issue
which the poets were to contest for the next twenty years,

that is, which was the better form for panegyric, the Pindaric and explosive style, or the smooth Virgilian epic, or narrative style. For some twenty years Pindar was preferred, but with the triumph of Addison's *Campaign* in 1704 the Virgilian mode prevailed. In modern terms, the differences might be described as those between the internal combustion engine, and the more powerful, better controlled and smooth operation of a steam locomotive.

What happened in the Pindaric imitations, often spelled Pindarick or Pindarique, is apparent in the productions of Joseph Harris, of which at least three are devoted, in part at least, to the war. What his "inflamed" brain produced has led to its severe condemnation, and may well have brought about Addison's sage remark that "those who paint 'em truest, praise 'em most." He is of course referring to heroic deeds. Without some acquaintance with these poems, however excessive and absurd, one is unable to estimate the cooler poems in the Virgilian style. Dr. Johnson, who showed a lifelong interest in war, as well as a detestation of it, remarked in his *Life of Dryden* that "The Occasional poet is circumscribed by the narrowness of his subject . . . Even war and conquest, however splendid, suggest no new images; the triumphal chariot of a victorious monarch can be decked only with those ornaments that have graced his predecessors."

It was not until the dazzling triumph of Blenheim, August 13 (2), 1704, that the poets had a subject that challenged them to find new images and new terms for their perorations. The tiny peasant village of Blindheim, on the upper reaches of the Danube, provided the scene. Its name was shortly transmuted into Blenheim, or Bleinheim, or ignored in favor of the more imposing Hochsted, also variously spelled, with its castle, which was to provide the scene for the culmination of the struggle.

Marlborough, Duke of, then Baron Churchill (1650-1722)

The Lord Churchill's LETTER *to the* KING.

1/2°: 1 page, 1 column, prose. No pub., n. d., but presumably late 1688. Christ Church, Oxford copy used. BM copy dates Nov. 23, but assuredly pr. later. Pr. with some variations in Lediard I, 75-6 and Sir Winston Churchill I, 299-300. Addressed to King James II, and left for him on November 23, 1688, when Churchill left his service for the reasons given in the letter, that is, his allegiance to the Protestant cause and "the inviolable Dictates of Conscience." Opens:

> SIR,
> Since Men are seldom suspected of Sincerity when they act contrary to their Interests. . .

Lord Churchill's agitation of spirit may be seen in the ambiguity of this statement. This version was used in the next item, the German translation, as is shown by the presence of "imaginable" in the phrase "the greatest personal Obligations imaginable." In the Lediard-Winston Churchill versions the adjective is missing. Both claim to have used the manuscript at Blenheim Palace. The German reads: "der durch die höchste Verbündnisse die man sich einbilden kan."

The *Letter* in English stands as the first printed item bearing the name of Churchill, Marlborough to be. The German translation is published in a pamphlet along with other letters from Prince George and Princess Anne and the Prince of Oranien (Orange). All are concerned with Marlborough's defection. Sir Winston notes that the letter "was found wrapped in another written by Prince George of Denmark, no doubt at the same time under Churchill's advice."

2   The title of the German pamphlet reads as follows:
Etliche/ aus Engel=und Holländischer in Hoch-teutsche
Sprache übersetzte/ sehr nachdenckliche *Briefe und Reden/*
An den König und Königin in Engelland/ Einer von dem
Printzen GEORG, der Andere von der Princessin ANNA aus
Dänemarck/ und der Dritte vom Lord CHURCHILL, Worbey Ein
Auszug eines Schreibens aus EXON, von dem Eyd/ damit sicj
Edelleute selbsiger Orten dem Printz von Oranien verbunden/
Benebst einer sehr nachdencklicken Rede des Lords de La
MEERE an den gesammten Adel in Cheshire, als sie zu=Knokes-
ford in gemeldeter Provintz versammlet [*sic*] gewesen. Am-
sterdam/ Gedruckt bey Joachim Noschens seel. Erben. A.
1689.
    4°: *A*-*B*⁴; 8 pp. unmbd. BM copy used.

1690

3   October 4 *ca.*

A *Full and True Relation of the Taking of CORK*, by the
Right Honourable the Earl of *Malborough* [*sic*], Lieut: Gen.
of their Majesties Forces: Together with the Articles of
their Surrender.
Licensed Octob.   Dated at the Camp before *Cork*   *MALBOROUGH*
    4. 1690 J. F.   this 28*th* of *Septemb*. 1690   *TERRON*
                                                         RYCOT.
LONDON, Printed for *Langley Curtiss* near *Fleet-bridge*.

1/2°: 1 side, Colophon at bottom. 62 lines of text.
Prose. BM copy used. Opens:

    "Last Night we received the joyful News of a Surren-
der of *Cork*, and the Perticulars [*sic*] of that Seige [*sic*],
which were as followeth.
    "On the 20th of *September* 1690. the whole Fleet sent
with the Earl of *Malborough* [*sic*] having made the Coast
of *Ireland* towards Night, lay by, and next Morning by
break of day they stood in the Harbours Mouth."

Gives details of the fighting, September 23-29, and
terms of capitulation. Perhaps the first imprint dealing
with Marlborough by name. The taking of Cork and Kins-
sale soon became topics for the panegyrists.

BM lists "Another edition" *Re-printed by the Heir of
Andrew Anderson: Edinburgh*, 1690, s.sh. fol.

1700

January 9

[Cobb, Samuel (1675-1713)]

Poetae Britannici. A POEM, Satyrical and *Panegyrical*.
[4 lines Horace] *LONDON*, Printed for *A. Roper* at the
Black-Boy, R. Basset at the *Mitre*, both in *Fleetstreet*;
and Sold by Mr. *Jefferies* Bookseller in *Cambridge*, MDCC.
2°: A²B-G²; t.p., *bl.*, *iii-iv*, 3-26, 28 pp.

Two short poems, "Addressed to their Friend the
Author," by W. Dove and W. Worts on *iii-iv*. 915 lines,
couplets. Folger copy has '9 *d*. 1699 Jan 9' also MS notation "by Mr. Cob of Trinity College Cambridge." Folger
and TxU copies used. Morgan C342 lists the title only,
with authorship unidentified. It is to be noted that Cobb
wrote the poem while he was a student at Cambridge. The
poem is reproduced, but only in its final form, from
Cobb's *Poems on Several Occasions* (1707), in the *Augustan
Reprint Society* Series 2, No. 1, 1946, ed. Louis I. Bredvold. This version is revised. Of the original 915 lines,
767 are retained: 109 are deleted, 21 are altered, but
only six positive revisions of material appear.

While the poem has no specific allusions to Marlborough, it does introduce William and military panegyric.
It traces the development of poetry from Classical and
Biblical beginnings, with the emphasis on heroic measures
and elevated style. The poem culminates with a prophecy
of fame for Queen Anne's son, the young Duke of Gloucester.
However, his death on July 30, 1700, only six months after

publication of the poem, obliged Cobb to add a note of apology in the 1707 revision: "Here the Author laments he prov'd so bad a prophet."

The importance of the poem lies in its mention of a considerable number of panegyrists: Pittis, Brown, Settle, Blackmore, following the great tradition of Chaucer, Spenser, Shakespeare, Beaumont and Fletcher, Ben Jonson (as "Johnson"), Milton, Cowley, Dryden, as well as the Restoration dramatists, Etherege, Wycherley, and Congreve. "Harmonious Waller" is particularly noted:

> As Squadrons in well-marshall'd Order fill
> The *Flandrian* Plains, and speak my vulgar skill,
>
> 497-8

anticipates a basic theme of military panegyric. Also favorable is a notice of Montague's description of "Boyne's swelling and purple Fields" which are stained "with hostile Blood" (11. 758-9). Because of the particular celebration of the recently deceased Dryden, and the contention for the position of being his successor in heroic verse, the lines on Blackmore have particular interest. Of Dryden he says:

> Here, Syren of sweet Poesy receive
> That little Praise my unknown Muse can give.
> Be thou immortal, nor harsh censure fear,
> Tho' angry *Bl*[ackmo]*re* in Heroick jear [*sic*].
> A Bard, who seems to challenge *Virgil*'s flame,
> And next in height, would be the next in name.   697-82

Blackmore is uneven, compared to his Roman model.

> Like *AEolus*, high *Bl---re* sometimes raves.
> We grant he labours with no want of Brains,
> Or Fire, or Spirit; but he spares the pains.   694-6

This haste will be a common feature of the panegyrics that are rushed to press as Marlborough's victories whip most every poet into a frenzy of praise; but Cobb urges that Virgil, the Mantuan, did not show the faults of hasty writing. By allusion, Blackmore's epics are reviewed. His *Satyr against Wit* had appeared November 23, 1699, as Luttrell notes.

The emphasis on epideictic verse leads to the conclud-

ing picture of King William listening to the "loud-sung
Triumphs of his Warlike Years" (ll. 886-7). William rewards the poets "with Honour and with Gold." It is on
this heroic note of praise of courage in battle, which is
associated even with the youthful prince, who follows in
his Uncle's steps, that this initiatory poem concludes.
Of course the prime expression of such prowess was to be
the Duke of Marlborough.

1701

May 24

Of WAR. A POEM. Being an ENCOMIUM on the Bravery of the
English Nation, both at Sea and Land. With a particular
Description of the FLEET. *Written at the Command of a
Person of Honour*. Arma virumq; Cano, &c. *LONDON*, Printed
for *John Chantry*, over against *Exeter Exchange* in the
Strand, and Sold by *John Nutt*, near *Stationers-Hall*, 1701.
    2°: A^2B-C^2D^1; t.p., *bl.*, *iii-iv*. Dedication in
prose, drop-t. on p. 1, 1-10, 14 pp., 262 lines, couplets.
TxU copy used. Brett-Smith Luttr., '24 May.' Morgan D330.
Advertisement of books sold by Chantry bottom of p. 10.
    The Dedication "To the Right Honourable, HENRY, Earl
of *ROMNEY*, &c" following fulsome apologies for *not* apologizing, envisions his lordship "at the Head of the bravest
Regiment of Men that are this Day in the World: all bold
and resolute *Britons*." Explains use of astrological symbols as appropriate in a poem on the opposition to
"Tyranny and Universal Monarchy." Opens:

    Awake, ye lazy Powers of Peace, awake;
    Hark, hark, the noisie War. your Temples shake.

Tributes to William III, as Nassau, and Liberty. Mars
smiles on "Nassaw, his Illustrious Son."

    It is Resolv'd, the Starry Gods agree,
    And Heav'n proclaims a War for Liberty.   12-13

7

The "Gallick Tyrant" appears with the train of war, making devastation. The English under Nassaw bravely resist. Most of the poem is devoted to descriptions of the satyrs in action as deities. The navy under sail occupies 182-210. The King, embodying goodness and justice, shines like Sol in the concluding lines. No reference to Marlborough, but the panegyric expresses the mood prior to his taking command on the death of William the following year.

6   October 20.

ADVICE TO Great Britain, &c. A POEM. *By a hearty Lover of his Country.* [ornament] *LONDON.* Printed for *Richard Mount*, and sold by *J. Nutt* near Stationers Hall. 1701.
    2°: *A*-B², t.p., *bl*.3-8, 8 pp. A POEM, p. 3. Wmk. lion erect in crowned circle. 125 lines, heroic couplets. Univ. of Leeds has fine paper copy, wmk. fleur-de-lys in shield. Morgan D8.
    Horn-Luttr. Copy. '3 *d*., 20 Octob.' Also Luttrell writes on title 'For Union agt. France.' Filled in *L*[ewi]*s* and *S*[pai]*n*, p. 7. Opens:

> A Time there was, e're Itch of Pow'r began,
> Or many Millions Vassal were to One.

This moderately Tory poem shows how ambitious men have disturbed the pristine harmony and peace. Urges gratitude to Nassau (William III), and proper rewards for those who serve the country. Appeals to English naval power against Louis XIV's ambitions. A propaganda piece, with slight literary power. Most striking passage urges use of English privateers against the "Num'rous sculking Train" of their French equivalents. Urges rewarding them with their prizes and laurels too. The beat is quite in Defoe's manner, and the opening lines suggest the tone of his *New Discovery of an Old Intreague* (1695). Thus:

> But *Albion*, Thou thy Happiness would'st own,
> In *Nassau*'s wearing thy uneasy Crown,
> Were you as wise, as you're ungrateful grown.

But if, in spight of His great Pains and Care,
A most Unchristian King will force a War,
And that not only *Europe* he'd enslave,
But o're the World a sole Command would have,
Let All, to curb his daring Insolence,
Forthwith Unite, and bravely make Defence.   29-41
                                                  passim.
The poem concludes with a warning against destruction of
the nation by "Male-contented Subjects." Thus Rome and
Carthage fell.

Consider This, and strive, e're too too late,
To free your selves from like unhappy Fate.   124-5

1702

7   March 31 *ca.*

Marlborough, Duke of (1650-1722).   Then Earl of Marlborough.

The Speech of his *Excellency* the *Earl* of *Marlborough,*
Ambassador Extraordinary and *Plenipotentiary* from *Her*
Majesty of *Great Britain,* to their High and Mighty Lord-
ships the *States-General* of the *United-Provinces* of the
Low Countries, 31 March 1702.
     1/2°: 1 side, prose. Reprinted in Lediard, *Life,*
1736, I, 141-3.
     The speech impresses upon the Dutch Queen Anne's de-
termination to continue the Union with them following the
death of William IIId. She "is ready, from this Moment"
to concur by sea and land in the alliance against the
power of France; and Marlborough is empowered to concert
with the Dutch in the necessary operations.

8   April 22.

Phillips, Samuel (fl. 1705)

England's Glory: A Congratulatory POEM ON THE CORONA-
TION, AND Happy Accession of Her Majesty to the Crown.
By *Samuel Phillips*, Gent. *Non est Mortale quod opto*.
LONDON: Printed, and to be Sold by *John Nutt*, near
Stationers-Hall, 1702.
    2°: A^2B-D^2; t.p., *bl. ii*, *iii-iv* 'To the Honour-
able Anthony Blagrave, Esq;' sgnd. '*Samuel Phillips*,
One of the *Seniors* of *Merchant-Taylors School*'; 5-16,
drop-t. on 5, 16 pp., 259 lines, couplets. NY Pub.
copy used. Luttr. date from Haslewood. Morgan E381,
as well has five other poems, 1702-3. The dedication
addresses Blagrave as a learned man, seeking to restore the splendors of the reign of Augustus, always
a possible slight at William III. Has approached him
on the encouragement of friends. Opens:

     Soon as *Aurora* left old *Tithon*'s Bed,
     And all black Mists of Sable Night were fled.

The classical-allegorical tone is maintained throughout,
in priase of Anne's ascension, April 23, 1702, O.S.
Thus Phillips's poem was published the day prior to
the Coronation. No reference to Marlborough. His
relation to the Tory interest, which is apparent in
Phillips, and the fact that the first full evidence
of his military and diplomatic skill appear later in
the year. Two allusions to Ormond, ll. 179 and 184,
also show Tory leanings. In 1703 Phillips published
Britannia Triumphans: a *Dramatic Entertainment* on the
Departure of the Duke of *Ormond*, while on the 19th of
June, 1702, he alludes to Dryden and Cowley.
     Nevertheless, a passage on Mars (ll. 175-85)
recognizes the military stance of the new reign in
which Marlborough became the Mars, "the mighty Arbiter of War." See No. 18.

9   April 24.

Barbon, Dr. [no dates]

Magna Britannia Triumphans: Or, the Coronation of the High

and Mighty *Anne*, by the Grace of God of *England, Scotland, France* and *Ireland*, Queen, Defender of the Faith, &c. who was Crowned at *Westminster Abby*, on *Thursday*, the 23d of *April*, 1702. [Wood engraving 6 3/4" by 10 1/2" of the coronation in Westminster, the galleries crowded with the Parliament and the Ministry at the side, with Anne in the center, and a winged angel above.] *LONDON*: Printed and are to be sold by *E. Mallet* next the King's Arms Tavern on the *Ditch-side* near *Fleet-street*. 1702. Price 2 *d*.
1°: 1 side, 3 columns, 113 lines, couplets. First section of 63 lines sgnd. "By Dr. *Barbon*.' The *Te Deum*, 70 lines. MH-Luttr. copy used, '2 *d*. 24 April, 1702.' Not in Morgan. Opens:

> When *Glorious Anna*'s happy Reign began
> And, its due Course, the *fam'd Succession* ran.

A pastoral mood opens the poem at Anne's accession. March is more summer-like than May. As the ceremony begins:

> *See, British Ladies*, thro' the World *renown'd*
> For *Matchless Beauty* walk the *dazling Round*:   20-1

Still Anne surpasses all, in her "sparkling Gems" and rich Crown. While Marlborough is not identified, martial preparations are noted.

> *Hark*! How her *Drums*, a dreadful March prepare
> Whilst *She leads on*, the *Goddess* of the *War*!
> Her *Glorious Conquests*, stretching far and wide:
> *Denmark* and *She*, shall the whole World divide.   53-6

Denmark is of course Anne's consort and husband. The *Te Deum* opens:

> To thee, O Lord, we chearful praises Sing,
> And duely [*sic*] own thee for our Sovereign King.

This portion is entirely religious, as an appeal for divine favor.

May 1.

Dyke, Ann [no dates]

The Female Muse. A POEM ON THE CORONATION Of Her Sacred

Majesty Queen *ANN*.   *LONDON*, and are to be Sold by *J. Nutt*
in *Stationers-Court*, near *Stationers-Hall*.   1702.
   *A*² B-C²; t.p., *bl*., *iii-iv* Ded. 'To the Right Hon-
ourable, *John* Earl of *Marlborough*, one of Her Majesties
most Honourable Privy Council, Captain-general of Her
Majesties Forces in *Flanders*, and Knight of the most Noble
Order of the Garter.' sgnd. Ann Dyke. 1-7, *8*, 12 pp.,
drop-t. p. 1. 156 lines, couplets. Bodley copy used;
Morgan E171.
   Dedication opens:

> "MY LORD, Being well acquainted with the
> glorious Character Your Lordship hath through
> all Europe, makes me presume to beg Your Pro-
> tection for the first Fruits my Muse hath
> ventur'd to the Censure of the World. . ."

Aside from begging forgiveness for "this poor scribble,"
the statement gives no personal clues nor indication of the
author's identity or claims on the then Earl's favor. The
poem opens:

> Once more our most dear indulgent Heaven,
> To heal our Griefs, this brave Cordial's given.

Literary interest appears in the effort to rouse Congreve
and Row[e] to sing instead of "scribling Fools," (37-40).
While the verses do not offer more than fulsome praise
for noble Anne, there is a military tone. Noble warriors
spring from her inspiration, and the Queen "brings conquests for succeeding Years." Only one specific allusion
to Marlborough appears:

> Go on brave Souls, who never were out-done,
> Nor need you fear while such a General leads you on.
> 116-17

This appears to be the first panegyric related to
Marlborough. Prince Eugene, who of course still outranked
him, and the Duke of Ormond were the focus of attention
from the poets.

1   June 3.

ENGLAND'S TRIUMPH, OR AN OCCASIONAL POEM ON THE Happy
Coronation of ANNE Queen of England, &c.
    1/2°:   1 side, verse, 3 column beneath large woodcut.
No pub., n. d., Luttr. copy at MH used by favor of Mr.
Foxon. '1 *d*. 3. June. 1702.' Morgan E21. Opens:

> Brave Subjects of *England* rejoice and be glad;
> Come cheer up your Spirits and be no more sad.

The ballad verse assures all enemies of English might that
though she has lost a "good Prince and a Hero of Fame," the
gracious Queen will be a worthy successor. So bumpers are
raised of "Canary" wine to her honor. No specific reference to Marlborough, who was still the Earl of Marlborough
till late in the year, appears, but a military tone pervades the poem. Line 23 asserts that "Our Cannon shall
rattle, our Trumpets shall sound."
    The engraving, 8 1/2 by 10 inches, depicts an ideal-
ized Queen Anne, enthroned beneath a canopy of state, with
kings, princes, and nobles on either side. A kneeling
figure of Europia cries, "God save the Queen," while female   ?
figures of Religion, with an open Bible, and Justice, with
a sword, draw the curtains to reveal the new sovereign.
Thus continuation of the military policy against France is
emphasized. A small insert depicts a crowned sovereign,
presumably the Emperor, who has arrived by ship, being
welcomed by the Queen.

2   November 19.

A POEM ON THE Late Glorious Success of His Grace the Duke
of Ormond at VIGO. By the Authors of *BRITANNIA's LOSS*.
LONDON. Printed, and are to be Sold by *J. Nutt* in Sta-
tioner's Court near *Stationers-Hall*. MDCCII. Morgan E373.
Under E531 lists *Britannia's Loss*: a Poem on the Death of
England's Caesar [William III] written by the Author of
Albion's Glory, *J. Nutt*, 1702. *Albion's Glory* is similarly
described as by the Authors of *Britannia's Loss*. Morgan
E16, cites another ed., 9 pp., 1702.
    2°:   *A*-*C*²; t.p., *bl*., 1-9, *bl. 10*; drop-t. on p. 1.

12 pp. Horn-Luttr. copy used. '4 d. 19. Novemb.' Wtmk.,
CSB and vague design. A note on Wrenn copy attributes to
Dennis. 'Finis' has E for F. 153 lines, couplets. TxU,
CtY. Opens:

> Near *Albion*'s Clifts [*sic*] a pleasant Vale there lies,
> That forms a Prospect of the distant Skies.

Pastoral mode used. Menalcus comes to recite Ormond's
deed to the shepherds and they dedicate the day to rural
sports in his honor. He invokes the nymphs to carve the
hero's name on trees and to pipe and sing his god-like
actions. Ormond charges like a Lyon, like Mars, or a
wolf. The Spaniards in vain hope for success. Alexis
urges Menalcus to recite Ormond's lineage, which he does.
Ormond sprang from warlike Oss'ry, terror of the French,
who forsook beds of down for cold, moist camps. Cloris
urges adorning Ormond's brow with flowery chaplets, of
violet, primrose, and daffodil. Then she urges him to
sing Pastora, i. e., Lady Ormond's charms. Seeking aid
from Spencer (Spenser), he does so, asking an heir to
Ormond's name and fame. Florimel now imagines he sees
the arrival of Ormond, the joyful, wondering throngs.
Ormond modestly receives the applause, "And only glories
in bright ANNA's Cause!" Anne and Ormond are the general
sound. Coridon concludes the poem as he recalls how his
father knew Ossory, Ormond's sire, and his gallant acts
against France. Though he died young in battle, Ormond
carries on his fame. "When he commands who would refuse
to die?" Loud huzza's from all, "And Hills and Dales did
Ormond's Name rebound." (1. 153)

Obviously a mildly Tory piece, interesting as the
first to employ pastoral for panegyric. Coridon is evidently the author, but no identification has been made.

13   November 21.

[Harris, Joseph (c. 1650-c. 1715)]

LUZARA. A Pindarique ODE ON Prince EUGENIUS OF SAVOY: And
His Late VICTORY over the *French* and *Spaniards* in ITALY.

14

Most Humbly Dedicated to His Grace the Duke of Somerset.
[2 lines Virgil]   *LONDON*, Printed and Sold by *B. Bragg*
at the *Blue-Ball* in *Ave-Mary Lane*. 1702. 415 lines in
pindarics. Haslewood identifies and dates. MH, CtY, CLU,
BM. No Luttrell copy. Horn copy used.
   2°: A²-D²; t.p., *bl.*, *iii-iv*, 1-12, 16 pp. Ded.
sgnd. 'J. H.' Wmk. Foolscap and B. HMC Rept. 12, III,
78 prints letter from Harris to Sir Thomas Coke, at St.
James's, appealing for aid for his wife and children. Has
sent this "book" and another on the Duke of Marlborough.
Requests return if cannot be helped, so may present to some
other eminent person. See Nos. 20 and 29, 1703.
   Effusive dedication to Somerset, Master of Queen Anne's
Horse and Chancellor of Cambridge, and "even at the Helm of
State." Opens:

> Hail Great *Eugenius*! More Renown'd
> Then [*sic*] *Macedon's* Victorious Prince.

Eugene did not overcome soft persons, nor Parthians. His
deeds such as gave immortality to mighty Heracles. Darkness falls on the battle scene on the Po. Uproar of mount-
ing seas, a "bloody Hurry," but Eugene

> With vigilant Care
> His labouring Combatants survey'd
> And where the Battle totter'd, lent his timely Aid. 116-18

His courage as of Agamemnon forces Catinat and prouder
Villeroy to yield, though Vendosme seeks to rescue them.
Eugene addresses his victorious army, "I lead ye now to
Death or Victory," and inspires the whole body. His lieu-
tenants fight with Rinaldo's and Tancred's flame, or as
Ascanius foiled Mezantius, and David, Goliah. Three hours
of battle, then darkness. Vendosme's false claims of vic-
tory to save his credit set Versailles rejoicing in vain.
May valiant Eugene live on as "Terror of usurping France."
May his eagles prove as invincible as Jove's, by Roman
consuls not outdone, and with surname of Neapolitain and
Milanois.

14   November 27.

02

THE RETRIEVEMENT: Or, A POEM, Distinguishing between the
Late and the Present ADMINISTRATION. Being An Offering
of Thanksgiving for the Glorious Progress of Her Majesties
Forces by Sea and Land [ornament]   *LONDON*, Printed for
John Nutt. 1703.
    2°: A^2 B-C^2 D^1: t.p., *bl.*, 1-10. Drop-title on p. 1.
Pp. 8-10   To the *Queen* with drop-title, signed. 'Dread
Sovereign for You.' 175 lines. Horn-Luttr. copy used. On
p. 8 Luttrell smudges "g" in "shinging" to make "shining."
MS. '4 d. 27 Novemb.' Lower portion of the "3" in 1703.
smudged out to make 1702. CtY, Morgan F329, *WL*, Dec.
Opens:

> Pamper'd in Kentish Meads with pickled feed
> All Beasts grow Rampant of the factious breed.

This poem is important as the first full tribute to
the Duke of Marlborough, even though, as a Tory piece, it
also praises Rook and Ormond. The theme of retrievement
of course reflects on William III, who had not succeeded
in recovering the ancient honor of England. Condemnation
of the zeal of the Kentish Petitioners, five against 500
counsellors of state, opens the poem. This introduces
the theme of amassing wealth through war. England was
ridiculed and "the more she rais'd, was still the more
in Debt." They turned England against France, and for
it we have not one citadel or port. Urges that hearts
entirely English should command.

> That *Marlborough* (whose praise we should rehearse
> In Pindars high unimitable verse.
> Whose former Conduct did at once prevail
> 'Gainst *Cork* and forced the impregnable *Kingsail*.)
> Might Head th'united Hoasts [*sic*] and in one Siege
> Take *Venlo*, *Ruremond*, *Stevenswart* and *Liege*.   73-8

While retrieving of English honor lists Marlborough first,
Rook, Lake, Bembo, Whetstone, as naval commanders follow
as curbers of French insolence. The section 'To the
QUEEN' praises her as surpassing Elisa, who "Sunk the
Armado," for Anne has taken both the Armado and the Flota
too.   This portion totals 37 lines.

16

15 December 30.

[H., W.]

THURA BRITANNICA, a Congratulatory POEM to Her Sacred
Majesty Queen ANNE And the WHOLE REALM, For the Late
SIGNAL and HAPPY Success of Her Majesty's *Forces* both
by Sea and Land. By *W.H.* [4 lines in Latin unsgnd.]
LONDON: Printed for *Benj. Tooke*, at the *Middle-Temple-
Gate*, in *Fleetstreet*. 1702.
2°:   hft. A^2 B-C^2 D^1; C for B; D for C; *bl.*, t.p.,
bl. i-iv, 1-9, *10 bl.*, 14 pp. Drop-t. on p. 1. 182
lines, couplets. Morgan E222. CSmH, TxU-Luttr. copy
used. MS. '4 *d*-30. Decemb.' *WL*. Jan 1703. Opens:

> Fair *Albion's* Sons your tuneful Notes advance,
> To shew your Conquest over *Spain* and *France*.

Luzara's field answers the French *te deums*. Thanksgiving
no selfish aim; it reflects the blessings of a female
reign. The fairer sex can move powers above, as Venus
with Jove and Neptune for her son Aeneas. Anne conquers
with charm, as Hispania is bribed with Gallic gold. Louis
XIV more interested in getting a kingdom, "or a king restore." Portacarero took his guilded bait. Europe's
weakness and distress; northern Belgia and Austria shiver.
Only the British queen is undaunted. Anne summons her
council, especially Notingham [*sic*]. The Royal Prince
convokes the British and Dutch brigades, "to form a vast
Campaign." Ormond next, of princely valor.

> From *Thames* to *Rhine*, and the admiring *Po*,
> Resounds the praise of God-like *Marlborough*.   144-5

Marlborough compared to Achilles. Rooke repairs late loss
by victory at Vigo, in naval battle "whose Spouting Fiery
Vomits frighted Worlds above. . .From every Peer, to ev'ry
rural Swain." All shall lie more securely under "Anne's
effectual war, than others peace."
    Author unidentified beyond initials. A moderately Tory
poem, perhaps by a churchman. Recognizes claims of both
navy and army.
    Morgan E222 mentions "another edition, 11 pp. folio,"
but since gives 9 pp. for the actual 14, this possibly an
error.

16   Blandford, Marquess of (1688-1703)

Ad Reginam.   10 lines in Latin in *Academiae Cantabrigi-
ensis Carmina Quibus Decenti Augustissimo Regi Welhelmo
III. Patentat; et Succedenti Optimis Auspiciis Serenissimae Reginae Annae Gratulatur.   Cantabrigiae, Typus
Academicis.*
        2°: A-Hh^2; fol. B, sgnd. *Joh. Churchill* Comitis de
Marlborough Filius Unicus, Coll. Regal. *1702.* Horn copy
used. Opens:

> *Anna,* Genus Regum; Quae jam tibit debita dudum
>   Sceptra per innumeros missa tueris Avos.

        Young Churchill was the pupil of Dr. Francis Hare,
at King's College, Cambridge, where he died of smallpox
a year later. Hare was made Chaplain General in recognition of his services, and became one of the leading figures in publishing accounts and defence of the Duke's
military career. See the author's study, "Marlborough's
First Biographer: Dr. Francis Hare," *HLQ*, XX, No. 2,
Feb., 1957, 145-62.
        The poem, while a conventional juvenile exercise,
appropriately stands at the head of over a hundred pieces,
most in Latin, but a few in Greek and Hebrew, of the volume. This tribute from an ill-fated son has never been
noticed by the biographers. Blandford's death occurred
on February 20, 1703, at the onset of a particularly
frustrating year. See Congreve's pastoral elegy on
Blandford, below, No. 33.

17   An *Essay* on *Prince Eugene's Success* in *Italy.* . . . A *Poem,*
1702.
        12 pp. Morgan B185 the only information on this
piece.

18   Phillips, Samuel, Gent. One of the Seniors of Merchant-
Taylors School. fl. 1705.

The German CAESAR. A PANEGYRICK ON Prince *EUGENE* of *Savoy,*

Relating to the Present Posture of Affairs in ITALY, Especially before MANTUA. By *Samuel Phillips*, Gent.
Praestat otiosum esse quam Nihil agere. LONDON: Printed,
and are to be Sold by *John Nutt*, near *Stationers-Hall.*
1702.
    2°: A-C² (A on p. *iii*); t.p., *bl.*, *iii-iv*; The
PREFACE, 1-8, 12pp. Drop-t. on p. 1. 168 lines, couplets. Not in Morgan or CBEL. MH copy used. Opens:

    WHAT! durst the *Frenchman* such a Sentence breathe,
    And Swear, *that he will* Mantua *releive* [*sic*]?

The *Preface* sgnd. 'Samuel Phillips, *One of the* Seniors
of Merchant-Taylors *School.*' The writer admits his youth
but has been encouraged by the "favourable Acceptance of
the Town." The reference may be to one or all three
other poems by Phillips published in 1702. Those dated
extend from '22 Aprill' of *England's Glory* to '14 June'
The Grove, or *Muse's Paradise*, both dated by Haslewood.
*England's Happiness; a Panegyrick on the Present Parlia-
ment*, 1702, like the *German Caesar* does not apparently
survive in a Luttrell dating.
    While the poem does not mention Marlborough, it dis-
plays the Tory attitude of celebrating Prince Eugene, and
the favoring of war in Italy and the Mediterranean over
Flanders. Identifiable events include the capture of
Villeroi, the French commander, at Cremona, January 31,
1702. In spite of the device of gaining entrance through
a dry canal (11. 22-5), Cremona eluded capture. Vendosme's
arrival, February 18, to replace Villeroi is implied. Admiral Benbow, called Bembow, and Ormond are also introduced, confirming the Tory bias. Since Mantua was still
resisting capture, the poem inconclusively contents itself
with predictions of the disgrace of Louis XIV, and the
restoration of the city's liberty through Eugene's prowess.
Taunting of Prince Victor Amadeus of Savoy, as "Base and
Mercenary," as he assuredly was, adds to the tone of a
poem that is little more than chauvinistic. It certainly
preceded Luzzara, August 15, for which both sides claimed
a victory. Neverthess, Eugene had succeeded in foiling
French plans.
    See No. 8.

19   THE HEROE IN MINIATURE; OR, AN Historick Poem on Prince
     EUGENE. *Veni, Vidi, Vici*. *LONDON*; Printed and Sold by
     J. *How*, in the *Ram-Head-Inn* in *Fanchurch-street*, and *B.
     Bragg*, at the *Blew-Ball* in *Avamary-Lane* next *Ludgate-
     street*, 1702. TxU copy used. Morgan E186.
         2°: A^2 B-C^2; t.p., *bl.*, 3-12, 12 pp. Drop-t. on p.
     3. 208 lines, couplets.
         Fame and Fury are heard in dialogue; Fury in italics.
     Fame opens:

         Darling of *Men*, and Patron o' the *Wars*,
         Envy of *Kings*, and Favourite of *Mars*.

The poet has extolled Eugene's glories and toils, and en-
rolled his name in his sacred scroll. Formerly he praised
Nassau's conquests in Hibernia, and now he is dead and
Eugene alone can replace him as subject for praise. The
poem is Whiggish and of course precedes Blenheim by two
years, thus preparing for Prince Eugene's share in that
crucial victory for the Allies in favor of Austrian control of Spain and triumph over France. Louis XIV is told
that he must give up hopes of universal sway.

         No more thy *Arms* must *Europe*'s Voice controul,
         Nor lord it over *Belgia*'s Fruitful Soil.   163-4

    The poem recognizes the role of panegyric and the
Virgilian model.

         Then since great *Actions* are the Poets Theme
         By them remitted to recording Fame.
         May from great *Virgil*'s Tomb some *Maro* rise,
         In Epick Verse to Mount him to the Skies.   183-6

This anticipation of Addison's role in the *Campaign* may
well have been some encouragement to that effort. The
anonymous poet concludes with the deploring of "barren
scriblers," and the failure of the poets to string their
harps in praise of William IIId who was "Revil'd while
Living, and when Dead unsung " (1. 200). Never have there
been two greater heroes than Eugene and Nassau.

20   H., J. M. A. (Joseph Harris, c. 1650-c. 1715)

Leighton-Stone-Air, A POEM. OR A Poetical Encomium ON
THE Excellency of its SOIL, Healthy AIR, And Beauteous
SITUATION. Together with some Historical Hints, both
Antient and Modern, on its Noble Prospects, and adjacent
Forrest of *Eppen*. Also a Pindarick ODE on Prince *Eugene*
of Savoy. Humbly Dedicated To the Worthy Encouragers of
the *Latin* Boarding-School, newly Erected in Leighton-
Stone; By the Author, *J.H. M.A. LONDON*, Printed for *A.*
Baldwin near the Oxford-Arms in *Warwick-Lane*. 1702.
     2°: A-K²; t.p., Preface 'To the Worthy Encouragers
of the SCHOOL.' 3-36, headline titles, *Leighton-Stone-*
Air, 991 lines, couplets; *Pindarick on Prince Eugene*,
pp. 37-9, 49 lines in 4 ode stanzas, total 1042 lines,
40 pp. BM copy used; Morgan E221, but no notice of the
Ode. See Nos. 13 and 29.
     While the poem primarily celebrates the school and
setting, where Harris was head master, it also is strongly
Whiggish. Many references of William III, as "Nassaw,"
·and specific recognition of England as champion against
France in defence of the Empire lead to one early reference to Marlborough:

Won by the brave *Nassaw*'s or *Eugene*'s Soul,
Or *Rook*'s dread Prowess, or fam'd *Marlborough*'s Sword.
                                                  239-40

The *Ode* on Eugene opens:

Hast, Potent Genius, Hast away!
The victim-*Gauls* a-wait, Thy Prey.

Prince Eugene is urged to conquer France in verses of no
distinction. Numerous marginalia in the main poem deal
with The Royal Society, Newton, Sir Thomas Gresham, astronomy, Harvey and the circulation of the blood, the
great country houses as monuments of English history from
William the First to the Third.

1   *Prince Eugene; A Pindarique*. Written by the Author of
the *Muses-Treat*. Printed for *Jo. Senex*, and Sold by *J.*
Nutt near *Stationers-Hall*, 1702.

2°: Single sig. A, p. 1. No t.p., only drop-t. top
p. 1, colophon bottom p. 4, pp. 1-4. 88 lines, irregular
ode. Advertisement of *The Muses Treat*, or a Collection of
Wit and Love, in several Miscellany Poems. Sold by *Jo.
Senex* against *St. Clement*'s Church in the *Strand, London*.
bot. p. 4. Not in Morgan. Opens:

> Wake! m'Ambitious Soul awake!
> Off théy drowsy Dullness shake.

Lambeth Palace copy used, the only known copy. Not in
Morgan.
    A kind of "advice to the poets" poem. Urges rousing
from dullness to hail the hero, the Marcellus of the times.
Give and win deathless fame for your pen and for the hero.
    An interesting note is an anti-feminist attitude
toward women:

> They leave a Blemish in the Mind,
> A solid and a lasting Stain behind.   11-12

    Honor alone is "the brightest Gem." For honor under-
took "illustrious Hazzards." No locus or information is
available for the *Muses Treat*.

22   Stapylton, John, Baronetti Filius, Magdalen Coll, Oxon.
Pristina Angliae Gloria restituta. Latin poem in vol.,
In *Epinicion Oxoniense sive Solennis Feliciter*. *Terra
Marique Gestas A Copiis Serenissimae Reginae ANNAE Contra
Gallos pariter ac Hispanos* A. D. 1702.
    2°: A^2 B-I^2; *bl., i-ii*, t.p., *bl.*, 36 pp. unumbd.,
wtmk "H" and small Lily. Folio sigs. F-*F2*, 48 lines.
Horn copy used.

> Dum Classis Undis stridet *Ibericis*
> Ambusta, & Auro dum rutilum Mare.

One of 13 pieces urging maintenance of William III's policy
at Anne's accession by war against French tyranny. Several
poems celebrate Ormond and his victory at Vigo. Not separ-
arely printed.

23   TE DEUM, OU, ACTIONS DE GRACES A DIEU Pour les Glorieux
Succez Des Armes de Sa Majeste Britannique, la Reine
ANNE. *A Londres*, par J. DELAGE, dans *Stationers-Cour*,
proche *Ludgate*. 1702. With 3 added *Stances, Sur l'Expedition de Vigos*, and 2 more *Sur l'Union de la France
avec l'Espagne. Te Deum* in ten 6-line stanzas, total
90 lines, couplets. NY Pub. only loc. Since two later
poems published by Delage in French are by Mr. Hullin,
this may well be another from his ardent pen. Not in
Morgan. Opens:

    O Dieu, dont tous les mondes recontent les louanges.
    Monarque Souverain des hommes & des Anges.

We have captured provinces and thrown Louis into alarm.
Stanza IV brings in the commanders at Blenheim.

    Eugene a conserve son poste en Italie
    Devant MARLEBROUGH, tout succombe, tout plie,
    Le Grand Prince de Bade, a fait trembler Villars. 19-21

Some details on the attack on Vigo bring in Ormond, who
took the Fort at Rondelle, and "invincible *Rook*," who is
animated into destroying the French vessels. The interest
in the poem lies in its evidence of a colony of French
exiles in London, and the awareness of Marlborough's growing importance.

1703

24   January 15.

Shute, James (no dates)

A PINDARICK ODE, UPON Her Majesties sending His Grace the
Duke of *Marlborough* to Command the *English* Forces in *Holland*, and His Graces being chosen Generalissimo of the
Confederate Army against the *French King*. [two Biblical
quotations] By JAMES SHUTE. *London*: Printed for the
Author, and Sold by *J. Nutt*, near *Stationers-Hall*, 1703.
      2°: A-C²; t.p., *bl.*, Dedication to Marlborough *iii-
iv*, 1-8, 12 pp. Horn-Luttr. copy used. Luttrell MS.
'4 d. 15 Januar.,' and a dash and '2' under 1703. Since
Marlborough set sail on May 5, 1702, 1703 date correct,
even though Luttrell continued to think of it as 1702.
BM, CSmH, MH, N, NjP, TxU. 10 stanzas of 164 lines, pin-
darics. Morgan F28, but incorrectly ascribed to John
Shute, Viscount Barrington.
      A distinctly Whiggish poem. Dedication alludes to
Marlborough's being chosen by William III for command in
Flanders and on the Irish expedition. Opens:

         Hear, O Celestial Hosts that shine so bright,
      You glorious Sons of the Eternal light.

The muse should not fear *Cimmerian* night nor *Libya's*
Strand. Queen Anne, with capacious mind and gentle influence, treads paths to victory. But Factions and Confusion
dwell in a "deep loathsome Cell." A Tri-form Monster
threatens destruction to our lands.
      Miltonic influence shows in praise of the leader con-
fronting all the Host of Satan.

         From Regions of eternal light
            Down, down they fall to everlasting night.   92-3

As Michael or Moses against Pharaoh, so Marlborough. Then
Joshua the Great, and Barak, Jephtha, and Gideon. Hails
Britannia's "happy Isles," safe ports, a "happy land."

Here Lucius, Constantine, Arthur, Alfred, Henry, Edward,
and wise Eliza make a constellation with Anna in the
midst. "Go, said She, "Thou chosen one," and Marlborough "went, he saw, and overcame." Marginal notes emphasize that the French fled before Marlborough.

Aside from the many Biblical allusions, Shute's
status as a spokesman for the church is apparent in two
earlier sacred poems, *Virtue and Science*, 1695, and *A
Sacred Poem*, 1689. He does not appear in CBEL nor DNB.

5   January 15.

[Tooke, Charles]   (no dates)

*To the Right Honourable Sir George Rooke, Vice Admiral of
England*, &c. At His Return from His Glorious Enterprize
near VIGO. 1702. [3 lines of Virgil] *London*: Printed
for *Benj. Tooke*, at the *Middle Temple-Gate* in *Fleetstreet*.
1702. Though dated 1702, the TxU-Luttr. copy, which is
used, identifies the poem as appearing early 1703. MS.
'15 Januar 1702/3.' Identification of the author as "Char.
Tooke" may suggest a brother, or close relative of the
publisher, or simply be an error. *WL*, Jan. Morgan E423.
  2°: A^1 B-D^2; t.p., *bl.*, 1-11, *bl.*, 14 pp. 223 lines,
couplets. Drop-title on p. 1. Opens:

        Amidst the loud Applause, which fills the ears
        Of Heroes and returning Conquerors.

The poet offers the praise of "an humble Muse," in
face of the acclaim of the populace, the Senate's thanks,
and the sovereign's choice. Poets, in praising, can only
secure for themselves the honor they pretend to give. Fame
must be pursued early in life. The strong and anticipatory bias of the poem in favor of growing Tory hostility
to Marlborough and the land war against France becomes
apparent. The theme of a nation winning victories, but
gaining nothing else from "pompous Conquests" is forcefully asserted. England is "proudly poor," though weakened by victories. The poet admits the fact of land

victories, but prefers naval conquests. Nature has set England on an island, surrounded by circling waves, and "walls of wood, circling castles," that is ships, protect her. Marginal notes cite specific ships and expeditions of Admiral Rooke. His flagship, the Eagle, and capture of the Smyrna fleet impel the poet to excesses of rapture. Rooke becomes godlike, as if Jove himself came down to earth in his form. Albion is freed from bondage; Astrea (Anne) reigns in peace. English courage inspired by an English prince has taken a town, Cales, and brought home Spanish galleons and the "wealth of *India* and the price of *Spain*" (1. 158).

Though unnamed, Marlborough and Eugene are depreciated in allusion to the rapid healing of the slight wounds that have been given to Spain and France. Rooke, on the other hand, invades "at once the Springs of Life." He has attacked the tyrant in his strongest hold, and has seized the very gold with which he bribes support from princes. Anne will now use this treasure to "rescue Europe, and redeem Mankind."

Toward the end of the poem one darker note is introduced. While "the World is ours, whilst you command," still a part of him can die. What women envy and men admire is by disease defaced, and his laurels are darkened with the loss, presumably of his wife. Nevertheless in the final lines, hope is seen in a son who may "Rival his mighty Father in Renown."

26   January

[Hare, Dr. Francis (1671-1740)]

An Exact Journal of the Forces of the Allies this Last Summer's Campaign under the Command of the Duke of *Marlborough* in *Flanders*. Sold by *J. Nutt*. *WL*, V, p. 60, Jan., 1703. Not in Morgan.

See same title below under 1704, No. 57. The writer has shown that Hare produced this journal of the campaigns, and that he employed much of the material in his, the first, life of the Duke. See "Marlborough's First Biographer:

Dr. Francis Hare," HLQ, XX, No. 2, Feb. 1957, 145-62.
See No. 112.

7   January 30.

[Bryan ?; Yalden, Thomas ? (1670-1736), Chaplain to
2d Duke of Beaufort]

The Temple of Fame, a Poem, occasion'd by the Late Success
of the Duke of *Ormond,* the Duke of *Marlborough,* Sir *George
Rooke,* &c., against *France* and *Spain.* Inscrib'd to Mr.
Congreve. Printed for *J. Nutt,* 1703. Price 6 *d.* 382
lines, couplets.
       2°: $A^2 B^2 C^1D^2$. *i-ii,* 1-12, 14 pp. Yale-Luttr.
MS. '30 Januar. 1703,' with '2' added under date. *WL,* Feb.
1703. H. Hills 8vo, 1709. BM, MH, CtY, TxU, Yale *1-2,*
3-15, *16 bl.,* 16 pp. CtY copy used. Morgan F442. Dobell
Anon.Cat. notes: "In the *Bibliographer,* IV, 93, Edward
Solly attributes this piece to Thomas Yalden, D. D., but
recently had a copy with inscription on title 'Wrote by
one Bryan a worthy Chaplain to Bp. of Norwich'." Morgan
C493, lists 1700 ed., an elegy on the death of Gloucester.
An H. Hills ed., 1709 reprints: The *Temple of Fame.* A
POEM. Inscrib'd to Mr. *Congreve.* [2 lines Latin] *LONDON.*
Printed and Sold by *H. Hills* in *Black-fryers* near the
Water-side. 1709, 16 pp. Horn copy used. Opens:

       Of *Namur, Cressy, Poictiers, Agincourt,*
       Too big for Truth, or Truth at best disguis'd.

Congreve is urged to praise new heroes, since "Vigo can be
an equal to the Boyn." A narrative line is established
with Fame, a wanderer in Homer's days, who seeks a shrine
or Temple. Flying in search, she finally comes to Albion.
She saw England confronting the "Boy of *Spain,*" and Lewis,
like a Canvas-Jove. The thunder of battle and the sale of
the Navy rouse her heart. They "cut the boom," at Vigo,
and put whole squadrons to flight. The returning Navy
waylays rich fleets, and with an unconscious mercenary
touch, Fame decides to build her Temple there, in England.
The heavily allegorical picture of the Temple embodies a

floor paved with eyes, nerves, sinews, broken bones and
arteries, and numerous figures, Despair, Humor, Calumny,
Deceit, and the like, enemies to true fame. The goddess
stands on a mountain above a wood of trees of all sorts
and uses, a green prospect, safe from croaking ravens,
serpents and toads. . .

> High o'er the Wood the Goddess rears her size,
> And hides her Tow'ring forehead in the Skies.   207-8

Her golden wings and silver trumpet are enhanced by an
allegorical scarf of babbling mouths across her arms, and
a plate of yawning ears which conceals her veiled breast.
      A warlike knight, identified in a footnote as Sir
George Rooke, arrives to the sound of victorious trumpets.
Since he leads and concludes a long recital of heroes,
from Brutus, Caesar, and Hengist down through medieval,
Tudor, and Stuart champions, it is clearly a Tory poem,
even though addressed to Congreve. The names are en-
rolled in the book of Fame. Particular attention is
given to the boy prince, the Duke of Gloucester, the
focus of the 1700 edition. He is depicted playing at
battle, riding his war steed, and winning pasteboard
trophies, of course with Marlborough as tutor.

> Fighting his sport, a Bloody Sword his toy,
> He acted Man ev'n while he Play'd a Boy.   318-19

Prince Eugene and Ormond both receive notice for heroic
exploits, but Marlborough is given only slight notice.

> But never *Annals* can presume to shew,
> Another *Ormond* or a *Marlborough*.
> Forgive my boldness, if your worth to raise,
> I make you but Competitors for Bays,
> Competitors are foils to one anothers Praise. 359-63

They are compared to two stout, fearless lions who chase
the herds and herdsmen. Others appear, but unnamed, "And
all fought well, for all were *English* born." The absurdities of chauvinism, rampant in later panegyrics, appear
here and in the picture of Rook, who when he sees his name
honored, exhibits a "Virgin Blush" as he closes the sacred

page of the volume of *"English* born" heroes.

February 6.

Wall, Thomas [no dates]

AN ODE FOR An Entertainment OF MUSICK ON HER Majesty's
Birth-Day, AND The Success of Her Majesty's Arms by Sea
and Land. The Night Performance before her Majesty at St.
James's. The Words by Mr. *Wall*. Set to Musick by Mr.
Abell. London, Printed for *J. Nutt* near *Stationers-Hall*.
1703.
    4°: A-C^4; hft., *bl.*, t. p., *bl.*, To the Queen's Most
Excellent Majesty, dedication sgnd. Tho. Wall,*v-vi*, 1-5,
bl.; t. p. Second Part, colophon 1703 *vii-viii*, 9-13, *bl.*
Advertisement (xv), *bl. xvi*. 24 pp. Pt. I, 39 lines; Pt.
II, 38 lines, 77 in all. Wmk. foolscap. Horn copy used.
Morgan F409.
    Dedication pure celebration of Anne's speeches, good-
ness and sincerity. The performers include Fame, Pallas,
Victory, Triumph, and Britain. Opens:

    Hark, *Britain*, hark! the loudest Trump of Fame
    Sounds abroad the Glorious Name
    Of thy Victorious *Female*'s sway.

    The allusion to female reign is tempered by Anne's
consort, who rules the main, that is, the seas. Anne,
under Heaven's guidance, declares her generous mind, for
Britain and for Europe's freedom. She must complete Herculean labors in "The Conquests of a Tedious War." The
second part, for another performance, praises Anne's
heroes and bold commanders, for their conduct in Flanders.
Marlborough in particular is implied though not named, the
emphasis being on Anne, and Royal George's mighty power.
Hastily printed, as is evidenced by misspelling *'ANNNA'*
(1. 34), P. 13, the piece presumably was published on or
near the Queen's birthday, February 6.

29   February

H., J. [Harris, Joseph (c. 1650-c.1715)]

ANGLIA TRIUMPHANS. A Pindarique ODE, On His GRACE, the
DUKE of *MARLBOROUGH*. And His Glorious Campaign in the
Spanish Low-Countries, Anno MDCII. Most Humbly Dedicated
to the Right Honourable JOHN GRANVILLE, Lieutenant-General
of the ORDNANCE, &c.   [Latin motto from Seneca] *LONDON*,
Printed for the Author, 1703.
      2°: A^2B-F^2; t.p., [errata on *ii*] Dedicatory Address
iii-iv, 1-19, *bl*.   24 pp. Dedication is signed 'J. H.'
WL, Feb., 1703. Morgan *F191a; and Wrenn catalog, attri-
butes to Hughes. 557 lines, couplets. TxU copy used.
Haslewood identifies author. Opens:

> So, having ended his Campaign in *Gaul*,
> Victorious Caesar back return'd to *Rome*.

The entire work is wretched stuff, quite justifying
the charge of C. E. Moore that "Hughes" takes first place
for "adulatory absurdity," even though Harris is the real
author. ("Whig Panegyric Verse," *PMLA*, XLI, 367, 1926.)
Three poems, styled Pindaric odes, precede this one, but
they are odes largely by virtue of very irregular line
lengths, useless inversions, and vacuous turgidity. In
the *Dedication*, after listing all of Granville's titles,
the author alleges that these reflect Queen Anne's recognition of men of Bravery, Wisdom, and Truth. Twice addressing his subject as "Sir," he professes to have had
his brain inflamed to poetry by Marlborough's successes
in "this last Campaign." Venlo was taken September 23,
1702. In the poem Marlborough returns in triumph, but is
concerned solely with renown, to "enlarge his Sovereign-
ess's Fame." Like Zenobia, Anne has been summoned to war
by Bellona.
      Europe is trembling and helpless before Louis's
rapes and savagery. "To Arms, to Arms," she cries, and
chooses Marlborough to bear them. He is commanded to
save Europe, while the French, wrapped in vain conceit
conceive themselves invincible. Soon, however, Boufflers
craves aid, and the young Prince Burgundy is sent. Allusion to a "kettle-drum Procession," is the only striking

detail. Marlborough's attack is irresistible, like a
cataract. "Nature, improved by Art," but feebly strives
to guard the fugitives (p. 7). Alexander, Hercules, and
Hannibal are brought in for comparisons. The Rhodian
walls stand high, but soon Venlo and Ruremond fall, their
barricades futile against Marlborough. Men once fought
gods, but Homer never dared let Thetis's son, that is
Achilles, attack such a fortress as Venlo (p. 10). Cutts,
in particular, and Huntington, Lorn, Dalrimple, Webb, and
Temple are mentioned in comparison to Greek heroes.

The most interesting passage is an allusion to panegyric, p. 12. Poetry is a "speaking Monument," and heroes
owe their fame to Homer, Pindar, Tasso, and presumably the
author. Marlborough is now shown, seeking not blood but
renown. He orders immediate attack, and by the "decorum"
of Cohorn's cannon, the way is made. Belgium is sad until
Marlborough charms and reassures her. On his return Anne,
like the Sun, receives him and returns the laurels which
he has won and presents to her. Her choice has been confirmed, "the English Arms in Pristine *Fame* restor'd," and
Marlborough's conduct has fixed the "sacred League,
'gainst *Spain* usurp'd." Astrea descends and presides as
Anne awards her hero "the highest Evidence of HER ESTEEM;
A DUCAL DIADEM." (ll. 553-4) Long may Marlborough live
to serve the best of queens, and may those who read his
story be inflam'd to acts of Glory when they see his name.
That name will be inscribed on pyramids, which will read:

"Great MARLBOROUGH's Name, who once *All* EUROPE sav'd."
See Nos. 13 and 20.

March 23.

ASTREA TRIUMPHANS. The *Temple* of *Gratitude*, and the
Trophies of VIGO; Being a Congratulatory Poem To His Grace
the Duke of ORMOND, On His Happy Accession to the *Lieutenancy* of the Kingdom of *IRELAND*. *LONDON*, Sold by *A. Baldwin*, at the *Oxford Arms* in *Warwick-Lane*, MDCCIII.
A-D^2; t. p., *bl*., *ii-iv* To Sacred Majesty, a prose
dedication, 1-12. 16 pp. 337 lines, couplets. Horn-
Luttr. copy used. MS. '6 d.' - Arabic '2' under III of

date, and '23 March.' No further markings. Wtmk. Lion and Unicorn ARMS. *WL*, March. BM, CtY (2). Haslewood March 23, 1702/3. Morgan F19.

Dedication on proper dispensation of favors by imperial power. "Desert should always precede preferment." Here rewarding "hardy Services," and a "long unbroken Chain of the most unshaken Loyalty." Opens:

> The Bright ASTREA now no longer driven,
> Exil'd from Earth to an embracing Heav'n.

A turgid poem with little theme or development. Effusive tribute to Ormond as the "plumed hero." Astrea is no longer exiled from Earth, and heroes are no longer requited with barren laurels and neglect. "Bright *Anne*" now reigns, "Good and Great," she rewards merit. Urania is invoked to inspire the poet, a bit incongruously, in view of the observation about Astrea. Nevertheless, the Muse of Astronomy inspires a passage addressed to the stars, "Ye spangled lights that deck the Heav'ns so gay" .(1. 44). They are asked if they have ever witnessed such a claim to honor as Ormond's. His triumphs in *Belgia* won Envy's homage, and Great *Nassau*, or William, as he is also called, gave tribute. That Ormond strove for honor, not rewards, is emphasized. His "Eagle plum'd her Wings, but not her Nest." He led to "blazing Vigo," and Urania cannot praise him too highly; Jove is transported.

But the picture is now shaded with recollections of destruction in Ireland, especially to Ormond's halls. But this spoilage by "hungry *Vultures*" could not shake Ormond's loyalty. Anne is gratified and she grants Ormond a commission sealed by her "*Guardian Angel*." While Albion rejoiced, "two Snaky Heads," (Spain and France), hissed hatred. Lewis looked on at a distance as the leader of "a *Feminine Troop*" advanced. Ormond crosses the Irish Channel, as thousands rejoice, to assume command -- "*Ireland*, thy Sceptre how shall ORMOND sway." Only one cloud shadows the glory, for Ormond, now reigning in Ireland, can no longer serve in the field, winning military honors.

The panegyric concludes with a final address to Urania, who has made it so easy to write. The poem is not the poet's, since "WIT is but GLORY's Echo." The poet

only thrusts in to give sound and air to the song of the
hero's deeds.

Vast Wreaths may twine, and won'drous Perfumes bring.
But Oh the Sweets must all from his own Garden spring.

326-7

1   1703, February-March

ELEGIA in Praematurum Obitum *Nobilissimi*, & *Maximae Spei
Adolescentis* JOHANNIS, MARCHIONIS *De BLANCFORD*. *Illus-
trissimi D U C I S* DE MARLBOROUGH FILII UNICI, mortue
Cantabrigiae dum Literis praeclaram operam datat. Die
20 Februar. *LONDINI*. Imprimebat *Richardus Janeway*.
Anno 1702/3. 52 lines Latin verse in 2 cols., each 26.
    1/2°: 1 side, 2 columns, black bands surrounding
whole, and dividing 2 cols. of verse and colophon at bot.
BM copy used. Also a copy on vellum. Opens:

    HUS adsint Sacrae, moestissima turba, Sorores,
    E gremio quarum raptus Alumnus obit.

A conventional and classical chiding of forces of Nature,
and lamentation for the House of Marlborough. Blandford
died at Cambridge on February 20, 1703, of smallpox, and
was interred in a splendid tomb in King's College Chapel.
His tutor, Dr. Francis Hare, was made Chaplain General of
the Forces, and became virtual head of the "public rela-
tions" team supporting Marlborough and the war. In this
role he also was Marlborough's first biographer, and his
compilations of fact largely at eyewitness and his inter-
pretations of Whig policy in pushing the War of the Spanish Succession is the real primary source for most subsequent accounts, from the early so-called "lives" to Lediard (1736) and down to Winston Churchill.

June 29.

THE HYPOCRITES. A SATYR. [Motto from Horace] *LONDON*,
Printed in the Year 1703.
    2°: *A*² B-G²; hlft., *bl*., t.p., *bl. iv*, 1-23, *bl.*

28 pp. 472 lines, couplets. Drop-title on p. 1. Wtmk. foolscap. Horn-Luttr. copy used. '8 d- 29. June.' MS. correction of 'miver' to 'miter,' p. 11, and names, such as Tate, Dennis, Ranelagh, Saint John filled in. Morgan F195, limited title only. BM, Bod.

No reference to Marlborough, but fills in background of political satire, and R[oo]ke appears, p. 17. Opens:

> They who have best succeeded in their Rhimes
> Have drest the Verse according to the times.

The zealot, "big with Verse, and fill'd with Godlike Rage" cries out for virtue, virtue which gives crowns to conquerors. Atheism and self-interest abound "Where busie Villains cant up Reformation." Rigby prates for reformation. All is turned to panegyric flattery of the court; there a wit is a gentleman. The playwright cajoles an honor from fools. Fool and fiddler from a foreign nation plus new scenes and songs; all things but wit make a play. Without quite the Swiftian intensity, the tone of the verse suggests the lampooning of Swift. The attack is on "greatness" and lordly haughtiness. The "needy Poet" fawns until his lordship falls from his high place; then he can denounce ambition, lust, and vanity, and even name names. The animosity here anticipates that of the satires on Marlborough after his fall from favor. The picture of

> The great luxurious Prodigals who dare
> Spend their own Wealth and Blood in Foreign War   211-12

who "drunk with Blood. . .revel in Wounds," are "lavish of Deaths, and greedy of Renown."

In allusion to William III, we learn that not long since Providence "refus'd our own, And fix'd a stranger Prince upon the Throne." Much of the verse has the clang of Defoe, especially here where the worship of the new is scored on.

> Then happy who his Pen could first unsheath
> To lash the darling Isle that gave him Breath;
> 'Twas paltry English, barb'rous Insulane,   ⎫
> Their Praise was wisely carry'd to the Main: ⎬
> But had it been a Native's time to reign,   ⎭

They'd ne'er have dar'd to vent their wicked Spleen,
And damn the Race of *True-born Englishmen*.   243-9

Next Blackmore, the BARD, comes in for mild notice; he
"attack'd almighty Wit," but was far from being the thing
"he wou'd lampoon." Wit, once upheld by Waller and Cowley,
may survive in Wycherley and Row[e]; although self-interest,
as with the parsimonious laureate, Tate, and which may
prompt Dennis to write in vain imitation of Pindar, sets
the tone. Is there no difference between a thief and the
man who judges him?

> Pacific P[eer]s, and desperate Men of War;
> Young charming S[eint] J[oh]n and a Murtherer.   319-20

(The words are filled in by Luttrell.) Finally the satire
turns to the merchant trade as the chief occasion for hy-
pocrisy. They import costly wines, fabrics, perfumes and
other encouragements to vice. A powerful, Hogarth-like
picture of the man of ill-got wealth now morose and dis-
eased and embittered, who now "Detests the Sin 'cause he
can do't no more," concludes the portrayal of hypocrites
in poetry and the men poets honor.
    The pertinence of the poem for Marlborough lies
largely in the passages on greatness and men of war; but
also in its inclusion of Blackmore, Dennis, Tate, Rowe,
and others of Marlborough's panegyrists.

July 2.

Congreve, William (1670-1730)

THE TEARS OF *AMARYLLIS* FOR *AMYNTAS*. A PASTORAL. Lament-
ing the DEATH of The Late Lord Marquis of *BLANDFORD*.
Inscrib'd to the Right Honourable the Lord *GODOLPHIN*,
Lord High-Treasurer of *England*. By Mr. *CONGREVE*. [Virg.
3 11.] *LONDON*, Printed for *Jacob Tonson*, within *Gray's-
Inn Gate* next *Grays-Inn-Lane*, 1703. WL, June. Clark-
Luttr. copy used. '4 *d*. 2 July.' Morgan F86. CtY, CU,
DFo, TxU.
    2°: π^2 A-C^2; t.p., *bl*. To the Reader *iii-iv*, 1-8,

drop-title p. 1, 12 pp. In "To the Reader" Congreve specifies the poem written for condolence, but publication has
induced him to have it printed correctly. He has recently
seen *A Satyr against Love* attributed to him, although he
had no previous knowledge of it. The poem opens:

> 'Twas at the Time, when new returning Light,
> With welcome Rays, begins to cheer the Sight.

The anguish of the Duchess of Marlborough at the death of
her only son is powerfully yet delicately portrayed in
pastoral terms. She appeals to the Nymphs and Sylvan Gods,
to the Sun and Winds, and Cruel Earth to relieve her pains.
Finally they voice their grief, while Echo multiplies each
mournful sound. At last tears come, and Amaryllis waters
the tomb of Amyntas. And Amaryllis saw, with wond'ring
Eyes,

> A Flow'ry Bed, where she had wept arise.
> . . . . . .
> For ev'ry Tear, that fell, a Violet grew,
> And thence their Sweetness came, and thence their
>   mournful Hew.   156-9 *passim.*

Future visitors to the tomb are urged to pause and drop a
tear and pluck some flowers in tribute to the dead Amyntas. Congreve has produced a fine expression of pastoral
elegy, and Blandford is interred in an equally fine tomb
in King's College Chapel, Cambridge.
See ELEGIA, No. 31.

36

1704 is the year of the inception of the full
stream of Marlborough panegyric. Only one poem, *Or-
mondus Redux*, dated by Luttrell as on April 22nd, had
broken the silence of the first half of the Blenheim
year. It also marks the virtual eclipsing of Marlborough's only important rival in the English armies,
even though it associates the Duke of Ormond with
Queen Anne as defenders of Europe's cause. That this
partnership was to be based on the victor at the
Battle of Blenheim, August 13, 1704, along with his
coadjutor in the Treasury, the Earl of Godolphin,
became apparent with the arrival of the thrilling news
on August 11, O.S.

The Blenheim documents begin at this point.

The presses poured out pamphlets almost as fast
as Colonel Parke galloped across Europe with the great
news. The first two to appear are German, preceding
his arrival at Dover. At Nürnberg, three days after
the battle, and at Leipzig, four days, the first gazettes appear. Adjusted dates are inserted for these.
The first English accounts are dated on the 11th of
August, which would of course be the 22nd, New Style,
to correspond to the Continental dating of events.
All English datings, unless otherwise specified, will
be Old Style, that is, eleven days earlier. Quite
possibly some foreign pieces have not been located;
but searches in Amsterdam, Vienna, and in some German
libraries, have not revealed any.

Panegyrics prior to Blenheim strikingly reveal
the uncertainties of the poets. Whig writers looked
for a successor to William III in prowess in arms and
also in sustaining the war against France and her ambitions in Spain in particular. Prince Eugene, as
champion of the Austrian Empire, receives repeated
tributes, as does the Duke of Ormond from Tory poets.
However, following the coronation of Queen Anne, it
soon became apparent that Marlborough was her chief
commander, and his successes rapidly established him
as the favorite of the pack of poets who quickly nosed
out political winds and subserviently praised the
favorites. Thus some poems devoted exclusively to
Eugene have a distinct significance for the career of
Marlborough, since he established himself as the leader
in the War of the Spanish Succession, and the two worked
together for the victory at Blenheim and later.

34   April 22.

ORMUNDUS Redux   An HEROICK POEM To His GRACE the Duke
of Ormond. On his Victorious Expedition to *SPAIN*. His
Auspicious Government of *IRELAND*: And Prosperous Return
to *ENGLAND*. [2 lines Virgil] *LONDON*: Printed for *J.
Nutt*, near *Stations-Hall*. 1704
       2°: π^1, A^2, B^2, D-E^2; t.p., *bl*., 1-16, 18 pp., drop-
title p. 1. Wtmk. foolscap and circled PS. Horn-Luttr.
copy used. MS. '6 d.-22. Aprill.' No further markings.
MH, CtY. 713 lines, couplets. *WL*, Apr.; Morgan G362.
Opens:

    Illustrious Prince! who best Your Martial Race
    By your own Valour do Adorn and Grace.

Old Ormond descends from the "bright Regions of Eternal
Day," and bids Ormond to serve Anne by going to Ireland.
That the earlier Ormond is compared to Enoch, translated
unchanged from Earth to Heaven, suggests a clerical
author. The rivers, Boyne and Shannon, no longer show
·the effects of destruction and blood. Ormond, now Albion's sad loss, is but lent to Ireland (Juvernia). The
Austrian Eagle is displaying her wings, bidding him to
come to her aid against the Vulture's (France) claws.
Allusions to the Spanish Succession and England's anti-
French policy lead to a picture of Ossory with bloody
sword; but, Ormond's victory at Vigo surpasses that of
his grandfather at Mons. Ormond is both the Jove and
Mars of Albion. Comparisons to Marlborough, who is
unnamed in the poem, are brought in with the retrievement
theme.

    England's ancient *Honour*, and true Martial Fire,
    Some may *Retrieve* but You Exalt much higher.   132-3

While this follows the allusion to Ormond's father,
Ossory, the retrievement of ancient honor had already
been associated with Marlborough.
    Ormond has proved that "action is the Life of Gov-
ernment," and that it is now apparent how the works of
Fame surpass poetry, and provide the best monuments.
They are "more lasting than the strong *Horatian* Verse."
(While this reverses the usual praise of poetry, it is

part of the convention of poetic modesty.) France and
Spain are compared to two royal stags that fight till a
fierce lion parts them. A lengthy passage condemns avarice, the thirst for gold, the curse of Nero and Cain.
Satan brought this curse to the new world, and Spain has
contracted it, along with France.

> 'Gainst Both these Powerful Foes no Power could stand,
> Till *England* took all Europe's Cause in hand.   279-80

Anne made Ormond her champion, and now Cales proved English valor against Spanish cowardice. Rota, Mattagorda,
San Victoria fall. The account of Vigo begins with dawn,
and is heightened with the sounds of naval battle, and
particularly by Hobson's cutting the boom, and momentous
choice as he breaks the protective barrier.

> Their *Hobson*'s Choice, was here to Burn or Drown,
> Or Piece-Meal mount the middle Region.   441-2

.Thus England is retrieved by Ormond; Anna and Ormond
jointly govern, he "little less than King." She sees
him on hills of slain maintaining British supremacy.
Aged Laertes and young Telemachus rush to pay tribute.
False political doctrines are condemned and put to shame
by Anne's greatness and goodness. The English fight for
honor, the Dutch and the Spaniards for gold (1. 630).
The strongly Tory poem culminates with a picture of
the returning hero, the rejoicing of the people, the procession to St. Paul's, the thanks and praise of the Senate, the flags and streamers filling the air to welcome
Ormond. He is depicted as being what Marlborough soon
after became, virtually joint-ruler.

> If Kings are Gods, such should their Vice-Roys be;
> And Ormond, Anna's Place does Best Supply.   642-3

After such suggestions there was little more than silence
on the Ormond theme, at least until he supplanted Marlborough as chief commander in 1712, after Marlborough's
dismissal from office.

35 [August 5 O. S.]
August 16, 1704

Umständliche Und Weiters ausgeführte RELATION Von der
herrlichen VICTORIE Welche die Hohen ALLIRTEN Gegen
Chur=Bäyern/ und die Frantzosen Am 13 Augusti dieses
Jahres/ glücklich erhalten.
4°: t.p., *ii-iv*, unsgnd., unmbd., 4 pp. No. pub.
BM copy used. Headline:

Nürnberg den 16. Augusti 1704

A factual account of the arrival of the message of
victory, although no location is given, beyond a reference to the Danube. The capture of the French and Bavarian officers, of Tallard, with his son and son-in-law,
and of many banners, and the death or capture of 19,000
of the enemy are mentioned. Concludes: "Dieses ist eine
so herrliche dergleichen man wenig in diesen raisonnabeln
.Frieden!" A paragraph on the siege of Regensburg on the
12th of August fills out the page.

36 [August 6 O. S.]
August 17.

Ausführliche RELATION Von der herrlichen und grossen VIC-
TORIE Welche die Käyserl. unde Hohe Alliirten Gegen Die
Chur=Bäyrische und Französische Armee/ den 13. Augusti
dieses 1704ten Jahrs in der Gegend Hochstädt bey Donawerth
erhalten. (large ornamental, long-necked Eagle at top, a
banner in its beak proclaiming victory, and a sword and
scepter in the claws.)
4°: prose text on three unmbd., unsgnd. pages; large
floral ornaments. No imprint. BM copy used.
A similar account to the preceding but with a headline:

Leipzig den 17. Augusti. 1704.

Not the same wording; Eugene is named before Marlborough.
The battles lasted till 7 in the evening, 16 to 18,000 men
were taken or killed; Tallard, it is asserted, was captured

"auf einer Kleinen Insul" by the Prince of Hesse-Cassel,
although actually it was his aide-de-camp who received
the sword of the conquered marshal. The emphasis of the
report is understandably German. The capture of both
Tallard's son and stepson is noted also.

August 11-14.

The earliest reports of Blenheim in the London Gazettes are included for their bearing on the flood of
panegyrics that ensued. The dates are Old Style, that
is in relation to considering Blenheim as on August 2nd.
Since the battle is customarily dated New Style, that is
the 13th, eleven days later, this must be borne in mind.
Luttrell's datings are also O. S. Thus the first panegyric, No. 42, is dated August 12 by Luttrell.

August 11.

The Daily Courant. Numb. 725. Friday August 11, 1704.
London, August 10. "This Afternoon Collonel Parke arriv'd
Express; with a Letter from the Duke of Marlborough which
(we are informed,) was address'd to my Lord Treasurer,
written by his Grace on Horse-back with a Black-lead Pencil, and imported, that his Grace desir'd my Lord Treasurer to inform the Queen, that the Army had join'd in a
great Victory, and that Marshall de Tallard and two other
French Generals were prisoners. . .in his Coach." Praise
of General Churchill's exploits, that is Marlborough's
brother, follows. The same issue carries an advertisement of the newly presented *Emperor in the Moon*, a play
by Aphra Behn, at Drury Lane, "with a new Prologue occ'd
by the good News of the great Victory over the French and
Bavarians." Of course this bit of verse could lay claim
to being the first panegyrical performance. The note was
delivered to Duchess Sarah, not Lord Treasurer (Godolphin)

41

38   August 12.

The Post-Man Numb. 1306.-Thursday August 10 to Saturday,
August 12, 1704. "On Thursday in the Afternoon Collonel
Parks [*sic*], Aide de Camp to his Grace the Duke of Marlborough, arriv'd. . .The News caus'd universal Joy in
this City. . .firing Cannon in the Tower, the ringing of
Bells, Bonfires, Illuminations, &C." Confusion over the
name of the messenger persists.

39   August 12.

The Flying-Post: or the Post-Master. Numb. 1447. From
Thursday August 10 to Saturday August 12, 1704. While
this is a brief account, and Parke's name appears twice,
it is the first printing of the famous Blenheim note alluded to in the *Post-Man*. A somewhat grudging Tory recognition of victory.
     August 13, Wednesday. The Lord Turnbridge arrived
here this evening. Pirated account of Blenheim and the
taking of Gibraltar. Marlborough's letter included for
the former. Edinburgh. Re-printed by the Heirs and
Successors of *Andrew Anderson*, Printer to the Queen's
most Excellent Majesty, *Anno DOM* 1704. BM copy used.

40   *The London Gazette*. Printed by Edward Jones in the Savoy,
1704. Numb. 4094, Thurs. August 10 to Monday August 14.
This is the official government gazette. Jones, the
second printer of the paper, held the post 1688-1706.
The account repeats that in the *Post-Man*, adding the
Continental date, "the 13th Instant, N. S." It includes
the Blenheim note, and the corrected information of its
delivery. "The Colonel brought a Letter to my Lady Dutchess, which his Grace had written on Horseback with a
Lead-Pencil." A later issue states that he was sent at
7 o'clock in the evening, after the Duke had been 16
hours in the saddle.

1   August 17.

Anne, Queen (1665-1702)

A Proclamation for a Publick Thanksgiving.   We do most
Devoutly and Thankfully Acknowledge the Great Goodness
and Mercy of Almighty God, who has Afforded Us His Protection and Assistance in the Just War, in which, for the
Common Safety of Our Realms, and for Disappointing the
Boundless Ambition of *France*, We are now Engaged, and
hath given to Our Arms, in Conjunction with Our Allies,
under the Command of *John* Duke of *Marlborough*, Captain-
General of our Land-Forces, a Signal and Glorious Victory over the *French* and *Bavarian* Forces at *Blenheim*
near *Hockstet* in *Germany*:   And therefore. . .We have
thought fit, by the Advice of Our Privy-Council, to
Issue Our Royal Proclamation, hereby appointing and
Commanding, That a General Thanksgiving to Almighty
God, for these his Mercies, be Observed. . .upon *Thursday* the Seventh Day of *September* next. . .*Anno R.*
Given at Our Court at St. *James*'s, the Seventeenth Day
of *August*, 1704.   In the Third Year of our Reign.   God
save the Queen [large letters].   *London*, Printed by
Charles Bill, and the Executrix of *Thomas Newcomb*, deceas'd; Printers for the Queens most Excellent Majesty.
1704.
        1°:   1 side, thick paper, 10 1/2 by 13 3/4 inches.
Coat of arms at top center, and large, embellished initial letter W.   This is the conventional format of
proclamations, and is included here for dating and
wording, which is frequently reflected in panegyrics.
Horn copy used.   Not in Morgan, but duplicate of main
title, G321.

August 12.

[Smallwood, James (fl. 1699-1709)]

A Congratulatory Poem   to His Grace the DUKE OF *MARLBOR-
OUGH*, ON His Glorious Success and Victories over the
French and *Bavarians*.   *London*:   Printed by *R. Janeway*,

and Sold by *B. Bragg*, at the *Blue Ball* in *Ave-Mary-Lane*.
1704. MH copy used; Adv. *D. Cour.*, No. 847, Jan. 1705.
Full title, and 'By Dr. Smallwood, Chaplain to his Grace
the Duke of Marlborough. Printed for John Isted and Sold
by B. Bragg, 6 *d*.'
     1/2°: 2 sides; single column, numbd. 70 lines, coup-
lets. MH-Luttr. copy MS. '1 *d*. 12. August. 1704.' No
other markings. Authorship identified as by Smallwood,
in article by R. D. Horn, "The Authorship of the First
Blenheim Panegyric," *HLQ*, Aug., 1961, pp. 297-310. It is
reprinted entire there, and also below, No. 66, *England's
Triumph*, Nov. 1704, pp. 90-92. Opens:

> Brave General, whose Conduct in the Field,
> Where-e'er You come, does Sprouting Lawrels yield.

Thanks to Luttrell's dating, we can establish that
the poem follows hot upon the gazette accounts, and is
interesting primarily for what it includes. "Astonish'd
Nations" wonder at this new victory of Blenheim which is
even more glorious than that which they have just heard
of, that is Schellenberg which opened the way. At Marlborough's birth "auspicious Constellations" of stars sang
in their spheres, that he had come to free nations from
a bloody tyrant. He is seen as threatening haughty
France. He stands as men did at Azencourt, and will go
on to revive the British name. No details of the battle,
such as the Danube drowning and capture of Tallard, appear,
since they were not available prior to this publication in
the papers on the same day. The tribute concludes with
hope that Austria may respond with honors, now that her
Eagle has been aroused and replumed. May more victories
come that will bring "A Peace. . .which by Just War is
sought."
     The emphasis on a war policy as the best means to
controlling Louis XIV and bringing peace for all Europe
is evidence of the Whig character of the panegyric.
Arber lists two sermons by Dr. Smallwood, in February
and April, 1699, III, 106, 135; and Luttrell records the
thanks of the House of Commons, voted "for her sermon
yesterday," *Brief Relation of State Affairs*, Thurs. 6
April, 1699, IV, 502.

3   August 19.

Defoe, Daniel (1660-1731)

The REVIEW of the Affairs of FRANCE: Purg'd from the
Errors and Partiality of the *News-Writers* and *Petty-
Statesmen* of all Sides. Saturday, August 19, 1704, Numb.
48, pp. 205-7. Horn copy of Vol. I used. See Facsimile
ed. for locs. Morgan V334.

   Defoe was in Scotland, and thus denied the triumph
of a scoop, or even early proclamation of Blenheim, although he had urged upon Harley the propagandistic value
to him of news of a military victory. Here, only six
months after the first issue of the *Review*, was a victory
of which Defoe could write, "the Greatest, most Glorious,
and most Compleat Victory that I can find in History for
above 200 years past." No one could rejoice more than he,
the author of the paper. He notices the drowning of the
French cavalry in the Danube, supplies statistics on
prisoners taken, and very astutely comments on the difficulties the French will have in remounting cavalry, since
all their horses have been bought in Germany, Switzerland,
Flanders, and England. With characteristic practicality
and sagacity, Defoe hopes that the Allies will not be made
over-confident by the victory. France has never been put
on the defensive before, and "as a good Peace is the end
of all War," he hopes the King of France will offer good
terms. In spite of his restraint, he asserts that Blenheim is "not only the greatest Action, but has the greatest Consequences of any in the Memory of Man."

   The report in the *Review* is Defoe's first contribution to Marlborough panegyric. It was followed by at
least three major pieces and various minor ones as well
as the faithful reporting of the Duke's activities in the
field of diplomacy.

August 19.

Clare, R. (no dates)

THE ENGLISH HERO: OR, THE *Duke of Marlborough*. A POEM,

Upon the late Glorious Victory over the *French* and *Bavarians*, at *Hochstetten*. Dedicated to Her Grace the Dutchess of *Marlborough*. LONDON Printed, and are to be Sold by *B. Bragg*, in *Ave-Mary-Lane*. Price *Two-pence*. MH, CtY, BM. MH copy used. Haslewood-Luttr. copy supplies date. *P-Man*, Aug. 17-19, This day is publish'd. *WL*, Aug., 1704.

A^2 B^2; t.p., *bl*. To her Grace the Dutchess of Marlborough, sgd. R. Clare, *bl*., 1-4, 8 pp., text 83 lines, couplets. Not in Morgan. Opens:

> Rouze up, ye drowsie Mortals! at the Call
> Of *Victory*'s Triumph, to Rejoice us all.

In addition to identifying Hochsted, as Hochstetten, in the title, the poem is first to include many specific details, particularly the Danube drowning and capture of Marshal Tallard. The French "...in Disorder fly,"

> And court the *Danube* in their Misery,
> Who can no other Succour let 'em have,
> Than yield her Billows up to be their Grave,
> *Bavaria*'s quite undone, and *Tallard* he
> Is taken Prisoner by his *Enemy*.   46-50

The main feature of the poem is emphasis upon Anne's role in the victory, in her choice of the leader and in her own virtue and piety. While this can hardly be seen as detraction from Marlborough, it did become a strong Tory attitude later. Presumably Clare is a conservative cleric from the tone of the poem.

45   August 29.

Defoe, Daniel (1660-1731)

A HYMN TO VICTORY. *LONDON, Printed for J. Nutt*, 1704.

$4°$: $a-G^4$ H^2; *i-viii*, 1-52, 62 pp., 1040 lines, couplets, varying length. Sec. ed. adv. *Review*, Sept. 9. Another ed. printed 2 columns, 12 pp. BM and Horn copies used. "By the Author of the True-born Englishman" added to the title, A^4-F^4; *i-viii*. 1-36, 44 pp. in the *True Collection*, 1705, II, 118-84. The unmbd. *To the Queen*, as its concluding lines show, is obviously added as an afterthought.

The poem is in three sections: I, *To the Queen*, 123 lines; II, *The Hymn*, 860 lines; III, *To the Duke of Marlborough*, 57 lines, total 1040. Drop-title for each part. No. wtmk. Horn copy used of 36 page ed. sgnd. in MS on title, 'Daniel D:Foe' in what may be Defoe's script. Uncut. Morgan G147, Moore 85, Foxon D31-5. Both first and sec. eds. pr. by J. Nutt, and verso of t.p. of the latter are 14 lines Latin verses sgnd. J. C., "*In Celeribam. Victoriam apud Hochstett in Germania.*" One ed. pr. in 2 cols., 4°, no pub., 12 pp., 1704. Foxon reports 3 copies of the piracy in Edinburgh, and suggests printed there. In *Rev.*, V, 49, Defoe, referring himself as champion of truth, remarks, ". . .and how many Satyrs have I had level'd at me for a Poem call'd *A Hymn to Victory*, only because it paid some Respect to the Duke of *Marlborough* and the QUEEN." BM, Bod, BPL, CtY, CSmH, IU, NYPL, TxU. Others in Moore.

To the Queen, sgnd. 'De Foe,' p. vii, opens:

Madam, *The Glories of your Happy reign*
Are seal'd from Heav'n, and Hell resists in vain.

This portion, largely in italics, hails "Female Glories" which may break the usurping chains of France. Ransomed nations bow to Anne, as Marlborough conquers in her name.

*Th'*Imperial Throne your pow'rful Troops restore,
Spain seeks from you her rich Peruvian Shore.   61-2

This portion concludes with a strikingly Defoesque passage on his grievances.

The Humble Muses *now their Tribute pay,*
And sing the Joys of the Triumphant Day.
And now, the meanest of the inspir'd Train,
Supprest by *Fate, and* humbl'd *with Disdain,*
From all the Joys of Art and Life exempt,
Debas'd *in Name, and cover'd with* Contempt,

.   .   .   .

He sings the Glories of your happy Reign,
And humbly then retreats Disconsolate *again,*
Under the Blast of Personal Pique *to die,*
Shaded from all the Blessings of your Eye   112-29
                                passim.
                    De Foe.

The *Hymn* opens:

Hail VICTORY! *Thou Stranger to our land;*
Thou coy, long-courted Mistress of Mankind.

The poem primarily celebrates the English fighting man,
and the return of Victory, known at Cressy, Agen-Court
and Poictiers (1. 57), but now "the Whore of War," and
unknown in England. Even young Nassau was unable to win
her, and she left for France, since the Dutch would not
"defray the Charges of her Train" (1. 148). But at last
Britannia called her over, under William. Traitors and
cowards were startled; these are the men that banished
victory, and made William fight in vain. Party politics
are seen as the "Parties decide the Nation's Doom: Fighting Abroad's a Jest, *The Wars at home*" (11. 205-6).
Political intrigue in "the war at home" dominates Defoe's
interest, till p. 15, when "Marlbro'" is introduced at
Schellemberg [*sic*].
    Instead of description of battle Defoe expatiates
on the English fighting man.

An *Englishman* has something in his Blood,
Makes him love Fighting *better than his Food*;
He will be sullen, lay him down, and die,
If he cannot *Come at* his Enemy:
But, *let him loose*, you fill his Soul with Joy,
He's ravish'd with the Thoughts of *Victory*.   403-7

The French excel at trickery and bribery; but now Tallard,
who had won glory defeating Germans, is asked how he likes
the English fighting spirit. Blenheim, though unnamed, is
reflected in *Danubius*, which provides a "courteous Death"
for the French. An earlier allusion to the defeat of the
Thirty Squadrons who courted the waves (1. 489) is no less
chauvinistic. Bavaria (Max Emmanuel) and Prince Eugenius
are brought in for examples of despicable and glorious

actions respectively; but Fame is adjured to repeat no
more names. It is the army that gets the praise.

> *Never* was Battle better fought,
> *Never* was Vict'ry longer kept in doubt;
> .   .   .   .   .   .
> *Never* was braver Army *better beat.*   786-91 *passim.*

The *Hymn* proper concludes with a picture of Marlborough
calm and sedate in battle; but more direct notice is taken
in the third section, *To the Duke of Marlborough* (pp.
34-6). This portion is preceded by "CONCLUSION," and an
opening address to "SIR,"

> In ancient Time, a far less Fame than yours
> Transpos'd their Heroes *into Heav'nly Powers.*

Marlborough is told that the Glory of his deed *"Stamps
Medals* in the Hearts of *Englishmen"* (1. 15). His battles
establish new peace at home.. The dangers he encounters
on the Rhine and Danube make England more secure. Faction and Party fly before his name. Defoe concludes,
"Let them that Prize you more advance you higher," and
signs his initials 'DF.'
    The *Hymn to Victory,* actually three poems, is the
first of Defoe's three major poems on Marlborough. See
The Double Welcome, No. 95, 1705, and *On the Victories
in Flanders,* No. 153, 1706. Defoe's full attitude toward
Marlborough is implicated in his view of politics, war,
and England's welfare. See *Review,* Aug. 19, No. 43.

6   *ca.* August

Cobb, Samuel (1675-1713)

The Portugal Expedition. To which is added Dr. *G*[art]*h's
Epigram* on the Same Subject, *Ah integro faecinum nasci-
tur ordo.* Virgil. By Mr. *COBB. LONDON:* Printed for
R. Basset, at the *Mitre* in *Fleet-street*; and Sold by
John Nutt, near *Stationers-Hall,* 1704. Price 2*d.*

A^4 A2 only sig.; t.p., *bl.*, 3-8. Main poem, pp. 3-5, 51 lines, couplets. BM copy used. Morgan G113. Opens:

> At length Auspicious Blasts are Heard to blow,
> From Icy Lakes, and Mountains cloath'd with Snow.

The Austrian Prince is urged to set forth with swelling sails. The poem is largely devoted to invoking propitious winds. Anna's breath inspires, but no action is described. Suggests written and published before the great battle. A Latin translation follows, pp. 6-7, *In Caroli* III. *Iter Lusitanicum*, 24 lines. Dr. Garth's Epigram, p. 8, is in 6 lines, for which Cobb supplies a Latin translation. Opens:

> *Pallas* destructive of the *Trojan* Line.
> Raz'd the Proud Walls, tho' built by Hands Divine.

Advs. of books bottom p. 8. No references to Marlborough, but the naval campaign in the Mediterranean was part of his total strategy.

47   (Sept 7, *ca.*)

The QUEEN's *Thanksgiving Hymn*, in *St. Paul*'s Church, for the *Glorious Victory* obtain'd at *Blenheim*, near *Hockstet*, in *Germany*, on the 13th of August, 1704. [Judges V:12, 1 line]   *London*, Printed for *William Turner*, at the *Angel* at *Lincolns-Inn Back-Gate*, and *J. Nutt*, near *Stationers-Hall*. 1704. Price 2 *d.*
    4°: *i-ii*, 3-7, *bl.* 8 pp. Ind. U. only copy. Used photostat. 82 lines. Not in Morgan. *The Invitation* opens:

> O magnifie the Lord of Hosts with ME,
> Sole Author of our *Glorious Victory.*   Psalm 34

A conventional, but enthusiastic, celebration of Blenheim. The *Hymn* proper opens:

> With Joy, let all the People Clap their Hands;
> This Tribute, now, our Gratitude Commands.
>
> Psalm 47, 1

Every stanza paraphrases a Scriptural passage from the
Psalm. Credit is given to God as the choir sings glory
to His praise. The concluding *Acclamation* opens:

> Thou, Blest, forever, be the Lord of Hosts;
> The God who *England* Loves, in whom *She* boasts.

A *Doxology* in 6 lines concludes the whole.

8   September 7.

The Royal Triumph: A Poem. To Her most Excellent *Majesty*
Queen Anne, On Her going in State, to St. *Paul's* Cathedral,
to return Thanks to God, for the Success of Her Majesties
Arms, in Conjunction with the Allies. *London:* Printed by
R. Tookey, and are to be Sold by *S. Malthus* in *London-
House-Yard*, at the west End of St. Paul's.
   2°: 2 sides, 1 column. 2 pp., 47 ll. Hymn-ode
style, alternate and random rhyme. MH-Luttr. copy used.
Only copy known. Not in Morgan. Opens:

> Hail, *Britain*'s Queen, and Empress of the Sea!
> The World's Protectress, hail!

Strong Biblical emphasis and Tory tone. Marlborough is
compared to Barach, and Queen Anne to Deborah, Hester, and
Judeth [*sic*], who treads on the Gallic Holophernes's head.
As they pass through the triumphal Temple Bar archway the
statue of Elizabeth can look upon her, and if she could
speak would admit that "You and your *Rook*, have Her and
her *Drake* out-done." Concludes on the theme of the Spanish Succession,--"To You the Emp'rour owed his Crown, You
made his Son a King." Inclusion of the Danube drowning
is evidence of this detail having been established as one
of the hallmarks of the victory. Here it is significantly
associated with Egyptians drowning in the Red Sea upon the
escape of the chosen people. As "th'*Egyptians* perish in
the flood,

O're which their Leader stretch'd his Hand.
Miriam her thankful Voice to Heav'n did raise;
It was a Woman sung the Hymns of Praise.
So, whilst Great Marlborough thro' the Danube drives
   The Armies of our Foes,
     'Till the choak'd [*sic*] Stream the Bank o'erflows,
Our pious QUEEN to Heav'n the Glory gives.   21-7

49   September 9.

ON THE DUKE of *MARLBOROUGH*'s *Victory.*

Published in *Post-Man: And the Historical Account*, &c.
No. 1312. From Thursday Sept. 7 to Saturday Sept. 9,
1704. 35 lines, couplets, and among the earliest allusions in verse to the Danube drowning at Blenheim. Preceded by note:

> The Muses have so much used themselves to Hyper-
> bole's and other high-strain'd Figures, that they
> have long ago been banish'd from History, where
> matters of fact ought to appear in their greatest
> simplicity, without any Ornament. . .This paper
> being an account of the daily transactions in the
> World, we have avoided to meddle with Verse, ex-
> cept when upon great occasions, and if ever we had
> reason to dispence [*sic*] with our Resolution, sure
> we may be allow'd to do it at this time, when all
> the World rings with the praise of the Duke of
> Marlborough. This Muse is altogether a Stranger
> to us, but she has so civilly requested a place
> in our Paper, to Sing the Glory of this Great Man,
> who has rescu'd the Empire, that we could not
> deny it. . .

The poem opens:

> Fame Sound thy Trumpet! Sound forth Marlborough's Name,
> Let rescu'd Germany with joy proclaim,
> And France with Terror own, His never dying Fame.

At Marlborough's advance, Suabia raised her drooping
head. Heaven had designed that Britain give law to balance Europe and her states. She smiled on the "Glorious
March."

> This well concerted March owes nought to Chance,
> Baffles the Troops and Politicks of France.   15-16

Haughty Lewis is repulsed by the sword which, as a note
indicates, Charles the 3d has given to the conqueror.
With this he rescues Europe and the Empire.

> Such Glorious Acts the Muses shall Rehearse,
> In lofty Numbers, and never dying Verse,
> T'instruct the Age to come, to whom they owe their
> Peace.
> Your Battels they hereafter shall indite,
> And draw the Image of Our MARS in Fight,
> Of sinking Squadrons tell, Batallions flying,
> The Fields and Danube too fill'd with the dying,
> A Captive Marshal, an Electorate forsaken,
> An Army slaughter'd, and an Army taken!
>
> Thus to your Fame Posterity shall bow,
> And pay the same Applause, as we do now.   25-35

50   September 12

Sherlock, Dean William (1641?-1707)

A Sermon Preach'd before the *Queen*, at the Cathedral
Church of St. *Paul, London*, On the *Seventh* of *September*,
1704. Being the Thanksgiving-Day for The Late Glorious
Victory obtain'd over the *French* and *Bavarians* at *Blenheim* near *Hochstet*, on *Wednesday* the Second of *August*,
by Forces of Her Majesty and Her Allies, under the Command of the Duke of *Marlborough*. By *William Sherlock*,
D. D. Dean of St. *Paul*'s, Master of the *Temple*, and Chaplain in Ordinary to Her Majesty. Publish'd by Her Majesty's Special Command. London: Printed for *W. Rogers*,

53

at the *Sun* against St. *Dunstan*'s Church in *Fleetstreet*.
MDCCIV.

4°: A^4 B-D^4; hft. p. 1, *bl.*, t.p., *bl. iv*, 1-26,
bl., 32 pp. Running title as headline throughout. Horn
copy used. Adv. in the *Post-Man*, No. 1316, Sept. 9-12,
as printed for W. Rogers and Thos. Knaggs, at Knight's
Bridge Chapel, and Pr. for J. Barnes. Morgan G429.

Inclusion of this sermon is to indicate this is another type of printed tributes to Marlborough, even
though this intensely Tory sermon barely mentions him.
All attention is turned to the text from Psalm 11, st.,
viii, on the rewards of righteousness. Only one mention of Marlborough, p. 24, and to no others by name.
The deeds of heroes are the evidence of God's justice
and rewards of virtue in service of the Crown. Breaking
the power of France establishes that "it is in vain for
any Prince to Affect an Universal Empire while an *English Queen* sits upon the Throne." Reference is made to
the gazettes and prints, and to the glory attaching to
Marlborough's being entrusted with such a mission by her
Majesty and her Allies, "as glorious an Action, as any
upon Record."

51   September 16.

By a Lady. *A POEM to Her GRACE the Dutchess of Marlborough*. Occasion'd *by the late Glorious Victory obtain'd
by his Grace the Duke of Marlborough*, over the *French*
and *Bavarians* at *Hochstet*. Written by a LADY. *LONDON:
Printed for Abel Roper, at the Black Boy in Fleetstreet*,
MDCCIV. Luttr. MS. '16 Septemb.' 321 lines, couplets.

2°: A^2 B-C^2; t.p., *bl.*, 1-10, 12 pp. 10 reversed
to read *01*, To Her Grace the Dutchess of *Marlborough* as
drop-title p. 1. Fleur-de-lis wtmk. NN, OCU, WL, Sept.
1704. Horn copy used. Has 'Agrippina' in contmp. MS at
end. Morgan G322. Opens:

Pardon me, Madam, if in humble strain,
I sing the Glories of a Female Reign.

Celebrates female reign, and also the retrievement of the
honor of Edward's days. Marlborough freed Belgium, and
now goes to the aid of Caesar, that is the Empire and
Austria, on Ister's (the Danube's) banks. Troy is now
in ruins, except as it survives in Homer's fire. Churchill's valor demands equal poetic tribute; but poets now
serve lewd passions and bow to faction.
　　　Military themes open with siege of Liege. Marlborough is seen as mild in victory, not delighting in blood.
A mild Tory case is apparent in praise of Ormond and Rook,
but the poem goes on to Blenheim.

　　　Loose in the Air a thousand Ensigns play,
　　　And Spears like Forrests intercept the Day.　　222-3

A new detail is noted in that Marlborough commands the
squadrons of horse, and his brother the foot. The Danube
drowning is quite effectively introduced.

　　　In num'rous Squadrons Swimming Men and Horse,
　　　Obstruct the Stream, and stop the Rivers Course. 270-1

Tallard meets defeat and the Noricians, that is Bavarians,
run for hiding. The poet now directs her muse to turn
from the hero to the Queen. "Heaven approves the justice
of her Arms." Long may her People bless her gentle sway.
May "Envy, Strife, and Faction cease, And Crown her Days
with everlasting Peace." (320-1)
　　　The defensive tone of the poem, urging the justice of
the war as seeking security and lasting peace, is its most
prominent feature. It betrays no evidence of a feminine
pen, and may well be one of those poems which were inscribed as "By a Lady" though having a masculine author.

2　　　September 18.

Johnson, Charles (1679-1748)

A Congratulatory VERSE, To Her Grace, the Dutchess of
MARLBOROUGH: On the Late GLORIOUS VICTORY, Near HOCH-
STET in GERMANY. *August* the 2d 1704. [6 lines Horace]

LONDON; Printed for *Robert Battersby* at *Staple-Inn Gate*, against the Barrs in *Holbourn*. 1704. MH-Luttr. MS '3 d. 18 Septemb.' No other markings.

2°: t.p., *bl.*, PREFACE to the READER, *ii-iv*, 1-4, no sigs.; *i-iv* 1-4, 8 pp. Colophon rptd. bottom p. 4. Printed for *Robert Battersby*, at *Staple-Inn-Gate*, in *Holbourn*. 1704. The poem is signed: "Grays Inn. I am Your Graces, Most Obedient, and Most Humble Servant, Charles Johnson." Also a drop-title on p. 1 is addressed "To the Most Illustrious Princess, *Sarah*, Dutchess of *Marlborough*." *Post-Man*, Sept. 16-18, 1704, 'This Day is publish'd.' 108 lines, couplets. Morgan G263. Opens:

> MADAM, amidst the numerous crouds that wait,
> Your happy HERO to congratulate.

The preface expresses the poetic convention of modesty. The poet does not feel equal to celebrating such a great action, including the retrieving of ancient English honor. He quotes: "The HERO's Acts transcend the Poets Verse." He is presenting only a "Grateful Spark of that Fire of Joy I could not conceal."

This is the first of three poems which Johnson wrote on Marlborough's victories. Since he went on later to make some reputation with his definitely Whiggish plays, he may be recognized as second after Defoe in the line of panegyrists with some reputation. An article by M. M. Shudofsky, *ELH*, X, June, 1943, notices only two of the poems and makes only slight recognition of Johnson's political emphasis in his writing.

The poem opens with more on the poet's sense of inadequacy -- "were my Verse but equal to my Zeal." He needs Ovid's softness, Virgil's and Homer's nervous strength. Then he urges his Muse to celebrate Marlborough's great actions, a hero born to "vindicate the Liberty of Man." Soldiers are taught by their great leader, and Bavaria feels his power. "Ask the insulted *Danube*'s Crimson Flood," leads to the now well-established drowning episode of the Household squadrons of horse.

> Ask the insulted *Danube*'s Crimson Flood,
> Who dyed her bright transparent Streams in Blood.
>
> 37-8

The French Household Troops hide their dishonour in the
wave. The Whig note of liberty is reiterated, in the
rescue of "injured Europe," and the rescue of Germany.
The remainder of the poem mixes allegorical figures of
Envy, Joy, and Echo, or 'Eccho' as Johnson spells it in
all three of his poems, with allusions to battle. More
important is the introduction of a Miltonic note. Envy,
after she spits out her hate of Marlborough, "Then casting round her baleful Eyes, she flew," and withdraws from
battle, a distinctly Miltonic image. The poet expresses
the hope that Envy will no longer curse England, "And
Meditating Secret Mischiefs."
      The poem concludes with scorn for France and her
Salique law, now that Queen Anne has shown her superior
force. Johnson also disdains France's Salique law in
The Queen in the following year 1705.

September 18.

THE VICTORY. A POEM. In Two PARTS. I. To the QUEEN.
II. To the Duke of Marlborough. *LONDON*: Printed and
sold by *Benjamin Bragg*, in *Avemary Lane*. 1704. Price
Sticht 6d.
      2°: A-C^2; t.p., *bl*., 3-12, 14 pp. Drop-t. p. 3,
and for Part II, p. 11. CtY, MH, *WL*. Sept. 1704. Horn-
Luttr. copy used. MS '6d. - 18 Septemb.' No other markings. 252 lines, 212 in couplets. Morgan G485. Opens:

   Madam,
      Inspir'd by You, what can our thoughts restrain?
   To Sing the Trophies of Your Happy Reign.

Part I praises Anne against tottering France; her conquests on the banks of the Danube surpass all the glories
of William III. With his death, Spain and France conspired, along with Bavaria's Elector, against Vienna;
but "As Brave a Man as 'ere the Empire knew," that is
Prince Eugene, opposed them. After slaughtering thousands of Turks, he conquered at Buda and Belgrade. Eugene
is triumphant in battle, but hard pressed, till heroic

Marlborough comes, sword in hand, to his rescue. The
poet urges the Nine Muses to inspire his verse, and does
rise to the challenge of Blenheim where Tallard fought,
till Marlborough overcame him and his fifteen generals.
The banks and waves of the Danube strike terror into the
enemy's face. "Amidst the Courteous Stream they faintly
Dy'd." The Imperial Eagle bows to Marlborough alone, by
him saved from the power of France.

The Tory tone is apparent in urging Eugene's claims,
and in the conclusion where Anne is described, a "Blessing. . .from the Supream Authority of Heaven," that is
favored by Divine Right (p. 10). Let us reflect on her
glories and how she conquers factions at home.

The Second Part, 40 lines in ode style, hails the
godlike hero. He overcomes Tallard, and submits his
forces to the Danube, "to exalt Great *Anne*'s Triumphant
Name." He is urged to go on to further great victories,
but is reminded "Anne was still the Royal Word; That
Victory again to Us restor'd." The emphasis upon Queen
Anne's role over Marlborough's is another distinctly Tory
feature.

54   September 30.

Ivoy, Colonel (Frederick Thomas Hongest d'Ivoy)

A Full and Impartial Relation of the Battle fought on the
13th of August [N. S.] in the Plain of Hochstette, between
the Villages of Pleintheim, Overklaw, and Lutzingen, etc.,
by an Officer who was in the Engagement. *London*: (Sold
by J. Nutt, near Stationer's Hall.) Price 1s. 6d. Adv.
in The *Post-Man*, No. 1323, Sept. 28-30; in *London Gazette*,
No. 4058, Sept. 28-Oct. 2. Same title Sold by David
Mortier Bookseller at Erasmus's Head, near the Fountain
Tavern in the *Strand*, *Post-Man*, No. 1325, Oct. 3-5. The
Post-Man, Oct. 5-7 identified as being "Exactly drawn by
Collonel Ivoy, Quarter Master General under the Duke of
Marlborough." Also adv. in the *Flying Post*, Oct. 17-19.
    4°: A-E^4; 1-19, prose account. By courtesy of
Peter Smithers, M.P. Morgan G204.

5   September 30.

Prior, Matthew (1664-1721)

A LETTER TO Monsieur Boileau Depreaux [*sic*]; Occasion'd
by the VICTORY at *BLENHEIM*, 1704. [3 lines Hor.] *LONDON*,
Printed for *Jacob Tonson*, within *Gray-Inn* Gate next *Grays-
Inn Lane*. 1704.
   2°: A²-C²; t.p., *bl*., 1-10. Full t. rptd. as drop-
title on p. 1. 183 lines, couplets, 12 pp. Luttr. MS
'30 Septemb.' BM, Bod, CtY, CSmH, MH, TxU. Morgan G390.
Opens:

   Since hir'd for Life, thy Servant Muse must sing
   Successive Conquests, and a happy King.

   This piece is remarkable for several features. Not
only is it a good.expression of "easy Mat's" genius, and
thus the first and only witty panegyric, it is also the
first Blenheim poem from Tonson's press. Previous productions had been predominantly by John Nutt or Benjamin
Bragg; but now at least a. dozen, more moderate and better
printed productions reflect a higher status for the great
victory in national eyes. While in the 1704 folios the
lesser printers used a good format and paper, they still
admitted errors in printing and other evidences of hasty
production.
   Prior twits Boileau on his problems in having to
"loudly boast" of his sovereign with laurels, "Whatso'er
they cost." What can he say about one day in which a
single English subject broke the proud column built up
over sixty years? He suggests that *Bavaria's* Stars may
be accused," and that "Fate mistook tho' LEWIS order'd
right." This irony is followed by witty deploring of
the difficult names for a poet to put into rhyme: Wagen-
hen, Arnheim, and *"Wurtz*---who could mention in Heroic
Wurtz?" Anne has sent more harmonious names from the
Tweed and Thames to conquer, Hamilton, Lumley, Palmes,
Ingoldsby, and above all 'Marlbro.' He grants to his
"old Friend old Foe," that verse makes difficulties as
compared with prose. Military facts and figures are not
poetic, as a sample shows.

> In one great Day on HOCHSTET's fatal Plain
> FRENCH and BAVARIANS Twenty Thousand slain;
> Push'd thro' the DANUBE to the shoars of STYX
> Squadrons Eighteen, Battalions Twenty-Six:
>
> . . . . . .
>
> Tell me, is this to reckon or rehearse? 54-64
> A Commissary's List, or Poet's Verse? *passim.*

Anyone who can sum up Lewis's loss in rhyme could make Newton's books fit with Dryden's style.

Prior, on his side, would sing Arms and a Queen. He would summon all the muses to his aid, and depict her as attended by the gods of war and love, by nymphs and tritons, and Thames would rise with anchor and silver oar to complain of the enslavement of his brother streams by the Seine, for the Maes, the Waal, and Rhine and Saar all feel the burden of oppressive war. Anne calls forth her general, without naming any bounty or proclaiming his worth. Obedient to her command, Marlborough leaves. Then descends to him the fairest child of Jove, with palm and lawrel, the figure of Victoria. She promises him greatness and fame.

> At Schellenberg I'll visit Thee again,
> And sit propitious on Thy Helm in *Blenheim's*
>   glorious Plain. 132-3

He sails to Belgia, which almost ceases to weep the loss of William. He sees half Germany combined with France; but this does not deter him. He goes into battle with the cry, "ANNE and *St. George*." The Ninth Victoria comes to the Hero, and the enemy recede as the Roman Eagle hears the victorious roar of the British Lion. Such thoughts, for there is no description of battle, make the poet wish to rise to Virgil's level; but "I ne'r was Master of the Tuneful Trade," he remarks. His small genius is inadequate; but he hopes he may some younger Muse incite to let France know "As we have Victors we have Poets too." Though we may quarrel at home, we can join forces against the arrogance of France. The poem concludes:

> Whilst MARLBRO's Arm eternal Lawrel gains,
> And in the Land where SPENCER sung, a new ELISA
>   reigns. 182-3

Although Prior's name frequently appears in later panegyric, his poem did not meet the occasion. He had "strenuously sought Marlborough's favor," according to Charles K. Eves, *Prior*, pp. 190-2; but Halifax turned to Addison for proper celebration of Blenheim. *The Campaign* came from Tonson's press ten weeks later. Except for this poem, only Prior's has enjoyed the advantages of modern editorial study. In their edition of *The Literary Works of Matthew Prior*, H. Bunker Wright and Monroe K. Speaks (Oxf. Pr., 1959), I, 220-6, supply variants between the 1704 folio and the numerous changes in the 1709 and 1718 collected editions. The number of lines is increased from 183 to 201, most of the changes being for improvement of the versification, for clarity or for euphonious effect. Though it provides an interesting study in the "correct," substantive changes are slight.

October 5.

Ivoy, Colonel

The True Plan of the Battel fought at *Pleintheim* near *Hochstet* the 2d of August 1704, O.S. Exactly drawn by Collonel Ivoy, Quarter Master General under his Grace the Duke of *Marlborough*, and curiously engraven on 2 Copper Plates near 2 foot square, where by the true plan may be distinguish'd from all Counterfeits. With a Full and Impartial Relation of the whole Action, and exact References to the Plan. Written by Coll. *Ivoy*, N.B. The several Batallions and Squadrons distinguish'd by their proper Colours. Sold by J. Nutt near Stationers-Hall, and David Morier Book and Mapseller at the Sign of Erasmus Head in the Strand. Price 1s. 6d. Adv. in *Post-Man*, No. 1331, Tuesday, Oct. 7 to Thurs. Oct. 9. Not in Morgan.

HLS Copy

57   October 13.

[Hare, Francis, D. D. (1671-1740)]

An Exact Journal of the Campaign in Germany for the Year
1704 under Conduct of his Excellency John Duke of Marlborough. . .giving an Impartial Account of the Two Famous
battles of *Schellenberg* and *Blenheim*, London, Printed for
J. Nutt, near *Stationers-Hall*, 1704.
    4°:   64 pp.   BM.   Used Sec. Ed. Horn copy.   T.p., *bl.*,
To the Reader *ii-iv*, 1-74.   Morgan H284. *Daily Cour.* Numb.
780, Sunday, Oct. 14, 1704.   'Yesterday was publish'd.'
Text used extensively in Hare's *Life and Glorious History
of John Duke of Marlborough*, 1705.   See article on this
cited above, "Marlborough's First Biographer: Dr. Francis Hare," *HLQ*, XX, No. 2 (Feb.) 1957, 145-62.   No summary
of the content of the prose pamphlets and accounts is
given here.   For further details see Aug. 16, 1705, No.
112, Sec. Ed., as *The History of the Campaign in Germany*,
No. 90.   Except for the gazettes, this is probably the
first printed description of Blenheim.

58   October 17.

A FULL and Impartial Relation of the BATTLE Fought on the
13th of August, 1704. N.S. In the Plain of HOCHSTETTE Between the Villages of *Pleintheim* and *Lutzingen*, Wherein,
The Army of the High Allies, under the Command of his
Grace the Duke of *Marlborough*, and Prince *Eugene* of *Savoy*,
obtained a most Compleat and most Glorious Victory over
the Combin'd Forces of the Elector of *Bavaria*, and the
Marshals of *France*, *Tallard*, and *Marsin*.   By an Officer
who was in the Engagement.   *LONDON*: Printed for *Ben
Bragge*, in *Avemary-Lane*, 1704.   Price 6 *d.*
    2°:   A-E²; t.p., *bl.*, 3-19, *20*, drop-t. on p. 3.
Prose.   Adv. *London Gazette*, No. 4058, Sept. 28 to Oct.
2, 1704; *Post-Man*, No. 1323, Sept. 28-Oct. 3, but also
has No. 1330, Oct. 14-17, 'This day is publish'd.'
Morgan G204.
    A strictly technical and factual account, apparently

by an adjutant. Some phrases and considerable detail
duplicate Hare's account in 1705, No. 57 preceding; but
this appears to be an independent account. The spelling
Pleintheim, for Blenheim, is rare. It is used in a manuscript record of the entire campaigns of Marlborough,
from 1702 through 1713; but the officer who wrote it had
not yet taken to detailed description such as appears
later. He has the terse phrase, "Fought the Battle of
Plentheim, & lay in the Field of Battle all Night." The
manuscript, 408 folio pages, was purchased by the author
through a dealer from the Earl of Lonsdale's Library. It
includes much concrete information, officers of the day,
passwords, or paroles, marching orders, injunctions
against marauding, courts martial, and extended description of later actions. Since the compiler is not identified, it was presumably an adjutant.

October 21.

Mareschall *TALLARD*'s *Aid-de-Camp*: His Account of the
BATTLE OF BLEINHEIM. IN A LETTER Written by him from
Strasburg, to Monsieur de *Chamillard*, a Minister of State
in *France*; and intercepted, and sent over to a Foreign
Minister, residing in *England*. Wherein Some passages of
that Memorable Day, are more fully and impartially related, than in any Relation yet made Publick. *Both in*
French *and* English. *LONDON*, Printed, and Sold by *John
Nutt* near *Stationers-Hall*, 1704. Price 6 d. Horn copy
of *The Second Edition; with a Letter from the Adjutant
of the* Gendarmerie, *to Monsieur de* Chamillard. August
the 28. 1704. *N. S.* Adv. in *Post Man* No. 1332, Oct.
19-21, 1704, plus three later issues.
    4°: *A* B-F², D not signed; t.p., Adv. of Ivoy's
Exact Plan on ii, *1*, 2-18, 7-10, 24 pp. Morgan G466.
    This prose account is marked with much precise de-
tail of the battle, and is innocent of the chauvinism
that infects most military accounts. While the French
gendarmerie repulses the attack on their stronghold in
Bleinheim, as it is called, the enemy is credited with

plenty of courage. Marsin's troops need to be awakened
from their "FATAL DROUSINESS!" In the defeat *"Our Troop-
ers fled, and our poor Batallions were cut in pieces."*
Many are forced into the Danube, accepting drowning
rather than capture. Marlborough is named only once, in
the strategy of using a prisoner, Mons. de Nonville, to
persuade the French to surrender and save their lives.
A certain amount of recrimination, particularly between
various divisions of the French army, is apparent, particularly in the second item, the adjutant's of the gendarmerie. He observes that "the Mareschal de *Tallard*
had no kindness for us," although on being taken prisoner he honored the gendarmes with some compliments.
Both letters are given in English translation, followed
by the originals in French.

60   October 24.

R., R.

Epinikion Marlburiense. BLEINHEMIANUM: 2° August 1704.
Non Sine Clade.   PARLAMENTO Pio Convento 24 *Octobris* 1704.
     2°: A²; t.p., *bl.*, *iii*, 1-5; 8 pp.   95 lines.   To
the Most Illustrious *John* Duke of *Marlborough*, Captain
General of the Queen of *England*'s Armies Abroad, &c., p.
iii, sgnd. 'R. R.' in large letters. Not in Morgan.
Bodleian copy only one located. Used by courtesy of the
Bodleian Library. No advs.
     Although the title is in Latin the address to Marl-
borough and the poem are in English. R. R. calls his
piece a "Stripling Essay," and it is so grammatically as
well as poetically. He offers it "towards Acknowledgment
of many Favours from you [Marlborough]." He states that
Marlborough's grandfather "was long Imprison'd, and his
antient fair Estate long sequester'd for Loyalty to our
Queen's Grandfather." Yet Charles II appointed him to
protect the nation and its religion; he was by Turenne
"enter'd into Arms," he protected Queen and Consort at
the "happy Revolution," and is now "Declared General;"

and now he has "redeem'd not only *England*, but all *Europe*
also by a Stratagematical Victory." The poem opens
without drop-title:

> Before the Queen o' th' *French* was grown Mis-spired
> By th' *Cardinal*, And by his Torch was Fir'd.

England was at ease till the Queen opened Pandora's box
and released Louis the Monster. He swore he would gnaw
into the church, fracacie [*sic*] the islands, and enslave
all. The poet names nineteen regions, from Holland to
the Indies, urging them to speak out against the Levia-
thans. He fears only bullets and honesty. Marlborough,
chosen by the Queen and Parliament, prayed, then charged
and rescued Prince and Empire; haughty Tallard was
forced to succumb. Crowds of French cowards chose
Pharaoh's death to escape him. Marlborough, victorious,
prayed and cried, ". . .to God's Name be Glory." Now he
is bringing home the ensigns of France, and is welcomed
as preserver of the crown. It may be the first pun on
the name -- "Our *Churches Hill*, still may our *Churchill*
Guard" -- but neither this nor another monstrous pun
serves to lift a dull poem. The piece concludes:

> Dis-sheath'd, I'le Stand or Fall, *Huzzah* Your Fame,
> And hope this LOU*p*, you'll *Tallardize*, or Tame.
> Tho' I can't reach what to your Glory's due,
> My Sword shall make out, what my Pen can't do. 92-5

It should be noted that the date on the title-page is not
that of publication. The line, *"Welcome, In-Laurell'd
SIR,"* suggests that it may have been issued on the Duke's
return to England in December.

November 4.

S., R., Capt.   (Richard Steele, 1672-1729)

An imitation of the Sixth ODE of *Horace*, beginning, *Scri-
beris vario fortis.* Apply'd to his Grace the Duke of

MARLBOROUGH. Suppos'd to be made by Capt. R. S. First pr. in *The Diverting Post*. From *Saturday* October 28, to *Saturday November* 4, 1704. 30 lines, octosyllabic couplets. Sec. ed. in *Oxford and Cambridge Miscellany Poems*, (1708), ed. Elijah Fenton., Pr. for Bernard Lintott, pp. 319-20. Identified in Table of Contents as "By Captain Steel." Also in *Odes and Satires of Horace*, 1715 and Thomas D'Urfey, *Wit and Mirth; or Pills to Purge Melancholy*, 1719, III, 351. Not in Morgan.

Also printed in *The Occasional Verse of Richard Steele*, Oxf. Pr., ed. Rae Blanshard, 1952, 14-15. Opens:

> Shou'd Addison's immortal Verse,
> Thy Fame in Arms, great Prince, rehearse.

An appeal to Addison, as master of epic, that is, heroic, verse, to celebrate Blenheim, the proud Bavarian's fall, "And in the *Danube* plunge the *Gaul* (the French)." The poet does not dare attempt praise of Marlborough or the Queen. His muse is equal only to "trifling cares," and instead of battling troops can "paint the soft Distress and Mien," and the "little Follies of the Fair." He concludes:

> A slender stock of Fame I raise,
> And draw from others Faults, my Praise.

While the importance of this slight piece rests primarily on its being the work of Steele, it is significant as calling attention to Addison as the proper poet for Blenheim. While it precedes the *Campaign* by six weeks, Addison was probably already at work on that poem.

62   November 6.

[Browne, Joseph]   Ascribed to William Oldisworth (1680-1734)

Albion's *Naval Glory*, or Britannia's Triumphs: A POETICAL ESSAY Towards a Description of a SEA FIGHT. Occa-

sion'd by the Late Engagement BETWEEN THE *ENGLISH*, *DUTCH*, and *FRENCH* FLEETS in THE Mediterranean SEA, August the 13*th*, 1704 [2 lines Virgil] *LONDON*, Printed in the *New Exchange* in the *Strand*; and Sold by *Benj. Bragg*, in *Avemary Lane*, 1705 (Price Six Pence.)
2°: A^1 B-D^2; t.p., *bl.*, *iii-iv*. To the Right Honourable Sir George Rooke, ...Shovel, ...Leake, ...Dilks, Wishart, Jennyngs; *bl.*, 5-16, 16 pp. No wmk. Drop-t. p. 5; Errata bot. p. 16. Haslewood-Luttr., Nov. 6; *D. Cour.* No. 804, Sat. Nov. 11, 1704. 'Newly publish'd.' 280 lines, couplets. Bod. copy used. Not in Morgan. Opens:

I sing the Pride of *Albion*, and the Pow'r
That guards our own, and threats the *Gallick* Shore.

No allusions to Marlborough appear, since the poem is in the Tory tradition of playing up Rooke's victory at sea against the Duke's on land. It may be noted that the date, August 13th, is New Style, and that the corresponding date for Blenheim is the 2nd, eleven days earlier; or taking the customary dating of Blenheim, the 13th, the victory at Gibraltar would have the corresponding date of the 24th.

[Browne, Joseph] Ascribed to William Oldisworth. Redaction of the previous poem. A Poetical ESSAY ON THE *Last Sea-fight with the* French *August* 12. 1704. *State Miscellany Poems by the Author of the 'Examiner'*, 1715, II, *58-71*. 246 lines, couplets. TxU copy used. This is a shorter version of *Albion*'s *Naval Glory*. The poems ascribed to Oldisworth are reported by Foxon as by Joseph Browne. Vivid pictures of the "floating Citadels" in combat in "seas where Romans sailed" (ll. 100-1).

Here Legs and Arms in wild Disorder flie
While furious Flames amidst the tackling fly;
This way they run to prop the falling Mast,
Men leave't to save the sinking Ship with haste:

Here a Broad-side has pour'd a Deluge in,
Than at the Pump they work with all their mein,
To pour the Sea into the Sea again.   104-10

At the conclusion

fierce Artillery proclaim
Great ANNA's Glory and Immortal Fame.   225-6

64   November 21.

Denne, Mr. Henry, Trinity College, Cambridge (fl. 1704)

Marlborough: AN Heroic Poem. By Mr. *DENNE*. [2 ll. Horace, 1 line Virg.] *LONDON*, Printed by *W. Downing*, and are to be Sold by *B. Bragge* at the *Blue-Bell*, in *Avy-Mary Lane*. 1704. Dedication 'To His Grace the Duke of Marlborough' sgnd. Henry Denne.
   4°: A^2 B-D^4; t. p., *i-iv*, 1-24. Drop-t., p. 1.
Adv. *Flying Post* or *Post Master*, Numb. 1490, Sat., Nov. 18 - Tues. 21, 'This Day is publish'd.' 28 pp. 855 lines. Only copy known at Newberry Lib., Chicago. Used by courtesy. *WL*, Dec. Not in Morgan.
   The Epistle Dedicatory effusively praises Marlborough as "Hero of the dawning Century." We feared slavery from the union of France and Spain; but Schellenberg and Blenheim have changed all to dazzling serenity. Her Majesty's choice of a leader whose "triumphs will be a Propagation of Arts, and Britain become the Academy of *Europe*" is praised. Holland and the Empire rejoice and acknowledge Marlborough's claims to gratitude. Opens:

Fame, for a while, 'till *British* Arms appear,
Is silent; but then spreads the *Gallic* Fear.

Fame follows the British cross, although false rumors of victory set France to vain rejoicing. Louis is exposed as Magnus, the grand imposter, abetted by wily, shifty Richelieu. Magnus threatens the Empire, but Marlborough, an English Scipio, crosses the Rhine and Danube. He is

accompanied by many leaders, Cutts and Eugene alone being
named. The signal given, the brazen cannon roar, "And
Rings of curling Smoke expel the Day."
    Blenheim and the drowning of the French are presented
largely by abstract references to flames and conquest. As
poetry this is one of the flattest of the panegyrics, conventional in form and detail, and strikingly devoid of
concrete references, aside from a few names. One possible
innovation is the introduction of the "advice to a painter"
device at two points."

> Paint *Marlborough* in Sweat, and Dust, and Blood,
> Paint him as you wou'd paint the Martial God,
> Or as *Nassau* when thro' the *Boyne* he rode.   687-90

The Danube drowning is equally vague and colorless:

> The Marshall [Tallard] drove by Terror to the Waves,
> Sees Squadrons sinking in their watry Graves.   714-15

The poem, praising both Marlborough and Eugene, is not
notably partisan, though High Church. It places emphasis
on the humiliation of Magnus and Marshall Tallard. Only
defeat and death lie ahead for Magnus, and praise from
"infernal Laureates" who will extol his reign "In Hellish
Numbers, and Satanic Verse."
    The last, page 24, uses smaller type to crowd in
extra lines. Again the drawing of an elaborate symbolic
design is urged.

> Compose a Circlet for your Hero's Brow,
> From numerous Laurels which his Arms bestow.
> Let *Liege*, and *Schellinburg* [*sic*], and *Ulm*, and *Bonn*,
> *Augsberg*, and *Munich* by his Conduct won,
> A Martial Crown for *Marlborough* prepare,
> But let brave *Blenheim* have the sovereign share.   818-23

The poem concludes with an injunction to British historians to show Marlborough as "their utmost strain," and he
is urged to complete British fame, winning battles and
defeating the politician,

> 'Till rescued *Europe* shall proclaim Thee Great.   857

Denne's rather prodigious effort, whether or not Godolphin expected much from it, assuredly could contribute to his conviction that Blenheim deserved a better poem.

65   November 28.

Wine, John   (fl. 1704)

A Welcome to VICTORY.   A Congratulatory POEM On the Success of Her MAJESTY's Forces in *Germany*, under the Command of his Grace the Duke of *Marlborough*.   With an AFTERTHOUGHT On *The Late Engagement* at SEA.   *LONDON*. Printed in the YEAR. 1714.
     4°:   *i-iv*, A-K^2; L^1; t.p., *bl.*, To the Most Illustrious, Serene and Mighty *Princess*, ANNE, etc. sgnd. 'John Wine.' 1-42, *bl.*, 46 pp. 708 lines, mainly couplets, but opens with ode style. *The Introduction*, 4 stanzas, 60 lines, an Acrostick to Anne and Marlborough, and the *After-Thought*, 124 lines. Welcomes the fair nymph Victory back from France to dwell in England and be a companion to Princess Anne. Folger and Newberry Lib. copies used. The only ones known in libraries. Not in Morgan. The poem proper opens:

         Who can be silent, when the jovial Round
         With loud *Huzza*'s, and joyful *Shouts* resounds?

The poem could only intensify the sense of inadequacy in Blenheim panegyric. Clichés, flat imagery, and obvious rhymes abound. Marlborough's name is a terror to the foe; his mighty merits deserve the utmost praise. Even so his light is dimmed by Anna's, that "great Nursing Mother of the Universe" (1. 176). Anti-Jacobite sentiment appears in a satiric passage denouncing those who shelter under the Queen's protection but still grudge her what right and birth entitle her to enjoy. May they "on some *loathed, stinking* Dunghill dy [*sic*]" (1. 278).
     A Tory interest in deflating Marlborough's honors is operative and is apparent in Section 18 which praises

Ormond. Five lines hymning his virtues, and each beginning with his name, set the tone. He is generous, illustrious in race, valiant, great, and brave. Furthermore
he first won honors under Nassau, that is William III,
an honor which was more properly Marlborough's. Ormond
is the terror of Spain and the pride of Ireland. Cutts
next is praised for courage and prowess, and then Marlborough again. The gazettes are reproved for understat-
ing his claims. "Tho' Blab-tongued *Fame* was here so
sparing too" (1. 369).

Finally the poem approaches the great actions. Germania shrieks for help, and the long, long march begins.
Fully satisfying neo-classical distaste for low words,
the verse does little to describe battle, although Shellenberg is named, since "Heav'n pre-ordan'd it." Tallard
appears, his whole life directed toward arms.

Near to the Banks, where Ancient Danaus flows,
A strong and advantagious Camp they chose,
Nature and *Art* contribute utmost Aid,
And every Thing is to Advantage laid,
Their stronger Camp the Marshy Grounds defend,
And Rivers round their Guardian Waters send.   469-74

But Churchill, Tunbridge, and Cutts, undaunted, only gain
fresh laurels from these obstacles. In the description
of Blenheim, this is almost the first poetic effort to
ignore the drowning of the French squadrons. The effect
is that of baroque illustration.

And now the Bloody *Action* doth begin,
Of death and Horror an amazing Scene.
Trumpets and Drums the Heroes Hearts inflame,
And Thundring *Vollies* do the Fight proclaim,
.   .   .   .
From *Gaping* Wounds a Crimson Flood doth rise,
And dying Groans and Shrieks do rend the troubled
                                             Skies,
Repulse, Repuls'd; Attack, Attackt they are,
Whilst Vic'try doth for neither side declare. 491-507
                                         passim.

71

Now Eugene, though hard pressed, sends aid to Marlborough, and for this deserves eternal fame; the two heroes share equal laurels. This conception of the shared victory, essentially true for Blenheim, marks a new note, but also a Tory detraction of glory from the English leader. In the closing lines Holland is reminded that she should record Marlborough's name "*to Ever-lasting Days*" (1. 564).

Wine, who seems much given to afterthoughts, now intersperses four short pieces, a Conclusion in ode style of 20 lines which invoke the Queen's happiness and lasting peace, and three Acrostic pieces, on Anna Regina, on her Majesty's Motto, Semper Eadem, and on Marlborough. These are conventional, but the After-Thought on the late Engagement at SEA, addressed To the Queen, is something else. Any allusion to the conquest of Gibraltar had become a reflection on the land policy and triumphs of Marlborough. Actually, there is little thought in the poem, and no reference to Rooke or other proper names. "By Land *Your* Armies, and *Your* Fleets by Sea," and a reference to "*shatter'd Ships*" are the only specific allusions to the naval victory.

The extreme rarity of this piece is attested by the fact that only recently did a copy come to light. It is now in the collection of Mr. Peter Smithers, M.P. The writer had been offered a copy when happily another turned up, and a microfilm from this, the Folger copy, was used. It is also listed in *WL*, VI, Nov., p. 702. An adv. in *Post-Man*, No. 1349, Sat. Nov. 25-Tues. 28, 'This day is publish'd.' Adds 'Sold by S. Malthus in London-house-yeard.' Price 1 s. Where is to be had the Ghosts of King William and Queen Mary, Price 6 d. each."

66   November 29.

S., J. [James Smallwood (fl. 1699-1709)]

England's *Triumph; or the Glorious Campaign in the Year 1704.* Containing An Exact Account of all the memorable Transactions that have happened by Land and Sea; as

Sieges, Battles, Sea-Fights, Skirmishes, Marches and
Counter-Marches of Armies, Successes, and Victories, in
Flanders, the *Empire, Savoy, Italy, Portugal, Spain* and
other places. With the Letters and Declarations of the
Emperor, Kings, Princes, and great Generals. The Result
of Councils of War and other Councils.

More particularly of the forcing of the Lines of the
Enemy at *Donauwert*, and the glorious Victory obtained by
his Grace the Duke of *Marlborough*, in Conjunction with
the Confederate Forces, over the *French* and *Bavarians*,
at the famous Battle of *Hochstet* and *Blenheim*. The Siege
of *Landau* and Traarback. The taking *Gibraltar*, and the
Defeat of the *French* Fleet by Sr. *George Rook*, &c. With
a Poem on his Grace the Duke of *Marlborough*. LONDON:
Printed for *N. Boddington*, at the *Golden Ball*, in *Duck-
Lane*, 1704. Price 1s. Folding plate of Marlborough, in
plumed hat and armor on prancing steed, with tents and
battling troops in background; t.p., *bl.*, Preface to the
Reader *iii-iv*, 1-175. The Preface is sgnd. I. S., al-
though Morgan G406 and BM 'Cat. incorrectly state it as
T. S. This correction, along with the inclusion of
James Smallwood's poem, *A Congratulatory Poem* To His
Grace the Duke of *Marlborough*, pp. 90-2, and other evi-
dence establishes Smallwood as author. See No. 42 above,
August 12. Smallwood served as chaplain to Her Majesty's
Foot-Guards, both on the great march and at the victory.
Internal statements in the account confirm this fact. He
provides a detailed summary, using Hare's Journal and
other sources.

Adv. in *Daily Courant*, No. 819, Wed. Nov. 29 'This
Day is Publish'd.'

November 30.

[Chapman, Richard, M.A., Vicar of Cheshunt (fl. 1698-1735)]

Le Feu de Joye: OR A BRIEF DESCRIPTION of Two most Glorious VICTORIES OBTAIN'D BY *Her* Majesty's *Forces and those
of Her Allies*, OVER THE *French* and *Bavarians*. In *July*

and *August*, 1704 at *Schellenbergh* and *Blainhaim* [*sic*]
near *Hocksted*. Under the Magnanimous and Heroick Conduct
of His Grace the Duke of *Marlbrough* [*sic*]. A POEM. By
a *British* Muse. [3 lines Virgil] *LONDON*: Printed by
Freeman Collins for *W. Henchman*, at the *King*'s *Head* in
Westminster Hall. 1705.
    4°: A⁴-D⁴, D⁴ (D1 for C, and D2 for C2); t.p., *bl.*,
iii-vi; 1-26, 32 pp. Errata p. 26. Drop-t. p. 1, wtmk.
small fleur-de-lys. BM, IndU. Both copies used, but notations in Indiana copy important. *iii-iv* "To the Right
Honourable Sidney *Lord Godolphin*, Lord High Treasurer of
ENGLAND. Knight of the most Noble Order of the Garter,
And on the Lords of Her MAJESTY's most Honourable Privy
Council." Dedication, 27 lines, couplets; poem 455 lines,
couplets. To His Grace, 68 lines, couplets; total 550
lines. Morgan H160. Dedication opens:

> My LORD,
>   When I had done what my rude Passion strove,
> To shew my Duty, and express my Love.

Associates Godolphin with Marlborough in serving Queen
Anna. "The Nerve of War is Treasure, and the Soul Is
Courage." Serves Anne as Burleigh did Elizabeth.
    Authorship identified by the suggestion in a nota-
tion in the Indiana copy. Former owner, T. Park, writes
that William Cowper ascribed the poem to Chapman. He
adds: "No production that I have seen affords so many
specimens of the Bathos in poetry as the present. Cowper first introduced it to my notice in a letter which
contained the two marked passages at pages 19 to 21."
On the title page he adds that "Cowper seems to have
thought that the Author's name was Chapman." The matter
is completed by examination of Cowper's letter to Park,
first printed in the volume of Cowper's Private Correspondence, ed. by the Rev. T. S. Grimshaw, V, p. 147,
1835. There Cowper speculates concerning Chapman's
Homer, that the author "cannot surely be the same Chapman who wrote a poem, I think, on the battle of Hochsted, in which when I was a very young man, I remember
to have seen the following lines:

> Think of two thousand gentlemen at least
> Each mounted on his capering beast,
> Into the Danube they were pushed by shoals.

It was these lines, incorrectly quoted by Macaulay, since
he presumably took them from Cowper's misquotation, that
provoked his memorable remark that Godolphin was "morti-
fied, and not without reason, by the exceeding badness of
the poems which appeared in honor of the battle of Blenheim. . .One of these poems has been rescued from oblivion by the exquisite absurdity of three lines." The poem,
without the association with Cowper and Chapman, is stud-
ied in "Addison's *Campaign* and Macaulay," *PMLA*, LXIII, No.
3, Sept., 1948, 886-902, by the author. Opens:

> Musing one Night in Bed what I shou'd do
> To feed my Flocks, (and pay my taxes too).

This opening, poetically absurd, does establish the problem of the costs of war. Marlborough is urged to fight
to renew Britain's natural treasure, and to go even beyond the Danube. The English Genius gives this command
in a dream-vision from which the poet awakes. A march
of 600 miles follows to Schellenberg, near Donawert,
both names associated with the subsequent victory at
Blenheim. Primrose, Web [for Webb], Ferguson and Rue
[that is Rowe], "whose blood was sav'd for Blenheim,"
lead the attack. Others are mentioned and then the poem
proceeds to the most extended account of Blenheim that
had been attempted, for all its absurdities. The French
are "encamp't upon a rising Ground," in a superior situation. Eugene is on the English right, in command of
the German forces. Tallard, opposing him, commands the
enemy's right, and Marsin the left, with Bavaria's Duke.
Marlborough speaks to his troops in a long address,
praising Queen Anne's virtue and justice and denouncing French perfidy. "Let us fight, or die. . .for Liberty." Loud acclamations follow, which suggest that
Chapman knew *Paradise Lost*.

Churchill's deeds, we learn, are crowned by Blenheim,
with Lumley, Palmes, North and Gray, Ingoldsby, Wood, and

others. Following seven lines, all opening with "Thunder
and Lightning," he is portrayed:

> And now our Gen'ral's even Temper shew'd,
> Was here and there, and ev'ry where i' th' Crowd;
> Where Bullets whistle, or where Cannon roar,
> Whose well-steel'd Bands before 'em rent and tore;
> Now to the Right the useful Word he gave,
> And then the Left, the Center helpt to save.   316-21

The Danube drowning supplies the famous and notorious
passage:

> But sure I am, no Pen can here express
> This lively Scene, in its own nat'ral Dress.
> Suppose Four Thousand Gentlemen at least,
> And each Man mounted on his cap'ring Beast,
> Arm'd Cap-a-pee, Equipt from Head to Foot,
> With all the Marks of Honour clad to boot,
> Should at an Instant, in a Body Roll,
> And plunge into the Deep, their violent Soul. 378-85

Fifty lines are devoted to the cries and shrieks of the
dying and their desperate efforts to save life if not
honor. This misery produces worse sounds than screeching
owls, croaking frogs, howling wolves, or dogs or lions,
or even the Irish o'er their dead. "Not Infants squeal,
poor Wife's moan, or eagles squawling, snakes hissing,"
not cries of shipwrecked sailors or lost travelers can
equal the sound. The poem concludes with the comparison
to toppling a tall pine, something of an anticlimax.
Lines to Marlborough praise him along with the usual
classical list, Caesar, Alexander, and Epaminondas, and
assure him he will be welcomed home by singing British
youths and maids. It remained for the *Campaign*, now certainly virtually completed, to satisfy the officials of
the government, and to celebrate the day of the hero's
return to London.

8   December 1.

Dennis, John   (1651-1734)

Britannia Triumphans: OR THE EMPIRE Sav'd, AND *EUROPE* Deliver'd. BY THE Success of Her Majesty's Forces under the Wise and Heroick Conduct of his Grace the DUKE of MARLBOROUGH. A POEM, by Mr. *Dennis*. *Ab Jove Principium Musae*. Virg. *LONDON*: Printed for *J. Nutt* near *Stationers-Hall*. 1704.
8°: A^8 B-K^8, *i-xvi*, 1-72, 88 pp. Ded. to "Her Most Sacred Majesty ANNE," *ii* sgnd. Adv. in *London Gaz*. No. 4076, Thurs. Nov. 30-Mon. Dec. 4; *Rev*., Dec. 16 also; *Post-Man*, Nov. 25-28 adv. Copies at BM, MH, CtY, ICN, MU. 1381 lines, blank verse. Morgan G162.
    Repr. in *The Select Works of Mr. John Dennis*, London, Pr. by *John Darby*, 1718. 2 vols. I, 151-218, without the *Preface*. 'On the Battle of Blenheim,' headline on every page. Opens:

    Up, Rouze your selves, ye Nations, praise the Lord,
    Sing, ye deliver'd Nations, to your God.

Then addressing the high God of Revenge, Dennis appeals for inspiration. Immediately he hits upon the Danube drowning as his focus, comparing himself to Moses Appealing for aid against the Egyptians, or the Prophetess who invoked the Kishon against Jabin:

    As Hoary Danube, with indignant Waves
    Swallow'd the Gallick and Bavarian Hosts.   45-6

Three times he calls on his Soul to sing, aided by the Angels and the Church, above and below, praises of William and successor, Queen Anne, champion of Liberty and Faith, of "distress'd Virtue." He alleges that he is writing under the Queen's "majestick Patronage, This Song Begun at thy Command so strictly given" (ll. 129-30). Dennis is plainly attempting expression of those "enthusiastick Passions," as described in his *Grounds of Criticism in Poetry*. Written in the same year, 1704, it carries his demand for an impassioned poetry, a poetry fired by religious enthusiasm. Inevitably he is drawn

to Milton, whose sublimity he emulates. In a picture
seeking terror, he portrays Germania, daughter of Rome,
bound, threatened with rape, and allegorizes the Danube
calling on the Rhine for aid. Germania, the Empire, does
not need to call for aid, for from Britain come the rugged
Saxons, sent by Anne who alone sends aid to give "the
lab'ring Nations Peace." The deliverers come from the
land of "Fair Liberty," and meet Eugene who, reflecting
his meeting with Marlborough, exclaims he had never seen
such soldiers before.

> For only *Britons*, of the Race of Men,
> Their Liberties entirely have maintain'd.   303-4

Addressing Austria, the poet deplores that Philip had not
joined with Elizabeth in friendship. He invokes nations
that profess the Christian faith to sing together (410 f.).
     He now comes to Marlborough, Anne's chosen leader.
"But who shall paint thee, Wond'rous Chief?" Marlborough's "sweet attractive Majesty invites. . .Calm are his
thoughts, his gestures, his majestic brow." The love of
Fame urges him, severely curbed, always obedient to cool
wisdom's voice, "Far, far above the Tempest's stormy
Rage." The whole picture, from line 347 to 555, emphasizes Marlborough's calm, his foresight, poise in battle,
yet his amazing swiftness in action and above all rapidity
in making decisions. Dennis shows that Marlborough designs two campaigns, like an artist. Inspired by lofty
motives, he leads his English to Schellenbourgh, the important pass at Donawert, key to Bavaria. Like the eagle
that looks at the Sun, he, "with calm considerate Soul,"
looks at the foe. His troops stand unmoved while he marshals them, even though Bavarian cannons tear into their
ranks.

> Their mangled Trunks divided from their Limbs:
> Yet all their dauntless Spirit they retain.   623-4

Apostrophe abounds as the great, sacred Day of Blenheim
is addressed. Then the furious soldiery and Britannia
are urged to recall the victory which led to the Danube's
"swallowing down his impious Prey" (1. 699). The Danube

and the field of battle are hailed. The flower of French
soldiery, proud of its successes, is presented, proud in
their junction with the Bavarians. Then the British come
marching, fresh from the triumph at Schellenbourgh, inspired as champions of justice, truth, and liberty. The
foe is encamped on Blenheim's field, and again this spot
awakens poetic raptures. It surpasses Canne, Bleury, and
Landen.

> But heark! [*sic*] The Goddess gives the dreadful
> Charge,
> I hear th' enchanting Sound, I feel its magick Pow'r.
> 967-8

The result is an outpouring of exclamations and inflated
imagery of clouds and thunder and sounding drums as Nature
and embattled men are mingled. Description of the battle
dominates 200 lines of verse, 1100 to 1300. The French
squadrons attack, and drive the English horse back. Ca-
lamity threatens; but Marlborough, supported by his
brother Churchill, by Lumley, Villiers, Erle, Ingoldsby,
Orkney and Cutts, immortal heroes all, finally turns the
tide. Such fervor is chauvinistic in the extreme, and
Marlborough's summoning of aid from Eugene at the crucial
moment goes unnoticed. Not only the British troops, but
the very Danube is stirred to furious action, and once
more the now famous scene of drowning is invoked.

> But tenfold Horror drives them headlong on!
> Down, down, ten thousand take the fatal Leap,
> And plunge among the Waves; the *Danube* raves,
> And calls his stormy Billows to the Spoil,
> His stormy Billows to the mighty Spoil
> Drive on, advancing with a hideous Roar.
> Ten thousand Warriors rolling in the Flood,
> Horses and Men reverst midst scatter'd Arms,
> And floating Ensigns on each other plunge,
> Drive one another drowning to th' Abyss.
> And with tremendous Prospect strike the Eye. 1252-62

Inevitably Dennis compares the scene to the Hebrews and
the Red Sea swallowing the Egyptian enemy. If only he

could paint all the cries, grief, rage, shrieks, and
horror "Not *Milton*'s wondrous Piece should mine transcend," (1. 1285) "nor Michael Angelo's stupendous
Work."

Now the battle is over, and the poet addresses Glorious Death, the ultimate conqueror. Had Death foreseen
the hecatombs of dead that Marlborough would raise he
might have spared Blandford, the Duke's dead son, "He
was so good, so charming, and so great" (1. 1314). This
theme is developed in the pathos of Marlborough's loss,
which is shared by Anne and Britannia. The Whig note of
recognition of family sentiment is developed in a picture
of Anne as the Mother and her people as her Children who,
even in death, bring a blessing and are now praising God
in Heaven. It is the strong assertion of Whig doctrines,
rather than poetic power, that gives the poem importance.
Religion, the family, liberty, and ultimate and lasting
peace are its themes.

E. N. Hooker notes that Dennis wrote the poem during
the summer and that it "seems to have attracted the attention of Marlborough, Buckinghamshire, and Godolphin,
and to have been in part responsible for Dennis's appointment, on June 6, 1705, as a waiter to the custom house."
Op. Cit., p. 37.

69   December 5.

Ivoy, Colonel.

The PLAN of the Fortify'd Camp of the French and Bavarians
at Schellenberg, near Donawert, here they were attack'd
and routed by the Duke of Marlborough and Prince Lewis of
Baden. With a full and impartial Relation of that Fight
and Victory, and the Order of Battel of the Confederate
Army; the Foot, Horse, and Dragoons being distinguish'd
by their proper Colours. Price 1 *s*. Sold by J. Nutt near
Stationers'Hall and David Mortier Book and Mapseller at
the Sign of Erasmus Head in the Strand. Where may also

be had the true PLAN and Relation of the Battel of Hochstet by Coll. Ivoy. Price 1 *s*. 6 *d*.
    Adv. in the *Post-Man*, No. 1352, Sat. Dec. 2-Tues.
Dec. 5, 1704. See September 30, above, No. 54.

70   December 9.

A *Lunenburgher* General His Circumstantiated and Full
ACCOUNT of the BATTLE OF BLEINHEIM. WHEREIN What passed
that memorable Day, as well on Prince *Eugene*, as on the
Duke of *Marlborough*'s side, and the true *Humane Causes*
of that great VICTORY, are Impartially Related. To which
is added, Prince *Eugene*'s Letter to the King of *Prussia*,
upon Occasion of this Battle. LONDON: Printed, and Sold
by *John Nutt* near *Stationers-Hall*. MDCCV. Price 6*d*.
    4°: A-F^2; t.p., *bl*., 3-24. Drop-t. on p. 3. Advs.
at end of Nos. 60 and 69, as below. Adv. with three
stars in the *Post-Man*, No. 1354, Dec. 7-9, 1704. The
title is given almost in full, including the references
to Eugene and his Letter. Adv. *Post-Man*, No. 1366, Jan.
23-25, 1705, which may be actual date of publication.
Adv. with *True Plan*, Tallard's *Account* and Defoe's
Double Welcome. Advertisements of three Nutt publications bottom of p. 24, A Plan of the Battle of Hochstet
. . .drawn by Coll. Ivoy; A Plan of the Fortified Camp
of the *French* and *Bavarians*; Mareschal *Tallard*'s *Aid-
de-Camp* His Account of the Battle of *Blenheim*. Both
in French and English. The Second Edition, Horn copy
used. Morgan H274, but as 10 pp. Not in BM.
    This is another allegedly original account that
largely transcribes the *Life and Glorious History*, by
Dr. Francis Hare. See the writer's article, "Marlborough's First Biographer: Dr. Francis Hare," *HLQ* XX,
Feb., 1957, 145-62. It may be added that the two main
authorities, Serjeant Millner and Thomas Lediard, both
also largely pirate Hare's account. This fact had not
been detected when the article was published, and it
should be observed that the December advertisement cited
above would place the Lunenburgher General's account

earlier. The author must have had access to Hare's journal. He also is interested in calling attention to
Prince Eugene's important role in Blenheim as is apparent in the title and the appended letter. The writer
uses the spelling 'Bleinheim' which is probable evidence
of the pamphlet's not having been by Hare, even though
it draws very largely on his account, or at least duplicates it.

71   December 9.
The Seat of the War in Flanders, Brabant, Cleve and Co-
logne, in 6 large sheets, 8 more maps, Rhine, Bavaria,
etc. Sold by Mr. Mortier Book and Mapseller, Erasmus
Head.
      Adv. in the *Post-Man*, No. 1354, Thursday, Dec. 7 to
Sat. Dec. 9, 1704. No copy known. Not in Morgan.

72   December 14.

Addison, Joseph (1672-1719)

THE CAMPAIGN, A POEM To His Grace, the DUKE of *MARLBOROUGH*.
By Mr. *ADDISON*. [4 lines of Claudian] *LONDON*, Printed
for *Jacob Tonson*, within *Grays-Inn Gate* next *Grays-Inn
Lane*. 1705. 476 lines, couplets.
      $2°$: A^2, B-G^2; hft., *bl.*, t.p., *bl.*, 1-23 [unmd. p.
Tonson advs.], 28 pp. Various papers used. Star wmk. in
Folger copy may be unique. Normal wmk. 'Dp.' One of Horn
copies has p. 31 for 13. BM, Durham, MH, CtY, TxU, CSmH,
Clark, Horn (3) and others. Morgan H5, 1705. Sec. ed.
essentially same description, except for insertion 'The
Second Edition' between motto and colophon on t. p., and
smaller type for 'Campaign' and larger for 'Poem' in half-
title. Both second and third eds., 1705. Wmk. 'ML.'
Drops. adv. of 15 books third ed. Aside from Addison's
final revisions, main differences in reduction of total

pages *iv*, 20, that is to 24, and insertion of two Latin
quotations in the motto, from Livy, *Hist Lib.* 33, the
latter of 5 lines. The principal added passage describes
the gentleman who bears the burdens of sustaining liberty
against injustice and tyranny. The page of advertised
items is omitted also from the Third Edition. Wmk. 'WC.'
For full description see Robert D. Horn, "The Early Editions of Addison's Campaign," *Studies in Bibliography*,
U. Va., III, 1950-51, 256-61. It is there established
that while six Tonson editions in all appeared, and that
most editions derive from the Tickell edition of Addison's *Works*, 1721, the First for primacy and Third for
finality are the only significant versions. Since the
writer made a census of copies, it may be mentioned that
19 in all were located, three in the hands of the writer.
Copies at the BM, MH, CY, TxU, CSmH, while the Clark copy
is labeled as Luttrell's, both the inscription and hand-
writing do not seem to be his. No certain Luttrell copy
has been found, except for the Latin translation, which
is labeled as "13 Februar., 1708/9." However, Haslewood
supplies the date 'Dec. 14, 1704.' This and subsequent
editions are listed in their proper years. Opens:

> While Crouds of Princes Your Deserts proclaim,
> Proud in their Number to enroll Your Name.

The poet is transported by a "theme so new" and great.
Emperors and Queen Anne herself hail the victory. The
poem treats war with restraint, and places the emphasis
on the great march, "an Iliad rising out of One Campaign" (1. 12). Threatened by France, the nations turn
to Britain, for there true worth is recognized. As soon
as spring breezes come the march begins. The Moselle is
reached, and the God-like leader already has his scheme
in mind. Crossing the Rhine, they move steadily east-
ward through clouds of dust. At length Prince Eugene
comes to an interview with Marlborough. They join in
mutual friendship. As the hounds pursue the hunted deer,
the soldiers strain toward the fight. "The Immortal
Schellenberg appears at last" (1. 106).
The battle is opened at sunset, and the rows of

brass cannon fail to daunt the British soldiers, though
"many gen'rous *Brittons* meet their Doom" (1. 155). The
commander is warned not to risk his important life. They
gain the pass and move on to Donnawert, "with cannons
doom'd to batter Landau's Walls" (1. 104). France's doom
is now certain, and her troops will seek shelter behind
the Rhine. They are confronted with a man of "Unbounded
Courage and Compassion join'd" (1. 219), such as make the
hero and man complete. Marlborough had long striven to
win the enemy by diplomacy, but now he must unloose his
forces to ravage the land with sword and fire. This allusion to the policy of devastating the Bavarian lands
is one of many which make the poem the most detailed and
accurate. The wrathful soldier,

> A Thousand Villages to Ashes turns,
> In crackling Flames a Thousand Harvests burns. 229-30

The soldiers are loathe to obey the commands and the
leader grieves; but the time and the day have come.

> Behold in awful March and dread Array
> The long extended Squadrons shape their Way! 259-60

They press through fens and floods and reach the height
of battle. Here the poet calls on his muse for greater
effort. Lines 279-92 embrace the famous Angel simile
and the picture of a calm, self-possessed Marlborough,
who "pleas'd th'Almighty's Orders to perform,
        Rides in the Whirl-wind and directs the Storm."
Now the rout begins, and the Danube drowning is depicted.
Thousand of steeds, standards, and soldiers lie in the
Danube's bloody whirlpools and are swept away by the
rolling billows. The French give up their banners with
tears. Tallard, humiliated in defeat, is pictured as
losing his only son in the battle, which was not the case.
He is urged not to blame fate for the defeat in which
"fam'd *Eugenio* bore away only the Second Honours" (11.
349-50). The battle is over, but the victor continues
to conceive great designs. He drives the French beyond
the Rhine where they escape from further conflict. Austria's young monarch, Achilles-like in grace, is now

instructed by Marlborough in the siege of Landau. Then,
enlarged with titles and conquests, the British chief
marches back to Belgium, freeing Treves and taking Traerbach as he goes. King Louis trembles as he sees "The
Work of Ages sunk in One Campaign" (1. 449).

The poem concludes with the observation that Marlborough's exploits shine in their own light, "And those
who Paint 'em truest Praise 'em most" (1. 476). Unquestionably the *Campaign* quickly proved itself the most popular and successful panegyric to date; and it continued
to win applause and ultimately established itself as the
finest tribute to Marlborough's genius. It is perhaps
not a great poem, but it is a highly appropriate summary
of the march and battle and a fine tribute to a great
field general. That it was issued on December 14, 1704,
the Thursday of Marlborough's return to London, inevitably suggests that its printing was hastened for that
event. The writer has shown evidences of at least two
typesetters and its title-page of 1705 confirms premature publication. Nevertheless it is free of misspellings aside from variant forms of 'Britain,' 'Britannia,'
and 'Briton' with two t's in the B-C sheets. 'Echoing'
is spelled 'ecchoing' in line 242, and is corrected in
all editions subsequent to the three folios. As will
be shown, the poem was frequently praised and cited in
subsequent panegyrics, and critics from Steele to Dr.
Johnson commented with more or less favor, the Angel
simile being the crux of most discussions. A portion
of it will establish Addison's perception of Marlborough's foresight in strategy and his calm in battle
tactics.

'Twas then Great Marlbro's mighty Soul was proved,
That, in the Shock of Charging Hosts unmov'd,
Amidst Confusion, Horror, and Despair,
Examin'd all the Dreadful Scenes of War;
In peaceful Thought the Field of Death survey'd,
To fainting Squadrons sent the timely Aid,
Inspir'd repuls'd battalions to engage,
And taught the doubtful Battel where to rage.
So when an Angel by Divine Command

85

With rising Tempests shakes a guilty Land,
Such as late o'er pale Britannia past,
Calm and Serene he drives the furious Blast;
And, pleas'd th'Almighty's Orders to perform,
Rides in the Whirl-wind, and directs the Storm. 279-92

The *The Campaign* quickly established itself as the
prime expression of the English muse at Marlborough's
great victory, is familiar from the early accounts down
to modern biography. Numerous poets refer to it and
Addison. That it is also the most interesting biblio-
graphically is apparent in the numerous editions, the
three folios and an Edinburgh quarto in 1705, a Latin
translation in 1708-9, and the editions of Tickell and
others. Addison received the post of under Secretary
of State, succeeding John Locke, and a significant determination of his entire career in diplomacy and public affairs. Although his fellow Whigs, Defoe and Blackmore, jibed at his financial success, it was the praise
of envy, and 18th Century critics and poets recognized
the signal success of the poem in the history of panegyric. That even A. C. Guthkelch knew only the first two
folios, and was unaware of the Third, in which Addison's
final substantive revisions appear, is significant of
the rarity of items, and the limited knowledge of Marlborough panegyrics in general. He based his text, as
have other editors, on Tickell's 1721 edition in Addison's *Works*. That even the eminent historian and bibliographer, W. T. Morgan, was unaware of the first appearance of the poem in 1704, prevented his placing it properly. He numbers it H5, for 1705, though actually it
was issued on the day of the Duke's triumphant return
to London. This assuredly adds great interest to it as
a monumental tribute, and also it helps to explain evidences of haste in printing, and even in finishing it
off for publication.

73   (*ca*. December 14)

D'Urfey, Thomas (1653-1723)

On the Battle of Blenheim.   In *Wit* and *Mirth; or Pills
to Purge Melancholy*, III, 347, Printed by W. Pearson for
Jacob Tonson, 1719.   The poem consists of 3 stanzas,
each 8 lines; 24 lines.   Opens:

> The conqu'ring Genius of our Isle returns,
> Inspir'd by *Ann*, the *Godlike Hero* burns.
> Retrieves the Fame our ill-led Troops had lost,
> And spreads reviving Valour thro' the Host.

No evidence of immediate publication, and since poems on
Marlborough's return continued to appear on into the January following, there is no assurance of its having appeared in December beyond Lediard's association of it
with the *Campaign*'s appearance.

The poem is also reprinted by Lediard, as follows:

Anon.   *On the Duke of Marlborough's Victory at Hochstadt
in 1704.*   10 lines, couplets, on Marlborough's return.
Quoted by Lediard, *Life of Marlborough*, 1736, I, 437-8.
Lediard prints this and a portion of Addison's *Campaign*
as "a Couple of the most celebrated" tributes.   This
piece is "one we find inserted in *Tom Brown*'s Works."
Lediard may have believed it to be Brown's, but since that
poet died June 16, 1704, it cannot be by him.

4   December 21

Robins, Jasper   [no dates]

THE Hero of the Age: OR, the Duke of *Marlborough*.   The
Three Parts. I. Pindarick.   II. Heroick.   Being a Descrip-
tion of the late Battel at *Blenheim*.   III. An Ode. ----
Tibi Brachia contrahit Ardens Scorpio.   Virgil.   *LONDON*,
Printed: And Sold by *Benjamin Bragg* in *Avemary-Lane*.

1705. (Price Six Pence.)

2°: 2 B-G²; t.p., *bl.*, *iii-iv*, To the Right Honourable *Harriot Godolphin*, 24 lines, couplets; 1-7 The Hero
of the Age: or, Duke of *Marlborough*, 140 lines, couplets;
II, no drop-t., 8-21, description of Blenheim, 284 lines,
couplets; III, An ODE, 53 lines. Total 501 lines. Adv.
the *Flying Post*, No. 1503, Tues. Dec. 19 to Thurs. Dec.
21. 1704. 'Yesterday was publish'd.' But No. 1504 has
'On Thursday last was publish'd.' The *Daily Courant* Dec.
23, Sat., has 'On Thursday last was published.' Adv.
repeated Dec. 26-8, and later notices add, "Being a Description of the late Battel at Blenheim" after Heroick.
Not in Morgan. Dr. Williams Lib. copy used. The only
one known.

Dedication opens:

With Awe beyond Expression, I entreat
Your Leave to lay this off'ring at your Feet.

Compares Marlborough to Tamerlane; notices he is father
of Lady Harriot.

I. The Pindarick opens:

When *Europe*'s sav'd, in Silence can we sit?
Nor each present his grateful, humble Muse?

The highly rhetorical description appears to be based on
the *Gazette* with its account of Marlborough's note to the
Queen. The Germans and English meet, casting fear into
the hearts of the French who remember Cressy and Poictiers. Marlborough is pictured on his horse, contemplat-
ing the field (1. 255-71), while Eugene leads his faithful bands. Europa trembles, but the goddess of Freedom
cheers the army, as the battle begins. Charges and
countercharges take place with Cut[t]s and Hesse pressing on. Marlborough sends his brother, General Churchil[1], to the aid of Eugene. Thus the honor of the
battle is seen as dominantly English and the Duke's. His
conduct of the fight is as the soul moves the body, so
he moves calm and serene in the fight. Finally Marlborough leads a reserve force to a morass that Tallard had
thought impassable. The French are overcome, and

the Danube drowning becomes the main feature as in many
poems.

> Thousands of Horse remain'd unbroken yet,
> But saw the Horror that their Fellows met,
> Yet Quarter desperately declin'd to crave;
> These *Marlbro'* push'd into *Danubius* Wave
> And Man and Horse they plunge into the watry Grave.
> Were *Shakespear* living, and had then stood by,
> *Shakespear* had wanted Words for this Dread Day.
>
> 386-92

This early singling out of Shakespeare as the prime heroic
poet is more remarkable than the verse. As the horse gasp
and drown, and the "Screaming Death and Hellish Noise" of
battle suggests the Day of Doom, it becomes apparent that
Robins might well have some living under the shelter of
the Church. Following the account of Tallard's surrender
and his finding safety in Marlborough's "Hospitable Chariot," the concluding ode links the names of *Ann* and *Marlbro'*. While he is compared to Hannibal at Cannae, she
raises prayers and offerings to Heaven - *"First Fruits
and Tenths* she gave" (1. 34).

5 December 21 f. (?)

Sandby, James, Chaplain to Marlborough (fl. 1700-1704)

An Account of the last Campaign in Germany. Under the
Command of his Grace the Duke of Marlborough. By J.
Sandby A. M. Chaplain to Her Majesty's Train of Artillery,
and Secretary to General Churchill, &c. Printed for A.
and J. Churchill at the Black Swan in Pater-Noster-Row,
and Edward Castle at Charing-Cross.
 Adv. in *Daily Courant*, No. 835, Mon. Dec. 18 to
Thurs. Dec. 21. "There will shortly be publish'd." Not
in Morgan and no later advertisement appeared. Possibly
publication was forestalled by competing accounts. Interesting as associating Churchill family of publishers

with celebration of the Duke's achievements. No copy is
known.
   Murray *Dispatches*, III, 611-12, prints letter Marlborough to Harley recommending Sandby, "one of our chap-
lains, who has been my brother's secretary for some years
past," for a post "suitable to his merit and character."

76   December 30 *ca*.

Oldmixon, John (1673-1742)

A Pastoral POEM on the VICTORIES at *Schellenburgh* and
Bleinheim; Obtain'd by the Arms of the Confederates, under
the Command of his Grace the Duke of MARLBOROUGH over the
French and *Bavarians*. *With a large Preface, shewing the
Antiquity and Dignity of Pastoral Poetry*. *By Mr*. OLDMIXON.
Sylvae sint Consule Dignae. Virg. *LONDON*, Printed and
Sold by *A*. *Baldwin* at the *Oxford-Arms* in *Warwick-Lane*,
1704.
   2°:   a^2 A-F^2, H-O^2, t.p., [Errata on *ii*], To Her
Grace the Dutchess of Marlborough, sgnd. J. Oldmixon, *iii-
vi*, Preface *vii-xxx*, 1-28, 58 pp.   4° size, and so called
by Morgan G358.   428 lines, couplets. Pastoral dialogue.
Bodley, InU, NY Pub. copy used. Largely reprinted as *A
Chain of Providence*, August, 1705, No. 111. Morgan G358.
   The Dedicatory Preface, approaching the Duchess
"from an awful distance," apologizes for his Rural Muse,
which is incapable of flattery. There is little but flattery for the services to her majesty of the Duchess and
her Hero. Whether the Preface or the poem is the more
important depends almost entirely on the reader's interest. Oldmixon was a leader in the Whig attacks on Prior,
and became involved with Arthur Maynwaring, Defoe and
others as a distinctly political and unpastoral figure.
He opens with the point that heroic acts deserve tribute,
and especially Marlborough's. Other conquerors, Alexander and Caesar, have found their country free and left
if enslaved. Louis XIV has won sycophantic flattery by

no acts at all and the exhibition of lawless ambition.
Now he suffers defeat on the Danube.
That Oldmixon could be provocative is apparent in
his comments on poets who have sung Blenheim so poorly.

> I am far from thinking I can do so illus-
> trious an Action Justice, I ought to have been
> frightened by the success of most Writers, who
> have hitherto attempted it, had our Soldiers
> fought no better than our Poets write upon 'em,
> we should have had very little to rejoice over
> but our *Victory* at Sea. Yet instead of discour-
> aging, this embolden'd me to do as I saw others
> had done before me: Comforting myself, that if
> I cou'd not do better 'twas impossible to do
> worse. (pp. *ix-x*)

Perhaps he can at least be lost in the crowd of those for
whom the subject has been too hard, and he does hope that
some genius will arise to treat the British Hero in terms
worthy of the British Muse. In all this Oldmixon is affirming his strong Whig leanings, both in demand for
praise for the leader of Whig causes and in the stress
on English liberty.

The remaining twenty-four pages of the Preface are
devoted to a discussion of pastoral, particularly in defence of its use for heroic themes. The previous claim
that a Caesar demands a Virgil, implying as it might,
not only the epic but the pastoral poet, is put to good
use. Oldmixon cites classical precedents for shepherds
as doing something more than "Billing and Cooing, Sigh-
ing and Sobbing" (p. *xi*). He quotes Dryden's translations, especially of the passages on Pollio, and Theoc-
ritus's *Pharmacentria*. Pastoral, especially in the eclogue, affirms that the rural muse is the most ancient
of all. Rapin places it as earlier even than satyrs,
elegy, or the ode. All this has been well discussed
by "the ingenious Author" of the Preface to Dryden's
Virgil. Both Rymer and Boileau have urged imitation of
Virgil who has proved that the eclogue is capable of elevation (pp. *xi-xvi*). In the early days shepherds had

the care of their flocks but also of the state. Three
of them were leading founders of monarchies. Kings held
both crook and scepter, and Fabricius was called from
the plough to be placed at the head of the Roman Empire.

Discussion of the term *idyll*, as applied to Theoc-
ritus, leads to comment on blank verse. "In Complais-
ance to the Tast of the Age, we have left off writing in
Blank Verse, waiting till a second *Milton* shall finish
what the first began, and shake off the barbarous Yoke
. . ." (p. *xviii*). Oldmixon concludes with a comment on
shepherds talking at what has been called undue length,
and defends the practice again by classical examples.
He uses English names for Queen Anne and Marlborough,
again as did Virgil with Pollio, Varus or Gallus (p.
xxiv).

In the poem proper while Thyrsis and Menalcus are
conversing, wise Menalcus does most of the talking in
what amounts to little more than conventional panegyric.
His two long speeches, one 153 lines and his concluding
discourse in 189, total 342 lines, which added to the
opening dialogue means that Menalcus dominates the poem
throughout. The sentiments are again entirely Whig,
celebration of Anne as champion of human rights and
liberties, extending them from her native Britain to all
Europe; her champion, Churchill, affirming the superior-
ity of British arms and courage; the humiliation of venal
and tyrannical Louis XIV. The pastoral tone opens and
closes the poem.

> Oh Father of the Field! whose artful Strains
> Sweeten our Sorrows, and relieve our Pains.

Thyrsis addresses venerable Menalcus, urging him to sing
praises of Churchill by Sabrina's stream. Queen Anne,
for whom "*Collin* touch'd his golden Lyre," brings a comparison between Elizabeth and Spenser, and introduces
the technique of marginal identification of places and
persons. Marlborough's refusing contributions offered
by the Bavarians introduces the theme of his incorrupti-
bility. Some names go unidentified. Mopsus, who, "kind
to Discord," has railed at Caesar; Maevius, "lewd in

Life, and Infamous in Song," are of the kind who will re-
vile Menalcus's "loyal Song." Only Sacheverell is identified, as "the Mad Prophet on the Ouse." A golden time
of peace and cessation of faction and "Frantick Zeal" are
predicted to follow this iron time of war. Thyrsis assures him that the French tyrant is now bound to Anne's
chariot wheels, groveling in the dust.

Menalcus launches on the first of his two long
speeches, even though his Muse feels inadequate. He
praises Anne's choice of "Churchill, Her Belov'd, Her
bravest Chief" (1. 204). Swiftly the hero marches to the
Danube. But first Donawert is won, and *"Gauls to British*
Valour yeild [*sic*]," as Churchill leads the battle. The
muse here pauses to lament the death of Strephon, a poetic
youth who was slain. Thyrsis' lament for Strephon well
sustains the pastoral mood, and then follows Menalcus'
long, final discourse in which he summarizes Blenheim,
where Churchill is accompanied by Eugene who has never
failed to conquer.

And now the moving Squadrons joyn, and now
'Tis Darkness all Above and Death Below.
The Bellowing Cannons tear the Vaulted Shoar,
And more than Imitate the Thunders roar.   322-5

Clouds of smoke, lightning flashes bring chaos; but amid
it all Marlborough rides "with cheerful Patience," distributing his commands. The Danube drowning terminates
the action, as "the scatter'd Host. . .Leap down, and in
the foamy Waves are lost" (1. 356). With his brother,
General Churchill, holding the enemy at bay, Marlborough
spares them further losses and even evil Tallard is
spared. "The Wrinkled Tyrant," Louis XIV, is urged to
think on the shame of his captured troops. The poem concludes with the recognition of the many who should be mentioned, "Wise Godolphin," Candish (Cavendish), Pembroke,
who serve the throne in the Ministry. In the pastoral
shades and coolness of the evening, "Night spreads her
Sable Mantle ore the Skies," and the shepherds return to
the village and their beech fire where they pass the bowl,
and hearty shouts hail Anne and her Hero's Healths.

See also Oldmixon's *Iberia Liberata*, 1706, and *The Life and History of Belisarius*, 1713.

The remaining 1704 items are listed alphabetically, but all seem to fall in the latter months of the year and most are broadside ballads.

77 *Britain's Joy* For the *Noble Victory* obtain'd by their Forces over the *French* and *Bavarians*, August 13th, 1704. To its own proper Tune.
   1/2°: ballad in six 8-line stanzas, 48 plus 4, but 4 more cropt in only listed copy, sig E, Library of Scotland - Foxon. Foxon Xerox used. No pub., n.d. Not in Morgan. Opens:

> Hark, I hear the Cannon roar,
> Ecchoing from the *German* Shoar.

The brave news has come that Marlborough and Eugene have bridled the French invaders with "*Scots* and *English* Courage too." Mildly chauvinistic and pro-Scots. Eugene broke the French array; and Tallard and thousands yielded to the valiant Britons. Let us drink a health to our Queen -

> And pray for her long Happy Reign,
> And her Enemies Confusion.

A Whig touch appears in a reference to the Emperor of Germany, who "With all his Popish Heresie," could not free his lands from French intrusion.

78 [Krook, Enoch and Daniel Kroon]

DEN ROEMRUCHTIGEN ZEGENPRAAL VAN DEN VELDSLAG BY HOOGSTET; *OORLOGSSPEL*. Versierd met verscheidene Vertooningen,

Zang, Dans, Konsten Vliegwerken. DOOR YVER BLOEID DE
KUNST. [allegorical emblem]   TO EMSTELDAM, By de Ers-
gen: van J. LASCAILJE, op den Middeldam, op de hoek van
de Vischmarkt, 1704. Met Privilegie. Authors(;) names in
script, late hand.
    12mo 40 pp. Printed uniformly with similar produc-
tion on Ramillies and Oudenard, 1706 and 1709, Nos. 189
and 295 below. A coll. of plays at Amsteldam Shouxbourg
Theather, 1669-1750. Lib. Cong. only copies known. Text
in 12-syllable lines and songs. Mixture of characters,
Dutch generals and citizens, rivers, and abstract virtues
and vices all appear allegorically denominated. "Marlbourg" and Eugene appear, as well as French commanders,
but only silently. Descriptions of Schellenberg and
Hochstet justify the label 'Oorlogsspel' or war-play. In
spite of its allegorical features, much more of a dramatic piece than any English play, most certainly than
the productions of Tate. Not in Morgan.

Die aus Blenheim Hochstädtischen Greffen. . .Angekommene
schwäbische Fama, welche mitbringet das Frankreich,
Bäyern und Cölln beschehene Weheklagen uber die
schleunige Veränderung ihres Glücks. . .nebst einer
grossmüthigen. . .resolution des gefangenen Frantzösischen. . .Marschals de Tallard [in verse]. 4°, Cölln,
1704. Morgan G 60. Only ref. No copy located. Next
entry appears by title to be the same.

Die auss dem Parnasso auf der Post angekommene Poetische
FAMA, *Oder Das von Franckreich/ Bayern und Cölln besche-*
hene Weheklagen/ über die schleunige Veränderung ihres
Glucks/ und vorgehabte DESSEINS, *Nebst* einer Grossmüthigen Ergebung zur Gedult des gefangenen Frantzosischen
Generals Mons. de TALLARD. No pub., n.d., 4°, 2 pp. BM
copy used. 28 lines hexameter couplets. Pr. in Gothic
type. Opens:

95

Gedrucht in dem beglückt= und Wunder=vollen Jahr/
Darinnen Franckreich sein Concept verrucket war/

A satire in which a hypothetical Frenchman bemoans the
fate of Louis XIV's armies and allies. The doggerel in
which French mispronunciations of German words are apparent is similar to that of No. 81 following. After the
opening statement that the French plans have been upset
comes a shriek of mingled anger and obscenities. The
English are charged with being ganz Barbar, Cruel, Horrible, böss," that is entirely evil. An allusion to
"fatal Schelenberg" [*sic*] after a reverse two years
earlier, dates the poem as in the summer of 1704. The
successful campaign in Spain, with the liberation of
Barcelona, is noticed. The French spokesman is struck
to the heart by the defeats. He ends the poem with the
observation that German soldiers eat and drink and take
booty, while the poor French go in rags.

Der Teutsche frist and saüfft/ holt immer Beute ein
Die arm Frantizoss die muss nur Berenäuter seyn.

81 Des Frantzösischen Marechalls De TALLARD Jammer-Klage/.
    wegen der bey Höchstädten am 13. Augusti 1704. gegen die
    hohe Reichs-Alliirten verlohrnen Schlacht/ and selbt
    eigenen Gefangenschafft.
        4°: No sigs.; t.p., *ii-iv* unmbd., 4 pp. No pub.
    Eighteen 6-line stanzas, nmbd., n.d. 108 lines, rhyming
    in couplet form. BM copy used. Not in Morgan. Opens:

              Mort, diable, c'en est fait,
              Cette chose neme plait,:/:
              Hilff mir/ Sainte Genevieve,
              Die Pariss so offt anrieffe/
              Und bekam bey Theurung brod;
              Bitt für mich in dieser Noth!

        As in No. 80 a doggerel verse reflects the French-
    man's attempts at German words and expressions. Tallard's
    lament reviews the events from his receiving three orders

to go to Dillingen, Schellenberg, and the disaster on the
Danube. The poet thinks he must have an Angel in his
favor. Not only Marcin, but ten or more generals, his
son and son-in-law, and 30,000 men have been taken prisoners. The Marshal bemoans hów the news will strike
Louis XIV; furthermore it will go to England and to
"mutter ANNA."

However crude, the verses are interesting as giving
a German reaction to Blenheim and the defeat of France
and Bavaria. Though undated, the publication seems to be
soon after the battle.

Dux BRITANNICUS, Or the DUKE of MARLBOROUGH.   a POEM.
By a Shrewsbury Scholar. Together with a Prophecy in
another Hand. [2 lines Latin] *Salop* Printed by Thomas
Jones. 1704. Used unique copy in Trent coll., BPub.
    4°: *A*⁴ A2, *1-4*, 5-8, 8 pp. Drop-t. on *4*. To the
Reader *ii-iii*. The poet apologizes for his youth and
lack of ability, justly, as the poem is written in an
ungrammatical, crabbed style. He says the bookseller
insisted that the poem should have come from a Master,
rather than a Scholar. The poem concludes with a "Vale"
and two lines of Lucretius: "Amidst rough Wars how can
verse smoothly flow." Not in Morgan.

The poem is in 94 lines, couplets. Drop-titles "On
the Glorious Victory, Obtained by His Grace the Duke of
Marlborough." Opens:

> May *Marlborough* such loud Acclamations see
> In peace; as those that brought his Victory.

Since the poem makes no detailed allusions to Blenheim,
and is hastily written and printed, it may well be among
the earliest. While it urges that Marlborough be crowned
with glory and honored with columns and bastions, the emphasis is on Anne's outdoing Elizabeth, and on Marlborough surpassing her Drake. Albion's two queens have overcome two empires. Allusions to classical figures and
poets dominate, Caesar, Alexander, Scipio, but "What arms

of theirs cou'd Claim such Victory" (1. 22). They fought
with bows and battering rams, but Marlborough fights with
Heaven's and Jove's thunder. Elizabeth's Drake alone can
supply a comparison. The poem concludes with urging
Marlborough to possess the French "shore," cut the ac-
curs'd Tyrant, so as to be "all *Europs* [*sic*] peace, all
Europ's [*sic*] Liberty."

    A Prophecy is added, p. 8. It consists of 8 lines,
couplets with an anapestic lilt.

> When a Church and a hill to the Danube advances.
> Then near to its Ruin the best Cock of *France* is.

The Prophecy is actually a conundrum, playing on "three
against five," and is interesting for its tribute to Marlborough's Duchess as "the Wit of *St. Albans*," who will be
a princess, and who shall make her spouse "father of
three." Also, it concludes with an allusion to its having been found under ground, "By one who was lately in
Packingtons pound." The Prophecy is reprtd. in *Poems on
Affairs of State*, 1707, IV, 16.

83   The French King Distracted; or, His *Sad Lamentation*, For
the late Defeat of his Forces in *Bavaria*, by the Duke of
Marlebrough [*sic*]; The loss of Marshal *Tallard*, and his
two other Generals that were taken Prisoners. *LONDON*,
Printed for *C. Green*, near *Fleet-street*. 1704.

    4°: A^2, *i*, 2-4, 4 pp. TxU copy used. Colophon
bottom p. 4. The only copy known. 108 lines, couplets.
Not in Morgan. Opens with 'WHHT' for 'WHAT':

> What must I do alas, I am undone!
> Here's New *La Hague*; I've lost my *Rising Sun*!

Although written after Blenheim, a rather dull satire.
King Louis appeals to Madame Maintenon for a cordial, and
is obviously ill.

> In *Savoy*, things go with me very bad;
> In *Italy*, Affairs do look but sad;

In *Spain*, I fear much Blood and there's a Curse;
I fear my Grandson I must take from Nurse.   24-7

Europe laughs, Cologn despairs, Mantua complains, and
Modena weeps; his Holiness groans in spirit.

The *Dauphine* Raves, as he reads the Express,
And curses *Marlborough* and the Prince of *Hess*. 83-4

The court is in confusion. "The *Pope* and Devil have
left me in the lurch" (1. 103).
The poem concludes with Louis XIV sick and apprehen-
sive over England's fame and his own loss of France.

4 *Oxfordshire*. Printed in the Year MDCCIV. Price 1 *d*.

2°: 2 pp., 92 lines, colophon bot. p. 2, couplets,
satire. Bodley only copy known. Not in Morgan. Opens:

Perusing the LIST of the *Tackers* in Print,
And carefully marking what Members were in't.

Satirizes the nine Tackers' lukewarmness toward the Blenheim victory. The poem must have come late in 1704.
Trevelyan, *Ramillies*, p. 16, quotes the opening 17 lines,
describing it as "an election song," and provides a full
discussion of the action of William Bromley and the Oxford group in supporting a tack. Since this action involved attaching the Occasional Conformity Bill to the
Land Tax, the effect would have been to obstruct the war.
Oxfordshire is a strongly political poem, strikingly reflecting the embroilments between the Whig and High Tory
factions. Marlborough's identity is only implied by
allusions to Blenheim, and the addresses to the Queen
hailing the victory. The inconsistency of the Tacker's
plot with these addresses, in sending out verses whose
chime "turns to Burlesque all *Addison*'s rhyme," and
urging the Union with Scotland all appear as themes.
In general tone and competence the poem is not

unworthy of Defoe, who was now working with Harley, and
who suggested luring the High Tories into supporting the
Tack and thus exposing themselves. Reflections of the
emerging hostility among political factions, within the
Tory party as well as between Whig and Tory, make this
poem important. Hope is expressed that Queen Anne may
find the means of reuniting the country, as Henry VIII
"joined the Roses."

> Who knows but our *Ann* may by Heav'n be Decreed
> To Close the wide Wounds of a Nation that Bleed?

Thus, as conquering a second time, she by her sweetness
will attain a "Victory Equal to *Blenheim* Success."

The year 1705 was the year after Blenheim. Not only did it not produce another comparable victory, it marked a year of disappointment for Marlborough. While the poets and the nation continued to exult during most of the year, he saw his plans for a vigorous following-up in a march up the Moselle toward Paris fade. Instead he was beset by Dutch reluctance to take risks, and even German treachery in the surrender of Trèves to the French. Aside from Marlborough's passing the French lines, a kind of symbolic triumph, there was little to show, and the whole situation was aggravated by the Margrave of Baden's refusal to come in support of Marlborough's forces, using an infection of his foot as explanation, the famous "Margrave's toe." In August, ironically in the region of Waterloo, Marlborough was again frustrated, this time when he had every advantage in numbers and position, and could anticipate another Blenheim. But again the Dutch commander Slangenberg dampened his hopes out of jealous spite.

With such a year, panegyrics could be only a carry-over of the celebration of Blenheim. Poems by Smallwood, Cobb, and Wesley appeared, while later Oldmixon and others celebrated the forcing of the lines. Otherwise Defoe, Fitchett, and other poets were confined to the Queen's birthday, the Thanksgiving for Blenheim, and such topics. Tory sympathizers lay in wait, courting the Queen's favor or at most venturing to deplore the lack of a victory, and explaining Blenheim as a lucky, or even rash, accident.

Disappointed in his hopes for a campaign on the Moselle, with a movement toward the French capital at Paris, Marlborough was forced to content himself with the adroit maneuvers involved in passing the supposedly impregnable French line of fortifications connecting Antwerp and Namur. French efforts to retake Gibraltar were checkmated, with considerable element of luck, and the Earl of Peterborough succeeded in capturing Barcelona. Although this last event proved to be of negative value, it did achieve a kind of glory for Peterborough which was exploited later by High Tories who urged his claims against those of Marlborough.

The main events of the year were those of parliamentary and ministerial intrigue and controversy. A series of events which were essential to prosecuting the War involved various bills, the Queen's dissolution of Parliament, and a General Election in which the Tories were thoroughly beaten. Their favorite Occasional Conformity Bill had been defeated in the effort to 'tack' it onto the Land Tax in the previous November. The vote was a resounding 251 to 134, but the Tackers continued their pressure till the General Election in the summer which routed them even further. Trevelyan remarks that the elections "decided the fate of Europe and of Britain" (*Ramillies*, p. 30). For these reasons Marlborough pamphlets and poems are not confined to celebrations of battles. Such victories depended heavily upon support at home, upon Godolphin and bills of supply. Thus politics, war, and poetry continue to be inextricably intertwined.

[Smith, Edmund (1672-1710)]

Untitled: "Janus, did ever to thy wond'ring eyes."

1/2°:   I side, 1 column. No pub., n.d. Lehigh copy
used. BM, MH. 43 lines, ode style, 4 stanzas, nmbd. in
Roman. Reprtd. in The *Works* To which is prefix'd a Character of Mr. *Smith* by Mr. *OLDISWORTH*. Printed for Bernard Lintott, between the *Two Temple-Gates*, 1714, 8vo.,
pp. 93-4, as ODE for the Year 1715. 44 lines in four
stanzas. Not in Morgan. Opens:

> Janus, did ever to thy wond'ring eyes,
> So bright a scene of Triumph rise?

The poet asks whether Greece or Rome ever wore such laurels as Marlborough's arms have won. In the second stanza the Danube floods, bringing in the classic subject of
the drowning of the French forces. A mildly Tory slant
appears in the third stanza, with an allusion to Admiral
Rook's extending Queen Anne's sway "O'er the seas." The
poem concludes with a vindication of the war against
France in the name of freedom.

> Now Janus with a future View
> The Glories of Her reign survey
> .   .   .   .   .   .
> ANNA conquers but to free,
> And governs but to bless.

January 2

[Smallwood, James   (fl. 1699-1709)]

A Congratulatory Poem to his GRACE the Duke of Marlbor-
ough, &c. Upon his Safe Return to England, after the
Glorious Victory obtain'd by the English and *Germans*
under his Conduct, over the *French* and *Bavarians* at the
Battle of Hochstet in Germany, A. D. 1704.   LONDON,
Printed by *R. Janeway*, for *John Isted*, at the *Golden
Ball*, over against *St. Dunstan's Church* in *Fleetstreet*,

and sold by *B. Bragg*, in *Ave-Mary-Lane*, 1704. Price 6 d.
Half-title, t.p., drop-title, p. 1. 271 lines, couplets.
    2°: *A*^{2} B-D^2; *i-iv*, 1-12, 16 pp. Date and author-
ship identified in *Daily Cour.*, No. 847, Tues. Jan. 2,
1705. See author's article, Smallwood, above, No. 42.
Lehigh, MH, BPL, CSmH, DU. Penciled "By Dr. Smallwood"
on MH and DU copies. Morgan G321. See also "A Sermon
Preach'd July 15," No. 109 below. Opens:

> As *Caesar* at the end of each Campaign
> Return'd in Winter still to *Rome* again.

Britain welcomes her hero as did Rome. Vollies of cannon,
feu-de-joies, "rattle through the skies," like the sound
of battle on Danube's banks. Marlborough is compared to
William III at Steenkirk and Landen; as graceful on his
horse as Alexander. "Composure all *without*, all Heat
within" (1. 81). Or like stout Aeneas meeting Turnus and
the Queen of Carthage. He is both God of battle and of
Love. Next to him is his brother, rough in battle, the
two like Castor and Pollux (11. 111-16). Then other
heroes, Cutts, Lumley, Wood, Orkney, Ingoldsby, are
praised.

> Long was the waving Contest stoutly try'd,
> And mutual deaths exchang'd from either side. 131-2

Tallard's fate is to fall at English hands, but he flees
in shame. The Danube drowning is compared to Homer's account of Xanthus.

> And, who 'scaped *Fire*, were in the Water lost:
> Th'*astonished* River, choak'd up with the Dead,
> Debarr'd of passage, rear'd his Crimson Head.
> .   .   .   .
> The *Danube*, purple *Danube*, I attest,
> What num'rous Heaps into thy Waves were prest
> O'er thy steep Banks more headlong Squadrons roul'd
> Than little *Xanthus* in his *Brook* cou'd hold;
> Confus'd in light they bear each other down,
> And *following* Crouds help *former* Crouds to drown,
> Horses and Men together tumbled lye,
> *Meeting* that Death, from which they fain wou'd *fly*.
> 165-77 *passim*

Smallwood, not yet knowing of the Danube drowning in his, the first, panegyric, returns to the theme. Marlborough is compared to a Lion, hunting herds to their death in a river, to an eagle forcing exhausted birds into the sea, and to avenging Gabriel forcing rebel angels into the depths of Hell. So the enemy before Marlborough.

> Into the Streams Heels-over-head they fall,
> The wide-mouth'd River gapes, and swallows all.
> Haste then, triumphant River, haste away
> To *Buda*, *Belgrade*, and the *Euxine* Sea:
> Bear down the Ecchoing Name of *Marlborough*,
> To ev'ry Town, to ev'ry Region tell
> What Shoals of *French* into thy Bottom fell.   200-6

The drowning theme is continued with Biblical parallels. Pharaoh's locusts drove numbers to rush into the waters. When Queen Deb'rah was beset by rash Jabin's forces, the river rose, and Kishon swelled and swept them away. Similarly now for Queen Anna and her hero Barak.

Two more themes, both Whiggish, remain. In retrievement of the ancient honor, Edwards and Henrys are surpassed. "Our *Old Sires* look on" smiling to see themselves outdone by their sons (11. 253-4). Pride in female reign, which could be either Whig or Tory, leads to contempt for France's Salique Law. "A Woman over *France* in time may Reign" (1. 265). Finally Smallwood exults in the fact that not only the foreign enemy, but one at home as well, has been vanquished -- "*Faction*, that Homebred, English, Teeming Fiend" (1. 267) has been subdued. While it was common for either side to deplore faction, the allusion is to political obstruction to the war, and even disgruntlement at Marlborough's victories, a theme to be pressed hard, down to Swift's *Conduct of the Allies* (1711). In one great action Marlborough has struck all the Hydra's heads at one blow, thus uniting the English to go ahead and "ballance the Globe" and give law to "distant Climes." The balance of power policy is adumbrated in an Anna "poizing Empires in her equal Scales," and Milton is echoed in the closing picture of Marlborough:

> And you, Great Sir, with *Flaming Sword* in Hand
> As th' *Angel Paradise*, Protect our Land.   280-1

87   January 2.

[Phillips, John (1676-1708)]

BLEINHEIM, A POEM, Inscrib'd to the Right Honourable
ROBERT HARLEY, Esq; LONDON, Printed for *Tho. Bennet*,
at the *Half-Moon* in St. *Paul*'s Church-yard.   1704.
Drop-title, p. 1.
     2°: A^1 B-F^2 G^1; t.p., *i*, *bl.*, 1-22, 24 pp., no wmk.
Second issue has Errata bottom p. 22.   493 lines, blank
verse.   M. G. Lloyd Thomas, *Poems of John Phillips*, xxi,
cites Luttrell copy as '1704/5.'   Advs. in The *Post-Man*,
No. 1362, Jan. 2-4; and *Daily Cour.*, Jan 2.   Morgan H347.
     Ibid.   2°: same except for insertion of 'The Second
Edition' on title, correction of two errata, change of
period to comma after Bleinheim in drop title, and addition of incorrect parenthesis after "Load," p. 2, 1. 8.
'Snows' changes to 'Frosts,' p. 4, 1. 20.   No wmk. Dated
Jan. 13-16 in *Post-Man*.   Also 18-20.
     Ibid.   2°: same except for insertion of 'The Third
Edition' on title.   All corrections and erroneous parenthesis as in second edition.   No wmk. Adv. *L. Gaz.* No.
4601, Feb. 26-Mar. 1.
     Ibid.   H. Hills octavo piracy, 1709.   16 pp.   Horn
copies of all eds. used.   Available in coll. eds.
     The poem was commissioned by Harley and St. John,
and written at the house of the latter, as a retort to
Addison's *Campaign*, which establishes its Tory point of
view.   While Saintsbury describes it "as that most terrible of failures, an unconscious burlesque" (*CHEL*, IX,
204), it is preceded only by Charles Johnson in use of
blank verse, and it was popular in its day, which is
one of the virtues of panegyric.   Opens:

> From low and abject Themes the Grov'ling Muse
> Now mounts Aerial, to sing of Arms.

While the martial acts of "*Britain*'s Heroe" provide the
theme, address is made to Harley on whom the country's
weal depends, and upon whose hourly councils Anne depends.   Marlborough's name appears only once, as 'Marle-

borough,' while eleven times he is referred to as Churchill. Godolphin is praised for supplying funds for the
war, as did Elizabeth's Burleigh. Little attention is
given to the great march. Soon Eugene joins the English
forces and Churchill, whom Anne has chosen as leader.
The French utter jovial taunts, and Tallard voices insulting questions concerning British courage.

No notice is taken of the preliminary victory at
Schellenberg; pages 7 to 14 are devoted to Blenheim
proper and here are bloody and violent scenes. In general the Tories professed shock at the cruelties of the
war they deplored. Here the Miltonic blank verse surges
with grisly imagery.

> Now from each Van
> The brazen Instruments of Death discharge
> Horrible Flames, and turbid streaming Clouds
> of Smoak sulphureous; intermix't with these
> Large globous Irons fly, of dreadful Hiss,
> Singeing the Air, and from long Distance bring
> Surprizing Slaughter; on each Side they fly
> By Chains connex't, and with destructive Sweep
> Behead whole Troops at once; the hairy Scalps
> Are whirl'd aloof, while numerous Trunks bestrow
> Th'ensanguin'd Field.   143-53

While mangled limbs and clotted brains and gore dominate,
Philips does bring in one new touch, the well-aimed can-
nonball that shot his horse from beneath Churchill. Also
Eugene's bringing vital aid at the crucial moment in the
battle, a favorite Tory theme later, is brought in, as
Ajax aided Laertes's son. The Danube drowning, as the
French leap into the "wide extended Flood," is equally
baroque and classically embellished with a grisly Hydra.
Marlborough's clemency and British concern over loss of
life now balance the savage portrayal of battle. Two
Youths who might have been leaders in war are seen walk-
ing together in the underworld, Anne's son and Marlborough's, both of whom died young.

Now the Muse returns to earth, to contemplate the
triumphs of England's conqueror. Canon [sic] fire, the

shouts of crowds, and the congratulations and awards from
princes of Prussia and the Empire are contrasted with the
miseries of Louis XIV, for whom even Boileau's harp is now
incapable of providing cheer. Devastated lands and cities
are the lot of the defeated enemy, while Albion enjoys
peace and security. The war is deplored as "wasteful
Strife" since the Iberian succession is still undecided
(1. 362). The natives are uncertain as to whom to obey,
while Eugene ravages their land and Sweden and Russia send
forces to fight. In Poland also civil broils reflect contention for the crown. Only in England is peace, and from
there Queen Anne sends her Churchill to aid injured realms
and peoples. And in the now usual Tory touch, Rook "rides
O'er the Lab'ring Main," to fight the Gallic navy.

Philips concludes with a tribute to St. John, the
"English Memius" who is too preoccupied with war-making
to sing victory himself, and at whose "delicious Rural
Seat," he is writing. Eventually Churchill will be celebrated in St. John's "Sublimer Verse," and "latest Times
shall learn From Such a *Chief* to Fight, and *Bard*, to
sing" (1. 494).

88   January 2.

Cobb, Samuel, M. A. Cambridge (1675-1713)

HONOUR RETRIEV'D. A POEM Occasion'd By the late Victories obtain'd over the *French* and *Bavarians* by the Forces
of the Allies, under the Command of his Grace the Duke
of *MARLBOROUGH*. [3 lines Claudian] By Samuel Cobb, *M.A.*
LONDON: Printed for *William Turner*, at the *Angel* at
Lincolns-Inn Back Gate, and *John Nutt*, near *Stationers
Hall*. MDCCV. Price 1 *s*. Adv. Theodore Gouston's translation Aristotle's *Art of Poetry*, bot. t. p.; drop-t., p.1.
    2°: A^2 B-G^2; hf. t., t.p., *bl.*, *iii-iv*, 1-24, 28 pp.
Wmk. foolscap. 622 lines, couplets. *Post Man*, No. 1362,
Jan 2 to 4, 1705: "There is now publish'd Philips' Blein-
heim and Cobb's Honour Retriev'd." BM, MH, CtY, TxU, ICN,
CSmH. Huntington Lib. copy used. The 1707 ed. in *Poems
on Several Occasions*, pp. 227-64, corrects numerous

errors, and introduces others. Only a few substantive
changes. Drops "Honour Retriev'd" from title. Enlarged
1709, 1710 eds. Morgan H93. Opens:

> Scarce had we time allow'd our thanks to yield,
> For bloody *Schellenberg*'s Victorious Field.

The news of new conquests inspires the poet "with a
Pierian rage." If only Churchill, that is Marlborough,
would deign to approve him no monument could surpass his
efforts. The political situation is described with the
usual emphasis on a tyrant French monarch. In a vision
he is misled into despising the Allies, and Mazarin and
his marshals abet this delusion. It is not till p. 14
that the meeting of the armies and the great conflict
of "Blenheim" is reached.

> When *Tallard*, strengthen'd with a numerous Force
> Of fresh Batallions, and of *Household* Horse
> Comes pouring like a Torrent; such a Host
> Deserv'd our Swords; the best which *France* could
> boast.   360-3

Amidst the ninth hour of battle, Prince Eugene rebounds
to his fourth attack, and with the English leader in the
thickest of the conflict, the battle is turned. Wood
and other generals participate. The cry of "Queen Anne"
is heard, and the Angel Asariel addresses the Danube. As
a result the drowning takes place. The proud *Gens d'
arms* and their horses are flung into the boiling stream.

> With idle Swords some think to ward the blow
> Of Billows breaking on their Heads below;
> Others, despairing, rowl their ghastly Eyes
> Tow'ards highest Heav'n, and blame the cruel Skies.
> 503-6

If only England properly appreciated such a victory, as
the Senate and the Queen have! United minds alone can
defeat France. Brief tribute is paid to naval victories,
though Gibraltar is not specified. The long poem concludes with a prophecy of Marlborough's appearance in
France in the ensuing year. Heaven will produce miracles,

And Fate confirm the Promise of the Muse.   622

Cobb's tribute has limited poetic appeal, but added
to the *Poetae Britannci* of early 1700 and *The Female
Reign* in 1709, he established himself as one of the most
productive panegyrists.   Shorter pieces signalize Ramillies and other events.   That he should be among the first
to exploit the Whig doctrine of honor's being retrieved,
and later that of a woman as sovereign, is particularly
notable.

89   January 6.

His Grace the Duke of *Marlborough*'s Welcome into the City
of *London*:   Printed and Sold by *H. Hills* in *Black-fryers*.
        1/2°:   1 side, 2 columns.   Foxon-Crawford only ref.
Bottom cropt, perhaps cutting off date.   Portrait of
Marlborough in oval at top.   56 lines, couplets.   Not in
Morgan.   Opens:

        Thrice welcome home, thou Mighty Conqueror
        From Forreign Ward, to thy Native Shore.

Marlborough, as Queen Anne's agent, saving religion at
home and the liberty of Europe abroad.   Tribute to

        . . .valiant *Cuts* that led the English on,
        And shar'd the honor was at Blenheim won.

The poem hails future campaigns and victories.

        For never was such a Vic'try seen,
        Nor such a General, for such a Queen.   55-6

90   January 9.

THE HISTORY OF THE CAMPAIGN IN GERMANY For the Year 1704.
Under the Command of his Grace *JOHN* Duke of *Marlborough*,

Captain General of Her Majesties FORCES. WITH AN Impartial Account of the Two Famous Battels OF *Schellenberg* and *Bleinheim*; AND LISTS of the Kill'd, Wounded and taken Prisoners. From the Time of his *GRACE*'s Setting out, to his Return to *Whitehal* [*sic*]. *Si placuit semel, haec iterum repetita placebit LONDON*: Printed for *J. Nutte*, [*sic*] near *Stationers-Hall*, 1705.

4°: A-K⁴, L⁴; t.p., *bl.*, *iii-iv* To the READER, 1-48, 41-74 (pp. 41-8 rptd.), 82 pp. An extended ed. of *An Exact Journal of the Campaign in Germany*, 1704, No. 57 above. Also a pamphlet with the same title, except as *A Compleat History of the last Campaign*, etc. Both adv. *Daily Cour.* Numb. 853, Jan. 9, 1705 as 'There is now publish'd.' Horn copy of the *History* used. Morgan H284.

In the prefatory 'To the Reader' the anonymous writer speaks of having received several letters from foreign parts, and the pamphlet is composed of gazettes and letters. Except for the prefatory material it contains nothing original.

Flying-Post, Nov. 27-9, 1705, adv. as pubd. by *B. Bragg*, with the addition of forcing the lines.

1   January 16.

THE BATTLES. A POEM. On the late Successes of Her Majesty's ARMS by SEA and LAND. [5 lines Prior, *Carmen Saeculare*: "*The Muses only can Reward his Care.*"] *LONDON*: Printed for *John Nutt*, near *Stationers-Hall*, 1705. Adv. *Daily Cour.* No. 860 as 'Yesterday was publish'd' on January 17. Advs. *Rev.*, No. 99, Feb. 13, 20, and almost continuously thereafter for some time.

2°: A-*D*²; t.p., *bl.* 2, 3-13, 10 for 14, 11 for 15, 16 unmbd., Adv. of Dennis's *Britannia Triumphans* on *16*, 16 pp. Drop-t. on p. 3. 244 lines, couplets. BM copy used. Dr. Williams (2). TxU. Foxon has Luttr., "16 Januar. 1705/4." Morgan H41. Opens:

> Ye Sacred Muses whose Exalted Lays
> Best speak our Wonders, best express our Praise.

The Muses are implored to aid the poet's song in praise
of Anna, "Soul of Righteous War" (1. 9). She has appointed Marlbro, reviver of the martial fire of the
chiefs of old. Also, under Anna's great consort, i.e.,
Prince George, another hero (Rook), shows England's
right to rule the sea. The poem, while primarily celebrating Blenheim, gives four pages to Rook and the navy,
linking Vigo with the victory on the Danube. Retrievement of ancient honor is developed by reference to Cressy
and Poictiers. Then William, who attempted only what
Anne achieved. The most unique feature is the recognition of the role of the panegyrists. First Prior, for
his praise of William and Marlborough.

> ADDISON Imitates the happy Choice;
> DENNIS and TATE and all the tuneful Train,
> Sing the New Wonders of the *Great Campaign*.   79-81

Anne sends Marlbrô, who embarks for Belgium. "He went,
he saw, he bravely overcame" (1. 105). The Gallic general (Tallard), sought to flee, and pass the Danube, but
is captured and forced to resign his sword to Marlborough. Bavaria, also, mourns her "violated Faith."
The remainder of the poem praises Rook by name.
Vigo is described in very general, though gory, terms.

> The trembling *Spaniards* from the neigh'bring Shoar,
> Fear once again a *British* Lady's Pow'r.   210-11

While Godolphin is praised for supplying Marlborough's
"shining Troops," who are "with Exactness paid," the poem
clearly in its title, *The Battles*, and its praise of Rook
inclines to Tory sentiments.

> Infernal Envy can't Disguise
> Thy long successive *Triumphs* o'er the Seas.   161-2

Rook is welcomed home from victorious battle and receives
the thanks of the Prince, the Queen, and the Senate, who

employ him in council. This pointed praise of the Senate
is a new element in political panegyric.

> By *Them* we Act, by *Them* we Tribute raise,
> And what's a juster Tribute than *Due Praise*.   234-5

The poet returns to the Queen at the close, since she
"does my young unpractis'd Muse inspire," and links the
two heroes in the final lines.

> Happy, for ever Happy be *Thy* Reign,
> May MARLBRO's mighty Arm the State sustain,
> And ROOK Command the warring Castles on the spacious
> Main.   242-4

2   January 18.

Tate, Nahum (1652-1715)

THE TRIUMPH, or *Warriours Welcome*: A POEM on the *Glorious Successes* of the *Last Year*. With the ODE for the
New-Year's Day. 1705. By Mr. TATE. Poet-Laureat to Her
MAJESTY. [Latin prose motto. *P. Arb.*] *LONDON*, Printed
by J. *RAWLINS* at the Bible in St. *Paul's Alley*, Sold by
J. *Nutt* near *Stationers-Hall*. 1705.
  4°: *A*⁴ B-E⁴; *i-iv*, 1-29, 22, 30, 30' [i.e. 32], 36
pp. MH, Horn copy used. *Apology* to FAME, 29 lines, coup-
lets. The WARRIOURS Welcome, &c., 324 lines, couplets;
The TRYUMPH, 182 lines, couplets; The ODE for the *New-
Years* Day, 44 lines, ode. Total 579 lines. TxU, Clark,
CtY, BM. Adv. *Post-Man*, No. 1365, Jan. 16-18; 18-22.
Ibid. Same title with The Second Edition inserted on t.p.
  4°: *A*⁴ B-E⁴; *i-iv*, 1-28, 32 pp. MH, Clark, NY Pub.,
InU, Col. Morgan H430.
  Opens [*ii-iv*] *Apology to Fame*, italics.

> *Forgive, O Gen'rous* Fame, *a tim-rous Muse,
> That long your Desp'rate Service did refuse.*

The author, because of injuries and age, feels inadequate

to the efforts of epic poetry, and the fields of young
adventurers. But now, Schellenberg and Blenheim demand
that he welcome the brave warrior home in triumph. The
pomp, the inspiring sight, the trumpets, transport the
muse to attempt a "new and daring Rhapsody." This portion is 29 lines. *The Warriours Welcome* is 324 lines,
pp. 1-19. *The Tryumph* [*sic*], pp. 20-9, is 182 lines.
All are in couplets, with frequent triplets and an occasional octosyllabic line. The *Ode* is 43 lines. The
total of verse is 578 lines. *The Warriours Welcome*
opens:

> O For a Muse of Flame, the Daring Fire
> That *Blenheim*'s Battling Warriours did inspire.

Even the paper should blaze with martial fire, and the
Hero halt after Schellenberg and Blenheim. Young Ammon
and Julius Caesar are recalled. As indicated in the
margin, Mr. Waller is quoted: "Heroick Deeds, Heroick
Thoughts infuse." The conqueror creates a Muse, but
Maro's too modest and Homer too cold. Let Spencer, i.e.
Spenser, rise from fairyland and Milton "soar his loftier
Paradise," but valor mounts still higher. Boileau must
sing Tallard and defeat. "ANNA's the Word," reflects
the slogan of Blenheim (1. 107).
     The Elector of Bavaria is pitied, as victim of
French perfidy, when he might have won renown with Eugene, as next to Marlborough (125-40 *passim*). But how
praise Blenheim, "theme of Wonder and Delight"?

> What Parchment *Blenheim*'s Battle can contain?
> Have you a Scrowl [*sic*] to cover *Blenheim*'s Plain?
> From *Hassael-brook* to *Hockstet*, Front and Flank
> From *Aghberg*'s wond'ring Wood to *Danube*'s bloody
> Bank.   173-7

Because "one Muse *Worthy a Conq'rer's Name*" soared, would
you expect another to do so? We can only attempt the feat.
Stretch the canvas and paint the picture. Even if the
main figure is set down, how about all the rest? "Down
with your Pallet, Dauber, and Despair (1. 216)." The

theme goes beyond history to romance. The bard pales at
the effort, and the poem turns to a lament for the dead.
Then thoughts of Landau and of Gibraltar and "floating
war" revive the muse, rather tactlessly since the poem
was written to celebrate Marlborough. He now undertakes
the second main portion, *The Tryumph*, specifically on
Marlborough's return. Opens:

> Where beauteous *Greenwich* views, with graceful Pride,
> Her Charms reflected in the Chrystal Tide,
> There *Britons*, on your *Thames* proud Banks, behold
> Fame's Chariot blazing all with Gems and Gold.

The pageantry of allegorical figures and ensigns celebrate Schellenberg and Blenheim's Fame, and Britannia
and the royal emblems invite Europa to hear, while music
plays martial movements to express the conquests. The
Danube drowning is noticed.

> Till *Danube*'s Stream, choak'd to a *Stygian* Lake,
> Thro' plunging Squadrons can no Passage make.   50-1

The singers, from their seat on a barge, celebrate Britannia, Father Thames, Matthew Prior's poem to Boileau on
Blenheim, Augusta, the peers, the Pride of Albion, the
Palace, Prince George, and would have sung the Queen, had
not "the listening Nymphs of *Greenwich* Groves struck in"
(1. 131). Even so, the muse praises her, in advance of
her birthday, which is specified as February 6 in the
margin. Marlborough lands and advances to the Queen's
"Wain," but avoids the praise, which is drowned out in
the noise of cannon firing and the shouting.
      The *Ode* for *New-Year's Day*, Performed to Musick be-
fore Her *Majesty*, opens:

> From Fates dark Cell to Empire call'd,
> Ah how forlorn must I appear.

The New Year laments that there is nothing remaining for
him, and since this was the year of the Margrave's Toe
and general frustration of Marlborough's hopes to invade
France and end the war, it is highly prophetic. The poet

invokes long life for the Royal pair; Albion and Europe
will be safe with such a general. In this production
Tate fully establishes his claim to be the laureate of
absurdity; but the national ecstasy at the victory
seemed to call forth every type of excess, not least
from the poets.

93   January 19.

Wesley, Samuel (*c*. 1666-1735)

MARLBOROUGH; OR, The Fate of Europe: A POEM. DEDICATED
to the Right HONOURABLE Master *GODOLPHIN*. By *SAMUEL WES-
LEY*, M.A. [ornament] *LONDON*; Printed for *Charles Harper*,
at the *Flower-de-Luce* over-against St. *Dunstan*'s Church
in *Fleetstreet*. MDCCV.
    2°: *A*[^1] B-D[^2]; t.p., *bl.*, *3*, 4-12, 12 pp.; pp. 10-12
marked '9-11'; drop-t. p. 3.   525 lines, couplets. Clark-
Luttrell copy dates '19 Januar., 1704/5.' BM, NjP, ICN,
CSmH copy used. Morgan H464. Thomas Hearne's *Colls*., I,
49-50, prints a long letter in which Wesley relates his
sufferings at hands of the Dissenters, barns burned, cows
stabbed, and income shrunk to one-half. Also, he has
been turned out of his brief chaplaincy under Col. Lepell,
which was his reward for writing the poem. See also
Hearne, Oct. 10, Dec. 3, and 23. Hearne is of course
violently Tory, taking delight in describing all Whigs
as fanatics and in stressing Marlborough's concern for
money, and later the delays in building Blenheim House
and the Marlboroughs' loss of position. The poem is not
overtly Tory, though conservative. Opens:

    Th' *Eternal*, who the *Fates* of *Empires* weighs,
    And with Impartial Eyes the World surveys.

God sees the growing arrogance and power of France, whose
people worship Lewis rather than Himself. He sends the
angels Prudence, Fortitude, Celerity, and Secrecy to Marlborough who is brooding in his tent over the fate of

Europe. Aided by Eugene in particular, and also by the
Princes of Baden and Hesse, he now marches to the Danube.
Tall ramparts, deep trenches, and rows of cannon con-
front him. Then a phantom from Hell comes to the French
camp, scorning Anne as comparable to Elizabeth. "Must
then a *Woman* crush our rising State!" He attacks, but
Michael intervenes.

Blenheim is largely accounted for by reciting the
courage of the English leaders, Cutts, Ingoldsby, Mordant,
Orkney, North, and of great Eugene.

> Of Troops, Brigades, and Wings the rest take care,
> But MARLBOROUGH alone is *every where*;
> As PRUDENCE bids, the *various Battle* views,
> Like *Nature*, what is lost by *Time* and *Death*
> Till COURAGE calls, her *well-known* Voice he hears,
> *Erect*, and *greater* than himself appears.   255-60

The Danube drowning again provides the culmination of the
battle.

> What thousands *plung'd* in *Death* their *Lives* to save,
> And sought glad *Refuge* underneath the *Wave*:   292-3

Even though squadrons are lost, the "kind *Gazettes*" re-
pair the loss and raise new paper-squadrons. On the
other hand, it seems faint praise to say that from "one
long *Campaign*" the reward is some dukes and a few towns
(1. 309). Europe should now sue for peace and France condescend to part with Germany. Even so, "We merit *Chains*,
if *France* agen [*sic*] we trust," since Louis's oaths cannot be just.

Marlborough is now returning via Belgium, to provide
calm council in state affairs. "Nothing deny'd, where
He's th' *Embassador*." He is praised for humanity, dex-
terity, clemency, and other virtues, the Great Spirit
that moves the whole army. His victories come with a
rush, like those of Alexander. Britannia rears her head
and speaks at length, urging her sons to end noise and
strife and learn to love. She says her Senates will
frustrate France's design (1. 400). Anna reigns justly,

subduing tyrants. England is blessed with her generous
hand and Marlborough's peace, and "with *Eternal Verdure*
bless'd" (1. 522).

94   January.

Albion's Triumph: Or The *Roman Bravery*: a Congratulatory Poem to the Duke of Marlborough. . .Blenheim. Sold
by S. Malthus, 1705. *WL* Jan. 1705. No copy known. Not
in Morgan.

95   January 22.

Defoe, Daniel (1660-1731)

THE DOUBLE WELCOME. A POEM to the DUKE of *MARLBRO'*.
[ornament]   *LONDON*: printed, and sold by *B. Bragg*, at
the *Blue-Ball* in *Ave-Mary Lane*, 1705.

       4°: A-D^4; *i-ii*; t.p., *bl.*, 1-30, 32 pp. Foxon D6;
Morgan H127. BM-Luttrell copy dated '4 *d.* 22 Januar'
with '4' under 1705 in MS.
Ibid. LONDON. Printed in the Year 1705. Horn copy used.
       A B2 [for A2]-C-D^4. Drop-title p. 1. Foxon D7 says
some have E for D1. No wmk. Variant copies also MH, BPub.
Copies also InU, CtY, LU, *et al.* The poem is listed in
Rev., No. 89, Jan. 9, and *Lee*, 65, cites this date. *Rev.*
No. 93, Jan. 23; *Post-Man* and *Daily Cour.* cite as Jan.
22. Repr. in *True Coll.*, II, 1705, pp. 169-85. 508
lines, couplets. Opens:

    My Lord,

       The Muse that by Your Victory's Inspir'd,
       First sung those Conquests, all the World admir'd.

Defoe's claim of being author of the first panegyric is

inaccurate. Samllwood and R. Clare, Nos. 42 and 44, preceded him. Since Defoe was not in London, even his first
report in the *Review* was delayed till August 19 (see No.
43), a week after Smallwood's, the first effort. Though
"scorch'd by Party-Fire," he has always scorned to flatter,
even though he has sung to Kings. Satire has been his
talent, and Truth his song. He has never praised any but
William and Marlborough, the one at Boyn and Namur, and
the other at Schellenburgh and Blenheim, or Hocksted.
    Now he quickly summarizes the march from Breda,
across the Maese, Moselle, and Rhine. The French are
puzzled, not foreseeing the Danube as the place of conflict. "We at a Distance knew the Design," but were "a-
mazed at the success." Now Defoe urges that all the sons
of Rhyme speak up, as they did for Augustus. He will
only hail the conquest, but not the "how," that is the
details. Addison has done this, though for pay.

> Let *Addison* our modern *Virgil* sing,
> For he's a Poet fitted for a King!
> No Hero will his mighty Flight disdain
> The *First*, as thou *the Last* [Defoe] of the
>   Inspir'd Train;
> *Maecenas* has his modern Fancy strung
> And fix'd his Pension first, or he had never sung.
>   179-84

Addison has never known envy and party spleen. "No humbling Jayls has [*sic*] pull'd his Fancy down" (1. 176).
Let Addison, then, describe how Marlborough conquered,
and struggle with such names as baffled Boileau, perhaps
an allusion to Prior's poem on Blenheim.
    Defoe returns to his great interest, political
strife and factionalism at home. The remainder of the
poem is a mixture of powerful satire and an appeal to
Marlborough to restore order. For this he deserves a
Double Welcome, for Double Conquests, and Double Joy.
In an allusion to his recent *Consolidator*, Defoe scores
on the High Church party.

> Con---dators to *Consolidate*
> And *Tack* or T----rs to their own dear Fate.   316-17

Defoe also censures foppish beaus and cowards who buy commissions and strut themselves. They will now be discredited as Marlborough has made war mean *fighting*. William
restored heroism after "Thirteen Ages past," and Marlborough is the last. That Defoe primarily has in mind the
Occasional Conformity Bill becomes evident. Bills and
Pulpit War create strife. High Church and Sacheverel,
their leader, "a Noisy, Sawcy, Swearing, Drunken Priest"
(l. 384), fight for plunder, as Marlborough does for
peace. "They *damn the Lords* because they *damn'd the
bill*." Marlborough is urged to screen the Church from
wild absurdities, and to bring peace at home through moderation.

> Thus, Sir, the Nation's Guardian you'll appear,
> Abroad suppress, at Home prevent the War;
> Anticipate our Factions in their Growth,
> And smother Feud beneath the Arms of Truth.   499-502

96   February 1.

A TRIP TO NOTTINGHAM WITH A CHARACTER OF Mareschal *TAL-
LARD* AND THE French-Generals. *LONDON*: Printed, in the
Year MDCCV.
    2°: A^2, B-D^2; t.p., *bl.*, 3-4, 3-14, 16 pp.   3-4
rptd., drop-t. on p. 3. Clark-Luttr. copy used. '6 d.
1 Febr. 1704/5.' MS fill-in of words by Luttrell. CtY.
592 lines, couplets. Morgan H428.

> Half tir'd with Drinking, Dull-plays, and the rest.
> *Miss* quite out of Humor, the Town grown a Jest.

In this bored mood the poet departs from his punk on a
picaresque trip which involves all the usual inns, merry
drinking, casual encounters, and bedroom adventures. The
first night he spends at St. Albans, the second at an
unidentified inn where the presence of two beds leads to
a strange episode. At St. Albans the fat landlord supplies good claret and manifests that his landlord is the

Duke of Marlborough. The Queen, Prince, and Duke are
loyally toasted. The sedate pace of the poet's horse,
the low-bowing landlord at the Lyon Inn, and the many
glimpses of English life of the day produce a rich, often
racy, Hogarthian quality.

At Nottingham, the complaisant presence of Tallard
and the French officers, who pay well and are courteous,
raises the question of why they are enemies. Some cry
treason for treating them well; but the landlord geni-
ally defends them, and the poet joins Tallard in a hunt.
While there are allusions to the Occasional Bill, tack-
ing, and the Scots, there is slight political bias.
Tallard is such an ordinary fellow it seems difficult
to see how Marlborough could gain honor from capturing
him. The poet decides to go to Litchfield to see how
the French prisoners are faring there.

See No. 100, March 1, 1705.

7   February 2.

Great Britain's Triumph. *A triumphal Arch*. Illustrated
with the Battle of *Schellenberg* and *Blenheim*. Description of *Standards* and *Colours*. Account of the Procession
from the Tower to Westminster Hall. . .To Perpetuate the
Memory In All Families throughout *England* &c. Of His
Grace *John* D. of Marlborough. London, Printed and are
to be Sold by *S. Malthus in London-house-yard* near St.
Paul's at the *Kings Head* in the Savoy *Church-yard*, and
by the Booksellers. Price Two Pence. Bsd., prose. MH-
Luttrell copy used. '2 *d*. 1 Febr. 1704/5.' Not in
Morgan.

Large cut of triple columns, devices, soldiers,
banners. Lists French officers taken prisoner and gives
accounts of the two victories. Blenheim & Hochstet,
right, and Schellenberg and Donauwert, left.

98   February 6.

A *Prologue* to the *Court* on the *Queen's Birth-Day*   1704
London: Printed for *J. Tonson*, 1705. Not in Morgan
     1/2°: TxU-Luttrell copy 'Febr. 6, 1704/5.' CSmH,
MH, Clark, Crawford. 40 lines, couplets. *D. Cour.*,
Thurs. Feb. 8. "This Day is published" - "on Her Maj-
esty's Birthday." Opens:

     The Happy Muse, to this high Scene preferr'd
     Hereafter shall in Loftier Strains be heard.

The poet will turn from war on vice and folly on the
stage, that is the comedy and satire, to undertake nobler
themes. By British Councils the Christian world has been
freed.

     The fierce Foe was pre-ordain'd to yield,
     And then the Battel won at BLENHEIM's Glorious Field.

99   February 6.

A DIALOGUE BETWEEN THE *French Standards* in *Westminster-
Hall*, AND THE *Guns* on the *Tower-Wharf*, ON THE ANNIVERSARY
OF Her Majesty's Birth, Suppos'd to be Occasioned by their
then Firing. [ornament] *LONDON*: Printed for *John Wick-
ins*, and Sold by *J. Nutt*, near *Stationers-Hall*. 1705.
     2°: *A*²B-C²; t.p., *bl.*, 3-12, 12 pp., drop-t. on p.
3. MH-Luttr. '4 *d.* 6 Febr. 1704/5.' Only copy known.
204 lines, couplets. In dialogue form. Morgan H139.

          STANDARDS.
     Sons of Thunderer, and *Bellona's* Care,
     Heraulds of Death, and Gyants of the War.

The French standards politely inquire as to the occasion
of the "pleasing Joy" of their thundering. The Guns respond that their exulting Roar" is for the event on the
Danube. The Standards reply that they know that Albion's
joys increase, and that her land is not invaded by war.

In turn the Guns modestly speak the blessings of Eng-
lands's isle.

> While Marlborough's Arm the Conquering Sword Sustains,
> And New-reap'd Lawrels strow *Bavarian* Plains;
> While yet New Scenes the *Gallic* Champain's yield,
> And growing Honours spread the Future Field;
> While *Britain*'s Floating Castles Sovereign Ride,
> And Her large Empire o'er the Sea decide.   35-40

The exchange turns only slightly to argument as the Standards loyally insist that their leader, Louis XIV, will
yet prevail. The Guns retort:

> The Ard'rous Zeal (though Dutious) ye express
> Your hapless Monarch's ills can ne'er Redress;
> Your Vows and Prayers are sent to Heaven in Vain,
> Nor can avert his Fate, or Ease his Pain.
> As well might *Tallard*, and the Glorious Train
> Of *Marlborough*'s Captives, (won on *Blenheim*'s Plain)
> O'er Slain Battalions dream of High Commands,
> And Fancy Conquests in Confederate Lands.   125-32

The poem concludes with the Guns reciting a peroration to
the Queen's birthday (11. 147-204) in which Phoebus,
Philomel, and Neptune are urged to join the joyous celebration. The verse seems to be superior to many panegyrics despite its conventional terms.

0   March 1.

A TRIP TO LITCHFIELD WITH A CHARACTER OF THE *French* OF-
FICERS there. *By the Author of the Trip to* Nottingham.
LONDON: Printed, in the Year MDCCV.
     4°: *A²*, B-C²; t.p., *bl.*, 1-12, 14 pp. Clark-Luttr.
copy used. '4 *d*. 1. March. 1704/5.' Words filled in by
Luttrell. Also CSmH, *WL* Feb. 1705. 412 lines, anapestic
couplets. Not in Morgan. Opens:

Now Muse, grown acquainted with Country Air,
In suitable Meetre [*sic*] my Progress declare.

Seeking further grottoes and adventures, the poet rides
directly from Nottingham, No. 96 above, to Litchfield.
He arrives late, but at an inn where a beautiful hostess
who, though married, supplies an adventure quite in the
picaresque style. He puts his purse of gold in her charge
and recovers it through her husband's innocent blunder.
Riding on, the next morning, he falls in with a merry
wedding party, plump bride in sugar-loaf hat and green
fittings, a lusty groom, and a jocular, ale-bibbling
assemblage of country folk. Healths to the Queen, Marlborough, the Fleet, to next summer's successes are politically tolerant, although a sturdy country Toryism
might be detected. The French officers are so gallant
that only our women could conquer them!

101 March 1 *ca*.

[Pittis, William (1674-1724)]

A HYMN TO NEPTUNE: Occasion'd by the late Glorious Vic-
tory obtain'd on the Height of *Malaga* by Her Majesty's
Royal Navy, under the command of Sir *George Rooke*, Vice
Admiral of *England*, &c. [4 lines Horace]   *LONDON*,
Printed for *R. Basset* at the *Mitre* over against *Chancery-
Lane-End*, in *Fleet-Street*, 1705. Price 1 *s*.
    4°: A-F^4; t.p., *bl.*, *ii-viii*, 1-40, 48 pp. Verse
Dedication "To the Right Honourable Sir *George Rooke*,
Vice-Admiral of *England*; And one of Her Majesty's most
Honourable *Privy-Council*," *ii-iv*, 38 lines, couplets;
Prose Preface, *vi-vii*; Advertisement of book printed for
R. Basset and Errata, *viii*. 701 lines, in 37 stanzas,
two nmbd. XXX, no XXXIII. *Flying Post*, No. 533, Feb. 27-
March 1, 1705. Morgan H222. CSmH copy used.
    The Dedication, which precedes the Preface, opens:

> While every Breast is full of your Applause,
> That joins in Monarchy's or Merit's Cause.

This support of the monarchy strikes the Tory note. Pindar's lofty manner is urged as none too good for the "noble Subjects." The defence of Rooke against detractors and the "Censures of the Factious Crowd" (1. 23) provides the occasion of the poem as much as the Admiral's exploits at Malaga. Albion's and Rooke's foes are foes of the Muse.

The Preface versifies the necessity of such a poem as being manifest to any reader. Public rejoicings at the late victory at sea attest to the triumph at Gibraltar. Still some industriously omit Rooke's name in public addresses. "I wonder they did not leave out the Duke of *Marlborough*'s too, since he is also for the Monarchy and the Church Establish'd." The statement concludes with the assertion that not all Englishmen are ungrateful. The catchword "No" leads to the poem, but p. *viii* with the advertisements and Errata intervenes. The poem opens:

> NO, 'tis in vain, not all their Factious Arts,
> Made use of to debauch our hearts.

Not these, nor the "little Tricks, and Whiggish Lies" (1. 7) will prevent our esteem for "such a Man." Soaring above Envy the Muse addresses Neptune, the "trident-bearing Deity." That the poem is relatively amateurish and conventional is soon apparent, and it warrants no detailed analysis. The usual themes of a modest muse, unequal to the great task, and the ungrateful treatment of a national hero dominate it. *O*[rmond] is represented as having had too much of the credit for Rooke's triumphs (St. VII). "Dastard *C*[ole]*pe*[p]*er*" and his friends at *Mercer*'s-Hall, and the "party hireling *Tutchin*" (St. XI) are noted as particularly obnoxious. To be sure, Rooke did not conquer at le *Hogue* alone. Hopson's great exploit in making way through the boom (St. XVIII), as well as various commanders, mentioned later, had their share.

Marlborough appears, primarily as a devastator, in St.
XXV.

> Danubian Plains saw the Grim Tyrant stalk
> And with huge Strides o'er slaughtered Armies walk,
> > Saw him at *Marlborough*'s Command
> > > Depopulate the Land,
> > And make the *Gall* [*sic*] before him fall,
> And sue for Mercy from his Conquering Hand.   309-14

While Rooke is credited with corresponding devastation
at Sea, the onus for the destructive aspects of war is
placed on the Duke. Plainly, though he has had a great
victory, Rooke's does more credit to England.
     Little detailed description of either naval battle
or the siege of Gibraltar appears. All Art and Nature
can do is overcome. Rooke bears his bloody flag, as if
two bulls were clashing. Shovel led, with Leak next, and
Bing, Dilks, and Wishart, all playing their parts. Due
credit is given to a brave foe, and the *Toulouse*, a
French ship, even escapes as night falls. Rather surprising praise to the "God-head of Neptune" is given, and a
grateful Senate's thanks crowns the deed. Even so, Rooke
has encountered so much ingratitude that sometime he may
decline to come to England's rescue, a threat which reminds the poet of Troy and Achilles, and also produces
a strongly political and highly inarticulate conclusion,
as of Achilles:

> Who but for him, had Conquer'd mourn'd the Conquest
> of their Foes.

This over-extended and confused final line, properly terminates a poem that is more tendentious than poetic. This
is perhaps the first poem to introduce the specific political label of Whig. It shows the advent of controversy in
connection with Marlborough's career, since the charges
are actually against those who favored his policies.
     Neptune is hailed as having seen Rooke's triumphs,
and is urged to speak. Feuds and differences of opinion
should vanish in face of victories, and those who have
curbed the pride of France should be welcomed. While

Rooke was in *O*[rmond]'s fleet, he conquered on his own.
His victories crowd in so fast that "we know not which
to fix on to Command" (1. 135). The French king commands his fleet to go and destroy the English fleet, but
instead they flee. Yet there are those who would give
credit to others than Rooke.

> Such as is Dastard *C*[ole]*pe*[p]*er*,
> That Writes, and makes a mighty stir,
>   To let us see,
> There are not many greater Fools than he.
> Except his Friends at *Mercers-Hall*, a Scandal to
>   the Fur.
> And gives it in large Folio under's hand,
> He durst not any but *Law Tryals* stand.[1]

Tutchin and Party rancor are also noticed, and
O[rmond] who could not have pursued the French without
Rooke's earlier blow. Neither booms, nor chains, could
stop him and his leader Hopson. A dubious pun appears:
"But when the Prince of Birds a Quarry finds" (1. 255).
Description of naval battle, the seas turning red with
blood, and gold from the Spanish loot, attempts little
in the way of the usual detail.

Perhaps the emphasis is intentionally on the greater
horrors of land battle, and Marlborough's devastation and
depopulation of Bavaria (p. 26). Shovel leads the van,

---

[1]An allusion to Colepeper's alleged insult to Rooke
and his encounters with several antagonists. The episode
is cited by John R. Moore, *Defoe, Citizen of the Modern
World*, 1958, pp. 129-32, 173. Since Colepeper had been,
though inept, attorney for Defoe and also had been one of
the Kentish Petitioners, an interesting and complicated
relationship is involved. The Folio mentioned is *A True
State of the Difference* Between Sir *George Rooke*, Kn^t and
William Colepeper, Esq; Together with an Account of the
Tryal etc., *London*, Printed: And Sold by the Booksellers
of *London* and *Westminster*. MDCCIV, fol., *i-iv*, 1-44, 48
pp. Horn copy used.

by Defoe

with Leak close behind. The French admiral's *Soleil
Royal* is overwhelmed when "two from five bear off the
Prize" (1. 563). Bing, Dilks, and Wishart also are de-
serving, and Jennings is alongside the leader. Otherwise all glory goes to Rooke. The poem culminates with
a strong appeal that Rooke's patience not be overstrained.
While he has received the thanks of the Queen, the Nation,
and the Senate, some enviously decline thanks. It may be
hoped that "wearied with abuse," Rooke may never refuse
to "guard a base ungrateful Shore." Those who have rejected him may be like the Greeks imploring Achilles to
forget his resentments and lead them again.

102 March 19.

Johnson, Charles (1679-1748)

THE QUEEN: A Pindarick ODE. [4 lines Horace] By Mr.
Cha. Johnson. *LONDON*: Printed for *Nicholas Cox*, at the
Golden Bible without *Temple-Barr*. 1705.
    2°: A^2 B-G^2; hft., *bl.*, t.p., *bl.*, *i-iv*, Drop-t.
p. 1. Errata bot. p. 23. 1-23, *24 bl.*, 28 pp. No wmk.
MH, TxU, Sutro, *WL*. 505 lines, ode tone but largely ir-
regular couplets. MH copy used. This is the second of
Johnson's three Marlborough panegyrics. See No. 52,
September 18, 1704. Morgan H228^d. Opens:

        Touch, my Muse, thy jarring String,
          In joyful Lays address to Sing.
    Britannia's Empress be the mighty Theme.

Whig ideas are strongly reflected in praise of Albion's
Queen, who reformed a vicious court, and married a Danish
prince. Sadness at the loss of her son gives way to
praise of "Germanick Marlbro'." Invoking Pindar's rage
and fire, the poet approaches the great subject of Anne's
triumph over the "vast Leviathan" of France (1. 150).

> The Great Destroyer now,
> Does to Female Vertue owe
> His everlasting Overthrow.   162-4

Anne draws the sword for Liberty, and sails to Belgick
shores. She gives power to Churchill, her hero. His
acts "Transcend the weaker Power of Verse" (1. 276).
Bavaria bleeds and its country is in flames as "*Marlbro*'s sure Victorious Sword" (1. 368) deals its blows.
Blenheim is described largely by allusion to classical
victories and heroes. Marlborough, Eugene, and Cutts
fight in the flames and smoke. "Anna, Britannia's Empress, was the Word" (1. 454). This use of the Queen's
name as slogan is confirmed in the *Full and Impartial
Relation*, 1704, p. 4, though Prior has it as *Anne* and
St. *George*. For the third time the Danube drowning comes
in for notice.

> To shun the glorious Death with Shame,
> They plunging dye the rapid *Danub*'s [*sic*] Stream:
> The eager flying Troops crowd hard to have,
> E'er 'tis too late, a charitable Wave.   442-5

Tallard's despair and the slaying of "his only Son,"
which was not the case, and his being taken captive,
leads to exultation for the Roman Eagle and the British
Lion. The poem closes with an angry Apollo, who descends to denounce the inadequacy of the poet's efforts
since it is above the power of verse to celebrate Anne's
eternal glories. He must himself descend and immortal-
ize

> Great *Anna*'s Name,
> *Marlbro*'s Sword, and *Bleinheim*'s Fame.   504-5

The second of three panegyrics by Johnson. In this poem
he exploits the entire body of Whig doctrines.

103 March 26.

Fitchett, John   (No dates)

THE Hero Reviv'd; OR, A POEM ON THE Glorious Success and
Victories obtain'd by the Duke of Marlborough At *BLEIN-
HEIM*.   By *JOHN FITCHETT*, A. B. of *Cambridg* [*sic*].   *Sem-
per honos, noménq; tuum, laudésq; manebunt*.   *LONDON*,
Printed for *John Barnes* at the *Crown* in the *Pall-Mall*.
1705.
     2°: A^2 B-C^2; t.p., Dedication *i-iv*, 5-12, 12 pp.
TxU-Luttrell copy, '4 *d*. 27 March.'   Wmk. Amsterdam-Arms.
Dedication "To the Right Honourable Francis Godolphin,
Esq; Coferer to her Majesty's Houshold [*sic*].   This POEM
is humbly Dedicated by the AUTHOR."   TxU only loc.   Adv.
Daily Cour. No. 918.   'Mon. Mar. 26, 1705. 'This Day is
publish'd.'   Luttrell notes date of purchase, rather than
of publication.   284 lines, couplets.   Not in Morgan.
Opens:

> As when in antient Times to mighty *Jove*
> Men did on Altars their Devotion prove.

The poet dares to praise *Marlbro*'s name,

> Altho' ambitious *Westley*'s daring Muse
> Does more than we can say, or think, produce,
> A Draught of Glory, and the Hero's Dues.
> So covetous his eager Verses seem
> In handling to monopolize the Theme.   10-15

No other panegyrist than Samuel Wesley is mentioned, but
it is recognized that there is no need for bards to
jostle each other, as the space is immense, like the sky
where planets rove.   Mention of Jove, Briareus, Pelion,
and Ossa, and later classical allusions reflect Fitchett's Cambridge training.   Marlborough and Apollo dif-
fer only in name, as what the god does in appeasing the
gods the earthly hero does in smoothing over factional
differences (p. 7).   Marlborough's victories are beyond
praise, and will set the standard for all future triumphs.
     Instead of extended description of Blenheim, the

poet stresses the sinister animosity of the French and
Bavarians, and their generals. Their conspiring is contrasted with Marlborough's openness and good nature. The
massy cannon create convulsions, but this does not dismay
the English chief. He comes like a Lion against a herd
of stags. He is asked to "recite the various Movements
of enraged fight"; but it is the morale of battle rather
than its actions, that is considered. "How," the poet
asks, "can the Spawn of Cots," that is cottagers, used
more to mattocks than guns, perform as they did at Hochstet? The British souls "take fire," and like a monster
wave overwhelm the cowardly French. They pour vengeance
on the foe, and the Danube drowning alone is suggested
in the eight hours of severe fighting.

> Twisted in *Danube*'s Bowels they expire,
> And soft Destruction is their last desire;
> *Danube*, late witness of their haughty Pride
> Now does their treble Cowardice upbraid,
> And triumphs o'er them with unusual Tide.   266-70

In conclusion, the Muse is urged to open the "Scrouls of
Fame," and enroll the names of Churchil [*sic*], Cutts, and
Ingoldsby. These are excelled by only one, Anna. William
looks down in joy and wonder to see "The tott'ring World
so well upheld by You" (1. 284).

4   March 26.

Barnes, Joshua (1659-1712) Regius Professor of Greek at
Cambridge.

EPINIKION [in Greek, in Latin] EPINICIUM, Super Invictis-
simo Duce MARLBORAEO, Quie *Bavarorum* & *Gallorum* Exercitus,
In Agris *Blenamamaeis*, Profilgavit; *Anacreonticum Josuâ*
Barnes Auctoro. Horn copy used. The title means victory
song, and the poem of 80 short lines is preceded by a
prose dedication, pp. *vi-xii*. This EPISTOLA DEDICATORIA

combines effusive praise of Marlborough and Blenheim,
with allusions to Queen Anne and Tallard. It is signed
and dated March 26, 1705. The *Epinicium* opens:

> Lyricus Poeta *Teius*,
> Ut ad alta Tecta venit
> Ducis Ille Marlboraei.

The poem is only of anecdotal interest. It appears in
the octavo volume *ANACREON* TEIUS. It includes full-page
engravings of Barnes, Marlborough, and Anacreon, a Latin
life of Anacreon, a list of Barnes's works, and an Index,
as well as the Latin translation of Anacreon's poems,
opposed to the Greek originals.

Trevelyan, *Ramillies*, p. 8, relates the alleged in-
cident of Barnes's recognition from Marlborough. The
Duke is reported to have said to St. John, Secretary of
War,

> "'Dear Harry, here's a man comes to me and talks to
> me about one Anna Creon, and I know nothing of
> Creon, but Creon on the play of Oedipus, prithee
> do you speak to the man.'
> "Mr. St. John said the Duke never gave the man any
> money, but he was forced to pay him."

The anecdote is quoted as the kind of absurd evidence
brought to support the charges of Marlborough's avarice.
Dr. Johnson's comment is more authentic, if not any more
complimentary to Cambridge professor Barnes. Writing of
Addison's dedication of *Rosamond* to the Duchess of Marlborough, he remarks that it was, "as an instance of servile absurdity, to be exceeded only by Joshua Barnes's
dedication of a Greek Anacreon to the Duke." Birkbeck
Hill ed., *Lives*, II, 89.

105 April 23 *perf*.

Steele, Richard (1672-1729)

The Tender Husband: or, *The Accomplish'd Fools*.

The play has a number of references to Blenheim and the "General," although Marlborough is not named. It introduces satire on the thirst for factual detail. As the Niece remarks: "I would fain hear an exact description of it [the war] -- Our publick Papers are so defective."

)6   June 5.

Goldwin, William (1683-1747)

Great Britain: Or the HAPPY ISLE. A Poem. [1 line Virgil] By *William Goldwin*, A. B. Fellow *King's College* in *Cambridge*. LONDON, Printed for Fr. Leach and sold by B. Bragg at the Blue Ball in Ave-Mary Lane, 1705. Adv. *Post-Man*, No. 1417, June 2-5. 'This Day is publish'd.' Rptd. June 19-21, 'Just publish'd.' Morgan H180. CtY, DLC, Yale copy used.
   2°: 302 lines, couplets. *A* B-C, D2; t.p., *bl.*, 3-12, 12 pp. Drop-t. p. 3, p. 12 labeled 10. Opens;

> To Sing of *Albion's* Great and Happy Isle,
> Amply enrich'd with Fruitful Nature's Smile.
> Of Mighty Kings and Mighty Battels fought,
> And Laurels fresh from Rescu'd Empires brought:
> Of *Anne's* Successful Days, and *Marlbro's* Fights,
> My Virgin Muse attempts its daring flights.

Goldwin used three spellings, Marlbro three times, Malbrough, and finally the correct Marlborough, p. 10. ·The Duke's exploits provide his subject:

> How *Malbrough* Fought, how haughty *Lewis* Fell,
> When *Suabia* view'd, at *Hochstet's* Fatal Plain. 14-15

Even the Russian Czar came to learn the arts of war from Nassau, and also how to govern. Also George decrees that English ships plough the seas, and Rook obliges (11. 80-90 *passim*). But Anne favors trade. The poem returns to Marlborough, as "whole Squadrons thro the *Danube* [are] pusht" (1. 112). Replete with Classical allusions, the poem is still Whiggish and adulatory of Anne's policies. At her "Retrieving Hands" a drooping Church stands out in purest lustre (1. 270). Lewis unhappily declines in power, years and glory. In honor of Marlborough, "Great *Ann*, a Lasting Pile" (i.e. Blenheim Palace) advances.

On April 27, 1706, Goldwin also published EUROPE, A POEM, No. 139 below. This poem follows the monumental, epideictic style, combining classical allusions to Rome, with Caesar and Virgil's *Aeneid*, and praise of England's line of rulers and the prosperity that feats of arms and trade have brought. Marlborough and Blenheim are repeatedly noticed. England's isle is blessed with "A Fertile Soil, a Fierce Couragious Race" (1. 19). While the Whig policy of trade is approved, the praise of Rook and the capture of Gibraltar suggest some Tory interest. In an essentially conventional poem, little that is original is likely to appear. An allusion to the breeding of horses for Blenheim reflects the price in agriculture.

> Fat Pasturage for Warriors Prancing Steeds,
> Such as Proud *Greece*, and Fruitful *Argos* breeds;
> Such as whole Squadrons thro the *Danube* pusht,
> And *Gallia*'s Pride with Trampling Fury crusht. 110-13

Descriptions of battle are confined to the "sullen Drum" as it sounds "the Triumph of the last Campaign" (1. 222). Verrio and the painting of battle, as of Blenheim and Gibraltar, are noticed. The challenge to Rome is seen not only in Marlborough, who is "more than Caesar," but in the poetic celebration of victories.

> Tho *Phoebus* seems our Northern Isle to shun,
> We boast a *Prior*, and an *Addison*;
> Whose lofty soaring flights advance to sing
> A rising *Princess*, and a falling *King*.   239-42

Enumeration of the glories of William I, Henry V, Elizabeth, and finally William III and Anne, serve to bring out England's fame. The themes of Retrievement of ancient glory and of Female Reign are brought in, both con-

134

firmed when "Brave *Churchill*, made the Ballance rise"
(1. 279). With his aid Anne can command the world.

07 July 14.

[Buckridge, Bainbrigg (fl. 1705)]

On Her Majesty's *Grant* of *Woodstock Park*, &c. To His
Grace the DUKE of MARLBOROUGH, 1704. In a LETTER to
Signior Antonio Verrio at *Hampton-Court*.
2°: 2 pp., no pub., n. d. 54 lines, couplets.
Identified in HMC, 6th Report, 1877, p. 391, Sir Henry
Ingilby, Bart. Papers, Ripley Castle, York. Letter July
14, 1705, B. Buckridge to Ralph Palmer, enclosing some
verses he had written "On Her Majesty's Grant of Woodstock to his Grace the Duke of Marlborough, 1704. In a
Letter to Signior Verrio at Hampton Court." Quotes
first 2 lines of p. 2 of printed version, and closing
line, 35 lines in all. This suggests the record made
from the printed version, since the total is 54 lines.
Previously recognized printing is 1709 reprint in J.
Nichols, *Select Coll. of Poems*, V, 165-6, 1782, 54 lines.
Mary Tom Osborn, "Advice to Painter Poems," 1949, had
found no earlier version than 1709 reprint in *Poems
and Translations by Several Hands*, etc. By the Late
William Walsh, 1714. Also pr. entire in Lediard's *Life*,
III, 436-7, as "excellent lines." No author given. Pr.
in J. Nichols, *Select Collection of Poems*, 1782, V,
165-6. Not in Morgan. Opens:

> Renown'd in Arms, when Mighty Heroes rise,
> Th' Immortal *Muse* in lasting Numbers try's.

Poets usually transmit the hero's fame, but Marlborough
disdains to wait, and "The *Royal Gift* display's [*sic*]
a nobler View" (1. 15). Here amid Elysian shades, eternal peace and pleasure will reign. Woodstock will no
longer mourn her Plantaganet whom Chaucer sung, nor Wil-
mot (Rochester). Here Verrio's pencil will portray

Schellenberg, camps assaulted, battle, flying coursers, surrendering squadrons, groans and shouts. Verrio is instructed to depict the hero in his victorious Carr, Albion rejoicing, the Danube streaming purple, and the swift Rhine transporting prisoners and trophies to England. Then they will "haste to the rising and the Setting Sun." Allusions are to Louis XIV and Queen Anne as well as to the rivers.

108 July 15.

The British Caesar; or the History of the Glorious Achievements of John Duke of Marlborough. Sold by J. Nutt, 1705.
     WL only reference. July 1705. No copy located. Not in Morgan.

109 Smallwood, James (*fl.* 1699-1709)

A Sermon Preach'd before his Grace the Duke of *Marlborough* in the Camp at *Ulierberg-Abby*, near *Louvain*, in *Brabant*, July 15, 1705. Just after Passing the *French* Lines. By James Smalwood [*sic*] Chaplain to Her Majesty's Foot-Guards. Publish'd at the Request of the *General Officers*. *London*: Printed by *T. Mead* for *Andrew Bell*, at the *Cross-Keys* in *Cornhill*. MDCCV. See Nos. 42, 66 and 86. Horn copy used. Not in Morgan.
     This sermon is included because of Smallwood's contributions to Marlborough panegyric, and its particular association with the Duke.

110 August.

The Confederacy: or, a *Welcome to Victory*; a *Poem* on the several Successes of the Confederate Forces under

. . .the Duke of *Marlborough*. Sold by A. Baldwin, 1705.
WL only ref., Aug., 1705. Not in Morgan.

11   August.

[Oldmixon, John (1673-1742)]

A Chain of Providence; OR the Successes of the Prince
and Duke of MARLBOROUGH On his Forcing the *French* Lines.
Virtus omni obice major. LONDON, Printed and Sold by
A. Baldwin at the *Oxford-Arms* in *Warwick-Lane*, 1705.
The only copy known, at the Bodleian, is used. However,
it presents problems. The *Chain of Providence* occupies
five pages of signature A and B, and ends with catchword 'This.' However, next page opens with 'But' and
the balance of the poem consists of pp. 4-28, the remaining sheets of Oldmixon's *Pastoral Poem on Schellenburgh
and Bleinheim*, 1704, No. 76. Since both are printed by
Baldwin, it may be assumed that the conjunction was in-
tentional, and the 94 lines of the *Chain* make a proper
introduction to the pastoral. Details appear below.
    2°: A-B² (one p. missing of B), I-O²; t.p., *bl*.,
1-5, 4-28, 32 pp. Morgan H79; see below. *WL*, August
1705.
    The *Chain of Providence*, 94 lines, couplets, pro-
vides a pastoral mode, suitable to Oldmixon's original
poem. It opens:

    'Twas when the bright Guide of Day had driv'n
    His mounting Steeds to the highest Round of Heav'n.

Nature, the great Mother, and Flora, warmed with Phoebus'
fire, responds with a hymn of gratitude. But as the
Nymphs and Pomona seek shelter in a sylvan dell, they
hear the distant sounds of battle. Barred from Albion's
shore by the Imperial Sway of Glorious Anna, the clangor
and cannon fire can be heard. The added theme of forcing the French lines in Brabant is dealt with, pp. 4-5,

and the theme of English security rather neatly duplicates the earlier poem. Marlborough's action in passing
the lines which linked Antwerp and Namur is interpreted
as victory in which he finds compensation for his inability to persuade his allies to accept the action on the
Moselle. The *Chain* portion ends:

> Thus enter'd to the fair *Brabantine* Plain
> No more of our *Moselle* Lost hopes complain:
> Fate has not chang'd the Conquest but the Scene. 92-4

The catchword 'This' and lack of a period after 'Scene'
suggest further extension of the poem; but now the pastoral Thyrsis begins, p. 4: "But Sighs of Happy or Unhappy Loves" (1. 43 of the *Pastoral Poem*). The dialogue
between Thyrsis and Menalcus is discussed, No. 76 above.
While the *Chain* does provide a valid introduction for the
working off of the original *Pastoral Poem*, no reference
is made to this. Of course the beginning with sig. I
occurs primarily from the omission of Oldmixon's long
discussion of the pastoral mode in the original *Preface*,
which is not included.

In view of the fact that the action specified in the
title occurred in the latter part of July, publication in
August was fairly prompt, and this may account for the
production. It combined two virtues, a timely celebration of Marlborough's newest success, and the putting on
sale of unsold copies of Oldmixon's *Pastoral Poem*. On
the other hand, Morgan says: "A poem (15 pp.) on Marlborough's success against France follows." Since he describes the poem correctly, at least to the casual glance
as 28 pp., this statement is puzzling. He may well have
seen some other copy than that in the Bodleian. Furthermore, *WL* ascribes the poem to B. Bragg as publisher, and
if this is correct, other copies, perhaps of the complete
Chain by itself, may have appeared.

With the portion of the *Pastoral Poem*, the total
number of lines is 479, since the first 42 are not retained.

12   August 16.

[Hare, Dr. Francis (1671-1740)]

The LIFE AND GLORIOUS HISTORY of *John* D. and E. of *Marlborough*, Prince of the Empire, Captain General of the
Confederate Forces, &c. CONTAINING A Relation of the
most Important Battles, Sieges, and Negotiations manag'd
under His Auspicious Conduct, both in the Wars of *Flanders* and *Ireland*; With a full and particular Account of
the ever Memorable Battles of Hockstet and Schellenberg
in *Germany*.
          As also His March to the Moselle in 1705. His re-
turn to the *Netherlands*, and forcing the *French* Lines
near *Tirlemont*; With other Remarkable Passages from his
first Advancement in the Court of King *Charles* II. to
the present Time.
          LONDON: Printed for *J. Chantry* at *Lincolns-Inn
Backgate*. Price 1 *s*.
          12°: B for A, B-H, I; engraving by Van Der Gucht
of Marlborough in oval with 'John Duke Marlborough' below, *bl*., t.p., *bl*., drop-t. p. 5, 5-192. Adv. *Flying-
Post*, No. 1605, Tues. Aug. 14 to Thurs. Aug. 16. 'This
day is publish'd.' Horn copy; only one known. An expanded Sec. Ed., 1705, 214 pp. in Clark Lib. BM has
what seems to be a pirated portion of 16 pp. Adv. Not
in Morgan. See the writer's article, "Marlborough's
First Biographer," *HLQ*, XX, No. 2, Feb., 1957, 145-62.
          Hare, as a reward for being tutor to Marlborough's
son, the Marquess of Blandford, and attending on his last
moments, was made Chaplain-General of the forces. He
became the central figure in the group supporting the
Duke's interests, and produced numerous pamphlets himself
in 1710-12, when Marlborough was under attack from Swift
and others. Sir Winston Churchill recognizes his position. In comparing his retinue with the splended en-
tourage of Louis XIV, he remarks: "What a pitiful contrast to the style in which the Great Monarch took the
field! No mistresses, no actors, no poets, no painters,
not even a historian -- except the chaplain, Dr. Hare"
(I, 413). Being unaware of the *Life and Glorious*

History, Churchill was unable to estimate the extent of its bearing on his comment. Actually Hare's little book became the basis for all the early lives, including Churchill's earliest anonymous sources, and the indispensable Lediard (1736), the first full-scale posthumous biography. Even the earlier *Compendious Journal* of Serjeant John Millner, in 1733, like Lediard, directly transcribes largely from Hare. The *Life* opens:

> 'T were worth a particular Enquiry, How *England* came to Breed so Great a Soldier as his Grace, the present Duke of *Marlborough*; (if I may venture on the Terms) in the unactive, lazy Reign of a Prince, under whom he pass'd his Youth.

As with all of Hare's writings on Marlborough, he is defensive of his patron, but he also has the facts. Not only did he travel with him in the field, serving the religious needs of a commander who began the day with religious services; he continued to uphold the reputation of Marlborough throughout his career.

113   September

Pritz, Johann Georg.

DE SERENISSIMA atque POTENTISSIMA PRINCIPE ANNA, Magnae Britanniae, Franciae & Hibernia REGINA, Fidei Defensore &c. POEMATION; Cui Subnectitur In Expeditionem gloriosissimi Dvcis de MARLBOROUGH, Qua Fossas Brabanticas feliciter perrupit, ELEGIA. Auctore IO. GEORGIO PRITIO, Lipsiensi, SS. Theologiae Doctore, Et sacrorum apud Schlaizenses in Variscis ANTISTITE, Mensa Augusto, A.O.R. CIƆI D CCV   *LONDINI*, Prostant apud IONAM BOWYER, ad insigne Rosae Ludgate-street, juxta Coementerium D. Pauli, MD CCV.
2°: A² B¹; t.p., *bl.*, 3-6, 6 pp. Lambeth Palace

copy used; only one known. Poem to Anne 40 lines; to
Marlborough 38 lines, 78 in all. Not in Morgan.
Dated and identified in Thomas Hearne *Collections*,
I, 49, Sept. 28 (Fri.) 1705. "George Pritius has writ
a silly Poem in Latin in Praise of the Queen, & the D.
of Marlborough." Shows Pritius and a group from Ham-
burg coming with letter to Dr. Hudson, Librarian of the
Bodleian, where Hearne was his assistant. Opens:

ANNA tuae Mater patriae, primara mundi
Foemina, vel summis anteferenda viris.

The verse of both poems is notably conventional, as is
the form. The Queen is praised for her role as the first
woman in the world, and as restorer of the glories of
Elizabeth's reign. "Talis, credo, fuit, quam vinam
reddit, ELISA" (1. 15). All Europe, freed by her, rejoices, and Gaul is trampled under foot. Similarly, Marlborough is hailed as the invincible conqueror, and his
feats and glories will never be surpassed.
Certainly both pieces are highly rhetorical, but they
appear to justify Hearne's label as being "silly" only
when viewed in terms of his Tory bias. Pritz's other
works were printed mainly in Germany.

14   September

The D[utc]*h* POLITICS EXAMIN'D: or, The DANGER of a *De-
fensive* War to the CONFEDERATES. In Reflections on the
Duke of *Marlborough*'s Letter to the S[tate]s General of
the United Provinces, as well as on those of Mons. *D'
Auverquerque* and D----s of S----s, on the Subject of not
Attacking the *French*. Also some Remarks on a Letter from
Altea, inserted in the *Post-Man*, Sept. 1. *LONDON*:
Printed in the Year 1705.
    4°: A^4B-H^4; t.p., *bl*., 1-54, 56 pp. Drop-t. on p.
1. Prose. Horn copy used. Morgan 149.
    This vigorously written pamphlet is concerned with

the restraints imposed upon Marlborough by the Dutch Deputies, and the Duke's letter protesting this action. The
writer insists on his friendliness toward the Dutch; but
wishes to defend his country and her "greatest Glory, the
Duke of *Marlborough*, against those, who either by Ignor-
ance, Malice, Envy, Revenge, Fear, or mistaken Interest,
have endeavor'd to stop the Progress of his Victories,
and delay, by that his settling the Liberty, and Peace of
Europe on a sure, and lasting Foundation" (p. 2). Letters
and arguments are given in favor of Marlborough's breaking through the French lines. It reveals Marlborough's
frustration in a fruitless year of campaigning, and also
the animus of Tory opposition.

115   September 6-8.

THE Thanksgiving. A POEM. By a late Officer in the Army.
LONDON, Printed and Sold by Benjamin Bragge, In Ave-Mary-
Lane, 1505 [*sic*] [1705]. Price 6 d. *Post Man*, No. 1404,
Thurs. Sept. 6-8. 'Just publish'd.' Morgan H434. Bodley copy used. 375 lines, couplets.
     The Thanksgiving ceremonies honoring Blenheim took
place on September 7, and this propagandistic poem provides a relatively brilliant picture of the military life.
It pays tribute to the Queen, the planning and strategy of
the campaign with reflections of natural beauty and pas-
toralism that are striking if not highly poetic. That it
was written by an officer is apparent in the pictures of
troops, in batallions and squadrons, parading prior to
the campaign. Anne is challenging the "mighty Tyrant,"
Louis XIV, who is ravaging Europa. Opens:

     Now the warm Sun compress'd the fruitful Womb
     And she [the Earth] grows big, with the fair
                                   Spring to come.

Spring invites to war abroad, and British blood boils up
with martial fervor. Each soldier learns to obey, "in
order to Command." Each sentry could be a captain, and

each captain could command a host. All seek fame, they
have heard of Schellenberg and Hochstet (Blenheim).
They leave for Belgium, the sails fill as Zephyr
swells them, while Tritons and Nereids play about and
Neptune awakes. Heaven applauds a "just war." The
Belgians crowd the shore with music and huzzahs. "Full
Goblets crown great Marlbro's Health." The French fleet
disappears. Then as the Sun shines warmly, the soldiers
and Belgian maids seek the shade. This invitation to a
somewhat gay soldier's life may reflect problems in recruiting, and is certainly unique in panegyric. It is
the military man's view of the soldier's life, and the
writer justifies it by allusions to Marlborough himself.
While it may be rather daring to recall the gay, Restoration youth of the Duke, it is another relief from the
usual panegyric tone. "Sing of his Loves and Triumphs,"
he says, for he won the love of Almeria with a "person
form'd with every grace." Next Marlborough and his
chiefs are shown planning their campaign, calmly and de-
liberately. The Dutch descend the Maese and the British
the Moselle, a strategy that allayed French suspicions
of the real plan. Only Germany is lethargic, endanger-
ing the scheme; but Marlborough invades the bowels of
France. The French camps, cannon, equipage are in a
sad state; granaries and cities are empty alike. In
contrast Austria shows a vigorous spirit. "The Imperial
Eagle does her youth renew."

16   November 8.

[Pittis, William (1674-1724)]

TWO CAMPAIGNS in One PANEGYRICALL ESSAY Upon his Grace
The Duke of *Marlborough*'s Successes in the Years 1704
and 1705, and his fine House of *Blenheim* now building
at his Mannor [*sic*] of *Woodstock*, lately given him by
Act of Parliament, for his Great Services. To which is
added, The Fifth Ode of *Horace*'s Fourth Book, turn'd into

English by way of Imitation, and humbly address'd to his
Grace, instead of *Augustus*, to whom it is dedicated in
the Original. *LONDON*, Printed for *J. B.* and Sold by *B.
Bragge* in *Avemary-Lane*. 1706. Price 6 *d. Post-Man*,
No. 1552, Tues. Nov. 6 to Thurs. Nov. 8, 1705. This con-
firms 1705 pr. 'This day is publish'd.' BM copy used.
Ryland, Manchester, MH, TxU, HMC, Postland MS., V, 200
ascribes to Pittis. Morgan I391.

    4°: A-E^4; t.p., *ii bl*, 3-39, *bl*. 40 pp. The prose
Essay, pp. 3-33; the poem, nine 6-10 line stanzas, pp.
35-9. 64 lines, ode.

    The prose *Essay* is definitely panegyrical. It is an
act of presumption and zeal. "But you have oblig'd all
Mankind by your Victories." It is not enough that Queen,
Parliament and the poets have expressed praise; the greatest recluse should also join in the chorus, even "the
meanest" (p. 4). Marlborough's actions and achievements
under *Conde* and *Turenne* are more than enough to dazzle.
He joins in himself the eloquence of Cicero, the polite-
ness of Balthasar Castillo, and the generalship of Caesar.
"The Action at *Donawart* [*sic*], will justify that this is
no Romance; for you sav'd there more Kingdoms and Princi-
palities in less time, than an *Eagle* or *Fame* itself, with
all its Plumes, could fly over" (p. 7). Marlborough has
received laurels with true courtesy and modesty. "Never
was such Self-denial in a Soldier" (p. 9).

    Numerous classical allusions to Hannibal and Caesar
in particular, stress Marlborough's glory. The Danube
will dim the memory of the Rubicon, and swell with Pride
(p. 13). If he would permit himself one defeat, calumny
might speak out. He could have overrun all Bavaria, but
he conquered only what was worth the effort. He did
force the French lines, achieve new glory. His cheerful
soldiers do impossible things as soon as ordered. His
looks are "a presage of Victory" (p. 20), and even the
lands he conquers and his prisoners admire him. He does
have enemies, and these conspired to prevent his further
progress into France. "The *Mosell* had been Witness of
as great Exploits this Campaign, as the *Danube*" (p. 22).
Discussion of the nature of a Hero, and further classical

documentation lead up to Blenheim House. That structure
will preserve the memory of Marlborough's achievements
for any who might be ungrateful enough to forget.

> . . .the Parliament of *England* have done much
> more Honour to the Nation, in bestowing the
> Mannor of Woodstock, &c. upon you, in Recom-
> pence of your Services than they have done your
> Grace. (p. 27) The Fabrick is as stupendious
> as the Actions, which your *Grace* has arrested
> the Astonishment of the World with; and the
> Contrivance, Texture, and Beauty of it, will
> not only gain your Name, that Immortality it is
> design'd for, but the Architect will come in for
> a share of it. (pp. 28-9)

This suggestion of approval for the unidentified Vanbrugh
reflects the already festering opposition to the building
of Blenheim Palace. At this time only the foundations
had been laid; but Pittis may well have viewed the model
at Kensington Palace. His suggestion that "the Palace in
all probability will occasion more Victories," was more
prophetic than he could realize. That Sir Winston Churchill was to be born there is only one case in point. That
the Palace issue was the real subject of the essay becomes
apparent. It concludes with comparisons to Versailles,
and the hope that Marlborough will continue to advise the
Empire wisely and then return home to "be a Guide to our
Parliaments, as you have been a leader to our Armies"
(p. 33).
   The poem opens with two lines from Horace's original,
then

> O Born! when Heav'ns propitious deign'd to smile,
> Thou best and bravest Champion of our Isle!

The hero is urged to hasten his slow return, as men crave
the spring, or a fond mother her son, they long for him.
Oxen plough the fields, Ceres yields crops, and the land
is free from Gallia's naval threats, through Marlborough's
care. Who fears the French, the grumbling Scot, Bavarian

plots or the Hungarian or Swede "If *Marlborough*'s free from Harms?" (1. 42). Healths are drunk to Marlborough's health and England's happiness and security. Two Latin lines from Martial are appended. See No. 101.

117 November.

EPIGRAMMATA Anti-Gallica. Sive Epigrammata quaedam quibus conscribendis duerent. Occasioni. Et Pugna ad *Blenheim*, & Vallum in *Flandria* Perreptum. [4 lines Martial,
two quotations] *LONDINI*, Prostant Venales apud *B. Bragg,*
in vico dicto *Avemary-Lane. MDCCV.*
    2°: A^2 B-D^2; t.p., *bl.*, *iii-iv*. Praefatio, 1-11,
12 bl., 16 pp., drop-t. on p. 1, Errata p. *iv*. Bod. copy
used. CtY. *WL* Nov. 1705. Not in Morgan.
    Twenty epigrams of varying length, total 218 lines.
Opens:

> Materiam illorum Vates non viribus aequam
>   Sumunt, *Bleinheimi* ut praelia magna canant.

The epigrams include: *In Praelium Bleinhemense, Loquitur
Danubius ad Gallos in fluvium ruentes, In Milites Gallos,
Ludovicus Exclamans,* and the like. The majority deal
with Marlborough and the war.

118 December 1.

LIBERTY. A POEM. [7 lines Virgil] *LONDON*: Printed for
Tim Goodwin, at the *Queen*'s-*Head* against St. *Dunstan*'s
Church in *Fleetstreet.* MDCCV. Horn-Luttrell copy, '4 *d.*
1. Decemb.' used.
    2°: A^2 B-C^2; t.p., *ii bl.*, 3-11, *12 bl.*, 12 pp.
Drop-t. on p. 3. Wmk. FB (or DO) and Arms. Copies MH,
BPL, TxU, CtY. 187 lines, couplets. Morgan H263. *Post-
Man,* No. 1556, Nov. 29-Dec. 1. Opens:

Hail Beauteous Goddess! Hail Harmonious Pow'r,
Whose happy Influence Mankind adore!

Homage is paid to Liberty who dispenses blessings on the
meanest subject. The goddess keeps a peaceful court,
particularly in "frozen Climes," while, strangely, in the
regions of the friendly Sun, she is less to be found, for
there priest-craft and tyranny dominate (p. 4). Italy
in particular wakens rage and pity at her plight. There
architecture, sculpture and painting abound. Bernini,
Guido, Coreggio, Titian and Raphael are praised for every
art and virtue (p. 6). In music, Pauluci and Corelli are
noticed (p. 7).

  Yet still the People's wretched, still complains;
  For Tyranny through all Italia reigns.   97-9

Their sumptuous palaces are prisons, to bind "the poor
unthinking Multitude." Their paintings described the
"Priesthood's Cheats. . .to make Men Bigots"; and music's
charms debauch the mind since reason does not prevail
(p. 8). Our British arts, our learning and laws, lend
an ear to virtue in distress, guard our liberties, and
curb usurpers.
  Such blandly stated Whiggish claims for virtue and
justice under Right Reason summarize Locke, Addison, and
the praise of William III, who as Nassau disengaged England from servile chains, restoring happiness and "liberty and Empire" to a grateful isle (p. 10). Devonshire,
Leeds, Shrewsbury, and Dorset are praised as supporting
liberty. The poem concludes with praise of Queen Anne,
"Thou O great *Protectress* of this *Isle*," and her servant
Marlborough.

  What Great Design soe're thy Councils form,
  Marlbro' with Resolution will perform.
  To him, next You, our Safety we allow;
  The *Rescu'd Empire* do's its Freedom owe.
  Still may th'imploring World Indulgence find;
  Still may You Both go on in Pity to Mankind.   182-7

147

119 December 14, after.

[Cockburn, Catharine Trotter (1679-1749)]

A POEM On His GRACE the Duke of Marlborough's Return from
his *GERMAN* Expedition.
    2°: *A*-*B*^{2}; t.p., *bl.*, drop-t. on p. 3. 3-8, 8 pp.
Price Two Pence. BM copy used. Not previously identi-
fied as Mrs. Cockburn's. Repr. in Thomas Birch ed. of
The Works of Mrs. Catharine Cockburn, London, J. and P.
Knapton, 1751, 2 vols. I, 561-4, 97 lines, couplets.
"On his Grace the Duke of Marlborough's return from his
Expedition into Germany, after the Battle of Blenheim,
1704." Not in Morgan. Opens:

> Assist me, sacred Muse! The man I sing,
> Who does to *Britain* fame, to *Europe* safety bring!

Boast to France, but still restrain your power. It would
ill suit a female hand to wield warlike weapons. No need
to display Marlborough's glories as even France will proclaim them. They must compare him to Caesar and Alexander. But Marlborough shows no thirst of power, like
them. "He but destroys to save" (1. 38). Anne's glories
outshine Marlborough's. Her fate is to check lawless
Louis, using Marlborough whose combination of majesty,
sweetness, and tempered mind she saw. Europe's princes
are grateful.

> Monarchs,, by him supported, bless her choice,
> Deliver'd nations join their grateful voice;
> Exulting Britain proud of giving birth
> To such a subject, foremost of the earth,
> Waits with triumphant joy his near return.   78-82

But Marlborough shuns applause and defeats all "pompous
expectation."
    In the prefatory *Life*, I, *xxvi-vii*, Birch says:

> The victory at Blenheim, which exercised
> the pens of Mr. *Addison* and Mr. *John Phillips*,

whose poems on that subject divided the admiration of the public, according to the different
parties of the writers tempted Mrs. *Trotter* to
write a copy of verses to the duke of *Marlborough*, upon his return from his glorious campaign
in *Germany*, in *December* 1704. But being doubtful
with respect to the publication of them, she sent
them in manuscript to his grace; and received for
answer, that the duke, and duchess, and the lord
treasurer, *Godolphin*, with several others, to
whom they were shewn, were greatly pleased with
them; and that good judges of poetry had declared,
that there were some lines in them superior to any,
which had been written on the subject. Upon this
encouragement she sent the poem to press; but it
was not published till a month after it was
written.

This statement is largely paraphrased from a letter of
Mrs. Trotter/Mr. Burnet, February 19, 1705, which is
printed in the *Works*, *op. cit.*, I, 190. She also recounts
the death of Locke, and Addison's being rewarded with his
post in honor of the *Campaign*. See No. 149.

Pending determination of date, the following are listed
alphabetically by titles.

20   *Advice* to Mr. *Vario* the Painter. *A Poem* on the Defeat
of the *French* and *Bavarians* by the *Confederate Forces*,
Commanded by his *Grace*, the Duke of *Marlborough*. London:
Printed by *R. Tookey*, and are Sold by *S. Malthus*, in
London-House-Yard, at the West End of *St. Pauls*.
      1/2°: 2 sides, single column. 4 lines, couplets.
Foxon-Crawford copy used. Not in Morgan. Opens:

> *Vario*, no more thy Sacred Skill prophane,
> To show how Fabl'd Gods with Gyants fought.

Truth alone claims the name of history. Such mighty
truths the German plans relate.

> Or Danube's Billows to the Ocean told,
> When stain'd with Gallick and Bavarian Blood,
>   they rowl'd.

Horror in all its shapes, the pangs of the dying, clouds
of dust from flying armies, must appear. Next "the charging Cuts," but mainly

> .   .   .   . paint the Glorious *Marlborough* now,
> Paint Bravery in his Eyes, and Counsel in his Brow.

Paint him like Pompey and Caesar, then

> .   .   .   . with Universal Voice
> We'll Praise the Nation's Hero and the Monarch's
>   Choice.

Mary Tom Osborne, *Advice-to-a-Painter Poems*, 1633-1856,
An Annotated Finding List, Univ. of Texas Press, 1949.
No. 57. Cites four Queen Anne examples, all Marlborough
panegyrics. See Nos. 107, 138, and 273 below. Cites MH,
TxU for 1709 reprint; says probably written early 1705,
but knows no copy. The reprint has no pub.

121   Conduit, John (1688-1737)

Manuscript poem. "A copy of Verses on Mr. *Philips*'s Poem
on the Victory at Blenheim Occasion'd by the Vote of the
House of Commons to do Somewhat to perpetuate the Duke of
Marlborough's memory. By J. Conduit, a *Westm*. Scholar.
To the Commons." Appears in folio copy of Philips's
poems, written in imitation of typography. See M. G.
Lloyd Thomas, *The Poems of John Philips*, Blackwell, 1927,
pp. *xxxii-iii*. 30 lines, couplets. Volume owned by H. F.
B. Brett Smith.

> Ye can't a Monument more lasting raise
> Long to perpetuate your CHURCHILL's Praise.

122   The D[utch] Deputies. A SATYR. *Quid non Batavia fecit.*
       LONDON: Printed in the Year 1705. Another ed. has A
       Satyr Occasioned by the Opposition made to the good In-
       tentions and Fair Opportunities the Duke of *Marlborough*
       had to prosecute the Advantages he obtain'd over the
       Enemy by forcing their Lines in *Flanders*.   Price 6 d.
       Sold by the Booksellers.
              4°: A^2 B-F^2; t.p., *bl. 2*, 3-24, 24 pp., drop-t. on
       3. BM, Camb., DT (uncat.), CtY. Morgan H148.   Yale copy
       used. 328 lines, couplets.   Opens:

              Now, Satyr, raise thy forked Sting, strike Deep;
              Let all *Circe's* Charms lull thee to sleep.

       The writer is extremely bitter against the Dutch, who are
       called "Sons of Mud," a degenerate race sprung out of mud
       and slime, worshippers of Mammon, base water-rats, and
       the like. Their freedom has cost seas of blood, and Eng-
       land has secured it for them.

              Their Populace they to Sedition move,
              For we have well deserv'd their Peoples Love.
              There's none but *D--men* but wou'd have comply'd,
              None wou'd have less our *Marlbro's* Fame deny'd.
                                                           307-10

       Admission is made that the Dutch did help at Blenheim,
       and from this they reaped profit; but now "they Doubt
       and Stop that Conqu'ring Hand," persistently "obstruct-
       ing the vast Designs of *Marlborough's* thoughtful Soul"
       (10-13). Nothing is overlooked. The Dutch fast and
       pray in *"John Calvin's Covenanting* Way"; it is hoped
       that Dutch wives may bully and cuckold their husbands;
       may their bellies and purses be empty; the Dutch wage
       open war with fame and wit. There is no excuse for any
       reprieve for them; for their stopping of the Duke's
       advance has made them friends to Rome and France.
              The poem reveals the animus of arch Tories such
       as Swift served with perhaps better satire but little
       less venom.

123   Settle Elkanah (1648-1724)

Eusebia Triumphans. The *HANOVER* SUCCESSION TO THE *Imperial* CROWN OF ENGLAND, AN *Heroick* POEM. *Pro aris & focis.* *LONDON*, Printed for the Author. MDCCV.
2°: *A*² B-P²; hft., t.p., *bl.*, *Preface*, *v-xvii*,
Poem, 14-58, Latin on left p., English on right. First
ed. 1702; used CSmH; 1705 ed. with additions on Marlborough; used Folger ed. Horn copy. 1709, same plates except for t.p. and 58, for 59, on last English p. of
1705. 1709 t.p. *Eusebia Triumphans.* THE PROTESTANT
SUCCESSION As now Establish'd, and Inviolably Secur'd,
By the Happy UNION of the IMPERIAL CROWNS of GREAT
BRITAIN. An *Heroick* POEM, etc., as in 1705. The change
of sub-t.'s significant. 640 lines, couplets; 831 lines
in 1709. Other eds. 1711, 1715. Morgan E449. DFo,MH,NjP.
    Preface "To the Lords and Commons of GREAT BRITAIN,"
supports The Act of Settlement as the crowning work of
the never-to-be-forgotten Champion of *English* liberties,
the Great NASSAU." Providence and divine justice are
associated with the "Transport of the Victorious Banners
of *England* to the very Banks of the Danube." Thus Marlborough's victory is firmly linked with Whig policies, in
opposition to *jure divino*, and in support of the establishment and William's actions.   Opens:

        When midst the Myriads of his Angel Train
        The Great IMMORTAL in his boundless Reign.

The Latin:

        IMMENSI supra Myrias cum subdita Regni
        AETERNUM, aeterno cantuque genusque colendum.

God, as the great "Architect," the "Founder" and "great
Dispenser," established a universe based on government
and law, and Nassau and "darling Hanover" (1. 130) were
given to sustain these. The Thames and also *Oxon*, Bodley, the Isis, all join in praise of Hanover. This
rather bold championship of the Hanoverian succession
dominates the poem. William and saintly Queen Mary, as

well as Anne, are praised; but Eusebia is part of the inauguration train of Hanover.

The expansion of the poem in 1705, 11. 580-640, takes account of Blenheim in "the far stretch't *Danube*'s watry Bed" (1. 618), and the raising up of the Austrian eagles. Britannia has "given the World an *ANNE*, and *ANNE* a *MARLBOROUGH*" (1. 629). William at the point of withdrawing to heaven, like Elijah, bequeathed to Anne "the leading Chief." The praise of Marlborough is not excessive, but his role in supporting justice and peace and the Hanoverian Succession is clearly defined.

In pardonably proud vindication of his prophetic support of the Hanoverian line, Settle added a further 191 lines to the 1709 edition which hailed the Union with Scotland as supporting the Protestant Succession. Anne is more positively noted, and Britannia is seen as giving new Marlboroughs "t'endless Worlds" (. 779). Settle also supplied one of the many elegies on the death of the Duke in 1722. See No. 528.

Hullin, Mr.

ODE, *Sur Les Glorieux Succes* De MONSEIGNEUR LE DUC DE MARLBOROUGH EN ALLEMAGNE. Par Mr. *Hullin*. [2 lines Virgil] [Ornament] *A LONDRES*, par *J. DELAGE*, dans *Stationer-Court*, proche Ludgate, Amen-Corner. 1705. 2°: A^1, B-C^2; t.p., *bl*., 3-10, 12 pp. Drop-t. on p. 3. 27 6-line stanzas, 162 lines. Manuscript copy in Blenheim Library. Lambeth Palace copy used. Not in Morgan. Opens:

Dans les soudains Transport que m'inspire ta Gloire, *Marlborough*, je medite un Hymne de Victoire.

Hails Eugene and Marlborough, gaining victory in one month. Footnote on fooling the French by feint toward the Moselle. Urges support and rescue for the Cevennois. "*BLENHEIM* Bourg si fameux" (1. 97) hails Marlborough's triumph. At close Hullin admits his birth as a French citizen, but the tyranny of Louis XIV has made him praise Marlborough.

Hullin, a religious writer, presumably a cleric, also had DISCOURS CHRETIEN contre LES IMPIES. A Monsieur **** Par Mr. HULLIN. J. DELAGE, 1704, 29 pp. This is purely religious verse. BM copy used.

125 A KIT-KAT C---B *DESCRIB'D*. *O Monstrous Moderation!* [cut of head and shoulders of man in ecclesiastical hat and cloak, half a bishop's mitre and half dissenter] *London*, Printed in the Year 1705.

4to. A2 on p. only sig.; t.p., *bl.*, 3-8, 8 pp. Five books, "lately publish'd," and "All sold by *B. Bragg* in *Ave-Mary-Lane*" bot. p. 8, drop-t. p. 3. Prose, with 20 lines doggerel verse, pp. 7-8. CSmH copy used. Opens: "Is an *Ens Rationis*, a mere *Imaginary Being* in every Body's Apprehension but his *own*." Kit-Kat took a meaningless name to disguise his real purpose. His godfather was J[aco]b T[onso]n, a young Hannibal, who wars on learning. This anti-Whig pamphlet brings in Marlborough in association with party policies and Addison. Morgan H240.

> He stands up for Liberty and Property, as if he
> dar'd fight for it; but had rather the Duke of
> *Marlborough* should take that Task off his Hands,
> for he had much rather judge of *Addison*'s *Poet-*
> *ical History* of the Battle of *Blenheim*, than be
> in it, and fitter to write the Second part of the
> *Campaign*, than to make *One*. (p. 5)

A verse portion, without separate title, opens:

> A Kit-Kat's *Compos'd of Ill Nature and Breeding*,
> *Of* Immoderate Follies, tho' Moderate *Reading*.

The Kit-Kat is opposed to Rook as head of Fleet Royal, another touch of Whig partisanship that is the theme throughout. Its sponsorship of Vanbrugh's new Queen's

Theatre is noticed. The poem is quoted by Robert J. Allen, *The Clubs of Augustan London*, 1933, pp. 234, 237.

26 [Forbes, William, of Disblain]

A PIL for Pork-Eaters: OR, A SCOTS LANCET FOR AN *English Swelling*. 4 lines Cowley, "Curs'd be the Man. . .
who thinks it brave And great, his Countrey to enslave";
2 lines Claudian, 2 lines Ovid. [Ornament Scotch
thistle] *EDINBURGH*, Printed by *James Watson*, in
Craig's Closs. 1705.
    4°: A^4, A2 reprtd., pp. 3 and 5, B^2; t.p., *bl.*,
3-12, 12 pp. Advertisement on pp. 3-4. Morgan cites
another ed., 8 pp., 1705, H342. Also similar title, A
PILL for Pork-Eaters, and Observations Made in England
on the Trial [*ca.* 1705], H350. No copy known, but see
below.
    Often attributed to Alexander Pennecuik, the Younger (d. 1730), as in DNB, which also cites the *Complete
Collection*, 1756, in which it is ascribed to Pennecuik.
See William Brown, *Papers of the Bibl. Soc. of Edinburgh*,
VI, 117 f., 1906, for discussion.
    NLS, CtY, both cropt. Horn copy used. 207 lines,
couplets. Advertisement opens: "Be it known to all
true honest hearted *Scotsmen*, That *England* is now turn'd
Bully; and Commands you in the Name of *Dependency*, to
beware how you stand any more upon your *Privileges*. . ."
Expresses scepticism about the proposed Union of Scot-
land and England, and denounces the scandalous libels
of rogues, including "their *Newgate* News-monger *Dyer*."
The primary occasion of the satire is the Darien scheme
and the trial of Captain Thomas Green in March, 1705.
Poem opens:

    Heavens! Are we such a servile Nation grown,
    Beneath our Ancestors so vastly thrown.

England, aside from telling Scotland she has no right to
choose a successor to her present Majesty, is guilty of

arraigning Scottish justice and laws and of making
"Three Villains Lives a Nation's Cause" (1. 7). The
execution of Green and two others to appease Scottish
resentments, and thus save the Union, thus opens a
strongly biased poem. England's offenses are the issue.
"Insolent and pround like Hell" (1. 28), she is charged
with numerous crimes. Her luxury and foppishness are
noted; while great *H*[amilto]*n* is held up as "our noblest
Patriot" (1. 76). The day when a Scottish king assumes
the English scepter is cursed, and Bannockburn is recalled as an occasion for vengeance. Heroes, such as
Wallace, Douglas, and the Bruce, fought the English
with courage. The poet is strongly opposed to the
Union with England.

> When Swans grow Black, and Ravens shall grow White
> Proud *England* then with *Scotland* shall unite. 165-6

The poem concludes with a strong note of resentment for the slighting of Orkney and the Scottish share
in Blenheim. Men that served there can now serve
against hated England. The warlike "Pills" will purge
English insolence.

> Then to our Aid, let's call our Forces strait,
> Who gave to *England* such renown of late;
> The *English* were the Conquerors proclaim'd,
> While injur'd *Scots* were to Oblivion damn'd:
> Yet had not ORKNEY and our Troops been there,
> Who in these Victories claim such a Share;
> Few Trophies then to *England* had been brought,
> Nor *Shelenberg* and *Blenheim* so well fought. 170-7

The call is made for unbribable patriots, such as
S[altu]*n*; then England, to her cost, will learn what
Scotsmen can do. Highlands and Gillikrankies will rifle
Lombard-street, and the English will be terrified into
acceding to the Scots, for, to quote the concluding line,
"The *Scotch* we find, will be Oppress'd no more."
Trevelyan summarizes the entire situation of the
Darien episode and the execution of Green and his two

companions, in relation to the Union, *Ramillies*, Chap.
XIII. The poem supplies further evidence of the immense range of Marlborough literature. Morgan H350,
from its title as cited above, seems to be a reply from
the English standpoint, and presumably has no Marlborough significance.

27 Swift, Jonathan (1667-1745) ?

A *Parody* on the *Recorder* of Blessington's *Address* to Her
Majesty Queen Anne. 42 lines, couplets. Sir Walter
Scott, *Works*, XII, 257-9. Scott accepts on internal
evidence, as does Elrington Ball. Williams, *Poems*, III,
1075, rejects, maintaining "there is no good ground for
the metrical parody to be by Swift, although he was still
associated with the Whigs." On the other hand, aside
from several editors, R. P. Bond accepts the piece as by
Swift, and publishes it as No. 14 in his Register of
English burlesque poems, *op. cit.*, p. 252. Even so,
while stating that the poem deals with Marlborough, he
quotes only the passage which appears in Elrington Ball.
Scott prints the *Address*, pp. 255-7, and states that it
was presented January 17, 1704-5. That it is ponderous
and fair game for parody is apparent. As an Irishman,
William Crowe takes satisfaction in the presence of his
countryman in the forces of

> your gallant, enterprising general, whose twin-
> battles have, with his own title of Marlborough,
> given immortality to the otherwise perishing
> names of Schellenberg and Hogstete: actions
> that speak him born under stars as propitious
> to England as that he now wears, on both which
> he has so often reflected lustre, as to have
> now abundantly repaid the glory they once lent
> him.

The current Tory attitude is mildly reflected in recognition of the capture of Gibraltar. Swiftian irony marks

157

the poem, whether or not it is the true voice, and the
anapestic beat is one of his modes. The verse opens:

> From a town that consists of a church and a steeple,
> With three or four houses, and as many people,
> There went an Address in great form and good order,
> Compos'd, as 'tis said, by Will Crowe, their Recorder.

The account of Blenheim is lively for all its levity.

> We have heard with much transport and great satis-
> faction
> Of the victory obtain'd in the late famous action,
> When the field was so warm'd, that it soon grew hot
> For the French and Bavarians, who had all gone to pot.
> But that they thought best in great haste to retire,
> And leap into the water for fear of the fire.
> But says the good river, Ye fools, plague confound ye,
> Do you think to swim through me, and that I'll not
> drown ye?   13-20

The Danube appears to resent the trampling of his banks
as much as the venality of the French.

> So it plainly appears that they are very well bang'd,
> And that some may be drown'd, who deserved to be hang'd.
> Great Marlbro' well push'd: 'twas well push'd indeed:
> Oh, how we adore you, because you succeed!   25-8

Predictions of the end of the French empire conclude the
poem.
    Not in Teerink.

128 *The Perkinite Jacks*: Or, a new *Ballad* on the *Tackers*.
Printed in the Year MDCCV. No pub.
    2°: pr. in 2 col. *ca* 120 lines, bsd. ballad satire.
Morgan H343. No copy located.

> We have no great Cause to be vaunting
> Of *Marlborough*'s Triumph so brave.

29   [Gery, John, Christ Church, Oxford (no dates)]

A POEM TO HIS GRACE THE DUKE OF MARLBOROUGH, ON THE Glorious Successes OF THE LAST CAMPAIGN.   [2 lines Horace]
Printed in the Year MDCCV.
    $2°$: π^1 A-C^2 $*^1$; t.p., 1-13, $bl.$, 16 pp., drop-t.
p. 1. TxU copy used. BM copy has notation 'By Mr. Gery
C C C Oxon.' Wrenn Cat. ascribes to Mandeville. 322
lines, couplets. Morgan H176. Gery is not in DNB nor
CHEL. Opens:

    O thou renown'd in War, whose Godlike Deeds
    No *Brittish* Youth without a Rapture reads!

The poem is not distinguished by any feature, except perhaps the comparison between "Bleinheim" and a surgical
operation to release matter from a swelling. The march
to the Danube, the preliminary victory at Schellenberg,
which is not named, and the final great clash of forces
at Blenheim are indicated but not described with any
specific details. Marlborough in combat is shown as
fierce, impetuous as a huge rock rolling down a mountain.
The Danube drowning is noticed, the Ister dyed

    By Streams of hostile Blood, with friendly Waves
    The plunging Rout from Farther Vengeance saves.
                                              195-6

    A comparison of Marlborough to Julius Caesar follows
the question as to why his worth has not been previously
noted. The poet falls back on the old theme of his inadequacy to such a great subject, for an adequate treatment demands both Fancy and Judgment, both fury and correctness. A tribute to Admiral Rook and Gibraltar, ll.
247-66, is quite consistent with Gery's being at Oxford,
one of the strongholds of Toryism. He apologizes for
this, asking Marlborough to "spare a Line, That sacred
is to other praise than thine" (ll. 269-70). Return to
his great deeds and hailing a grand future for Britannia
and Queen Anne's arms hardly rescues the poem from near
oblivion. No notice is taken of Addison or other more
successful poets.

130 Manley, Mrs. Mary de la Riviere (1663-1724)

The Secret History of Queen Zarah, and the Zarasians;
Being a Looking-glass For ----- -------- In the Kingdom of Albigion. Faithfully Translated from the
Italian Copy now Lodg'd in the *Vatican* at *Rome*, and
never before Printed in any Language. *Albigion*,
Printed in the Year 1705. Price Stitched 1 *s*. Price
Bound 1 *s*. 6 *d*. Prose satire on Marlboroughs.
    8vo: Part I. T.p., To the Reader 22 pp.; Text
1-119. Drop-t. p. 1.   Part II. Same title and
prices. T.p., The Preface, 6 pp., text 9-141; drop-t.
p. 9. Total pages 284. Morgan H281 gives another ed.
16mo, 1705, 1711. French eds. 1708, 1711, 1712, 1745.
French ed. attributes to Sacheverall.
    Extremely vicious satire, using allegorical names:
Duchess Sarah is Queen Zarah; Marlborough is Hippolito;
Queen Anne, Aliania; William III, Aurantio; Godolphin,
Volpone, etc. Marlborough's early sordid amours; but
rises to highest pinnacle of honor. It may be added
that evidence for the more sordid amours is largely
from Mrs. Manley's dubious accounts.
    Facsimile editions of four of Mrs. Manley's "nov-
els" have been published, with Patricia Köster as editor, *Facsimiles and Reprints*, Gainesville, Florida,
1971. These are: *The Secret History of Queen Zarah*,
I and II, 1705; *Secret Memoirs and Manners Of Several
Persons of Quality*, Of Both Sexes. From the New ATA-
LANTIS, I and II, 1709; Memoirs of EUROPE, I and II,
1710; and *The Adventures of RIVELLA*, 1714. The editor
supplies brief notes and a convenient Key to *Queen
Zarah*, as well as an Index to the whole series. The
Marlboroughs appear in the *New Atalantis*. See Nos.
286, 332.

1706

This is perhaps the most productive year for panegyrics on Marlborough's successes, with not only his
second great victory at Ramillies, but also the triumph
of English policy, largely his, and English financial
subsidy in the victories of Eugene in the Italian campaign. The taking of Turin, although no British soldiery
were involved, "was a triumph of our island policy," as
Trevelyan remarks, *Ramillies*, p. 141. Although Morgan
specifies only six Marlborough pamphlets as appearing in
1706, he treats those of Defoe, Dennis, Charles Johnson,
and a few others under names of authors, or titles.
Actually no less than forty-five did appear, and considerably more associated items. Furthermore, the negotiations for the Union with Scotland were reaching their
final stages, November and December being the critical
months, even though the preliminary endorsement of the
Treaty was signed by all but a few of the Commissioners,
on July 22, 1706.

Thus, to cite Trevelyan again, 1706 was an *annus
mirabilis*, the highest point in Marlborough's fortunes,
and as 1707 was to show, in his hopes of completely defeating France and the armies of Louis XIV. After 1706
the surge of panegyric began to decline, reviving somewhat with fifteen poems honoring Oudenarde in 1708, but
thereafter giving way to a flood of satires equal in
quantity bo the panegyrics of Blenheim and Ramillies.
Since the latter victory fell on May 23, or May 12 in
England, O. S., panegyrics could not appear till after
that date. In this instance, as will appear, Defoe was
probably the first in the field of celebrants.

131 January *ca.*

Tate, Nahum (1652-1715)

Britannia's Prayer For The *Queen*, By Mr. *Tate, Poet
Laureate* to Her *Majesty. London:* Printed for *John
Chantry*, at the Sign of *Lincolns-Inn-Square* at *Lincolns-
Inn-Back Gate.* 1706. Price Two Pence.
2°: 88 lines, ode. E. K. Broadus, *The Laureate-
ship*, Oxf. Pr., 1921, p. 96, "probably written after
one of Queen Anne's frequent attacks, January, 1706."
Poems on Affairs of State, IV, 129-31, 1707. Morgan
I380. See No. 188. Opens:

> How justly now I might aspire
> To mighty *Pindar*'s Force and Fire!

Very conventional praise of Anne as more sacred than
the Muses, the best of sovereigns, whose equal never
rose. Long may she survive, but may she be assured of
"everlasting Welcome," when she does "go."

> While You remain, our World is blest;
> When You remove ---- I leave the rest
>   To be in Sighs Exprest.

The Marlborough significance in a stanza on Anne's Triumphs. The poet through Britannia, prays:

> Not for increase of Wealth, more *Blenheim*-Spoils;
> More Trophies of her Hero's Toils,
> To hear her Naval Thunder roar,
> Alarming all th' *Atlantick* Shoar.   55-8

Like all of Tate's deplorable tributes, this safely
steers between Whig and Tory sentiments, without mentioning either, and avoids poetic importance with
fascinating consistency.

32   January 8.

Defoe, Daniel (1660-1731)

A HYMN TO PEACE. Occasion'd, by the two Houses Joining
in One ADDRESS To the Queen. BY THE Author of the *True-
born English-man*. *LONDON*: Printed in the Year, 1706.
4°: *A* as *B*, B-G⁴, H⁴; t.p., *bl*., 3-60, 60 pp.
Pp. 51-60, 196 lines, CONCLUSION TO THE QUEEN. Total
1048 lines, varying lengths, couplets. Half-t. p. 3.
Moore 109 and Foxon D19 have as Printed for John Nutt,
but Lee 79 and the copy used lack pub. BM, IU, N, CtY,
and Clark copy used. Foxon reports BM-Luttr. as Jan. 8.
Notes no external evidence for Defoe's authorship. Morgan I108. Opens:

> Hail Image, of th'Eternal Mind
> The only perfect Blessing of Mankind.

Advertisement in the *Review*, 12 Jan., and Lee's
admiring acceptance might seem to validate Defoe's
authorship. Nevertheless, the poem marks a striking
shift from the enthusiasm for Blenheim and Marlborough
in the poems of 1704. Lee notes the "loftiness of
thought and vigour of expression" in the lines to the
Queen; but neither he nor Moore notes the strong anti-
war sentiments. No reference is made to Marlborough
nor to any other military figures. The pertinence of
the poem is negative. War is seen as the product of
man's fury and insatiable ambition which produces
"Feuds and War" (1. 153). Tributes to Union, the
"sister of Peace" (298) and jibes at High Church figures, as well as the general style are all in the Defoe
manner.
     On July 19 a pirated edition of Defoe's longest
poem, *Jure Divino: A Satyr*, appeared. The genuine edition in folio soon followed. A long Preface, Verse to
the Author, and a verse Introduction. All are rich in
reflections of Defoe's character, as is the poem. It
is a mixture of satire on the High Tories and summaries
of political history and theory. At the end of Book XII,

the last, Marlborough is praised for his services. Allusions to Blenheim and later military episodes, such
as the siege of Landau, appear; but apparently the poem
was completed too long before the Battle of Ramillies
for the surge of elation that this victory brought,
even though its publication followed by over six weeks.

133 January 26

Oldmixon, John (1673-1742)

Iberia Liberata: A Poem. Occasion'd By the Success of
Her Majesties Arms in *Catalonia, Valentia*, &c. Under
the Command of The Right Honourable *Charles, Earl* of
Peterborough and *Monmouth*, General of Her Majesties
Forces in *Spain*, and Joynt-Admiral of the Royal Fleet.
[2 lines Horace] *London*: Printed for *Anthony Baker*,
at the *Unicorn* next *Serjeants-Inn-Gate in Fleetstreet*;
and Sold by *John Nutt*, near *Stationers-Hall*. 1706.
Price 1 *s*.
    8°: *i* A-K⁸; t.p., *bl*., Verse Dedication "To the
Right Honourable the Countess of *Peterborough*," sgnd.
'J. Oldmixon' *x*, 76 lines, couplets, as *Epistle Dedicatory, iii-x*, text pp. 1-58, with drop-t. on p. 1, and
running title on each page; 70 pp., 1025 lines, couplets;
pp. 59-70 *Remarks on the Preceding Poem*. Horn copy used.
Morgan I207, but not identified as by Oldmixon. The
dedication, on Love and Beauty, is flattering only, but
concludes with the hope that Mordaunt may ever conquer,
and his son also have a glorious career. The poem
opens:

        Again, my Muse! for Lofty Flights prepa[re]
        To Sing the Triumphs of th'*Iberian* Wa[r].

The poem, unlike Oldmixon's pastoral on Blenheim, No. 76,
attempts heroic measures. The *Remarks* opens with a discussion of the genres, especially as appropriate to a

theme second only to Blenheim. The poem deals with
Mordaunt, i.e. Peterborough, as swift conqueror of Barcelona. Tributes to Anne and William III and condemnation of monsters Faction, among them "mad Sachev[erel]l,"
and "the vile Apostate W[e]s[le]y" (ll. 209-10), reflect the mixing of satire and panegyric styles. The
Universities are also condemned for encouraging rebel-
lious attitudes. The point is that the new victory
should bring about harmony at home. Addison is praised
for his *Campaign*'s lofty numbers and Dennis for his effort, though neither is named except in the notes. Even
though it is a theme for a Homer or Virgil, the poet
proceeds.

The British troops march for Barcelona, and soon
overcome Montjuich, the main fortress, although Hesse-
Darmstadt is killed. The assault on the ramparts brings
the greatest effort at battle poetry, with the roar of
cannon from Shovel's fleet added. Clouds of sulphur
smoke, flying globes of fire, dusky air, and explosions
over the city produce an impression quite like the engravings of the period in which curving lines trace the
flight of cannonballs (ll. 511-34).

> A gloomy Cloud as thick as Ancient Night
> Ascends, and baleful Lightnings blast the Sight,
> And Darkness gone, a hideous Scene's disclos'd,
> And Naked to the Foe the City stands expos'd.
>
> 529-32

Not William himself could free the world as Anne has
done. It remains only to pay tribute to great leaders.
Churchill is cited as the first, with Blenheim and the
more recent forcing of the French lines on the Dyle.
"By *Churchill*'s Courage and *Godolphin*'s Care" (l. 781)
England and Europe are assured peace and security. Mordaunt is urged to go on further conquests in Spain, and
the poem concludes with tributes to government leaders:
Cooper, Somerset, Candish, Pembroke, Spencer, Montague,
Wharton. By their aid Charles IIId will be placed on
his proper throne and the young French usurper Philip

displaced. The fight against faction and the lewd dis-
turbers of the state deserves a better muse. The abrupt conclusion is somewhat compensated for by the
Remarks which identify places, names, and events.

134   February 6 *ca.*

Fenton, Elijah (1683-1730)

To the *Queen*, On Her Majesty's *Birth-Day*. By Mr. *Fen-*
ton. *London*: Printed for *Benjamin Tooke* at the *Middle-*
Temple-Gate in *Fleet-street*. n.d. Morgan I152. No sigs.
T.p., *bl.*, 3-4, 4 pp. 49 lines, couplets. BM, CSmH
(Luttr. "6 February"), LP copy used. Opens:

> From *this* Auspicious Day Three Kingdoms date
> The fairest Favours of indulgent Fate.

The scepters of Europe turn to Anne as victor and friend.
What can now prevent her Red-Cross Banners from waving
over the Seine? She conquers to restore, not destroy.
Justice waits on her word. The future will gain new
temples of faith and increased commerce under the Southern stars. Feuds expire and arts revive. Heaven favors
Anne, "And Golden Plenty covers all the Plains" (1. 49).

135   February 7.

Kremberg, James [no dates]

England's Glory: A POEM. Perform'd in a Musical Entertainment BEFORE HER MAJESTY, ON HER Happy BIRTH-DAY.
[ornament] *LONDON*: Sold by RICHARD HARRISON at *New-*
Inn Gate in *Witchstreet* without *Temple-Bar*. 1706.
      2°: A^2 B-C^2; frontispiece engraving, descr. below,
t.p., *bl.* iv, v-vi TO THE QUEEN, sgnd. James Kremberg,

1-6, 12 pp. Morgan I145.
    Bodley-Luttr. copy used, '6 *d*. 7. Februar' also a
'5' inserted under 1706, and second '6 *d*.' on frontispiece. The engraving, fully described in the text,
supplies the principal feature. It depicts a crowned
pyramid on which appears "ANNA REGINA" etc. The pyramid is wreathed in ivy and supported by a handsome Lion
and Unicorn. At the bottom, three circles, the left
labeled *Barcelona*, the right *Gibraltar*, and the center
Blenheim appear. The cities are represented by charts,
but Blenheim depicts a battle scene. Each has its
phrase, that for Blenheim being "TERROR INIMICORUM."
The tribute to the Queen states that Kremberg, "tho' a
Foreigner" pays tribute, and has "composed the musical
parts of the following Poem."
    The text is 149 lines including the characters who
sing and dance. The verse opens:

> Bellona *appears in a celestial Machine, and
> sings as follows:*
>   Lov'd *Britannia*! Heav'n allows Thee
>   All her rural Blessings here.

The significance of the Queen's glory resting on Blenheim, as well as on the victories in Spain, is obvious.

56   February 21.

[Philips, John ? (1676-1708)]

Cerealia: *An Imitation of Milton*:   [2 lines Petronius]
London, Printed for *Thomas Bennet*, at the *Half-Moon* in
St. Paul's Churchyard.   1706.
    2°: *A*² B-D². Half-t., *bl*., t.p., *bl*., 1-10, 12 pp.
Drop-t. on p. 1. *L. Gaz*., No. 4203, Mon. Feb. 18-21,
1705/6. 'This Day is Publish'd.'   207 lines, blank verse.
Morgan I317.
    The theme of the poem is wine and ale as giving

victorious strength to England's Warriors. Blenheim is
brought in on p. 3 as Fame wings up from "Ensanguin'd
Ister's reeking Flood." She sounds a golden trump three
times after flying swifter than the gerfaulcon trussing
the quarry, or "Hern, or Mallard, newly sprung from
Creek" (1. 31), and assembles the gods who listen. The
tone is mock-heroic throughout.

> There SHE relates what CHURCHILL's Arm has wrought,
> On *Blenheim*'s bloody Plain. Up *Bacchus* rose,
> By his plump Cheek and Barrel Belly known.
> The pliant Tendrils of a Juicy Vine
> Around his rosie Brow in Ringlets curl'd;
> And in his Hand a Bunch of Grapes he held,
> The Ensigns of the God! with ardent Tone
> He mov'd, that straight the Nectar Bowl shou'd flow,
> Devote to CHURCHILL's Health, and o'er all Heav'n.
>   42-50

M. G. Lloyd Thomas, edition of Philips's Poems, accepts
as by him, but notes one copy with Fenton's name.

137   March 5 *ca.*

Granville, George, Baron Lansdowne (1667-1735)

The British Enchanters: Or, No Magic Like Love. A
Dramatick Poem. As it is Acted at the *Queen*'s *Theatre*
in the *Hay-Market*, By Her Majesty's Servants. *D. Cour.*
No. 1203, Feb. 22, adv. for performance the 23d.
Printed in the Year 1710. However Allardyce Nicoll
gives playing date as Feb, 1705/6, and says publ. 1706
anonymously. *Post-Boy*, No. 1688, Mar. 5-7 as 'Lately
publish'd.' 5-act drama, with numerous choruses and
songs. Horn copy used. Concludes with scene of the
Queen amidst all the Triumphs of her reign, Anne denouncing War and presenting Liberty. Freedom and Peace
appear in a vision of the future, and the final act is

set in "Urgandar's Bower of Bliss. Being a Representation of Woodstock-Park." Elizabeth Handasyde sees this
as a Tory compliment to Marlborough. Morgan W206.

38   March 16.

Harison, William (1685-1713)

Woodstock Park. A POEM BY *WILLIAM HARISON*, Of New-College,
Oxon. *Habitarunt Di quoque Silvas*. Virg. Eclog. 2.
LONDON, Printed for *Jacob Tonson*, within *Grays-Inn* Gate
next *Grays-Inn* Lane. 1706.
     2°: A^2, B-C^2; t.p., *bl*., 1-10, 12 pp., drop-t. on
p. 1. 369 lines, couplets. No wmk. A second ed. pre-
cisely same except for insertion of 'The Second Edition
Revis'd' between motto and colophon. Two ostensible
errors are the only changes: 'those' for whose, p. 1,
1. 23, and "Splendour' becomes Splendor, p. 8, 1. 19.
No substantive changes. BM, MH, CtY, TxU, Lehigh, CSmH,
Clark for first ed.; Foxon cites TxU, CtY for the second
ed. Horn copies of both eds. used. Haslewood-Luttr.,
'6 *d*. 16 *March* 1705/6.' *D. Cour.*, No. 1212, Sat. Mar.
16, 1706. 'This Day is Publish'd.' Pr. in Dodsley Coll.
V, 201-17, but with "Vanbrook's Fame" becoming "Vanbrugh's
frame [*sic*]," p. 5, 1. 9. Spence, *Anecdotes*, pp. 352-4
reports that Addison said: "This young man, in his very
first attempt, has exceeded most of the best writers of
the age." Addison recommended Harison for the post of
one of the secretaries for the plenipotentiaries at the
Treaty of Utrecht. The poem is superior to most. Morgan
I182. Opens:

     King Heav'n at length, successfully implor'd,
     To *Britain*'s Arms her Hero had restor'd.

Marlborough's return meets with loud applause, and

     The Poets sung, tho' *Addison* alone
     Adorns Thy laurels, and maintains his own;

In him alone, Great MARLBOROUGH is seen,
Thy graceful Motion, and Thy godlike Mien:
Each Action he exalts with Rage divine,
And the full *Danube* flows in ev'ry Line.   7-12

Deserved as this tribute is, it would need no strong
sceptic to see how Addison could comfortably praise the
youthful poet. He goes on to associate gods and men and
the Olympic games. Only Woodstock could vie with Greece
as an adequate spot, a hunting scene, the hounds pursu-
ing the deer; and anyone familiar with Blenheim Forest
can agree that England offers no more engaging place for
"Nature, to display her various Art" (1. 74). With a
comparison of the hunted deer to kings, Harison apologizes to Denham for emulating his art. This leads to
Chaucer, who was allegedly born at Woodstock, and to
Dryden, who is censured for attempting to modernize
Chaucer. The tale of Rosamonda's amour with Henry II
brings in the medieval palace, now in ruins, and Vanbrugh.

Ev'n *Vanbrook*'s Fame, that does so brightly Shine
In Rules exact, and Greatness of Design,   164-5

would fall into ruin had not the architect also
"adorn'd the Stage." The context suggests that the
change to "Frame" in the Second Edition is a genuine
correction.
It might be wished that Harison had supplied more
topographical detail. Even so, especially in mytho-
logical and historical associations, he follows the
model of Denham's *Cooper's Hill* closely and effectively.
Queen Elizabeth, who spent some time at Woodstock, is
brought in; but decidedly the most interesting passage
involves panegyric poetry. Professing inadequacy to
the theme of Blenheim, Harison says:

Themes so exalted, with proportion'd Wing,
Let *Addison*, let *Garth*, let *Congreve* sing.   274-5

He is struck by the new Woodstock that is to arise, that
is, Blenheim Palace. He views the foundation, which in
the spring of 1706 was all there was to see. Construc-

tion was painfully delayed by poor stone which had been
"flying" off with frost, to the delight of ill-wishers.
Harison's optimism made the poem welcome to Addison and
the Duke's supporters; not excluding Queen Anne.

> Rise, glorious Pile, the Princess bids thee rise,
> And soon assert thy Title to the Skies:
> Where she presides all must be nobly Great,
> All must be regular, and all Compleat.   303-6

The decoration is imagined with "successful *Kneller*" as
painter, depicting Marlborough on a rising ground among
his squadrons, prepared to strike the decisive blow.
France defeated, Spain seeking Austrian government, and
all indebted to Anne's "mild Councils" terminate the poem.

> Whole Kingdoms shall be bless'd, all Europe free
> And lift her Hands unmanacled to Thee.   364-5

Until the summer campaigns of 1706, and the victory at
Ramillies, there was little to celebrate except memories of Blenheim.

Mary Tom Osborne, *op. cit.*, No. 120 above, states
that Thorn Drury mentions owning a Luttrell copy.
"Notebooks" in Bodleian Library.

9   April 27.

Goldwin, William, of King's College, Cambridge (1683-
1747)

EUROPE.   A POEM.   By *William Goldwin*, A. B. and Fellow
of *Kings College* in *Cambridge*.   [1 line Horace]   *LONDON*,
Printed, and Sold by *A. Baldwin*, in *Warwick-Lane*, 1706.
BM-Luttr. copy used; the only one known.   '6 *d*. 27
Aprill.'   Haslewood has '22 Aprill.'
    2°:   *A*, B-D²; t.p., *bl.*, 1-13, drop-t., p. 1.
'Humbly Dedicated to the Right Honourable the Lord
Keeper.'   *14 bl.*, 16 pp.   Not in Morgan or CBEL.   363

lines, couplets. Opens:

> Tho *Europe* Groans, distress'd with Clam'rous din
> Of Wars, injurious to the Peaceful Nine.

His Muses undismayed, the poet surveys the sad scene of
war and death. He "presumes to view *Europe*'s Princely
Courts," even though he is confined to rural and pastoral scenes, i.e. Cambridge. In turn various countries
and leaders are dealt with, though in conventional terms.
The Tory bias of the poem is apparent in its extensive
praise of Eugene (11. 81-109) as "bravest Hero" as well
as in the limited notice of Marlborough and Godolphin.
Several references to Queen Anne, and a cautiously favorable attitude toward Hanover appear. Louis XIV, hated
by his subjects, appears, as does the War of the Spanish
Succession. Praise of Peterborough (11. 261-8) includes
recognition of his dubious role, "by private Foes con-
temn'd," and

>   His daring Soul,
> Tho baulkt by sad delays, the War supports
> With Resolution firm, true *Brittish* Peer,
> Deserving best Rewards, unenvy'd Praise.   265-8

It is only at the close of the poem that Goldwin
recognizes the role of Marlborough and his treasurer,
even though he has plainly shown that war they have been
conducting is the crucial event in the Europe of the day.
Of Marlborough he says:

> Behold! A Mighty *Duke*, of Graceful Mien
> With Virtues fit for Camp or Court endow'd;
> *Marlborough*, Favour'd Peer, in Valour clad,
> Best Armament, recounting Triumphs gain'd,
> Triumphs ineffable, by Publick Thanks
> By Royal Grants, and *German* Honours paid.   339-44

Godolphin is noticed for his "subtle Policies," and the
trust that he inspires for his management of finance.
    In view of the extreme rarity of Goldwin items, and
the scarcity of information about him, it is worth noting

that he became Master of Grammar Schools, in Bristol, as is evidenced in Morgan *R260a. There he preached a sermon before the Society of Merchants, "On the Honourableness, Usefulness, and Duty of Merchants," at St. Stephens Church, which was published in 1715. *An Hymn to the Redeemer*, 1703, suggests religious interests, as well as a *Thanksgiving Sermon*, preached on December 31st, 1706, and published in 1707. Both these are in the BM Library. His *Great Britain*: or, *The Happy Isle*, 1705, No. 106 above, is the only other piece of importance for Marlborough.

40   April 30.

[Vernon, James ?]

CORONA CIVICA. A POEM, To the Right Honourable the Lord-Keeper of the Great Seal of *England*. *Moribus ornas, Legibus emendas*. Hor. *LONDON*, Printed: And Sold by *John Nutt*, near *Stationers-Hall*. 1706.
        2°:   *A*, B-C^2; t.p., *bl.*, 1-12, 14 pp. Drop-t. p. 1. 476 lines, couplets. Lambeth Palace copy used. Williams Lib. had; Clark-Luttr., '30 April.' 'A fulsome flattering piece, in commemoration of him and all ye Whig party.' Morgan I397 ascribes to Mr. Vernon, but James Vernon, envoy at Copenhagen, reports from there in January, 1706, to Harley. H. M. C. *Portland*, IX, p. 120, and Trevelyan, *Ramillies*, p. 60. Opens:

        My LORD,

            WHEN on some antique *Medal*'s dimmer Brass
            Corrosive Juices fret the minted Face.

The reference is to cleaning medals, and Cowper is reminded that his patriotic virtues are similarly revealed when the tarnish of spite and spleen is removed. His noted eloquence is praised, and compared to that of Cicero. Classical allusions and comparisons abound in the poem, many obscure. Some twenty-six names are treated including the five Lords of the Whig junto, and other leaders of that party. Unfortunately almost nothing in the way of political issues appears, such as the Tack, the Occasional Conformity Bill, and the Union. "Harmonious *Halifax*" is given credit for maintaining "a needful War in Foreign Lands" (1. 182). Hartington is compared to Caesar, but is not noticed for his remark anent Ashbey, the cobbler, that "I think the liberty of a cobbler ought to be as much regarded as of anybody else: that is the happiness of our constitution." Sunderland is compared to Brutus, and Newcastle is noted for the wealth of Crassus, the bravery of Julius, and the courtesy of Pompey. In view of this indulgence in classical associations it is not surprising that Marlborough and Godolphin are given short though favorable notice at the close of the poem. Actually credit for victory is accorded more to the Lord Treasurer:

> *Blenheim* ignoble, *Donawert* unknown,
> No purpler Names than *Agincourt* had shown,
> Perhaps the Frontier *Rhine* our Arms had past,
> But in th'exhausted *Empire*'s ravaged Waste,
> Want in the glorious March a Barrier cast,
> The *Troops* unpaid stopt their victorious *Course*,
> Flaggy their Muscles, and unnerv'd their Force.
> 446-52

Although the poem is written as a flattering Whig production, the reminder of naval triumphs, along with Blenheim, assuredly qualifies the already limited praise of Marlborough.

141   May.

The Honour of England Revived by his Grace the *Duke* of *Marlborough*. Sold by *B. Bragg*. The only notice in *WL*, VIII, May, p. 318, 1706. Not in Morgan.

142   May 2.

JOSHUA: A POEM In Imitation of MILTON: Humbly Inscrib'd
to the Duke of *MARLBOROUGH*.   Occasioned By Mr. *Stephens*'s
LETTER To the Author of the *Memorial of the State of England*.   [3 lines Horace]   *LONDON*:   Printed for *John Lawrence* at the *Angel* in the *Poultry*, MDCCVI.   Horn-Luttr.
copy used.   '10 d. 2 may,' uncut.   Foxon has only one
other loc., OCU.   569 lines blank verse.   Morgan I260.
    2°: A^2 B-G^2; hft., *bl*., t.p., *bl*., *v-vi* untitled
Comment,   drop-t. p. 1,   wtmk. Arms and S, 1-22, 28 pp.
Adv. *Post-Man*, No. 1607, Tues., Apr. 30-Thurs., May 2.
'This Day is publish'd.'
    Preliminary comment.

        "The ensuing Lines were put together some Months
past. . ."

Occasion of the poem is support of Marlborough -

    . . .had not the *Heroe* been of late very impudently,
    tho' indeed sorrily, attack'd by an Epistolary Au-
    thor; who never yet was so happy as to be through-
    ly [*sic*] pleas'd with any thing; and, either through
    sourness of Temper or Neglect of his imaginary
    Merits, has more than once signaliz'd Himself in
    affronting the Highest Authority.   Nor wou'd the
    sly insinuations of this Spiritual Antagonist have
    deserved any other Treatment than Contempt; were
    they not too industriously us'd by a Discontented
    Party to give a more plausible Air to their unreas-
    onable Clamors.

This statement shows how the career of Marlborough had
been drawn into the satirical arena.   The writer adds
that Marlborough's character will rise above those in
the *Iliads* and *Aeneids*.   He hopes that the behavior of
those "Monsters of Ingratitude" who have treated Marlborough as Themistocles, Scipio Africanus, and Belisarius were treated will not prevail.   Nothing bur gratitude, unanimity, and love are needed to make England the

happiest of nations. The author hopes to help toward
this harmony. The poem opens:

> Of Glorious ARMS, and of their Blest Effects,
> *Empires* upheld and Furtive *Crowns* Retriev'd.

Praise of Queen Anne, who has surpassed even Elizabeth,
is the prime theme. Elizabeth looks down with approval
on this exponent of "Albion's grandeur in a Female
Reign" (1. 27). Factions have been subdued and William
III, Atlas of a tottering world happily replaced. The
name of Joshua does not appear till line 22, and, while
its application to Marlborough is apparent in an allusion
to "*Danubian* Waves" in line 226, Marlborough is not named
till line 378. His role in giving repose to Europe and
checking Gallia's boundless pride plainly identifies him,
and there is little of Biblical allegory. Eugene appears,
"tho' oft repuls'd On *Blenheim*'s Plains" (1. 268), as a
mild retort on those who ungratefully seek to detract
from Marlborough's part in the great victory.

Description of battle, adulation of Queen Anne, and
poetic imagery strongly suggest that the author is
Charles Johnson, who had established his position as an
ardent supporter of Whig policies. In *The Queen*, six
weeks earlier, numerous parallels appear, and Johnson's
anticipation of John Philips in Miltonic imitation appears in *Ramelies*, *A Poem*, about five weeks later. Among
verbal resemblances are: "fiery Meteors" and "lawless
Fires," in *The Queen*, and "lawless Meteors" in *Joshua*,
both as metaphors for the boundless passions of Louis
XIV; "damps" as a repressive of poetry, as in Johnson's
The Queen, "the melancholy *Thought* wou'd damp the Muses
Flame," and in *Joshua*: "May no just Damps. . .eclipse
The Dazling Beauties of thy Mighty *Theme*"; and "jarring
world" for the state of Europe, in *The Queen*, Anne lifts
the sword to "give the Jarring World a solid Peace," and
in *Joshua* the sacred awe of the Empire "holds the jarring
World in happy Poize." More extended treatments of Fe-
male Reign, Old Time in *The Queen* and "swift Revolving
Time" in *Joshua* embracing historic events, and the manner

of use of mixed Classical and Biblical allegory all
strongly point toward Johnson as a possible author of
the poem.
A rare, that is unusual, tribute to Peterborough,
as the *"Petroburgian Heroe"* (1. 516) brings in recognition of naval successes. The poem concludes with the
Whig celebration of the practical fruits of victory:
"Expiring *Commerce* shall augmented rise" (1. 554), and
Arabian spices, Persian silks, and noble metals will be
brought in British keels as "import secure." "Swift
Time shall lead on His Auspicious Years," and repose,
love, joys for England and Grateful Europe will affirm
that the world is "Thrice Happy in so Good, so Great a
QUEEN" (11. 563-9 *passim*).

RAMILLIES

The great victory of Ramillies fell on Whit-Sunday,
May 23, N. S. 1706. Since the reports and poetic tributes, largely printed in London, are dated Old Style, it
is important to think in terms of May 12, O. S. as the
dating of the battle in England. The spelling Ramillies
is used by Trevelyan, but numerous variations appear:
Ramellies, Ramelies, Ramilly, *et al.*, as well as the
Latin *Ramillia*. Extracts only are given of the first
reports.

43 May 16.

2°: 1 p. issued as 'Postscript to the Flying-Post,'
No. 1796.
An Express Arriv'd this Evening from his Grace the
Duke of *Marlbrough* [*sic*]. The Duke of Marlbrough the 21

O. S. advanced with the Confederate Army, and without
the least Notice to the Enemies Force; gave a sudden
on set, who being unprovided for such an unexpected attack, were totally Defeated: *'Tis credibly reported
that he kill'd above nine Thousand upon the Spot; and
took between four and five Thousand Prisoners, amongst
which were at there [sic]* computed to be about four
Hundred Superiour Officer [sic] together with all their
Artillery and Baggage: a more particular Account we hope
to have by the next Holland Mail: Colonel Fox being this
Evening gon [sic] with an Express to the Queen.
  *But having this Intelligence from very good Hands
we question not but we have obliged the Publick for this
Good News.*
  Printed by *A. Snoden*, in *Carter-Lane*, near *Doctors'
Commons*. Use of large type, italics, and frequent errors
convey the excitement.

144 May 23.

Post-Man, No 1616, Tues., May 21-Thurs. May 23.

  *On Saturday next will be publish'd, An Exact Plan
of the Battle of Ramellies as brought over by Captain
Pit. Curiously ingraven on a Copper Plate. Printed
for R. Smith under the Royal Exchange, and J. Raund at
Seneca's Head in Exchange Alley.* *P-Man*, No. 1617, May
23-25, 'This Day is publish'd.' *D. Cour.* May 22, short
title.

145 May 21.

Defoe, Daniel (1660-1731)

AN ESSAY ON THE Great Battle at Ramellies. By the AUTHOR
of the *REVIEW*. *LONDON*, Printed in the Year, MDCCVI.

1/2°:   2 sides, 1 column, both sides, 128 lines,
blank verse. Clark copy used. Pr. in *Rev.*, III, 242-4,
May 21, 1706 (*Facsimile Book* 7). The dates of the separate folio and of the printing in the *Review* are assumed
identical. Not in Morgan. Opens:

> Say, *Britains*! felt you nothing in your Souls,
> No *Anxious* Thoughts, no *Trembling* deep Concern?

The only specific allusion to the battle, but the first
appearance in verse, is the reference to Marlborough's
having his horse shot from under him. It is in italics.

> *Britannia's Fate was touch't in Marlb'rough's* Fall
> The Horse, *crush't with th'unusual pond'rous Weight*
> *Of rising Glory*, fell beneath the Load;
> That like *Antaeus*, touch't by *Mother-Earth*
> He might *with doubled Strength* renew the fight.
>   35-9

Defoe inquires rhetorically of "sons of Terror" what they
felt at this event, and of his own Numbers how they can
represent the emotions of the moment. All this is left
in doubt, and the poem rises perhaps only once more when
he urges Louis XIV to make peace terms. Raised to Fame's
summit, there is no place to go but down.

> *Obey the Caution*. Now shake Hands with Fame,
> See thy bright Trophies fade, by Marlborough's *Fire*
> *Scorch't*. And as sulphureous Vapours blasting kill,
> Thy Lillies dye, struck with the pointed Dart
> Of a superior Glory.   78-82

The poem is in fact an essay on policy, an editorial asserting that the world expects France to make terms, and
"Barter Liberty for Peace" (1. 126). The sentiments are
less Whiggish than generally humanitarian and libertarian
against French tyranny. Nevertheless, pressure to conclude the war was strong on the Whig government; hence
Defoe's theme. In comment, Defoe says he has

> given Vent to my own Thoughts in the following
> lines. I know some People will miss the Jingle,

and like the Pack-Horse that tires without his
Bells, be weary of the Lines for want of Rhyme;
but the Subject has so much Musick in it, I
doubt not it will make amends for the Chime. . .
I suppose nobody will imagine, I have been many
Days about them; and When I assure them they are
the Birth of three Hours, they will first of all
excuse their being somewhat incorrect; and
secondly, acknowledge the Subject very inspiring.

Cf. Defoe's *On* the *Victories* in *Flanders*, etc., *Ibid.*,
Thurs. June 27, No. 153.

146 May 21.

The *Flying Post*, No. 1729, May 21, quotes Marlborough's
Letter to the States General on his plan to pass the
Dyle, but that the French saved him the trouble. "The
Generals, Officers and Soldiers, did all that was hu-
manly possible in the Glorious Battle." The captured
cannon, colours and prisoners are summarized. *L. Gaz.*,
May 5, Marlborough has ordered two days of rest for the
troops, and has gone on to Brussels. Also, he has ap-
pointed "tomorrow" for the Thanksgiving, i.e. June 1,
N. S.

147 May 31.

[Browne, Joseph]

THE Royal Prophetess: or *ISRAEL*'s TRIUMPHS OVER JABIN
King of Hazor. An *Heroick POEM*. Written after the Manner of the Antients. And now Publish'd upon the occasion of the Unparallel'd Success of Her Majesty's Forces,
under the Command of that Great Captain of this Age, His
Highness and Prince the Duke of *MARLBOROUGH*. *London*,

Printed: and Sold by *A. Baldwin*, at the *Oxford Arms* in
Warwick-Lane, 1706. Price 1 *s*. Clark-Luttr. copy used,
'10 *d*. 31 May.' *Post-Man*, No. 1619 Tues. May 28 to
Thurs. May 30, 1706. 'Tomorrow, being Friday, will be
publish'd.' *WL*, May, VIII, 319. Not in Morgan.
    8ᵛᵒ: *A*⁸ B-G⁸; t.p., *bl*., Preface *iii-iv*, Verse 'To
the Author,' 14 11., *v-vi*, text 1-48, 52 pp. 902 lines,
couplets. Reprtd. in *State and Miscellany Poems*, partly
by Oldisworth, 2 vols., 1715, II, 72-110. On the basis
of this inclusion the poem is often attributed to Oldisworth. The *Preface* says it is the work of several years.
The poem deals with the principles of epic poetry, which
require, not bombast of words, but sublime actions. English, next to Greek, is held best for epic, and couplets
the superior form, preferable to Spenserians. Romantic
actions are below the dignity of epic. It is the greatest absurdity to deviate from the Rules.

   To the Author on His Heroick Poem, sgnd. J. William, A.M.
     What Muse has fir'd thee with Poetick Rage,
     That thou outstripst the foremost of the Age.

The poet surpasses Homer's lays, Virgil's purity, and
Milton's fire. He happily combines Wit and Piety. Shows
no awareness of Marlborough.
    The Poem opens:

      When Pious *Joshua* Israel's People led,
      After the Mighty Prophet had 'em fed.

There are no references to Marlborough or Queen Anne, and
only the general character of Joshua as military leader
and national hero justify the publication of the poem on
the occasion of Ramillies. Strangely, only one anachron-
ism appears in the entire 48-page poem, an allusion to
the court painter Varrio. It appears in an account of
the decoration of the Temple.

    A Lordly Dome rais'd up its Antique Head,
    Which o're the Centre of the Building spread,
     .   .   .   .
    There *Varrios* Skill in shining Colours lives,

> And there Immortal *Joshua* survives.
> There you may see the Radient [*sic*] Beamy Sun
> By Man's soft Pencil, Artfully out done.   145-8

Deborah in the role of chooser of the champion of her
people against Jabin and the Amorites, suggests Queen
Anne only in the situation. No allusions to parallels
appears, except possibly one reference to "blest Liberty," and the very general allusions to Jabin as an
insatiable tyrant. Readers might apply these to contemporary persons and events, but the poem does not.
The poet and his publisher simply seized on the victory
as a fortunate inducement to purchasers.

148   June 1.

An ODE On the *Duke* of *MARLBOROUGH*: *London*: Printed
for *Egbert Sanger*, at the *Post-House* near *Temple-Gate*
in *Fleetstreet*. 1706. (Price 2 *d*.)
       1/2°: Foxon-MC only loc. Reptd. in *Poems on Af-
fairs of State*, IV, 25-7. 75 lines. 6 stanzas of varying line length. Not in Morgan. Opens:

> What Pow'r of Words can equal Thy Renown,
> Illustrious God of War? What Muse can raise
>   Numbers sufficient to Thy Praise?

Who can praise Churchill? Only one of his line, Sunderland alone, for "She shares alone the Godlike Hero's
Fire" (1. 7). Marlborough has shown Lewis, at Schellenberg and on "*Bleinheim*'s Fatal Plain," that injured Nations should have their rights restored. Classical
heroes, Pompey, Caesar, Anthony, blush at their inferi-
ority to the hero who "gain'd Immortal Fame at *Rammelies*" (1. 51). How depressed are the bards when they
behold

> The British General, with greater Ease,
> Vanquish the Nation's Enemies.   75-5

182

149   June 5.

[Cockburn, Catharine Trotter (1679-1749)]

On his GRACE The *Duke* of *Marlborough*, A POEM. *London*:
Printed for *John Morphew* near *Stationer*'s *Hall*, 1706.
Adv. *Daily Cour.*, No. 1292, June 5. Horn copy used. 68
lines, couplets. No wmk. Clark. Reprtd. in Mrs. Cockburn's *Works*, 1751, II, 566-7. Not in Morgan. Opens:

> Durst thou attempt to sing of Blenheim's Plain,
> Too strongly mov'd the Transport to restrain,
> (Nor Marlborough did thy humble Verse disdain)?

The theme demands a Sappho, yet "the worthiest Theme
needs least the Poet's Art" (1. 13). Marlborough might
seem fictional. Unlike Virgil's heroes, he is faultless.
Unlike Aeneas, he is not moved by vengeance. Who would
not think the poet was trespassing on the historian in
depicting him? His hero's life was contracted into one
campaign, and now doubters must yield to the "Glories
of Ramillia's Field" (1. 57). The very rudeness of the
praise attests to its truth, for "wild Barbarian Worship,
proves the Deity" (1. 68).

150   Marlborough, Duke of (1650-1722)

His Grace the Duke of Marlborough's *Letter to the Rt.
Hon. Mr. Secretary* Harley, *together with other Letters
which passed between his Grace and the Deputies of the
States-General and the Three States of* Brabant, *the
Magistrates of* Brussels, &c. *Published by Authority.*
Printed by *M. Jones* in the *Savoy*. 1706 (*Price 2d.*)
        1/2°: 4 pp., 1 side, 2 columns, no sigs. TxU copy
used. Not in Morgan.
        Only the letter to Harley is repr. in Murray, II,
538-9. It is printed in one broad column, and Murray
has an additional short paragraph on the war in Spain
and Portugal. The versions are identical except for

details of spelling and punctuation.

The letter is dated: "Camp at *Grimburgh*, May 28, 1706." It is Marlborough's official report on Ramillies. Murray alters "write" to "wrote" and heads the letter as *Camp at Grimberg, 28th May*, 1706. Opens: "I hope Colonel Richards will be with you in a day or two with the good news of our victory over the enemy, which by the events appears to be much greater than we could well have expected. . . ."

151   June 11.

Johnson, Charles (1679-1748)

RAMELIES. A POEM. [2 lines Virgil] *LONDON*: Printed for *Ben. Bragg* at the *Black Swan* in *Pater-Noster* Row, 1706. Luttr. dates 'June 11.' *D. Cour.*, No. 1296, June 10, 1706. 'This Day is Publish'd.' No. 1297 'Yesterday was Publish'd.'
    2°: A^2 B-D^2; t.p., *bl*. To the *Right Honourable* the *Lords* And others of *Her Majesty*'s *Most Honourable Privy Council*. This *Poem* is most humbly Inscrib'd, By their most obedient and devoted Servant, *Cha. Johnson*, text, pp. 1-12, drop-t. p. 1. 16 pp. Only the Lambeth Palace copy has author's name, printed in later. Bodley has. 375 lines, blank verse. Morgan I213. Bodleian and Lambeth copies used. Opens:

> Hail Goddess to our Isle propitious,
> Since ardent Virtue by thy Name Inroll'd.

Aside from a few details in Defoe's poem, this is the first extensive tribute to Ramillies. It is also one of the first poems to make use of Miltonic verse, and is the third and last of at least three Johnson Marlborough panegyrics by this minor dramatist and Whig pamphleteer. In sturdy Whig allegiance he praises Nassau, that is William III, and his Herculean opposition to Louis XIV and his bribery and spying through "the shining mischief

Gold" (1. 22). The poem ends with Anne as the Female
Warrior, powerful through self-conquest. Louis's fall
has been like Satan's and now even Blenheim's field is
transcended by Judoign, another name for Ramillies.
The battle is extensively described following introduction of 'Churchill,' whose aide is torn from him
by a cannon shot (1. 146). Villeroy is seeking vengeance for Blenheim and Tallard. With rolling eyes, he
addresses his soldiers in epic style, and "a sudden
Murmur as the hum of bees" runs through the camp (1.
188). The night before the battle the aged Dyle rises
from his oozy couch and addresses the hero encourag-
ingly. Marlborough leaps from his bed, the trumpet
sounds, and the battle is on. Twice he rallies the Belgians against the multitude, among whom Tallard's young
son rides foremost. (This may be a reminder to those
who thought it was his only son who fell at Blenheim!)
The heroic death of Bringfield, Marlborough's aide, is
signalized; he is struck down at his side, and is
"Eterniz'd by his Death" (1. 122). Orkney, Murray and
Wood are compared to classical heroes. The broken
enemy "recedes" on all sides,

> while eager Hast[e]
> Pushes the Horse on their own flying Foot,
> Mangled in Heaps, Confounded, Disarray'd,
> They meet that Death they fly.   310-12

Some preaching of Whig doctrines is worked in:

> Princes should be their Countries common Fathers,
> Their Peoples Guardians from licentious Tyrants.
>   333-4

Anna, her mind bounded by triumphant virtue, is finally
seen shining as the "Goddess of Liberty" (1. 349). The
writer's suggestion that Johnson may be the author of
the anonymous *Joshua*, No. 142 above, is reinforced by a
concluding tribute to the Mediterranean branch of Marlborough's total plan, which is anticipated in the hailing of the "Petroburgian Heroe" in that poem. Here the

"joyful Catalans" resound

> Her grateful Praise, by valiant *Mordaunt* led,
> Or in *Iberias* Plains unweary'd, bold,
> *Gallway*, from *Lusitanian* Shores conducts
> The *British* Heros, them not *Syrius* heat,
> Nor tedious Marches over arid Plains,
> Combust by torrid Rays too near the Sun,
> (Tho' us'd to temper'd Heat, and milder Climes)
> Dismay: When Glory calls, and *Ann* Commands.   356-63

Johnson at least had noted certain Miltonic features
such as appear in this passage.

152   June 18.

A LETTER to Mr. PRIOR occasion'd by the Duke of *Marlborough*'s Late Victory at *Ramilly*, and Glorious successes
in *BRABANT*.   [4 lines Horace] LONDON: Printed By *W. D.*
for *Edmund Curll* at the *Peacock* near *Devereux*-Court
without *Temple-Bar*; and Sold by *Benj. Bragg* at the *Raven*
in *Pater-noster-Row*.   1706.
        2°: A^2 B-C^2; t.p., *bl.*, 3-12, 12 pp. 190 lines,
blank verse. ICU-Luttr., '18 June'; *D. Cour.*, No. 1307,
June 22, 'This Day is publish'd.' CU copy used. Morgan
I321.   Opens:

> Shall MARLBRO' still new Victories obtain?
> And shall the Muse be wanting to his Praise?
> Exert, O PRIOR! thy melodious Voice,
> Convince the World, tho' forceful *Dryden*'s gone,
> A Poet still remains, whose lofty Verse
> Can in just Numbers, *Arms* and *Conquest* sing.   1-6

The new wonders in the gazettes, crowds in coffee houses,
and ladies looking Ramilly in the maps, are all evidence
of the need of a poet. How can Prior forbear to write,
he who celebrated the great Nassau in his *Carmen Saeculare*. Marlborough supplies Nassau's place, and now he

is seen, surrounded with foes. His wounded steed falls,
but as the French exult, he is rescued by his men and
fights with redoubled fury.

> And now the War in all its Fury flows,
> The neighing Coursers with the Trumpet warm'd,
> Press forward on the Bit, and Paw the Ground
> With restless Feet, impatient of the Rein.
> See, with what Fierceness the Batallions join,
> In dread Array on the decisive Plain.   54-9

Mounted "on a second Steed," Marlborough speaks to his
fainting troops, reminding them of Blenheim and calling
on Europe's safety and Anna's glory to inspire new efforts. Bringfield's death is lamented, but now the
French flee in terror, pursued by the British cavalry.
  Auverquerque, second in renown to Churchill, and
Argyle, who saved Marlborough, are praised. Then the
shame and misery of the Bavarian Prince and Louis XIV
are reviewed. What trophies shall be raised? Only
Anna's favor can suffice, "Still constant to Herself,
and *still the same*" (1. 182). From her foreign princes
can learn to reign. She was born to restore injured
nations and curb the tyrant.

53 June 27.

[Defoe, Daniel (1660-1731)]

On the Victories in *FLANDERS*, and THE THANKSGIVING at St.
PAUL's. Pub. in The *Review*, III, 307-8, June 27, 1706.
Facs. Bk. 7, No. 77. 62 lines, couplets. Pr. as *Daniel
Defoe*'s *Hymn for the Thanksgiving*, London: Printed for
the Author, 1706.
    1/2°. Moore, No. 119.

> When *Israel*'s Army pass'd the Dreadful Stream
> To Conquer *Canaan*; *how did Nature dream!*

The river withdrew and even the Sun stood still when

"*Joshua* THE MARLBRO's of those wondrous Days" (1. 11)
attacked Canaan. The poem takes on the tone of a hymn,
or psalm, rejoicing as the English Joshua makes France
tremble. Humbled cities crowd in surrender, Ghent, Antwerp, Ostend, Newport.

> *Listen, ye Nations*, to the mighty Song,
> And view at distance *the Illustrious Throng.* 43-4

English fame is restored by Marlborough's sword, as a
Queen commands, who is "Humble, Merciful, and Kind" (1.
55). No flattery here, for "Truth forms her Crown, and
Liberty her Reign" (1. 62).
  See Defoe's earlier poem, May 21, and the undated
ballad "Now is the Time," which, while attributed to the
Author of the *True Born Englishman*, seems doubtfully his.

154 June 27.

ON THE VICTORY AT RAMELLIES   A PINDARIC. *Arma, Virumque Cano*, --- Virg. [ornament] LONDON Printed: And
Sold by *Benj. Bragge* in *Pater-Noster Row*, over against
Ivy-Lane, 1706. Ind.U-Luttr. copy used. Only one known.
'4 *d*. 27 June.'
  2°: t. p., *bl.*, 3-12, 12 pp., A²-C. 191 lines,
uneven length, ode couplets, 15 stanzas. Morgan I333.
Opens:

> Awake, awake, my *Lyre*,
> And Thoughts Immortal as thy Theme inspire.

  The poet urges his infant muse to celebrate Marlbro's acts, as "Scourge of GALLIC Tyranny." The exceedingly conventional and banal verse hardly merits his
claim to producing "Monuments of never dying *Verse*"
(1. 18). Lewis, the French tyrant, is depicted as conspiring with the forces of Hell to propagate a "damn'd
Design" of revenge for Blenheim. He calls up his "chief-
est" men, and the sun rises on the glorious day. Sounds
of battle, bombs, bullets, and shrieks of dying soldiery

mark the threat of a French triumph. The English and
Dutch are driven back. At this point, however, Marlbro' moves to the head of his troops. The French cry
out that he is a god, and the fortunes of war are reversed.

The classic episode of Marlborough's being unseated
from his horse, with Bringfield's rescue of him at the
expense of having his head blown off by a cannon-ball,
is recited. However, Bringfield is represented as being
merely wounded! Marlborough is referred to as "Donawert"
in a rare effort to supply him with a hero's title. No
other concrete details of the battle appear, and the
poem concludes with the hope that France may be forever
obscured, and that Europe may live in peace. Austria
and Anjou will no longer fight, nor Spain live in dread
of tyranny. The poem concludes:

> While ALBION's *Grandeur* will for ever shine,
> With such a GENERAL, and such a QUEEN.   290-1

Frequent errors mar the poem. Aside from its lack
of poetic value, nothing but its rarity distinguishes
this outpouring of the muse.

5   July 4.

Wagstaffe, W[illiam]   (1685-1725)

RAMELIES: A POEM, Humbly Inscrib'd to his GRACE, the D.
of Marlborough.   By *W. WAGSTAFFE*, Gent. of *Lincoln* College, *Oxon.*   [2 lines Virgil] *LONDON*:   Printed for *T.
Atkinson*, at the *White-Swan* in St. *Paul's Church-Yard*,
1706.

2°:   A-C^2; t.p., bl., 3-12, 12 pp.   Drop-t. on p. 3.
Horn copy used.   Leeds U, MH.   MS. corrections.   370
lines, couplets.   Morgan I400.   Opens:

> BLEINHEIM e're while at ev'ry turn appear'd,
> And MARLBROUGH's Praises number'd by each Bard.

189

The Muse is urged to sing "A Second Hocstet" (1. 10).
Fame boasts she made Louis great, but now his lease is
up. Marlborough deserves a vast reward; "Woodstock's
too little" and he hates to take the gifts the grateful
kingdoms offer (1. 116). Bringfield welters on the
ground, glorious in death (1. 137). In Paris, where
ladies enjoy luxuries, the news arrives, but Chamillard,
the French Minister of War, tries to keep the news secret. Since he had written to Villeroi that he attributed Blenheim "to chance alone," and he had a "mediocre
opinion" of the capacity of the Duke of Marlborough,
the ironies were delicious, if not developed by Wagstaffe.

The latter half of the poem is devoted to two long
speeches, from a despairing Louis and Marshal Tallard.
Louis wishes he had died young and glorious, like Ammon
(Alexander); and Tallard, prisoner in Nottingham, laments Lutetia's (France's) fate. Had General Wood only
pushed on "a second General in Chains wou'd rave" (1.
357). Wagstaffe reflects the grudging Tory state of
mind, but also the desire to be on record as praising
Anne's triumphs. It is one of the poorer poems, though
sumptuously printed on fine paper.

156   July 6.

Prior, Matthew (1664-1721)

AN ODE, Humbly Inscrib'd to the QUEEN. ON THE Late Glorious Success of HER MAJESTY'S ARMS. Written in Imitation of *Spencer*'s Stile. [4 lines Horace] *LONDON*:
Printed for *Jacob Tonson*, within *Grays-Inn* Gate next
Grays-Inn Lane. 1706.
π1 A2, B-F1; hft., *bl.*, t.p., *bl. The Preface*,
v-vi, 1-18, 24 pp. Running title on each page. No wmk.
350 lines in 35 10-line stanzas. BM, Bodley, MH, CtY,
CSmH, Clark, TxU, *et al.* Horn copy used. See No. 152.
Morgan I322.

In view of Prior's eminence as well as the critical content, the *Preface* has value. He first thought
of the "Warmth of an Ode" and had Horace's Ode IV, 4 in
mind, and he has imitated the great strokes in that poem.
However, he has turned to "our great Countryman *Spencer*"
for the stanza. Actually Prior's stanzas are 10-line,
each ending with a couplet. He repeats the legend of
Troynovant, that is the founding of London by a descendant of Aeneas, and makes interesting observations on
Spenserian archaisms. He finds both Horace and Spenser
poets of great imagination and mastery of the sublime.
He praises their diction and imagery, and their mingling of morality with the story. Professing to have
returned to poetry for this piece, he promises that "I
will neither trouble him the reader with Poem or Preface any more, 'till my Lord Duke of *Marlborough* gets
another Victory greater than those of *Blenheim* and
Ramillies." The ·poem opens:

When Great *Augustus* govern'd Ancient *Rome*,
And sent his Conqu'ring Troops to Foreign Wars.

Horace "set battle in Eternal Light" (1. 8). Similarly
Spencer praised Eliza's achievements. But what about
Anna? "What *Poet* shall be found to Sing Thy Name?"
(1. 24). The poet feels himself too mean, but if the
Queen deigns to smile he will follow Horace and Spen-
cer in heat and style.

The poem is not unworthy of Prior. Marlborough is
called from calm councils to battle by Anne's command.
Bavar, that is Bavaria, gasps at his swift arrival, but
determines to seek vengeance for Blenheim. Auverquerque,
who has drawn William's sword, and the Dutch forces are
particularly noticed. Momentarily the French exult at
Marlborough's fall, but he remounts at once. The enemy
attacks are repelled and *Blenheim*'s Fame again is in
Ramillia known" (1. 170). Tributes to *Anne* who chose
Marlborough, and who is "The Woman Chief" and Master of
the War, show Prior's intent of serving Whig policy.
He hails England as *Troynovante*, new-found Troy, and
associates numerous chiefs with those from the Middle

and Elizabethan ages. The final eight stanzas are devoted to anticipating a triumphal column, higher than
Trajan's, upon which will stand a statue of Queen Anne.
She will command the fleets to strive until "the young
Austrian on *Iberia*'s Strand" shall set his foot (1.
283). This token of victory in the War of the Spanish
Succession, in which Blenheim and Ramillies are the
twin stars, leads to detailing of the rich symbolism of
the column. Vigo, Gibraltar, and Barcelona, in Spain;
Blenheim in Bavaria; and now Ramillies in Flanders,
would appear. Masses of swords, helms, pointed spears,
standards, from Crecy to Ramillia, would summarize
British victories. The British Rose, the Northern
Thistle, and the Irish Harp would appear. Prior's Muse
asks only the humblest position, low down on the base
of the statue.

> Who durst of War and Martial Fury Sing;
> And when thy Will appointed *Marlb'rough*'s Hand
> To end those Wars, and make that Fury cease,
> Hangs up her grateful Harp to Everlasting Peace.
> 347-50

Prior's *Henry and Emma, A Poem*, Upon the Model of
The Nut-Brown Maid, seems to be at about this time.
June 27 was appointed as the day of Thanksgiving for
Ramillies. In the poem, The Queen of Beauty, follow-
ing the triumph of Love, calls upon Mars to have Fame
exalt her voice:

> To sing her Fav'rite *Anna*'s wond'rous Reign;
> To recollect unweary'd *Marlbro*'s Toils.

She goes on to say: "From every annual Course let one
great Day" be set aside for sport and celebration.
This may refer to the day of Thanksgiving for the Gaul
"thrice-Vanquish'd" by the British Soldier, *i.e.* Marlborough.

57   July 20.

AN EPISTLE TO *Sir* Richard Blackmore, Kt. On Occasion
of the Late Great VICTORY in *BRABANT*. *London*, Printed
for *John Chantry*, at the sign of *Lincolns-Inn-Square*,
at *Lincolns-Inn* Back Gate, 1706. Price 2 *d*.
     2°: A²; drop-t. on p. 1, 1-4, 4 pp. Colophon
bottom p. 4. MH, TxU. TxU copy used. Foxon cites
Luttr. date, Walpole-Bute copy, '20 July. 1706.' *Wrenn
Cat*. V, 108. Morgan I 46. 78 lines, couplets. Opens:

> Oh *Blackmore*! Why do'st thou alone refuse
> To grace *Ramillia* with thy noble Muse,
>
> .   .   .   .
>
> How canst thou answer to *thy self* and *Fame*
> A Victory like this ---- without *thy* Name?

Without Narcissus Luttrell's note, "A banter on Sir
Richard," this is plainly satirical, although this fact
seems to have been concealed to Mr. Albert Rosenberg,
Sir Richard Blackmore, U. Nebraska Press, 1953, p. 88.
     Sheffield goes on to praise Blackmore as William's
poet, as Augustus had his Virgil. But, he insists,

> So vast a *Genius* and so large a Mind
> Can never to *One Heroe* be confin'd.   21-2

Allusions to Blackmore's treatment of King Arthur, and
to his epic *Eliza* (1705) only intensify the irony of
over-praise. What if ten thousand sick should die, the
rhyming doctor's tribute to Churchill must be produced.
Tate has said somewhat, but "He has his *office* not his
Muse obey'd" (1. 38). Prior, in Spenser's style, has
reflected more honor than he has given. Lesser poets
have contended.

> *De Foe*, as ever, Execrably bad,
> Throws out a Hasty *Poem*, wrote like Mad.
> 'Twas the first-born, and welcome in *our Mirth*,
> Tho' not *One Muse* assisted at its birth.   47-50

If only Blackmore will write then "All will silent be,"

and his account of Ramillia will distance the whole
poetic tribe (1. 64). If he can waken Blackmore's muse,
some share of glory will be his!

158   July 24.

B----y, Mr. [No dates]

An ODE Occasion'd by the *Battle of Ramellies*. By Mr.
B----y. Printed and Sold by the Booksellers of *London*
and *Westminster*.
        2°: 1 p., single column, no pub., n. d. TxU.
Rprtd. in *Poems on Affairs of State*, IV, 48-9, 1707.
28 lines, octosyllabic couplets. An ode only in name.
Not in Morgan.

        How will the grateful Senate praise!
        What new recording Pillars raise!

The Romans immortalized their heroes in monuments and
verse, and also deified them. Had they had a Churchill
they would have shadowed half their deities with his
obelisk. Pharsalia would have vanished before Blenheim
and Rammelies. Britain's hero never gains a conquest
but to free the enslaved. Thus from his race the Fair
may claim a title to Beauty's fame. "Rich in Lip! a
Cheek! a Hand! Or any Charms of Sunderland" (11. 27-8).
This tribute to the second daughter, Anne, may provide
the best clue to Mr. B's identity. Similar sentiments,
as well as brevity, suggest that another Ramillies piece,
undated, may be by the same author, even though he is
called *Dr*. Brady.

159   Brady. Dr. [No dates]

On the Duke of Marlborough. By. Dr. Brady. In *Poems
on Affairs of State*, IV, 459-60, 1707. Three 6-line

stanzas, 18 lines.

How, Glorious *Marlbro'*, shall we sing thy Praise?
How shall we match thy Laurels with our Bays?
What Muse can stretch her Wing o'er *Blenheim*'s Plain,
Ramillia's Field, and all the Grand Campaign?

Anyone attempting adequacy in verse to his fame would
need to have Marlborough's "generous Fire." Then our
times would surpass the Augustan age. Even Maro would
be surpassed, as Rome's best sons are by him. That this
piece is nearer to being an ode, or at least lyric, suggests the possibility of some interchange of titles with
the preceding poem. Conceivably the author is Dr. Nicholas Brady (1654-1726), chaplain to William III and
Queen Anne. His metrical version of the *Psalms of David*
and *Proposals* for blank verse translation of Virgil's
Aeneid attest to his combined religious and classical
interests.

60   July 23.

Blackmore, Sir Richard (1654-1729)

ADVICE TO THE POETS. A POEM Occasion'd by the Wonderful
Success of her Majesty's Arms, under the Conduct of the
Duke of *Marlborough*, in *Flanders*. *LONDON*: Printed by
H. M. for *A.* and *J. Churchill*, at the *Black Swan* in
Pater-Noster-Row. MDCCVI.
       2°: A-H²; t.p., *bl.*, 763 lines, couplets. 3-34,
34 pp. Errata bottom unnumbered p. *35*, MH, IU, TxU,
Clark-Luttr. Adv. *L. Gaz*. No. 4247, July 22-25. 1706.
'23 July.' Morgan I 45. IU copy used. Sec. Ed., 1706;
considerably revised, in *A Collection of poems on Various Subjects*. Printed by W. Wilkins, 1718, 2 vols., pp.
3-24. UC copy used.
       In this lengthy poem Blackmore not only responds to
the challenge to deal with Ramillies; he also treats of
the problem of panegyric and scores on some of his
enemies. It is an important item in the war of the

195

poets. It opens:

> Oh! let the Conqueror stop his swift Career,
> A while the Foe, a while the Poet spare.

The exhausted muse is following the swift warrior, to the Danube.

> For *Blenheim* was a Theme too bright, too strong
> For any Rapture, any master Song.   58-9

And now Ramellies presents new, great challenge. The muse feels weak, but the will is strong. Mercenary wits, who write for bread, and writers of pretty prologues and sonnets are warned off (ll. 183-6). Only the few are worthy, Prior, Congreve, Granville, Stepney, Walsh, and Hughes are mentioned, with Summers and Montague to preside and correct. (Fictitious names for these are substituted in 1718.) A poem, strong as Woodstock's towers, must be built, and decorated with painting and sculpture, or verbal equivalents.

The poem now takes on the manner of "Advice to a painter" poems, lines 327-572, when he subdues the fire of description and takes the lyre of lyric ode celebration. Drawing inspiration from Michel Angelo and Raphael, Blackmore envisions battle scenes, and then the destruction of a monument in Paris, as it breaks "with the Thunder of *Ramillia*'s Plain" (l. 465). After the victory, Marlborough is described entering Brussels to receive surrender of Belgian towns. Following an Angelic vision, the ode portion, lines 635-748, presents the now conventional shouts of triumph and mingled allegory and baroque decor of clouds, shimmering light, and imagery of grief and destruction for the enemy. Blackmore's strong Whig convictions pervade the poem, which terminates with a tribute to Anne, "By all good Princes lov'd, and by all Tyrants fear'd" (l. 761).

Of course this poetic attempt is central to a body of verse and satire associating Blackmore with Marlborough. Whether or not Blackmore took Buckingham's "encouragement" of July 20th seriously, he supplied a note of unconscious hilarity to the heroic theme.

61   August 6.

Phillips, John, Milton's Nephew (1631-1706)

The VISION Of Mons. *Chamillard* Concerning the BATTLE of
RAMILLIES: And The *Miraculous Revolution* in Flanders
Begun, *May* the 12*th*. 1706.   A POEM.   Humbly Inscrib'd
to the Right Honourable JOHN Lord *SOMERS*.   *By a Nephew
of the late Mr. John Milton.*   [5 lines *Par. Lost*, Lib.
vi, applied to Flanders and Spain.]   *London*:   Printed
for *Wm. Turner*, at *Angel* at *Lincolns-Inn-Back-Gate*,
1706.
        2°: A^2, B-C^2 D^1; hft., *bl.*, t.p., *bl.*, drop-t.
on p. 1, 1-12, 16 pp.   504 lines, blank verse.   InU,
TxU copy used.   *WL*, August, 1706.   Morgan I1318.   Opens:

    One Ev'ning e'rst the Moon unveil'd her Light,
    And o're the Dark a silver Mantle threw.

Chamillard, French Minister of War, lies under a canopy
restlessly reviewing state affairs.   He falls asleep and
sees a vision of spectral figures, mangled limbs, and
clotted gore impregnating the fields of "Dreary *Judoign*,
and Dry Ramillies" (1. 25).   When morning comes he
hastens to Madam Maintenon, Louis XIV's mistress, and
tells of how two successive visions of an old hag and
a colossus prophesied destruction to France.   He saw the
Gallic Host, but then the British leader rose up to challenge it, who, though severe, "None seem'd to have a
cooler Head, or warmer Heart" (1. 181).   Maintenon pro-
tests but the vision is supplanted by battle, gory and
terrible.   Marlborough calmly sits on his horse in the
midst of it.   Scarce three hours passed, Miltonic hours,
with "baleful Eyes" and "high Disdain Mix'd with Obdu-
rate Pride, and stedfast Hate" (11. 308-10).   Auver-
queque and Murray are seen along with Churchill, and
Bringfield falls gloriously.   The poem concludes with
tributes to Queen Anne, allusions to Blenheim, and rejoicing that Marlborough conquers so fast "where now a
WOMAN reigns" (1. 473).

162   August 13.

[Philips, John (1676-1708)?]

A Panegyrick Epistle, (Wherein is given An Impartial
Character of the present ENGLISH POETS)   To S. R----
B---- On his most Incomparable Incomprehensible POEM,
call'd *Advice to the Poets*.   [1 line Virgil]   *LONDON*,
Printed, and sold by *B. Bragge* at the *Black Raven* in
Pater-Noster Row.   1706.
        2°: A^2 B-C^2; hft., *bl.*, t.p., *bl.* drop-t., p. 1,
1-8, 12 pp.   No wmk.   136 lines, couplets and ode.   Adv.
in *Post-Man*, No. 1660, Tues., Augs. 13-Thurs. 15.   Horn
copy used.   Foxon has CLU-Luttr.   Ascription to Philips
contested by M. G. Lloyd Thomas.   De Maar attributes to
Philips on basis of a note from Fenton to Joseph Newton:
"I should be mighty obliged to you, if you could get me
a copy of his verses against Blackmore."   Blackmore had
satirized Philips in *Advice to the Poets* (ll. 191-6).
"No more let *Milton*'s Imitator dare Torture our Language. . .with Numbers harsher than the Din of War."   Morgan I 47.   Opens:

        Permit an humble Muse to sing thy Praise,
        Thou everlasting Fund of Rhime and Lays.   13-14

Blackmore surpasses Virgil, who achieved only "One
Heroic Poem," "*Arthur*'s, *Job*'s, *Eliza*'s" (l. 7), with
verse of born perfection, and as "Lasting as *Marlb'ro*'s
Deed, and as *Ramillia*'s Plain" (l. 20).   Blackmore's
comparison of Marlborough to Constantine, and the role
of S[ommers] and M[ontague] as critics are noticed.   But
suddenly his poem takes an upward flight and abrupt turn,
that is into ode.   "Nothing Prophane e'er match'd it here
below" L. 79).   Then a bevy of poets, some identified,
others indicated by a single initial, succeed.

        How *Addison* excels in th'Epic Strain,
        Learn from his finish'd Poem, his *Campaign*.

This is the only poem specified, but Wicherly [*sic*],
Stepny [*sic*], Prior, Congreve, and Southern and Row are

named, while G[art]h and G[ranvi]lle are readily identifiable. All this seems to lead to the passage defending John Philips, though unnamed.

> Then (tho' rejected by our heav'nly Bard)
> *Great Milton*'s *Imitator* shall be heard.   122-3

The muse will remain unknown, with Rhimer [*sic*] and
Walsh to preside over his "strong but *factious* Lay."
    While Blackmore continued to exploit the theme of
Marlborough's victories, down to 1708-9, this is the
final association in 1706.

63   August 15.

Congreve, William (1670-1729)

A PINDARIQUE ODE, Humbly Offer'd to the QUEEN, On The
Victorious Progress of Her MAJESTY's Arms, under the Conduct of the Duke of MARLBOROUGH. To which is prefix'd,
A DISCOURSE on the PINDARIQUE ODE. By Mr. *CONGREVE*.
[6 lines Horace] *LONDON*: Printed for *Jacob Tonson*,
within *Grays-Inn* Gate next *Grays-Inn* Lane. L706.
    2°: π^1, A-C^2, D^1; t.p., *bl.*, *Discourse on Pin-
darique Ode ii-vi*, drop-t., 1-10, 16 pp. BM, CtY, TxU,
Clark, CSmH. Horn copy used. Morgan I 85. No Luttr.
located. No wmk. Pindaric ode, 140 lines, in stanzas
7, 7, 14 lines. Morgan I 75 gives same for Chester-
field, but with cross-ref. to Congreve.
    In the *Discourse* Congreve stresses the hitherto
unrecognized regularity of Pindar's Odes. He points
out the abundance of irregular odes, including Cowley's
which fail to see that, within each poem, regularity
should be preserved in Strophe, Antistrophe, and Epode.
These reflected the movement, counter-movement, and
stationary position of the chorus in chanting the ode.
While this function is now obsolete, a pleasing structure is still inherent in the stanzaic pattern. In this
ode he follows the first of Pindar's Pythics, which

happily is short, thus atoning for the length of the
introduction. Opens:

> Daughter of Memory, Immortal Muse,
>   *Calliope*; what Poet wilt thou chuse
>   Of *ANNA*'s Name to Sing?

With the Muse's aid, even he, humblest of poets, may
dare to sing Anna's praises. He strikes the lyre, and
the music reminds of *"Spencer* sweet, and *Milton* strong,"
and the lay that raised humble Boyn above Tiber. Anne,
of mighty mind, mercy and pity, servant of the common
good, is praised.

> *ANNA* Her equal Scale maintains,
> And *Marlbro* wields Her sure deciding Sword.   83-4

Now he sings Marlborough's triumph on the Ister, the
classical name for the Danube, that is Blenheim. If he
could sing Blenheim, what art could go on? How can he
proceed to Ramillia's Day? Fear unstrings the lyre,
and admiration stops the song. He can only urge Marlborough to go on to further great conquests till Europe
is freed. With universal peace restored, rewards far
above his trophies and spoils will come to the hero,
"Thy QUEEN's just Favour, and thy COUNTRY's Love" (1.
140).
   The poem is strictly lyrical throughout, beautifully controlled, and in some ways a better example of
Pindar's style than later examples. Congreve's association with the Whig leader is reflected in the hearty
tributes to the governmental policy and Marlborough's
splendid service to Queen Anne. Extensive footnotes
document the classical terms, Cannae being compared to
Blenheim, Pharsalis surpassed by Ramillies, and the like.

164   August 29.

A Modern Inscription to the Duke of Marlborough's FAME:

A Poem. Occasion'd by an Antique, In Imitation of
Spencer. With a *Preface* Unveiling some of the *Beauties*
of the *Ode* which has pass'd for Mr. *Prior*'s. [1 line
Juvenal] London: Printed in the Year MDCCVI. Clark-
Luttr. copy has '18 Septemb,' but adv. in *Daily Cour.*,
No. 1365, Thurs. Aug. 29, 1706, as "This Day is Pub-
lished." Also the description in *Post-Man*, No. 1681,
Thurs. Oct. 3 to Sat. Oct. 5, 1706, has, 'Sold by B.
Bragg at the Raven in Pater-Noster-Row.' TxU copy used.
MH, CtY, CCU. Morgan I262, Sept. 1706.
    2°: a, b, c², B-C²; t.p., *bl.*, *iii-xii*, 1-4; 5-8
Latin translation, 91 lines.
    The *Preface* expresses the ironic view that Prior
intended a "Banter" in his Spenserian imitation. By
quoting and precise line references it goes through
Prior's *Ode to the Queen*, No. 156, above, and points out
flaws in logic, grammar, and rhetorical features. It
achieves both satiric and critical effects. The poem
opens:

    As of his Faction's Downfal [*sic*] P[rio]r sings,
    His Muse attempts to rise with broken Wings.

The satirist deplores the use of "dull antiquated
Words" by France's partisans, while Marlborough conquers
anew. It had been thought that Liberty was dead in England with the death of William III. This poet hailed
his horse Sorrel as his Pegasus. The *Top Croakers* of
the sword and gown (1. 25) have been discredited by
Marlborough and Anne, who is "Heav'ns peculiar Care."
The *Immortal Man*, that is Louis XIV, must admit that a
Woman's deathless fame doth his suppress. England is
too sincere to deal with those who have no fear of future consequences. William saw this, but was forced to
sheathe his sword, which is now brandished by Marlborough, "the Scourge of Tyrants, and Support of Kings"
(1. 93).

165   September 5.

> *To His Grace the Duke of Marlborough* On His Late Suc-
> cesses in *Flanders*. London: Printed for *Egbert Sanger*,
> at the *Post-House* near *Temple-Gate* in *Fleetstreet*. 1706.
> (Price 2 .)
>   1/2°: 60 lines, couplets. MH-Luttr. only loc.,
> 'Septemb. 5, 1706.' Reprtd. in *Poems on State Affairs*,
> IV, 1707, pp. 77-8. Not in Morgan. Opens:

> > Whilst You, my Lord, with an extensive Hand,
> > O'er distant Provinces hold a wide Command.

Marlborough is still sweeping up the Belgian towns in
the aftermath of Ramillies. No specific episodes are
brought in, and the poem concludes with the image of
Andromeda being released from her chains, that is
Europe by Marlborough, who is now presumably Perseus.
One of an increasing number of broadside tributes and
satires. The main purpose appears to be to point out
to the Dutch the need for a more favorable response
to British aid.

> Three mighty People rais'd from sad Distress,
> The *Po*, and *Danube*, and the *Rhine* confess.
>   .   .   .   .
> Replete with Joy, the grateful Dutch shall tell,
> How *Antwerp*, *Brussels*, mighty *Menin* fell.   23-8
> *passim*.

166   October 14.

Paris, Mr., of Trinity-College, *Cambridge*. Morgan has
"[John?]." [no dates]

RAMILLIES A POEM, Humbly Inscrib'd to his GRACE the DUKE
of *MARLBOROUGH*. Written in Imitation of *Milton*. By Mr.
PARIS of Trinity-College, *Cambridge*. [2 lines Pliny]
LONDON: Printed for *Jacob Tonson*, within *Grays-Inn* Gate

next *Grays-Inn* Lane. 1706.
2°: A^2 A2, B-C^2; t.p., *bl.*, 1-10, 12 pp., drop-t.
on p. 1. No wmk. 363 lines, blank verse. Morgan I306
has another ed. L., 1708. Horn copy used, MS. 'Enterred'
on t.p. Opens:

Of *Britons* Second Conquest, and the Man
That Twice has triumph'd o'er the *Gallick* Arms.

This opening suggests the near-parody of *Paradise Lost*.
The Miltonic features are largely rhythmic and little
of sublimity appears. The poet invokes Milton's muse
to sing "great ANNA's gentle and triumphant Reign" (1.
29). The Sun had scarce made its planetary circuit
twice after *Bleinheim* before this second victory came
to distress *Lewis*. Burning for revenge, he calls his
forces and addresses them, urging that Bleinheim was a
"foul Overthrow" by adverse chance or some evil star's
influence. Marsin and Villeroy are prepared to serve
him, and their army marches in battle array. Marlborough is joined by Batavian and Danish troops. He addresses them briefly, seeking "a second *Bleinheim*" with
no dread of the superior force of the enemy. The battle
is described in the usual terms, dusky clouds, horses
and riders in gore, shouts, and the roar of cannon.
But where is Marlborough?

Swift as the Light'ning Glimpse he wings his Way
Impetuous, nor can ought restrain his Course
Where Danger calls; o'er Heaps of prostrate Slain
He rides intrepid, not regarding Death
That covers all the Plain in hideous Hue.
. . . . . Ball from Hostile Tubes,
Instinct with Motion from the Nitrous Grain
Inflam'd, with dismal Hiss play round his Head
Innocuous, the Messengers of Fate,
Part single, part with Chain connexive link'd
In conjugal Destruction. Thrice his Steed   239-51
Sunk under him.   *passim.*

Night falls, and battle ends. But now victory sends

thrills from town to town. Churchill, Auverquerque must
be praised, and, alike victorious, Mordaunt and Galloway,
and Eugene. For further tribute the poet resigns "The
mighty Task to tuneful *Addison*" or "*Prior*'s artful Song"
(ll. 332 ff). In their lines Nassau triumphs still and
Churchill at Bleinheim and Ramillia. In conclusion the
poet draws the moral that "'Tis better to be lov'd by
a gentle Prince, Than fear'd by a Tyrant" (ll. 356-7).
Marlborough will return to shouts of triumph and such
favors as only Anna can repay.

> To thy unerring Choice we *Churchill* owe,
> To his victorious Arms the World's Repose.   363-4

167   October 24.

[Daniel, Richard] [no dates]

The British Warriour. A POEM. In a LETTER TO HIS EXCEL-
LENCY The Lord Cutts, Occasion'd by the late Glorious
Success of Her Majesty's Arms. [2 lines Horace] *LONDON*,
Printed for BENJ. BRAGG at the *Raven* in *Pater-Noster-Row*.
n. d.
    2°: A^1 B-D^2 E^1; t.p., *bl.*, 1-14, 16 pp., orna-
mental band and drop-t. on p. 1. 314 lines, couplets.
No wmk. Morgan I 53 speculates 1705, but an allusion to
Ramillies proves date. *D. Cour.*, No. 1413, Thurs. Oct.
24, 1706. 'This Day is publish'd.' *Ibid.* No. 14, 21,
28, Jan. 1, 1707. Ascr. to Daniel in Lintott's *Misc.*
Poems and Translations, 1720. Horn copy used, uncut,
sewn. Opens:

> The *British* Muse in *Chaucer* first began,
> All Nature list'ning to the wondrous Man.

Not only the first association of Chaucer with Marlborough
panegyric, but also a striking affirmation of his role as
a source for English poetry. The tree he planted took
root and from it came Milton, Spenser, Shakespeare and

Ben Johson, at least in tragedy.

> *An Eden lost and won, a Fairy Queen,*
> *A Moor to Doubts betray'd, and lofty Cataline.*
>
> 12-13

After this formidable group came also the School of Wit,
in satire, and presumably comedy.

> Wit then all lovely and Gigantick stood,
> Like the large Sons of Men before the Flood;
> The well-pleas'd Muse confess'd a strong Embrace,
> And teem'd an Off-spring of a Manly Grace,
> Whose vast Athletick Limbs, and wondrous Fire
> Still own'd the brawny Vigour of the Sire.   14-19.

By contrast, modern, puling Witlings have shown an ebb
of judgment, "and a Flux of Rhime," and have choked the
press with "unhallowed Ballads." These reflections on
the line of Marlborough panegyric are plentifully justified -- "A *Churchill* they to *Withrington* debase -- and
the vigorous swing of the satire suggests more to come
than actually develops.

> Departed Chiefs who were in Battel slain,
> Are rais'd from Death to be destroy'd again;
> Who cursing Pen and Ink, less fearful stand,
> Of their brave Foes, than of the Writer's Hand.
>
> 32-5

The poem does provide an interesting game in detection
of unnamed panegyrists, first Sir Richard Blackmore,
"A knighted Bard," who has "Deafned [*sic*] with sturdy
Verse the listen'ng Crowd." He but affords,

> A swoln and windy Timpany of Words. . .Rumbling
> he mounts. . .Down drops with heavy Wight [*sic*]
> to Earth again. . .Murthers his Patients, and
> his Readers too."   36-50 *passim*.

Next is the Oxford author of an imitation of Milton, presumably Wagstaffe with his *Ramelies*, No. 155
above. While both *Joshua*, possibly by Charles Johnson,

and *Ramellies*, certainly his, are in Miltonic blank
verse, Wagstaffe is described as "of Lincoln College,
Oxon." on his title. The unnamed poet has by witch-
craft invoked Milton's ghost, with disastrous results,
as Wagstaffe's assuredly are.

> Sonorous Bard, what happy Accents throng
> Around thy Lips, and thunder from thy Tongue!
> What racking Throws afflict thy lab'ring Brain,
> We see with Wonder, and we read with Pain.   60-3

If he would justly imitate Milton, he is urged to make
Satan the hero of his poem, and a footnote notes that
Dryden said that "*Milton* made the Devil his Hero." No
other theme could be worthy of such a poet!
   The third, and final, example of bad poetry is an
imitator of Spenser. Gothic type is used for the ital-
icized words.

> A *douty Piece* came pricking o'er the Plain
> In *auncient Guise I weet*, and *Spencer*'s Strain,
> Of Fancy nice disdain'd our modern Mode,
> Stept out a Ballad, tho' *yclipt* an Ode.

Like Durfey's Dame of Honour, and dressed in an Elizabethan farthingale and ruff, "From *Sternhold* all her
shining Phrase she drew," and "Speaks others English,
but forgets her own." Prior's *Ode to the Queen*, No.
156 above, had come on July 6th, and was not identified as his. The review of panegyrists comes with:

> Thus all their Arts our lesser Poets use,
> To force a Genius, and provoke a Muse,
>   86-92
> And still are Witty----at the Reader's Cost. *passim*.

But in Cutts the poet finds a worthy prospect, and
the remainder of the poem is devoted to Marlborough's
glories and a final urging Cutts to sing them. "A thousand Graces" affirm his "Title to the Muse's Arms" (ll.
95-6). Following pictures of the vengeful Bavarian and
the invincible Marlborough serving "mighty *Anna*" the

Muse of Cutts is urged to "do the Heroe right" (1. 301).
Only he can please Apollo, as Achilles charmed Homer's
fires.

One Master-Work remains to crown the Scene,
Whilst *Anna* claims the Beauties of your Pen;
Rich Fancy with unerring Judgment join,
And add their Coul'roing [*sic*] to some just Design;
. . . .
Untouch'd by Time, unknowing of Decay,   302-10
Fix'd as the Triumphs of *Ramillia*'s Day.   *passim.*

Unquestionably this piece displays a facility in
witty rhyming that is beyond the average, and it raises
questions about Cutts' position in poetic tribute even
though he did not appear to have produced the "Master-
Work" requested of him. Three advertisements of works
"Lately Publish'd" appear at the bottom of p. 14. None
relates to Marlborough. Cutts (1661?-1707) produced
various panegyrics and an elegy "On the Death of the
Queen," 1695. See CBEL, II, 280.

68 *The British Ode: To His Grace the Duke of Marlborough.*

2°:   *i-ii*, 1-14, 16 pp.
Morgan G73; Dobell *Cat.* XVIIIth *Century Verse*, 1933, No.
2397. In Welsh. No copy known. Not in Welsh National
Library. Lintott Misc. Poems, 1720, and Welsh Bibl.
Soc., July 1948.   Opens:

Gwyd i chod y fawr levydianen en Duk a Marlboro.

69 October 30.

[Mr. Bolton] [no dates]

B., J. *Prince Eugene: An Heroick Poem* on the Victorious

Progress of the Confederate Arms in Italy under the Conduct of his Royal Highness the Duke of Savoy, and Prince
Eugene. By J. B. of Christ Church College, Oxon.
Printed for *J. Morphew* and the Booksellers of London and
Westminster, near *Stationer*'s *Hall*. Price 6 *d*. Adv. in
Daily Cour., No. 1418. Wed. Oct. 30, 1706. 'This Day
is publish'd.' But the *Post-Man*, No. 1734, Tues. Feb.
4-Thurs. Feb. 6, 1707, 'This Day is publish'd.' This may
be a second edition, or possibly selling off of unsold
copies. The Texas copy, which is used, has the following title page, dated 1707, but almost certainly is the
same poem. Not in Morgan.

Prince EUGENE: An Heroic Poem On the Victorious
Progress of the Confederate Arms in *Italy*; under the Con-
duct of his Royal Highness the Duke of SAVOY, and Prince
EUGENE. [6 lines Horace] *London*: Printed for *Edmund
Curll* at the *Peacock*, without *Temple-Bar*; and *Egbert
Sanger*, at the *Post-House*, at the *Middle-Temple Gate* in
Fleetstreet. 1707. See No. 207.

2°: *A*², B-C²; t.p., *bl.*, 1-12, 12 pp., drop-t. on
p. 1. Morgan J 71 [Mr. Bolton], 229 lines, couplets.
The poem opens:

> O! lend, *Pierian Virgin*, lend your Air,
> You that o'er Music's Pow'rful Force preside.

The poet longs for Maro's sweetness, Prior's excellence,
Garth's melting harmony, and Milton's sense, to sing Anne
and Eugene. While Anne is queen and "Conqu'ring MARLBRO
does our Armies lead" (1. 32) France's Hellish stratagems
and tyranny are not to be feared. "The Plains of BLEN-
HEIM and RAMILLIA," still damp with human gore, attest
to Britannia's power. Marlbro, like Alcides, rides
among the cohorts. This acknowledgment of debt to him
being disposed of, the theme of the poem, Eugene's conquests, is brought in on page 4. As he approaches the
battle which freed Turin, he craves Milton's muse, and
a footnote specifies *Paradise Lost* as "An Heroick Poem"
(p. 6). Battle is described as a "Horrid Din," with
thundering cannon, clash of arms, and the groans and
cries of dying soldiery.

Never was *Battel* with more Conduct fought,
Or *Victory* so great, so cheaply bought.   143-4

No French commanders are named, but this victory freed
Italy and did much to sink French glories and hopes.
Heaven favors British arms.

Thus did we *Blenheim* and *Ramillia* win;
Thus Conquests follow MARLBRO', and EUGENE.   185-6

The poem culminates with anticipations of victory and
peace, of the Austrian ruler restored in Spain, and even
the Angels rejoicing in Heaven and Astrea will return to
earth, virtue will reign everywhere, and vice will no
longer molest the world.
    An advertisement of four works "Newly Publish'd"
appears at the end. Included are *A Letter to Mr. Prior*,
No. 152 above, Addison's *Remarks on Italy*, and Garth's
Dispensary. All are sold by Sanger.

170   November 5 *ca*.

Tate, Nahum (1652-1715)

A Congratulatory Poem on the Right Honourable EARL
RIVER's Expedition. Written by Mr. Tate, Poet Laureate
to Her Majesty. London, printed and Sold by *B. Bragg*
at the *Raven* in *Pater-Noster-Row*, 1706.
    4°: A^2-B^2; *1-2*, 3-8, 8 pp. Adv. *Post-Man*, No.
1695, Sat. Nov. 2 to Tues. Nov. 5. Day not specified.
Not in Morgan. TxU copy used. Opens:

   The modest muse presumes not to enquire.

71   November 14.

[Tickell, Thomas (1685-1740)]

OXFORD: A POEM. Inscrib'd to the Right Honourable the

Lord *LONSDALE* [2 lines Horace] Printed for *Egbert Sanger*, London: the Post-House at the *Middle-Temple-Gate* in *Fleetstreet*. 1707. Adv. in *Post-Boy*, No. 1797, Tues. Nov. 12-Thurs., Nov. 14, 1706. 'This Day is publish'd.' *Daily Cour.* has Nov. 14, 1706, 'This Day is publish'd.' Lehigh copy used. Morgan J448.
    2°: *A*² A2, B-C; t.p., *bl.*, 1-10, 12 pp. Drop-t. on p. 1. 470 lines, couplets. Opens:

> Whilst You, My LORD, adorn that stately Seat,
> Where shining Beauty makes her soft Retreat.

Lonsdale is at Lowther Castle; but the poet is at Oxford where all youths write poetry, his the humblest. The Marlborough connection in the nice topographical poem is pervasive. 'Vanbrook' is referred to, and in the Sheldonian Theatre,

>   in equal Verse,
>   The youthful Bards their Godlike QUEEN rehearse,
> And sing the Plains of *Hockstet*, and *Judoign*. 59-61

The Bodley suggests security, and "No more we fear the Military Rage" (1. 76). A review of Oxford poets, many taught by Aldrich, includes Philips, who "Sings with that Heat, wherewith his *Churchill* fought" (1. 263). Other Marlborough panegyrists, Codrington, Steele, Trapp, and Harison, with his *Woodstock Park*, and "ev'ry Muse was fond of *Addison*" (1. 289). It is clear that education at Oxford benefits from the security gained by Marlborough's military achievements, and profits from studies of ancient heroes. On Lonsdale the poet says:

> And now your Cheeks, with Warlike Fury, glow,
> Whilst, on the Paper, fancy'd Fields appear,
> And Prospects of Imaginary War,
> Your Martial Soul sees *Hockstet*'s fatal Plain,
> Or fights the fam'd *Ramillia* o'er again.   384-8

Oxford is a place of green retreats, a haven of poets, "inspir'd like Athens." But even now we hear the World own "Those Fictions by more wond'rous Truths out-done" (1. 434).

Frowd, R., Gent. [no dates]

A POEM On Prince *Eugene*'s *Victory* Over The Duke of
Orleans. Humbly Inscribed to the Commissioners chosen
for managing the 250000 *l*. remitted to Prince *Eugene*,
and the rest of the Honourable Subscribers to that
Loan. By *R. Frowd*, Gent. *London*, Printed for *Isaac
Cleave*, next to *Serjeants Inn* in *Chancery-Lane*, 1706.
2°: *A-B*^{2}; t.p., *bl*., 3-8, drop-t. on p. 3, 8 pp.
'Price Four Pence' at end. TxU-Luttr. copy '4 *d*. -
20 Novemb.' 136 lines, couplets. Not in Morgan.
Opens:

> At length old Time brings forth th' important
> > hour,
> That sets a period to the *Gallick* Power.

Louis has ravished lands, stolen crowns, and spared
neither "Fraud nor Force." Europe is trembling in
fear, hardly daring to oppose him anywhere.

> Till to her Aid illustrious *Churchill* rose;
> And great *Eugene* by his Example taught,
> With the same Courage, the same Conduct fought:
> Else *France* had yet retriev'd her former Blow,
> Had curst the *Danube*, but have blest the *Po*.
> > 16-20

Eugene saw Turin besieged, Savoy in distress, and
grieved. He calls his troops to arms, to go beyond
the Po. In vain luckless Orleans comes to oppose him.
The French defenses of floods and mountains are in
vain. Eugene and Orleans rush into combat like "Lyons."
The slaughter of dying men chokes the Po, and the Doria
nereids gasp for breath.
Victory is won, and choirs of birds and Zephyrs
sing in celebration. What happy Muse can relate the
day of blood and Eugene's glory?

> None but *Apollo*'s self can justly praise:
> His Voice alone is for their Triumph fit,
> Immortal Valour claims Immortal Wit. 135-7

173   November 26.

[Clay, Stephen (no dates)]

AN EPISTLE FROM THE Elector of Bavaria TO THE *FRENCH KING*:   After The BATTEL of *RAMILLIES*.   [4 lines Ovid] *LONDON*:   Printed for *Jacob Tonson*, within *Grays-Inn* Gate next *Grays-Inn* Lane.   1706.
       2°: π^2, A-F^2; hft., *bl*., t.p., *bl*.   To the Right Honourable *William Cowper*, Esq; *Lord Keeper* of the *Great-Seal* of *England*, *iii-vi*, Epistle, 1-16, 304 lines, couplets; To the Duke of Marlborough, 17-20, 56 lines, total 360 lines, 28 pp.   No wmk.   Horn copy used; sgnd. in MS Rob: Alard (?) and 'Enterred,' p. 17. Running titles throughout.   *D. Cour.*, No. 1441, Nov. 26, 1706.   'This Day is publish'd.'   Clark copy has "Mr. Clay of the Temple."   A. R. Waller ed. of pr. works attributed to Prior.   Bod (2), Worcester; CSmH, NjP, TxU (3).   Morgan I320 attribs. to Prior, but cites Clay.
       Dedication is flattering to Cowper: "Our General has not signaliz'd himself more in the Field, than Your Lordship has done in the Courts of Justice."   Has sought to imitate Ovid, though has "been Censur'd by some of his friends for leaving the Study of the Laws for that of Poetry."   His Lordship deserves comparison to Sir Thomas More, Lord Verulam, and "what is a far greater Honour, my Lord Sommers."   Poem opens:

       If yet, Great SIR, your Heart can Comfort know,
       And the Returning Sighs less frequent flow.

The Elector is subjected to the painful reminder of Anna, Marlborough, *Ramillia*; but he disclaims all blame, and urges Louis XIV to remember the load of shame he bears.   What language can he find to heal the "raging Anguish" of Louis?   Before the battle he had imagined the British chiefs as prisoners, and Paris had celebrated prematurely.   The battle began well, had "only MARLBRO, not been there!" (1. 73). He arrived and turned the battle.   Though he fell, batallions rushed to his rescue, and "some friendly Hand" met death in his rescue.   After Ramillia, he went on to Ostend, Brussels, Ghent, Antwerp, taking all.

Grateful *Germania* unknown Titles frames,
And CHURCHILL writes among her Sov-raign Names.
168-9

Now he envies even Tallard, and urges Louis to cease
wars and slaughter. Schellenberg and Bleinheim have
shown Marlborough to be irresistible, and Ramilia has
exhibited his contempt for death. The Elector recalls
his own glorious youth, rescuing Austria and overthrowing the Turk, but now all his glories are blasted.
Lamenting his losses, he concludes by asking excuse
for his ravings but insists that

    No Suff'rings shall my Firm Alliance End,
    An Unsuccessful, but a Faithful Friend.

The portion *To the Duke of Marlborough* opens:

    Pardon, Great Duke, if *Britain*'s Stile delights;
    Or if th' Imperial Title more invites.

The poet deplores the failing of his muse, forced to
write at a distance, and in "mournful Lays," since
peace and liberty for Europe still elude and deny her
"weary Champion" the retreat and ease he has deserved.
The poem is mainly on Woodstock, as Blenheim Palace
and park were then called. He urges the woods to grow
fast and "Yet rising Tow'rs for your new Lord prepare"
(1. 27).

    The Pleasing Prospects and Romantick Site,
    The Spacious Compass, and the Stately Height;
    The painted Gardens, in their flow'ry Prime,
    Demand whole Volumes of Immortal Rhime.   32-5

There from his godlike race "Four beauteous *Rosamonds*"
will adorn the bower, while Marlborough, the Great
Eagle, with the wars over will build his spacious nest
in some proud tree and lie basking all day in the warm
Sun. If associating Marlborough's four celebrated and
beautiful daughters with the mistress of Henry II,
Rosamund Clifford, is not the height of tact, it at
least recognizes the well-known historical associations with Woodstock, already signalized by Harrison.

JUDOIGN.   A POEM ON THE Late VICTORY IN BRABANT.
London: Printed, and are to be Sold by *B. Bragge*,
at the *Black Raven* in *Pater-noster-Row*.   1707.   Price
One Penny.
      No sigs.; t.p., *bl.*, (2) 3-4, 4 pp., drop-t. on
2.   102 lines, couplets.   Clark-Luttr. copy '14 Dec.
1706.'   Foxon cites only Clark copy, which is used.
Morgan J263.   Opens:

> Rise Sacred QUEEN, *Apollo*'s Darling Muse,
> And Martial Numbers thro' my Soul diffuse.

After eight lines of invocation for the Muse's assistance, the poet goes immediately to his subject, that
is an engagement associated with Ramillies, here, as
often, named for one of the adjacent rivers, Judoign.
Eugene had suffered a setback in Spain from Vendosme,
and the French are confident.

> *Judoign* their left, *Mehaign* receives their Right,
> Assur'd of Conquest, and prepar'd for Fight.   26-7

Battle is described swiftly, roaring cannon, clouds of
smoke, and hills of gasping soldiers.   Marlborough,
superfluously identified in a marginal note, revives
his troops and overcomes the French.

> Ten Thousand Souldiers [*sic*] on the Plain they leave,
> A Loss they never, never can retrieve.   63-4

Also ten thousand captives are taken; it is all like a
flooding river.   Only night saves the French from further
destruction, and Anna is praised as ruling over haughty
Lewis.   While handsomely set up, this piece shows signs
of hasty printing in some misspellings, such as *timerous*
and *artempt*.   Judoign was a minor action involving the
surprise capture of some French troops in a defile following Ramillies.   Brabant is the area north of Flanders,
in Holland.

175 December 17.

Chase, John [No dates]

An ODE on the SUCCESS OF Her Majesty's Arms, Under His
GRACE the Duke of MARLBOROUGH. *By* J. Chase. [1 line
Horace] *LONDON*: Sold by *John Morphew*, near *Stationers-
Hall*. 1706.
    2°: A^2 B-C^2; t.p., *iii-iv*. To the Right Honourable
JOHN, Earl of *Leicester*, &c. 5-12, 16 pp., drop-t. on
p. 5. Folger-Luttr. '17 Decemb.' Morgan I 74. Only MH,
DFo, TxU, which is used.
    The Dedication apologizes for first effort "where
the Best have fall'n short"; but the poet offers this
piece in acknowledgment of many favors. It is signed
'John Chase.'
    The poem consists of 19 ode stanzas, each of 12
lines, 228 lines. Opens.

    I never slept on fam'd *Parnassus* head,
    No artful, or well-Natur'd Muse,
    Did e're her pleasing Rage infuse.

A strongly Whiggish poem, the ode opens with William III
and his efforts to free Europe. He was an Atlas whom
Anne now replaces. Lavish in praise of Marlborough,
Chase urges that there is no need to turn back to Rome
for heroes. Marlborough is "All that is Wise, or Generous, or Great" (1. 97). He combines the virtues of
Caesar and Brutus, and Blenheim surpasses the battle of
Fabius against the Carthaginians. He turns back French
greed and tyranny, as Belgium knows. But at the thought
of describing Ramillie [*sic*] or Hocsted the Muse is held
back. "*Marlbro*'s bold March no narrow Rules confine"
(1. 205). Continental rivers welcome his standards;
Nature confesses his power, and the poem concludes with
an attractive picture of a river pouring out its waters
onto a wide plain, an image possibly of encouragement to
increased powers for Marlborough.

176 December 23.

D'Urfey, Thomas (1653-1723)

A NEW ODE. Or, DIALOGUE Between *Mars*, the God of War, and *Plutus*, or *Mammon*, the God of Riches. Perform'd in an Entertainment made for his Grace the Duke of *Marlborough*, the Nobility, and General Officers, by the Right Honourable the Lord Mayor, and the Honourable the Court of Aldermen, at *Vintners-hall*, in the City. The Words by Mr. *D'urfey*, Set to Musick by Mr. *Weldon*, and Sung by *Elford* and Mr. *Leveridge, Decemb*. the 19th, 1706. *LONDON*. Printed by *Fr. Leach*, for the Author, and Sold by *B. Bragg*, at the *Raven* in *Pater-noster-row*, 1707.
     2°: no sigs., pp. 1-4. Colophon bot. p. 4. Adv. p. 4, "To-Morrow will be Publish'd, The Trophies, or *Augusta*'s Glory. A Triumphant Ode, written by Mr. *D'urfey*." TxU copy used. 92 lines, in ode movements, with instruments indicated. Morgan J*172ª. Opens:

> *Mars*. From Glorious Toyls of War,   *With Violins*.
>   With Dazling Honours, brought from far.

The chink of coins is all but audible as Marlborough is rewarded for the victory at Ramillies. The "Cordial Coin" is also sent over the Alps in support of Prince Eugene, who enjoys a generous share in the poem. Concluding duet summarizes objectives, bringing Gallia down, driving Philip from Madrid, and even banishing spleen from Scotland, for the problems at home were as pressing as those of the war abroad. The poem is dated by the adv. of *The Trophies*. See next entry.

177 December 24.

D'Urfey, Thomas (1653-1723)

The Trophies: or, Augusta's Glory, a Triumphant Ode, made in Honour of the City, etc. and upon the Trophies taken from the French at the Battle of Ramellies. (Adv. in *Daily Cour*., No. 1467.) Printed by Fr. Leach, for

the Author, and Sold by B. Bragg. 1707. Dec. 27. 'On
Tuesday was publish'd,' (i. e. Dec. 24).
    2°: *A*2 B-C2; t.p., *bl. iii-iv*, 1-15, *16*, 20 pp.
WMK. MF. Not in Morgan.

78   December 30.

Dennis, John (1657-1734)

The BATTLE OF RAMILLIA: or, the POWER of UNION, a POEM.
In Five BOOKS.   By Mr. *DENNIS. LONDON*, Printed for *Ben.*
Bragg at the *Raven* in *Pater-Noster-Row*, 1706. *Post-Man*,
No. 1116, 26-28.   'On Monday next will be publish'd.'
Daily Cour., No. 1469, Mon. Dec. 30 'This Day is pub-
lish'd.'   Reprtd. in The Select Works of Mr. *John Dennis.*
In Two Volumes. *London*: Printed by John Darby in *Bar-*
tholomew-Close. M.DCC.XVIII. I, 219-320.   2040 lines,
blank verse. BM, MH, CSmII, ICN. Wmk Horn on Shield.
Morgan I128.
      Dedication to Lord *Halifax.* Expresses obligations
and acknowledges favors received.
      The *Preface*, not published in *Sel. Works.*   In
Hooker, *Critical Works*, I, 394-5.   Denies this is a true
epic, but in the epic manner. Has used 'machines' because of the greatness of the subject. Anticipated
criticisms are answered by appeal to Boileau's "L'esprit
n'est point ému de ce qu'il ne croit pas," and his use
of fictions. Thinks of writing a Pindarick on Quintus
Flaminius between whom and Marlborough "a very just parallel may be drawn." The poem opens:

        Of *Belgian* Provinces, by Union's Pow'r,
        Deliver'd in *Ramillia*'s Plain, I sing.

With spring the Confederate troops assemble near Tongeren.
A vision of Satan appears, which is compared to Louis XIV,
as he addresses his followers. He reminds them they promised to overturn the Heavenly kingdom, where liberty and
law would rule, rather than men. Miracles are seen at
Blenheim when Marlborough turned the battle by "his

Godlike Presence" (11. 180-90 *passim*). Lewis is a man
after Satan's heart, but he must be supported against a
Woman! Following this long speech, Discord appears,
daughter of Lucifer and a dire fiend so terrible that
only he dares look upon her, and he is stupefied, like
Laocoön in the statue. Her long exhortation completes
Book I, as she urges the fiends to action against the
religious English Queen, and her servants, Marlborough
and Godolphin. In Book II Discord meets the old hag,
Night, and they fly to Lewis's couch, where with the
Maintenon, he shirks his duty. She urges him to action.
Discord reminds him of Blenheim, and the threatened loss
of Spain, while England and Scotland are preparing to
unite their strength and Godolphin is allaying faction
at home. She persuades him to send troops to the Rhine.

Book III opens at dawn. Discord, in person of
Bavaria, comes to Villeroy and calls attention to the
congregating Confederate forces. He asks what gives
them their spirit, and Villeroy, expressing good Whig
doctrine, replies:

> From Liberty, the Mareschal strait replies,
> 'Tis from the Bravery of the *English* Troops,
> Who with immortal Liberty inspir'd,
> And with the Love of Glory all inflam'd,
> Infect the Nations with their noble Fire.   III, 68-72

Discord recognizes that God rules the world, and that
Marlborough must be overthrown tomorrow. He gives a
discouraging picture of Marlborough at Blenheim. Villeroy exclaims at Discord's generous description of the
hero's godlike qualities when in England he has so many
detractors.

Book IV is devoted to Heavenly scenes and Angelic
actions. Christ asks for a volunteer, and an Angel
descends to Marlborough's tent, and informs him of the
morrow's battle. The pictures of Angelic hosts are
carefully labored, but hardly touch the intended sublime; hence the entire poem fails of its purpose. Marlborough's self-control is evidenced, even as the Angel
reminds him of Blenheim and the terror the French anticipate. He is assured of a special glory in Heaven.

Book V presents the Battle of Ramillies, though with
not more than the usual features, especially Marlborough's
horse being shot from under him, the momentary exultation
among the enemy, and the heroic death of Bringfield.
Battle is primarily allegorical and Christian detail and
imagery more a matter of Angels than of gunfire. Death
appears in all his alleged terror, but the hero rejects
him disdainfully. He "wants the Pow'r to strike," even
though his parent Discord urges him on. Throughout the
poem memories of Blenheim are much more prominent than
details of Ramillies. It ends suddenly after the fall of
Bringfield, with the moral tag:

Thus Discord and the *Gaul* were forc'd to yield
To *Marlb'rough* and to Union's Sacred Pow'r.   V, 306-7

The importance of the poem is largely incidental
and negative. It is a huge poem in the new Miltonic vein
of imitative blank verse, and it is devoted directly to
Marlborough and one of his great victories. It is a
companion piece to Dennis's Blenheim poem, *Britannia Triumphans*, and both have had expert notice from E. N.
Hooker, though without recognition of their position in
the vast mass of Marlborough tributes. As verse they distinguish themselves chiefly by their deficiencies, exhib-
iting the features of epic without its sublimity and
power.

79   December 30.

[Cunditt, Mr., of Eton and Trinity College, Cambridge]

A POEM Upon the Late Glorious Successes, &c. Humbly In-
scrib'd to His GRACE the DUKE of *MARLBOROUGH* [2 lines
Juvenal] *LONDON*: Printed for *Jacob Tonson* within
Grays-Inn Gate next *Grays-Inn* Lane. 1707.
    2°: A-C²; t.p., *bl.*, 1-10, 12 pp. Drop-t. on p. 1.
No wmk. CSmH-Luttr. '4 *d*. 30 Dec. 1706,' InU, OCU, CtY.
Two Horn copies and CSmH used. 373 lines, couplets. Not
in Morgan. Opens:

Oh! when together will one Age afford
A hero to perform, and Poet to Record.

Troy was warbled by "ev'ry Tongue," Alexander had only
poor Chaerilus, and only with Augustus and Virgil were
warrior and poet matched. Now we have Marlborough, and
"the Heliconian springs are dry" (1. 32). Europe hoped
that Bleinheim would end the tyrant's menace, but he has
revived for new campaigns. A striking picture of the
peasant torn from his cottage, fields lying fallow,
choked by thistles, as the peasantry again go to war,
is painted in. Addison strung his viol for Bleinheim
(1. 87), but now there are new conquests. "Bois'trous
Hotspurs" abound, and Marlborough is again sedate in
battle. Happily he escapes death. No description of
battle is given. Instead "wretched *Bourbon*" and *Rich-
lieu* are noticed with contempt. The British Ministry,
Godolphin, Cowper, Sommers, Hallifax, Manchester, St.
John, and Ormond of Vigo are noticed. Finally Eugene,
"the Terror of the *Turkish* Plain" (1. 332) leads to a
conclusion on the blessings of Anne's reign and the
peace which all shall conspire to bless,

And Faction only in this Strife be seen,
Who most shall Prise to great a Chief, so
good a QUEEN.   372-3

180   Tate, Nahum (1659-1726)

Song. For the Performance of Musick at *York-Buildings*,
December the 31st, 1706. By *Nahum Tate, Esq.* Her Majesty's Poet Lauriat [*sic*]. Printed in *The Muses Mercury*,
ed. John Oldmixon, Vol. I, No. 1, For the Month of January, p. 7. CtY copy used.

O Whither will thy Triumphs Spread,
Britannia, injur'd Nation's Friend?

Chor.
With MARLBRO's each Campaign Renew'd,
And still the Glorious Game pursu'd.

Blenheim (Once the Blazing Dame
And Brightest in the List of Fame)
Sees her Lawrels spring Again
In Ramillias honour'd Main.

81   December 31.

A LETTER From the B. of S--- to the A. B. of *Paris*.
Dated *London*, Dec. 31. 1706. No pub., Foxon queries
Edinburgh. n.d.
    1/2°:   2 sides.   51 lines, couplets.

> Since News at *Paris* grows so wondrous scarce,
> Pray give me leave to send you some Verse.

A satire expressing satisfaction in English triumphs and
Anne's reign, and that "Marlborough makes the next Campaign." Eugene is assisted with coin. Louis XIV declines in power.

> So shall he sink, the *British* Prophets tell,
> As they do of the Union now in hand
> That *Britain* shall the World Command,
> And wretched *France*, shall be glad to pray
> That God would send another ANNE to sway.

Morgan J285 cites 1707 ed., and suggests Bishop of Salis-
bury.

2   [Cavendish, William, Duke of Devonshire (1699-1755)]
Matric. New Coll., Oxon., 30 May, 1715.

AN ALLUSION to the Bishop of *Cambray*'s Supplement of
HOMER. Printed in the YEAR MDCCVI.
    2°:   no sigs.; *1* 2-4, 4 pp.   BM, CtY, TxU. Texas
copy used.   147 lines, couplets. Not in Morgan. Opens:

> *Cambray*, whilst of Seraphic Love you set
> The noblest Image in the clearest Light.

Approves Cambray's piety in spite of Rome. He is even
more sublime in sublunary subjects, as in *Telemachus*.
Deplores tyranny by one man, even when celebrated in
equestrian statues.

> Oh Liberty, wish'd for too late, when lost,
> Like Health, by those that want thee, valu'd most.
>
> 61-2

England's laws assure freedom while other kingdoms boast
of their servility.

> While Streams of Blood the Continent o'erflow,
> Red'ning the *Maese*, the *Danube*, and the *Po*.
> Thy *Thames*, auspicious Isle, her Thunder sends
> To crush thy Foes, and to relieve thy Friends.
>
> 78-81

He has a vision of a building by the Thames where a
monster rules and horrible crimes are committed, and
people are tortured to "improve their Faith." He awakes
and hails Anna's reign, to free Europe and save the sinking Empire. At her name the phantom disappears. Nothing
directly on Marlborough, but celebrates the War of the
Spanish Succession, and supports the Protestant, anti-
Catholic spirit that animated the war. Reprtd. as *The
Charms of Liberty*, 1709. Cambray was Francois de Salig-
nac de la Mothe Fénelon.

183 Curieuses Lamentiren/ Eines Frantzösischen Musquetiers/
Uber die durch die Heldenmüthige Thaten des Weltberühm-
ten Duc de Marlborough Wider die Frantzosen in Braband
glücklich erhaltene VICTORIE. No pub., n. d., but is
1706.
  4°: no sigs., t.p., *ii-iii*, *bl. iv*. 48 long lines
of German verse. Text and title all in Gothic. Ornamental band top p. text. BM copy used. Morgan I257.
Opens:

> O Buger Allemang/ Holland=und Engels=Mann
> Der uns der gross Affront wieder hat gethan/

The Frenchman complains at the German conquests,
and denounces the English as barbaric and cruel.

Du bist jetz gar Barbar/ Cruel/ horribel. böss
Du gibst uns arm Frantsoss/allseit nur Schläg und
Stoss   29-30

From Schellenberg to Brabant the English have attacked;
also in Barcelona and Madrid, the French have suffered.
Without food or forage, how can they carry on a war?

84 Eine wahrhafte *Neue Zeitung*/ Von der hissigen und bluti-
gen *Schlachte*/ unweit Beyern vogegangen zwischen der
Französich=Spanischen/ under den Herzogen von Bäyeren
und Villeroi gestandnen Armeen einerseiths/ Und Der
Englisch=und Holländisch veründeten/ under dem Herzog
von Malborug und dem Grafen von Obertuch gestandner
Armee anderseits/ den 23tgsten Tag Mey/1706. Im Tohn:
Wie das Vogelgesang. Samt einem schönen *Discurs=Lied*/
zwüschen dem Herzog vom Marlborug und dem Herzog Maxi-
milan [*sic*] Emanuel auss Bäyeren. Getrukt zu Augspurg.
4°: no sigs., no nmb.; t.p., *ii-iv*, 4 pp. No pub.
Verse in 20 8-line stanzas, 160 lines; the *Discurs=Lied*
32 lines, dialogue. Total 192 lines. Not in Morgan.
Opens:

Komt her/ und tuht anhören/
Ihr lieben Christen=Leuht.

On the 23d of May "Malbrug" encountered the French in
Brabant, with severe firing from 1 to 4 o'clock. Many
French regiments were ruined, 70 standards and banners
were taken, and 60,000 men were overcome.
The *Discurs=Lied* opens:

König Ludwig euch sey klagt/
Wie bin ich so übel plagt.

The Bavarian ruler thus bemoans his fate in suffering a
third attack from Marlborough. Each speaks in turn, with
Marlborough assuring the Bavarian that he fully deserves
the defeats. The whole is printed in Gothic type.

185 The GLORY of the Confederate Arms Illustrated in a Bla-
zonry Description, and 35 Standards, taken from the
French and Bavarians in the Famous Battle of Blenheim,
by the forces commanded by his Grace the Duke of Marlborough; with the Inscription to be put on a marble
pillar to be erected at Hochsted. Printed on a sheet
of imperial paper. London, Sold by Christopher Brown at
the Globe at the West End of St. Paul's, 1706.
    Morgan I 173 only ref. See No. 259 for same title.

186 GRATULATIO IN ILLUSTRISSIMI Principis ac Ducis MALBURI-
ENSIS, Post AEstatem Gloriosissime Exactam, In Urbem
Reditum, *Anno* 1706. *OXONII Habita.* *LONDINI*: Venditur
apud Johannem Morphew prope Bibliopolarum.
    4°: A^4 B-D^4; t.p., *ii*, Gratulatio p. *iii*, *iv*, 1-23,
24, 28 pp. Drop-t. p. 1. Latin prose. BM copy used.
Morgan I 258.
    The account summarizes the political background and
the alignment of powers involved in the war. Allusions
to Schellenberg, Blenheim, and Ramillies appear, but,
aside from an allusion to the Danube drowning, the piece
is more in the manner of one of Dr. Francis Hare's pamphlets championing Marlborough and the war than the
strict congratulatory statement that the title implies.

187 Maidwell, Lewis   (No dates)

MAJESTAS imperii Britannici.   The Glories of GREAT
BRITAIN Celebrated in   LATIN POEMS by Mr. *MAIDWELL*.
Paraphras'd in ENGLISH By Mr. *TATE* Poet-Laureat to Her
MAJESTY.   Part I.   *London*, Printed in the Year 1706.
    4°:   A-C^4, D^2; *i-vi*, 1-22, 28 pp.   BM copy used,
Bod., CtY.   Three poems.   Morgan I 381.
    The Dedication, sgnd. 'N. Tate' is "To the Right
Honourable CHARLES Earl of Carlile."   States that for
many years Carlile's father was a patron of Tate's, of
Maidwell's (?).   Wmk. fleur-de-lys on shield.   Pp. 1-4
VOTA BRITANNIA . . . Serenissima Regina, transl. by

Tate as *Britannia's Prayer for the Queen*, &c. 88 lines, ode. Opens:

> How justly now might I aspire
> To mighty Pindar's Force and Fire.

Printed separately as follows:

88   Tate, Nahum (1652-1715)

Britannia's Prayer for the QUEEN. By Mr. Tate, *Poet Laureate to Her Majesty*. London: Printed for *John Chantry* at the Sign of *Lincolns-Inn Back Gate*, 1706. Price Two Pence.
    2°: 2 sides. Rprtd. *Poems on Affairs of State*, 1707, IV, 129-31. See No. 131.
    The third poem, pp. 17-18, is of Marlborough interest. Its title is Vaticinium Pacis. Quae cito Confirmabitur sub Auspiciis ILLUSTRISSIMI *DUCIS MARLBURGENSIS*, &c. Opens:

> Quatuor EUROPAE Gratissima Flumina Coel,
>   Exorant Miseris Rebus adesses JOVEM.

Tate translates as: A PROPHECY OF PEACE, To be speedily Ratified by the Auspicious Conduct of the most Illustrious D. of Marlborough. Opens:

> Four Noble Rivers, *EUROPE*'s Pride,
>   To Her and to the Stars Ally'd,
> Their Favourits [*sic*] Once but now Distress'd,
>   In joint Complaints to *JOVE* apply'd.

The rivers appeal for the peace specified in the title. Their banks have lost their beauty. The poem is in 68 lines, ode style. The second poem, to the Duke of Newcastle, is of no Marlborough significance.

189 [Krook, Enoch and Daniel Kroon (no dates)]

HET VERLOSTE BRABAND EN VLANDEREN, DOOR DEN VELDSLAG BY
RAMMELLIES; OORLOGSSPEL, 1706. Remainder of description
identical with the poem on Hochstet, No. 78 above. Lib.
Cong. copy used. Same form and style with figures and
rivers associated with Ramillies. See No. 295. 40 pp.
Not in Morgan.

190 Graauwhart, H. (no dates)

Ter Eewiger Gedagtenis Der HEERLUKE OVERWINNIGER Door de
HONDGENNOTEN op de Wapenen van VRANKRYK, Onder den Seegen
des Almagtigen behaald: In het Jaar 1706. No. pub. Atlas fol., 15" by 20". Large copper plate engraving at
top, 9" by 13 1/2", of battle of Ramellies, between two
columns. Allegorical figures of Battle and Victory at
sides. Medallions of Marlborough, Eugene, and Marshal
Ouverkerk top center.
    The text is in three columns, lower half. Prose
account of great battles in 1 and 3; verse in center
column.
    Bodleian, Firth B 33. An example of the elaborate
pictorial contributions to panegyric. 44 lines of verse.
Not in Morgan.

191 A Hymn to St. *Tack*; Sung at the *Election* of the New Vice-
Chancellor of Oxford. Printed for *John Morphew* near
Stationers-Hall. Price 2 *d*.
    1/2°: 41 lines in 3 stanzas, printed on both sides.
Morgan I 205. Opens:

        What tho' the GREAT, the HIGH ALLIES
        Had sunk for want of due Supplies?
        EUGENE and SAVOY had been lost
        With all the Towns on the *Ligurian* Coast.

A satirical ballad, attacking the Whigs and their alleged

opposition to the established Church.

Tho' RAMELLIES had never been,
We had a nobler Conquest seen.

The ballad ends with:

And now we may Hope for Glorious Days Agen,
And once more Ridicule both CHURCH and QUEEN.

92   Durston, John (no dates)

ILLUSTRISSIMO DOMINO, ET HEROI VERE MAGNANIMO, JOHANNI,
Duci *MARLBORIENSI*. DE *Gallis* & *Bavaris ab ipso, pugna
ad Blenheim inita, strenue debellatis*, EPINICIUM. Hoc
summa cum Observantia & humiliter offert JOHANNES DUR-
STONUS, *Ecclesiae* Misserdonsis *in Comitatu Rector*.
     2°:   no sep. t.p., 1-4, 4 pp. 48 lines, Latin
tribute. Lehigh copy used. Not in Morgan. Opens:

Atonitus tandem respirat *Phoebus*, & inquit,
O docti vates, *Aonidumque* Chori.

A routine tribute, emphasizing the Danube drowning
of Tallard's forces. The people rejoice in one voice,
praising Anne and the English Alcides, i.e. Heracles
(Marlborough).

93   MARLBOROUGH. A POEM; Occasion'd by the EXPLOITS OF THAT
Famous General. Ne dubita nam vera vides. Virg. *DUB-
LIN*: Printed by *S. Powell* over-against the *Crown Tavern*
in *Fishamble-Street*, for *Thomas Shepheard* Bookseller in
Dames-street, near the *Horse-guard*. 1706.
     2°: A^2 B-G^2; *i* hft., *bl*., t.p., *bl*., 1-23, *bl*., 28
pp. Not in Morgan. Cambridge U. copy used; only one
known. 496 lines, couplets. Opens:

The taking of one poor Town in Ten Years Time,
As handl'd, by a Son of the Sublime.

The poem is largely turgid in style, and confused as

between allegorical and historical elements. The theme
of Marlborough, his personal heroism and great victories,
emerges occasionally, but not brilliantly. The allegory
rests largely on allusions to classical gods and heroes.
Allusions to Bleinheim, as it is spelled, and Ramilly are
positive but without any original ideas or sense of im-
mediacy. An allusion to a poet who would surpass "dusty
Arthars" [*sic*] possibly alludes to Blackmore's ponderous
epics. An allusion to the Danube drowning, and several
references to Prince Eugene "Proud after *Marlborough* to
enroll his Name" (1. 241) do not retrieve a poem that
seems to have little to dignify it except that it was
published in Dublin, presumably by an Irish bard. Real-
izing his limited powers, he cries out for a "great Bard"
with a fire to equal Marlborough's, but this is only one
of the many conventions of a poem that is nothing but
conventional.

194   *A New* ODE, Being a *Congratulatory Poem* on the Glorious
Successes of Her Majesty's Arms, under the Command of the
Auspicious General his Grace the Duke of *Marlborough*.
Set to Musick by Mr. Jer. Clark. To be Perform'd by the
Best Masters on Friday the 20th of this Instant at Seven
a Clock in *York-Buildings*.

        1/2°: 2 sides, 1 column. 29 lines, couplets, with
chorus, in italics. Foxon xerox. Not in Morgan. Opens:

> Hail Happy Queen! Born to Heal and to Unite
> Our private Hearts now melt into Delight.

A purely lyric piece, hailing the Danube, Mosell, Maes,
and Rhine victories, and calling for 'Io's' for Queen
Anne, who holds the scales of justice for Europe.

195   Jeffreys, George (1678-1755)

On Blenheim House and *An Ode on the Battle of Ramillies*,
1706. See under date 1754. See No. 577.

96   [Defoe, Daniel attrib.]

Now is the TIME: A POEM.   By the Author of the True Born
Englishman.   *LONDON*, Printed in the Year, 1706.   No pub.
      1/2°:   2 columns.   25 4-line stanzas, 100 lines,
ballad.   Not in Moore.   Morgan I 112.   Clark copy used.
Opens:

> If *M----h* could curb the King of *France*,
> And lead the Tyrant of *Versailles* a Dance,
> Then *Now*'s *the Time*, since his late Victory,
> To humble *Lewis* for his Villany.

Defoe's authorship is made doubtful by Stanza 12:

> If we would have the *Observator* and
> *De Foe*, two factious R----gs rid of the Land,
> Then *Now*'s *the Time*, when Acts in Print are seen
> For Idle Vagabonds to serve the Queen.

Flanders, Tallard, and coarse allusions to Madame Maintenon
are among the themes that bring on the title refrain.

7   Steele, Sir Richard (1679-1729)

PROLOGUE to the University of OXFORD.   Written by Mr.
Steel, and Spoken by Mr. *Wilks*, *London*, Printed for
Bernard Lintott at the *Cross-Keys* near to *Nanda*'s Coffee-
House near *Temple-Bar*.   1706.   (Price 2 *d*.)   Foxon-MC,
Crawford only ref.
      1/2°:   22 lines, couplets.   Not in Morgan.   Reprtd.
in *Muses Mercury, or Monthly Miscellany*, 1707, p. 208.

> As wandering Streams by secret return
> To that capacious Ocean . . .

> We less adore their more exalted Vein,
> And must expect a *Blenheim* or *Campaign*.

See Rae Blanchard, *Occasional Verse of Steele*, p. 45.
Reprints the broadside of the Chatham Library, Manchester.

Notes pp. 92-3 show that the passage of five lines on the
poems of Philips and Addison were excised in the 1707
edition. *WL*, June-July, and adv. *Daily Cour.*, 4 July.

198 Ward, Ned (1667-1731)

A Poem on the Happy Success of His Grace the *Duke* of
Marlborough in Forcing the *French* Lines. In *Collected
Works*, 1706, Third ed., 1718, pp. 207-11, 8vo. Poem is
81 lines, couplets.

> Long did *Nassau* his *Belgick* Valour try,
> By *English* Arms to curb *French* Tyranny.

Ironic commentary on William III's failure to do more
than chase the French, bomb Brussels, and burn St.
Malloes. Marlborough in two campaigns, at moderate cost,
has retrieved "that Honour fourteen Years had lost" (l.
18). Anna's virtues, joined with his courage, have
settled domestic jars, and transcended the exploits of
Elizabeth. Capel and Essex won fame but couldn't equal
Marlborough. Terror of enemies, champion of the Empire,
friend to Hungarian Protestants, scourge to Bavaria, and
sting to France, he has won the worship of *Hogen Mogen*,
i.e. the States General, and is beloved and feared abroad.

> Thy Glorious Actions fill the World with News,
> And are the only Themes of ev'ry Muse.
> With Mirth and Joy thou dost whole Nations fill,
> The World seems stagnated when you stand still.
> *Blenheim* and *Hochstet* witness your Success,
> And this more dang'rous Vict'ry does no less. 66-70

Marlborough achievements surpass those of Caesar, Fabricius, and Alexander. "But *Marlborough* conquers all in
conqu'ring one" (l. 81). Trevelyan quotes 10 lines in
Blenheim, p. 419.

99 Warton, Thomas, Sr. (1688?-1745)

To Mr. ADDISON, Occasioned by his Return from *Hanover*
with the Lord *Halifax.* Written 1706. Pr. in *Poems on
Several Occasions,* 1748, pp. 167-72. The poem is included here because of its emphasis on the Blenheim
theme. 77 lines, couplets. Not separately printed.

> O for a Muse of Fire and lofty Style,
> To hail Thee welcome to thy native Soil!

Halifax did not sail till at least later than August 10,
but there are no allusions to Ramillies by name. Instead
we have:

> But happier *Marlbrô,* when fierce Winters come,
> And *Anna* calls her conquering Hero home;
> Finds here your Muse his matchless Acts rehearse,
> While *Danube* choakt with Dead o'erflows the mighty
> Verse;
> He more than sees what you so warmly write,
> And gladly thinks himself again in Fight;
> Again his Sword, imperial Gift, unsheaths,
> And dauntless all around distributes Deaths,
> With secret Pleasure vanquishes again,
> A second *Blenheim* boasts, a more compleat Campaign.

Since Ramillies was often called a "second Blenheim,"
Warton is discreetly avoiding specific reference to the
battle which had not brought forth a second *Campaign.*
Warton pictures himself wandering along the Cherwell,
thinking of the "Monarch of Poets," and hoping that he
will not again leave his native land.

0 To REGINA be the Mutual Cry. A New SONG. Set by Mr. Pur-
cell. London, Printed and Sold by *J. Morphew,* near Stationers-Hall, 1706. (Price 1*d.*)
    1/2°: 1 side, 12 lines, rambling rhyme. Not in
Morgan. Opens:

> To our Arms by Land and Sea's
> O'er the *Danube* and the *Mease,*

Healths are to be drunk to Galloway, to Rook, and "to
the more successful Duke," that is Marlborough. Next
year if we gain another victory we'll drink it in
'champaign.'

201 [Browne, Dr. Joseph (no dates)]

VOLPONE, OR THE FOX: By Way of FABLE Very Applicable to
the Present Times. London, Benj. Bragg. 1706. No Luttr.
copy known.
      4°:   t.p., 1-19, *20 bl.*, 20 pp. Morgan I 60.
MH, CtY, ICU, Clark. Rprtd. in *State and Miscellany
Poems*, 1715, II, 41-57 without subtitle. 329 lines.
TxU copy used.   Opens:

        In Times of Yore, when Brutes were Speakers
        And Men were only reckon'd *Sneakers*.

The Fox is Godolphin and Marlborough a "neigb'ring Lyon,"
who with his Dame (Sarah) combine to control the sovereign and the country. The sly Dame and the Fox connive
while the Lyon is in the field. All but the first 16
lines are a dialogue between the Fox and the Lyoness.
She has gained great wealth, as has her husband, and
also shows subtle knowledge for sly diplomacy. Although
the Geese, i.e. the people, are shy of her, she manages
them as well as the political parties. The only concrete allusions are to the Tack, and possibly one by the
Fox to a Swan that has sung for him, and who "told me he
expected pay" (1. 180). He plans to mock the Wolves, the
Tories, by 'sparking' "Among the Racers at New-Market"
(1. 144). At the end they are planning to win favor with
both the Wolves and the Geese, and also to be faithful to
the Hind, that is the Church.

1707

This was an interim year for Marlborough's fortunes,
and those of the war. Ramillies had awakened great expectation for the following year. Marlborough hoped to
answer criticisms that he had been pushing the land war
unduly by a combined land and naval action against Toulon.
However, his plans were thwarted by the failure of the
Emperor to cooperate, and the prodigious victory of his
own nephew, the Duke of Berwick. The latter's stunning
victory over the Earl of Galway at Almanza* led to the
supreme irony that Marlborough's nephew commanded the
opposing army. Even the forces of Nature seemed unfavorable, as Admiral Shovel lost his life and a considerable naval force in the mists among the rocks of Scilly.
In passing one can recall Addison's celebrated *Spectator*
26, of March 30, 1711. After noting poets without monuments and monuments empty of poets,

> Which had been erected to the Memory of Persons
> whose Bodies were perhaps buried in the Plains
> of *Blenheim*, or in the Bosom of the Ocean,

he muses over Admiral Shovel's pompous and absurd monument in Westminster Abbey. Here a "plain gallant Man"
is represented in the figure of a periwigged beau, an
example of tastelessness which could serve as a comment
on absurd poetic panegyric as well as for funerary
sculpture.

The one genuine triumph for the year was the final
ratification of the Act of Union with Scotland, on May
1st. After long months of delicate, often savage, nego-
tiation and maneuver, it was accomplished, though to the
complete satisfaction only of the Hanoverians. Trevelyar
justly acclaims this event and the Battle of Blenheim as
the two supreme moments in Queen Anne's reign.

---

*Trevelyan quotes a ballad on Almanza, *Ramillies
and the Union with Scotland*, p. 300.

202 January 1.

[Walsh, William (1663-1708)]

·ODE for the THANKSGIVING DAY. *LONDON*: Printed for *Jacob Tonson* within *Grays-Inn* Gate next *Grays-Inn* Lane. 1706.
     2°: *A*1 B-D2, E1; t.p., *bl*., 1-14, 16 pp., drop-t. on p. 1. Wmk. "WC," pp. 13-14. *D. Cour.*, No. 1471, Jan. 1, 1707, 'This Day is publish'd'; *L. Gaz.* Jan. 2. ICU has MS attrib. to Walsh. BM, MH, CtY, DFo, TxU, ICU, Clark, CSmH, NjP. Horn copy used. 40 6-line stanzas, 240 lines, ode style. Morgan I 404. Opens:

> Begin, my Muse, and strike the Lyre!
> Begin! and lofty Lays inspire,
>   That fading Fame prolong!

Poets have sung Ramillia, but here will be a picture of "the whole Campaign" (1. 12). With this possible allusion to Addison's Blenheim tribute, we are reminded that again, as at Blenheim, French and Bavarian troops are joined for revenge. They move slowly, but the Britons advance with impetuous fury, resolved to make the enemy know what it is to be free men. Like the flooding Po is the tyrant's rage, and Eugene and Savoy sweep down from the Alps to free Turin. It is like Andromeda, freed from the monster by Perseus; and Eugene exults over Orleans, Marsin, and Feuillade. Next Barcelona is liberated and young Anjou feels the impact. A footnote calls attention to an eclipse of Louis' sun. Next Galway marches to Madrid, against general, the Duke of Berwick; but Rivers comes and disperses the enemy. The achievements of Eugene in Italy, and of the Earl of Galway in Spain, obscure Ramillies. Walsh may not entirely prove the value of stanzaic, ode patterns for narrative; but he concludes with a spirited celebration of "ANNA's Glory" that inspires both the Muse and "ev'ry Chief."

> She Chains th'Oppressor, and She Frees th'Opprest.
>   240

203   January 2.

[Wycherley, William (1640-1715)]

On his GRACE THE DUKE OF MARLBOROUGH. *LONDON*: Printed
for *John Morphew* near *Stationers Hall*. 1707. (Colophon bot. p. 4.)
      2°: no sigs.; pp. 1-4. Drop-t. on p. 1. 54 lines,
couplets, in First Ed.; but reduced to 43 lines in *Posthumous Works*, I, ed. By L. Theobald with Memoir by Major
R. Pack; same in Montague Summers ed. of *Complete Works*,
IV, 231-2. Haslewood has '2 Jan. 1706/7.'
      P & C-Luttr. copy '1 *d.*, 2 Januar. 1706/7.' BM,
Clark, CSmH, CtY. Used all copies. Clark has "By Mr.
Wycherley" under title. Morgan J499. Opens:

      Swift as his Fame, o'er all the World he flies,
      Follow'd by Friends, as shun'd by Enemies.

A conventional poem. Britain's Chief vanquishes cities,
is merciful as he is brave, risks his life, "His Foes and
Friends to save." Marlborough shows Roman virtues of calm
courage and self-restraint, unlike the "fierce hot Ministers of State." "What wonder *Marlbro'* by these Virtues
rose" (l. 47). Such virtues made Aeneas, "first a Hero,
then a God."

      Both were alike by Goddesses Inspir'd,
      By *Venus* he, as you by *ANNA* fir'd;
      Yet with this diff'rence each in Fame shall live,
      He Fought to Gain an Empire, ---You to Give.   51-4

      The poem is included, with additions and some changes,
in the *Posthumous Works*, 2 vols., 1728-9. Repub. Montague
Summers, *Works*, IV, 231-2. 6 lines added to opening, viz.:

      Heroes have still, when from the Wars they come,
      Bin [*sic*] pleas'd to let the *Lyre* supply the *Drum*.
      I but a feeble Harmony can raise,
      My Art and Hand too weak to touch your praise!
      Yet I've a common Right, as *England*'s Son,
      To thank you for the wond'rous things you've done.

Such turgidity and sing-song rhythm can be of interest only
in that Pope edited the second volume, and it was with such

badly recalled and monotonous stuff that he was compelled to struggle as adviser to the aged poet.

204   January 6.

Rowe, Nicholas (1674-1718)

A POEM upon the Late *Glorious Successes* of Her *MAJESTY*'s
Arms, *&c.* Humbly Inscrib'd to the Right Honourable the
Earl of *GODOLPHIN*, Lord High-Treasurer of *ENGLAND*. By
N. ROWE, Esq; *Extremum redisse pudet*. *LONDON*: Printed
for *Jacob Tonson*, within *Grays-Inn* Gate next *Grays-Inn*
Lane. 1707.
     2°: A^2 B-F^2; hft., *bl.*, t.p., *bl.*, 1-20, 24 pp.
Drop-t. on p. 1. Wmk. "WC." *L. Gaz.*, No. 4294, Thurs.
Jan. 2-Mon. Jan. 6, 1707. 'This Day is publish'd'; *D.
Cour.*, Jan. 6 crossed out for 7, 'Yesterday was pub-
lish'd.' *WL*, Dec. 1706. BM, Bod, CtY, CSmH, Clark,
ICN-Luttr. 'Januar. 1706-7.' 489 lines, couplets. Horn
copy used. Morgan J405. Opens:

> While Kings and Nations on thy Counsels wait,
> And *ANNA* trusts to thee the *British* State.

His humble muse invoked, while the crowds hail the hero.
Also Heaven's inspiration is sought, since it is Anne's
source of virtues. By Heaven she is taught to trust
Godolphin at home and to "send Victorious CHURCHILL
forth to War" (1. 31). The first half of the poem is
devoted to Spain, urging action on a once noble, imperious state that fought the Moors. Charles of Austria
against Philip of Bourbon, justice against tyranny, reminds of the War of the Spanish Succession. Most tributes place the emphasis on Marlborough. Philip's shame,
the futility of ambition, and the wastefulness of battles,
lead Rowe to think of the happy youth of the poet (11.
150-63 *passim*).
     Ramillies and Marlborough are the subject, 11. 187-
386, while the remainder of the poem turns to Eugene in
Italy and the freeing of Turin. Rowe comes as near as
anyone to the style of his fellow Whig, Addison; his poem

moves easily, and in the description of Ramillies attains
to some spirited battle poetry, to be sure with the fash-
ionable neo-classical features prominent.

Thick Dust and Smoak in wavy Clouds arise,
Stain the bright Day and taint the purer Skies:
While flashing Flames like Light'ning dart between,
And fill the Horror of the fatal Scene.   217-20

Bellona thunders in her car, and the sound of a raging
flood is heard by distant shepherds. In the midst is
Marlborough, escorted by Liberty with her silver shield,
and Victory, like Jove's eagle, flies overhead. Such was
Ammon at Arbela, as painted by Le Brun, as a marginal
note specifies. The effect is distinctly that of the
allegorical depictions in the engravings of Marlborough
and some of the decorations already being planned for
Blenheim Palace. The poet anticipates vast rewards from
Europe and a "proud Column" to Marlborough and Victory
in every city and land (ll. 279-8). Bards will bring
their verse, and Rowe, plainly preferring peace, looks
forward to a happy Britain. Marlborough's return, delayed by unfavorable winds, finds happy response, especially from his second daughter, the Countess of Sunderland, with her sparkling eyes and blooming cheeks.
Her husband's political position in the government seems
to attract the poets more than that of Henrietta and the
others of the four beauties. A peroration to Anne, who
has succeeded William, brings in the usual images, of
liberty, security, repression of tyranny, the public
good, etc.
        One triumph yet remains, and Eugene in Italy,
fighting in a river country, the plains of Lombardy,
occupies lines 387-450. Presumably Rowe did not intend any reflection on Marlborough; but his tribute
nicely anticipated Eugene's visit to England three years
later when Marlborough's status was increasingly precari-
ous.

05   January 11.

[Fenton, Elijah (1683-1730)]

An ODE to the SUN for the NEW-YEAR.   [6 lines Horace]

237

LONDON: Printed for *Jacob Tonson*, within *Grays-Inn* Gate
next *Grays-Inn* Lane. 1707.
2°: hft., A^2, bl^2, B-D^2, E^1; hft., bl., t.p., bl.,
1-13, *14*, a p. of Advertisements of Tonson pubs.: 5
Marlborough poems: Prior, Congreve, Rowe, [Cunditt], Mr.
Paris; titles as above. Wmk. 'WC'; none on D sheet.
Horn copy used. DFo, CtY (2), MH, IU, TxU (2), Clark-
Luttr. 24 10-line stanzas, numbered in three's, 240
lines. Rptd. in *Poems on Several Occasions*, 1717, pp.
1-17. Morgan J189. Opens:

> Begin, Celestial Source of Light,
> To Gild the New-revolving Sphear.

The Sun is invoked to bring a splendid new year, and
Anne is titled Gloriana. Marlborough is brought in
throughout, first l. 54: "The *Heber* had a *Mars*, a
CHURCHILL *Thames*," his just lawrels, l. 70, Blenheim
and Ramillia (l. 100). Clio, muse of history, will offer
such brilliant records that posterity will doubt them.
Lines 151-240 are entirely on Churchill and his achievements in bringing quiet to the Belgian states, retrieving
the Austrian crowns, and defeating Bavaria and France.
Phoebus, that is the Sun, saw him lead his Britons forth.

> The wand'ring Ghosts of Twenty Thousand slain
> Fleet sullen to the Shades, from *Blenheim's*
>   mournful Plain. 179-80

Britannia must wipe her dusty brow and put on Bourbon
lawrels. Having risen to the ecstasy of the ode, the
poem in its final stanza hails Blenheim Palace, at Woodstock.

> And *Woodstock*, let his Dome exalt thy Fame,
> Great o'er thy *Norman* Ruins be restor'd;
> Thou that with Pride does * EDWARD's Cradle claim,
>   **The Black Prince*
> Receive an Equal Heroe for thy Lord.
> Whilst ev'ry Column to Record their Toils
> Eternal Monuments of Conquest wears,
> And all thy Walls are dress'd with mingled Spoils,

Gather'd on Fam'd *Ramillia*, and
High on thy Pow'r[1] the grateful Flag display,
Due to thy QUEEN's Reward, and *Blenheim*'s Glorious Day.
230-40
[1]"Pow'r" is changed to "Tow'r" in 1717 *Poems*.

206 [January 23]

Abel, Mr. (No dates)

A SONG on his Grace the Duke of *Marlborough*'s happy Return into *England*; This is to be Sung this Day, being
Thursday the 23*d* of January, 1707; by Mr. *Abel* in the
Tennis-Court. No pub., n.d.
2°: 3 stanzas, 19 lines. Foxon-Crawford xerox
used. Not in Morgan. Opens:

> Fame thy loudest blast prepare
> Sing the Hero's Deeds in War;
> Trumpets Sounding, death Surrounding.

Marlborough not named, but his heroic deeds induce the
elations of a conventional song to the British sons of
glory. Fears are over, danger is gone, Fame gives what
life denies.

207 February 6.

B., J. [J. Bolton]

Prince Eugene. See No. 169, October 30, 1706. *P. Man*
adv. of same poem, No. 1734, Tues., Feb. 4 - Thurs. Feb.
6, 1707. 'This day is publish'd.' The 1707 issue, by
Curll and Sanger, is described there for easy comparison.
No copy of the 1706 ed. known.

208 February 6.

[Tate, Nahum (1659-1726)]

Song. For New-Year's Day, 1707. By the Same.
In Oldmixon's *Muses Mercury*, No. 2, pp. 27-8, February
6, 1707. A tribute to Anne, Union; Marlborough's
"Mighty Work is Done."

209 March 5.

Addison, Joseph (1672-1719)

Fair Rosamund: an Opera. Inscrib'd to her Grace the
Duchess of Marlborough. 3 lines Virgil's *Aeneid*. *LONDON*,
Printed for *Jacob Tonson* within *Grays-Inn* Gate next
Grays-Inn Lane. 1707.
      4°: 36 pp. March 5.
Performed Drury Lane, Mar. 4; repeated Mar. 15. Music by
Thomas Clayton. Morgan W1.
      The Marlborough relation lies in the Dedication to
his Duchess, and the setting at Woodstock with the associ-
ations with Blenheim Palace. Act III, scene 1, presents
Henry II asleep, and visited by two Angels, the guardian
spirits of British kings. The First Angel:

                    Looke up and see
            What, after long revolving Years,
                    Thy Bower shall be!
            When Time its Beauties shall deface,
            And only with its Ruins grace
            The future Prospect of the Place.
                Behold the glorious Pile ascending!*
                Columns swelling, Arches bending,
                Domes in awful Pomp arising,
                Art in curious Strokes surprizing,
                Foes in figur'd Fights contending,
                Behold the glorious Pile ascending!

      *Scene changes to the Plan of *Blenheim* Castle.

David Green's splendid volume, *Blenheim Palace*, London,
Country Life Lmtd., 1951, should be consulted for infor-

240

mation on the building of the vast tribute in stone and gardening. The Plan appears on p. 54, showing only the foundations. Certainly, as a successor to his *Campaign*, aside from some burlesque quality that anticipates Gilbert and Sullivan, Addison's opera was all the failure poetically that it was theatrically at Drury Lane.

210 March 4.

[Harris, Joseph (*c*. 1650-*c*. 1715)]

H., J. M. A.

MARLBORIDES, SIVE Bellum Britannicum. CARMEN HEROICUM Lingua Romana Susceptum. Liber Primus. Ab Authore J. H. A. M. Scholae Grammaticae commensalis in Vico Leighton-Stone in Comitatu Essex. Moderatore. [1 line each Ovid and Cicero] Prostant Venales apud Johannem Darby in Divi Bartholomaei Quadrungalo Typographum. An. M. DCC. VII.
2°: A-H², I¹, t.p., *bl.*, *iii-iv* Argumentum Libri Primi, 1-30, 34 pp. 921 lines, Latin verse, numbered. Errata p. 14. *D. Cour.*, No. 1523, Tues. March 4, 1707. 'This Day is publish'd' and March 5 'yesterday was publish'd.' Bodley copy used. Not in Morgan. Opens:

Arma virumque cano redivivi Stammatis Angli,
Quem Deus, adversi post tot distrimina Belli.

Marlborough, presented as "Dux mirabilis" in the 'Argumentum,' is followed in his campaign, with references to Blenheim, Ramillies, Schellenberg, but the poem is primarily an heroic imitation in which the main figures, including Louis XIV and Anne, as well as the German leaders and Marlborough, deliver oratorical statements. Frequent marginal notes identify the speakers. The poem mainly contributes, along with others in Latin, a new dimension to Marlborough panegyric but one of limited appeal. It is impressive mainly by sheer magnitude, and no continuation seems to have appeared. See Joseph Harris's *Leighton-Stone Air*, 1702, No. 20.

211 March 7.

[Gardiner, Mrs. E. (no dates)]

A POEM Occasion'd by the Late *THANKSGIVING*. By a Lady.
[ornament] *LONDON*: Printed for *R. Burrough* and *J.
Baker*, at the *Sun* and *Moon* in *Cornhill*, near the *Royal-
Exchange*. 1707. Horn-Luttr. copy used. '3 d. 7.
March,' '6' under 1707. 227 lines, couplets.
    2°: A^2 B-C^2; t.p., *bl.*, 3-12. Wtmk. 'F' and slen-
der Cannon. MS of this poem in Long Library, Blenheim
Palace, 10 pp., addressed to 'Madam,' i.e. Duchess Sarah.
Sgnd. 'To Her Grace the Duchess of Marlborough.' Morgan
J374. Opens:

> Could a woman's pen attain to *Dryden*'s wit.
> And reach that Flight of Thought with which he Writ.

Admiration for Dryden and apology for being a woman lead
to happy, glorious days to come and "*Heroes* deckt with
never-fading Bays" (1. 35). Anne is recalled as going
to the Temple, on a winter's day, her piety so apparent,
that Juno and Venus lay their feud aside. The loss of
her son by the Queen was "the greatest Trial could on
Earth be made" (1. 93). But Anne, like the best of
Christians, accepted her grief, and has opposed irre-
ligion and Popish tyranny (p. 7). Her obedience to her
husband is also praised, even though she is the sovereign.
    Marlborough enters, 1. 151: "Now Sound ye Men of
War, your Trumpets Sound." Trophies are to be raised
to Marlborough and babes and sucklings taught to pro-
nounce his name. Thoughts of Aeneas lead on to Cupid
and Mars, who welcomed his birth, presenting a shield
and bow. He has put generals to flight - "From *Blenheim*'s Battle they may see their Fate" (1. 198). With
a cause so righteous and a Queen so pious and just, pen
and rhetoric are inadequate to express the thoughts of
the poet. She concludes with invoking from Heaven an
immortal crown for Queen Anne. A finely printed, but
less impressively conceived and written tribute. The
author seems to have been at the Thanksgiving.

212   March 27.

Glanvill, John, of Lincoln's Inn (1664?-1735)

A POEM, Occasion'd by the SUCCESSES of the PRESENT WAR:
and Calculated for the Beginnings of the Present YEAR.
By JOHN GLANVILL of Lincolns-Inn, Esq; [2 lines Virgil,
1 Horace] LONDON, Printed: And Sold by J. Morphew, near
Stationers Hall. MDCCVII.
        2°: A² B-C²; t.p., The Preface i-ii, 1-10, 12 pp.,
drop-t. on p. 1. MH-Luttr. '25 March.' TxU, Clark.
CSmH copy used. 'London, Printed for Egbert Sanger.'
Wmk. Amsterdam Arms. Daily Cour. No. 1597, Thurs. March
27, 'This day is publish'd.' 444 lines, couplets. Not
in Morgan.
        The Preface remarks that the poem threatens to be-
come as long as the war itself, and apologizes for writing. It was composed, except for a small, earlier part,
in the previous January. Experience will show whether
previous efforts have satiated the taste of the Town.
The poet is both inspired and discouraged by Clarendon's
dignity and style. Glanvill has had eye trouble which
has led to idleness and a return to poetry. Exceptions
will be taken to the poem, but it must speak for itself.
The poem opens:

        Years have their Glory, Ages have their Fame,
        (As their fair Suns shone with a brighter Flame.)

Times are distinguished by great events, wise councils
and sublime deeds. How many have an Actium, a La Hogue,
or Vigo; or Agincourt and Cressy, or the events on the
Granicus or Boyne? Elizabeth made her people happy and
great; William taught "where to War and how to Fight"
(1. 42). He made his France her Spain, and now Anne
has the opportunity to win glory, especially with Churchill. French caution and the coolness of others deterred Churchill; but Austria was threatened. Alexander
anticipated Churchill in long marches, but for him Schellenberg at least offered resistance (1. 148). No ramparts, dangers, Danube streams, or other obstacles could
stop the British. Churchill shines like Alexander in
that fair year, of Blenheim, of Landau restored to

Germany, Traerbach freed, and new fame for British arms.
But soon another year will be born, in which Eugene
shall have his hour. It is like the poet who, after a
fine flight, sinks momentarily, only to regain his
height and strength. Such was it in going "From *Bleinheim*'s summer to *Ramillia*'s spring" (1. 234), of course
from August to May.

No description of battle is attempted, but Ramillies is signalized by comparison to "a poor Nymph" who,
in spite of good resolutions succumbs to a second seduction. The only detail is the General, that is Marlborough, lying prostrate on the ground, and his swift
recovery. No reference is made to Bringfield. It is
weary work to take every town and fortress; but in
Italy Eugene wins a Bleinheim and Ramillia both at
Turin. Godolphin is praised for his work, for "To
guide the Treasure is to rule the War" (1. 305). Mordaunt at Barcelona, and hapless Galway, have their turn;
but the poem returns to Marlborough, the "happy Commander," his four daughters, and Blenheim Palace rising to
the skies as a "massie lasting Trophy" (1. 352). Finally
the Queen, the source of all justice and glory, is recognized. Janus enters, since March 25 was regarded as
the beginning of the new year, Old Style, and anticipations of a brilliant future with more victories and
final peace.

> May *Churchill* his own Conq'ring Steps pursue,
> And others Emulous pursue 'em too.
>
> . . . . . .
>
> May thus our fleet too its *Ramillia* gain,
> And *Shovel* prove the *Marlb'rough* of the Main. 413-18
> *passim*

It is hoped that the Iberian war will grow strong. Particular hopes for the Scottish Union are also expressed,
clear indication that security and peace at home were
seen as essential to military success abroad.

> At home may the same wise and good Design
> Two Kingdoms and Two Kingdoms Wishes join.
> Let not the Marriage, like a Marriage, do,
> And make us one the more to make us two;

But calm let either *British* Nation learn
What is their mutual, and their great Concern.
420-5

May fair Religion love "a Moral Fame," may Faith reveal
some Charity, "And teach Humanity, as well as Zeal" (1.
440). Then may Anne set a standard for times to come.
As might be expected, Glanville produces a Tory poem in
which, though acknowledging Marlborough, attention is
diverted to Eugene and Queen Anne.

213 April 7.

[Harison, William (1685-1713)]

On His *Grace* the *Duke* of *Marlborough* Going for *Holland*.
In Imitation of the third ODE of the First Book of *Horace*.
Caesarem Vehis. *LONDON*: Printed for *Jacob Tonson*. 1707.
(Price 2 *d*.)
    1/2°: 1 side, single col. Drop-t., and colophon
bottom p. 2. 42 lines, couplets. *Daily Cour*., No. 1605,
Mon. April 7, 1707. 'This Day is publish'd. (Price 2 *d*.)'
Also No. 1621, Apr. 25. 'Tomorrow will be publish'd.'
Thus publication possibly April 26. No wmk. Horn copy
used. Foxon only LSA, Crawford 1ocs. 42 lines, couplets.
CBEL ascribes to Harison. Morgan J307.
    Marlborough went abroad primarily to confer with
Charles XII of Sweden. Since his letters show that he
was held at Margate from March (12) 23 to the (20) 31st,
sufficient time for producing the poem by April 7 is
allowed. It opens with an address to the ship.

        Thrice happy Barque, to whom is giv'n
        The Pride of Earth, and Favourite of Heav'n.

Marlborough is to go via Belgium to "Councils yet suspended" upon which depend Europe's fate. It was a bold
man who tempted the seas and fought in foreign climes,
despising his own welfare for the public good. Patriotic spirits are urged to support him and to combine "To
lift the baffled Claim of RIGHT DIVINE" (1. 26) and to

distinguish the subject from the slave. This is a war
for Freedom to "shock the Pow'r of Hell, and Pride of
France" (1. 36).

214 May 1.

[Pix, Mary (1666-1720?)]

A POEM. Humbly Inscrib'd TO THE *LORDS COMMISSIONERS* FOR
THE UNION OF THE TWO KINGDOMES. *LONDON*: Printed; and are
to be Sold by *J. Morphew*, near *Stationers-Hall*, 1707.
        2°: *A*² A3, B²-C¹; t.p., *bl.*, 1-8, 10 pp. Drop-t. on
p. 1, A POEM UPON THE UNION. Horn-Luttr. '4 *d.*, May 1.'
Uncut, sewn. Morgan J373. Xerox placed in BM. Wmk.
cross with ball tips above three circles with letters
H R and W, one in each circle. 214 lines, couplets.
Foxon reports a presentation copy from Mary Pix to Lord
Somers, MR-C. Also CSmH copy with dedication sgnd. 'John
Powler,' but this properly belongs to his "On the Queen's
Most Glorious Victory." Opens:

        Hail, fragrant *MAY*, thou glory of the *Spring*,
        To thee, the Shepherds all their Tributes bring.

Seasonal atmosphere, pastoral peace, maids and youths
wreathing garlands of daffodil and violet, turtle-doves
singing. Ancient bards have made May divine, but theirs
not half so sweet as this one which honors a pious Queen,
whose exemplary life is a blessing to this Isle.

        What Scenes of coming Joy this *UNION* shows,
        Since you have fixt the *Thistle* to the *Rose*.   35-6

Anne's work is greater than that of Henry, who joined the
Roses, or of James, who brought the crown of England but
could not blend the kingdoms into one. The Northren [*sic*]
Albans are urged to rejoice and spread the sails of commerce. The project of a hundred years has been consummated by wise Godolphin, "and all beyond the *Tweed* made
British Ground" (1. 56). (During 1707 France was intrigu-

ing to invade Scotland.) Heaven provides guardians for Britain's Isle. *"Marlbro*'s Name, *Talbot*'s of Old, exceeds" (1. 63). While this is the only allusion to Marlborough, the importance of the Union in the protracted struggle with France lies behind the entire poem. "We praise, we wonder at his vast Success, Till his next Conquest makes the first seem less" (1. 70).

The rest of the poem presents the heroes who brought about the Union, Queensborough first, then a list of Scottish and English "councellors": Argile, Seafield, Montross, Mar, for Scotland, and Pembroke, Somerset, Newcastle, Kingston, Sommers, Hartington, and Boyle, for England. The faithful Senate with its "belov'd Speaker" and particularly the "mighty *EMPRESS* of the *British* Land" (1. 175) are hailed. Their action will serve to *"Ballance Power"* and Anne's very name will subdue whole armies. The stately Piramids of Egyptian monarchs have crumbled, but Anne's acts will last. Long may she live and *"Britain's* scepter Wield" (1. 214).

Since the poem appeared on the day the Union was finally signed, it is another example of the close following of political events by the panegyrists. Harley, who had a considerable share, is not mentioned. Mary Pix's principal literary contributions were twelve plays written between 1696 and 1706.

15   May 8 *ca.*

[Tate, Nahum (1652-1715)]

A Panegyrick Epistle upon the Lord Treasurer *Godolphin*, in Latin and English, which artificially comprehends all the different Verses and Odes of *Horace*; with Annotations explaining the same. Sold by *Tim. Child* at the *White Hart* in St. *Paul's Church-yard*, and J. *Morphew* near *Stationers-Hall*. Adv. in *Post-Man*, No. 1778, May 8-10, 1707. 'Just publish'd.' Only ref. Morgan J445, which ascribes to Tate. No loc. known.

The PATRIOTS of GREAT BRITAIN: A *Congratulatory Poem* to
Those Truly Noble and Illustrious PEERS who happily
United the Two Kingdoms of *ENGLAND* and *SCOTLAND*, under
the Auspicious Government of Her most Sacred Majesty
Queen *ANNE* &c.   [2 lines Ovid and Virgil] *LONDON*: Printed
by *R. J.* and Sold by *J. Morphew*, near *Stationers-Hall*.
1707.
    2°: *A*² B-D²; t.p., *bl.*, *iii-iv* To the *Reader*, 1-12,
16 pp. Drop-t. on p. 1. '6 *d.* 14. May.' *Post-Man* 17
May. Horn-Luttr. Morgan J30. No adv. known. Wtmk.,
foolscap. 239 lines, couplets. The poem opens with a
Prologue to the Queen.
    To the *Reader*. Alludes to Cicero's observation that
"There are two Qualifications requisite in Men that are
of Great Power to advance a Nation, saith Cicero, *Wealth*
and *Prosperity*." We owe so much to these Great Patriots
that acknowledgment demands an encomium. Precedent is
cited from Cyrus, and four lines of Horace are quoted.
The technique of the poem is to footnote, by letters of
the alphabet, from the Classical poets, Virgil, Horace,
Ovid, Martial and Lucan, each point made. There are 86
of these footnotes running throughout; 84 are classical
quotations. The poem opens:

       How shall my *Muse* express thy *Pow'r* or *Praise*,
       Whose Godlike Gifts are *Crowns*, and *Peaceful Days*.

Anne has assumed a Triple Crown, in the Act which makes
it that, "This *Union* looks so much like a Work Divine"
(1. 29). Caesar and Alexander were too weak to bear up
the World. Now realms are taught to unite. This brings
the only reference to Marlborough: "For *Marlborough*
Conquers not to *Gain*, but *Give*" (1. 57); but about 26
lines are devoted to his service which "make a Second
Mars of *Churchill*'s Name" (1. 75). He is also specified
in a marginal note, as are four other figures, though
only the Dukes of Queensbury and Argyle are named. Presumably these and the Lord Chancellor and Lord High
Treasurer are the patriots who are the subject of the
poem. The passing of winter, and the advent of spring
call for dedication of the Happy Day (1. 210). Return

to Queen Anne, the real source of the happy events, concludes the panegyric. It must be admitted that the
Latin quotations are rather forced.

217   May 22.

[Oldisworth, William (1680-1734)]

THE BRITISH COURT: A POEM. Describing The most Celebrated Beauties at St. *James*'s, the *Park*, and the *Mall*.
The Ladies Characteris'd. 1. The Duchess of Marlborough.
[29 in all are named and numbered.] *London*, Printed for
Samuel Bunchley, and Sold at the *Publishing Office*, in
Dove-Court, near *Bearbinder-Lane*, 1707. *D. Cour* , No.
1644, Thurs., May 22, 1707, 'Just publish'd.' BM, HD, ICN.
    2°: A^2 B-D^2; *i-ii*, *1-2*, 3-14, 18 pp- Advertisements
verso t.p. BM, ICN, HD, Lehigh copy used. Sec. Ed. adds
four names to total 33, 2 pp., total 20 pp. Drop-t. on
p. 3. Horn copy of Sec. Ed. used. *A*, B-D^2; *i-ii*, 3-16,
18 pp. Morgan J79 lists Sec. Ed. only. Bod., CtY, TxU,
Kinsey Inst., InU. 290 lines; wmk. foolscap. Identification through reprint in *Misc. Poems* of Oldisworth,
1715, p. 205. The Dutchess of *Marlborough* is No. 1.
Opens:

> Give my *Genius*, fill'd with soft delight
> Of Beauteous Forms, blest Images of Light.

After a safe tribute to Queen Anne, whose court the ladies
adorn, they are treated conventionally, with all the feminine graces included.

> Go on, my Muse, next to *Minerva*'s smile,
> *Minerva*, the bright Goddess of the *Isle*,
> The happy Partner of Great *CHURCHILL*, place
> Where *Beauty* still maintains a Pleasing Face,
> After she blest the World with such a God-like Race.
> So tenderly are both touch'd ev'ry where.
> The Gods were pos'd themselves to make this Pair,
> And show four *Heroins* [*sic*] equally as Fair.   44-51

The poem presents the familiar features of a beauty contest. Its importance is perhaps mainly in reflecting the paucity of great subjects in 1707, with all due compliments to the Queen Anne beauties of course. It brought an anonymous reproof, *Advice* to the Author on a Late POEM, Entitled, The *British Court*. Printed for the Booksellers of *London* and *Westminster*, 1707. Price 2 *d*. Bsd., 2 pp., 16 3-line stanzas, 48 lines, couplets. "For shame give o'er, And Write no more."

218   July 9-16.

A Compleat History of the Wars in Flanders, Italy, Spain, Portugal, and on the Rhine. Containing a Particular Account of the Glorious VICTORIES and memorable SIEGES, during Her Majesty's Auspicious Reign, under the Command of the Illustrious Prince, John Duke of MARLBOROUGH, Lord PETERBOROUGH, and the Earl of GALLWAY: with the Several SEA-FIGHTS, and acquisitions in the Mediterranean, West Indies, etc. *Printed and Sold by P. Parker*, 1707.   183 pp., 12 mo. Equestrian portrait of Marlborough, plumed hat, cannon, standards below. Morgan J306. BM, CSmH.
      Prose account. No refs. to poems. Tells of Marlborough's honors, the grant of Woodstock Park.

219   July 31, or earlier.

Escourt, Richard (1688-1712)

Britain's Jubilee. A New Congratulatory *Ballad*, on the Glorious Victories obtain'd by the Duke of MARLBOROUGH, over the *French*: Written by the Famous Comedian, Mr. *Escourt*, and Sung by him to most of our Nobility, with great Applause. *London*, Printed and Sold by *H. Hills*, in the *Black-fryars*, near Water-side, For the Benefit of the Poor, 1708. Published with *Windsor-Castle*, No. 244 below. MC. Morgan K450. TxU copy used.
      BM has separate printing for *J. Morphew*, n. d.,

called *A New Copy* of a *Ballad*.   Presumably later.   Has
only 10 stanzas; omits first two.   8VO: pp. 15-16.
12 4-line stanzas with refrain, 60 lines, ballad.

> You tell me *Dick* you've lately Read,
>   That we are beaten in *Spain*;
> But prithee Boy hold up thy Head,
>   We'll beat 'em twice for it again:
> With a fal la la la la la la la la la la la, &c.

The defeat in Spain is Almanza, April 1707, a triumph
for Berwick.   Still we have in Johnny Marlborough a man
who can beat the French.   He has eight Fair Daughters:
Lady Rialton, Bridgewater, Sunderland, Mount-Hermer.
The Younger four are: *Hochstet*, *Schellenburgh*, bright
Blenheim, and Lady *Ramillies*.   To make "thy hopes" more
strong they belong to the Queen of *Great Britain*, he is
urged.

20   August 18.

Grubb, John (no dates)

The British Heroes: OR, A NEW BALLAD In Honour of St.
GEORGE, &c.   By Mr. *JOHN GRUBB*, School-Master of *Christ-
Church, Oxon*.   [2 lines Horace]   *LONDON*, Printed: and
are to be Sold by *John Morphew*, near *Stationers-Hall*:
and *H. Clements   Oxford*.   1707.
        4°:   A-B^4; t.p., *bl*., 1-17, *bl*., 20 pp.   385 lines,
in 12 stanzas of varying length.   Adv. in *Daily Cour.*
No. 1719, Mon. Aug. 18, 1707.   'Tomorrow will be publish'd.'   Aug. 19, 'This Day is publish'd.'   BM, Bod,
MH, CtY (3).   Yale copy used.   Not in Morgan.   Opens:

> The Story of King *Authur* [*sic*] old
> Is very memorable.

The poem has no evident relation to Marlborough,
but in view of its title may embody cryptic references.
The figures presented are hardly British heroes, except
for King Arthur.   Following him come "Tamerlain,"

Achilles, Thalestris, Hannibal, and others. Footnotes
identify references to Oxford 'characters,' a letter
carrier, a one-eyed fiddle-maker, a certain Lord L--ce
who broke down the bridges at the Revolution, a butcher,
a cook, and an ale-house keeper all of whom added to the
local color of Oxford. If the intention was simply to
celebrate such individuals as associable with St. George,
the poem is no less obscure. It has none of the usual
features of mock-heroic, such as scenes of combat, and,
though long, offers no matter to quote for poetic effects
or for allusions to the events of the war. Its inclusion
here rests solely on the title, which would induce anyone
who did not examine it to think that Marlborough would be
one of the heroes.

221 September 4.

Maynwaring, Arthur (1668-1712)

A manuscript poem on Ramellies. Enclosed in a letter,
dated September 4, 1707, to Duchess Sarah, on the day
of Maynwaring's taking the post as her secretary. Manuscript in Blenheim Palace Library. He writes:

> I will content myself with saying that you shall
> always find me very different from most secretaries
> you have known in one respect, which is that I shall
> never care how much I am employ'd nor how well I am
> paid.

The poem is 135 lines, couplets. No pub. identified.
Opens:

> While, madam, with a mild yet warlike Reign
> You bless your Subjects, your Allies maintain.

The goddess Victory comes from Flanders, bearing a palm.
She speaks 68 lines, each marked in the left-hand margin
with a single quotation mark. These are not retained here.

> I come, She says, in England to proclaim
> An Action worthy of Eternal Fame.   10-11

The lines are marked by more exultation than explicit
detail. Schellenberg and Blenheim are noted first, but
strangely with no naming of Marlborough. He is the
'leader' or 'Captain' of the victors.

> Think how he led the valiant Britains [*sic*] on,
> When D'arco fled, and Schellenberg was won;
> When freeing Nations that your Arms enslav'd,
> Think how on Blenheims Plains the Fight he gain'd
> With Gallick Blood the wandring Danube stain'd.
>
> 44-8

Successive captured cities are named: Brussels, Louvain,
Bruges, Courtray, and Ostend, taken in three days, whereas she formerly held out for three years. Victory flies
away, and now Liberty speaks (ll. 85-106). She gives
Anne the main credit, as commanding the battle, and hails
England as the land of liberty. The poet resumes for the
final 29 lines, stressing particularly Anne's role as
representing "Female Reign":

> But, Madam, you, by this amazing Warr,
> Revenge that bold injustice to the Fair:
> Who thought your Sex unworthy to Command
> Now falls the Victim of the Female hand!   124-7

Not a distinguished effort. Presumably written soon
after Ramellies, as is suggested by the absence of the
Duke's name in a poem later given to his Duchess.

2 October.

Colepeper, William (d. 1726)

To his Grace the Duke of Marlborough, on the foregoing
Verses. By William Colepeper, Esq.
   6 lines in ref. to a 6 line motto, "Gallus semper
Gallus," By the same, i.e. T. D. author of a *Pastoral.*
Occasion'd by the Marriage of a Lady [the Duchess of Rich-
mond] *And a Colonel of the Army* [Thomas Howard]. Pr. in
Oldmixon's *Muses' Mercury*, No. 10, p. 229, Oct., 1707.
See No. 101, f.n.

223 October 23.

TO HIS GRACE THE DUKE OF MARLBOROUGH. No pub., n. d.
    1/2°: 1 p., 1 column. MH-Luttr. '1 *d*. 23. Octob.
1707.' The only known copy. Also adv. *Daily Cour*., No.
1775, Thurs. October 23, 1707. 'This Day is publish'd.'
26 lines, couplets. Not in Morgan. Opens:

> Haste, great Commander, to our longing Isle,
> And meet your Country's Thanks, and Prince's Smile.

Since the new victory excels any previous success, Marlborough should not repine that every year does not supply
a victory. Don't blame the timorous Gauls for flying,
since you always conquer them.

> Can it be that after *Blenheim*'s Blow,
> And that which they at *Ramileis* [*sic*] did know,
>   11-12

that they foresee inevitable defeat from you? Not only
do they fly, they rear bulwarks of defence, knowing they
are not safe while you are near.

> But haste, great Man, haste o'er the Ocean Home,
> Since this Year's Action is in Belgium done.
>   22-3

It is time you take your place in Britannic Council
where you are as great as in the field.

224 November 8.

On the UNION of the *Two Kingdoms*, of ENGLAND and SCOTLAND.
As Represented in One PARLIAMENT. *London*: Sold by *Benj.
Bragge* at the *Raven* in Pater-noster-Row. 1707. [Colophon
bot. p. 2.]
    2°: MH-Luttr. '8 Nov. 1707.' 34 lines, couplets.

> When *Blenheim* and *Ramellies* wond'rous Fields,
> To ANNA paid, what Gory Conquest Yields.

Anna sees the German states separated, where if they were

united they could conquer the world. We, all nations,
owe Liberty to different reigns, but Union we owe to
Anne, "all must come from YOU" (1. 12). Britains, go
conquer and free all states. Like bundled arrows no hand
can break, in Union we are irresistible.

> O Harley! O GODOLPHIN, Babes unborn
> Shall Sing, your Labours for your Country done,
>   21-2

how you overcame faction and made your Mistress loved by
all countries as Marlborough subdues them.

> With open Arms, ye *Senators* receive,
> Your Brothers, from beyond the Ancient *Tweed*   27-8

for there will be no more discord at home, and you will
be able to conquer and extend Liberty to your foes abroad.

> But view the ‡QUEEN whose Eyes with Lustre shine,
> And tell, the future Glory of Her ISLE.

‡ *Going to the House to meet them.*

25   November 27.

The GOTHIC HERO: A Poém; to the Memory of Charles 12th King
of Sweden . . . the glorious restorer of the Protestant
Religion in Silesia, from Popish Usurpation, and arbitrary
Power. London: Printed for B. *Bragge* in *Pater-noster-
Row*, 1708. Price 6 *d*. Adv. *Daily Cour*., No. 1809. Tues.
Dec. 2, 1707. 'This Day is publish'd.' Morgan K180
states "Luttrell noted on his copy the price and the date,
27, November, 1707." Haslewood also has '27 Nov. N.S.'
Here Luttrell anticipates an advertisement. No copy
known. Marlborough met with Charles XII, April 16. See
Lediard II, 166-7.

6   December 4.

An Essay on the Character of his Grace the Duke of

Marlborough. In a Letter to a Gentleman in *Portugal*.
Printed for R. Kanplock at the *Bishop*'s *Head* in St.
Paul's *Churchyard*. Adv. in *Daily Cour.*, No. 1811,
Thurs. Dec. 4, 1707. 'This Day is publish'd.' No copy
known. Not in Morgan.

227 Brookes, Henry (no dates)

DAPHNIS. A Pastoral POEM. To the Most Illustrious His
Grace the Duke of *MARLBOROUGH*, &c. Most humbly Dedi-
cated. By *HENRY BROOKES*, M. A. Rector of *Camerton* near
Bathe in the County of *Somerset*: And Chaplain to his
Grace the Duke of *Devonshire*. [11 lines of Horace] *LON-
DON*, Printed by *J. Darby* for *Bernard Lintot* next *Nando*'s
Coffee-house in *Fleet-street*, M.DCC.VII.
   2°: A^2 B-C^2; t.p., *bl.*, 3-11, *bl.*, drop-t. on p. 3,
284 lines, couplets, 12 pp. NNC, CSmH copy used. Not in
Morgan. Opens:

> *Damon*.   Well met *Alexis*! 'tis a glorious Day
>   The brightest and the sweetest of the *May*.

But a savage Chief, ravenous as the Wolf and wily as the
Fox invades the pastures. The last great shepherd, who
resisted, died and Pastora (Queen Anne) has inherited his
sword and sceptre. To Daphnis (Marlborough) she has assigned the command, and now the foe trembles and runs.

> This *Ramillies* can tell, now famous place,
> That saw the Slaughter, and the fatal Chase;
> To *Britain*'s Glory, and the *Gaul*'s Disgrace.   74-6

Damon, in sleep, had a vision of a great disturbance and
battle in the forest, and then of a brilliant Leader,
graceful, tall, unafraid. Alexis says, it is no dream,
the news of Ramillies has arrived, and Daphnis is the
leader. He says Damon should sing the event, but Damon
insists only Virgil could do so, or Addison.

> Or matchless Addison's high-soaring Verse,
> Immortal Blenheim when he did rehearse.   168-9

Daphnis has won thanks from Pastora for defending her throne, but has had too few honors at home, while being graced with "Foreign Honors." Who can adequately praise him? And "high-born *Celadon* that rules the Main" (1. 217). Pastora's reign will glide smoothly, and Daphnis will no longer have to "cross the briny Main" (1. 265), for peace will prevail, and "madding Sons their Factions shall forbear" (1. 273). Grateful *Britains* [*sic*] never will forget their preserver, "Or think his *Blenheim* a Reward too great" (1. 283). This plea against criticism of the vast extent and cost of the Palace reflects the changing attitude toward Marlborough whom the poem attempts to justify.

28 Mackqueen, John, Minister at St. Mary's in Dover (no dates)

A Divine and Moral Essay on Courage, its Rise and Progress; with some reflections on the Causes of British Valour, and more particularly on the Victory of Ramellies. London, sold by John Morphew, 1707.
    4°: Morgan J301, only ref.

9 *An Epistle to Charles Montague.* Earl of Halifax. Writ upon the Occasion of the Signal Successes of Her Majesties Arms in Last Summer's Campaign. *London*: Printed for Sam Crouch. . .Tim Goodwin. . .Thos. Fox, 1707.
    4°: A-E3[4]; t.p., *bl.*, 3-38, *39-40 bl.*, 40 pp. Dobell Cat. of Lit. of the Restoration, No. 1135. Says "looks like Tate production." Note on p. 6 ref. to Dryden: "By your poem called *The Man of Honour.* . .and by your Fable of *The Pot and the Kettle*, &c., you have kept the most prudent dissenters from joyning with the Papists against the Church, and baffled Mr. Dryden's books in behalf of the Church of Rome." Morgan J179 gives part of title only. Says a verse production. MH only copy.

The *Fifteen COMFORTS* of a DUTCH-Man. *Written by the Author of* the DUTCH-CATECHISM. [ornament] *LONDON*:

Printed in the Year, MDCCVII.
    8vo: A^2; t.p., 2-8, 8 pp.   Drop-t. on p. 2.
Coarse paper.   Headline title for each comfort; errors
in printing, 156 lines, couplets.   Horn copy used.   "I
have seen another copy," Mr. Percy Dobell wrote in sending this copy.   Foxon lists ten or more poems with "Fifteen Comforts" titles, as of Cuckoldry, a Lawyer, a
Widower, of Single Life, of Whoring, of Matrimony, etc.
Not in Morgan, who has only one, *The Fifteen Comforts of
a Scotch-Man*.   Written by Daniel D'Foe in Scotland.
London: *Printed in the Year*, MDCCVI.   Moore 143, who
cites only Bodley copy.   Morgan: *150a, but doubts by
Defoe.   Lacks *Dutch-man* poem.
    All of the poems of this minor genre exhibit a tone
of varying degrees of coarseness and obscenity.   This one
is concerned with Marlborough throughout, especially with
the advantages of the war to the Dutch allies.   Not in
Morgan.   Opens:

The First Comfort.

You may talk of haughty *France*, and boast of *Spain*,
And tell us of the poor *Bavaria*'s Gain,
That perjur'd Villain, who soft betray'd
King *William*'s Council, for which he was paid,
By cursed *Lewis*.

But since Great-Britain is our faithful friend we Dutch
will aid in defending Europe and Holland's right.   Jacobites may prate in vain, for England will own no Prince
of Wales, and "*Anne* the true Religion still will own"
(1. 29).   Bavaria was puffed up with victory.

A while, till *Marlborough* with his Army came,
And blasted all his Trophies strait with shames,
The *Dutch* and *English* by their brave Designs,
At Schellenberg did beat them from their Lines.   33-6

Hochstet is then brought in, as the Fourth Comfort, with
the Danube drowning as the prime feature.   Tallard and
Marsin are defeated,

and into the Flood
Of swift *Danube*, to dye with *Gallick* Blood,
Squadrons into the rapid Flood did throw.   51-3

and made Tallard beg for his life, "in any ENGLISH Goal"
[*sic*]. The Jacobites and the French are heavily damned,
and in the Sixth Comfort, Marlborough joins with Auverquerque against them, here and in the Seventh Comfort,
where Schellenberg and Bleinheim are again brought in.
Prince Eugene enters at this point, but the honors go to
Marlborough, who is welcomed at Brussels, Antwerp, and
Ostend. In the Twelfth Comfort, "a second Fight of
Ramillies (1. 123) is threatened. Naval battles are mentioned in the Fourteenth, and a promise is made that
"Next Year we *Hollanders* will lead poor *France*" a dismal
and fatal dance.

For Royal *Anne*, her sacred awful Name,
Throws on her Enemy perpetual Shame;
And may Her Majesty ne'er sheath Her Sword,
Till it do's Peace to *Christendom* afford.   152-3

In spite of its lack of artistic, or even satiric,
importance, this piece does embody basic principles of
Whig policy, and thus holds to a loyal defence of the
war. The *Dutch Catechism* does not appear in Morgan, and
has not been identified.

1 *The Several Qualities* of the *British Court*, Characteris'd.
D. of Marlborough, L. Orford, Godolphin, Ormond, the Lord
Chancellor, L. Hallifax, E. of Pembroke, E. of Sunderland,
D. of Somerset, L. Granby, D. Newcastle, L. Hartington,
D. of Devonshire, L. Kingston, D. of Richmond, L. Mor-
daunt, E. of Lindsey, L. Stemford, L. Sharton, L. Ortland,
L. Summers. London, Printed in the Year 1707.
     8°:   pp. 1-8.
Adv. *Daily Cour.*, No. 1644, Thurs. May 22, 1707. Cf.
companion poem to The Ladies. Morgan J424. Listed also
in C. N. Greenough and J. M. French, *Bibl. of the Theo-
phrastian Character*, 1947, p. 161. Evidently a deriva-
tive from the procession of court beauties, *The British
Court*, No. 217 above.

1708 is above all the year of the great victory
at Oudenarde, July 11th, N. S., and the third, and
final, wave of panegyrics. That the identified authors are confined to such as Gildon, Tate, and Eusden,
with the remainder of anonymous and inferior nature,
is significant. The victory was splendidly achieved,
but the political tide was turning. Mrs. Masham was
already at work against the Duke and Duchess, and all
the factors of backstairs intrigue and treachery were
setting about subversion of all that Marlborough had
achieved.

Morgan specifies only seven poems on Oudenarde,
but actually thirteen appeared, including two in 1709.
It was a year of theological and doctrinaire controversies, leading up to the Sacheverell episode. Most
of the poems were in fact concerned with Marlborough,
and military matters. That John Phillips's *Cyder* was
the only poem of any note to appear, the Marlborough
pieces notwithstanding, gives an indication that the
muse was at best awaiting new inspiration.

32   January 1, *ca.*

Tate, Nahum (1652-1715)

The SONG for the New Year 1708.   Set by Mr. Eccles Master
of Her Majesty's Musick.   The Words by Mr. Tate, Poet-
Laureate to Her Majesty.   No pub.
      1/2°:   1 side, 31 lines, ode.   Not in Morgan.   Foxon-
Crawford only loc.   Opens:

>   See how the New-Born Season Springs!
>   High Entring on auspicious State,
>   On Smiling UNION, Golden Wings;
>   See the Blessings that He brings,
>   EUROPE's Freedom, Tyrants Fate.

Trophies and spoils "due to" Anna's prayers and Marlborough's martial toils have won fresh lawrels, like those
of Blenheim and Ramillia.   Nor less renowned is his last
campaign.   A Grand Chorus of four lines concludes the
song, hailing new wonders and blessings.

33   January 29.

A POEM Inscrib'd to *Lieut. Gen. Ingoldsby*, Occasioned by
his Going to IRELAND.   On the *Glorious Successes* of *Her
Majesties Arms* and *Councils.   London*:   Printed, and Sold
by *John Morphew*, near *Stationers-Hall*, MDCCVIII.
      2°:   *A*¹ B-E² F¹; t.p., *bl.*, 3-19, *20 bl.*, 20 pp.   No
drop-t.   425 lines, couplets.   Wmk. lion on crowned seal
and 'H P.'   Adv. *Post-Man*, No. 1876, Sat. Feb. 21 - Sat.
Feb. 28.   1708.   'Just publish'd.'   Horn-Luttr. copy used.
'6 *d.* 29 Jan.' and on title 'A Silly Whiggish Poem.'   MS.
corrections pp. 8, 10.   CtY, IU, OCU.   Morgan K215.   Opens:

>   SIR
>   As by some wond'rous Sympathy appears
>   Our future Fate, in mighty Hopes or Fears.

Actually, a poem on Marlborough, with no allusions to Ireland, and only a belated reference to Ingoldsby in the

final two lines. While most of the Whig leaders are mentioned, the poem is not "silly" in the political sense so much as the artistic. It does not achieve clarity and point; but then Audenard lay ahead and at the moment there was little to celebrate. William III and the Danube, that is Blenheim, occupy the first half, with Liberty being the key word. To Marlborough the poet says:

> The Banks of DANUBE Eccho to your Fame,
> And BLEINHEIM never shall forget your Name.
> The DANUBE freed, sure must some Bard inspire.
> With +VIRGIL's Language, and with HOMER's Fire;
> Fit to describe the Place where MARLB'ROUGH stood,
> And how he drove his Foes into the Flood.   33-8

+Our best Poems on that Subject, being understood by few besides our selves.

Plainly the Whigs do crave another Blenheim as much as a poet to praise it. Names of Blenheim heroes are recited: Crowther, Meridith, Cadogan, Wood, Webb, Orkney, Lumly [sic], Churchill [Marlborough's brother], and 'You,' the only allusion to Ingoldsby till the end of the poem.

The poem turns to political matters in a general way, urging an end to faction and the preservation of liberty, and naming leaders: Sommers [sic], Hartington, How, the Major General, Cowper, Mordaunt, Wharton, the Mountagues, the Duke of Newcastle, Spencer, Somerset, and Godolphin, whose sobriquet of Volpone is deplored. A compliment to Marlborough's four beautiful daughters is achieved by associating them with English rivers. The poem is scattering, and at the close does invite Luttrell's derision in its tribute to the Union. Thetis, daughter of Jove, comes ashore and speaks. She praises Godolphin's victory over the hydra of faction, Anna's command of the seas, and, with a return to Marlborough's daughters, she prophetically assigns a victory to each, leaving only one so unassociated. Schellenberg, Blenheim, Ramillies appear, with only Audenard missing, since it was not to be consummated till the following May. Thetis promises that Marlborough's sword will restore liberty and peace in Europe, whose children will come to Blenheim, the Palace,

to boast they have seen the Conqueror (1. 404). Marlborough is to no isle confined; Jove owns Anne's cause
and blesses her sending her hero forth to conquer, to
help the oppressed and give laws to tyrants. The poem
ends: "But yonder see, your INGOLDSBY appear," and
Thetis turns to ambient air, and disappears.

In spite of Luttrell's partisan contempt, the poem
preserves considerable insight into the political atmosphere at the time. It is one of a very few Marlborough
panegyrics to which he attached such a critical comment.

34 *ca.* April 25-30.

Sarah, Duchess of Marlborough (1660-1744) and Arthur Maynwaring (1668-1712)

ADVICE *to the* ELECTORS *of* GREAT BRITAIN, *occasion'd by the
intended invasion from* FRANCE. *LONDON:* Printed in the
Year 1708. 4 pp. in folio.

Formerly attributed to Defoe, Morgan K120, who reports a quarto Edinburgh ed. 1708, repr. for the heirs
of A. Anderson. BM Cat. and Moore's *Checklist* as well
as CHEL *et al.* also have Defoe. BPub. copy used.

Sarah had sent a present of money to Defoe in 1705;
but no evidence appears for her having collaborated with
him in the *Advice to the Electors.* Snyder (*HLQ*, XXIX,
No. 1, 1965, 53-62) shows that Maynwaring sent her a
draft of the pamphlet, and that she responded with a
draft from her own hand. He concludes, however, that
it is impossible to determine which passages belong to
either of the two authors. At one point the "True Principle of the Tories" is specified as "to profess Passive
Obedience and Non-Resistance, to set up an Establishment
opposite to Liberty, void of Property. . .in short make
a Government as absolute and lawless as possible." An
equally succinct account of Whig policy tempts to the
suggestion that it may have come from Sarah's sharp pen.

The true Principle of the Whigs is to maintain
the Religion, Liberty and Property of their

Country; and to have a just concern for the
common Good and Welfare of their Fellow-
Subjects. To keep the Monarchy within its just
Bounds, and secure it with Laws from Tyranny at
home, and with Forces given by Parliament from
the Danger of a foreign Power. To reverence
and esteem good Church-men, yet tolerate Dissenters; and in a word to keep our Constitution
as it now stands between the two Extreams of
Arbitrary Power, and a Common-wealth.

France is naturally represented as the great threat
to these good things, and while Marlborough is not named,
the voters are urged to elect representatives who will
"bring a Consciousness of the War with Honour and safety"
(p. 4). The pamphlet concludes with a strong warning
against "the deplorable Misery" that the recent opponents of the Scottish Union will bring on themselves if
they fail to protect their civil and religious rights.

235 April 29.

The Flight of the Pretender with Advice to the POETS, a
POEM, In the Arthurical,--Jobical,--Elizabethecal Style
and Phrase of the sublime Poet *MAURUS*. Printed for Bernard Lintott, at the Cross-Keys between the Two Temple
Gates in Fleet-street. Price 2 d.
    8°: A⁸; t.p., Preface *iii-vi*, 1-8, *9-10 bl.*, 16 pp.,
drop-t. p. 1. 266 lines, couplets. Adv. in *Post-Man*,
No. 1895, Tues. April 27 to Thurs. April 29, 1708. 'This
Day is publish'd.' MH, DFo, TxU, Clark. Morgan K48.
Horn copy used. Also an edition by H. Hills, 1708.
    The *Preface* combines satire on the Scottish efforts
of the Pretender and his monkish supporters, and the epic
pretensions of Maurus, that is, Sir Richard Blackmore.
Nothing is done to elucidate this inept conjunction of
Popish plots and a prime Protestant-Whig spokesman. The
significance of the production in relation to Marlborough
lies almost entirely in Blackmore's continuing role as
defender of the War policies. Opens:

Oh! *thou Pretender* stop *thy* swift Career,
A while the *Fleet*, a while the Poet spare.

The detailing of young "James III's" attempted invasion
is replete with sharp satiric strokes, on Forbin, the
admiral of the French fleet, on Admiral Byng's pursuit,
and the humiliation of taking refuge at Dunkirk. An
ironic call for a poet to celebrate this inglorious
adventure brings in Blackmore.

> *Beat up for Volunteers* who Rime for Bread,
> *Whose* unfledg'd Muses, *no* high Subject dread.
> *All* the inferior Race *that* can indite,
> A *sorry* Prologue, or a *Poem* write;
> All *that* can raise a Shed, *let them* presume,
> To Frame a Palace *and* erect a Dome
> Once more let *Arthurs Ballad-singer* dare,
> Torture our Language to *oblige* our Ear.   54-61

The poetic "Pretender" lacks nothing "but Design and
Sense" as he "Plies hard the Pump, and labours every line"
(11. 68-72 *passim*). The war is brought in with the flight
of Gallia's troops, and the sounds of triumph from Flanders, but Marlborough is not named.

56   May 13-15.

Hill, Mr. (no dates)

The Invasion, a Poem to the Queen, by Mr. Hill. Printed
for T. Bickerton, at the Golden Flower de Luce in St.
Paul's Churchyard, price 6d.
     Adv. in *Post-Man*, No. 1903, Thurs. May 13 to Sat.
May 15, 1708, as 'Just publish'd.' Only ref.
     Ostensibly deals with the Pretender's ill-fated
effort. Not certainly related to Marlborough. Not
in Morgan.

237 May 22.

[Blackmore, Sir Richard (1654-1729)]

The KIT-CATS. A POEM. *Tantae Molis Erat* [ornament]
LONDON: Printed for *E. Sanger* and *E. Curll*, at the
Post-House at the *Middle-Temple-Gate*, and at the *Peacock*
without *Temple-Bar*. 1708.
2°: A^2 B-F^2; t.p., *bl.*, 1-19, *bl.*, 22 pp. Lehigh
and Clark copies used. Clark-Luttr. '22 May.' BM, CtY,
MH, TxU also have. Morgan K49. Three H. Hills eds.,
two 1708, one 1709; reprtd. in 1718 ed. of *Works*, with
stylistic and mechanical changes. The three Hills eds.
show variations in sigs., but also addition of two short
anacreontic imitations by the Marquis of Normanby, i.e.,
Buckingham, 'The Picture' and 'The Coquet Beauty,' pp.
14-16. These three in MH, CtY, TxU, CSmH as reported by
Foxon. Horn copy of No. 1 used. Blackmore's 'Advertisement' verso of t.p. appears in folio ed., contrary to
Allen, *Clubs of Augustan London*, p. 45, and is thus of
interest. Not in octavo Hills eds., but in 1718. Blackmore states: "This Poem was writ some Years ago. . .
not design'd for the Press." He is now publishing it,
"having Reason to believe it will otherwise come abroad
by means of that Copy." The poem of 365 lines, couplets
in all eds., opens:

> I Sing the Assembly's Rise, Encrease and Fame,
> That condescends to honour *Kit-Cats* Name,
> Whose Pride, like thine, O *Rome*, from small
> Beginnings came.

No allusions to Marlborough, but general recognition of
the Whig tradition and support of William III's policies,
Anne's continuation of it in the war, and the obligation
of Kit-Cat poets to celebrate it. An allusion to "poor
Devil Brown," who seems still alive though starving, suggests that the writing was before June 16, 1704, the date
of Tom Brown's death (1. 236). The poem links *Macflecknoe*
and the *Dunciad*, and is far from contemptible, as is recognized by Richmond P. Bond, *English Burlesque Poetry*, pp.
257-9. Blackmore has one more significant contribution to

Marlborough panegyric. See the *Instructions to Vander Bank*, 1709, No. 273, for a summary of his role *in toto*.

38   May.

Gay, John (1685-1732)

WINE A POEM. [2 lines Horace] *London*: Printed for *William Keble*, at the *Black-Spread-Eagle* in *Westminster-Hall*, MDCCVIII.
     2°: A^2 B-D^2; t.p., *bl.*, 3-16, 16 pp. Bodley, TxU.
Morgan K175. 278 lines, blank verse. H. Hill ed., 8vo:
t.p., *bl.*, 3-11, with pp. 12-16 *Old England*'s *New Triumph*: or, The BATTEL of *Audenard*. A SONG. No. 263.
Horn copy used. Opens:

     Of Happiness Terrestrial, and the Source
     When human pleasures flow, sing *Heavenly* Muse.

After noting how wine has inspired heroic poets, Virgil and Horace, and orators, such a Cicero (Tully) and Demosthenes, Gay deplores that John Philips has sunk to cider for his stimulus.

     Had the *Oxonian* Bard thy Praise rehears'd,
     His *Muse* had yet retain'd her wonted height;
     Such as *of late* o're *Blenheim*'s Field she soard [*sic*]
     Aerial, now linger in *Ariconian* Bogs
     She lies inglorious floundering. . .   120-4

Gay evidently did not know of Philips's *Cerealia*, No. 136 above. Being Tory in sympathies and associations, Gay could not lavish praise on Marlborough; but Blenheim is noted in a tribute toward the close.

     The Hero MARLBRO next, whose vast Exploits
     Fames Clarion sounds, fresh Laurels, Triumphs new
     We wish, like those *HE* won at *Hockstets* Field.   231-3

Toasts are drunk to the Prince Consort, and members of the government, Devonshire, Godolphin, Sunderland, and Halifax.

The poem concludes with a touch of *Trivia*, as the company breaks up at midnight. The streets are silent from the rumbling noise of coaches, and only the cries of linkboys to be heard. The score is paid,

> And Homeward each his Course with *steady* step
> *Unerring* steer'd, of Cares and Coin bereft.   277-8

239 July 14.

A Copy of Verses Occasion'd by the late Happy Victory in FLANDERS. Pr. in the *Observator*, No. 44, Fri. July 9th to Wed. July 14th. 1708. Pp. 3-4. 19 lines, couplets. Not in Morgan. Opens:

> Hark! How FAME's *leaden* Trumpet *hoarsely* sounds,
> As if it *felt*, not *told* lost Gallia's wounds.

The hopes of France are dead. The drooping Lilly sinks, while lawrels crown the "*thistled* Rose." The victors' shouts thus reflect the success of the Scottish Union. The fogs dissolve before the Sun's "Rays of *Two*," i.e. England and Scotland (1. 19).

240 July 16.

On the *Duke* of *Marlborough*'s late Success.

Pr. in the *Observator*, No. 45, Wed. July 14th to Fri. July 16th 1708. Pp. 3-4. 26 lines, alternate rhyme and couplets; varying line length, in ode style. Opens:

> Illustrious Guardian of our Nation, when
> Will thy Herculean Labours Cease?

Exultation over Louis XIV and his generals who have been frustrated in their ambitions. Marlborough will not stop till Heaven has blessed his toils with glorious Peace. Such publication in the newspapers increases, especially when the satirical war heats up. It is impossible to list all.

241   July 17.

The Battel of Audenard.   A POEM.   Occasion'd By the Glorious Victory obtain'd over the *French* near that Place,
the 11th of *July*, 1708, N.S. by the Confederate Army
under the Command of his Grace the Duke of *Marlborough*,
Monsieur *D'Auverquerque*, and Prince *Eugene* of *Savoy*.
With the *Characters* of the General Officers, who were
present in the Engagement.   [ornament]   *LONDON*, Printed:
And are to be Sold by *J. Morphew*, near *Stationers-Hall*.
1708.   Price Six Pence.
        2°:   A-C²;   t.p., *bl.*, *iii-iv* The *PREFACE*, 5-12, 12
pp., drop-t. on p. 5.   322 lines, couplets.   *Obs.* VII,
No. 44, July 14-17, 1708.   Here Luttrell date is late.
P-Man, No. 1925, Thurs. July 15-Sat. July 17, 1708.   Clark-
Luttr., '6 *d.* 20. July' used.   Only loc.   Morgan K315 as
10 pp.   Also Horn copy of H. Hills ed., also July 17, 1708.
Same title and text but with *London*, Printed and Sold by
H. Hills, in the *Black-fryars*, near Water-side, For the
Benefit of the Poor.   1708.   T.p., *ii-iii* The *Preface*,
4-15.   Added on [16] *Jack Frenchman*'s *Lamentation*, see
No. 243 following.
        The *Preface* opens with the usual apologies.   The
birth and education of the poem were not a matter of more
than three days.   No divine inspiration here.   "If Poets
were like Prophets, we of the chiming Tribe should do
well enough. . .but the Age of Possession is over. . ."
The writer believes such poems are favorable to the
health and welfare of the State, since soldiers, who
serve it, are desirous of an illustrious character.   They
crave having their glory transmitted to posterity.   Lucan
is quoted to show we have the custom of celebrating heroes.
Although "these Sort [*sic*] of Rewards are now in a great
Measure grown out of Fashion". . .he has made an essay at
perpetuating the Memory of those general officers who have
lately been of such high service.   He hopes that amends
for his imperfections will be made by "abler Pens."   The
poem opens:

        Coelestial Maid, now touch thy Golden Lyre,
        And Numbers sing, which CHURCHILL's Arms inspire.

The hero makes the poet; but what power can write of

Marlborough's acts? Even Milton's verse could only "soar
so high" (1. 13), while Marlborough made Fate stand sub-
servient,

> Who Blenheim's Plain with slaughter'd Heroes fill'd,
> And at *Ramillies* mighty Numbers kill'd.   25-6

Churchill fights to save, and where illustrious Nassau
could not defeat the Gaul, he wins the honors. After
six long years of war, British troops invaded Flanders
and the Rhine. Only Almanza stopped them. Still the
enemy giant rose like Antaeus, stronger than before.
The "too feeble Works of *Audenard*" (1. 124) offer little
obstacle, nor do the forces of Vendosme. Successively,
Lumley, Wood, Ross, Orkney, Withers, Cadogan, Campbell,
Stairs, Temple, Sabine, and finally the Prince of Hanover, George II to be, are reviewed for their heroic
qualities and share in the victory (11. 175-308). An
allusion, in a marginal footnote, to Dryden reflects
the taste of the anonymous poet, as the poem suddenly
concludes with an image of "the last Trumpet."

    Since this is virtually the first specific and im-
portant effort in honor of Oudenarde, and one of the
most ambitious, it is unfortunate that the poet remains
unidentified. Auverkirk and Eugene, though mentioned
in the title, never appear, and it may be said that the
poem did not fully carry out its implied intentions,
even though it does signalize a considerable body of
officers. An incidental interest attaches to it from
the statement of Thackeray that he could recall the
line attached to General Webb, "like Paris handsome,
and like Hector brave," as being "from a contemporary
poem called 'The Battle of Oudenarde' which my uncle
had, but on which I have not been able to lay hand."
Actually it is line 257 which he quotes. See Gordon
Ray, III, p. 447. Aside from Addison's, and occasionally, Prior's, Philips's, and Congreve's poems, the
vast mass of Marlborough panegyric has received very
rare notice, particularly in view of the richness and
precision with which it follows his career and the
main events in the political life of Queen Anne.

242 July 16.

Gaynam, J. (no dates)

MARLBOROUGH Still CONQUERS OR UNION hath got the Day. A
POEM upon the late VICTORY. London, Printed for *D. Rogers,*
and sold by *J. Morphew*, 1708. (Price 6 d.)
2°: *A²* B-C²; *1-2*, 3-12, 12 pp. *D. Cour.*, '16 July.'
BM, Lehigh, Morgan K116.
Ibid., title includes *Upon the late VICTORY* obtain'd by
the Prince and Duke of MARLBOROUGH; *And* UNION *of the Two
Kingdoms.* [5 lines, Livy] *London:* Printed by *H. Hills*,
in *Black-fryars*, near the Water-side. 1708.
8ᵛᵒ: t.p., *bl.*, To the Author of this Excellent
POEM, *iii-iv*, 29 lines, signd. 'W. B.,' couplets; poem
5-16, 16 pp., drop-t. on p. 5. 316 lines, couplets, in
three Parts. Also opens with 12-line Induction, with two
other passages totaling 345 lines in all, in italics.
Horn copy used. Opens:

Lolling upon the Ground, as Stragglers do,
Whose Pockets thin, and thinner was my Show.

The poet falls asleep under a willow and foresees the
future may repeat the past.
Part I opens:

ZEAL always looks a-squint, tho' now and then
Throws off that Mask, but puts it on again.

Part I summarizes the struggle between Catholic and Protestant doctrines, from Henry VIII and "good Queen Bess"
down through the Stuarts to Anne, with the struggle for
power, Passive Obedience, and Popery the themes. Now
that Glorious Anna is on the throne, and "UNION in Her
Glory keeps the Door" (1. 110), religion is no longer
vain pretence. Part II continues the theme of Union
and Moderation as providing love and peace. Factions
disappear, and tyrants are in confusion.
"When She commands, Great Marlborough doth obey"
(1. 163), and calm in battle makes nations happy. With
Blenheim he first taught the French to run, and now, apparently with Oudenarde, he has gained the complete

victory which he was previously denied. His prisoners
shout that they find more mercy with him than with their
tyrant king.
     Part III continues the subject of Anne's just reign,
with virtue and Marlborough as her strength. She has established the "*Ballance of Power*" and *Great-Britain* dispenses blood and energy throughout the world. England
enjoys:

> Unheard-of *Miracles*, before unknown,
> Which cou'd be done by none but ANNE alone:
> She scarce hath left us Room ought to require;
> May *Sarah's Blessing* crown *Her Hearts Desire*. 316-17

     This somewhat inferior piece still fervently associ-
ates Marlborough's victories with the Scottish Union, ascribing the blessings of peace and security to their
working together under Anne's wise guidance. While Morgan calls it the usual panegyric on the Duke and attack
on Louis XIV, it is distinctly motivated by political
concern for close identification between the two principal members of the union that has brought about Great
Britain, and Britain's greatness.

243 July 17.

Jack Frenchman's Lamentation. An Excellent New Song, To
the Tune of *I'll Tell Thee Dick*, &c. London, Printed for
John Morphew, 1708. Also pr. with *The Battel of Audenard*,
Hills 8° p. *16* as "A New Copy of Verses." Ballad. BM,
Rothschild, MH, TxU, CSmH, Clark, *et al*. Horn copy of
Hills ed. used. First ed. 1/2°: 1 side, 2 columns, 78
lines, in 13 6-line stanzas. Engraving of battle top of
p. 3. BM copy used. Morgan K406. Attribs. to Swift.

> Ye Commons and PEERS,
> Pray lend me your Ears,
> I'll sing you a Song (if I can)
> How *Lewis le Grand*
> Was put to a Stand
> By the Arms of our Gracious Queen *ANNE*.

On Oudenarde, and two of Louis XIV's grandsons, who having hidden in a steeple to watch the battle, flee on advice of Vendosme. By contrast, young Hanover fought on foot even when his warhorse was shot. In Spain they won Almanza, but the French dream of success is dispelled by Marlborough, for "'tis *Bleinheim* wherever he comes" (1. 60). Lewis is perplexed as to what general next. Tallard, fattened on good Nottingham ale and beef and pudding, we could let out; but the losers would still lose.

This was one of the most popular of all the ballads that began to pour out from 1708 on. Reptd. in Dryden-Tonson Misc., VI, 250-4, 1709, 1716. Also rptd. as *Jack Frenchman's Defeat*, 1/2°, Morphew and Hills eds., 1708. BM copy has large woodcut, 5" x 8" at top, depicting Louis XIV's two grandchildren with the Pretender on a tower, safely watching the battle. The poem is in 14 6-line stanzas, 84 lines. No pub., n. d.

244   July 22.

Gildon, Charles (1675-1724)

Libertas Triumphans, A POEM, OCCASION'D BY The Glorious VICTORY obtain'd near *Odenard* by the Forces of the ALLIES under the Command of His Highness JOHN Duke of *Marlborough*, and Prince of the Sacred *Roman Empire*, and the Velt-Mareschal *Auverquerque*: On the First of *July*, 1708, [2 lines Claudian] *LONDON*, Printed for *Tho. Bullock*, at the *Rose* and *Crown* near *Holbourn-Bridge*; and Sold by *J. Morphew*, near *Stationer's-Hall*. 1708. BM, MH, CtY, ICN, CSmH-Luttr. '22 July.' Adv. *Post-Man*, No. 1930, Thurs. July 29-Sat. 31, 1708. Yale copy used.

2°: A² B-E²; t.p., *bl.*, *iii* To His Highness George Augustus, Electoral Prince of *HANNOVER*, Duke and Marquis of *Cambridge*, Earl of *Milford-Haven*, Viscount *North-Allerton*, Baron of *Tewksbury*, &c. and Knight of the Most Noble Order of the Garter. . .This POEM is most Humbly Inscrib'd and Dedicated By *His most Humble and Devoted Servant*, Charles Gildon; *iv* The PREFACE; 5-20, 24 pp. 705 lines, couplets. Morgan K179.

The *Preface* is written "according to the Mode," but it purports to introduce a poem out of the common road wherein planlessness, inundations of similes, and wantonness of injudicious fancy are to be found, where they are monstrously clapped in by our Modern Poets, "like Mr. Bays." Gildon compares his freedom from these to Homer. "If the Reader expects to find any Noisy and confus'd Descriptions of the Battle he will be disappointed." Only Virgil has barely succeeded, after Homer, in battle poetry. He manifests that he has taken great care with the design, and regrets his failure to do full justice to the young Prince, whom "all True *Britains* will ever pray for." He opens:

An impious Doubt did oft my Mind invade,
And to vain Wand'rings my Thoughts betray'd.

The doubt is whether Providence or Chance rules the world, and especially the affairs of men. But the fall of Lewis has assured him that it is Providence that prevails. "Blenheim, Ramilly, and Turin weigh him down" (1. 63). In despair he addresses Madame Maintenon in a speech of 112 lines which amply demonstrates the turgidity of the poem. The King reviews Marlborough's victories. Wherever he appears the French troops "retreat with one consenting Fear" (1. 114), and Eugene and Mordaunt, Earl of Peterborough, have added to the humiliation. All this had come from a Woman. He recalls "Pucel," that is Jean'Arc, who turned France's fortunes and freed her from foreign domination. He asks Maintenon to do the same, and then falls into a trance.

The "old Crone" Maintenon revives her lover-King, and then reads him a 49-line lecture on courage. She points to Rome retaliating against Carthage when all seemed lost; and she shrewdly urges that he use arts against the English which will probe their vices, "disjointed Int'rest, and the Thirst of Gain" (1. 246). That this wily attack does not succeed in his poem does not deny Gildon's Maintenon the claim of being a shrewd counsellor. She makes a swift flight to the haunt of Arbitrary Power, which is located in a deep chasm in a lofty, barren mountain allegorically and improbably set in the

heart of France. This Gildonesque Hell is later balanced
by a radiant Hill on the Thames where Anne dispenses justice and peace. Here is the court of Lucifer and a noisy
train of abstractions: Oppression, Rapine, Slaughter,
Atheism, Pride, Luxury, Slavery and blind Avarice being a
few. They welcome Maintenon joyously, and she responds
with a long speech demanding their support of her King,
who has employed them all. A hideous figure, Tyrannis,
then rears up and speaks 72 lines in which he particularly denounces Liberty and Common-wealth. Aroused, the
sponsors of evil hearten France, and in Almanza a setback
of English hopes is achieved. Even so, with return to
the English antithesis of Hell, Anna, Liberty, and Union
triumph. In Odenard a new great victory affirms English
hopes and defeat for the Hydras.

> See Warlike MALBRO', and the Brave EUGENE,
> And the NASSOVIAN AVERQUERQUE, Serene
> In all the Tempests of the War.   651-3

That Gildon's efforts attain to nothing remotely comparable to Homer, or Milton, is evident, and it is just as
well that he absolved himself of any obligation to describe a battle. He concludes with a tribute to Prince
George: "A NATION's Genius in ONE *mighty soul*" (1. 676).
George will benefit from a Heav'n-born Muse, which alone
can give a deathless name. Just rewards will secure him
the services of a bard, not identified by Gildon; but
one can observe an ironic anticipatory tribute to Pope,
unconscious of course. Hell's black troops flee before
the Prince, and Liberty prevails in this Whiggish and
rather disastrous effort at heroic poetry.

245   July 31.

WINDSOR-CASTLE: A POEM Inscrib'd to the *Immortal Honour*
of our most Gracious Sovereign ANNE Queen of *Great Britain*, *France*, and *Ireland*. Sold by B. Bragge. Adv. in
Post-Man, No. 1931, Sat. July 31-Tues. Aug. 3, 1708; No.
1936, 14-17; also in *Obs.*, No. 48, July 28-31. 'This

Day is publish'd'; No. 49, July 31-Aug. 4, 'This Day is publish'd.'
    A-C². Also pr. by *H. Hills*, with identical title, 'To which is added, BRITAIN's JUBILEE. A New Congratulatory *SONG*, &c. [1 line Latin] *LONDON*, Printed and Sold by *H. Hills*, in the Black-fryars, near Waterside, For the Benefit of the Poor. 1708.
    8ᵛᵒ: T.p., 2-16, drop-t. on p. 2. 16 pp., 432 lines, couplets. Morgan K450. BM, CtY, MH, TxU, CSmH, Clark, Horn (2 copies) used. For *Britain's Jubilee* see No. 219, 1707. Opens.

> After Great *Nassau* taught this Nation War,
> And led them out with conduct, and with care.

At Landen the field was covered with the slain, and "None will exceed Immortal William's Name" (1. 14). Then Anne rose like a Sun, and lives as queen and virtuous wife to Royal George. In Windsor Castle she reigns, a castle described largely in terms of its spacious and lofty hall, with paintings by Verrio, of William and other English kings in battle. Commerce abounds on the Thames which flows by, and Windsor Park provides the beauties of Nature. Here Anne meditates on the ravages of Louis and France. She falls asleep, and in a vision sees a towering Angel-bard, who instructs her to assemble the council and declare that her sword shall curb France's power. Her leader is to be Churchill; he will exalt her fame. "To *Marl'brough*'s Genius, *Burgundy* must bow" (1. 254). Anne awakes and at Westminster addresses the Council. While one opposes, consent is given to her choice of the leader.

    Marlborough speaks, deploring "that proud ungrateful Race," who have opposed him. A young Peer supports him but an aged one, named *Maroc*, counsels caution. Anne fervently urges war, however bad it may be, as necessary, and the poem concludes with a harmonious resolve to send Marlborough and his forces against the enemy. "While *Britain* slept" (1. 417) Anne saved her, and now again she and Marlborough will do the same.

    The poem has some of the features of Denham's model, but it is less a topographical-architectural poem than

the title implies. Actually it is a Marlborough panegyric, with the common Whig emphasis on Queen Anne and her
policies.

No copy has been located for a title which Morgan
lists, K132, but it may be listed here for its association with Windsor Castle. The item is A DIALOGUE between
Windsor Castle, and Blenheim House. . .a Poem, London,
1708. Morgan describes it as octavo and as a "panegyric
upon the Duke of Marlborough."

246 August-September.

Tate, Nahum (1652-1715)

A Congratulatory POEM To His *Royal Highness* Prince *GEORGE*
of DENMARK, Lord High Admiral of *Great Britain*, upon the
Glorious Successes at Sea. By *N. Tate* Esq; Poet-Laureat
to Her Majesty. *To which is added* A Happy Memorable SONG
&c. *LONDON*, printed for *H. Meere* for J. B., sold by R.
Burrough and J. Baker, and J. Morphew, 1708.
     4°: A-E^2; *1-3*, 4-18, *17-18*. No wmk. *WL* July 1708.
C, InU, MU.
     Also *London*: Printed by *Henry Hills*, in *Black-fryars*,
near the Water-side. 1708.
     8VO: A; t.p., 2-10; drop-t. on p. 2, *Postscript*
11-13; The ballad, 14-16, 16 pp. Morgan K 414. Horn copy
used. 229 lines, couplets. No certain dating, but falls
between Oudenarde and Prince George's death, October 28,
1708.

     Bless'd *Prince*! in Whom the Graces seem combin'd
     To raise the sinking Glories of Mankind.

The poem is about as labored and often absurd as most of
Tate. He professes a rural muse, which still returns to
court. He hymns the Queen's birthday, George's conquests,
the defeat of the Pretender, and the like. The poem is
of course concerned with Prince George, and much of it
deals with the hapless effort to land the Pretender, and

Admiral Byng's successful naval intervention, all in
March. The Prince is -

> The Leading Light, that fir'd Her Sons of Fame;
> From Hence *Marlburian*, and *Eugenian* Flame.   17-8

While this is the only allusion to Marlborough in the
poem, he also appears in the *Postscript*. This portion
consists of more of Tate's pussyfooting and flattery of
royal persons. More interesting is an allusion to his
mentor, Dr. Gibbons, to whose learning and judgment he
is most obliged, and who is rewarded with nine lines
wherein he professes to have been taught more than Horace and Roscommon knew, and apologizes for deserting the
classical road. He does defend celebrating worthies of
one's age and nations, "because it is doing Justice to
living Merit, and Transmitting its Glorious Example to
Posterity." He also alludes to "a fresh and signal Victory by the Conduct and Bravery of his Grace the Duke of
Marlborough" along with the two earlier naval successes
of the year. Eight more lines of verse on the royal
couple bring Tate's laureate effort to a close.
 Prince George's appointment as Lord High Admiral
was made by Anne, at her ascension, along with Marlborough's as Captain-General.

247 August-September.

A Happy Memorable Ballad, On the Fight near *Audenarde*,
between the Duke of *Marlborough*, of *Great-Britain*, and
the Duke of *Vendome*, of *France*. As also the strange and
wonderful manner how the Princes of the Blood-Royal of
France were found in a Wood. In allusion to the *Unhappy
Memorable Song* commonly call'd *Chevy-Chace*.
 2°: 1 p. Wood engraving of battle scene at top
beneath title, and a vertical band of nine miniature engravings between 2 cols. verse. *LONDON*: Printed by *J.
Bradford. Fetter-Lane*, n. d. Not in Morgan. Yale has
undated bsd. printed for John Morphew.
 The ballad is printed, pp. 14-16, with No. 246,
Tate's *Congratulatory Poem*. Broadus, *The Laureateship*,

assumes this also is by Tate, but this seems very doubtful. It looks more as if Hills wished to fill out his
sheet, and perhaps to add a lure to the purchaser beyond
what Tate's name could boast. Morgan K414, published by
H. Hills.

    8vo, 22 4-line stanzas, 88 lines in all, ballad
style. Opens:

> God prosper long our gracious Queen,
>   Our Lives and Safeties all,
> A woful [*sic*] Fight of late there did
>   Near *Audenard* befal.

Marlborough has driven the French in defeat when two
French princes fall at his feet. He sends them up in a
nearby church spire, to watch the fray. After the battle
they go to the woods to cry, where the Duke again comes
upon them. With a reference to the courage of the Prince
of Hanover in the battle the poet refrains from following
this pitiable tale further.

248   August 13.

AUDENARDE. A POEM, Inscrib'd to the Right Honourable the
EARL of *Bridgwater*. [2 lines Virgil] *LONDON*, Printed
for *Harry Clements* at the *Half Moon* in *St. Paul*'s Church-
Yard, 1708.

    2°: *A* B-C²; t.p., *bl.*, 3-12, 12 pp., drop-t. on p.
3. No wmk. 222 lines, couplets. Horn-Luttr. copy used,
'4 *d*. 13. August.' HD, InU, OCU. Morgan K314. Opens:

> Leave for a while, MY LORD, th'Affairs of State,
> And all the Business that attends the Great.

The anonymous poet urges his lordship to admit some diver-
sion, to listen to the account of war and its successes,
of Netherlands restored to Charles of Spain, the prod-
igies of Churchill's sword. Since the latter was his
father-in-law, Bridgwater being husband to Marlborough's
third and favorite daughter Elizabeth, interest is added
to a poem that is at least not an absurdity.

Audenard is properly seen as restoring the balance
lost at Almanza, with the victory of Marlborough's nephew, the Duke of Berwick, who proved to be France's most
successful antagonist to the Duke. Fortune had been
favorable, but suddenly came the reversal.

> Forget the Slaughter of *Almanza*'s Plain,
> And *Berwick*'s Fortune in the Fields of *Spain*;
> Forbear the wild Engagements to relate
> Of *Fourbin*'s Squadron, and *Britannia*'s Fleet.   30-3

But *Marlbro'* enters the scene with his "unconquered Soul";
the Gaul feels the shock grievously.

> Nor *Blenheim*, nor could *Ramilly* alone,
> Retrench the vast Enlargement of his Crown,
> But AUDENARDE's designs his Fall compleat,
> And *all united*, finish his Defeat.   50-3

Marlborough and Eugene, again united, with others quickly
overcome the foe, but the poet attempts no description of
the battle. Rather he alludes to Homer and heroic poetry,
and calls on the poets to continue to celebrate heroic
actions. Of the great leader, Marlborough, he says:

> Or *Garth* shall paint him in his matchless Strains,
> Or *Congreve* speak. the Language of the Swains:
> *Parnassus* daily shall advantage gain,
> And *Addison* compose his next *Campaign*.   187-90

Meanwhile the warriors will appear at court, and the
beauties of Marlborough's house shall adorn it. Bridgwater's Countess and the Countess of Sunderland are mentioned.
    The poem concludes with praise of Anne and the assur-
ance that under her wise government faction, prejudice,
and spite will no longer corrupt the muses.

> In vain the Scriblers the Contagion spread,
> And strive to scandal only for their Bread.   216-17

The immediate thrill of the news of Audenard has plainly
passed, and the lagging state of poetry is apparent in
the persistent tendency to look back to Addison's *Campaign*

as the model of panegyric, and to call for a comparable
production. It did not come. Addison remained silent
and aloof.

249   September 3.

THE BATTLE of *Audenarde*, being an Intire Victory over the
French, by the Duke of *Marlborough*, and Prince *Eugene* of
Savoy; the 3*d*. Day of *July*, 1708. *LONDON*: Printed and
sold by *Benja. Bragg*, *Pater-Noster-Row*, 1708. Price 1 *d*.
    2°: 1 side, 2 columns, fine print; large engraving
of embattled cavalry with pikes and a compass, at top.
MH-Luttr. copy used. MS. '1 d. - 3 Sept. 1708.' Trimmed
on right edge. Not in Morgan. Opens:

> I should give a Relation of the Battle; but
> seeing I have no particular one, think it better
> to let it quite a lone. Should I infer what has
> been already publish'd, I should give Offence. . .

The anonymous writer points out that both sides make undue claims, and that even sovereigns are not to be trusted.
The reader can then only read both and make up his own
mind. An amusing account is given of the bromides of reporting.

> For while on one Side they cry nothing but A
> *signal Victory*, A *complete Victory*, a *Victory*
> that *obscures* and *effaces* all *former* Victories,
> A *Defeat* which the Enemy will never be able to
> *recover* we hear the *contrary* Party coolly say-
> ing they *beat*, *They drove* us from our *Posts*. . .

Particularly the issue as to who maintained the field of
battle arises, and the French reports on this point are
challenged. A recently printed letter written by a
French apologist for the Duke of Vendosme is alluded to,
and a supposititious version is offered. In this the
French commander's errors are reviewed. The effect is
to establish a clear victory for the English. Marlborough is never mentioned, nor any British commanders; but

thc piece is definitely pro-Allies in its review of the
battle of the pamphlets and pens.

250 October 20.

On the Taking of Lisle, &c.

Pub. in the *British Apollo*, Vol. I, No. 72, Friday October
15th to Wednesday, October 20th. 1708. 26 lines, couplets. Opens:

>   At length the *Blow* is struck, all *Gallia* feels
>   The *Blow*, at which *Her Haughty Monarch Reels*.

The enemy is superior in all but fight. The trump of
Fame grows hoarse proclaiming the name of great Marlborough round the globe. How shall we raise trophies to "invincible Eugene"? Great Boufflers and his men fly to more
secure barricades when they come, and yield the glory of
the day to "our Champion."

251 November.

A POEM On the DEFEAT of the FRENCH ARMY AT THE River
SCHELD, And Raising the Siege of BRUSSELS, BY HIS Grace
the Duke of *Marlborough* and Prince *Eugene*. [ornament]
London, Printed by *J. Read*, behind the *Green-dragon-
Tavern in Fleetstreet*. N. d.
    4°: A2 on p. 3 only sig.; t.p., *bl*., 3-8, 8 pp.
Drop-t. p. 3, with '&c' added following. Foxon reports
a copy printed by '*J. Morphew*. 1708/9.' 148 lines,
couplets. Bodley copy used. Only one known. Not in
Morgan. Opens:

>   A Muse in Arms inspire my willing Pen,
>   To Sing the Deeds above the reach of Men.

Marlborough is not identified, except in the title,
a fact which along with the misspelling of Schelde as

Scheld, might suggest that the printer is responsible for the title. Actually Eugene is mentioned once, 1. 40, and then as the potential victim of Louis XIV's poisoning schemes. Actually French perfidy, now humiliated in defeat, is the theme of the poem. "And *British* Truth [may] strike *Gallick* Falshood [*sic*] dead," 1. 9, represents almost all of the British sentiment. Louis XIV, particularly for his slaughter of Protestants, and as the "bold Tyrant," provides the focus. Oudenarde appears in only a few lines:

> Be Witness *Schelde*, that twice in one Campaign,
> Thy clearer Streams run Purple to the Main,
> Blushing with *Gallick* Blood, a due Reward
> For those who will a faithless Tyrant guard. 95-8

Similarly the siege of Brussels, also in the title, receives only one line: "Whilst proud *Bavaria* from, rich *Brussels* fled," 1. 117, and the Belgian cities taken also are briefly noticed:

> *Lisle* thou hast lost, with all thy strength of Arms,
> Which faithless *Ghent*, and *Bruges* fresh alarm. 103-4

Aside from the faulty rhyme, which provides further suggestion that the author was not a native Englishman, it may be observed that Marlborough won his third greatest victory at Oudenarde, in retaliation for the French seizure of Ghent and Bruges, and that the long siege of Lisle was a key element in this threat against Paris, even though he was forestalled from marching on to the French capital. Brussels fell November 28, 1708, which event helps in dating the poem.

52 November 16.

Welsted, Leonard (1688-1747)

A POEM, Occasion'd by the Late Famous Victory of AUDENARD. Humbly Inscrib'd to the Honourable ROBERT HARLEY, Esq; by LEONARD WELSTED, Gent. [3 lines Virgil] LONDON: Printed

for *Benjamin Barker* at the *White-Hart* in *Westminster-Hall*, and Sold by *J. Morphew* at *Stationers-Hall*, 1709. Price 6 *d.*
    2°:   ² B-C², *i-ii*, 1-10. Clark-Luttr. '16 Novemb. 1708.' 377 lines, couplets. IU, CtY, Lehigh copy used. Morgan L441. Opens:

> O for that Heaven'ly Voice, that pierc'd so high,
> As bore ELIZA to her Native Sky.

This appeal, plus a similar allusion to the poet who sang "the Immortal BOYNE" initiates a conventional poem. However, Welsted was only 19 and this seems to have been the maiden effort of his muse. He praises Marlborough who disdains stealing castles; "by Arms he conquers, and by Force he gains" (1. 59). He supports justice. The battle is described, though without specific detail. Marlborough is seen "Calmly distributing his wise Commands" (1. 144). His particular genius in improvising movements of troops during the battle is noticed. George II cheers Britannia with his heroic bearing and conduct which is compared to "young Harry" overcoming Hotspur (11. 172-210). Like Scipio, Marlborough adds Vendom [*sic*] to the line of Tallard and Villeroy, of defeated French commanders. A pastoral tone and picture of Blenheim Palace, to which the hero retires, complete the poem.

253 December 7

Wilson, Bernard (no dates)

ALDENARDUM CARMEN Duci *Marlburiensi*, Datum, Donatum, Dedicatumque. *Anno* Salutis Humanae, 1708. [4 lines Latin motto, unsgnd.] *LONDINI*: Impensis *H. Clements*, ad Insigne Lunae Falcatae in Coemiterio D. *Pauli*.
    4ᵗᵒ: A-C⁴; t.p., *bl.*, 3-23, *24 bl.*, 24 pp., drop-t. on p. 3. 295 lines in Latin verse. Wmk. fleur de lys on shield. BM-Luttr. copy used. '3 *d.* 7 Dec. 1708.' Foxon reports BM fine paper copy with name. ICN, *WL* Jan. 1709. Morgan K313. Opens:

Vandomus Gallorum acies, arma arma frementes,
Undique disponens, laeta spem fronte serenat.

Descriptions of battle and allusions to Blenheim and
Tallard, but the poem mainly portrays Marlborough in
the gloom and horrors of combat.

54 December 8.

On the Taking of the Citadel of Lisle, &c.

Pub. in *Brit. Apollo*, Vol. I, No. 86. From December 3d
to Wednesday Dec. 8th. 1708. 21 lines, couplets. Opens:

Triumphant Heroes, MARLBOROUGH and EUGENE,
When will you terminate the *Glorious Scene*?

Winter, with its dark, sullen damps and threatening
storms, cannot allay their thirst for glory. France, the
dancing nation, and Lewis and Maintenon cannot withstand
them. In vain they toil and fortify. Heaven smiles on
your brave actions, and makes the tyrant disgorge his
spoils.

The following items, for which no precise date
has been discovered, are listed alphabetically by
title. That the number of such items increases in
1708 and after is evidence of two factors, the increase in the number of broadsides, for which the
newspapers seldom supply dates of advertisements,
and the great and rapid increase in the number of
satires as the Tory intrigue, particularly against
the War and Marlborough.

5 Characters of the Great Men of the Age, Done in Prose
and Verse after the Manner of Boccaline in his *Parnassus*. By several Hands. No pub.
Morgan K84. "Includes a characterization of
Marlborough."

256 The DEVIL of a Whigg: or Zarasian Subtilety [sic] De-
     tedted: done from the Original by a Fellow of the Insen-
     sate, or the Society of the Unthankful Club at Bologna.
     32 pp., 8VO, London, 1708.
          Morgan K130 only ref. A satire on the Duchess of
     Marlborough, as Sarah was by now well established as
     'Zara.'

257 The French Invasion. To the Tune of Prety [sic] Parrot
     say, &c. London: Printed in the Year, MDCCVIII. 6
     stanzas of varying length, 66 lines. 1/2°: 1 side,
     ballad. DT, CSmH. Not in Morgan.

               Have you heard of late,
               How Affairs of State?

     Rather coarse, colloquial ballad. Has allusion to Blen-
     heim, for which "let every Bumper fill," and defense of
     English honor. A drinking song to England's Glory. The
     ill-fated expedition that was intended to put the Pre-
     tender on English shores, and a bibulous expression of
     English chauvinism provide the slight subject matter.

258 The French Pride Abated; or A Friendly Admonition to
     Lowly Humility. The Words by Tho. Durfey. To a New
     Tune. Printed for S. Deacon in Guiltspur-Street.
          1/2°: 4 16-line stanzas, 64 lines, n. d. Satire,
     pro-Marlborough. Six lines of music inserted with
     Stanza I. BM copy used. Not in Morgan. Opens:

               Grand Lewis let Pride be abated,
               Thy Marshals have all had a Foyle.

     In Stanza II allusion is made to Marlborough's "Hoch-
     steting" the French army; but in Stanza III, an allusion
     to General Webb's victory at "Winendale" on September 28,
     1708, proves that the song belongs to the later date of
     1708 or later. In the fourth stanza the promise is made
     of further "marching and charging" in a winter's campaign

under "Great *Marlborough* and glorious *Eugene*" (1. 59).
Lille had fallen, and the subsequent investiture of
Ghent justified the abatement of French pride. The
events are outlined in Sir Winston's Chapter 27, 'The
Winter Struggle.'

59   The Glory of the Confederate Arms. Set forth in the late
     Glorious Victory Obtain'd over the French near *Audenarde*
     in *Flanders*; under those two mighty Generals Prince Eu-
     gene of Savoy and the Duke of Marlborough, killing 10000
     Men on the Spot; taking 12000 Prisoners, with all their
     Cannon, Baggage, and Ammunition, and above Standards and
     Colours. Together with a pleasant new Copy of Verses
     between an English Soldier and a French Soldier on the
     Battle. To the Tune of Marlborough's *March*: or, *Paris*
     Gazzette [*sic*] say. LONDON: Printed by J. Bradford at
     the Bible in Fetter-Lane 1708. Engraving at top of
     battle scene and horsemen on either side.
          1°: 2 sides, verse in 2 columns, followed by long
     prose account in letter to 'Noble and Mighty Lords'; giv-
     ing account of the battle. A segment of a military jour-
     nal of the march of the armies follows, dating from
     March 8, but including the Battle of Oudenard, March 11,
     N.S.
          The ballad consists of 8 10-line stanzas, 80 lines
     of varying lengths. The English and French soldiers al-
     ternately utter their sentiments in contrasting exulta-
     tion and despair. See No. 185 for same title. Morgan
     I 173.

               Eng Soldier. Monsieur prithee say,
                             Since you've lost the day,
                             How still you've learnt to run away,
                             Dreading British Valour?

     The Frenchman responds with admissions of defeat, and the
     refrain "Oh fatal! fatal Day!" which runs through most of
     the stanzas. Eugene and Marlborough are hailed as fellow
     commanders, and a toast in tribute to them concludes the
     ballad.

260 THE Great Heroe, and the Little One: OR, A DIALOGUE Between Prince *Eugene* & Marschal *Boufflers* On the Surrender
of *Lisle*. *Dublin*. Re-Printed by C. *Carter* in Fish-
shamble street, 1708.
    4°: A, 1-4, 4 pp. Drop-t. only; colophon bottom
p. 4. DCL copy used. Dublin and Edinburgh reprints.
Foxon knows of no original pr., though the "Re-printed"
implies one. Not in Morgan. 109 lines, couplets. Opens:

> Eugene and Boufflers, *now Contending are,*
> *For rival Glories in the Lists of War.*

Ten lines of introduction, in italics, followed by
dialogue in which the two generals exchange sentiments,
marked more by courtesy than factual details. It is apparent that the final surrender of December 9th has not
yet occurred. Boufflers says he is still in possession
of the town and citadel. Even so, he anticipates the
necessity of surrender although he insists at the close
that his forces will "out-face dispair [*sic*]." Marlborough is not named, even though his army supported the
siege, and he in fact took over the siege upon Prince
Eugene's being wounded.
    The siege of the great fortress of Lisle (Lille)
was of course the key to Marlborough's plans for marching on Paris. Since he and Eugene differed on the possibility of such an action without first taking the
fortress, the bearing of the poem on Marlborough's
career is plainly cool, if not hostile. The verse is
devoid of any distinction, and the poem is marred by
numerous errors. The vapid quality of the verse may
be illustrated by two lines from Bouffler:

> Believe, Sir, that I'm not reduc'd so low,
> As that I'll yet a tame Submission show.   45-6

261 Deane, John Marshall [fl. 1708]

A JOURNAL of The Campaign in FLANDERS, A.D.-M.DCC.VIII.
Including THE BATTLE OF OUDENARDE, AND THE SIEGE OF LILLE.
BY JOHN MARSHALL DEANE, Of the First Battalion [*sic*] of

Foot Guards. NOT PUBLISHED. 1846. x,69. A motto from
Fluellen and Henry V. is included, and the phrase "Not
Published" is intended to indicate private publication
of only 75 copies. The work was edited by the Rev. John
Bathurst Deane, a descendant of the author, who was a
private soldier in Marlborough's regiment. He appears
to have died not long after the year 1708, to which his
vividly detailed account is confined. He is considerably
quoted by Churchill. While his manuscript waited till
1846 for publication, it seems appropriate to include it
at this point.

The editor draws evidence from the manuscript that
Deane was a Christian soldier, and certainly his deploring the use of "hellish" devices such as boiling oil,
pitch, and the like by the besieged at Lille supports
this view. It is gratifying to notice that Private Deane
shows the affection and admiration of Marlborough's
troops toward their commander. He describes the actions
of 1708 as "a long, tiresome, troublesome, mischievous
and strange, yet very successful campaign"; but with considerable misspelling such as was common to commanders
as well as honest, plodding foot soldiers such as Deane.
Copy used by courtesy of the Library of Congress.

2 [Smith, Edmund (1672-1710)]

ODE. No pub., n.d. Apparently on the recovery of Prince
George, who finally died October 28, 1708. Foxon-Craw-
ford. Not in Morgan.
    1/2°: 1 side, 1 column. 24 lines in 4 stanzas.
Opens:

    Ormond's Glory, *Marlborough*'s Arms
    All the Mouths of Fame employ.

Rejoicing everywhere, but tempered by concern over Prince
George. He revives, and future triumphs are anticipated.

    Mighty George, the senate's care,
    The people's love, great *Anna*'s prayer!   10-11

With his momentary recovery, the refrain of the opening
lines is repeated. Pr. in Anderson, Chalmers, and
Nichols anthologies.

263 *Old England's New Triumph*:   or The Battel of *Audenard*.
A SONG. *LONDON*. Printed for *A. Baldwin* in *Warwick-Lane*,
1708. Price a Half-Penny.
      1/2°: ballad; 2 sides, 2 columns. 22 6-line stanzas,
132 lines. Also pr. with 1709 H. Hills ed. of Gay's *Wine*.
Morgan *K309a. Opens:

>   Ye *Britons* give ear
>   To my story, and hear.
>   How *CHURCHIL* [*sic*], the Chief of Commanders.

A spirited ballad, with the French princes watching the
battle from the church tower, the humbling of Vendosme,
and particularly exultation over the High Flying Tories,
who last year complained of no battle's being fought.
Not in Morgan.

>   There's now no more Hopes,
>   Of *Lewis* thy Troops,
>   Once valiant, and fearless of dying,
>   Will e're stand again
>   The brave *Briton*'s Men,
>   They have got such a habit of Flying. St. XX, 116-20

This is an early example of the flood of such drinking
ballads, pro and con, that Marlborough's career evoked.

264 The Rival Duchess, or Court Incendiary, in a Dialogue between Madame Maintenon and Madam M[arlborough].
      8ᵛᵒ, 32 pp. 1708. Morgan K263 only ref. Presum-
ably prose. No loc.

65 The Thanksgiving SONG: Or the Horse and Foot-Race at
OUDENARD. *London*: Printed for *J. Morphew* near *Station-
ers Hall*. 1708.
    1/2: 1 side, 12 6-line stanzas, 72 lines. Not in
Morgan.

> As I told you before
> You would never give o'er,
> Old *Lewis*, your Bouncing and Cracking;
> 'Till *Marlborough*'s Battoon
> Crack'd Yours and Phil's Crown
> And to the De'el sent you both Packing.

BM copy used.

56 *To the Duke of Marlborough*. By an Anonymous Author.
From Steele's Collection. In J. Nichols's *A Select
Coll. of Poems*: with Notes, IV, 31-2, 1780. 56 lines.

This year is notable for an increasing proportion
of satires, and corresponding hostility toward the Duke
of Marlborough and his Duchess as well. Little significant panegyric appears; rather there is an appeal for
an Addison and deploring of the quality of verse. The
Battle of Malplaquet, September 16, 1709, a bloody,
costly victory for the Allies, marks almost the final
success of Marlborough in the field. The Siege of
Bouchain, in 1711, was a great achievement, but lacking the dash and deployment of mobile forces. Malplaquet was an autumn battle, whereas Blenheim fell in
the summer, August 13, and Ramillies and Oudenard in
the spring with the latter being followed by a winter
activity in Belgium. Actually the name Malplaquet does
not appear in titles, Blaregnies and Taisnieres, or some
version of that name, being used instead, the latter
perhaps more frequently. Because of its appallingly
bloody character, and the increasing tide of opposition to Marlborough, this fourth great victory received
slight notice from panegyrists, but plenty from the
satirists. Most of these were in fleeting broadsides;
the flood of handsome folio panegyrics dwindled and disappeared until their revival with Marlborough's death
in 1722.

67 January 15.

Britain's Wish for the Duke of *Marlborough's* Return. An
Imitation of the Fifth Ode of the Fourth Book of Horace.
Inscrib'd to his Grace the Duke of Marlborough. Sold by
B. Bragge. Price 6 *d.* Adv. in the *Observator*, VII, No.
96, Wed. Jan. 12-Sat. Jan. 15, 1709. Listed as the
"Tenth Part of Poetical Reflexions, Moral, Comical,
Satyrical &c. on the Vices and Follies of the Age," No. 9.
There were 10 parts in all, sold separately at 6 *d.* each.
Not in BM Cat. or Morgan. No copy located.

68 February 15 *ca.*

Marlborough, Duke of (1650-1722)

The *Duke* of *Marlborough's* LETTER To the *Parliament*.
LONDON: Printed for *J. Smith*, near Fleetstreet. 1709.
1/2°: prose, 1 side. Badly printed, but evidence
of public interest. Bod.; TxU copy used. Not in Morgan.
Opens:
"HHS [*sic* for His] Grace the Duke of Marlborough
has done such eminent and Signal Service to the Government" that it would fill a large volume. "*As for Instance*, the *Famous Battel*, and Glorious Victory. . .his
Grace obtain'd over the Numerous French Army at Odinard
. . .while the Flower of their Army were Eye Witnesses
of it, without striking a Stroke." Refers to forcing the
French from the Scheld and taking Ghent and Bruge, raising the siege of Brussels. The Letter, dated February
13th at Brussels, is printed entire in Murray, IV, 441-2.
It expresses the Duke's satisfaction in the vote in Commons, and in his services to the Queen and his country.
He concludes: "I shall never think any pains or perse-
verance too great if I may, by God's blessing, be instrumental in procuring a safe and honourable peace for H. M.
and my fellow-subjects."
See No. 270 for March 3.

269 February 22.

An HEROICK ESSAY upon the UNEQUALED VICTORY Obtain'd by
Major-General Webb over the *Count De La Motte*, at WYNEN-
DALE. [ornament] *LONDON*, Printed, and Sold by *A. Baldwin* in *Warwick-Lane*. M. DCC. IX. Adv. *Daily Cour.*, No.
2286, Feb. 22, 1709. 164 lines, couplets.
       2°: A^2 B-C^2; t.p., *bl.*, 3-11, *bl.*, 12 pp. Drop-t.
on p. 3. Headline "An Heroick Essay" on top of each page.
TxU copy used. Morgan L168. Opens:

> *DELIA*, who once of Courts and Empires sung,
> The Lofty Muse subdu'd to Rural Song,
> Where silver *Medway* glides the Shades along.

A pastoral opening of twenty-two lines presents the Goddess of Love, her hair trailing to the ground, caresses
Mars, and then addresses Delia, who is ostensibly the
real poet, even though much of the remainder of the poem
is spoken by the Goddess. Quotation marks head each line.
       Delia is told that Webb is "as *Eugene* Brave, as *Marl-
bro'* Fortunate" (1. 28), an indication of Tory emphasis.
Inaccurate reporting of Webb's victory had been falsely
used against Marlborough; hence the allusion to being
"fortunate" rather than courageous and foresighted is a
slur. Webb's brilliant victory, on September 28, 1708,
assured passage of a convoy of munitions to the siege of
Lisle. On the French side, such troops as had been
spared "from *Blenheim*'s fatal Day" are massed to attack
the convoy.

> "*MARLBRO*'s good Fortune here stood at a gaze,
> "Dreadfully anxious how to tread the maze,
> "Fear'd this the Crisis of his Happy Days,
> "Th'Event the Factious *Britans* [*sic*] wait to see;
> "For *Lisle* untaken *Oudenard*'s no Victory.   60-4

Webb's triumph surpasses Alexander's, and even Marlborough thinks it "too big for War" (1. 86).
       The taking of Lisle and the spectacle of the French
king groveling are fruits of Webb's victory. As panegyric,
the poem is far from the worst; in the history of the form
it has interest. On direction from the Goddess, Delia
speaks eighteen lines, which identifies the author as

female and mentions several poets. She says:

"Unequal to the mighty Task my Muse,
"A Woman's Song (bright Goddess) they refuse:
"Cou'd ev'n *Orinda*, *Sappho* live again,
"*Sappho*, *Orinda*, they wou'd now disdain.   129-32

Even more interesting is allusion to Addison and Steele,
though not by the full name.

"For Notes so sweet young *Ad---son* was raised,
"He was rewarded too as well as prais'd.
"Ingrateful *St----le* forgets his former State,
"And former Friends, in his new Change of Fate;
"Nay, Critick D[ennis] in his declining Age
"Indulg'd, may leave turmoiling for the Stage. 133-8

Protesting that she is in a mournful state, Delia urges
that Addison be given the task to celebrate the victory,
to which the Goddess replies:

"Already to great *Marlbro'* he has sung,
"Nay every Muse for him the Lyre has strung.
"To Power like his new Trophys still are rais'd;
"Who can the most Reward, they mostly Praise. 148-51

The poem concludes with the claim that no new hero can
ever exceed Webb's triumph; no future hero will dare to
"rank his own with WEBB's Immortal Name" (1. 164).

70   March 3 *ca*.

Cowper, William, Lord Chancellor (*c*. 1665-1723) and
Marlborough, Duke of (1650-1722)

The *Ld. Chancellor's Speech* to the *Duke* of *Marlborough*,
and His Grace's ANSWER. *LONDON*: Printed for *T. King*
near *Fleetstreet*. n.d.
     1/2°: prose, 1 side, 36 lines, no wmk, torn edge.
Prose report, hastily printed with errors, such as inverted type. Horn copy used. Only copy located. Not
in Morgan. Opens:

"On *Tuesday* the 1st Instant, near Two a Clock, in
the Afternoon, his Grace the Duke of *Marlborough* came
through the City of *London* from *Flanders*, his Duchess
Sitting in the Coach with him, being heartily Welcom'd
all the Way by the joyful Shouts and Acclamations of the
people" The Peers unanimously ordered the Lord Chancellor
to express their thanks for his services, "particularly
for the Famous Victory over the *French* Army at *Audenard*
Commanded by the Princes of the Blood of *France*. That
taking of Lisle, passing the Scheld, relieving Brussels,
and reducing of Ghent and Bruges were acknowledged. The
Duke's ANSWER follows, in the third person. He was extremely sensible of the great honor, and thought no pains
too great if he might be instrumental in "procuring a
Safe, Firm, Lasting, and Honourable Peace for Her Majesty
and his Fellow Subjects."

Interest attaches to the document in that later in
the year Cowper stood in opposition to Marlborough's request to be made Captain-General for life.

271   March 8.

G., T., physician (fl. 1698 f.)

Scipio Britannicus: The Scourge of *France*. An Heroick
Poem, inscrib'd to the Immortal Glory of his Grace John
Duke of Marlborough, Prince of Mindelheim, &c. Also a
Latin Poem Annex'd To the Christian Hannibal, the most
Illustrious Prince Eugene of Savoy, &c. Sold by *B.*
Bragge in Pater-Noster-Row. Price 6 *d.*

Adv. in *Daily Cour.*, No. 2299. Tues. Mar. 8, 1709.
'This Day is publish'd.' Foxon rpts. Supplement gives
'for tomorrow' as by 'T. G.' Physician in Essex. *Ibid.*,
Mar. 10. 'Just published.' No copy known. Not in
Morgan.

T.G. also is credited with *Edeo Ophiambos*: being
England's Triumphs, 1698.

272   March 9.

The BEASTS in Power, or Robin's Song: with *An Old Cat's
Prophecy*. Taken out of an old copy of Verses, suppos'd
to be writ by John *Lidgate*, a monk of *Bury*. *London*,
Printed in the Year 1709.
        8VO: T.p., *bl.*, 3-4 *The Preface*, the poem 5-8,
drop-t. on p. 5. 155 lines, couplets. Satiric fable.
Morgan L30. *Preface*: the poet is at a bookseller's
buying some books. There he sees nine editions of Tom
Thumb, De Foe's Works, Jack Hall's *Life*, and the New Art
of Cookery. He observes that the Beasts are the passions,
and the work a moral piece. Actually it is anti-Marlborough satire. Opens:

        One that had in her Infant State,
        While playing at her Father's Gate,
        Seen, and was most hugely smitten
        With a young Dog and dirty Kitten.

The girl, Princess Anne, takes in the cat and dog when
she comes of age. They become domineering and evil. The
Dog joins a Wolf in ravaging the flocks he was set to
protect. Robin sings, revealing the perfidy of dog and
cat, saying they should be hanged. The Dog is Marlborough, the Cat his Duchess, and Robin is Harley. The
verse pr. in Anderson, Chalmers, *et al.* Robin-Harley
warns the Queen that the Beasts are stealing her sheep.
Morgan L30 calls this "a delightful satire." See *The
Eagle and the Robin*, 1709 below, No. 292.

3   March 10.

Blackmore, Sir Richard (1654-1729)

Instructions to Vander Bank, A Sequel to the *Advice to
the Poets*: A POEM, Occasion'd by the *Glorious Success*
of *Her Majesty*'s ARMS, under the Command of the Duke of
MARLBOROUGH, the last Year in *Flanders*. [ornamental
design] *London*: Printed for Egbert Sanger at the Post-
House in Fleetstreet. M.DCC.IX.

297

2°: A^2 B-C^2; t.p., bl., 3-12, 12 pp., drop-t. on
p. 3. 518 lines, couplets, both eds. H. Hills ed., 16
pp. 8vo, 1709. Horn copies of both eds. used. Also
reptd. with considerable changes in 1718 ed. of *Works*.
Clark-Luttr. copy '10 March.' Morgan L45. Opens:

> Have all thy Bards, *Britannia*, spent their Vein? ⎫
> Not one rich Genius left that can sustain ⎬
> Th' expensive Task of *Marlbro*'s last Campaign? ⎭

If the poets are exhausted, then the makers of rich
arras, in silk and golden threads, must undertake to
portray the victories, and "For *Blenheim*'s lofty Walls
the Work design" (1. 22). Not Classical heroes, but
modern, are to be shown. A spirited, though rather blood-
thirsty outlining of an equestrian battle picture of the
Duke follows, prancing horse, martial mien, with Fame and
Victory hovering overhead in clouds of battle smoke. This
becomes painfully realistic.

> Show Warriors quiv'ring in the Pangs of Death,
> Rolling their Eyes, and gasping out their Breath.
>   55-6

In a succession of imagined scenes for the Belgian artist
Vander Bank to weave, Blackmore achieves something more
graphic than panegyric had fallen into. The poem embraces all of the major victories and sieges, and brings
the conqueror home for a reception with an arch of triumph
and a column in his honor. Poetry still occupies a lowly
place.

> Then let the Bards in humble manner stand,
> With Distichs, Sonnets, Prologues in their Hand,
> In *Marlbro*'s Praise: 'Tis all, alas! we know
> That from their dry exhausted Springs can flow. 355-8

While Blackmore has not produced a great poem, he has
produced an impressive assemblage of all the imagery and
allegorical symbolism of war, liberation, and triumphant
justice.
Steele, in *Tatler* No. 3, April 16, 1709, pictures his
group going from the playhouse to the coffee-house, and
amusing themselves with Blackmore's poem, of which the

full title and extensive description are given. Blackmore is not named, and the satire is directed more against
the low state of poetry than his particular efforts. Poets
may now be instructing calico makers in the art of presenting scenes on petticoats. "Do you think there is a
girl in *England*, that would wear any Thing but *The Taking*
of Lisle or *The Battle* of Oudenarde?" Cf. Mary Tom Osborne, *op. cit.*, Nos. 107 and 120 above, *Advice to Mr.
Vario*. This is the last of four "painter" panegyrics
cited by Dr. Osborne, though of course it was to a weaver
of tapestry.

74   March *ca.* mid-month.

Aubin, Mrs. Penelope (fl. 1708-21)

THE WELCOME, A POEM TO HIS GRACE THE Duke of *MARLBOROUGH*.
[2 lines Horace; 5 lines French, La Doct. de Moeurs]   *By
Mrs*. AUBIN. *LONDON*: Printed for *John Morphew*, near *Stationer's-Hall*. 1708.
        4°: A-B^{4}C^2 cropt, t.p., *ii-iv*, 5-19, *bl.*, 20 pp.,
257 lines, couplets. DCL copy used; only one known.
Not in Morgan.
        Aubin, Penelope, fl. 1721. CBEL knows her only as
writer of minor plays and fiction. The work is dated
1708, which is O. S., but must have come after Marlborough's return on March 3, O. S., permitting the '1708'
date. Opens:

        From distant Climes, and long Fatigues return'd.
        To *Britain*'s Joyful Shoars, who trembling Mourn'd.

Marlborough's arrival is signalized, transporting Britain;
the crowd stands gazing on the beach, aged and young en-
tranced. Beyond a reference to her "blushing Muse," the
poet gives only slight clues to her status or identity.
She invokes the aid of "mighty Homer" (1. 76), but with
no apparent response as the verse is hardly heroic, let
alone Homeric. A single sample should suffice:

More than *Ulysses*, in Wise Councils skill'd,
A GOD, both in Council, and the Field;
Whom to Describe, thy Eloquence I want
Expressions seem too weak, and Numbers scant:
Great *Virgil*'s Softness, and sweet *Ovid*'s Stile,
To speak Great *Marlborough*, Wonder of our Isle.
Faintly, Alas! Thy shining Virtues must be shown,
Since Admiration, we by silence must make known.

                                              88-95

It is not to be wondered that this poem seems to have
survived in only one copy, as it lacks value as poetry,
or even as a tribute of welcome. No descriptions of
battle are attempted, and only the hide-and-seek maneuverings following Oudenarde, with such names as Soignes,
Helchin, and Dender, remind the reader that warfare is
involved at all. The enemy fades away, and "the Mounted
Cannon roar not" (1. 219). Where so little is attempted
failure can scarcely be alleged. No climax is attained,
and only one Homeric simile is introduced, but with little
effect. Marlborough in the concluding lines is urged to
live long, "with all the Favours crown'd, that ever Man
possest" L. 255), but his survival could hardly derive
from such verse.

275 April 2.

[Earbery, Matthias (fl. 1709-22)]

THE BATTEL OF OUDENARDE. A POEM In Two CANTO's. [2 lines
Latin, unsgnd.] *NORWICH*: Printed by *Henry Cross-grove*,
MDCCIX.
       2°: P2, *A*² B-E²; *bl.*, *iii* To the High and Mighty
Princess ANNE OF *Great Britain*, *France*, and *Ireland*,
QUEEN, Defender of the Faith, This Poem Dedicated. . .;
bl., *v* nmbd. '*iii*'; drop-t. for each Canto, pp. 5 and 13.
To the Right Honourable CHARLES Ld. Viscount *Townshend*,
Baron of *LYN-REGIS*, Lord Lieutenant of the County of *Nor-
folk*. . .Presents the poem to Townshend, not knowing why

this age has produced more Great Captains than Great
Poets. *vii-viii* The *Printer* to the *Reader* (see below);
the poem pp. 5-20, 24 pp., 468 lines, but misdated, ascribed to Laurence Eusden, but Griffith questioned this.
Foxon reports MH copy with name. Horn-Luttr. copy used.
'6 *d.* 2. Aprill.' Clark has. Morgan L312, but erroneously also K316.

    "The *Printer* to the *Reader*
        "Gentle Reader, I have observ'd Four Things
very hard to be found in these Days, *viz.* a Panegyric
without Flattery, a Satyr without Malice, a Prophecy
without Enthusiasm, and a Poem without Obscenity or Pro-
faness [*sic*]." The writer hopes his poem free from these
faults of poetical fiction. "Some ingenious Men do con-
fidently affirm, that the *Spanish* Monarchy was ruin'd by
Don Quixot, the Good Old Cause by *Hudibras*, the *Rye*
Plotters by *Absolom* and *Achitophel*, the Army on *Hounslow-
heath* by *Lilly-bullero*, and the whole system of Popery by
the *Country* and *City Mouse* of *Montague* and *Prior*." He is
not sure, "but if the Poetic Tribe could banter the *French*
out of the Honour of Fighting for Honour, the *Britains*
for Liberty, the *Dutch* for Trade, and the *Germans* for Pay,
it would be a very great work," and a step toward "General
Peace." The piece shows considerable skill at banter, and
deals with political parties and the fate of one "Mrs.
Church" in the conflict for power among Papists, High and
Low Church, and other groups. The poem falls below the
promise in this address. It opens:

    What Man with Thirst of glorious Acts would burn,
    Till *Prior*'s Muses to the Court return?

Yet he will sing the events of France's fall. In an extended picture we are shown French conquests, and Louis
XIV utters a long discourse to his grandsons to relieve
his "*Blenheim*-Pain." Churchill's valor is revealed and
France's plight since he is irresistible. He is inter-
rupted by young Berry, who outlines a hope that Churchill
may be overwhelmed by their numbers, and that via Scotland they may overcome English projects, and their Te Deum
be sung in St. Paul's.
    Canto II, though promising to detail events, is domi-
nated by visions of Angelic figures and abstract reflec-

tions of war. Her soldiers approach conflict "as if their Hands were clean," and yet their land produces the poisonous juice of *Toland*, *Hobbs*, or *Blount*. The poem is not very effective politically, certainly not as military panegyric. Its main interest lies in its being printed outside London and its reflection of moderate religious views. Oudenarde is reviewed, particularly in its termination by the coming on of night in which the French slink away.

> Amaz'd at this the *Brittish* Army stands,
> And drops the Laurel from her bloody Hands;
> The *French* the Signal knew, and haste away,
> Bless the dark Night, and curse the conscious Day.
>
> 465-8

276 April 5 *ca.*

The Progress of Valour: A Poem. Humbly Inscrib'd to His Grace the Duke of *Marlborough*. [3 lines Virgil] *London*, Printed for *A. Baldwin*, in *Warwick-Lane*, 1709. Price Two-Pence.

    8VO: *i-iv*, 5-16, 16 pp. 267 lines, couplets. InU, Clark, CtY. CSmH copy used. Morgan L248. Adv. in *Post-Boy*. No. 2068. Tues. Apr. 5, 1709. 'Just Publish'd.' The Publisher to the Reader: "The following Lines coming to me by an unknown Hand" and showing great genius, and love of country and of the Duke of Marlborough, "thought it my Duty to make them Publick." Opens:

> Whilst Saturn rul'd the awful World in Peace,
> And Golden Ages did the Nations bless.

Then virtue prevailed, till Jove came, and Fame's loud voice enticed to war. The War with the Gyants brought a race of heroes: Alcides, Achilles, Aeneas; then Alexander, Caesar, and then valor flew from Rome to Britain. What muse can sing them all, William the Conqueror, the Plains of Cressy and Poictier, Edward, till mighty Nassau came, "To purge Religion from the Clouds of Rome" (1. 185). All leads up to Marlborough. The Danube streams and plains of Ramilly tell of his exploits.

> Let a swift Cannon-Ball the *Hero* meet,
> And fall a Suppliant at his Feet.   249-50

A thousand fine things go undisplayed. Such mighty things require a stronger plume: "Immortal *Addison* must touch the Lyre," (1. 260) or Prior in verses like his *Phoebus.* This theme of the need for silent Addison to speak out is persistent and unsatisfied throughout Marlborough's career.

277 April 7.

Newcomb, Thomas, of *Sussex* (1682?-1762)

AN EPISTLE from the DUKE of *BURGUNDY* to the FRENCH KING. [Mottoes in 3 lines from Hallifax and 2 lines from Stepney] By Tho. Newcomb, of *Stopham* in *Sussex. London*: Printed for *J. Tonson* at *Grays-Inn* Gate. 1709.
2°: A^2 B-C^2; t.p., *bl.*, *iii-iv* To the Right Honourable William Lord Cowper, Baron Wingham, Lord High Chancellor of Great Britain, &c. sgnd. 'Tho. Newcomb.' Drop-t. p. 1. Morgan L297. Horn-Luttr. copy '4 *d.* 7. April1.' MH, TxU (2). Deplores his inadequacy. No worthy picture can appear "'till some happy Genius, that directed our Armies to Conquer, shall finish his own Character, and his Nation's Glory, in the Description of Her Triumphs..." Drop-t. on p. 1, wmk. fleur-de-lis. 1-8, 12 pp. The poem is in 107 4-line stanzas, rhymed a-b-a-b, 428 lines. It opens:

> SIR,
>   If yet unmindful of Ramillia's Field,
>   Her Fatal Plains are lost, and bleed no more;
>   If *Blenheim*'s Wounds forgot, *no Terrors* yield;
>   And *Danube* rolls along, a guiltless Shore.

Burgundy appeals to Louis XIV to permit him to win honors in amours, in softer wars, as the King has done. Nothing can stop the British Leader, and this has been the story since Cressy and Poictiers. The poem summarizes Marlborough's victories, stressing Blenheim and Ramillies, down

to Lille, and points out how French troops always flee
before him. The point of the poem is to urge Louis to
accept a peace, and to escape further punishment from
Marlborough.

> Before her numerous Squadrons croud the Field,
>   To save your All, let ANNA be Implor'd:
> To her resistless Troops your *Flanders* yield,
>   And cheaply buy your Peace, with *Spain* restor'd.
>   405-8

April 28.

278 Welsted, Leonard (1688-1743)

The Duke of Marlborough's ARRIVAL. A POEM. Humbly Inscrib'd To the Right Honourable LIONEL, Earl of *Dorset*
and *Middlesex*, &c. [1 line Virgil] *London* Printed for
J. Gouge, at the *Castle* in *Westminster-Hall*; and are to
be sold by *A. Baldwin* in *Warwick-Lane*. 1709.
    2°: A^2 B-C^3; t.p., *bl.*, *iii-iv* Dedication to Earl
of Dorset, sgnd. 'Leonard Welsted'; text 1-4, 12 pp.
Drop-t. on p. 1. 124 lines, couplets. Clark-Luttr. copy
used, '4 *d*. 28 April.' Morgan L440.
    Dedication seeks favor and patronage of Dorset
throughout. "...to this Name 'tis we owe that Ornament
of Verse and Pride of Poetry, the incomparable PRIOR,
who writes what none but he could excel, under whose
Encouragement he grew and flourished." The poem opens:

> Soon as Bleak Northern Winds had froze [*sic*] the Air,
> And made the *British* Hero cease from War.

The Dutch strive to keep him, but finally release him
with prayers, cursing the "hasty Winds that bore him
thence" (1. 11). He is addressed by an allegorical Holland, and urged to return soon, "since *Auverquerque* and
Orange are no more" (1. 27). The vessel traverses the
seas, accompanied by Nereids and Tritons, who sing of
Hochsted, the *Danube*, and *Ramillia*'s Plains, and then
Audenarde and Gallia's shame. The poem is largely given
over to goddesses and allegorical figures. After the hero
lands, Britannia's Genius addresses him, bearing the
Union Cross, the Northern Thistle and Rose joined. He

prophesies that "every Rising Bard the Man shall tell"
(1. 122). Not a very effective poem, but another contribution to a minor genre which might be called the
"Return" poem.

279 May 24

ALCANDER: A POEM, Occasion'd by the VICTORIES of his
GRACE the Duke of MARLBOROUGH. [ornament] *LONDON*:
Printed for *J. Morphew*, near *Stationer's-Hall*. 1709.
        2°: A^1 B-E^2 F; t.p., *bl*., 1-16; 17 Verses occa-
sioned by the foregoing POEM, *18 bl*., 20 pp. Drop-t. on
p. 1, errata p. 17. Wmk. FD on A^1; rest EB and Lion and
Unicorn Arms. 327 lines, couplets. Horn-Luttr., only
known copy, used. '6 *d*. 24. May.' No other markings.
Morgan L246. Opens:

> ALCANDER Wise by long Experience grown,
> Gave this Grave Counsel to his Youthful Son.

The old man advises his son to read Tillotson with care,
if he wishes to enter the Church, or to understudy Cowper,
with his wit and eloquence, if he thinks of Law. But if
neither Pulpit nor Bar appeal, he should not become a
vain and idle fop. The heroes of the days of Agincourt,
Cressy and Poictiers were not such, nor are they in Marlborough's troops. He reviews the famous list of victories, Schellenberg, Blenheim, Ramillies, Audenarde, and
the Scheld. Lewis is urged not to condemn his forces,
and the old theme of the Danube drowning is revived as
an inspiration.

> See! In the *Danube*, plung'd by Hostile Force,
> Horseman on Horseman rouls, and Horse on Horse,
> Brigade falls on Brigade ----------
> The River quickly felt the Mighty Load.   140-3

The Danube is astonished, but it hurries to the sea to
send the news to the Thames, Po, Tagus, and Rhine, and
of course the Seine. Blenheim surpasses Arbela and other
Classical victories. Praise goes from the victories to

London, and especially to St. Paul's Cathedral, to "*Wren*'s Immortal Praise," as it touches the sky with its "lofty Cupola" (1. 269). England and Queen Anne's glory are happily associated with learning and eloquence, and a considerable array of names: Tillotson, Cowper, Sommers, Stanhope, Moss, Fleetwood, Adams, Duke, Atterbury; the skill of Newton and Harris in science; in theology, Lloyd, Caven, Pearson, Burnet, Stillingfleet, and Tenison; and in state affairs Pembroke and Godolphin, who gives the soldier nerves. To Anne, he says: "Great MARLBRO' has enlarg'd the Bounds of thy Renown" (1. 306). The *Verses*, only 20 lines, are addressed to the Maker of the World and envision the future, and now his muse will "leave Blenheim and mount above the Sky."

280   May 25.

A Poem: 1. On the *Prospect* of *Peace*, 2 stanzas; II. The *Reverse*: III. The *Return*, 5 stanzas, four hailing Anne, the 5th on Marlborough.

> *Trophies* of *Praise* are also due,
> Great MARLBOROUGH to *You*.

He is urged to rest on his laurels, "the Greatest *Gen'ral* of the Age. In *Brit. Apollo*, Vol. II, No. 17, Fri. May 20th to Wed. May 25th, 1709. 31 lines.

281   July 22.

On the Taking of Tournay. 123 lines, couplets, Pr. in *Brit. Apollo*, II, No. 34, Wed. July 20th to Fri. July 22d, 1709.

> GREAT MARLBOROUGH -
> But thou hast drain'd our Language with   Fame,
> Nor have we *Epithets* to speak thy *Name*.
> Our *Silence* then will taller Trophies raise,
> Since 'tis not in our Pow'r to sing thy *Praise*.

282 July 25.

C., W. [William Churchill]

A POEM Humby Inscrib'd to His GRACE the *Duke* of *Marlborough*, Occasion'd upon his *Repeated Victories* in *Flanders*.
[2 lines Latin, unsgnd.]   Wrote in the CAMP by *W. C.* and
Officer of Major General *How*'s Regiment. *LONDON*:   Printed
for *Benjamin Bragg*, at the *Raven*, in *Pater-Noster-Row*.
MDCCIX.
    2°: A^2 B-D^2; t.p., *bl.*, *ii-iv* To the Right Honour-
able Lieutenant General CADOGAN; 1-12, 16 pp.   Drop-t.
on p. 1. Wtmk. Arms and T. B.   To Cadogan, 28 lines;
Poem, 400 lines, couplets, total 428.   Horn copy used,
marked in MS. "Enter'd," and pp. 235-50 nmbd. in MS.   Not
in Morgan. The Dedication opens:

> *Whilst Marlbro' waves, like Mars, his Conquering
>   Arms,
> And Eugene frightens Lisle with loud Alarms.*

Asks Cadogan to condescend to bear his lines "wrote in
Camp, to Godlike *Marlbro's* War" (1. 12).   Laments his
inadequacy to Cadogan's praise. The Poem opens:

> Ye tuneful *Nine*, that drink the purling Stream
> Of Silver *Helicon*, inspire my Theme.

The poet urges the Muses to review the book of heroes,
Trojan and Roman, down to Gustavus and Nassau. After
sufficiently establishing classical knowledge and precedent, the Muse fixes on Marlborough. Phoebus admires
Hochstedt's Immortal Field and Ramillia's Plain more than
the achievements of Hector and Caesar. Even so, further
classical allusions emphasize Marlborough's primacy.
Maro sang Arcadian kings,

> But *Lewi*'s [*sic*] Heads lopt off by Marlbro's Sword,
> A loftier Theme and hardie Task afford.   65-6

Two Kingdoms, France and Austria, confronted each other.
Germany was helpless as France seized Belgian towns. But
Queen Anne sends Marlborough and at Blenheim (W. C.
spells it *Blenhiem*), he makes the Danube surpass the

Xanthus. But France, undismayed, follows Richelieu's
and Mazarine's schemes; she deploys new forces in Belgium. These too are destroyed on the Judoigne (i.e. at
Ramillies).
Now Lewis listens to Maintenon and Vendome, who
drains adjacent garrisons. Marlborough "detects his Mo-
tions, and dreading his sword, Vendome stops at *Brain-
lelew*" (1. 194). He sends out strong parties to "amuse,"
that is baffle, Marlborough. But Marlborough follows
closely and encamps at Hall. Here the enemy decamp pre-
cipitately, and march away leaving their baggage. Paris
and factious Scots look on maliciously and celebrate an
anticipated victory. But Eugene now comes to join the
Duke. Cadogan is sent to attempt the Scheld, and Prus-
sians, Danes, and Hollanders advance with German cavalry,
of Saxony, Wirtemberg, and Hannover. The battle is
swift, and again Marlborough has a glorious Victory at
Audenarde. The battle is not named, but, without being
great poetry, or hardly poetry at all, the description
supplies details of maneuver and some of the tensions of
conflict, particularly the invasion of Belgian towns,
Webb's triumph at Wynendale (11. 337-8), and the Siege
of Lisle (11. 339-40). William Churchill, being a relative,* is not less inclined to set Marlborough in the
line of Classical heroes; he returns to Hannibal and
then to Cyrus and Philip of Macedon. The Duke's victories will assure Anne's recognition as the rightful
sovereign by French Lewis (1. 392), and peace for Europe
as well. Marlborough combines the bravery of Ajax and
the wisdom of Ulysses, for he "has Wisdom, Conduct,
Brav'ry Joyn'd in One" (1. 400).

---

*William and his brother Awnsham were sons of Marl-
borough's brother General George Churchill. Murray
Letters and Dispatches of Marlborough, from 1702 to
1712, 1845, V, 42.

283   September 1.

Cobb, Samuel (1675-1713)

THE FEMALE REIGN: An ODE, Alluding to *Horace*, B. 4, Od.

14. *Quae Cura Patrum, quaeve Quiritium*, &c. Attempted
in the Style of *Pindar*. Occasion'd by the wonderful
Successes of the Arms of Her MAJESTY and Her Allies.
With a Letter to a Gentleman in the University. By
Samuel Cobb, M. A. *LONDON*: Printed for *J. Woodward*,
in St. *Christopher*'s Church-Yard, in *Threadneedle-
street*. MDCCIX. Price 6 *d*.
    2°: A^2 B-D^2; t.p., *bl*., *iii-iv* sgnd. 'S. C.,' 5-15,
bl., 16 pp. Drop-t. p. 5. ICN, ICU, TxU. MH-Luttr.
copy used, '4 *d*. 1. Sept.' Foxon records "Present from
the Author 13 Sept. 1709" on MH copy. 304 lines, ode.
8° ed. Printed by *H. Hills*, and Sold by the Booksellers
of *London* and *Westminster*, 1709. A^8; t.p., *bl*., 5-16,
16 pp. Horn copy used. 302 lines, 14 ode st., ll. 127-8
missing; otherwise only mechanical alterations. Footnotes preserved. Morgan L81.

    In the *Letter* Cobb congratulates the Oxford Gentle-
man on the successes, leaving it for him to read about
them in the newspapers. They "will furnish noble Topics
for the Wits of the University, like Yours." He dis-
cusses the problems of imitating the classical ode, and
Rapin's remark that it is better to read Pindar than the
best critics. The Ode opens:

> What can the *British Senate* give
> To make the Name of ANNA live?

Painting and statues are inadequate for Queen Anne. She
is "Greatest of Princes" (1. 20), and has brought treble
ruin on false electors and perjured kings. Marlborough
is praised for Blenheim, Ramillies, and Audenard, and for
his courage and calm in battle; so also Eugene "his partner in danger and in fame" (1. 174). Eugene's victories
over the Turks are swiftly reviewed, and Webb's at Wynendale. The final Stanza XIV returns to the title theme.

> A FEMALE REIGN, like Thine
> O ANNA, *British* Heroine!
> To Thee afflicted Empires fly for Aid.   281-3

She brings peace, and doom to those who oppose her.
J. Nichols pub. in *Select Collection*, VII, with six

other Cobb poems. Calls attention of Dodsley to Dr.
Watts's remark that he "thought it the truest and best
Pindaric he had ever read." Also in Pearch, Suppl. to
Dodsley's *Coll.*, I, 78-90.

284 September 15 *ca.*

To the *Duke* of *Marlborough*, Upon the Late VICTORY at
BLAREGNIES. London: Printed by *E. Berington*, for *E.
Sanger*, at the *Post House* at the *Middle Temple-Gate*.
1709.
    1/4°: 2 sides, 1 column. BM copy used; Crawford.
7 4-line stanzas, 28 lines, alternate rhyming. Not in
Morgan. Opens:

>   Tho' bold the Muse, yet scarce she dares assay,
>   Too High th'Attempt for Her Advent'rous Wing.

The swiftness of Marlborough's sword and conquests made
it seem that Ramillies would stand as the utmost limits
of heroic fame. But never has virtue been so severely
tried. Since Blaregnies is a village in the field of
Malplaquet, this determines that this victory, though
unspecified, is in mind. Actually Marlborough was encamped at Blaregnies, and from there he dated his letters
to Boyle and Stanhope, on the 11th and 13th, announcing
the victory. This may well be the first panegyric on
Malplaquet. As has been indicated, these were very few,
and none used that name.

285 October 20.

A LETTER TO A FRIEND, Upon the *Successes* of the Year
M.DCC.VIII. [2 lines Claudian] [Handsome ornament, two
winged cupids' heads, beneath a formal basket of flowers
and butterflies] *LONDON*: Printed for *Tho. Ward* in the
Inner-Temple Lane, and are to be sold by *J. Morphew*
Stationers-Hall. 1709.
    2°: A^1 B-D^2; t.p., *bl.*, 1-12, 14 pp., but perhaps

Half-t. missing. No drop-t. No wmk. 507 lines, couplets. Horn-Luttr. '4 *d*. 20 Octob.' Adv. in *Tatler*, No.
83. Tues. Octob. 18-20; No. 90, Nov. 3-5. Morgan L230.
Opens:

> SIR,
> Tho' *Flandria* calls our Glorious Chief away,
> And envies *Britain* scarce a Months short stay.

There will be new conquests, but since his friend wishes
to learn about the war, he will attempt a "plain Story,"
even though he is neither warrior nor poet; he is a
stranger to the combining of Spencer and Horace used by
Prior to sing of Marlborough.

The year begins with the attempted invasion of Scotland by the Pretender. He is told he should go back to
amorous pursuits and Old Lewis to his scheming. Later
Marlborough awaits the French on the plain of Flanders,
and Audenarde is fought. Marlborough and Eugene again
fight together. The poet turns back to William and the
Boyne for comparisons. Next is the Siege and taking of
Lille (Lisle) in which Vauban's greatest defences are
overcome. Webb and Wynendale with Boufflers yielding
come next, and then Brussels is taken. The poet apologizes for offending his friend, but he must go on to the
end. The remainder of the poem praises Anne's virtue and
her inspiring of Marlborough. If the hero would leave
but one year without great deeds the muses might look
back and then try to catch up with him.

> Not *Addison* himself with *Virgil*'s Force,
> Nor *Prior*, seated on his *Pindar* Horse,
> Can stretch so far.   494-6

He concludes by apologizing for the rude draughts of an
inexperienced muse. The writer reveals his admiration
for Addison, by whom Marlborough and Eugene "shall for
ever live" (1. 200).

[Manley, Mrs. Mary de la Rivere (1663-1724)]

*Secret Memoirs and Manners of several Persons of Quality,
of Both Sexes.* From the *New Atalantis*, an Island in the
Mediteranean [*sic*]. *Written Originally* in *Italian.* London: Printed for *John Morphew* near *Stationer's Hall*, and
J. Woodward in St. *Christopher's* Church-yard in *Thread-
needle-street.* 1709. 8ᵛᵒ, vi, 246. Pt. II, 1709.
    Pubd. in 4 vols., with the *Memoirs of Europe*, 2 pts.,
as Vols. III & IV, (1710) in 1720. Vol. II was published
on October 20, 1709, Vol. III by May, 1710, I and IV in
November following. Dates given in the excellent article
by Gwendolyn B. Needham, "Mary De le Riviere Manley, Tory
Defender," *HLQ*, XII, No. 3, May 1949, p. 264.
    All the volumes continue the attack launched during
the elections in 1705, *The Secret History of Queen Zarah*,
etc. A Key is printed at the end of Vol. I of the Sixth
Edition, 1720. A mingling of amorous intrigues, political and military maneuvering, and more or less disguised
allusions to Marlborough and his Duchess, Godolphin, and
innumerable other personages make the typical Manleyesque
appeal to voracious readers. Both Marlboroughs are represented as ambitious, scheming, and avaricious. Some of
the juicy details appear to have come from the Duchess of
Cleveland, King's mistress, with whom Marlborough had an
affair quite as dashing and triumphant as his later military exploits. The importance of this and the other productions of Mrs. Manley lies principally in their relation
to Swift and the Tory propaganda of reaction which was opposed by Dr. Francis Hare, *q.v.*
    Morgan L243.

287   December 8.

Butler, Richard (no dates)

The British Michael, An Epistolary Poem to a Friend in the
Country, By Richard Butler, A. M. [7 lines Horace, Lib.
Ep. 1] *London*: Printed by *J. Matthews*; and Sold by

William Lewis at the *Dolphin*, next *Tom*'s Coffee-House in
Russel Street, Covent-Garden. MDCCX.
2°: A² B-L²; t.p., *bl.*, *iii-iv* Dedication; 1-39, *40
bl.*, 46 pp. Drop-t. p. 1, running t. *British Michael*,
left, and *Epistolary Poem*, right, throughout. Not in
Morgan.
    Adv. in Defoe's *Rev.*, No. 105, Dec. 6, through No. 127,
Jan. 28, 1710, 'for W. Lewis and Sold by J. Woodward and
J. Morphew. (Price 1 *s.* 6 *d.*)'; in *Tatler*, No. 104,
Dec. 6-8, 1709, "Printed by John Matthews and Sold by
William Lewis and John Morphew." 840 lines, couplets.
University of Michigan copy used. Also in BM. Not in
Morgan.
    The Dedication is addressed to four men, all Marlbor-
ough's sons-in-law: John, Duke of Montague; Scroop, Earl
of Bridgwater; Charles, Earl of Sunderland; and Francis,
Lord Viscount Rialton. The poet would like to dedicate
to Marlborough, but knowing his modesty, has preferred to
get "as near His Grace's Person, as he cou'd," and has
been unable to select any one of the sons-in-law over the
others. Hence he has addressed his poem to all four. The
poem opens:

    To You, dear *Damon*, long my faithful Friend,
    From Scenes of *Noise*, to *Silent* Shades I send.

Butler deplores the venality of the city where "Great Mens
Vices" and distractions "warp a Writer's Will" (1. 17).
He has promised to write an account of Churchill's life,
and as the poem progresses it becomes evident that he is
defending Marlborough's deeds against a sceptic. He makes
no apology for using the "less grave" way of writing in
verse as his friend has seen his early efforts in that
form. The sacred dress he wears, as a cleric of course,
forbids a lie. He has no ambitions, nothing to gain,
and will give a true account. Actually his poem is
weighted down with moralizing and superfluous similes in
the classical tradition; but he does supply estimates of
leading battles and the nature of conflict, which he
justifies in face of its bloody, violent character.
    He is praising Marlborough, not because of his success,
his wide command, nor the favor of public and Queen, but

because of his "true Worth." He once was amazed at
these great deeds, but closer contact has brought familiarity. He urges Damon to see Marlborough as truly
favored by Heaven. His Herculean labors have made him
great, but he is also truly good. Mars and Venus never
were so surely reflected as in his marriage. A vision
of his name on Fame's spire, and his seat on a diamond
throne while a chorus of Angels sings introduce the
theme of his godlike character, so popular with many
poets.

Now begins the summary of past deeds, looking back
to Hochstedt, that is Blenheim. With this victory the
Danube hid her head in shame, and Caesar owes his crown
to Marlborough's sword, that is the Empire was saved.
Then Audenard, the recent victory. Here the British
cross a stream too deep for horses and too swift for
men, to attack a greatly superior force. They waver,
but Marlborough arrives and turns the tide. Then the
poem returns to Schellenberg, to show that Marlborough
can be stopped neither by a river nor by a mountain.
The attack against the steep, formidable heights is
quite vividly recounted. Streams stagnate with blood,
flowers are crushed, and trees flattened by the storm
of battle. Again Marlborough's presence spells victory as he revives the will of the troops. Tournay's
wall and the siege of a city come next, and finally the
poet gives his greatest attention to Ramillies, the
great battle which proved that Marlborough did not need
Eugene. His sceptical friend has raised the question,
"What about Eugene?" This was of course a leading Tory
jab. The Duke is shown in battle after the clash of
armies which shakes the earth like an earthquake or a
thunderstorm. Marlborough remains unmoved, "something
Divine" in his appearance, and before his sword whole
squadrons fly.

Little is made of the theme of Michael, but the comparison is introduced in lines 628-35, where Marlborough
is hailed as the "MICHAEL of our Armies fight." The
long poem concludes with tributes to the four beautiful
daughters, although "the grave Robes" he wears dictate
against the poet's dwelling on their beauty, wit and
youth, nor on the "bright Consort of the HERO's Bed."

He makes a final appeal to Damon to become "a *Convert*, and a *Patriot* too," by accepting Marlborough (1. 816), and somewhat strangely, to see Marlborough as the father of the dead son.

> What MARLBRO' *was*, and *is*, with Wonder seen,
> Show what the bury'd BLANDFORD wou'd have been.
>
>   821-2

    This appears to be an appeal from a mild Tory to a more vehement one in favor of Marlborough, particularly on the basis of his entire career when his star was fading. Its absence from Morgan is evidence of its rarity, yet it is one of the handsomest productions, as printing, in the whole roster of Marlborough panegyric.

88 [Browne, Joseph (fl. 1706-14)]

THE CIRCUS: OR, *BRITISH OLYMPICS*. A SATYR ON THE RING in *Hide-Park*. *Sunt quos Curriculo Pulverem Olympicum. Collegisse juvat.* Horat. Ode. I. *LONDON*: Printed and Sold by the Booksellers of *London* and *Westminster*. 1709. *Price One Penny.*
    8°: A⁸; t.p., *bl.*, 3-4, Preface; 5-15, *16* Catalogue of poems printed and sold by H. Hills, 16 pp. Half-t. p. 5. Morgan L75, cites another ed. 1717. Also repr. in *State and Miscellany Poems*, II, 221-9. 300 lines, couplets. Horn copy used.
    The Preface expounds the satirist's situation, when prudishness and over-nicety are in vogue. Ironically professes intent to satirize those who seek reason and good sense rather than the dress and manners of the beaumonde. Opens:

> From vulgar Eyes, on Plains exalted high,
> Where noble Dust does in Confusion fly.

An allusion to Blenheim suggests perhaps written earlier, in 1705.

> Blush, Britons, then, that here you tamely yield
> The Trophies won on *Blenheim*'s dustier Field;

Where your brave Ancestors rejoyc'd to see
Honour retriev'd by their Posterity.
But see how soon the blooming Flow'r is gone,
With'ring beneath the Coldness of the Moon! 18-23

The poets grow heavy and dull, neglecting their natural
subject for love and fantasies.
While the poem is primarily a satire in which satirical portraits of fine ladies and gentlemen anticipate
Young and Pope, much later, it may portray Marlborough,
p. 11, as Manlius:

> *Manlius* thro' all the City does proclaim
> His Arms, his Equipage, and Ancient Name;
> For search the Court of Honour, and you'll see
> Manlius his Name, but not his Pedigree.   173-5

A reference naming Marlborough appears in 1. 250. Speaking of gaudy colors, the line states, "For House-Painting,
Marlb'rough is only known," an allusion that is inscrutable even in its context. The interest in the poem lies
chiefly in the role of Browne, and Oldisworth, to whom
the *State and Miscellany Poems* is usually ascribed, in
panegyrics and here in satire.

289 The Duke of M. Catechism. [large ornamental block M]
h *LONDON*: Printed in the Year, 1709.
    8vo: no sigs., t.p., 2-8, 8 pp. No pub. U Kansas
only known copy. Drop-t. p. 2, '*The Duke of* M----'s
Catechise' [*sic*]. Prose pamphlet. Cropped, with top
line of p. 5 missing. Not in Morgan.
    Crudely printed, with inverted letters and misspel-
lings. In a dialogue between Soldier and Countryman, and
'Answer,' who is the 'centinel' whom the Soldier passes
off as the Duke of Marlborough. The scene is at St.
James's.
    An interesting item as strongly favoring a peace with
the French tyrant. The style is marked by a hearty, rural
tone. Countryman has told his wife Joan of his desire to
speak with the Duke. He has "rid many a dirty Mile" to
see his Grace. He says he has "about 90 Pound a Yeor [*sic*]

Land of my own: I have paid 100 *l.* Taxes this War'.' (p. 4).
He details terms of the peace, particularly that Louis XIV
call home his grandson and free Spain, as well as surrendering much gold and the West Indies. Countryman returns
home to his plough well satisfied with the prospect, and
also with the disappointing of several Tory rogues who
are seeking to escape the "Press."

290 *The Life and History of John Duke of Marlborough, Prince*
of the Empire, Captain-General of the Confederate Forces,
containing several remarkable Passages, from his first
Advancement in the Court of Charles the 2d to this pres-
ent Time; and a Relation of the most Important Battles,
Seiges [*sic*]*, and Negotiations, both in the Wars of*
Flanders and Ireland; with full and particular Accounts
of the Battles of Hochstet, Schellenberg, and Ramillies.
The Third Edition. With the Addition of the Three last
Campaigns. . .Printed for Arthur Collins, at the Black-
Boy in Fleetstreet. Just Publish'd. *Post-Boy* No. 1274,
Thurs. Dec. 8-10, 1709.
     This advertisement the only information. No copy
known. The repeated editions suggest considerable popu-
larity. Not in Morgan.
     Another edition is described in *Post-Boy*, No. 2358,
Thurs., June 22 to Sat., June 24, 1710. The names of
Audenarde, Wynendale, and Blaregnies are added, as also
the statement: "Likewise some curious Letters, and
Pieces, relating to the Negotiations of Peace, never
before made Publick." Printed for A. Collins, at the
Black-Boy in Fleetstreet. Pr. bound, 1s 6d.

1 On the QUEENs *Most Glorious Victories* Over the French
KING.
     1/2°: 1 side, 1 column, no pub., n.d. BM, OCU, CtY,
TxU. 24 lines, couplets. Poem pr. in italics. Yale copy
used. Not in Morgan. Opens:

     The *Macedonian Youth*, whose *Mighty Name*
     Once fill'd the *Earth* with *Terror* and with *Fame.*

Alexander weeps at no more worlds to conquer, and then a
woman conquers him. So now Lewis yields up his honors
to a Woman, *i.e.* Anna.

> SHE *Conquers* only the Opprest to save,
> And *Scourges* Him that wou'd the *World* enslave. 23-4

292 G., H.

King, William (1663-1712) ?

The Eagle and the Robin. An apologue, Translated from the
Original *Aesop*; written Two Thousand Years since, and now
rendered into familiar verse. By H. G. *L. Mag.* With an
old cat's prophecy. Taken out of an old copy of verses,
supposed to be writ by John Ludgate, a monk of Bury. A
Poem. *London*, printed by *J. Read*, 1709. 8vo. Also H.
Hills and John Morphew eds., both 1709. Morgan L150 accepts what appears to be an ironic attribution as to
H[oratio] G[ram], Master of Laws; but Anderson, Chalmers,
et al. ascribe to King. The poem seems to be inconsistent
with King's other satires, in spite of the note in Chalmers, IX, 289-90, as Robin-Harley is harshly treated,
while the Eagle (Marlborough) is glorified. Chalmers ed.
used. 237 lines, couplets. Opens:

> A Lady liv'd in former days,
> That well deserv'd the utmost praise.

She admits a stranger who bears a wet, miserable robin,
and then finds that, after she has given the bird a home,
he drives out the others, the "party-colored" birds, gold-
finches and all. This hardly puts Harley in a good light.
On the other hand the Eagle only resists the Robin, "He
being the very soul of war" (1. 62). Robin takes a pen
and seeks to undermine the Eagle, who disdains him, and
spares him "for the lady's sake" (1. 99). The Robin does
injure an eye of the Eagle. The Eagle ranges far, winning many victories, and giving security at home. Robin
says:

Ungrateful I, that have so stirr'd
Against this generous, noble bird.   137-8

Thousands of jackdaws fall before the Eagle, none able to
withstand his power. He returns home, and the Lady says:

My faithful Eagle, hast thou then
My mortal foes destroy'd again?
Return, return, and on me wait;
Be thou the guardian of my gate.   222-4

The Eagle soars high, and all is secure for the Lady.
This seems to be altogether pro-Marlborough.

93   [Maynwaring, Arthur (1668-1712)]

The Royal Shuffler, or; *A New Trick at Cards*: Shewing
how the French King has been playing a Game at Picket
with the Allies, and had like to have won the Set, but
that P[rince] E[ugene] and the D[uke] of M[arlboroug]h
finding the Cheat, are resolv'd to begin the Game again.
London: Printed in the YEAR, 1709.
    1/2°:   1 side, 2 columns; 19 quatrains, alternate
rhyming stanzas, 76 lines. Morgan *L240b assigns to
Arthur Maynwaring.

Monsieur so long at Cards had Play'd,
    Upon the losing Hand;
That quite grown weary of that Trade,
    A New Game do's intend.

Audenard is allegorized as a game of cards, in which
Louis XIV and Torcy attempt to cheat. But Marlborough
and Eugene outwit them, and vow they will no more play
at cards,

But either by Arms to win the Horse
    Or fairly lose the Saddle.   75-6

294 *The Glorious Campaign*, or *Jannes tou ma aperdu ton
pucellage.* Carv'd in Gold Letters on the Gates of Tournay. In English, *She* never lost her *Maiden-head*. The
Tune of Ye *Commons* and *Peers*. No pub., n.d.
  2°: 2 columns, each 32, that is 64 lines. TxU. Not
in Morgan. Opens:

> A Lack a Day
> Poor Monsieur they Say
> Dispairs of the Title *Le Grand*.

Louis XIV's soldiers have run from Marlborough. Lisle,
Mons, Tournay are mentioned, and Boufflers may remember
that Namur surrendered.

> Were old *Lewis* dead
> Tho' your People want Bread,
> They'd all sing *Te Deum* for Joy.   62-4

295 [Krook, Enoch and Daniel Kroon (no dates)]

DE NEDERLAG DER SEINE, DOOR DEN VELDSLAG BY OUDENAARDEN,
'T BEMAGTIGEN VAN RYSSEL, EN VERSERE OVERWINNINGEN; *OOR-
LOGSSPEL*. 1709. Except for a slight change in publisher's address, identical with t.p. of piece on Hochstet,
No. 78, and Ramellies, No. 189 above. Identical form and
style but with Vendome, Boufflers, *et al.*, as well as the
silent figures of "Marlbourg" and "Eugeen." Again song
and dance and general rejoicing in Dutch style. 63 pp.
Not in Morgan. Lib. Cong. copy used.

296 Eusden, Lawrence (1688-1730)

On the Duke of Marlborough's Victory at Audenard, just
after the Loss of Ghent and Bruges. By L. Eusden of
Trinity-College, Cambridge. Pr. in Dryden-Tonson *Miscellany*, VI, 260-2, 1716 ed. 97 lines, couplets. Not
separately pub.
    Opens:

As in a starry Night, the lonely Swain
Watching his Flock, on the *Sicilian* Plain.

The pastoral note is significant, since the poem appeared only in Tonson's volume which included Ambrose
Philips's Pastorals as the opening item, as well as
Pope's, thus provoking a famous quarrel. Eusden's conventional tribute to Marlborough provoked no quarrels,
which was the case with all of his verse, at least until
his appointment to the laureateship, some nine years
later, stirred satire to some protestations. He remained
silent on Marlborough's death, even though he had produced at least three of the panegyrics to the champion
of Whig causes.

Eusden is dazzled by Marlborough's success with the
goddess Fortune.

Thou art afresh the Burthen of each Song,
The darling Subject of the tuneful Throng.
In vain, alas! they string the sprightly Lyre,
In vain great Actions can great Thoughts inspire.
13-16

The inevitable classical allusions, such as Marlborough's possessing the soul of Alexander and the prudence
of Caesar, and to Socrates, mingle with allusions to
Louis XIV and to the rancorous envy that has set the loss
of two towns, that is Ghent and Bruges, even over the
glories of Blenheim and Ramellies. The poem concludes:

Let no fantastick Wits thy Conduct blame
Nor Envy blemish o'er thy spotless Fame.
Thee *Anna* chose; in thee let all rejoice,
Since by new Wonders Heav'n confirms the
glorious Choice. 95-7

This was the year of the Sacheverell trial and the decline of Marlborough's fortunes. Although Sacheverell was found guilty on March 20, the fall of Godolphin, which resulted considerably from reaction against the Whig government stimulated by the trial, came on August 8th. Even earlier, June 14, the Earl of Sunderland was dismissed, to be succeeded by the Tory Earl of Dartmouth. The last meeting between Duchess Sarah and the Queen occurred on April 6, a distressing occasion in which Sarah sought vainly to assert her claims. Since the Duchess had promoted Sunderland for secretary of state, and since also he was the husband of her favorite daughter, the "little Whig" Anne, her aggravation was very great. The defensive account in her *Conduct of the Dowager Duchess of Marlborough*, 1742, pp. 238-45, has the advantage of reflection after the death of the Queen and the lapse of many years. The election which put Harley's moderate Tory government in power did not come till October, but by then the tide had clearly set against Marlborough and his fiery Duchess.

Militarily, the year was largely one of disasters in Spain and routine maneuvers for the Duke. Barely twenty entries appear, and none of the ecstatic panegyric of the great years. It was the pause before the storm. The sharp decline in pamphlets favorable to Marlborough was accompanied by a growing hostility which culminated in Swift's *Conduct of the Allies* and the coarse balladeering of the following year. Since the Sacheverell trial recoiled against the government, Marlborough as Godolphin's partner was associated with the disaster. A detailed study and bibliography of the affair may be found in Dr. Abbie Turner Scudi, *The Sacheverell Affair*, New York, Columbia Press, 1939, and in Geoffrey Holmes: *The Trial of Dr. Sacheverell*, London, 1973.

[Eusden, Laurence (1688-1730)] ?

The ENCOMIUM, A POEM: Humbly Inscrib'd to The Right
Honourable the Lord High Chancellor of *Great Britain*.
Occasion'd chiefly by The SUCCESSES of the Last Campaign,
and his Lordship's SPEECH thereupon to his Grace the Duke
of MARLBOROUGH in *the House of Lords*, by Order of that
Illustrious Assembly. [5 lines Horace] *LONDON*, Printed
by *J. Darby* in *Bartholomew-Close*, and sold by *J. Morphew*
near *Stationers-Hall*. 1710.
        2°: A^2B-C^2; t.p., *bl.* [ornamental band on p. 3]
3-14, 14 pp. Drop-t. on p. 3.   410 lines, couplets.
Wmk. foolscap.   Adv. in *Tat.*, No. 209, Tues. Aug. 8 to
Thurs. Aug. 10, 1710. Horn-Luttr. copy used, '4 *d.* 14.
March. 09' under 1710. CtY, TxU. The Wrenn Catalog
assigns to Laurence Eusden, but Prof. R. H. Griffith expressed strong scepticism in a letter to the author.
Morgan M225 assigns to Eusden. No other poem is assigned
to him till 1714. The poem opens:

        Long has injurious Satyr vex'd the Town,
        And lately Brightest Characters run down.

The dirt flung on "Fairest Merit" is only a libel without
sting. He will write encomiums to Marlborough's perfec-
tions that will make his muse proud. Again Britannia has
seen him come home victorious, having given the common
enemy her annual humbling. No one realized England's
strength or her purse's depth till now she has carried
on a war as long as Troy's. Golodphin in the treasury
has managed well:

        Himself sustaining no less weighty Load
        Of Cares *at home* than MARLBRO' does *abroad*.   55-6

Spring comes, with birds singing and vernal airs, and
again France's King seeks a commander, yet each tells
what he will do next summer, not what he has done. The
attempt to praise Marlborough is painfully encumbered by
the dubious and costly victory of Malplaquet. The battle
is briefly reviewed, its bloodiness recognized, and its
name given as Taniere, with the footnote "So call'd in

the *Gazette*" (p. 6).

> Methinks I hear (the Goddess now alarms
> My breast, and with unwonted Ardour warms)
> Loud deaf'ning Peals of Ordnance; and see
> Plattoons discharge their small Artillery:
> Drums beat, and Trumpets shrill Defiance sound,
> Now Balls of Missive Ruin whiz around:
> Anon whole Squadrons and Brigades engage,
> Wheel off a while, and then with double Rage
> Renew the Charge. Anon the dusty Plain
> Is strew'd with Carcasses of Thousands slain,
> And wounded more; O'er both with heedless Tread
> Intrepid Bands by Chiefs more fearless led,
> Urge on thro curling Smoke and bickering Flame,
> Encount'ring present Death for future Fame. 122-35

The poet envisions friend and foe lying quietly together in death, in "promiscuous Rout" in their harvest of slaughtered heaps "now reconciled." Whoever the poet was he comes near to real pathos, and does what he can to face up to the lamentable waste of life at Malplaquet. Now his muse quits the field, shocked at the sight, and, with a recollection of Schellenberg, turns to the problem of poetry. He thinks of Addison, Garth, and Spenser's imitator, i.e. Prior, as being the only poets equal to the task. The glories of one campaign have exhausted "*Addison*'s rich vein" and he lies fallow (ll. 153-7).

The remainder of the *Encomium* turns to masters of prose, since the poets have adopted silence as their tribute. Cowper, the eloquent Lord Chancellor, is praised for his recent eulogy in the House of Lords. Marlborough could ask no higher honor than to be praised by this man who is compared to Demosthenes. An Angel's tongue could add nothing to what he has said. He ends, therefore, in silent admiration.

298   April 16.

[Ward, Edward (1667-1731)] ?

BRITANNIA: A POEM. With all Humility inscrib'd to the

FIFTY TWO (not Guilty) LORDS. *LONDON*: Printed for *John Morphew*, near *Stationers-Hall*, 1710.
2°: A^2 B-C^2; t.p., *bl.*, 3-12, 12 pp. Drop-t. p. 3.
Wmk. foolscap and small emblem. Dobell sold Luttr. copy
'4 *d.* 16 Aprill.' Clark copy has 'By Ned Ward the London
Spy,' in MS. Not listed by Troyer. Horn copy used. 214
lines, couplets. Morgan M95. Opens:

> O Fair BRITANNIA! Lovliest [*sic*] of the Sea,
> Thou Queen of Islands! Heroes! Worship thee.

Inclusion of the piece is justified by its vigorously anti-Marlborough motivation. He is not named, but
the lapse is the more significant by the stress laid on
the line of English heroes. The title alludes to the
final vote on the Sacheverell case in the House of Lords,
the 'Not Guilty' being the fifty-two Lords who voted
against the government which was sustained by a bare 69
votes for condemnation. The poem escaped both Dr. Abbie
Scudi and Geoffrey Holmes, which is the case with many
of the entries in this bibliography which are relevant to
important historical developments.
Britannia has been the victim of invasion by Roman,
Saxon, and Dane; the love-born Norman, as well as France
and Spain would have liked to attempt it. This is a
curiously disingenuous opening for a poem written by and
for High Tory, if not Jacobite consumption and sentiment.
Faction, meaning Whig faction, is condemned, and its great
opponent is, not Marlborough, but his successor as Captain-
General, the Duke of Ormond. He is presented as the "Bul-
wark of thy Isles, on Foreign Strands" (1. 28). With
ironic ineptitude the poet asks:

> Who'er in distant Lands, like him, has Honour sought?
> Or to a pitch so high, the *English Glory* wrought?
> 33-4

The answer, of course, as every reader would know, was
the Duke of Marlborough. To add insult to the sting, Ormond is then presented as "not coveting, or needing, Foreign Gold," which was an egregious hit at Marlborough's
alleged avarice and the impressive rewards he had received.

After this beginning it is simply a matter of listing Tory stalwarts, beginning with the Duke of Beaufort,
who, like Rochester, was to displace a Whig in the Lord-
Lieutenancy. In 1709 Mrs. Manley had bestowed the effusive Dedication of the *Memoirs of Persons of Quality* on
Henry, Duke of Beaufort. There is a probable allusion
to Marlborough as the "Hydra" in the assurance that Beaufort will tread out faction, "And *Move* and *Speak*, and
Look, the *Hydra* Dead" (1. 46). Nottingham and other
sturdy Tories are similarly praised, and of Lord North
and Grey it is urged that a statue be raised in his honor,
for "his brave Right-hand he lost," and "who can such
Monuments of Hockstet boast?" (1. 156). True, he led his
regiment at Blenheim, and the memory of the destruction
of the French and Bavarian armies might seem more impressive. At the end of the poem the poet expresses his
distress in being the victim of "slanderous Imputations,"
and of being "frightened and perplex'd" by Prosecution.
This could assuredly be Ned Ward, though here hardly
"facetious." Since the verdict was given on March 23d,
only three weeks elapsed before the appearance of the poem.

299 April 19.

[Defoe, Daniel (1660-1731)]

A Speech without Doors.
        Sibi id Negoti creditit solum Dari,
        Populo ut placerent quos fecesset Fabulas.
                                        Terent.
London, *Printed* for A. Baldwin *near the Oxford-Arms* in
Warwick-Lane. M.DCC.X. *Price Two Pence.*
        8°, pp. 3-20. Moore cites copies at BM, Bod, BPL,
DFo, MH, CtY, CSmH, NYP, TxU, and others. Morgan notes:
"Attacks Marlborough, charging corruption." (Actually
the poem attacks Sacheverell.) Defoe was shifting, in
service to Harley, his ground and attitude toward Marlborough. Morgan cites three London eds. and a Dublin ed.,
1710, one in 1711, and still another 1712, *q.v.*, M190.
        See same title under 1712, but concerning the

2-1/2%. Presumably Defoe expanded the pamphlet to fit
various political situations. Moore lists only one
title, for 1710, as above.

00 May 2.

Stubbes, George, M. A. (*fl.* 1710-31)

THE LAUREL, and the OLIVE: Inscrib'd to GEORGE BUBB,
Esq; *By* GEO. STUBBES, M. A. *Fellow of* Exeter-College *in*
Oxon. [ornament] *LONDON*, Printed for *Egbert Sanger* at
the Post-Office at the Middle Temple-Gate in *Fleetstreet*.
M.DCC.X.
2°: A^2 B-D^2; t.p., *bl.*, *iii-iv* Verses *To the Author*,
1-12, 16 pp. To the Author, 48 ll., the poem 387 ll.,
total 435 ll., couplets, uncut sewn. Wmk. RH and Arms.
Horn copy used. Clark-Luttr. '2 May.' MH, TxU. Adv.
Post-Man, Apr. 29-May 2. Morgan M674.
To the *Author*, signed Geo. Bubb, opens:

As when Love's smiling *Queen* her Dovelets reins
To meet her *Hero*, red from *Phlaegra*'s Plains.

Fulsome praise of Stubbes. Interesting for allusions to
poets. He is "Sweet as smooth G[ar]th, and bold as nervous Y[oung]." Lasting fame for Marlborough is predicted
from only two poets, Harrison and Addison.

Again the *Hero*, and the *Poet* shines,
In gentler *Harison* soft *Waller* sighs,
.   .   .   .
Whilst *Addison* records, and *Churchill.* fights.   42-5
passim

Stubbes' poem is even more fervently "poetic" than his
friend's straining for elegance and pastoral delicacy in
imagery and allusion. It suggests a carry-over of the
Platonic platitudinizing of the School of Friendship initiated by the 'Matchless Orinda.' It is distinctly an
effort to avoid some of the penalties of occasional poetry.
Hence it deals with a sylvan scene:

E'er bright *Aurora* streak'd with Rose the East,
Or glowing Clouds her purple Flight confess'd.

It is a dawn of sweet-scented showers and glittering
sunshine. The poet seeks the murmurs of a grove where
he reposes "beneath an Idol Oak." In such a grove
Chaucer listened to the elves by moonlight.

> *Emilia* hence inflames the Youth to come,
> And only *Emma* boasts more CHURCHILL Bloom.   30-1

Montague is mentioned as a poet, stirred by the Sybil who
mocks attempting bards:

> Till ADDISON once more the Trumpet try'd,
> That long unheard its Silver Blast deny'd;
> But now in louder Peals it Silence broke,
> Knew its own MARO, and for MARBRO' spoke.   40-3

Now in a vision, the thrilled poet sees the laureled
heroes, as "In shining Scenes tumultuous Glories rise."
Ninus, Xerxes, Ammon, and Alaric, and Cortez form a
strange procession of laureled heroes, which is later
balanced by an equally disparate group of the heroes of
the Olive — Cyrus, Scipio, Alcides, Nassau, Themistocles,
Perseus, and others, the "wrathless Warriors." Jove intervenes and the Olive-bearing group is victorious without
any battle. Victory, Union, and Liberty are allegorically
affirmed, for this is a Whig piece, and finally Marlborough is hailed as the wielder of Anna's thunder. The
Duke was engaged in the Siege of Douai when the poem appeared, while his Duchess was engaged in no less militant
actions at Court. The effect is at least ironic.

301 August 10, written.

S., H.

REASONS WHY THE Duke of *MARLBOROUGH* Cannot lay down His
COMMANDS, Deduced from the Principles of *LOYALTY, GRATI-
TUDE, HONOUR, INTEREST* &c. *In a Letter from the Country*

to a Friend in London. *LONDON:* Printed, and Sold by *J. Baker*, at the *Black-boy* in *Pater-Noster-Row.* 1710.
Price Two-pence. Colophon bot. p. 8.
    4°: A; drop-t. p. 1, 1-8, 8 pp. Prose. Morgan
M559 cites a cheaper reprt. in Dublin, 1710; French transl.
in C. P. A., 230, f. 285. Christ Church Coll., Oxford
copy used. Opens:

    SIR,
       Yours came to my Hand, with an Account of the
    late Changes at Court, and your *Concern for the
    Publick Safety, at this* unexpected *and* amazing
    Turn of Affairs, for so you are pleas'd to ex-
    press your self, tho' for what Reason I am yet
    to seek.

The author, H. S., dates this pamphlet *'Tonbridge, Aug.*
the 10th, 1710.' Since he refers to the dismissal of
Godolphin, which took place August 8th, immediate printing seems to have occurred. The occasion was national
anxiety over whether the Duke would retain his command
in Flanders. Public credit suffered, and pamphlets
against Marlborough appeared; but in compliance with his
promise to the States-General and to Prince Eugene, he
continued to command. To retain Anne's favor, he himself surrendered the gold key to the Stole, which his
Duchess had held. Lediard quotes a group of letters
relating to his actions and decision, and gives a good
summary of this crisis in Marlborough's fortunes (III,
95-104).
    The pamphlet develops the four principles stated in
the title. Marlborough's honor is upheld, but under 'Interest' his enormous income, with his wife's, is stated
at the startling sum of ₤ 104,000 per annum. Instead of
casting reflection on this, the writer simply advances
it as a cool argument against surrender of the Duke's
position. Toward the close he notices "the Poets that
are assiduous now-a-days in the Display of His Grace's
Heroic Enterprizes, and the difficulty they would have
in comparing him to Achilles were he to take the course
of resigning his posts."

302 *REASONS* why the Duke of *Marlborough* can't lay down his Commission, And Reasons for changing the M[inistry] and Dissolving the P[arliament]. At 2d. each. Adv. in *D. Cour.* No. 2785, Tues. Sept. 26, 1710. Not in Morgan. No copy known.

303 August 19.

Adams, Mr. (no dates)

The Brave Englishman: or the VISION. August 19, 1701, N.S. By Mr. ADAMS. Sold by *S. Popping* at the Black Raven in *Pater-Noster-row*.
   1/2°: 1 side, 1 column. 20 lines, couplets, plus 4 lines alternate rhyme, 24 lines. Bodley copy used; only one known. Not in Morgan. Opens:

   By *Ebro*'s Streams the *British* General sate,
   Revolving all the Affairs of War and State.

In a vision William III appears to General Stanhope, promising victory on the morrow and that he will free Spain. Let "Almanza" be the word. The battle of Almanza had been lost in the summer of 1707. This appears to be a commentary on the cry "No peace without Spain" of 1710. Its relation to Marlborough lies only in his alleged lukewarmness toward the Peninsular War. The victory at Almenara, July 27, 1710, could be seen as discrediting his policy.

304 October.

The Oxfordshire Election.

   1/2°: 1 side, 1 column. Satire. BM and Bodley. Morgan M492.

   We are told by the Town, that a Man of Great Note, For the sake of Lawn-Sleeves is turning his Coat.

Mainly a satire on Kennet. Satirizes Marlborough's influence.

> But now of late Days, the high Road to Promotion,
> Is to pay our Great *Duke*, not the Church your
> Devotion.   11-12

Refers to Godolphin as Volpone, and to Dr. Lancaster, Mr. Wright, Hoadley. The October election brought in Sacheverell. General Stanhope's defeat in Westminster is the subject of a bsd.: *The Glorious Warrior*: or, A Ballad in Praise of General Stanhope. Dedicated to all who have Votes for Parliament-Men in the City of Westminster. London, Printed for *S. Popping*, 1710.

05   November 7.

The Secret History of *Arlus* and *Odolphus*, Ministers of State to the Empress of *Grandinsula*. In which are discover'd the Labour'd Artifices formerly us'd for the Removal of ARLUS, and the true Causes of his late *Restoration*, and upon the *Dismission* of ODOLPHUS and the QUIN-QUIVIRATE. Humbly offer'd to those Good People of GRAND-INSULA, who have not yet done wond'ring why that Princess *wou'd change so Notable a Ministry*. [Latin 2 lines] Printed in the Year MDCCX.

8vo: A^8 B-E^8; t.p., *bl.*, *ii-iv* To the Reader, 5-37, *bl.*, (full title). Adv. *Post-Boy* No. 2416, Sat. Nov. 4-Tues. Nov. 7. 'This Day is publish'd.' 38 pp. Horn copy used of The Third Edition. Morgan M183. (Has also *Impartial Secret History*, 2 vols.) Extensive marginal identification of names in contemporary hand. Arlus is Harley; Odolphus, Godolphin; Fortunatus and Hautisara, the Duke and Duchess of Marlborough; Armilia, Ramillies; Lady Montia, Mrs. Masham, etc. Dr. Sacheverell, the Act of Security, and the Junto, all appear in this satiric account which belongs to the body of work from the busy pens of Mrs. Manley, Swift, and others, and the increasing attack on the Whigs and Marlborough as their chief obstacle to power. The writer purports to deplore the

conflict of Loyalists and Levellers, though finding the
former less dangerous. Harley of course replaced Godolphin as Lord Treasurer on August 8. Although Defoe came
back into Harley's service, there seems little reason to
attribute the pamphlet to him. Not the least interesting touch is the picture of Hautisara addressing the
Queen: "Lawrd! Madam, how can your Majesty let Things
run to these Extremities!" Since the "Lawrd" is stressed
and twice repeated later, it may give an indication of
Sarah's speech.

306   November 8.

Garth, Dr. Samuel (1661-1719)

A POEM to the Earl of GODOLPHIN. By Dr. G[art]h. Printed
in the Year MDCCX. No pub.
      1/2°: 1 side, 1 column. Morgan M251. MH, CtY,
CSmH, Clark, TxU. 32 lines, couplets. Pr. in *Political
Merriment*, pp. 94-5.

      Whilst Weeping *Europe* bends beneath her Ills,
      And where the Sword destroys not, Famine kills.
      Our Isle enjoys, by your Successful Care,
      The Pomp of Peace, amidst the Woes of War.

Godolphin unselfishly works for the welfare of the people.

      A People at their Ease is what you love:
      To lessen Taxes, and a Nation save.   14-15

The machine of state is moving smoothly, but now some
"sinister" Star contrives new schemes and calls Godolphin
from affairs. The poem concludes with the assurance that
though Godolphin is retreating for a while, "Your Globe
of Light looks larger as you set." Certainly this tribute to Marlborough's close associate and the father of
Francis, Lord Rialton, who married Henrietta, Marlborough's eldest daughter, has a healing quality, but Godolphin was to die on the 4th of September, 1712, without
returning to power. Marlborough's Duchess recorded the

fact in her Bible. See Sir Tresham Lever, *Life of Godolphin*, London, 1952, p. 252. Garth's tribute appears
in the *Works of Celebrated Minor Authors*, II, 236, 1749.

07 November 23.

Swift, Jonathan (1667-1745)

Examiner, No. 16, Nov. 23, 1710. Davis, 1940, pp. 19-24.
Dated as 1710, O.S.
    A Bill of Roman Gratitude and *A Bill of English In-
gratitude*. Swift contributed many papers to the *Examiner*,
but two in particular are devoted to Marlborough and the
strategy of terminating the war. Number 17, Nov. 23,
ironically defends England from alleged ingratitude toward
the great commander whose unequalled services are recognized. After stating the costs for Blenheim Palace, as
well as various offices and honors the Marlboroughs have
received, Swift gives an ironic summation of the costs
for a Roman triumph, £ 994 11 shillings and ten pence.
Twopence for a crown of laurel is the smallest and £ 500
for a triumphal arch the greatest. In contrast English
ingratitude toward Marlborough shows a total of £ 540,000,
Blenheim and Woodstock representing nearly half. Similar
irony attaches to The *D---e* and *D---s* of *M----h*'s Loss,
1712, No. 393 below.
    Swift's other notable Marlborough *Examiner* paper is
No. 28, for February 8, 1711 (No. 27 in the reprint).
See below, No. 321.

8 *The Age of Wonders*. To the Tune of *Chevy Chace*. Printed
in the Year MDCCX.
    1/2°: 1 side, 2 columns. 27 4-line stanzas, ballad-
satire. Strong Whig and pro-Marlborough sentiments. Pr.
in *A Pill to Purge Political Melancholy*, pp. 51-6, and
Political Merriment, pp. 103-8. Strong Whig and pro-Marlborough sentiments. Opens:

The Year of Wonders is arriv'd,
The Devil has learnt to dance;
The Church from Danger is retriev'd,
By Help brought in from *France*.

The ironic stanzas point out that the way to beat the
French is to pull Marlborough down; as a reward for retrieving English honor, spite is heaped on the Duchess
of Marlborough; the Treasurer, Godolphin, was just, so
the bank must be pulled down too. Several stanzas detail English "gratitude" toward Marlborough for facing
danger and winning victories, rewarding him by insulting
his family and stirring up the mob for the new election.
This is not the ballad of the same title listed in Morgan
M14. However, Morgan M768 lists *Wonders Upon Wonders* In
Answer to the *Age of Wonders*, 116 lines, in 29 stanzas,
a "peppery" Tory retort.

309 BELLISARIUS A great Commander and *ZARIANA* His LADY. A
    DIALOGUE. *LONDON*: Printed and Sold by *J. Morphew*, near
    Stationers-Hall, 1710.
    8VO: *i-iv*, 1-16, 20 pp. Adv. of *The Female Reign*
    bot. p. 16. Bellisarius in drop-t., p. 1 and text. Morgan
    M410; cites copy in Add MSS., 23, 904, *ff*. 73-84. 434
    lines, couplets; Moral Reflections on the Foregoing DIA-
    LOGUE, pp. 15-16, 6 4-line stanzas. Opens with The
    PREFACE, pp. *iii-iv*:

        I think it necessary to acquaint the Reader,
        that the following Dialogue was chiefly occasioned
        by the daily Invectives and scandalous Lampoons
        that are scatter'd thro' the Town, to sully Noble
        Characters, and eclipse the Glories of those Il-
        lustrious Worthies, to whose Fortitude and Fidel-
        ity, under the Providence of God, and Wisdom of
        Her Majesty, the *British* Nation owe the happy
        prospect of their approaching Felicity, as well
        as their present Security from a very trouble-
        some, also a dangerous Enemy.

The writer goes on to condemn the "groundless scurrilities"

that arise out of the printing houses, "like stinking Vapours out of Holbourn-Ditch." It is beneath the Great to take notice of these "pestilential Papers" nor should their fame suffer the least from such "ridiculous mis-representations of such loose and mercenary Pens." The poem opens:

ZARIANA

Welcome, my Lord, thrice welcome from afar,
And from the Toils and Dangers of the War.

Belisarius is of course Marlborough. The resemblances in courage, popularity with his troops, as well as a strong-minded, intriguing wife, and particularly the ingratitude both suffered, lead to many allusions associating them. This one is pro-Marlborough, and interestingly the only specific reference to pamphleteers is to the *R*[evie]*w*.

10   The Case of the British General. *Collected from several late Celebrated Papers: And laid down in* Two *Plain PROPOSITIONS.* To His GRACE the Duke of *MARLBOROUGH*, &c. Printed for *J. Baker*, 1711. *Price* 1 *d.*
1/2°: 2 sides. Morgan M411 cites a 1710 ed. CtY copy used. Prose satire. Opens:

My Lord! As every new Discovery in the Art of War seems of Right to claim Your Grace's Regards. . .

Satirizes Tory hostility toward Marlborough in face of his constant successes. Proposition I states that a British general must neither lie still nor win battles and take cities. Proposition II states that the true art and duty of a British general is to let the enemy "have the fatigue of beating our Armies, and taking Towns."
The only specific names cited are an appeal to the "multitude of modern Authors; particularly the late pious *Examiner*; the modest Writer of the *Post-Boy*; and the Author of *Reasons for Putting an End to the War.*"
The satire concludes with a paragraph in italics,

scoring on party rage and malice as distorting the truth.
"It puts out the Eyes and extinguishes the common Sense
of Mankind."

311 *The Court Lady's Tale*, Or, a Tale of the D---- of M-----.
Printed in the Year, 1710. No pub.
1/2°: 70 lines, couplets. MH only copy. Not in
Morgan. Opens:

Since Tales are such the new Mode of the City

After a long list of tales, the poem concludes:

Thus who is safe in defending the Church,
When all the World would leave it in lurch.
Therefore remember that Noble good deed,
And look to yourselves with great care and heed.
Now such you entrust with your good government
Lest when 'tis too late you do it repent.   64-9

The Tory cry of "The Church in danger" was associated with
Queen Anne politics and the conduct of the war. Anti-
Marlborough and pro-Sacheverell.

312 *The MOBB's Address to my Lord-----*
To the Right Honourable the Lord M----, with the Elect
Common Council of the City of L-----. The humble Address
of the Mobb, lately Commanded by Dr. S-----l, and unpun-
ish'd by Your Lordship, &c. Printed in the Year M.DCC.X.
1/2°, 2 pp. nmbd. Prose satire. CtY copy used, the
only one located. Morgan M413. However, Morgan says
"Very hostile to Marlborough, favorable to Sacheverell."
Actually the poem is addressed to the Lord Mayor and no
pertinence to Marlborough appears, at least beyond a
denunciation of books, pamphlets, sermons that "support
this dangerous War," since the satire is concerned with
the mob that seeks to undermine the Constitution. The
mob are tied down by his lordship, the doctor, and others
to Passive Obedience, and are ready to Hussa and Fight,

Burn, Murder. They give steady obedience to the doctor's
sermons and principles. Morgan may have had a work of
identical title, but since he supplies only a short title
for his entry this is indeterminable.

313   Hare, Dr. Francis (1671-1740)

The Management of the War. In a *Letter* to a *Tory Member*.
London, Printed for *A*. Baldwin, near the Oxford Arms in
Warwich Lane, 1710. Morgan M278.

Ibid., *The Management of the War* in a *Second Letter* to a
Tory Member. 44 pp., London, *A. Baldwin*, 1710. 2d, 3d,
4th eds., 1710; another ed. 42 pp., 1711. M279.

Ibid., *The Negotiations for a Treaty of Peace* in 1719 Considered. In a Third Letter to a Tory Member. 2 pts.,
I, *ii*, 49; II, 72 pp., 8vo. M280.

Dr. Hare made an impressive contribution to the flood
of political pamphlets in the years 1710-12. Since these
are identified in Morgan M278-80, and come largely in 1711,
they are only cited here and not fully described. They
are a very important part of the defence of Marlborough.
Hare had become the chief spokesman for the Duke, and
these pamphlets set forth clearly and forcefully support
of Marlborough and Whig policy. See Hare's *Life and
Glorious History of Marlborough*, 1705, No. 112 above.

14   Broome, William (1689-1745)

A Poem on the Seat of the War in Flanders, Chiefly with
Relation to the Sieges: With the Praise of Peace and
Retirement. Written in 1710. Humbly Inscrib'd to John
Holt, Esq., of Redgrave-Hall in Suffolk.

Poems on Several Occasions, London, 1727, 1739, 1750.
Chalmers, XII, 20-1. In *Poetical Works* of, Cooke's ed.,
n.d., pp. 19-25, 227 lines, couplets. Opens:

> Happy thou, *Flandria*, on whose fertile Plains,
> In wanton Pride luxurious Plenty reigns.

But Flandria is near France and "horrid War" invades her land.

> See the Britannic Lions wave in air!
> See mighty *Marlb'rough* breathing Death and War.
> From Albion's Shores at Anna's high Commands
> The dauntless Hero pours his martial Bands.   20-3

No specific battles are mentioned, but the roar and fury of war are emphasized, with death, mountains of slain heroes, and the horrid sound of drums and cannon-fire. The poet invokes the quiet of peace and contemplation. He is favorable to Marlborough, whose sword protects Anna's throne, but he wishes war to be chained and silenced. The tone and imagery of the poem suggest that much of it was composed later than 1710. It seems to have had no separate printing.

315   The PROPHESY or, *M*[asha]*m*'s Lamentation for *H*[arle]*y*. Translated from the Greek of Homer, London, printed for *Abel Roper* at the *Black Boy* in *Fleetstreet*, 1710. (Price 1 *d*.)

    1/2°. Morgan M285. No copy known.

> Now *Phoebus* did with Frowns the World Survey.

316   REASONS Why a Certain GREAT G---L Has not yet Receiv'd the THANKS Of either of the Houses of Parliament; AS ALSO A short ENQUIRY into those Eminent SERVICES which make it necessary in some Cast St----n's Opinion, why he should receive them, with some Conjectures on the Cause of our late Disappointments in *SPAIN*. *In a Letter to the Mayor of St*. Albans. Printed in the Year 1710. (Price 2 *d*.)

    8°: T.p., *bl*., drop-t. on p. 3 A LETTER TO THE MAYOR OF St. Albans. 3-16, sgnd. *Your assured Friend and Servant*, p. 16, 16 pp. Morgan M540. Horn copy used. *Wrenn Cat*.

attributes to Defoe, but the pamphlet is Tory and anti-
Marlborough and anti-Ministry throughout.

Opening with an allusion to Lord Haversham's ghost
and his bad influence, the writer mainly decries the
lavish rewards that the Duke and Duchess of Marlborough
have received. Not only is this contrary to practice in
Athens and Rome, but Blaregnies, that is Malplaquet, has
made all previous achievements a mockery. Acknowledgment
of great victories, such as Blenheim and Ramellies, has
been fully made. Marlborough is censured for the behavior
of some of his officers, who have drunk "confusion" to the
ministry. Allusions to *Examiners*, Hoadly, Bickerstaff,
and the like reflect the bitter contests of the beginnings of the effort to destroy the Duke. Most of the
arguments anticipate Swift's *Conduct of the Allies*.

The issue over distribution of military forces appears.

What remains for me to say, is, That whenever
it shall appear (as undoubtedly endeavors
will be made to make it out) that our late misfortunes in *Spain* owe nothing of their Rize to
such a vast part of our Forces and Treasure being sent to *Flanders*; that our present Successes
there are a Ballance for our losses elsewhere. . .

The piled-up sentences are normal for pamphlet writing, but they are lacking in the incisiveness of either
Defoe or Swift.

517 Sarah's Farewel [*sic*] to C---t: OR, A Trip from St.
James's to St. *Albans*. To the Tune of *Farewel Joy and
farewel Pleasure*. *LONDON*: Printed in the Year, 1710.
1/2°: 12 4-line stanzas, 48 lines. BM copy used.
Crawford. Ballad. Not in Morgan.

Farewell C[our]t and Farewell Pleasure,
Farewell all Things of Delight.

Sarah bids farewell to perquisites, Privy Purse, to Godolphin, Sunderland and Wharton and the Dear Cabal, and to

the Whiggish ministers. None of these is more than suggested by initials. The last stanza:

> Hither then my Dearest *Ion*[nn]*y*,
>   To thy *Sarah*'s Arms Repair,
> We'll for St. *Albans*, quit St. *James*'s,
>   Or for *Ble*[nhei]*ms* happier Air.

318 THE SPEECH OF THE Lord *HAVERSHAM*'s GHOST [Ornament]
LONDON: Printed in the Year, MDCCX. (Price Two Pence.)
    4°: A-B^2; t.p., *2*, 3-8, 8 pp. Another ed. (Price
One Penny) 8°: A^4; t.p., 2-8, drop-t. on p. 2. Different type. Horn copies used. Morgan 291.
    The Speech is addressed to "My Lords," and the Ghost
says death has taught him to see things in their true
state. (He had been a convert from Whig to Tory allegiance.) Hence he wishes to do justice to the Duke of Marlborough. The House is deliberating whether the Duke deserves thanks. What is his crime? Is it to make conquests without their orders? He recalls the rejoicing
after the first two campaigns, even though he was after
that put up to an annual libel of the hero. We were
satiated with victories after Ramillies. But Fault
Finders were turned loose, and

> To render his Grace odious to the People, that
> *Club* [which produces the *Examiner*] charges him
> with the Receipt of 240000 Pounds of the Publick
> Money, upon the account of *Blenheim-House*, which
> I may say, is no more his, than St. Paul's Church
> is mine. It is a publick Monument of the *British*
> Courage.

The remainder of the pamphlet contains a speech of Marlborough's old teacher, Marshal Turenne, praising him,
along with the ghosts of other defeated generals and
slain soldiers. Irony is poured on the charges that
disturb Marlborough's sleep, that he heads a dangerous
faction, and also on the senseless actions taken to restore credit and assure the Succession.

319 THE Swan Tripe-Club: [Gothic type] A SATYR, ON THE High-
Flyers; In the Year 1705. [1 line Juvenal; 2 lines
Garth's *Dispensary*] *LONDON*: Printed and Sold by the
Booksellers of *London* and *Westminster*, 1710.
        8°: A⁸; t.p.,   ., 3-16, 16 pp. Drop-t. on p. 3.
499 lines, couplets. Morgan M680. Same title attrib.
to Swift, 1377; two eds. 1706. BM Add. MSS. Horn copy
used.   Opens:

    How this Fantastick World is chang'd of late!
    Sure some Full Moon has work'd upon the State.

At a banquet Faction pits out venom, but the radiant Goddess of Victory has the last words.

    I sent the Goddess when *Victoria* came,
    And rais'd thee CHURCHILL to Immortal Fame,
    And *Hochstet*'s bloody Field advanc'd the *Hero*'s Name.
    By me he yet will more Immortal grow,
    When *Ramilies* and *Oudenard* shall know,
    His Arms Triumphant still against the *Gallick* Foe.
                                          459-64

The title is based on the Swan Tavern where the club
meets, Firedrake, a Senator; Grimbeard, a factionalist,
hater of Moderation; Nut-Brain, a Daggle Gown, from Dublin, an Irish locust; Sooterkin, Crab and Moon-Calf. All
are vividly etched pictures of political types. At the
close, following Victoria's speech, "immoderately Scar'd,"
they flee from the uneasy truths they have heard.

20 *Vulpone*'s TALE, Printed in the Year, 1710.
        1/2°: 1 side, 1 column. 56 lines, couplets. Satir-
ical fable. Morgan M736. Clark copy used. Opens:

    A Fox was out upon the pilfering Lay
    According to the Methods of his Kind.

Godolphin had been labeled as Volpone, and here as the
fox tries to lure the cock down from a tree. Then the
cock sees hounds in the distance, and the fox runs away,
even though Crafty Chanticleer says *"The General Peace
will save you"* (1. 40), The "Application," 12 lines,

341

concludes with the notion that one more year of war
will delude the public, Trade and Mother Church will
flourish, and the Fox will be safe, for "a Fox loves
to cram his Gut" (1. 54).

1711 is the year of strenuous Tory intrigue to end
the war by a secretly negotiated Peace. The French spy,
the Abbe Gaultier, in the beginning of the year, and
Matthew Prior, during the summer, went to Paris as agents
in the conspiracy. Swift's *Conduct of the Allies* is by
far the most influential and historically important pamphlet to appear. Because of the sharp increase in the
proportion of satire, a corresponding proportion of
anonymous pieces is apparent. That three should be identifiable as by Swift, with more to follow in the next
year, is evidence of his keen awareness that the war
could be ended only by the elimination of the 'Great Man.'
Dr. Francis Hare, chief spokesman for Marlborough, and
also a churchman, responded with three entries, and the
war on the Continent was reflected in the equally intense
pamphlet war at home.

The crux of the year was the siege and taking of
the fortress of Bouchain, called by Churchill Marlborough's "last conquest and command" (IV, 449). Churchill
points out that the Duke in after years took particular
pride in the fall of the last great fortress in the march
to Paris, even though the Tory strategy for the peace
prevented his capitalizing on it. The Blenheim tapestries, which he prescribed, provide a lasting record of
his preference for this victory. Bouchain surrendered
on September 12th.

321 February 8.

[Swift, Jonathan (1667-1745)]

The Examiner, No. 27, Thursday; February 1-8, 1711.
Temple Scott ed. IX, 174-80; Davis, *Examiner*, p. 80-85.
While allusions to Marlborough and the war run through
the paper, it is No. 27, along with No. 16, November
16-23, 1710, may well stand for all of Swift's prose attacks, outside of the *Conduct of the Allies*, November 27,
1711. The theme of the essay is avarice, which is duti-
fully and severely condemned. Marlborough is not named,
but a long letter, such as Swift would have liked to
write at the time of the first Triumvirate, is directed
against the imaginary person that Swift, in particular,
and the Tories in general, had evoked for the purposes
of discrediting him. "No man disputes the gracefulness
of your person; you are allowed to have good and clear
understanding. . .you are no ill orator. . .You have been
a most successful general, of long experience, great conduct, and much personal courage." This praise is followed by allegations that he is loved by neither patri-
cians nor plebeians, and, with great untruth, nor by the
officers and men of his own armies. The letter, called
by Gay a masterpiece, is perhaps Swift's most lucid summary of his indictment of Marlborough for an alleged
moral flaw that is at most ludicrously inept and exaggerated in view of his achievements and eminence.

322 September. 17

[Hare, Dr. Francis (1671-1740)] and [Maynwaring, Arthur
(1668-1712)]

BOUCHAIN: IN A DIALOGUE Between the Late *Medley* and *Examiner*. *Arms Virumque novis sustenat Famae Trophaeis*.
[ornament] *LONDON*, Printed for *A. Baldwin in Warwick-
Lane*. M.DCC.XI. Price 6 *d*.
    8vo: A-E^8 F^2; t.p., *bl*., 3-43, 43 pp. Morgan N262.
TxU copy used. A sec. ed., 1711, same collation. Copy

at CtY. The dialogue form is maintained throughout, though with *Medley* doing most of the talking. He insists that an express announcing the surrender of Bouchain arrived "last Night." *Examiner* is incredulous, but gradually accepts *Medley*'s account and his defence of Marlborough as not willingly prolonging the war. His great achievement in passing Marshall Villar's Ne Plus Ultra lines is detailed. The strategy involved is a triumph and the Duke's final stroke before his own downfall. He took particular pride in it, as have his biographers. Two of the tapestries at Blenheim Palace signalize Bouchain.

While the pamphlet has been ascribed to Dr. Hare, Oldmixon is authority for his report of its having been "revis'd and Publish'd" by Maynwaring. See his *The Life and Posthumous Works of Arthur Maynwaring*, Curll, 1715, p. 342. Marlborough was displeased with *Bouchain* and the retort upon it, No. 332 below. Churchill, IV, 452-3, quotes letters of the Duke to Sarah, and to Harley in October strongly condemning both. Since Hare was with him, and also in his confidence, it seems hardly possible that *Bouchain* could have been by him. Furthermore Morgan O289 cites a pamphlet by W. H., *A Modest Attempt to Prove Dr. H[are] not the Author of the Bouchain Dialogue, in a Letter to W. J.*, 1712, 8vo pp. *ii*, 36. Marlborough's resentment seems mainly directed against journalistic meddling during the critical negotions toward *i at* a peace, whatever he may have thought of them. The activities of Prior in particular are deplored, as well as is the notion of the surrender of Spain and the West Indies. Only allusions to the *Examiner*'s [Swift's] "Letter to Crassus" and allusions to Catiline, bearing on the fallacious charges of avarice might have been objectionable. See Herbert Davis ed. of *The Examiner*, Oxford, Blackwell, 1940, pp. *xxxii-iii*.

23   September 17.

The Duchess of Marlborough's Vision. London, no pub., 1711. Morgan N398, gives date, and says "a political satire." No loc.

To the Duke of *Marlborough*, on the Taking of BOUCHAIN.
LONDON: Printed for *W. H.* and Sold by *S. Popping* at
the *Black Raven* in *Pater-Noster-Row*:   and Enter'd ac-
cording to ACT OF PARLIAMENT, 1711.   (Price 1 *d.*)
      1/2°:   1 side, 1 col. 28 lines, couplets.   MH, LLP,
CSmH copy used.   A variant without pub. and date, but
with same number of lines, no exclamation point after
'Man!', and spelling 'Bleinheim' (1. 3) at BM.   Morgan
N397.   Opens:

> Great Glorious Man!   thus after Clouds shine bright;
> Thus thou break'st forth with new amazing light.
> *Blenheim, Ramillies*, widely spread thy Fame:
> But *Bouchain* shall Immortalize thy Name.

That the poem is defensive of Marlborough is shown in
line 5:   "Here, no Assistance from Great *Eugene*."   Aim-
ing the charges against the Duke was the claim that Blenheim owed more to Eugene than to his own prowess.   He is
shown to have broken the way to the Seine, and has suffered the difficulties of bringing bread and forage from
afar, as well as all the hardships of a "puzzling War"
(1. 10).   Marlborough has remained bold and sedate though
beset by envy at home as well as numerous foes abroad.
He has quelled both British and French envy, and has
braved death to serve and save England.   "Repenting *Faction* join in thy renown" (1. 22) shows more of hope than
truth.   He will be thanked in the English *Sanhedrin*, and
his glorious hand "must give the lasting Peace."   Marl-.
borough is being harshly criticized for allegedly prolonging the war, particularly for its high costs; and here
the poet defends him against these charges.
      The changes in the variant, presumably a piracy, are
largely ones of punctuation and italics such as a careless
printer might introduce.   In line 24, however, "Force to
thy Name shall a Discretion yield," becomes "Foes to thy
Name," a change that might come from dictation.   'Sanhedrin is misspelled as 'Sanhedium.'   An exclamation point
added to the final phrase 'Lasting Peace' does add emphasis.

325   October 4.   25 Sept

Hare, Dr. Francis (1671-1740)

The Charge of God to Joshua: In a SERMON Preach'd before
his *Grace* the Duke of *Marlborough*, at Avenes Le Sec, September 9. 1711, Being The Day of Thanksgiving for passing
the Lines, and taking BOUCHAIN.   By Dr. FRANCIS HARE, D.D.
and Chaplain-General of her Majesty's Forces in the *Low-
Countries*. *Enter'd according to Act of Parliament*. *London*, Printed in the Year M.DCC.XI.
        8vo:   A-C^4; t.p., *bl*., 3-4 The Publisher to the
READER, 5-24. Prose.   Horn copy used.   Has contemp. marginalia.   Important as preached in the field, and in view
of Hare's activities in pamphleteering for Marlborough.
The sermon cites Moses leading the Hebrews out of the
wilderness, and urges patience.   The victory assuredly
reflects the favor of God and Providence.   See the *Land-
Leviathan*, No. 361, Feb. 5, 1712.   Adv. *Spec.* CLXXXIV
(184), Mon. Oct. 1.   'Just publish'd.'   Bouchain was
taken Aug. 4-5.   Morgan N263.

26   [Swift, Jonathan (1667-1745)] and [Manley, Mary de la
Riviere (1663-1724)]

A *Learned Comment* UPON Dr. HARE's Excellent Sermon Preach'd
before the *D. of* Marlborough, On the Surrender of BOUCHAIN.
By an Enemy to PEACE. *Et multis utile Bellum*.   *LONDON*,
Printed for *John Morphew*, near *Stationers-Hall*.   (Price
2 *d*.)
        4°:   [A-B^8]; t.p., *bl*., 3-16, 16 pp.   Morgan N576.
Copy in San Francisco Pub. Lib. used.   Teerink, No. 538,
says Swift gave only suggestions to Mrs. Manley.
        Printed among Swift's works in most editions.   By
Herbert Davis in *The Examiner and Other Pieces Written in
1710-11*, pp. 259-72, but with the opinion that Swift gave
only suggestions.   He seems to underrate Swift's concern
with Dr. Hare.   In view of the shortness of the pamphlet
and the tone of the whole, it seems quite possible that
Swift is the author, as Temple Scott holds.   After

sarcastically alluding to the preface with its claim
that the text was printed from a text secured from a
friend, the writer comments on about a dozen specific
passages in the sermon, both from the angle of Hare's
incompetence as a writer of sermons, and the Duke's
allegedly dubious successes, and his request to be made
commander for life. Since Hare was in the field with
Marlborough's army, he could hardly have commissioned
publication directly. The interest in the pamphlet lies
in its being in the period of the *Conduct of the Allies*
as well as a number of other writings, such as *The Public Spirit of the Whigs*, 1714, which have allusions to
Marlborough and the peace.

327   November 27.

[Swift, Jonathan (1667-1745)]

The Conduct of the ALLIES, and the Late Ministry, in Be-
ginning and Carrying on the PRESENT WAR. [17 lines
Latin verse] *London*, Printed for *John Morphew*, near
Stationers-Hall. 1712. [pub. 1711] Second Edition is
dated 1711, also Third and Fourth, also 1711, 96 pp.
Full descriptions of all editions in Morgan N569.
Teerink No. 539.
      8°: A-F^8; t.p., *bl.*, *iii-iv* The *Preface*, *bl.*, 7-96,
96 pp. Horn copy of Sec. Ed. used. Adv. *Post-Boy*, No.
2581, Sat. Nov. 24-Tues. Nov. 27, 'This Day is publish'd.'
The Third Ed. in *D. Cour*. Dec. 1, 'Just publish'd.'
      Here, almost for the first time, is a pamphlet of
great importance and equal familiarity to scholarship.
In accordance with the principles of this bibliography
it will not be discussed in detail. The numerous editions present complicated bibliographical problems, but
more for Swift scholarship than for Marlborough. Suffice
it to say that with this one great blow Swift did more
than anyone or anything else to turn the tide of sentiment against the war. His concern is not with the facts
and truth, but with the Tory policy of ending the war. To
this end it had become apparent that only displacing the

Duke would serve. Thus the attack on the War, but also
on Great Men, especially military men, and most of all
the man whom he alludes to as only the G----l. Swift
does not here descend to the low and cheap allusions of
the verse satires, but adroitly calls in question a war
in which the English carry the greatest load and in which
the Dutch are of limited help. It is notable that in the
Preface he alludes to those who defend the Management of
the War, which is one of Dr. Hare's titles.

An excellent analysis of the *Conduct* may be found in
Michael Foot, *The Pen and the Sword*, 1957, 293-306.
Without being unjust to Marlborough, the soldier-com-
mander, he shows how Swift turned his genius to pulling
him down as the essential step in terminating an unduly
protracted war. To do this he assures his readers that
the war was being protracted to aggrandize one family,
the Duke's, and a small group of Whig profiteers. He
includes all the sensitive points, the alleged avarice,
the demand to be made general for life, and wider political issues, particularly the "no Peace without Spain,"
the Whigs' insistence that the throne of Spain be dis-
lodged from French control and restored to the Empire.
This, Swift shows, was not in the original program of
promises and policy.

8   December 24.

[Swift, Jonathan (1667-1745)]

The W[ind]*ds*[o]*r Prophecy. Printed in the Year, 1712.*
Three eds., two with the prophecy in mixed black letter
and Roman type. BM copy used. Morgan N589. Teerink
No. 327. Williams, Swift's *Poems*, I, 145-8.

2°: 1 side, 1 col., 26 lines, couplets. Prose introduction in two paragraphs.

The prose portion relates how the sexton unearthed
a leaden casket containing the poem which is offered for
the amusement of the reader. The extremely harsh lines
contain Swift's revenge on the red-headed Duchess of
Somerset, whom he calls 'Carrots.' He writes to Stella

Christmas Eve, 1711, about its publication, but has several
other references to the poem. Williams, *op. cit.*, supplies
some account of the Duchess, and Michael Foot, *The Pen and
the Sword*, 341-4, gives an excellent analysis of the enig-
mas which surround and fill the poem. Opens:

> *When a holy black* Suede, *the* Son *of* Bob,
> *With a* Saint *at his Chin, and a* Seal *in his Fob;*
> *Shall not see one New Years-day in that Year,*
> *Then let old* England *make good Chear;*
> Windsor and Bristow *then shall be*
> *Joyned together in the* Low-Countree.

These lines refer to Dr. John Robinson (1650-1723),
who was appointed Dean of Windsor, Bishop of Bristol, and
Lord Privy Seal. Marlborough is introduced as opposing
the Peace:

> *But spight of the* Harpy *that* crawls on all four,
> *There shall be Peace, pardie, and War no more.* 11-12

The piece is packed with bad puns and cryptic allusions reflecting Swift's deep animosity and party bias.
It concludes with an injunction to Queen Anne to keep Mrs.
Abigail Hill Masham "close" to her, and to bury "Carrots"
under a Hill (1. 26). The Duchess, sole surviving heir
and daughter of the last Percy, Earl of Northumberland,
was the leading Whig supporter and influence on Queen
Anne, in opposition to Mrs. Masham and the Tory interest.
See Trevelyan, *England Under Queen Anne*, III, 117-18. He
fully accepts the interpretation that Swift's greatest
personal frustration came from his circulation of this
poem, a view advanced by Deane Swift.
See same title below, No. 350, 1711, and 380, 1712.

329 Hare, Dr. Francis (1671-1740)

The Allies and the Late Ministry Defended against France
and the Present Friends of France, in Answer to a Pamphlet
entitled The Conduct of the Allies. In Four Parts.

350

Printed for A. Baldwin near the Oxford-Arms in Warwick-
Lane, 1711. BM and Horn copies used. Pt. I, *ii*, 46;
Pt. II, *iv*, 71; Pt. III, *iv*, 74; Pt. IV, *iv*, 84, 1711-12
For further bibliographical details see Morgan N261.
See No. 325 above.

30   Marlborough, Duke of (1650-1722) ?

D. of M----------h's Letter to Her M. *LONDON*: Printed
in the Year 17--.
      1/2°: 1 side, 1 column, prose. The date in the only
known copy, at TxU, is either smudged or simply incomplete.
It is almost beyond question 1711. Marlborough's response
to the Queen's letter of dismissal from his services is
dated January 1, 1712. Since he understandably flung her
letter into the fire, we have only his response. The
printed document cited above is certainly not his response
which is longer and quite different. In fact this statement, if it is authentic, must have come somewhat earlier.
It opens:

> *MADAM,* As I can never forget the many Obliga-
> tions of and Respect I lye under, for the signal
> Favours and Benefits heap'd on me, so I shall
> always confess my Life at your disposal, and
> Esteem nothing a greater Blessing than to have
> an opportunity of spending the remainder of it
> to do You Service.

He recognizes the charges of his enemies, but pro-
tests that he has always served the "best of Queens, the
most gracious of Women," and that he is loaded with
gratitude. The only detail giving a clue to the date is
a reference to his "having much rather you should be my
Sentencer, than depend on the fairest Trial, or the most
promising Defence." While he concludes with a "submission" and affirmation of being the queen's "Faithful, Tho'
unfortunate Subject," the letter seems dubious. It does
not appear in any of the historians from Lediard to Sir
Winston Churchill, nor in Murray's volumes. Furthermore,

351

the reference in the text to "Your M[ajesty]s" and the signature do not smack of a genuine letter. Whatever the
true situation, it is certainly a document of some interest in assessing Marlborough's state of mind in his elev-
enth "campaign," the only one which he failed to win.
Not in Morgan.

331 The Duke of MARLBOROUGH's Delight Or His Honours Cordial
Advice To His Fellow Soldiers. To a New Tune Licensed
according to Grder [sic, for Order]. No pub., n.d.,
coarse, uncut.
        2°: 80 lines in 2 cols., ballad. Clue to date in
Marlborough's stopping the appointment of Mrs. Masham's
brother, Jack Hill, to the colonelcy of a regiment, Jan.
1710. Not in Morgan. Opens:

                Set the Glass around
                about you have a care sir.

332 [Manley, Mary de la Riviere (1663-1724)]

THE D. of M------h's Vindication: In ANSWER to a PAMPHLET
Lately Publish'd, call'd [Bouchain, or A Dialogue between
the Medley and the Examiner.] [ornament] LONDON:
Printed for John Morphew, near Stationers Hall, 1711.
(Price 2d.)
        8°: A⁸; t.p., bl., 3-16, 16 pp. CtY copy used.
Morgan N389. This contribution to the running battle
between Swift, Manley and others against Dr. Francis Hare,
is accepted as Mrs. Manley's on the basis of suggestions
by Swift; but in content and style it is hardly distin-
guishable from the others. It opens with a slur on the
"stupidity and disingenuity" of the Medley, and maintains
that Marlborough has suffered little loss and less disgrace from the Queen. Dr. Hare is quoted directly, pp.
12-13, and other allusions to his Bouchain, No. 322,
appear. The pamphlet concludes with a firm appeal for
peace, even if the people cannot be let into all the
secrets leading to it. The precedent of a separate peace,

as made by the Dutch at Nimeguen, is cited, while assurance is given that not one step will be taken "in this
Affair, but what makes for the Glory of the QUEEN, and
the Happiness of Her Subjects."

33 *Oliver's Pocket Looking-Glass, New Fram'd and Clean'd*, To
give a clear View of the Great Modern COLOSSUS, Begun by
K. C---; Carry'd on by K. J----; Augmented by K. W----;
And now Finish'd, in order to be thrown down in the
Glorious R---- of Q. A------. [Motto 4 lines Eng. verse:
"So may the Man of ignominious Might."] Printed in the
Year 1711.
    8vo: *A* B-K^4; half – title, *bl.*, t.p., *bl.*, 1-78,
79-80 bl., 84 pp. Prose, satire. Horn copy used. Morgan N394.
    This satire is in the vicious manner of Mrs. Manley,
if it is not from her vitriolic pen. Any pretense of
civility toward a national hero, his great victories, and
his duchess, has disappeared. The Whig cry of ingratitude
toward Marlborough is quickly turned against him. Although his many victories are faintly acknowledged, he is
depicted as foul, ungrateful to James II, as merely lucky
in battle, and disgraceful in private behavior. The
Looking-Glass reflects him as in the line of Oliver Cromwell, its original owner.
    This preference of his country's true welfare over
a venal sovereign was dealt with by Hare in the 1705 Life,
and by every biographer down to Sir Winston Churchill.
Sarah is presented as Zara Shipton, another stroke from
the Manley-Bolingbroke-Swift-Wagstaffe group. Marlborough's lively activities as a Restoration Mirabel are reviewed. The Duchess of Cleveland appears as "*Harlotta
Villeria*, duchess of the Land of *C----ve*, who had the
Power to make him every Thing but grateful" (p. 16). She
provided his first step to power, while his sister, Mere-
tricia, as King's mistress, provided the next. Then came
marriage to Zara, daughter of Mother Shipton, a notorious
bawd. United in marriage, they are also alike in treachery
and ambition.
    Having blackened Colossus's character, it remained to

show him as a great commander, winning victories by luck
and command of the armies of most of Europe. The ironies
are Swiftian in severity and impact as the Duke is shown
working his way into the role of Cromwell, that is threatening to become a dictator. Blenheim is ignored, but
Ramillies is acknowledged, although the results could
have been gained, we are informed, without a battle the
year previous!

While Marlborough's request to be made Captain-
General for life came in the summer of 1709, it is here
revived as clear evidence of his insatiable ambition, and
it provides the culminating argument of the satire. He
is repeating *N[o]ll*'s tragedy, that is Cromwell's; for
". . .if a Subject can but fix himself in a Generalship
for Life, we know he may step afterwards to what Degree
he thinks fit, even tread upon the Throne at Pleasure
. . ." (p. 76). Admittedly Marlborough had overreached
himself. His request, along with Sarah's insatiable
thirst for power, wrecked them. Mrs. Manley had labeled
her as Queen Zarah as early as 1705, in her *Secret
History*, No. 130, and the resemblances between that work
and *Oliver's Pocket Looking-Glass* are extensive. That
they are both parts of a planned and persistent campaign
of attack, is evidenced by the republication of the *Secret
History* in a French translation in 1711, and again in
1712, as *L'Histoire Secrette de la Reine Zarah, ou la
Duchesse de Marlborough demasquée*, Traduite de l'Original
Anglais, *iv*, 295, Morgan B390. Summary of the total body
of the onslaught on Marlborough would fill a volume. Also
in 1711 appeared *Memoirs of Europe toward the Close of the
Eighth Century*, written by the *Translator* of the *New Atalantis*, 4 vols., 1710-11, Morgan N391. These were reissued
as Vols. III & IV with the *Secret Memoirs of New Atalantis*,
in 1710. See above.

The best summary of Mrs. Manley's role in the Tory
attack is the excellent article by Dr. Gwendolyn B. Needham: "Mary de la Riviere Manley, Tory Defender," *HLQ*, XII,
No. 3, May, 1949, pp. 254-88. This treatment is understandably sympathetic even to an outrageous woman.

34 *An Excellent New Song*, Being the *Intended* SPEECH *of a
Famous Orator against Peace.*
        1/2°:   1 side, no pub., n.d.   BM, MH, TxU, LLP.
54 lines, ballad satire.   First gives as 1711.   Morgan
N573.

>   An Orator *dismal* of *Nottinghamshire*
>   This forty Years let out his Conscience to hire.

10 preliminary lines precede the Speech.
        Coarse satire on the Marlboroughs.   The Duke shows
off his fine house, that is Blenheim Palace, and the
Duchess her purse of money.   The speech deplores making
a peace without Spain.   One line alludes to Defoe:
"*Daniel* we got from the Den of Lions."

35 *An Excellent New Song.*   To the Memorable Tune of *Lilli-
bullero.*   Printed in the Year M.D.CCXI.
        1/2°:   1 side, 2 cols., 13 4-line stanzas, plus re-
frain, 65 lines.   Morgan N202.   T.C., Dublin, Bodley,
Crawford, PU.   Allusions to Marlborough's being so far
away at the proroguing of Parliament.   Opens:

>   Oh! Brother Tom dost know the Intent,
>   *Lillibullero Bullen a la,*
>   Why they Prorogue the Parliament?
>   *Lillibullero Bullen a la.*
>   *Lero, Lero, Lero,* &c.

36 *Forty-One in Miniature*:   AN Elegiack POEM.   Inscrib'd to
the HONOURABLE *MATTHEW PRIOR*, Esq;   [2 lines Latin]
LONDON: Printed in the Year 1711.
        2°:   t.p., *bl.*, 3-15, *bl.*, 16 pp.   Drop-t. on p. 3
and line: *Emori per virtutem praestat, quam per dedecus
vivers.*   CSmH.   Horn copy used.   249 lines, couplets.
Opens:

>   Prepare, my Muse, the wond'ring World to tell
>   An Action, sad as Horrour, black as Hell.

This poem, more satire than elegy, raises many questions.
it has General Daniel Parke, the famous messenger of the
victory at Blenheim, as its subject. As Hortensio, he is
defended against his detractors; but who is the author,
and why is the poem given such handsome printing? That
it is a Tory piece is evident, in the dedication to Prior
and in the censoring of the Whig apologist, Abel Boyer,
the only writer to be named. All the details in its
slight story fit the picaresque career of Parke. He
serves Gloriana (Queen Anne) on the Isle of "Riga" (An-
tigua) in the Leewards. He is defended by a guard of
"auxiliary Negroes" but is assailed and taken from his
own house to be brutally murdered. The poet says it is
hard that he should be slain again in Britain, "Mur-
ther'd afresh, by Calumnies of Men," and by Bo[ye]r's
Pen (236-7). This is a strange reward for the valor he
displayed at "Schellenburgh" and on the banks of the
Danube. He lived from 1669 to 1710.

By far the most informative account of Parke's life
is to be found in Boyer's *Political State of Great Britain*, 1711, I, 335-40. Colorful episodes, largely missing
in DNB and Marlborough's biographers, begin with his
birth in Virginia as the son of a wealthy planter, his
marriage at 15 to a woman ten years his senior, the birth
of two daughters, desertion of his family to go to England, at 25, and there the seduction of the wife of a
member of the Life Guards, return to Virginia as a trader
in tobacco. He owned several ships, one of which on being
captured by pirates, led to a trial and the execution of
13 of 24 guilty persons. Parke stood for Parliament in
Hampshire, and was elected, only to be expelled for notorious bribery.

All this Defoesque activity preceded Parke's finally
going to Flanders as a volunteer. There his service to
Marlborough culminated with his being appointed as an
aide-de-camp to the Duke. If Boyer is correct, his career was blighted just as it was to brighten. A quarrel
with one of the Guards led to his leaving Marlborough's
service just prior to Blenheim. However, he stayed on
to serve in that battle. Then, when

> . . .he was just upon his departure for *England*,
> [he] humbly desired his Grace to favour him with
> a line or two, to acquaint the Queen with that

glorious Action. His Request was readily
granted: And thereupon, his Grace wrote, on
Horse-Back, with a Leaden Pencil, the following Note to his Duchess.

The famous note is quoted in full. In a marginal comment
Boyer states that Parke had not been commissioned as
colonel, but used the title which he had held in the Virginia militia. He further dims the glowing reputation
of the messenger of Blenheim by informing us of the good
fortune of Parke in acquiring "considerable Presents,
such as large Gold Medals, and Chains" in various German
towns en route to the Channel. Boyer leaves no doubt as
to the dubious morals of "Hortensio" and wastes little
sympathy on him for the violent death and the mutila-
tion of his body which were the consequences of his abuse
of authority. The author of *Forty-One in Miniature* was
less an enemy of Parke than of Boyer, and in the atmosphere of 1711, of the Duke. Unquestionably he cast an
ironic light on Marlborough's most glorious achievement,
or at least on the transmission of the news of the victory to the Queen.
    The trial and execution of the ill-fated Earl of
Strafford, May 12, 1641, seems little more than a Tory
parallel to Parke's death. Its bearing in the title appears to be the only pertinence to the fate of the bearer
of the news of Blenheim.

7 *The Fox Unkennel'd*; Or, The Whiggs IDOL. *By a Young
Nobleman of the University of* OXFORD. London, printed by
J. Benson in the *Strand*. 21 4-line stanzas, 84 lines,
ballad satire.
    1/2°: 1 side. Pro-Ormond and anti-Marlborough.
BM copy used. Not in Morgan. Opens:

        If Men are deem'd for Loyalty
        As Traytors to their Prince.

Great Ormond, eclipsed for a while, now shines forth as
an heroic soul. He never supported a Dutch Barrier Treaty,
nor sent his haughty wife to court votes to make him

"General for Life" (1. 44). He never made base deductions from foreign troops, nor fed on the soldiers' bread. He never let the French "Decamp, then form Excuses" (1. 58). Throughout Ormond is praised for not doing what is alleged against Marlborough.

338 He's *welcome Home*; or a *Dialogue* between *John* and *Sarah*. 1711.
        1/2°: 1 col. BM (2). Morgan N393. 78 lines, couplets. Opens:

        Wellcome Home, from Wars Alarms,
        Wellcome to my Longing Arms.

Favorable to Marlborough.

339 The IMPEACHMENT of His GRACE the D. of *Marlbro'*, On his Going Openly to Town, attended by many of the Nobility. No pub., n. d. Pr. on strip.
        1/4°: 1 side, 1 col. LAS-Foxon. 18 lines, couplets. Not in Morgan. Opens:

        Knows not your GRACE? when *Merit* soars too high,
        The *Object* but offends th' ungrateful Eye?

If the Duke had come incognito he would have discredited his enemies by making them guilty of envy at his modesty. When the infernal Powers defied the Omnipotent--

        The *Innocence* of *Michael* shockt 'em more
        Than all th' Artillery of Heav'n before.

        Marlborough returned on Epiphany Day, January 6, 1711, after passing the Ne Plus Ultra lines.

340 Blackmore, Sir Richard (1664-1729)

The Nature of Man. A Poem in Three Books. London, Printed for *S. Buckley*. 1711.

358

8vo *vi*, 113. Morgan N65. Also in *Coll. of Poems on Various Subjects*, 1718. Marlborough ref. Book II, 236-7, on Wit as native to the Island.
The Muses

. . . exhausted from continual Pains
In singing Marlbro's Toil, and great Campaigns,
They now sit silent to recruit their Veins.

41 *A Pair of Spectacles* for OLIVER'S *Looking-Glass Maker.* *LONDON.* Printed and Sold by *J. Baker*, at the *Black-Boy* in *Pater-Noster Row.* 1711. (Price 6 *d.*)
8vo: t.p., *bl.*, 3-46; added 'Books Printed for and Sold by J. Baker,' *iii-x* unmbd. All the items are anti-Marlborough satires and pamphlets, incl. *Oliver's Pocket Looking Glass.* 56 pp. Morgan N152. Says Stonehill ascribes to Defoe, but not in Moore. BM copy used.
Parallels the original by page and ref. and by paragraph, but in a muddy, heavy style. Doesn't get to specific charges till p. 40. Associates Marlborough with Cromwell.

42 [Oldisworth, William (1680-1734)]

Reasons for Restoring the WHIGS. *London*, Printed in the Year 1711. Price 6 *d.*
8vo: π'A-D⁴, F³, *bl.*, t.p., *bl.*, 3-38, 40 pp. Horn copy used. Prose pamphlet. Morgan N462.
The writing is so heavily satirical as almost to defeat itself. On p. 5 an allusion to Hare as "the *Confessor* to the *Army*, who knows so much of the *Management* of the *War*." Oldisworth was editing the *Examiner*, and Hare was one of the chief critics of the Tories and that paper as its spokesman. An ironic reference to "*Mr. Daniel de Foe*," p. 28, shows Defoe as still working for the Whig interest. Marlborough's victories are listed, but the satire is not directed against him.

343 *A Roman Story*. London, 1711. No pub.
Morgan N522. "Curious account of English politics, in
which Harley and Marlborough masquerade under thinly
disguised Roman names." *Wrenn Catalog* attributes to
Steele. Pickering & Chatto Cat. 155 lists. No copy
located.

344 [King, William (1663-1712)]

Rufinus, or on *Historical Essay* on the Favourite Ministry
under *Theodosius* the Great, and his son *Arcadius*. London,
1712. No pub.
8VO: 63 pp. Morgan N336. Prose attack on Marlborough. DNB says was printed 1711, though dated 1712.
To this is added a poem *Rufinus*, or the *Favourite*.
Imitated from Claudian. 330 lines, couplets. Less evidently a satire on Marlborough, but passages on the avarice
with which he was charged by his enemies are significant.
Opens:

> Oft, as I wondering stand, a secret doubt
> Puzzles my reason, and disturbs my thought.

The original harmony of Nature and the world, when piety,
faith, and justice prevailed is now disrupted by fiends
that darken the Sun and wreak havoc. The murder of Agamemnon, the blinding of Oedipus, and other classical episodes are introduced. Rufinus (Marlborough) is born, and
grows into a maturity of rapacious cruelty.

> Not dying patriots' tortures can assuage
> His inborn cruelty, his native rage:
> Not *Tagus'* yellow torrent can suffice
> His boundless and unsated *avarice*.   133-6

Passages seem to depict the erection of Blenheim Palace,
and Rufinus is ravished at the sight which appeals to his
Midas instincts. Nothing can satisfy his thirst for gold.
Even when a patriot comes to "assert a sinking *nation*'s
cause," he is not to be deterred from vengeance. Since
the noble Stilicho was the commander in the final stages
of Roman Britain, the Tory uneasiness and sense of

impending fate at the death of Queen Anne is discernible.
The poem of course displays party rancor rather than any
truth. It is reprinted in the anthologies of Anderson,
Chalmers, *et al.*, as well as in the *Works* of King, 1776
and 1781.

45   *A Short Narrative of the Life* of His *Grace*, *John* Duke
of *Marlborough*, from the Beginning of the *Revolution* to
this Present Time. With Some *Remarks* upon *His Conduct*.
By an Old Officer of the Army. *London*. Printed for
J. Baker at hte Black-Boy in Pater-noster-Row, 1711.
      8°:   A-E⁴ F³; t.p., *bl.*, 1-45, *bl.*, 48 pp., prose.
J. R. Moore assigns to Defoe on basis of bsd., *Plot or
No Plot*, but this seems unproved. See No. 373. Copies
at BM, Bod, NLS, UL, BPL, F, CSmH, IU, MH copy used. A
fine copy at San Jose State. Morgan N396, "No soldier
wrote this." The work anticipates *The Lives of Two Illustrious Generals*, 1713, which Churchill supposed to be
the earliest account. Both works are strongly loyal to
Marlborough, defending him throughout against the attacks of the *Examiner*. However, this is a vigorously
original recital of events, whereas the *Lives of the Two
Illustrious Generals* draws heavily on Hare's *Conduct* of
1712.

    Aside from summarizing Marlborough's career and cam-
paigns, *The Short Narrative* is devoted considerably to
defending the Duke against all charges, from those concerning Dunkirk to the current charges of misuse of funds, and
his conduct in command of the forces. Sir Walter Raleigh
and the roll of histories are cited as evidence of previous cases of ingratitude to famous generals. Morgan is
correct in saying that the author is "no soldier," but
there seems no reason to suppose that he is not an officer,
probably a chaplain in view of his classical learning and
Biblical allusions in his estimate of Marlborough's character. The word "contumaceous" does not sound either like
Defoe or what he might put into the mouth of an officer
(E 3).

346 [Defoe, Daniel (1660-1731)]

A Speech for the D[uch]*ess*. 1711. Morgan N159. Only
ref. Not in Moore. No loc.

347 *A Tail of J*[oh]*n and S*[ara]*h or, both Turnd out of
C[our]*t at Last*. Printed for John Arbor in Fleetstreet,
1711. BM copy used.
        1/2°: 1 side, 1 column. 64 lines, couplets. Not
in Morgan. A dialogue in pastoral vein between Damon
and Thyrsis. Opens:

    Damon.   Alas, the warlike Hero seems to grieve,
             That he his restless Toyls of War must leave.

The hero takes no pleasure in *Sa--ah*'s charms or joys of
peace. Thyrsis replies that he has won fame, conquering
like Mars, and that now to please Queen and country he
should give up war, so that trade and traffick may revive.

    He that's against a peace, Duke, Lord or Peer,
    He loves not Queen nor Church, the Case is clear.
                                                    51-2
Crudely printed. Apostrophe is reversed, but no misspellings.

348 *The Tale of a Disbanded Officer*. *LONDON*: Printed the
YEAR, M.DCC.XI.

        1/2°: 1 side, 1 column. 58 lines, couplets. A
fable in verse. BM copy used. Not in Morgan. Opens:

    The Birds reduc'd once to a Pop'lar State,
    Their King, and Lords of Pray [*sic*], Ejected sat.

The satire deals with Marlborough's situation, but seems
to favor him. As the Kite, he has won many battles for
the Birds. Now that he has had a bad campaign, they wish
to throw him out. The grave Parrot addresses "Mr. SPEAK-
ER" and asserts that "The *Stork*, or *Buzzard*, might have

done the same" (1. 20). The Linnet votes for the Swal-
low to take command, but the poem concludes with a 6-line
Moral. It points out that while those who would vote for
turning out may know best, but

> Tho' possibly another might Excell,
> 'Tis good for Folks to know when they are well.

                                          57-8

49 A TOAST For *A*--------*e* and *Robbin*, In the French WINE.
    London, Printed for *John Turnham* near *St. Paul's Church-
    Yard*, 1711.
    1/2°: 1 side, 1 column. 48 lines, couplets. BM
    copy used. Morgan N34. Opens:

> Great *A*----- be cautious and beware,
> Lest for thee and Robbin lie a hidden snare.

No specific reference to Marlborough, but the satire deals
with the war and the dangers of being deterred from pushing it through. French wines are subtly offered as a
bribe, and French spies are about. A striking example
of bad printing, full of misspellings and other blunders.
Queen Anne and Robert Harley are of course the subjects.

50 The Windsor Prophecy. Found in Marlborough Rock. London:
    Printed in the Year, 1711.
    1/2°: 1 side, 1 column. 37 lines, couplets. BM
    copy used. Foxon reports variant - 'Price One Penny.'
    Satire on ambitions of the Marlboroughs. Morgan N663.
    See No. 380, 1712. Opens:

> When *Stock* of *Wood* shall come to owe,
> Its New-born Name to MARLBOROUGH
> Believe it then, from hence shall Rise
> A PLANT, whose Boughs shall reach the Skies.

The birds strive with each other in the tree, Kites, Hawks,
and Vultures against the Dove's Prerogative. Still
Heaven's will shall prevail, and every side will "bless
the *Windsor Prophecy*."

The year is a laboratory for the study of political pamphleteering. What it lacked in quality, it atoned for in quantity. Morgan lists 748 entries, of which a considerable number are related to the great events of the year, particularly the secret maneuverings toward the peace. Quite as with the United States in Southeast Asia in the 1960's, it involved differences within parties as well as between them. It also involved face-saving strategies reflecting dubious elements of victories in combat and defeat in the myriad entanglements of diplomacy, economic rivalry, and the more human factors of a shifting social fabric. While the terms Whig and Tory serve for the broad differences in political attitudes, English society reveals many subdivisions and variations. From the Tory came the solid figure of John Bull, as articulated by Dr. John Arbuthnot, to stand as a permanent symbol of the English character. From the Whig side emerged a cluster of pamphlets from the pen of Dr. Hare, vindicating Marlborough, the policy of the war, and the difficulties of making a peace that would both satisfy Holland, the Empire, and also the various factions at home. Such writing is ephemeral, it is true, but it also embodies much that is useful to the historian who seeks to reconstruct the temper of the times.

Marlborough had gone abroad, in disgrace, and Godolphin had died, while Oxford was triumphant in the government over his old ally Bolingbroke. The latter was embittered over his being given only a viscount's title, and being denied the Order of the Garter. In short, 1712 was a year of deadly intrigues and bickering, lasting up to the Queen's demise. The visit of Prince Eugene, even with memories of his association with Marlborough at Blenheim, Oudenarde, and Malplaquet, was a disappointment, at least to Whig hopes. The tide had turned, and Swift and the enemies of Great Generals triumphed over them. The heroes of the past were now targets for vilification and shameful derision. It is significant that in creating

his Gulliver in the early 20's Swift should find occasion for allusions to Oxford and Bolingbroke, and certainly to the negative aspects of war, but not to Marlborough. Even whatever share he had in bringing about
the Treaty of Utrecht presumably is reflected in the
Queen's ingratitude for his seizing the French fleet,
an episode strikingly paralleled by Gulliver. He had
finally discovered what the Duke of Marlborough had long
known, that service is often rewarded with neglect, and
even exile. Hence even the aged Duchess could praise
the satire of the man who had done so much to destroy
her husband.

That the Marlboroughs accumulated vast wealth is
undeniable, as it is for so many members of the nobility. Much of this seems attributable to the Duchess's
fantastic energy and financial shrewdness. Certainly it
has nothing to do with Marlborough's service as commander
of the forces and as diplomat. The charges brought
against him were notoriously ill-founded, but they were
the subject of a lively pamphlet war, which is only one
of the phases of a conflict which the Duke deplored and
in which he participated only in the form of a public
address to his peers. Apart from the sparring between
Dr. Hare with Swift and Mrs. Manley, few names are identifiable. Unquestionably the war was dragging on into
complete futility. It did need to be terminated. The
only way this could be done was to blacken Marlborough's
name and reputation. Swift's part in this is the most
deplorable phase in the career of a great genius who
sought to "vex the world." Most of the writing remains
anonymous, which is perhaps just as well.

351 [Swift, Jonathan (1667-1745)]

A FABLE OF THE Widow and her Cat. *London*, Printed for
Philpot near *Charing-Cross*, 1711.
    1/2°: 1 p., 9 5-line stanzas, 45 lines, nmbd. Mor-
gan N574. Another ed. by Morphew, 1712, and a Dublin ed.,
n.d. Williams in *Swift's Poems* I, 151-4, prints with full
notes. He accepts it as by Swift "with some hesitation,"
since it is also ascribed to Prior and others. He notes
its relation to *When the Cat's Away*, No. 360, which is a
retort upon it. Almost certainly the poem was not printed
before early 1712. Teerink, No. 862, is "doubtful."
Opens:

> A Widow kept a Favourite Cat,
>   At first a gentle Creature.

When the Cat (Marlborough) has become fat he soon reveals
his true nature. He steals cream from the Widow (Queen
Anne), scratches her Maid (Mrs. Masham), and perpetrates
other outrages. Godolphin appears as the Fox.

> The Fox and he were Friends of old,
>   Nor cou'd they now be parted;
> They nightly slunk to rob the Fold,
> Devour'd the Lambs, the Fleeces sold,
> And Puss grew lion-hearted.   6-10

Although Marlborough is praised for his service in battle,
he is thrown out in disgrace, an action which had occurred
the previous December 30th. The poem makes the now customary charge concerning perquisites; but it is neither
extreme in its satire nor wit. At the close the Widow
exclaims:

> Tell me, Perfidious! was it fit
> To make my Cream a PERQUISITE.
> .   .   .   .
> Here, *Towzer*! -- Do him Justice.

Whether or not Parliament enjoyed being called Towzer, the
case had been concluded against Marlborough. The Fable is
soon followed by the quite superior, for satire and wit,
Fable of Midas, No. 362. It is also superior in venom.

366

352   January *ca.*

A Trip to Germany: or, the D. of *M-------h's* Farewell to
England.   Who With his *D---hess is going to live in* Germany *as a Prince of the* Empire.   *London:*   Printed by *J.
Read* in *White-Fryers,* near *Fleet-Street.*   [Colophon bottom of p. 5]   N. d. [1712]
      4°:   A; drop-t. only, 1-5, *6*, 6 pp.   133 lines,
couplets.   BM, CtY.   BM copy used.   Not in Morgan.   Satire
on Marlborough.   Opens:

      Are all my Lawrels come to this?'
      Farewell! Let Fame and Honour cease.

His name will be heard no more, his battles forgotten, and
only how he rose to fame will be recalled, also, how his
sister provided the first step by captivating royal James
II; how the Duchess of Cleveland aided in the next step,
and marriage to Sarah Jennings provided the final aid.
Now Mother Jennings' prophecy awaits to be confirmed to
determine his future.   Pages 3 to 5 recount the fable of
a Lyon who commands that all horned beasts be banished.
They flee in terror.   But Reynard, the Fox, stops one,
that is Marlborough, because he has only a "bunch of flesh"
on his forehead.   The latter insists this may grow into a
horn, and insists on fleeing.

      To *German* Courts let me repair,
      'Tis for my Health, the Change of Air.   105-6

He will have the friendship of Europe, of the Empire and
the Dutch in particular, and will reign in Mindelheim,
the princedom assigned to him in the Empire.   Thus, hoping
for Hanoverian Succession, and living in Hochstet's name,
he will be safe.   The satire is not decisive enough for
much force, nor sufficiently artful to conceal the factor
of ingratitude toward the erstwhile adored hero.

53   January 2.

An *Excellent New Song* Call'd the *Trusty* and *True Englishman.*
      1/2°:   2 columns, 2 sides.   No pub., n. d.   Foxon-

Luttr. '2 Jan. 1711/12.' 20 7-8 line stanzas, 160 lines. BM. Not in Morgan. Opens:

> Poor *England*'s Condition,
> By Sons of Perdition,
> Never was more in Danger.

A Tory, anti-Marlborough ballad. Whiggish ambition, the Austrian race, and "*M-----h*'s Grace" have brought England to a bad situation. It is, however, still too early to think of a peace.

354 January early.

PROLOGUE BETWEEN *FAME* and *ENVY*. The prologue to *The General Cashier'd*: Or, a PROLOGUE Between FAME and ENVY: As it was spoken before his Highness Prince *Eugene* of Savoy, at the Playhouse. *LONDON*: Printed for *J. Baker*, at the *Black-Boy* in *Pater-Noster-Row*, 1712. (Price 1 *s* 6 *d*.)
    1/2°: 2 columns, 75 lines, couplets. NYPub. copy used and only one known. Horn copy of Sec. Ed. of the play also used. The same, except for use of italics. Morgan W517. Opens:

> Fame)   Thou great disturber of Heroick Songs,
>   Parent of *Murder*, and the Hero's Wrongs.

In a strenuous debate Fame denounces Envy; but the latter insists that fame inflates heroes and creates jealousies, as with Caesar and Alexander. Similarly with William III, who freed the English people from slavery only to be rewarded with ingratitude. "Revil'd while living, and when dead unsung" (1. 68). Marlborough is not named, but the parallel is evident. He, too, despite heroic actions, cannot rise above "the Barren Scriblers Praise." Fame is urged not to "boast of his Darling Conqueror," but to go to some more grateful shore, "Where Merit and where Virtue may be heard. . .and meet a just Reward" (11. 74-5). The play was never acted, and has no direct bearing on Marlborough, although he was the "general cashier'd."

355   January 10.

[Defoe, Daniel (1660-1731)]

NO QUEEN: OR, NO GENERAL.   AN ARGUMENT, PROVING The
Necessity Her MAJESTY was in, as well for the *Safety* of
Her Person as of Her *Authority*, to Displace the D--- of
M---borough.   *LONDON*:   Printed, and Sold by the Booksellers of *London* and *Westminster*.   1712.
    8°:   A¹ B-F⁴ G¹; t.p., *bl*., 1-42, 44 pp.   Moore 227;
Morgan 0179.   BM, Bod, BPL, CSmH, CtY, IU, NYP, TxU, *et
al.*, Sec. Ed., 23 January, same collation; Moore notes
variant pagination.   Horn copy used.
    Defoe is writing under the influence of Harley, con-
stantly endeavoring to maintain the image of Marlborough
as completely loyal to the Queen and mindful of the immense returns he has enjoyed.   He shows Tory bias in
treating the "Juncto" and even the Dissenters harshly.
The Naval debt and the South Sea Bubble, as well as
other subjects are brought in; but the emphasis is
placed on the necessity for Peace, and support of the
ministry towards it.   Jacobite leanings are not revealed;
in fact, explicit anticipations of the ascension of the
House of Hanover are expressed, and the Elector is mentioned as a possible successor to Marlborough.   The claim
is made that the Duke will not be seriously missed, and
certainly that disaster will not befall the country at
his displacement.
    In the conclusion the alternative in the title,
either "No Queen or No General," is advanced as the only
retort to the faction that is using Marlborough for their
own interests.   They, Defoe says, include the "No[bili]ty"
and the generals and officers of the army.   He hints at a
second part which was not to appear; but the pamphlet
should stand as comparable to Swift's *Conduct of the
Allies*, not only as a factor in displacing Marlborough
but also as a document in expediency such as was demanded
of "mercenary scriblers."

356   January 15.

M. Manlius Capitolinus. *Printed in the Year* 1712. Date
bottom of p. 2.
1/2°: 2 sides, 1 column, no wmk., no pub. 4-1/2
lines Virgil precede 18 lines of verse in couplets.
Foxon reports a copy in larger type, 'Printed by John
Morphew 1711.' BM copy used. Not in Morgan. Luttr.
'15 Jan. 1711/12.' The title refers to Marcus Manlius
Capitolinus, a largely legendary figure of the 4th Century B.C., who was thrown from the Tarpeian rock. While
he actually seems to have aided the poor, his career is
credited with inordinate ambition. Resemblances to
Marlborough are striking: he left a great name after
conquering the Gaul, i.e. the French, and even aspired
to the crown. Even though the allegations were false,
Marcus Manlius suffered for them, just as Marlborough
suffered from false allegations of the Tories. Though
the Senate and the crowds heaped votes and adulation on
Manlius, so votes and ballads were heaped on Marlborough -

But 'twas too fierce an Ardor for Renown,
And was at once thy Trophy and thy Tomb.   17-18

See the next entry.

357   The FATE OF *M. Manlius Capitolinus*; Translated from Approved HISTORIANS. Ornament and date bot. p. 4, *Printed
in the Year* 1712. Ornamental band top p. 1, and drop-t.
only.
4°: A; *1-4*, 4 pp., no pub., prose. BM copy used.
No allusion appears to the preceding entry, but both
plainly bear on Marlborough in strong satirical vein. Presumably the prose piece is somewhat later. It depicts
Marcus Manlius as serving the emperor Marcus Furius Camil-
ius by resisting the Gaul. Associations with Marlborough
are overt in Manlius's inviting to his house members of
the *Junto*, aspersing Senators, and heading a dangerous
Faction.

But, when he appeared in Publick, he never forgot
to season his Speeches with the known Cant of

his Sense of the Miserys occasion's by the War,
his Concern for the Libertys of Free-born *Romans*, and *his* Continual Vows for Peace; tho' by
his *Creeping Motion* toward one, it was notorious, That the Design of *perpetuating* the War
was as *natural*, to him, as his *Avarice*.   (p. 3)

Moreover, Manlius hardens "several *mercenary
Scribblers*" to put the popular mind in a ferment, and
thus sway the giddy multitude to his purposes.   These
undoubtedly include an ambition to royalty.   The obvious moral is drawn: "That the Immoderate Desire of subverting the Constitution of one's Country, renders even
the Greatest Actions, not unregarded only, but Odious"
(p. 4).
    Again no specific allusion to Marlborough appears,
but none is needed in 1712.   Morgan 0427.

558   January 17.

[Hare, Dr. Francis (1671-1740)]

THE CONDUCT Of the DUKE of *MARLBOROUGH* During the Present
WAR.   WITH ORIGINAL PAPERS.   (4 lines Horace)   *LONDON*:
Printed in the Year M.DCC.XII.
    4°: A^4, B-Tt^4; t.p., *bl.*, 1-329, *bl.*, 332 pp.
Drop-t. p. 1.   'An Account of the Duke of *Marlborough*'s
Conduct in the Present War.'   Ornamental band at top of
p. 1.   Adv. *Protestant Post-Boy*, Numb. 59, Tues. Jan. 15-
17, 1712, 'This Day is publish'd'; also Jan. 24-6, and
Spec. 281, Jan. 22, 1712.   Horn copy used.   Morgan 0306.
    As the writer has shown, this work draws heavily on
Hare's *Life and Glorious History*, 1705, No. 112. Its purpose was to supply what was Hare's final estimate of
Marlborough's life, to reply to certain attacks, including *The Memorial to the Church of England* (p. 83), with
a concluding allusion to the Duke's request to be made
commanding general for life.   The criticism over the
2-1/2% and Marlborough's vast income are not considered.
Since the *Life and Glorious History* and the *Conduct* were

prime, though unacknowledged, sources for Lediard,
through him they influenced all modern biography of Marlborough, down to Churchill. See also the *Conduct of the
Dowager Duchess of Marlborough*, 1742, No. 561 below.

359 January 24 *ca.*

A SPEECH Without Doors, CONCERNING The *Two and a Half per
Cent*. *Jovis* 24 Die *Jan*, 1711, Resolved, That the *Two and
a Half per Cent* deducted from the Foreign Troops in Her
Majesty's Pay is Publick Money, and ought to be accounted
for. [ornament] Sold by the Book-sellers of *London* and
Westminster, 1712. Price Six-Pence.
     8°: A-E⁴; t.p., *bl. ii*, 3-40, drop-t. on 3, 40 pp.
Morgan O188 mistakenly ascribes to Defoe. See M190. Not
in Lee nor Moore. MH Business School copy used. Opens:

> *Mr. Sp----*. I have bestow'd some Time upon
> the R-p-t, I have given great Attention to the
> Debate, I have endeavour'd with my self to be-
> lieve every Charge against the Duke. . .I have
> weigh'd the Arguments on both sides, and the
> Result is, That no Nation in the Universe had
> ever greater Obligation to a Subject, than
> *Great Britain* to the Duke of *Marlborough*. . .

The writer, who might possibly be Dr. Hare, summarizes the entire case, noting the indebtedness of much of
Europe to Marlborough, notably for winning innumerable
victories, for which the use of the two and a half per
cent deducted from the money assigned for foreign troops
was used for intelligence of the enemy's actions and intentions. This was done with the full knowledge and consent of the allies as essential to victory. He shows
that the amount actually deducted has been exaggerated
by the Duke's enemies. Marlborough "has procur'd more
Benefits for his country than the Conquests of all our
Kings, from the first *William* to the last" (p. 39). The
only clue to authorship is the implication that the
writer was in Parliament (p. 15). The pamphlet has no
relationship to Defoe's, except for the title. See No.300.

360   January 31.

[Maynwaring, Arthur (1668-1712)] ?

When the Cat's *away, The Mice may play.* A FABLE, Humbly
inscrib'd to Dr. Sw----t.   [2 lines Latin, unsgnd.]   *LON-
DON: Printed for* A. Baldwin *in* Warwick-lane.   Price Two
Pence.
       2°:   not sgnd.; 1-4, 4 pp., colophon bot. p. 4.   18
5-line stanzas, 90 lines.   Extraordinarily handsome printing, ornamental band top p. 1, ornamental letter at opening.   BM copy used.   Inscr. in modern hand 'By John Gay.'
Teerink No. 1299 suggests Maynwaring, Prior.   Morgan 0557.
Opens:

>   A *Lady* once (so Stories say)
>   By *Rato* and *Mice* infested.

The poem is plainly a reply to Swift's *A Fable of the
Widow and her Cat.*   Also Swift alludes to it in his *Journal to Stella*: "A poem is come out to-day inscribed to
me, by way of a flirt; for it is a Whiggish poem, and
good for nothing."   He is writing on January 31st, the
day of publication of the poem.   It is Whiggish, which is
one reason for giving at least attention to the suggestion
in the Wright and Spears ed. of Prior's *Literary Works*
that Maynwaring might be the author.   As editor of the
Medley, which had directly opposed the *Examiner*, an ardent
supporter of the government against Dr. Sacheverell, and
particularly as secretary to the Duchess of Marlborough,
Maynwaring had ample motive.   Oldmixon, *Life of Maynwaring*, 1715, p. 40, quotes verses on the Occasional Conformity Bill, which are in the style of a fable:

>   Now Conscience is a Thing we know,
>   Like to a Mastiff Dog,
>   Which if ty'd up, so Fierce he'll grow,
>   He'll bite his very Clog.

The tone of these verses at least demonstrates Maynwaring's capability for the style and mode of *When the Cat's
away.*
       In the poem a Lady (Queen Anne) is persuaded to reject
her Cat (Marlborough) by Mrs. Abigail, and her Lapdog

(Harley) is restored to favour. But the mice and rats
return, and the Lady is induced by a former, trusted
serving maid (the Duchess) to restore her Cat. "Struck
with the Sense of Her Mistake," she resolves never to
give up the cat again. The poem perhaps had actually
been written in late 1709, when the conclusion would have
fitted actual events.

361 February 5.

The Land-Leviathan; or, *Modern Hydra*: in Burlesque Verse,
By way of *Letter* to a *Friend*. *Nec vult Pamthera domari*.
Quae Genus. [ornament] *LONDON*: Printed for *John Morphew*
near *Stationers-Hall*. 1712. Price 3 *d*. Drop-t. p. 5.
Adv. in *P. Boy*, No. 2611, Sat. Feb. 2-5, 'This Day is
publish'd.'
        8°:   *A* B-C⁴; t.p.,*b*l, 4-24. Pp. 3-4, Address to
"Sir," 18 lines, and the poem, 290 lines, both in octo-
syllabic couplets. [ornaments throughout] Morgan 0431.
MH, CtY, InU, ICU, TxU. Horn copy used. Preliminary
address opens:

        SIR.
            To You, my very loving Friend,
            I this Poetick Greeting send.

This portion is little more than disclaiming of attempting genuine poetry. At the conclusion of the whole he
remarks: "*Doggrel*'s my Province, not *Heroic*" (1. 289).
However, the satire shows considerable vigor and deft-
ness. It is a Tory piece, even though the author claims
to lean to neither extreme, and "in Opinion keep a Mean"
(1. 165). Satire on Marlborough is as leader of the Faction which constitutes the Leviathan, or Hydra. A Tory's
one, we learn, who is always for the Queen, wants Spain
but without forcing Philip, and who

        Respects, tho' not so much, his G[race],
        As Her who made him what he was.
        A Whig, per contra, does not care
        Who suffers, so we have a War.   136-9

374

He has converted from an art to a trade; he refers the
peace to their quondam majesties, the Junto; he is
"very loud" for Marlbro', but silent on "Anna." The
summation is that the satire is leveled against Low Church
and High Flyer alike, against Presbyterians, and Harley,
now *O*[x]*f*[or]*d*. That it comes from the group of which
Swift and Bolingbroke, and the *Examiner* are a part is
evidenced particularly in a cut at Dr. Hare.

> *H---re*, when, in hope to be a Bishop
> He does *Thanksgiving-Sermon* dish up.   264-5

He encourages boys to shed their blood against the
French.

> How bravely at *Taniere* they fell;
> How manfully they on were led,
> And follow'd to be knock'd o' th' Head.   271-3

See the Sermon, No. 325, Oct. 4, 1711, above.

362   February 14.

[Swift, Jonathan (1667-1745)]

The Fable of Midas. Printed in the Year, 1711. Variant
has 'Printed for *John Morphew* near *Stationer*'s-*Hall*, 1711.'
Foxon Bute-Silver has Luttr. date, '14 Feb. 1711/12.'
      1/2°: 1 side, 1 column. LLP, C, Crawford. BM copy
used. Morgan 0652. 82 lines, octosyllabics. Repr. Williams *Poems* and H. Davis, *Poems*, 1957, pp. 100-2. Teerink
No. 558. Opens:

> *Midas*, we are in Story told,
> Turn'd every thing he touch'd to Gold.

Nothing in Swift, except perhaps his coarseness, does him
so little credit as his attacks on Marlborough. Unsub-
stantiated vilification however wittily expressed, ultimately recoils on its producer.

This tale inclines the gentle reader
To think upon a certain leader;
To whom from Midas down descends
That virtue in the fingers' ends.
What else by perquisites are meant,
By pensions, bribes, and three per cent.   41-6

The piece merely asserts that Marlborough embezzled and
took bribes. It proves nothing but Swift's capacity
for relishing cruelty in political satire. Concludes:

And *Midas* now neglected stands,
With *Asses Ears* and *dirty Hands*.   81-2

363   February 19.

To the Duke of Marlborough in Disgrace. Pub. in *Protestant Post-Boy*, No. 73, Sat. Feb. the 16th to Tues.,
Feb. 19th, 1711/12. Pp. 1-2. Opens:

Go, Valiant Man, from Human Wrongs retreat,
Appriz'd of what must make your Fame compleat.

The poem is enclosed in an unsigned letter to the publisher, "written by a Friend of Mine who has made too
great a Figure in the Learned World not to give them
Imprimature." The writer claims to have held posts in
more than one kingdom.

364   February 21.

Prince Eugene's Welcome. London, Printed by Bernard Lin-
tott at the *Cross-Keys*. Price 1 d. N.d., adv. in *D.
Cour.*, No. 3231, Thurs. Feb. 21, 1712. MH, Clark, CSmH,
DFU, ICN-Luttr. dates '21 Feb. 11/12.'
    1/2°: 1 side, 1 column. Opens:

Great Britain, styl'd from Military Deeds,
Sympathic Welcome to Great-*Eugene* bids.

Stresses the full, harmonious cooperation between Eugene
and Marlborough, each a partner in the "Joint-stock
Vic'try." Eugene arrived the following day, February
22. Not in Morgan.

565   February (?)

Welcome to England, or a *Dialogue* between *Two Great Generals*, Relating to the *Peace*. 1712. No pub., fol. bsd.
Morgan 0229. No other information, except the comment
that CPA, 234, f. 202 is MS copy which contains a French
transl., *Arrivée duc Eugene en Angleterre, ou dialogue
entre deux generaux à l'occasion de la Paix*.
      The poem alludes to the open championship of Marl-
borough by Eugene, following his disgrace and dismissal,
December 21, 1711. The Prince arrived in London February 22.

66   February 22 *ca*.

[Wagstaffe, William (1685-1725)]

The Story of St. Alb[a]n's Ghost; or the *Apparition* of
Mother Haggy; Collected from the Best Manuscripts. Lon-
don, 1712. Prose pamphlet. H&L ascribe to Wagstaffe;
BMC to Swift; Wrenn Cat. to Defoe. Swift to Stella,
Feb. 22: ". . .to Ld Mashams to night, and Lady Masham
made me read to her a pretty 2 penny Pamphlet called the
St. Albans Ghost. I thought I had writt it my self; so
did they, but I did not." Fourth ed., pp. 53-75, in *Misc.
Works* of *William Wagstaffe*, 1726. Morgan 0714. Publica-
tion jointly with a complete Key to *Law is a Bottomless
Pit*, 1712. Haggite (Sarah), daughter of the witch Mother
Haggy, marries Avaro (Marlborough). Godolphin as Bacon-
face, Montague as Mouse, and other Whig leaders are ridiculed, but Avaro receives the main attack. He is rest-
less, talking of Merit, Hardships, Accounts, Perquisites,
Commissioners, Bread and Bread-Waggons.

See *Prince Eugene not the Man you took him for*,
1712, No. 415. The same names are used, and an even
more debased tone in attacking Marlborough.

367 February 23.

The History of Prince MIRABEL's Infancy, Rise and Disgrace; With the sudden Promotion of NOVICIUS. In which
Are Intermix'd all the INTRIGUES: As also the CHARACTERS
of the Old and New FAVOURITES of both SEXES in the COURT
of BRITOMARTIA. *Collected from the* MEMOIRS *of a Courtier
lately Deceas'd. London*: Printed for *J. Baker*, at the
Black-Boy in *Pater-Noster-Row*. 1712. Price 1 *s*. Part I,
adv. in the *Protestant Post-Boy*, No. 75, Feb. 23 (Sat.),
'This Day is publish'd.'
        8°: A^8 B-G^8 H^1; *bl.*, *iii-x* Introduction, 1-90,
drop-t. on p. 1, 100 pp.
        Part II, 8°: A-F^8; t.p., *bl.*, 3-80. Adv. *Protes-
ant Post-Boy*, No. 95, Apr. 8-10, 1712.
        Part III, 8°: A-F^8; t.p., *bl.*, 3-80. Adv. *Spec.*
Pt. I, 310; II, 349; III, 380. Morgan O175 assigns to
Defoe, on authority of Trent. Not in Moore. Horn copy
used; all parts 1712, with common Introduction.
        In the Introduction the anonymous author addresses
his friend, Palemon, and at the end promises that if it
succeeds, "the next Mail shall waft you over the Second"
part. This suggests someone in Dublin, or at least over-
seas. No further clues to authorship appear, and while
Mirabel is pornographically portrayed in his amorous pursuits in Part I, the portrayal is otherwise not as vicious as those ascribed to Mrs. Manley and Swift had been.
Mirabel's affairs with Chrysis and Libissa lead up to
Clavella, the Duchess of Cleveland, and finally he meets,
adores, and marries his Sarah Jennings, who is known as
Jenibella. While Mirabel distinguishes himself in arms
in Part I, he is also deprived of his offices by Auran-
tion (William III). These are restored in Part II, when
war breaks out, and he goes on to win his great victories.
Now his letters to princes and senates are introduced,
with much of their courtly and diplomatic tone preserved.

Politics are present in the description of the five
members of the Junto (II, 12-14), and in fact throughout.
Actually *The History of Prince Mirabel*, whatever its
original intention, turns out to be quite favorable to
Marlborough, and opposed to Harley and his tool Montantia
(Mrs. Masham). The Duke is noted for "Candour and Sincerity" and always acting "to the Glory of his Country"
(I, 89). After Blenia (Blenheim) he modestly avoids
notice and refuses to accept any honors without his
Queen's approval. His courage is shown in battle, especially at Ramillies, where his aide loses his life,
and most of the victories and sieges of his principal
ten years of campaigning are reviewed favorably. The
final page of Part III, printed in smaller type to
crowd in the account, confirms his patriotism, discretion, and his desire to terminate the war.

> . . .nothing could be more ridiculous and absurd,
> than to charge, with a Design to perpetuate the
> War, a Man who had in every Respect out-done the
> *Britomartian* (English) Wishes, and had done more
> towards a *good Peace* by his own Address and Abil-
> ity both in War and Peace, by his Conduct in the
> Field, by his interest with the Empress's Allies,
> by his Happy Temper to prevent or make up differ-
> ences, by his Dexterity and Wisdom, by his great
> Humanity and Sweetness of Behaviour, which was
> peculiar to him, by his Zeal for the Honour of
> his Mistress whom he serv'd with more Affection
> than most Men ever did a sovereign, and by his
> true Concern for the good of his Country, and
> the liberty of the whole Universe, in which he
> had few Equals.   (p. 80)

These qualities not only struck terror into his enemies,
but his many victories, marches and sieges, if, the
writer asserts, they served to prolong the war, "then
Prince *Mirabel* bid fair towards being a perpetual Le-
gato, not otherwise."
This exceedingly rare work, in its three parts,
stands as one of the most important and extended documents in the development of the reaction to Marlborough
and his career. In CBEL only the first part is recog-

379

nized, and this is ascribed to Defoe. Moore rejects as by Defoe, but wonders if it is not by a "twin" of Mrs. Manley, if not by her. This seems highly untenable, in view of the conclusion, as quoted above. Actually, this portion at least sounds more like Hare than any of Marlborough's detractors. See a retort on March 11, *The Perquisite-Monger*, No. 371 below.

368   March 6 to July.

Arbuthnot, Dr. John (1667-1735)

The five *John Bull* Pamphlets are fully treated by Lester M. Beattie, *John Arbuthnot*, Harv. Pr., 1935, pp. 33-189. Full description and accounting for these and their many derivatives are not attempted here. See Morgan 047. Marlborough, as Hocus, a "cunning attorney," is important only since the pamphlets are designed as part of the Tory drive toward overthrowing him and bringing the Peace. Beattie clearly establishes that they are by Dr. Arbuthnot, and not by Swift, as Teerink seeks to show. Unquestionably, however, there was much mutual stimulus and putting of heads together in the Scriblerus group and other Tory clubs.

   Law is a Bottomless Pit, Exemplify'd in the Case of Lord Strutt, John Bull, Nicholas Frog, and Lewis Baboon, Who spent all they had in a Law-Suit. Printed in a *Manuscript* found in the *Cabinet* of the famous *Sir Humphrey Polesworth*. 1712. Beattie and CBEL both give March 6 as first ed., with 5 other eds. 1712. The succeeding parts were similarly subject to numerous editions, and all were reprtd. Edinburgh, 1712. Part II, March 18; Part III, April 17; Part IV, May 9; Part V, July 31. For full titles see the works cited above. All parts were pubd. as *The History of John Bull*, 1712. That the work is sketchy and chaotic is admitted by Beattie and confirmed by examination. Only the two doctors G[ar]th and R[adcli]ff[e] are identifiable by name, and the satire is recognized as being light-hearted and inoffensive. Marlborough appears primarily in the first pamphlet, as having an affair with Mrs. Bull, that is the Whig government which was supporting his campaigns.

The less known *Art of Political Lying* (short title) has a passage alluding to Marlborough's avarice; but in general theme and point of view the work adds nothing to the John Bull pamphlets. It came at the close of the same year, 1712. Marlborough appears as "an old cunning attorney" but with no other specific traits.

Beattie properly urges caution in attributing works to Dr. Arbuthnot on purely stylistic grounds. In general he sees him as showing his characteristic geniality and tolerance toward the Duke. In fact his limited references to Marlborough's "avarice" suggest that he was mainly interested in the broad Tory policy toward the war. Morgan O46-7.

69   March 8.

Copy of the Paper Stuck upon the D. of *M-----s* Gate at St. James's on the 8th of *March*, instant, being the day of Her Majesty's Accession to the Crown.

1/2°: 1 side, 1 column, no pub., n.d. BM copy used, 32 lines, octosyllabic couplets. Opens:

> A *German* Prince of Noble Race,
> A very ancient Peer.

Margin MS noted, "John Churchill of Mindelheim."

After what might seem a favorable opening, the piece reveals itself as a biting satire on the Duke and Duchess Sarah. Punning on his title as Baron Sandridge leads to the observation that if knaves are given an inch they will take an ell. But God will smite "the *Great Leviathan*," and quash the Plunderers.

Those Plund'rers that delight in *War* will be scattered.

370 March 11.

*The True Copy of a Paper stuck upon the D. of M----'s
Gate* at St. *James*'s on the 8th of *March*, instant, being
the day of Her Majesty's Accession to the Crown. Printed
by *R. Mott* in *Aldersgate-Street*, 1712. LSA-Luttr., '11
March 1711/12.' MH, Crawford. The same piece with only
a few changes in punctuation and italics. It seems no
"truer." Morgan 0438.

371 March 11-13.

The Perquisite-Monger; or the *Rise* and *Fall* of *Ingratitude*, being One of the Stories which the Monks of *God-
stow* were formerly wont to divert Fair *Rosamond* with,
and which may serve to clear up Several Absurdities in
the History of *Prince Mirabel*. Made Publick, from an
Original Manuscript lately found in the Ruines of *Wood-
stock-Bower*. *London*: Printed and Sold by the Booksellers of *London* and *Westminster*. 1712. Price 3 d.
    8vo: t.p., *bl.*, 1-24. Morgan 0433. Says some-
times attributed to Swift. Adv. in *Protestant Post-Boy*,
No. 83, March 11-13, 1712. 'Just Publish'd.' Horn copy
used. Morgan 0433.
    While this piece might by its title seem to be a
retort on *The History of Prince Mirabel*, it makes almost
no direct allusions to that work, beyond the Prince
Mirabel of the title. Marlborough is now Artemidorus,
and the action is set in Persia with names such as Chos-
roes as Charles II; Mermeroes, James II; Statira, the
Duchess of Cleveland. For Duchess Sarah we have
Zaraida, which takes us back to Mrs. Manley's Zara. The
satire again follows through Marlborough's life and
career, though without any possibility of heightening
the love intrigues which are excessive in the earlier
work. The main emphasis is on the alleged perquisites.
The beginnings of the military career are rather closely
followed, though with repeated denials of any real courage
or "conduct" on the part of the Duke. He is called the
"handsome young *Persian*," by an admiring Mobodes (Turenne)

in a full account of the episode which won Marlborough
early notice from Turenne himself as the "young handsome Englishman," strangely serving the French under
the Duke of York.
   The marriage brings in Sarah's mother in a bad
light; Queen Anne is Annastasia, who finally throws out
her former friends. Any and every episode that could be
interpreted unfavorably to the Marlboroughs is introduced,
and the victories are slighted. The work concludes with
the recent dismissal of the Duke and Duchess from favor
and position. The role of Azarethes (Harley) and Berenice
(Mrs. Masham) in this notably Persian palace intrigue is
slighted in favor of emphasizing the alleged guilt of
Marlborough, to whom bribes are "perquisites."

> This was the End of that *Perquisite-Monger*,
> and the Justice that was put in Practice by
> that People, who had too true a Sense of the
> Nature of *Ingratitude*, not to distinguish it
> by a suitable Punishment.   (p. 24)

See *The History of Prince Mirabel*, No. 367 above. It
should be noted that this retort could have come after
only Pt. I, since the remaining two parts were not
published till April. Of course, the writer might have
seen the entire work in manuscript, but this seems un-
likely.

2 April 3-10.

A Miscellaneous Poem, Inscribed to the Right Honourable
The Earl of OXFORD, Lord High Treasurer of *Great Britain*, &c. [4 lines Eng. verse: "May never He by whom
the Muse is Scorn'd."] *London*: Printed for *J. Morphew*,
near *Stationers-Hall*. 1712. Adv. in *Examiner*, II, 19,
April 3-10, 1712. 'Just publish'd.' Morgan O315. Horn
copy used.
     2°: *A-B*²; t.p., *bl.*, 3-8, 8 pp. 204 lines, coup-
lets. Drop-t., p. 3. Opens:

> *Oxford*, to You, my Secret Muse inclines,
> Unmov'd by craving Interest, or Designs.

While the poem does not directly mention Marlborough,
it does concern itself with panegyric, especially military, and its being addressed to Harley is suggestive
of hostility toward the Duke and the War. Disclaiming
flattery, and even deploring satire, the writer credits
Oxford with critical skill, who "shall, with our Politicks, reform our Wit" (1. 23). He goes on to urge
judgment of poetry by the value, not the men, or authors.
Thus factions will be ended.

> Give Panegyrick, which loud FAME displays,
> When ill-performed, no Title to the Bays;
> But let, if weak the Flame, the noisie Style
> Upon the rash Discharger, back recoil,
> Had some of ours cloy'd *Alexander*'s Time,
> He'd shunn'd the Battle, to have 'scaped the Rhyme.
> We wrong the Hero, whom we shou'd commend,
> If Art and Nature, do not both attend.   35-42

The writer praises Waller and Boileau for "easie Words"
and "well-bred praise," and, in the ode, Horace and Dryden. Inclusion of Suckling, pastoral, satire, which
"shou'd be discourag'd," Milton, who could make Angels
seem natural, all confirm the title of a "miscellaneous"
poem. Marlborough is alluded to as the General, who is
brought to the Promised Land, but is not admitted there.
A Biblical passage on Moses, leads to a comment on fame.

> Then easily does fading Pomp resign,
> Impatient for the Land, where he may shine   }
> Without a Veil, and be all o'er Divine.

The poem plainly urges a departure from military panegyric, but with a "trembling Ray" to indicate the dawn of
a new poetry.

373   May 15.

A Plot or no Plot. London: Printed in the Year MDCCXII.
A second issue has same date with added '(Price 1 *d*.).'
TxU-Luttr. '15 May, 1712.'

1/2°: 1 side, 1 column. 52 lines, anapestic couplets. Edinburgh copy used; Edinb. has two; MH, Bodley,
Crawford. Morgan 0543. Opens:

>The Summons were sent, and without more ado,
>Away Troops the *Juncto* by Two and by Two.

At the head marches "the Great Duke, with his new Convert *Dan*" (1. 14). The Duke holds a session and makes
a speech proclaiming that he has caught Robin (Harley)
in a plot, and that he is dispensing orders from
O[rmon]*d*. *Bacon Face* and *Da-mi-Blood* are heard from,
and there is an allusion, "*Simile Garth* had his Son
and his *Nile*," which leads to remarks by *Daniel* (Defoc)
the spaniel, but he is unable to win them to his plot.
Two other members of the "Juncto," Mouse (Montague) and
Sigillo, are heard, but the whole remains obscure, both
in its satire on Marlborough and the representation of
Defoe as having become his ally. Moore regards the
latter as evidence of Defoe's authorship of the prose
account, *A Short Narrative*, No. 345 above, but he supplies no data in his *Defoe, Citizen of the Modern World*
to support this contention which was kindly made available in a letter to the writer.

4   May 30.

B-------d, W. (no dates)

Untitled poem in the *Medley*, Numb. XXVI, From Monday
May 26, to Friday May 30, 1712. 8 4-line stanzas, 32
lines, couplets. Pr. in italics. Opens:

>*Phoebus*, when I'd in Lyrick Verse
>Battles and taken Towns rehearse.

To Marlborough the poet says that he has spent his life
for England, raising her above the Continent, and filling her halls with trophies. He reveals that he has virtually translated one of Horace's odes to Caesar, and
that, though a Tory, he admires Marlborough, and the

Medley's defence of him against the *Examiner*. He anticipates prosperity and peace for France as well as England, since now she will keep her promises, since their
king has been subdued. Thanks to God and Anne will be
paid as "the Sun Shines out" (1. 25).

375 June 28.

A New Song upon One Who Never could be called a NON-
RESISTING GENERAL. Verse pr. in the *Observator*, Vol. XI,
No. 52, Wed., June 25 to Sat., June 28, 1712. 16 5-line
stanzas, each 4 lines plus refrain, 80 lines. Satirical
tone, but pro-Marlborough in response to satirical ballads against him. Opens:

> Most Men have an ambition,
>   In the dead Time of News:
> To tell of the Depositions
>   Of *Christians* and eke of *Jews*.
>   Against John Duke of *M-----gh*.

376 June 28.

An Excellent New Song, CALL'D The Full Tryal and Condemnation of *JOHN* Duke of MARLBOROUGH. [two staves of music]
No pub., n.d., 20 5-line stanzas, 100 lines. The only
date is for an 80-line version in the *Observator*, Wed.,
June 25 to Sat., June 28, 1712, Vol. XI, No. 52.
     1/2°: 1 page, 2 columns. See also same title but
with 'On the Huffing, Heathen, Covetous' etc., No. 448,
also *The Flanders Ballad*, 1713, No. 449. Morgan 0426
cites Wrenn Cat. which ascribes to Durfey. Certainly
one of the most popular ballads. Rptd. in *Political Merriment*, 1715, Pt. III, 66-70, and in *Pills to Purge State-
Melancholy*, 1715, pp. 161-4. Opens:

> I Now have an Ambition
>   In this great time of News.

The satire ironically disclaims against Marlborough's

"offences" in invading Germany, winning Schellenberg and
Blenheim, fighting Ramillies on Sunday, defeating the
French, and filling Westminster Hall with their banners
called "rags." Each stanza concludes with "cowardly,"
"covetous," "uncivil," John Duke of Marlborough, and the
like. They are laughing in France, now that he is out.

> He's broke and our Fears are all o'er,
>   Thus fell *John* Duke of *Marlboro'*.   99-100

This Whig ballad may be a retort upon *An Excellent
New Song* Call'd the *Trusty* and *True Englishman*, of January 2, 1712, a Tory attack, No. 353.

77   October 30, entered.

Tickell, Thomas (1686-1740)

A POEM   To his EXCELLENCY the LORD PRIVY SEAL, ON THE
Prospect of Peace. By Mr. *TICKELL.* [1 line Virgil]
LONDON: Printed for *J. Tonson,* at *Shakespear's-Head*
over-against *Catherine-street* in the *Strand.* 1713.
2°: A-F²; t.p., *bl.*, *iii-iv*, 1-20, 24 pp. Ded.
iii-iv. No wmk. Pr. 1712, as adv. *Post-Boy*, No. 2727,
Thurs. Oct. 30-Sat. Nov. 1, 1712. 'Just publish'd.'
Morgan P603 gives as 1712. Dr. John Robinson, Bishop
of London, was Lord Privy-Seal. Horn copy of 4th ed.
1713 used. 507 lines, couplets, 44 being of the dedication. Tickell's intention is apparent in the opening lines of the Dedication:

> *Contending Kings, and Fields of Death, too long,
> Have been the Subject of the* British *Song.
> Who hath not read of fam'd* Ramillia's *Plain,
> Bavaria's Fall, and* Danube *choak'd with Slain.* 1-4

He will raise a "gentler Note" and sing of Peace. He
sees returning heroes and disbanding hosts, while warring powers unite in friendly leagues. In compliment
to the Bishop of Bristol, almost the last churchman to
be given high public office, a Biblical reference to
Moses spreading plagues at God's command, is inserted.

Strafford, also, who with Bristol, went to Versailles
in January of 1712 to open peace negotiations, is
brought in. The poem proper opens:

> The haughty *Gaul*, in Ten Campaigns o'erthrown,
> Now ceas'd to think the Western World his own.

The disbanding of armies, veterans with their scars, the
shouts of joy, and the "gen'rous Fair" welcoming home
the brave heroes, all are detailed. Tickell perhaps adds
an Addisonian touch in the picture of the soldier's household, the fond wife weeping with joy over the husband as
he relates his experiences.

> Near the full Bowl he draws the fancy'd Line,
> And marks feign'd Trenches in the flowing Wine.   55-6

He describes the blowing up of forts and exploding mines
till his children turn pale and "beg again to hear the
dreadful Tale" (1. 60). Now eager youth seek out the
scenes of battle, from Belgium to Germany, and especially at the scene of Blenheim, where Stepney had placed
a stone to Anna's fame. The guide points out where Tallard surrendered and where the French household troops
fled. Once more the Danube drowning is described.

> Here *Marlborough* turn'd the Fortune of the Field,
> On those steep Banks, near *Danube*'s raging Flood
> The *Gauls* thrice started back, and trembling stood:
> When, *Churchill*'s Arm perceive'd, they stood not
>   long,
> And plung'd amidst the Waves, a desp'rate Throng,
> Crowds whelm'd on Crowds, dash'd wide the watry Bed,
> And drove the Current to its distant Head.   74-80

The scene fires the Briton's soul as does the artistic
portrayal of a rearing battle steed by Raphael or by
Kneller.

But the poet seeks less noble scenes, pleasant
ploughed fields, ivy creeping over shattered walls, and
grass and flocks safely reaching out where the mines ex-
ploded, that is, pastoral scenes. He denounces the tyrant who first enslaved subjects, and ambition which robs
the peasant and spearates lovers with cruel lust. Let

war be driven to far-off Scythia, away from England who
draws her glory from "pure Religion, and impartial Laws"
(1. 138). She stands amidst the waves, a fortress of
freedom through the proper use of power. Her merchants
now roam securely, from the Polar Bear to the tropics and
the regions of spices and gems.

   Tribute is paid to the heroes of battle: Churchill
first, then Webb, Lumley, Mordaunt, Campbell, Ormonde,
and even Harley, who has survived Guiscard's knife, and
Granville. Lines 218-85 develop a pleasant picture of
Marlborough finding rest and security at Blenheim Palace,
with its memories of Henry and Rosamonda, and also of
"old Chaucer" who warbles through the glades.   Strangers
from distant lands will come to contemplate the palace
and the work of painter and sculptor and tapestry-maker.
Perhaps some lovely boy of Churchill's race may one day
gaze transported.   Then the poem turns to Anne, who provides benevolent reign from the straits of Magellan to
Gibraltar, from Peru to India.   Through Harley's counsels
Dunkirk has been restored and its fort demolished, making
England more secure.   The Bishop of Bristol, as Lord
Privy-Seal, is again shown as an agent of justice and
the voice of Heaven, supporting the laws as the Church
rears her head.   The arts will receive the benefit of
"*Bolingbroke* the Muse's Friend" and Harcourt.   The
language will be controlled, and "*Grecian* Plans reform
Britannia's Stage" (1. 422).   Congreve, Rowe, and Addison, as the morality-encouraging Spectator, and also
Prior, Garth, Pope and Philips are cited as champions
of the arts, as Bristol encourages "Rules for just Thinking, and Poetick Laws" (1. 442).   The poem closes with an
allusion to Tickell's writing at Oxford, "Where sacred
Isis rowls her ancient Stream" (1. 452), and the resolution to urge on his soul "To woo the Muse, whom *Addison*
enjoy'd" (1. 461), even though he can pursue him only
at a distance, "and his Steps adore."

8   November 1.

[Sewell, George (1690?-1726)]

To his GRACE THE Duke of *MARLBOROUGH*, On the Report of

His Going into *GERMANY*. Printed for *E. Curll*, at the
Dial and *Bible*, and *J. Pemberton*, at the *Buck* and *Sun*,
both against St. *Dunstan*'s Church in *Fleetstreet*. 1713.
Price 2 *d*. Where may be had the following BOOKS, lately
Publish'd. (Four books are listed, by Cobb, Prior, J.
Watts *et al.*)

   2°: 2 sides, 1 column, 23 lines, couplets. Thorn
Drury-Luttr., 1 November 1712. Augmented to 25 and 28
lines in subsequent printings. Garth, R. Churchill and
others have been suggested as the author. Most of the
evidence is presented in an article alleging George
Sewell's authorship, by A. Rosenberg, *N & Q*, Oct., 1956,
429-31. Since he and Garth were both physician-poets,
there may have been some collaboration. See item 8 below. Rosenberg dates the poem September 30. Morgan
P377. Opens:

   Go, Mighty Prince, and those Great Nations see,
   Which thy Victorious Arms before made Free.

Marlborough is urged to view that "fam'd Column" whose
marble records his name and achievements. There every
country but his own, which has "Extoll'd his Conquest,
but Condemn'd his Name," may see. Still Marlborough is
untouched; he even blushes at his shameful treatment.
Disdaining to join party conflicts, he "proves, in
Absence most, *Britannia*'s Friend." In conclusion he is
compared to Scipio, who also incurred envy for his services to his country. Yet, even in exile, he was still

   Prepar'd, whene'er His Country's Cause requir'd,
   To Shine in *Peace* or *War*, and be again Admir'd.
                                            22-3

The prophetic note in these concluding lines became apparent on Marlborough's triumphant return.

   At least four reprintings in 1713, and six subsequently attest to the popularity of these verses. It
will be convenient to list them together. Detailed
descriptions are supplied below.

   1. The Curll broadside described above.
   2. *The Lives of Two Illustrious Generals*, 1713,
pp. 168-9, 25 11. In two added lines Marlborough "smiles

at Envy," but fears for the land he forsakes. See No.
434 below.
    3. *English Gratitude*, 1713. The first poem in a
collection. 28 ll., presumably the first version of the
complete poem. A triplet is added relating that, in going to other climes, Marlborough is leaving "Busy Tongues
and Lying Fame behind."
    4. Dive, Charles, *The Treasurer and the General*,
1713. Added, pp. 19-20. See No. 460 below.
    5. 'Philo Strategos,' *Churchill's Annals*, 1713.
Alteration in l. 15. See No. 461 below.
    6. Roscommon, Dorset, &c., Earls of, *Poems on Sev.
Occasions*, 2 vols., 1714. Eds. 1718, 1721, 1731, 1739.
Pp. 80-1.
    7. Parker, Captain Robert, *Memoirs*, 1747. 25 ll.,
pp. 200-1. The only verse in the book. Attributed to
Addison, as "elegantly set forth." This error is perhaps
the basis for A. L. Rowse's undocumented assiging of the
poem to Addison in *The Early Churchills*, p. 316, of which
he quotes 10 lines. No. 574.
    8. Garth, Samuel. The editor, F. Cogan, of Garth's
poems in the 1750 *Supplement* to the *Works of Celebrated
Minor Authors*, pp. 83-4, lists as by Garth. Also in eds.
of Garth's poems, by Johnson, Anderson, Chalmers.
    9. Cibber, Theophilus, *Lives of the Poets*, 1753.
Ascribed to Sewell, Vol. LV.
    10. Nichols, John, *A Select Coll. of Poems*, 1791,
VII. Lists as by Sewell on authority of Giles Jacob and
Theophilus Cibber. See No. 465 below.

9   November 4.

On *November* 4. 1712. The Anniversary of the Birth of
his Late Majesty, King WILLIAM the Third, of Glorious
Memory. [2 lines Virgil]
    2°: 1 side, 35 lines, couplets. BM copy used.
Morgan 0354 assigns to Jabez Hughes, but this may be a
confusion with an 8 pp. Latin poem perhaps same title
listed with it for 1715. Opens:

As with Cherubic Hosts and Choirs Divine,
In Songs of Joy triumphantly You join.

William is urged not to look down and see a similar un-
thankfulness to that which he experienced. In spite of
saving Religion, Liberties, and Laws, the modern Joshua
(Marlborough) is persecuted with calumny and ingratitude.

The same wild Phrenzy seizes us again;
Tasteless of Freedom, we invite the Chain,
Forget the Oppressions we so lately bore,
And seek that *Egypt* which we fled before.
The *Joshua*, who supply'd the Leader's Place,
When thou, our *Moses*, left'st this moody Race;
Who form'd, by thy Example, crown'd our Isle
With annual Victorys and Foreign Spoil,   13-20

and the dismal picture is completed with further evidences
of ungrateful behavior. But shortly the fascination will
break, and again the immortal name of William will be
revered. A strongly Whig poem, associating Marlborough
with the memory of William IIId, and the policies of both.

380   December 24.

Windsor Prophecy. Printed in the Year 1712. Price One
Peny [*sic*].
      1/2°: 1 side, 1 column, mixed couplets, largely
decasyllabic. Not to be confused with 1711 poems of same
title. 52 lines. BM copy used. Morgan O752. See No.
350, 1711. Opens:

There was a Fig-Tree on a rising Ground,
With a clear Riv'let at its Foot.

Birds shelter in the fig-tree; but one summer day they
leave it, and it catches fire, nearly burns, and loses
fruit and branches. Later some turtle-doves return to
the branches for shelter. The Kites would have drawn
them away to a neighboring oak, but they resolve to stay
in the fig-tree, in spite of wind and weather, "Resolv'd

tho' it was of its Honours stript, *They* and the *Fig-Tree*'d stand or fall together" (ll. 51-2). No specific reference to Marlborough, but clearly a satire on the war party, the hawks versus the doves. See Swift's use of the title, 1711, December 24, No. 328 above.

81 December 30.

Diaper, William (1685-1717)

Dryades: or, The *Nymphs Prophecy*. *A Poem*, By Mr. Diaper. [1 line Virgil, 5 Horace, and 6 from *Cooper's-Hill*] *London*: Printed for *Bernard Lintott* at the *Cross-Keys* between the *Two Temple Gates*, *Fleet-street*, MDCCXIII. Adv. *Post-Boy*, 27-30 Dec., 1712, 'This Day is publish'd.' 794 lines, couplets. In Complete Works, ed. Dorothy Broughton's notes show the poem has political allusions throughout, as well as tributes to John Philips, Prior, and Swift. No references to Marlborough by name, but definite allusions to his career. Morgan P203. Opens:

> Forgive, ye *Nereids*, if I sing no more
> Th' uncertain Sea, but choose the safer Shore.

The Tory theme of the need and difficulty of terminating the war is prominent.

> But Conquest now is stopp'd at ev'ry Fort;
> Bloodshed is cheap, and War becomes a Sport;
> In vain the Captains fall, the Heroes bleed;
> Fresh Victims to the Sacrifice succeed.   614-17

The parallel between the ten years of the Trojan War and the ten campaign years of Marlborough's wars is noticed.

> Now ten Campagnes, and Battles yearly won,
> Transfer no Kingdom, and no King dethrone.
>   But pitying *ANNA* ends the fruitless Toil,
> Blood shall no more enrich the *Flandrian* Soil.
> She, who maintain'd the War, must make the Peace.
>   629-34

393

This tribute is a typical Tory thrust at Marlborough,
reminding of his dependence upon the Queen and ascribing his victories to her wisdom. Later we learn that
she has enriched foreign powers and supplied the troops.
However true this may be symbolically, it was not Anne
who did the recruiting and led the troops on long marches
and fought battles.

382 P., D.

The Armies *Representation to Old* England. By D. P.,
at bottom.
    1/2°: no pub., n.d., 1 side, 2 cols., prose, but
with eight lines verse at the end. Not in Morgan. R425
lists a piece by D. P., a "country curate." BM copy
used. Opens:
    "We take this Occasion to let our Countrymen know
how heinously we resent their ungrateful Usage to our
Victorious Commander the Duke of *Marlborough*, whose Fame
and Character will far out-do those great Heroes *Alexander*, *Pompey*, *Caesar* and others. . ." While this is a
forceful and spirited defence of the Duke, for his courage, conduct in war, and particularly for his humane
treatment of his men, without the identity of the author
its bearing remains uncertain. The author insists that
if "we had been cheated of our *Allowance* in *Bread*, how
is it possible we should *Conquer?*" The concluding lines
are disappointingly insipid.

    Therefore we ought in Quietness to rest,
    Of all Generals Marlbro' was the best.

383 A BALLAD in *Honour* of the *Present Regency*. No pub., n.d.
    1/4° strip, 103 lines in stanzas. MH copy used.
Another version in CSmH, also 1/4° strip. Not in Morgan.
Allusion to Marlborough:

    There's the poor faithful Duke on whom Fortune don't
                                                      smile.

Fidelis sed infortunatus was the Duke of Marlborough's motto

384 THE Birth, Parentage, AND RISE OF *J*---- D. of M----,
Together with the REASONS, of his present Disgrace.
Arma virumque cano, &c. Virg. I'll tell the Tale, and
you may Judge the Case, Whether he's truly Great, or
vilely Base. With an Estimate of their former *Yearly
Income*, and their present Loss. *Entered in the Hall
Book according as the Act of Parliament directs.*
LONDON: Printed for *John Williams*, near St. *James*'s,
1712. Price One Penny. Not in Morgan.
4°: A⁴; t.p., *bl.*, drop-t. on 2, 2-8, 8 pp. CtY
copy used, cropt. Poorly printed, pp. 5-7 larger type.
Recites the now familiar tale of Marlborough's taking
advantage of royal favors, being King J---'s 'Darling'
and intimate with a succession of sovereigns whom he
betrayed. He is charged with betraying the secret of
Dunkirk through his "tattling" wife, and finally turning against even Queen Anne, holding that "She was a
Queen and no Queen." Page 8 consists of the printing
of the financial record of "The D---e and D---ess of
Ma----h's Loss" etc., as printed in the first edition,
without the perquisites of the 2-1/2% and the receipts
from bread and bread wagons. See No. 393.

385 *A Bob for the Court, Or, Prince EUGENE's Welcome.*
Printed in the Year 1712. No pub. TxU has another
copy in larger type, with Price one Peny [*sic*] added
to date. BM copy used. Not in Morgan.
1/2°: 1 side, 56 lines, alternate rhyme.

Bob sent the Dove that cross'd the Deep.

Anti-Marlborough, but makes show of welcoming Eugene.
Ironically insists that in spite of towns taken and battles
won, the Victors, that is the English, lose. A slur on
Marlborough,

Who whilst his Soldiers eat good Bread,
Himself liv'd on the Paring.
'Twas high Time then for Prior to pass
In search of Peace the train,
That *Britain*, loaded like an Ass,
At last might share the gain.

386 *The B----sh Embassadresses.* *Speech* to the *French King.*
4°: 70 lines, couplets. No pub., n.d., but probably 1712. LSA-Foxon only loc. Rptd. in *Political
Merriment*, III, 71-3. Not in Morgan. Opens:

> Hail tricking Monarch! more successful far
> In Arts of Peace, than Glorious Deeds of War.

Strongly pro-Marlborough. Anne's Embassadress comes with
news that will rejoice both Louis XIV and Rome. "For you
the Fighting *MARLBOROUGH*'s disgraced" (1. 20). Supplies
ironic account of events in England, where *Ox*[for]*d* is
chief of "the abandon'd Clan." In concluding 12 lines
the Tyrant, Louis, takes the Embassadress to his embraces
in bed. The Embassadress is presumably the Catholic
Church or Jacobitism, although the poem is not otherwise
allegorical.

387 December.

Marlborough, Duke of (1650-1722) and Godolphin, Earl of
(1645-1712)

The CASE Of his Grace the D--- of M---------. As Design'd To be Represented by him to the *Honourable House
of Commons*, in Vindication of Himself from the Charge
OF THE Commissioners of Accounts; in Relation To the Two
and Half *per cent.* *Bread and Bread Waggons.* *The Second
Edition Corrected.* Printed in the Year 1712. Price 6 *d.*
8VO: A-D⁴; t.p., *bl.*, 3-38, 38 pp. Drop-t. on 3.
Prose pamphlet. Sec. ed. Christ Church, Oxf., and 3d ed.
TxU, 16 pp., used. Morgan 0424 lists list ed., J. Smith,
1712, as well as 2d and 3d ed., and another 35 pp., 1712.

> When I first heard of the Proceedings before
> the *Commissioners* for taking the *Publick Accounts*,
> I was abroad and in the Queens service. . .

This candid and utterly convincing defence of himself against the malicious charges of peculation is reported to have been written by Marlborough with Godolphin's assistance. He mistakenly states that it was not

published till "some time after" (IV, 526). As it af-
fects Marlborough so deeply, Churchill quotes at length
(IV, 526-9) and for this reason no extensive summary
here is necessary. Marlborough follows the report of
the Commissioners, answering their charges point by point.
He shows that he was simply following established precedent in turning the 2-1/2% to the highly important purposes of secret intelligence, without which no campaign
can be conducted. He also shows that English soldiers
had received more and better bread than even the Dutch,
who were recognized as being well treated.

Lediard gives an extensive, well-documented summary,
quoting the *Report of the Commissioners* for the House of
Commons (III, 224-37), and *The Duke of* Marlborough's *Case
and Vindication of himself* entire (III, 242-60). The
style of the *Case* is a pleasant corrective for the tone
of slanderous vituperation that the satirists and pamphleteers were pouring out in 1712. The calm detachment
the Duke exhibited was impressively that which Addison's
picture of him in battle achieves.

88 THE COMPARISON OR Whiggish Fulsom Flattery Examplifyed
IN His G---- the D---- of M---- By Way of DIALOGUE Be-
twixt a WHIG and a TORY. Touching the Late Examination
of a Late G----l. *LONDON*, Printed, and Sold by the Booksellers of *London* and *Westminster* 1712. *Price 2d*.
    4°: A⁴; t.p., *bl*., 3-8, 8 pp. Prose pamphlet.
Morgan 0425. CtY copy used. The Tory urges the Duke's
alleged offences, his request to be made 'dictator' for
life, and especially the 2-1/2% and the bread perquisite.
Colossal figures are given, including costs and deficits
for the navy, of which his brother was in command. Of
course the Tory 'wins' the argument.

89 *The Congratulation*, Humbly inscribed to his Grace The
Duke of ORMOND. *Diu multumq; desideratus*. London:
Printed in the Year MDCCXII.
    1/2°: 35 lines, couplets. BM copy used. Not in

Morgan. Opens:

> At length propitious Heav'n begins to smile,
> And pours down blessings on her Fav'rite Isle.

No reference to Marlborough, but a strong implication of
his being the center of the overthrown Faction, and of
course the praise of Ormond is a distinct reflection
upon his career.

> But now *Britania* for your help does call,
> Her hopes are fixt on you her *General*.
> Press'd with a tedious and expensive War,
> She still grows poor by being *Conqueror*.   22-5

Ormond is called "Heav'ns *Vicegerent*," and, for appear-
ances, at least, the hope is expressed that he will advance Britain's standard to the heart of France. A good
summary of policy and the hope for an honorable peace
conclude the poem.

390 *The Consultation*. Printed in the Year, 1712.
     1/2°: 1 side, 1 column, 49 lines, couplets. BM
copy used. Not in Morgan. Opens:

> At Dead of Night when Midnight hags prepare
> To take their usual Tour thro' the Air.

At St. James's gate *Vulpone* (Godolphin) waits his "kind
Conductor, whom the deluded call 'Th' invincible Heroick
G[enera]l.'" The general, of course Marlborough, and
the treasurer conspire in their plight at being exposed
for financial peculations. This egregiously unfair attack
relates to events late in 1712, alleging that 'Dismal,'
the Earl of Nottingham, has been bought over by Marlborough. A deal had been made to support his Occasional Conformity Bill; but Nottingham saw the war's main purpose
the enthronement of the Austrian Charles on the Spanish
throne. See Trevelyan, *England Under Queen Anne*, III,
194-5, where Swift's "An Orator dismal of Nottinghamshire"
is quoted. The verses reflect the Tory view, and conclude
with a picture of the *Sun* (France, or at least the

Tories) brightening the scene so the Duumvirate of con-
spirators slink away "lest they shou'd be catch'd."

391   Clarke, Dr. Samuel

The Dedication of Clarke's ed. of Caesar's *Commentaries*
to his Grace, the Duke of Marlborough, in Latin and English. Tr. by R. T., London, Printed and Sold by *John
Morphew*, 1712. Price 3 *d.*
    2°: 15 pp. Morgan 0139. "Marlborough is likened
to Caesar."

392   THE D. of *M----*'s CONFESSION TO A *Jacobite* Priest: As
it was taken in Short-Hand the 6th of *February* last,
1711. And now Printed for the Satisfaction of the Publick. [large, crude woodcut of two separate figures,
the Duke kneeling before a gowned priest] *Licensed
according to Order*. No pub., n. d. If the dating in
title is O.S. the piece could be 1712. Morgan N393
gives as 1711. Since no internal evidence confirms, it
seems to remain uncertain. However, attacks on Marlborough had not reached the vicious stage by February of
1711, whereas they were distinctly in the spirit of this
piece by that date in 1712. U Kansas copy used; Bod. has
copy, but lacks title p.
    8°: sigs. cropt; t.p., 2-8, 8 pp., prose.
    This crudely printed satire adds nothing to the at-
tacks. At the close the Duke repudiates the Jacobite
priest as a "Canting Slave." Hence, while the usual
charges are made, of desertion of James II, currying
favor with William III, and the betrayal of Dunkirk,
that of Jacobitism can hardly be urged. Nothing is said
of the 2-1/2% nor of the allegations brought against
Marlborough toward the end of his career. In rejecting
the priest Marlborough says:

    Sir! I had thought to have been kind to you,
    and made you [to] have liv'd easily all your
    Life with your Family; but your stiff old

Jacobite temper, bars you from any Favour I
had design'd; go starve on with your *St.
Germain*'s Master.

He will send for Dr. *K*[enne]*t* for absolution. Since Dr.
Kennet had written a pamphlet against Sacheverell's sermon, and had refused to sign a Tory address to the Queen,
the politics of the piece is somewhat apparent. Even so,
it is a confusing and confused contribution.

393   The D---e and D---s of *M-----h*'s Loss; Being An Estimate
of their former *Yearly Income*. Printed in the Year,
MDCCXII. *Price One Penny*.
      1/2°: 1 side, prose. Sec. ed. "with additional
Observations," which includes the perquisites of the
2-1/2% and from bread and bread wagons, and a paragraph
on Anne's income as Princess of Denmark. Morgan 0439
lists as 4to. Sec. ed., different type, with 2-1/2% and
bread perquisites and note on income of the present queen
and Duke of Gloucester added. BM copies used.
      The matters which are stated to be "under Examina-
tion" provide the main differences between the two editions. Whereas the first estimates the total as Ł 62325,
the addition of receipts on Bread and Bread Waggons is
stated as Ł 63319 3s. and 7d., and that from the 2-1/2
per cent from the payments of troops as Ł 460062 10s. and
2-3/4. Since this is almost ten times as much as the
estimate in the first edition, the satirical import is
obvious. The satiric device of a pseudo-financial report
of course suggests Swift's *Bill of Roman Gratitude and of
English Gratitude*, *Ex*. No. 16, Nov. 23, 1710. See No. 307.

394   The D--- of M---- turn'd CONJUROR, or the History of the
Golden Apple. Licens'd and Entered according to Act of
Parliament, Printed for F. Cramphorn, in *Fleet-street*,
1712. Price One Peny [*sic*]. LSA-Foxon; also cites a
different printing without the statement on licensing,

Crawford.   Not in Morgan.

When *Juno*, *Pallas*. . .

Marlborough as Prince Avaro.

395   The *Duke* of *M-----h*'s VINDICATION.   In Answer to a Pam-
       phlet falsely so called.   *Dicite justitiam moniti*.
       LONDON, Printed for *A. Baldwin* near the *Oxford-Arms* in
       Warwick-Lane 1712.   Price 2   *d.*   Morgan 0307.
       8°: A^8; t.p., *bl.*, *iii-iv* Advertisement to the
       Reader, text 5-10, 16 pp., drop-t. on p. 5.   Bod, Horn
       copies used.   This is a reply to the ironic attack on
       Marlborough, No. 332 above.   Without much style, it shows
       strong Protestant zeal.   Marlborough's shift from allegi-
       ance to James II in favor of William III is defended.
       His career and campaigns, as well as the current situa-
       tion, are also favorably assessed.

396   Steele, Sir Richard (1672-1729)

       sgnd. *pseud.* 'Scoto-Britannus.'

       The ENGLISHMAN's THANKS To the Duke of *Marlborough*.
       [ornament] *LONDON*: Printed for *A. Baldwin*, near the
       Oxford-Arms in *Warwick-Lane*. MDCCXII..   *Price Twopence*.
       4to, prose pamphlet.   T.p., *bl.*, 1-5, *bl.*, 8 pp.
       Dated Jan. 1, 1711, and addressed to 'My Lord,' sgnd.
       at end 'SCOTO-BRITANNUS.'   Morgan 0632 states pub. in
       Spec., but this not the case.   Dr. Rae Blanchard reports
       reprinted *Daily Cour.*, 4 Jan., and in *The Political*
       Writings of Sir Richard Steele, 1715.   Blanchard reprts.
       in *Tracts and Pamphlets by Richard Steele*, Johns Hopkins
       Pr., 1944, Octagon Books, Inc., reprt., 1967, pp. 66-71.
       Yale copy used.
           The importance of the pamphlet rests, not only on
       its evidence of Steele's loyalty to Marlborough, but also
       to Whig policy.   He has heard with utmost consternation
       of the Duke's dismissal, "the Man Terrible in Battel, the

Scourge of Tyrants" (p. 4) as well as the "ministring Angel in the Cause of LIBERTY" (p. 2). No specific allusions are made to Swift and the attacks on Marlborough, beyond the concluding reference to love and loyalty in face of any "Shameless Ruffian" who would sully Marlborough's bright armor (p. 5).

397 A FUNERAL POEM UPON THE Much Lamented Death OF Lieutenant-General *WOOD*, Who Departed this LIFE at his House in *Kensington* the 17th of *May*, 1712. Humbly Address'd to Her MAJESTY. Written by a Female. *A. H. London*, Printed, and Sold by *John Morphew*, near *Stationers-Hall*. 1712.

2°: no sig. or cropped; t.p., *bl.*, The Dedication, prose, *ii-iii*, drop-t. on p. 5, 5-8, 8 pp., 88 lines, couplets. Morgan 0287. Folger copy used. Only one known. Opens:

> What Noise is this? Sure 'tis *Wood*'s Dismal Knell,
> It rings aloud, Eternally Farewell!

The poem is entirely funereal; no specific details appear, although Wood had a distinguished career in Marlborough's army, and commanded a regiment of horse at Blenheim.

Neither the Dedication nor the poem offers any very quotable passages. The self-abasing tone of the one, and the abstract, conventional tone of the other offer little. Wood is seen in universal combat.

> With a true Courage for his Countries Good,
> Waded thro' Fire and Smoke to Seas of Blood.
> Like a Fierce Lion seiz'd upon his Prey,
> And ne'er came off till he had gain'd the Day.
> In *Britain*'s Cause no Dangers did decline,
> Where his Heroick, Copious Soul might shine. 51-6

The chief distinction of the piece appears to lie in its rarity. Nevertheless, a poem celebrating one of Marlborough's commanders, in the year of his disgrace, may have an indirect bearing on his reputation. He is not named, nor is any overt slight apparent.

398   The Glorious Life, Character, History and Noble Actions
of that Famous Warrior *Prince Eugene* . . . Containing
the Case of his Grace the D--- of *M*[arlborough]. London,
1712. Morgan O226.
2°: sig. cropped, t.p., *bl.*, *ii-iii*, 5-8, 8 pp.
No copy located.

399   *The Grand Enquiry*, or, What's to be Done with Him? *London*,
Printed in the Year MDCCXII. Two eds., same imprint, but
one has Gothic type for sub-title. Morgan O429. BM copy
used; Clark has.
1/2°: 1 side, 2 columns, 105 lines, couplets.
Opens:

        When Beasts could every Office do,
        That Men of Business now pursue.

Satire on the continuation of the War, to the advantage
of the Leopard (Marlborough), and in spite of the "good
Lioness" (Anne). A fable, in which the poor sheep (the
English people) are starving, while the Leopard grows
rich. The Mastiff says that the Panther (Ormond) is as
brave as the Leopard. The Bull has brought the Olive
(i.e. Peace) home, and Members can look forward to Peace.

00   History of the Three Goddesses and the Golden Apple of
Prince Paris and Prince *AVARO*. Printed in the Year 1712.
Price a Peny.
1/2°: 1 side, 2 cols., 65 lines, couplets. BM copy
used. Not in Morgan. Opens:

        When *Juno*, *Venus*, *Pallas*, strove
        Which should Supream for Beauty prove.

Prince Avaro, that is Marlborough, is satirized for the
old charges of taking bribes, turning bread money to his
own use, and winking at deficiencies.

401 *The Humble Confession and Petition* of a *Whig* with his
Eyes Open. Dedicated to the D. of Marlborough. 1712.
48 pp. Morgan O356. Only ref.

402 Northey, Sir Edward

THE INFORMATION Against the Duke of *Marlborough*. AND
HIS ANSWER. *LONDON*, Sold by A. BALDWIN in *Warwick-Lane*.
Price 3 d. N.d. Prose pamphlet.
     8°: A-C^4; t.p., *bl*., 3-24, 24 pp. *Daily Cour.*
No. 3458, Tues. Nov. 11, 1712. 'This Day is publish'd.'
Morgan N449 gives as 1711; but 1712 seems more likely.
Morgan also has 1712, and a quarto ed. 1714; all eds.
24 pp. He also supplies the name of Sir Edward Northey
as author. Northey was the Queen's Attorney-General,
and thus presented the indictment. Marlborough's
Answer, pp. 12-24, is addressed to him.
     Marlborough is charged with having taken for himself
moneys from the 2-1/2% allowed for the employment of
foreign troops. As Churchill shows in his chapter "The
Peculation Charge," IV, 521-34, Marlborough's successor
the Duke of Ormonde was assigned the same allowance, and
used it for the same purposes, and this by the same government that had indicted Marlborough. See the next
entry, and particularly No. 387, *The Case of his Grace*.

403 *The Jewel in the Tower*. *London*, Printed in the Year,
M.DCC.XII.
     1/2°: 1 side, 2 columns. 12 4-line stanzas, 48
lines. 4 lines of music "For the Flute" at top. Rptd.
in *Pills to Purge State-Melancholy*, 95-7. BM copy used.
Not in Morgan. Opens:

          If what the *Tower* of *London* holds,
          Is valu'd more than it's [*sic*] Power.

Ironic on a brilliant jewel that once adorned the court,
more valuable than St. George's diamond. It was sometimes
worn by Marlborough, and the point seems to be that Marlborough should go to the Tower with the jewel.

404

404 *John the Bailiff*'s *Letter* to *Robin* the *Steward.*
     ca. 1712. No pub., n.d., fol., bsd. Morgan 0430 only
     ref.

405 F., J.

     A LETTER FROM A Curate of *Suffolk* TO A HIGH-CHURCH Member;
     Concerning the D. of M. and Mr. *W----le.* [2 lines Latin
     prose, unsignd.] *LONDON*: Printed in the Year MDCCXII.
          8°: π¹ A-E⁴; t.p., *bl.*, 1-46, 48 pp. Morgan 0236.
     Horn copy used.
          A vigorous defence of Marlborough, and in the final
     pages, of Walpole. In turn the duke is cleared of the
     charges against him for the bread perquisites, the 2-1/2%
     for foreign troops, and the allegations that he and his
     duchess had sold places in the court. It is shown that
     the money he received was such as any steward would con-
     sider as a fair share, and that it had gone for secret
     intelligence, that is spying on the French. Thus he had
     been enabled to win ten years of unbroken victories. The
     cardinals of France, Richlieu [*sic*] and Mazarine [*sic*],
     followed the same practice. Questions of the church lead
     to a long quotation from a sermon of Dr. South, based on
     the text: "Woe to them that call Evil Good and Good Evil,"
     pp. 29-38. The defence of Walpole occupies pp. 41-6, con-
     cluding the defence of the war policy. Complete denial is
     made of having stolen government funds. Walpole had been
     turned out in January, 1711, after the Tories had sought
     vainly to win him over to their side. False charges of
     peculation, of 35 million pounds, had been brought against
     him.

06   *Marlbro' Remov'd, or, The Sudden Downfal* [*sic*] of a *Great
     Favourite.* *London*: Printed in the Year, MDCCXII.
          1/2°: 1 side. Prose ending with 4 lines verse.
     Bodley copy used. Not in Morgan. Opens: "This surpriz-
     ing Removal of the Duke of M---h" calls for a serious pen
     to examine the reasons. Detached view, concluding that
     "Man should never rely upon Fortune." Verse ends:

The least Displeasure, flying from a Crown,
May from their Glory strangely toss 'Em Down.

407   Barber, Dr. (in MS.)

Untitled hymn, followed by a *Te Deum*. *Ca.* 60 lines.
Foxon-NN. Not in Morgan. Opens:

Near to the Sacred and Immortal Frame,

The poem censures France for ingratitude to Queen Anne:

For thee She Sheath'd the Terror of the Sword,
For thee she broke her General and her Word.

Anne has lost the honor and glory her arms have won.
She has:

Resign'd the Glory of Ten Years Reign,
And such as none but *Marlbro*'s Arm could gain.

408   Parnell, Thomas (1679-1718)

On Queen Anne's Peace. (Written in December 1712) Not
separately published.
   319 lines, couplets. Opens:

Mother of Plenty, daughter of the skies,
Sweet peace, the troubled world's desire, arise.

The poem reflects the shift of Parnell to the Tory
position, if not the death of his wife, both occurring
at about this time. It is a predominantly Tory piece,
though purporting to be humanitarian. It deplores the
ravages of war, and while not naming Marlborough, pays
a belated tribute to his greatest victories at the close.
The wars are seen as essential to England's security, but
as far from as glorious as they had been pictured.

Now twelve revolving years has Britain stood,
With loss of wealth, and vast expense of blood,

Europe's guardian; still her gallant arms
Secur'd Europa from impending harms.   19-22

Anne's prayers and Heaven's intent have properly humbled
Gaul with "War's destructive arm" (1. 44). It is not
Marlborough, but Oxford, now maneuvering with Lady Masham
for Marlborough's complete downfall, who is praised. He
is called to affairs of state, he and "graceful Bolingbroke." Peace restores the "comforts of a calm repose"
(1. 221). Peace returns, bringing plenty and the blessings of Traffic and Industry. The Arts and Sciences, and
the Liberal Arts too are invoked. Ormonde, Harcourt,
and Dartmouth are noticed, but with no poetic flourish.
These all supplant the reign of Discord, with train of
Horrors, Loud Threatenings, Ruin, Fierceness, and High
reddening Rage (11. 170-5). This occurs in "Flandrias's
soil, where camps have mark'd the Plain." It is surprising that Parnell notices Marlborough's victories; but he
is celebrating Peace,

> Thrice happy Britons, if at last you know
> 'Tis less to conquer, than to want a foe;
> That triumphs still are made for war's decrease,
> When men, by conquest, rise to views of peace;
> .   .   .   .
> Fam'd Blenheim's field, Ramillies' noble seat,
> Blaregni's desperate act of gallant heat,
> Or wondrous Winendale, are war pursued,
> By wounds and death, through plains with blood   312-15
>   embrued.   317-20

The poem concludes with satisfaction in Albion's risen
state, Gallia's broken condition, and an Austria restored.

09   Dive, Charles, Gent.

ON THE Duke of *MARLBOROUGH*. A POEM. By CHARLES DIVE,
Gent. *Extinctus amabitur Idem.* Printed for *E. Curll*,
at the *Dial* and *Bible*, against St. *Dunstan*'s Church in
Fleet-street. 1712. Where may be had an Epigram on the
SPECTATOR. Price 1 *d.* Not in Morgan.

1/2°: 2 sides, 32 lines, couplets. Two advs.,
foreign, *Works* of Boileau and satire of Petronius Arbiter.
TxU and Lambeth Palace; both copies used. Opens:

> As late I walk'd beside that Silver Spring,
> Where oft I've heard the Sister *Muses* sing.

Written in the pastoral vein, the poem laments Marlborough's downfall, as Venus mourned her Adonis. Marlborough, "seizing the *Wolf* was by the *Boar* destroy'd."
Ends:

> For ISTER's Wave no more shall *Crimson* flow,
> Nor shall thy Walls another BLENHEIM show.

See Dive's *The Treasurer and the General*, 1713, No. 460
below.

410   [Burnet, Sir Thomas (1694-1753)]

Our Ancestors as wise as we: OR Ancient Precedents FOR
MODERN FACTS, In ANSWER, to a LETTER from a NOBLE LORD.
[2 lines Budaeus] *LONDON*: Printed for *A. Baldwin*, near
the *Oxford-Arms* in *Warwick-Lane*. 1712. Price 6 *d*.
8°: A-D⁴, E¹; t.p., *bl*., 3-34, 34 pp. 3-4 A LETTER
from Ld---- to Mr. B-----., p. 5 The ANSWER TO THE LETTER.
Morgan 0116. BM copy used. Has MS note: "This Pamphlet
has no relation to the Peerage bill - it relates only to
the discription [*sic*] of the Duke of Marlborough." This
is essentially true, although the point of departure is
Queen Anne's political maneuver in appointing twelve
Peers to assure the change of Ministers and ultimate
peace. The pamphlet makes it clear that it was a stroke
against Marlborough, and a list of precedents for ingratitude toward famous generals is cited: Hannibal, Scipio,
Agricola, Raymond, and Sir Walter Raleigh. Marlborough
is defended in reasonable terms; but two pamphlets, *No
Queen or No General* and *The Representation of Albinia*,
are noticed with contempt.
    Mr. B----, who lives in the country, seems to have
more information than Lord ---- in town. Nevertheless,

the inquiry of the latter is quite pointed. "One Day we hear of twelve new Peers being made; another Day we hear of Lions that are all dead in the Tower, . . . a great D. will be impeach'd, etc." Since it is the Duke's being turned out that is the focus of interest, the pamphlet presumably dates early in 1713, which in Old Style could still be dated as 1712. It is signed as from "Your Lordship's Protestant Friend, and Humble Servant." The title is unmistakably ironic. Morgan 0116.

11 [Halifax, Charles, Earl of Montague (1661-1715)]

A PARAPHRASE On Part of the Fourteenth Chapter of *Isaiah*. In *English* Verse. Written on Occasion of the BATTLE OF RAMELLIES and the Following Successes. *By a Person of Honour*. [ornament] *LONDON*, Printed for *A. Baldwin* near the *Oxford-Arms* in *Warwick-Lane*. M.DCC.XII.
8VO: A4; t.p., *bl.*, 3-8, 8 pp. Wrenn Cat., III, 173, attributes to Halifax. Morgan 0290. TxU copy used. While the text deals with tyranny, the poem is strictly a paraphrase of Isaiah. The allusion to Louis XIV, the humbled French tyrant, is only implicit.

12 The PETTICOAT Plotters, or the D[uche]ss of M[arlborough]h's Club. London, 1712. No pub.
Fol., bsd., 1 p. Morgan 0533 Says found in CPA, and is satire on Duchess's attitude after losing her places at Court; touches on Godolphin, Sunderland, and Wharton.

13 The Pious Meditations of the Excellent Prince, John, the most noble D---K of M----gh, since he unfortunately lost his many great places under Her Majesty's Government.
Dobell Cat., 1934, No. 350. 4 lines, 8VO. Not in Morgan.

414 *The Portraiture of Oliver Secundus*, the *Modern Protector* in *Body* and *Conscience*. 1712. Morgan O434, bsd., prose. Only ref. See *Oliver's Pocket Looking-Glass*, No. 333 above, for satire on Marlborough as a second Cromwell, i.e. dictator.

415 Prince EUGENE NOT THE MAN You took him for: OR, A MERRY TALE Of a Modern Heroe. *Quis Furor O Cives! Quae tanta Licentia ferri! LONDON* Printed: and Sold by *J. Baker*, at the *Black-Boy* in *Pater-Noster-Row*, 1712. [Price Six Pence.]

        $8°$: A-F^4; t.p., 3-48, drop-t. on p. 3, 48 pp. In MS. 'Read' and identifications of names. Horn copy used. Prose pamphlet. Eight chapters. Morgan O227. Opens:

> The strange Notions the World hath conceiv'd
> of that famous Prince *Bonetto*, and the various
> Reports that is [*sic*] of him, the strange Descrip-
> tion of his Person, and the more unaccountable one
> of his Actions, with some other Occurrences of this
> Time remarkable, gives Birth to these Memoirs.

The style and satiric slights in this work associate it with the Mary Manley, Swift, Wagstaffe group. Prince Eugene as Bonetto, his mother as Heccat, Duchess Sarah's mother as Mother Haggy, and Marlborough as General Avaro, are the main figures to appear. The Duke's birth opens the picaresque story, and Eugene's arrival in England, 1712, concludes it, except for the final episode in which Eugene is swallowed up in a black cloud which wrecks his plans and those of the Belgians (i. e. the Dutch). The work is extremely scatalogical. Aside from vulgarities, its chief contribution is in the inclusion of several sets of verses. These include the conundrum "When an M and D with two C's shall by Joyn'd with an X" (pp. 6-7); the "Red-hair'd Girl" (pp. 12-14); the "Linsey Wolsey Apron" (p. 20); and an 82-line squib from the sword-bearer giving the menu for a dinner for Prince Eugene (pp. 39-44). Only the first two relate to Marlborough. An allusion to St. Alban's Ghost, p. 12, points to Wagstaffe as author.

The Red-hair'd Girl, i.e. Duchess of Somerset, concludes with a stanza on Sacheverell, and the line, "And
throws the D[uke] flat on his back." Of course many
Sacheverell pieces show the effect of his trial and the
fall of the Whig government on Marlborough's fortunes.

416 A POEM on Prince EUGENE. -- *Totos infusa per artus.*
Major in exigue regnebat corpore Virtus. *London*:
Printed for *J. Baker*, in *Pater-Noster Row*; 1712. Advs.
bot. p. 2 of two Baker pieces, viz. *Just Publish'd the
Second Edition of* Prince *Eugene*'s Daily Prayer; which,
for its singular Excellency, has been admir'd by all
Nations, and Translated into all Languages, and ought
to be Preferr'd, with his Immortal Glory, to all Suc-
ceeding Generations; with his true Effigies, curiously
Engraven on a Copper-Plate. Price 3 d. *To Morrow will
be Publish'd.* A Poem on the Duke of *Marlborough.*
Price 3. *d.* Sold by *J. Baker*, in *Pater-Noster-Row.*
1/2°: 2 sides, 1 column. 36 lines, couplets.
Clark copy used. Not in Morgan. Opens:

> So *Tydeus* look'd, when, single, He oppos'd
> The *Perjur'd Brother*, with his Guards inclos'd.

Though short in stature, Tydeus has slain fifty traitors.
So heroes are giants: "Heroic Spirits are of Heavenly
Birth" (1. 7). They exceed the level of mankind, as a
glass crowds sun-beams to a small point, with violent
heat. Such is the man Germany has lent "to bridle *France*,
and curb the Continent" (1. 16). Eugene, with an echo of
Denham's *Cooper's Hill*, is "Cool, but not Dull, and without Rashness, Brave" (1. 19). He could have equaled ten
Nestors at Troy.

> Go, Dauntless Prince, and stem the Gallic Rage,
> Act in one Year the Business of an Age.   19-20

Though Eugene has had a short span of years, the poem
concludes:

> H'has liv'd Three Hundred, who has fought like Thee.

411

417   Λ *Poem* on the *Duke* of *Marlborough*. Sold by *J. Baker*, in *Pater-Noster-Row*. Price 3 *d.* As adv. in preceding item. No copy known. Not in Morgan.

418   Prince *Eugene's Daily Prayer*. Also sold by *J. Baker*. Described in adv. above with A POEM on Prince *Eugene*. No copy known. Not in Morgan.

419   The QUEEN's and the Duke of ORMOND's New TOAST. Printed in the Year MDCCXII. Apparently another ed. as Morgan O40 adds *London*, Printed by R. Newcomb. No indication of pub. in first ed. Clark copy used.

      1/2°: 1 side, 1 column, 34 lines, couplets. Opens:

> Here's a health to the QUEEN, who in Safety does sit on
> The Throne of, and truly now Reigns in *Great Britain*.

Anti-Marlborough satire, since he would rule as *John* the Second. Ormond, his replacement, disdains to make sale of Commissions, to be bribed by Contractors, or make a Perquisite of the Bread's Chipping. Ormond, we are informed, will finish the strife "That ne'er could be ended by a *General for Life*."

420   *The Sense of the Nation* Concerning the *Duke* of *Marlborough*, as it is Expressed in Several Acts of Parliament, in the Votes and Joint-Addresses of both *Houses*, and in Her Majesty's Most Gracious Messages and Answers. *London*: Printed for *S. Popping*, at the *Black-Raven* in *Pater-Noster-Row*, 1702. Price Four Pence.

      8vo: A⁸ B⁶; t.p., *bl.*, 3-28, 28 pp. 1702 date clearly erroneous for 1712 in view of content. Morgan O435. Horn copy used.

      The pamphlet quotes addresses of 1702, but also 1704-6. The Grant of Woodstock Park, and a summary of events up to 1712 in fine print on the last page, prove 1712 date. Marlborough's dismissal, December 31, is mentioned "and the Conferences for a Peace were opened the

New Year." Supplies a relatively objective account, but implies Marlborough well rewarded, and Peace negotiations not initiated till after his downfall, which was not the case.

21 *The Sense of the Nine in Ten*, concerning the Late G[ener-al] and Late [Ministr]y, as it is Express'd in their Loyal Addresses to Her Majesty. *London*: Printed for *S. Popping* at the *Black-Raven* in *Pater-Noster-Row*, 1712. (3 d.)
    8vo, 24 pp. Morgan 0436. Ostensibly a reprint of the preceding, with corrected date.

22 *Soldiers Lamentation* For the Loss of their GENERAL. In a LETTER from the Recruiters in *London*, to their Friends in *Flanders*. To the Tune of To you fair Ladies, &c. Printed in the Year, MDCCXII. Pro-Marlborough ballad.
    1/2°: 2 sides. 20 7-line stanzas, 140 lines. Each stanza has refrain, "With a fa, la, la, la, la, la, la, la." Repr. in *Pills to Purge State-Melancholy*, 70-5. Not in Morgan. BM copy used. Opens:

>   To you, dear Brothers, who in vain
>   Have curb'd the Pride of *France*.

Reviews most of the campaigns and victories, but reminds that "you've lost your gallant *Marl----*."

Ibid. But subtitle 'In a Letter from the Officers in *Ireland*, to their Friends in *Flanders*.'
    1/2°: 1 side, 2 columns. In 16 6-line stanzas, nmd., 96 lines. No pub., n. d. (1712?) Opens:

>   To you, dear Brothers, we complain,
>   Who curb'd the Pride of *France*.

No refrain.
    Also another version 1/4 strip, with soldier's head at the top. Only 5 stanzas, and part of 6th, cropt. BM copy.

423 [Watts, Isaac (1674-1748)]

STANZAS To my Lady SUNDERLAND at *Tunbridge-Wells*.
London. Printed for *E. Curll* at the *Dial* and *Bible*
against *St. Dunstan*'s Church in *Fleetstreet*, and Sold
at his Shop in *Tunbridge-Walks*. 1712. Price 2 d.
    1/2°: 2 sides. BM copy used; has "Mr Isaac Watts,"
in MS, perhaps in Luttrell's hand, but no date given.
Has ad adv. as by Watts of "To his Grace the Duke of
Marlborough on the report of - - -" 24 lines. BM, Oxf.,
Camb. Not in Morgan. Opens:

> Fair Nymph, ascend to Beauty's Throne,
> And rule that radiant World alone.

The lines maintain that "not *Bleinheim*'s Field, nor
Ister's Flood," nor the French standards have such grace
as Spencer's (i.e. Lady Sunderland's) face. The Muse
faints at "what Pen and Pencils never knew," her charms,
which are more commanding than the warlike thunder of
Churchill's arms. Since she was his second daughter,
Anne, this is a double compliment to Marlborough.

424 *'Tis pity they should be Parted*: Or the FABLE Of the BEAR
and the FOX. *London*, Printed in the Year, MDCCXII. (Price
One Peny)
    1/2°: 10 6-line stanzas, 60 lines. A satirical
fable in which the Fox is Marlborough; the Bear, Godolphin;
Anne, the Lyon; and the Tories, the Tyger. Stanzas nmb.
BM copy used. Morgan O682. Opens.

                    I.

> *Bruin* and *Reynard* who had made,
> A Practice of the Pilfring Trade,
> Were in a Hen-Roost caught.

Anti-Marlborough, as Reynard and Bruin claim they have been
protecting abroad and at home, while they have been looting
for themselves. Ends:

> As both have our Destruction meant;
> *'Tis Pity They are Parted.*

25 To the DUKE. Written in his Absence, occasion'd from
the sight of some Defamatory *Libels* on Him. N.d., but
presumably 1712.
4to: A-D^4, 1-30 (31-2), 32 pp. Lacks t.p., hence
no pub., n.d. Not in Morgan. No separate title; drop-t.
p. 1. 456 lines, with a Postscript of 18 lines, total
474 lines, couplets. Opens:

> The Brave and Just, like to himself does give,
> Ready'st to dye, is fittest still to live.

No specific reference to Marlborough, nor to other
names or events. An exceedingly disappointing composi-
tion. Frequent cliches and solecisms in style suggest
an alien hand. While Marlborough's name does appear in
manuscript on the first page, it is in a modern hand.
Most of the clues to the "Duke" in the title seem to pre-
clude the poem's being addressed to Marlborough. "Had you
not own'd a KING for Syre" (1. 28); "Where tallest you,
but one, did firmly stand" (1. 90); these and a very few
other allusions suggest, perhaps the Duke of York, later
James II. An emphasis on naval references also points
toward someone other than Marlborough, if not the Duke
of York.
    Certainly the poem, though long, has no definite al-
lusions to Marlborough, and his exile. Further, the poem
is definitely conservative, if not positively Tory, in
tone. Only one concrete allusion appears. Following a
reference to "*Whiggs* Malice," is the passage:

> But *Whigg*! That Burlesque little paultry sound, ⎫
> In Ballad Verse, fit only to be found;   ⎬
> Where your great Name is Sung, it shoud [*sic*]   ⎭
>   be drown'd.   432-4

This seems a strange way to refer to the Whigs in 1712,
if that is the date of the poem.

6   *To* HIS GRACE the DUKE of MARLBOROUGH, A POEM. By a
Clergy-Man *of the* Church of *England*. No pub., n.d.
    1/2°: 2 sides. 109 lines, couplets, somewhat
varied. BM copy used. Morgan R356, but as 1715 (?).

Opens:

> May't please your Grace, in your Recess,
> T'accept the Muses last Address.

The poet has followed each campaign, for nine years,
with a poem, but in vain, a complaint that suggests
Richard Chapman or James Smallwood, both of whom wrote
repeated verses with little or no return. His status
as a Whig adherent is indicated by a passage complimentary to Blackmore, who celebrated Marlborough after
"sweetly singing *Arthur* and *Eliza*."

427 The Ungrateful World, OR; The Hard Case of a Great G----l.
No pub., n. d.
　　　1/2°:, 1 p., 1 col., o side. 48 plus 4 lines of Conclusion, 52 lines, couplets. BM copy used. Not in Morgan.
Opens:

> A village *Swain* secure from Wants,
> Had near his House a Bed of *Ants*.

A beast allegory. The Swain (the government, England,
Queen Anne) welcomes the Ants, since they aid his industry.
However, their Leader (Marlborough) and his Lovely Bride
(Duchess Sarah) become haughty, proud, and ungrateful to-
ward the Swain. The Swain, who had enriched and honored
them, resolves to root them out. He does so, and the
Leader loses his post as G[enera]l, and both he and the
Ants are losers in the end. The Conclusion is that

> Those who to Ambition make Pretence,
> And abuse the sweetness of an easie Prince,
> Find just Rewards, when they are doom'd to Fall,
> To be at once cast down and hurl'd from all.

A date may have been shaved, but is presumably 1712.

428 THE TRIUMPH OF ENVY: OR, THE VISION OF *Shilock* the *Jew*.
To which is prefix'd a Copper Plate, Engrav'd by the Best
Hands, from the Original done in *Holland*. [motto Old
Testament: "How are the mighty fallen?" etc.] *LONDON*:

416

Printed, and Sold by the Booksellers of *London* and *West-minster*. 1712. Price 6 *d*.
    8°: A-C⁸; Plate, half-t., *bl*., t.p., *bl*., 5-22,
bl., 24 pp. Morgan 0437. Folger copy used. Only one
known.

    In the rather handsome allegorical plate, Marlbor-
ough, supported by officers and army tents in the background, is offering his sword to a seated Britannia. A
winged Victory holds a scroll reading *"Virtus vincit
invidiam,"* while in the clouds overhead a demon rides in
a chariot drawn by dragons, surrounded by lesser demons.
Instead of explicating the plate, the pamphlet offers a
long explanation of an allegorical dream which depicts
some of the features of the plate. Though Marlborough
is not named, he is plainly the man on the Red Horse,
who comes to fight a Monster. A woman in Purple, who
is Queen Anne, touches him with her scepter, and her city
of Jerusalem is threatened. The Monster, with face of a
man, body of a tiger, and claws of a harpy (Louis XIV)
reaches east, north and south for conquests. The Man on
the Red Horse is victorious, and the Woman puts a gold
chain about his neck; and

      APOLLO, whose Melodious Tongue,
   Sweetly of *Arthur* and *Eliza* sung,

has in despair flung away his harp, and has written
'Advice' to all the other poets, an allusion to the
Advice to the Poets and Blackmore. Marlborough's brilliance transcends all poetic efforts. He is more than
hero now; whether at Woodstock, that is Blenheim Palace,
or St. Albans, he will merit Britain's praise. In the
country,

   Reflections there on wide *Ramillia*'s Field,
 On *Audenard*'s Plain, and *Blarney*'s Woods,
 On all Your Fights by *Flandrian* Floods,
  Will everlasting Pleasure yield.   85-8

    A clue to the date of the poem appears in a reference
to Tallard, the French Commander whom Marlborough had
taken prisoner at Blenheim. His release, December 1711,
had been opposed by the Duke. This event is interpreted
as an insult to him.

> Every Clown can guess,
> What's mean't by *TALLARD*'s Release, and your Recess.
> 75-6

Since Marlborough spent the summer at St. Albans, prior
to leaving England, the poem can be dated as coming in
1712. It concludes with an allusion to Heaven as continuing the war in spite of Marlborough's efforts toward
peace. The poem, however well intentioned, has almost
enough absurdity to suggest the indefatigable Dr. Richard Chapman as author. See his *Le Feu to Joye*, 1705,
No. 67. Not only was he a clergyman; he did follow
Marlborough's career with a tribute every year, or at
least nearly so.

"There was great Rejoicings in the *Temples* and the
TROPHIES of the *Monster* were set up in all the *High
Places*. . .for the Terror of the *Monster* was felt no more"
(p. 11). The plainest identification comes with a woman
of Tire, worshiper of the Man in Black, who influences
the queen. "She was named after the Name of *Nabal's*
Wife," that is Abigail. The allusion is of course to
Abigail Masham, and the remainder of the allegory depicts
the overthrow of the Man on the Red Horse by monsters of
Envy and Discord. Another clue might be the number of
enemies, given as "CCLXX and ODD." Actually in the vote
in Commons, the opposition to Marlborough was 232. On his
downfall the people weep, and "I saw sitting at his Right
Hand a Woman of Beauteous Form, and her Hair was platted
with Gold" (p. 17), obviously Duchess Sarah.

The author concludes by saying he has written what he
saw in his vision; but the allegory is too heavy and obscure to add much support to the fallen leader. The name
Shilock in the title is not repeated and seems to have no
relation to Shakespeare's Shylock, and certainly not to
the charges of avarice against Marlborough.

429   WE *are bravely served at Last* by the *Q*[uee]*n* and *P*[arli-
a]*m*[en]*t*. *London*, Printed by *J. Read* in *White-Fryers
Fleetstreet*. 1712. Morgan 0725. Ref. in *Bibl. Lindesi-
ana*, 1079, which states, "Writers rejoice in the downfall
of Marlborough, and the approach of Peace." Praises

renewal of credit, the Act for building new churches in
the London suburbs, and the Queen's charity to the new
clergy. Not in Morgan.

30 *Where's Your Impeachment Now?* or, the D---'s Safe Delivery. 1712
     1/2°: 1 side, 2 cols. Printed by John Bill in the
Strand. Price one Peny. 11 6-line stanzas, 66 lines,
ballad. Opens:

> *Bruin* and *Reynard*, who had made
> A Practice of the Pilfring Trad.

Anti-Marlborough beast-fable. Bruin (Godolphin), Reynard
(Marlborough) and a Lyon (Harley). The Lyon demands punishment for the others for chicken stealing. Bruin says
all his predecessors have been transgressors, and Reynard
that he "Abroad was Warring." The beasts insist that Reynard should be in the Tower, but that Bruin's faults be
remitted.

31 *WHIG* and *TORY:* OR Wit on Both Sides. BEING A COLLECTION
OF State Poems, UPON All Remarkable Occurrences, from the
Change of MINISTRY, to this Time: BY THE Most Eminent
Hands of both PARTIES. *LONDON*, Printed for *E. Curll,* at
the Dial and Bible against St. *Dunstan* Church in *Fleet-
street*, 1712. Price 2 *s*. 6 *d*. In Four Parts: each A-E^4;
i-ii, 3-40, 158 pp. Morgan 0731, R585. U Oregon copy of
Sed. Ed. used. Title of first ed. slightly different.
Notable for absence of poems on Marlborough and the war.
Only one allusion to Marlborough appears, and that is a
prose piece. The collections are heavily sprinkled with
doggerel pieces, many pro-Sacheverell, and, in spite of
the title, the "wit" is almost throughout anti-Whig. Dr.
Garth's Poem to the Earl of G[odolphi]n, No. 306, appears,
and also a response, ascribed to Godolphin, "The E. of
G---n to Dr. G----h, upon the Loss of Miss Dingle: In Return to the Doctor's consolatory Verses to him, upon the

Loss of His Rod," Pt. II, pp. 22-3. Morgan R585 lists
a reprint in 1715 under the title TORY Pills to Purge
Whig Melancholy. . .written in Defence of Church and
State. This ed. seems not to be enlarged, and certainly
the title is more explicit, in showing the anti-Whig bias.
     Case, *Bibl. of Miscellanies*, lists ed. 1712, 1713,
Nos. 254 (c) and (d). He also notes that this is a re-
issue of *Poems for and Against* Dr. Sacheverall, as is
also *A Tory Pill to Purge* WHIG *Melancholy*, 1715.

432 *The White-hall* PROPHECY, *Lately found under the Ruins of
     that Royal Chapel.* Printed in the Year MDCCXII.
          1/2°: 1 side, 1 column. BM copy used. Not in Mor-
     gan. Anti-Marlborough satire. The prophecy, engraved on
     a copper plate, alludes to financial matters in the gov-
     ernment, and is dated "CC D II M X," obviously a juggling
     of MDCCXII. Three heads of brass were also found with
     inscriptions reflecting on King William's designs on
     Dunquirque and winking at enormous losses in naval and
     merchant's ships. "And tho' you knew many Months before-
     hand of the Expedition of *Perkin* against *Scotland*, why
     did you send neither Men, provisions, nor Ammunition,
     for defence of Edinburgh Castle, till two days after the
     French Fleet were chased back." A pun on Churchill's
     name associates him with the satire.

With this first year of Marlborough's exile the
flow of both panegyric and satire abruptly tapered
off. Biographers of Marlborough and his career began
to write; but the principal literary efforts were devoted to the Treaty of Utrecht, and the consequent
peace. Addison's *Cato* and Pope's *Windsor Forest* were
not exceptions; but they do suggest that the muses are
returning even though the poets are as opportunistic
and uncertain as the political leaders. Steele turned
to Dunkirk, Gay celebrated rural sports, while Swift
occupied himself with such trivialities as Dr. Part-
ridge the astrologer, and the exciting episodes of
which he wrote to Stella in the *Journal*.

The succession of treaty settlements were finally
signed in March and April, but poems began to appear
before the treaty had been signed. Tickell was the
only notable name among contributors, except for Pope,
whose *Windsor Forest* was expanded into the best of all
possible peace poems. The Tories were enjoying an uneasy triumph; hence the poems on Utrecht largely reflect reaction against the war, or at least relief that
it was over. This meant such a deflation of heroes,
even such a great one as Marlborough, as marks modern
conflicts. Thus the poems on the Peace reflect more of
a triumph over the Whigs than of satisfaction in any
settlement with France and Louis XIV.

433 March 7, entered March 5.

Pope, Alexander (1688-1744)

WINDSOR-FOREST. To the Right Honourable *George* Lord
LANSDOWN. By Mr. *POPE* [3 lines Virgil] [ornament]
LONDON: Printed for *Bernard Lintott* at the *Cross-Keys*
in *Fleet-street* 1713
      2°: A-E; t.p., *bl.*, 1-18, 20 pp. Morgan P480.
BM copy used. Opens:

> Thy forests, Windsor! and thy green retreats,
> At once the Monarch's and the Muse's seats.

   While not mentioning Marlborough specifically, the
poem is a classic statement of Tory doctrines. The major
portion was written in 1704, as Pope says, when he was
sixteen years old. Thus it is contemporary with Addison's *Campaign*, and it has been alleged to be a retort
upon that poem. On publishing the poem, Pope added a
section on the Peace which gives the poem its ultimate
unity and full meaning. Professor Earl R. Wasserman,
The Subtler Language, 101-68, supplies a penetrating
correlation with Denham's *Cooper's Hill*, which he says
is "consistently and coherently political at the core."
Both poems develop the principle of *discordia concors*,
of unity in diversity, as both an aesthetic and political doctrine. "Harmony through conflict is essentially
a Tory doctrine. . .faith in political concord through
clashing equal forces of monarch and parliament. Whig-
gism, on the other hand, leans toward republicanism,
emphasizing the power of parliament and building on the
heterogeneous mass of the public." Pope uses Windsor
Forest, as Denham had the Thames, as a unifying symbol,
like Eden a microcosm of the ideal order of Nature.
The Whigs' pressing on with a crushing and bruising war
was Chaos-like.
   Swift, writing to Stella on March 9, says: "Mr.
Pope has published a fine Poem called Windsor Forest;
read it." This is his only reference to Pope in the
entire *Journal*. By adding the lines beginning "Hail,
sacred peace!" (1. 355) to a poem written eight years
earlier, Pope succeeded in producing the first poem on

the peace, and perhaps, as has been stated, the best of
all possible poems on the subject. Although the Treaty
had not yet been signed, the triumph of Tory policy was
assured. Father Thames could say:

No more my sons shall dye with British blood
Red Iber's sands, or Ister's foaming flood.   368-9

With this allusion to Spain and the Danube, Pope expresses a mild discrediting of Marlborough's campaigns.
Now the British swain can tend his flocks and reap the
grain in pastoral peace.

34   March 10.

M., C.

THE LIVES OF THE Two Illustrious Generals, *JOHN*, DUKE of
MARLBOROUGH, AND *Francis Eugene*, PRINCE of SAVOY. [3
lines Virgil] *LONDON*: Printed for *Andrew Bell*, at the
Bible and *Cross-Keys*, and *J. Phillips*, at the *Black Bull*
in *Cornhill*; And Sold by *John Baker* in *Pater-Noster-Row*,
1713.
        8°: engraved portrait of Marlborough, t.p., *ii bl.*,
Dedication to John Duke of Montague, &c, *iii-ix*, sgnd.
'C. M.'; 1-3 The Introduction, *4 bl.*, sep. t.p. for Marlborough; 5-174. The Prince Eugene portion is separately
titled, and has a corresponding portrait, pp. 175-283,
284 bl., 295 pp. Adv. in *Flying-Post*, No. 3346, Tues.,
March 10, 1712. 'This Day is publish'd. Price Four
Shillings.' Morgan P375. Horn copy used. BM, CtY, DCL,
TxU.
        'C. M.' states that he is the final compiler, but
that the bulk of the work was written by one who prefers
to remain anonymous. The dedication to John, Duke of Montague, a second choice, and the statement that his father,
Ralph Montagu, was friend to both generals, seem to leave
little doubt that Ralph Montagu (1638?-1709) is the
original author. Not only was he elevated to the dukedom
on the marriage of his son to Mary Churchill, Marlborough's
youngest daughter, March 2, 1705; he had shared with

Marlborough much of the licentious life of the court of
Charles II. Possibly it was recollections that he had
accepted largesse from Louis XIV, whereas Marlborough
was the only notable English leader to resist bribes
(Churchill I, 166-7), but also that they had both enjoyed
the favors of the notorious Duchess of Cleveland that led
to his deathbed injunction that his name be withheld.
Nevertheless, the original authorship is still in doubt,
while the identity of 'C. M.' also remains undetermined.
Some allusions suggest Arthur Maynwaring, secretary to
Duchess Sarah, as having had a share in producing the
Lives.

The *Life of Marlborough* has been given undue importance, not least in Sir Winston Churchill's crediting it
with being the "earliest of all Churchill's biographies"
(I, 241), and his citing it for his only source for early
biographical details. Actually the work draws considerably on Hare, No. 112, but it does add some authorial observations. Its use by Lediard, Wolseley, and others, as
well as by Churchill, provide its primary interest. It
is quoted generously in Abel Boyer's *Political State*, IV,
421-2, where are also quoted the verses "On the Duke of
Marlborough's Going into Germany," along with a jibe at
the *Examiner*. Assuredly the *Lives* were issued as part of
the campaign of defence of Marlborough, which centered
on Dr. Hare's writings.

The *Life* of Prince Eugene is singularly lacking in
details relating him to Marlborough. Even Blenheim is
given only two pages, 236-8, and is unnamed. Only one
reference to Marlborough appears, as "his good Friend"
(p. 265), then in disgrace and divested of power. The
Life concludes with a long extract from *Spectator* No.
340, in which Steele pays tribute to Eugene on the occasion of his visit to England.

The Life of Marlborough leaves him at Aix-la-Chapelle.
Since he wrote Sarah from this Belgian village, January 31,
1713, and then shortly left it to meet her, the terminal
date of the account can be determined. Its motivation as
basically a partisan pamphlet is apparent in the final sentences, in which the writer anticipates a near demise for
Marlborough:

I could wish, I had no Reason for such a
Surmize, but an advanced Age, a crazy Constitution, a Body worn out with continual Fatigues,
and a Mind impair'd with uninterrupted Trouble
and Ingratitude, cannot hold out very long
against the Assaults of Malice and Detraction,
that still pursue him in EXAMINERS, and other
tolerated, if not authoriz'd, Libels.   (p. 174)

35 April 9.

Trapp, Joseph (1679-1747), First Professor of Poetry
at Oxford, 1708-18.

PEACE. A Poem inscribed to the Right Honourable Lord
Viscount BOLINGBROKE. [3 lines Virgil] LONDON: Printed
for *John Barber*, on *Lambeth-Hill*; and *Henry Clements*, at
the *Half-Moon* in St. *Paul*'s Church-yard. MDCCXIII.
     2°: t.p., *bl.*, 1-22, 24 pp. 509 lines, couplets;
wmk. 'AC.' Adv. *Daily Cour.* '9 April, 1713.' Morgan
P516. Horn copy used. BM, CSmH, CtY, MH, TxU, *et al.*
Opens:

Then it is done! the wond'rous Work compleat!
Britain at last is Wise, as well as Great.

A Tory satire on Marlborough and the "boundless, wild Ex-
travagance of War"; but praises Blenheim as Hockstadt,
and its role in panegyric.

Yet *Hockstadt*, and th'ennnobled *Danube*'s Stream
Shall always live, the Poet's boasted theme.   32-3

Trapp pictures the stream choked with arms, blood, "And
Steeds and Squadrons tumbling in the Flood." Fame will
always honor the heroes of Ramillies, Wynendale, and even
Blarignia, i.e. Malplaquet; but greater even than military
heroes are those who "spar'd the Monarch we no longer fear"
(1. 55). They have saved England from her own victorious
arms, have overcome Faction's dark designs. The poet
thinks of romances and the tales of rescuing a princess
from a tower where a giant has immured her. What can

425

surpass this? Ormond, who has bravely suspended war,
"daring *not* to Fight."

Much of the poem turns on faction, that is the Whig
interest. Its victims are listed, Oxford first, of heroic zeal, braving Guiscard's attempt on his life. Next
great Harcourt, then St. John, now Viscount Bolingbroke,
combining all the gifts of body and mind, and Shrewsbury,
Hamilton, Bromley, and Bristol and Strafford, all of exemplary character and shining qualities. They have overcome Faction, and all England rejoices. In celebration
of the Peace, Anne goes to St. Paul's. The poem concludes with predictions for the future as a result of
the Treaty of Utrecht. In retort on the Whig championship of liberty, we learn that:

> *True Liberty* her Influence now shall spread,
> And long distress'd *Religion* raise her Head.   476-7

Vice, blasphemy, schism, all will disappear, and Britain
will forget her internal feuds, be truly brave and great
under "*ANNA* the Guardian of Mankind's Repose" (1. 516).
Lasting peace and happiness will bless the earth.

Vastly more interesting than this early tribute to
the peace, is the record of it in Swift's *Journal to
Stella*. Writing under the date April 1, he says of
Parnell, himself, and "Dartenuff" with whom he had dined:

> After dinner we all went to Ld Bol- who
> had desired me to dine with him, but I would
> not, because I had heard it was to look over
> a dull Poem by one Parson Trap, upon te [*sic*]
> Peace.

On April 2nd he continues:

> I was this morning with Ld Boling-- and
> he tells me a Spanish Courier is just come
> . . .I was prevaild on to come home with Trap,
> and read his Poem, & correct it, but it was
> good for nothing.

Thus, aside from Swift's contempt for bad panegyric,
we learn that he had some small share in this poem. Its
appearance, less than a week later, with the dedication

to Bolingbroke, of which apparently Swift had no anticipation, is evidence of the lack of complete candor between them. That Bolingbroke sought Swift's help in im-
proving the poem, shows him in an interesting light. At
last the secret intriguer for the peace could be revealed,
and even accept this handsomely printed tribute in his
name. "Dull poem" though it be, it is also one of the
most imposing examples of Queen Anne printing.

436   April 10, performed, Apr. 27 pub. first ed.

Addison, Joseph (1672-1719)

Cato. A Tragedy. As it is Acted at the Theatre-Royal in
Drury Lane, By Her Majesty's Servants. [6-line Latin
motto from Seneca, *Ecce Spectaculum dignum . . .* from *De
Divin. Prov.*] *London*: Printed for *J. Tonson*, at *Shakespear's-Head* over-against *Catherine-street* in the *Strand*.
1713.
        Five quarto publications in 1713, by Tonson. Morgan
W2 lists numerous subsequent eds. in the century with
others later. Morgan, using Swift as authority, dates the
first performance April 10, but all other evidence is for
April 14. Morgan supplies full summary of editions and
translations. Nine editions in 1713, of which five were
quarto, and the important Tonson ed. in *Coll. Works*, 1721
ff., are only part of the evidence of the extraordinary
popularity of the play. Peter Smithers, *Life of Addison*,
1952, pp. 252-61, supplies an excellent summary of the
response to *Cato*. Its then notable run of nine days, followed by further performances. brought commendatory verses
from Steele, Hughes, Young, Eusden, Tickell, George Sewell,
Ambrose Philips, and others. The significance for Marlborough relates to Addison's desire to avoid a partisan political piece, and the public insistence on finding political
points. Addison's intention of dedicating to Sarah, Duchess of Marlborough, was forestalled by his learning that
Queen Anne herself would be pleased at the honor; but it
shows his interest in the emigré family. The Whigs saw the
noble Cato, victim of political intrigues and viciousness,

as champion of liberty, and he supplies the alternatives
of "liberty or death" (11, v, 80). Juba was to the Whigs
the young Prince of Hanover. The Tories, in turn, saw in
the tyrant Caesar their enemy the Duke of Marlborough,
seeking to be made "general for life." Bolingbroke, from
his box, presented a purse of fifty guineas to Barton
Booth for "defending so well the cause of Liberty against
a perpetual dictator."

Certainly Addison had no intention of associating
Marlborough with Caesar. The relationship of his play to
Marlborough is primarily the general associations with the
Peace which was being negotiated at the time and Addison's
hopes for cessation of civil strife. He had declared himself as the impartial "Spectator" and it must be remembered
that most of the play had been written during his Oxford
years, prior to Blenheim and Marlborough's ascent to fame.
In November of 1714 Addison appended a verse dedication, at
least by implication, "To Her *Royal Highness* the *Princess*
of *WALES*." With some rather tasteless flattery of the
Hanoverian House, he includes the prediction that poets
of the future will no longer need to vindicate "endanger'd
rights, and liberty distrest" (1. 34). Of George I we
learn that poets will

> Describe his awful look, and godlike mind,
> And *Caesar*'s power with *Cato*'s virtue join'd.   41-2

However inept the application may be, the sentiment admir-
ably summarizes Addison's moral and patriotic purpose.
That Marlborough was thought of in connection with *Cato*,
and possibly its hero, is apparent in the next item.

437 *Mr. Addison turn'd Tory*: or *The Scene Inverted*, wherein
it is made to Appear that the *Whigs* have misunderstood
that celebrated Author in his Applauded Tragedy, call'd
Cato and that the Duke of M[arlborough]'s character in
endeavoring to be a general for life, bears a much greater
resemblance to Caesar and Syphax than the hero of the
play; to which are added some cursory remarks upon the
play itself. By a gentleman of Oxford. *London*: Publish'd by J. Baker, 1713.

4°:   23 pp.   Morgan P4.   Adv. in *Examiner* III, No. 46 may give some clue as to the authorship.

438 A POEM on the *Glorious Peace* of *Utrecht*, inscribed in the Year 1713 to the Earl of *Oxford*. London, 1713.
     Morgan P476. P474 almost same title: A Poem Dedicated to the Queen and presented to the Congress of Utrecht. Inscribed in the Year 1713 to the Earl of Oxford. London, 1713.

39 April 28.

Higgons, Bevill (1670-1735)

A POEM on the PEACE: Inscrib'd to the most Honble ROBERT, Earl of *Oxford*, and Earl *Mortimer*, Lord High-Treasurer of *Great-Britain*. [1 line Virgil] By Bevill Higgons, Esq; LONDON: Printed by *John Barber*, on *Lambeth-Hill*; and are to be Sold by *John Morphew*, near *Stationers-Hall*. N.d. [1713]
     A^2 B-E^2, half-t., *bl.*, t.p., *bl.*, 20 pp. Drop-t. on p. 1. 356 lines, couplets. Adv. *London Gazette*, April 28. Morgan P297. Horn copy used of first ed.
     An 8vo ed. as Inscrib'd in the *Year* 1713, pr. for *P. Meighan* at *Gray's-Inn Gate* in *Holborn* and Sold by the Booksellers of *London* and *Westminster*, 1731. (Price Six Pence). Wmk. CMT.
     2°: A-C^2 D^2, t.p., *bl.*, To Edward, Earl of Oxford *iii-iv*, Poem *1-19*, *bl.*, 24 pp., 336 lines. Dedication *iii-iv*, 1-19. Has note: "This Poem being entirely out of print, and falling into my Hands, I thought I could not do any thing more acceptable to the Town, than to renew their Pleasure Re-printing what they received with so universal Satisfaction when it was first published." This indication of a previous printing, and the immediacy of the events seem to support the 1713 date. Lehigh, TxU. Horn copy used.
     The poem opens with an address to Robert Harley, Lord Treasurer till his Dismissal on January 27, 1714. Opens:

>   While no Repulse thy Courage can abate,
>   Or Danger cool thy Zeal to save the State.

The Tory bias is at once apparent; in fact the Tory symbol
of oak leaves is brought in with the claim that all of
Albion's oaks could not supply sufficient decoration for
Harley's brows. The Whigs are a faction.

>   A Potent Faction, turbulent and bold,
>   With undisputed Sway had long Controul'd;
>   The Nation plunder'd to support their State,
>   And bought their Greatness with their Country's
>   Fate.   24-7

Britain, oppressed by wrongs and plundered, her treasure
spent and her blood spilt like water, now craves Peace as
the only cure. Only through escape from foreign "Leagues"
and bribery of never-satisfied nations, with their avarice
and rage of empire, can this be accomplished. This justification of a separate peace introduces Harley, who flies
to his country's aid and the Queen's relief. Although the
poem is addressed to Harley, the chief agent in the Peace
of Utrecht is shown to be Bolingbroke. The Almighty Power,
seeing Europe a prey to rapine, her cities razed, and the
land "manured with Blood," commands the Angel Raphael to
go down to Earth and direct Bolingbroke, or St. John
rather, to carry a message to the French monarch. He is
to tell him that Queen Anne is feeling "more pacifick"
toward him.

>   Let *Bourbon* know the certain Terms of Peace,
>   And shew the Means to make these Evils cease.   81-2

Raphael complies, and even borrows the form and appearance
of St. John which is so near to his own! Then he goes to
Versailles, where the king sits, oppressed with "gloomy
Cares." He states the conditions of peace. Austria will
continue to reign in Lombardy, Philip will rule the Spaniards, and leave his crowns to "his Asturian Boy" (1. 133).
These terms are accepted, and now factious men can "enjoy
the fruits of that Peace, they labor'd to destroy" (1.
144).
     The muse now returns to Harley, who in triumph is
compared to Columbus, courageous and indomitable in face

of doubters and contempt. As the terms of the peace have
been whitewashed, so now Harley's character is blandly
obscured in the joyous shouts of triumph, the firing of
cannon, and the anticipation of a splendid future for
England. All her rivers rejoice, the Thames, Tweed,
Trent, Ouse, Avon, the Severn, and particularly the Wye,
which was associated with the Harley family. Architecture
is brought in with all the Classical orders, to build London's churches and public buildings. Commerce will extend
to the South, the land of spices and precious gems. From
the straits of Magellan to India and Ceylon English sails
and sailors will reach out for new wealth. A striking
astronomical passage completes the picture of limitless
profit. The Moon, Saturn, with his "radiant Ring" unat-
tended, lonely Mars, Jupiter with his own moons, the Earth,
Venus, and even Mercury, whose identity is concealed in the
Sun's beams, are all reviewed in this celestial sojourn of
the muse. But now, exhausted by her great efforts she says
some nobler genius must continue the story, and "dauntless
fathom the dark Depths of Time" (1. 348). Granville alone
can do this, for he is the "lov'd Son of Phoebus," in whom
Art is Nature, and only skill in other poets. Only he can
sing "Immortal ANNE, and Her Immortal Reign."

That in 1731 Patrick Meighan should have the reprint
made under his own name is possibly more remarkable than
the poem itself. His prefatory letter to Harley's son,
Edward, Second Earl of Oxford, was presumably a bid for
notice and perhaps favors. It may also reflect the reaction against the Whig government and Walpole, which are
apparent in the *Grub Street Journal*, and the satires and
jibes of the Tory Scriblerus group of Pope, Gay, and
Swift. Advertisement in the *GSJ*, No. 72, May 20, 1731,
as published since the previous issue of May 13th, supports this view.

40   May 22.

[Oldmixon, John (1637-1742)]

ANNA TRIUMPHANS. A Congratulatory POEM on the PEACE. [3
lines Latin verse] *London*, Printed for R. *Gosling* at the

Mitre and *Crown* against St. *Dunstan*'s Church in *Fleet-
street*, MDCCXIII.
   A^2 B-C^2; *1-2*, 31-12, drop-t. p. 3, 14 pp. fol. 430
lines, couplets. Headline titles throughout. TxU copy
used; CtY, BM. Foxon-Brett-Smith-Luttr. '22 May.' Morgan P16. Morgan items P14-44 all relate to Anne, but
this one is closest to Marlborough interest. Many deal
with the Queen's death, though not remotely in the quantity of the near 50 elegies that signalized the death of
her sister, Queen Mary, in 1695. Opens:

> Whilst Heav'n alone, which laid the prosp'rous Train
> Of glad Success through all her happy Reign.

The poet, with religious emphasis, acknowledges divine
guidance for Anne, while vowing allegiance to her. He
asks his Muse to inquire the source of dissensions, blind
zealots, and faction under such a ruler. Factious rebels
are compared to screeching demons. On page 6 Marlborough's victories are reviewed, but with emphasis on Anne's
role as well.

> Thy General's Conduct must for ever own,
> Their vocal Reeds will speak his last Renown,
> Speak, whose victorious Troops he did Command,
> Poising the Scales of Empire in her Hand,
> Whose floating Castles storm rebellious Towns,
> And Flying Camps Retrieve Usurped Crowns:
> What Stratagems transported from afar,   ⎫
> Defeated *Tallard*, and the rough *Bavar*,   ⎬
> Enough to open, and conclude a War.   ⎭   142-50

Ramillia's rout and Audenard's revolting Vale are introduced, and a tribute to "Wonder-working Webb and *Winnen-
dale*" brings in this rival for acclaim. Considerable
space is given to Marlborough and Eugene in the siege of
Lisle. The poem is distinctly Tory in emphasis. It concludes by hailing the union of "*Gallia*'s Lillies, and the
British Rose," which brings the perfume of Peace. A pastoral note of peaceful fields and forests is introduced
as Britannia finds the good of Church and State prevailing.

441   September 11.

N., T.   [Thomas Newcomb (1682?-1762)]

PACATA BRITANNIA.   A PANEGYRICK to the QUEEN, On the
PEACE, and the interest of the *British* Nation.   By Mr.
T. N.   [8 lines Horace]   *LONDON*:   Printed for *R. Gos-*
ling at the *Mitre* and *Crown* against St. *Dunstan*'s Church
in *Fleet-street*, MDCCXIII.
        2°: A^2 B-C^2; t.p., *bl.*, 3-12, drop-t. on p. 3, 12
pp., 120 4-line stanzas, 480 lines.   Adv. bot. p. 12:
Anna Triumphans, a Congratulatory Poem on the Peace.
Printed for *R. Gosling* price *6* d.   MH copy used.   MS
mark at bottom t.p. 'Sept. 11. 1713.'   No authorization
is given.   Morgan 440.   Opens:

> In Ancient *Rome* thus *Great Augustus* rose,
> To conquer first, then give the World repose;
> While Wreaths like Yours the Hero's Temples bound,
> With Lawrels *Now*, and *Now* with Olive crown'd.

Since the rhyme of the stanzas is a,a,b,b, the effect
is essentially that of couplet verse.   Even so, the poem
fails to attain much momentum or to arrive at a very clear
statement.   The first half, some 280 of its 480 lines,
largely addresses the Queen.   She is beneficent, pitying
those who have fallen in battle on both sides.   Her personal sorrows in the death of her husband and son, as well
as William IIId and the handsome Earl of Scarborough are
mentioned (11. 45-9), with the point that sorrows are over.
Anne has conquered with her goodness as well as arms, and
now states will accept the position of subjects.   Few
specific events are noted, but the visit of the Czar of
Russia appears:

> See, while he visits *Albion*'s friendly Coast,
> The Hero forming, and the Tyrant lost!   241-2

Pertinence to Marlborough appears in comments on visits
to battle fields:

> Transported Peasants now in Raptures tell,
> *Here* Gaul *retreated, there* Bavaria *fell*;
> *His purple Banks here* foaming Ister *lav'd*,
> There Anna's *Troops expiring* Europe *sav'd*.   281-4

In the next stanza Addison is urged to paint the scene of
victories as Kneller has drawn it. Can Churchill's
wreaths inspire his muse? Thus Ramillia's Plain could
rival the Boyne. But since he declines the labor, only
Prior can assume the task.

Predictions of security for Iberia, for sea and land
while British fleets and troops prevail, prosperity and
trade, all are benefits of the Peaceful Britannia, which
is the title of the poem. This theme brings the poet back
to Queen Anne. The Earl of Oxford's fortunate escape and
recovery from the wound inflicted by Guiscard, noticed and
footnoted for identification, brings the ironic observation that the French, who once "his Fall decreed," now
should be grateful.

> To the Weak Steel she does her Freedom owe,
> The Trembling *Villain*, and the Failing *Blow*. 427-8

Marlborough panegyric as a whole was free of metaphysical
conceits, but Oxford evokes a notion that could hardly be
called anything else.

> Thus as Your Love exalts the Hero's Name,
> Sinking ador'd, and bleeding into Fame;
> His Blood shall like Applause with *Nilus* find,
> Which while it overflows alone is kind. 429-32

Return to the death of Anne's son, the young Duke of
Gloster, finds Anne assured that in conquering her grief
she has achieved the poise which has brought Britain freedom from discord! While this is remote from Marlborough,
it is to be noted that his victories are represented as
establishing England in the role of championing and maintaining the peace of Europe.

442 November 26.

[Sewell, George (1690?-1726)]

An EPISTLE from *Sempronia* to *Cethegus*. To which is Added
Cethegus's REPLY. [ornament] *London*: Printed for *John
Hommes*, near *Fleet-street*. (Price Sixpence.)

434

8vo: t.p., *bl.*, drop-t. p. 1; on p. 12 *Cethegus to Sempronia*, 3-22, 24 pp., 362 lines, couplets. MH-Luttr. copy used. Dated in MS. '26 Novemb.' CtY, TxU, Ind. Foxon questions attrib. to Sewell. Morgan P351. Opens:

Such Eyes as *Somerset*'s; Imperious Dame!
With mock'd *Ambition* fierce, and *red* with *Shame*.

A footnote identifies Somerset as the divorced wife of Essex, who had been married to the Duke of Somerset and became a favorite of James I, - "Condemn'd for the Murder of Sir *Thomas Overbury*, a violent, ambitious, intriguing Woman." The Duchess of Marlborough is Sempronia, and few satires paint such a picture of vengeful, power-hungry intriguing as she exhibits. Cethegus remains obscure, and is not Marlborough, who is briefly referred to as the conquering Germanicus. Sempronia addresses him as a dear friend, and urges the claims of her wickedness. She is determined to rule again, and attempt "What *Malice*, *Hell*, or *Woman* can effect" (1. 24). She resists exile to German soil, preferring as she says later to hide in "fair *Blanamia*'s Tow'rs" (1. 123). There she can enjoy the tapestries and paintings which celebrate "Germanicus's" arms. She deplores the fact that the building of Blenheim Palace has stopped, and curses the Peace. "Yet, My *Cathegus*, yet some Hope remains," she cries. "All is not lost. . . Unconquerable Hate, and stedfast Pride." The allusion to Milton associates her with that poet of Whig policy.

Though not a distinguished poem, the piece provides interesting puzzles for the student of satire. Hortensio (Harley) and Serena (Mrs. Masham) are recognizable, as is an allusion to Volpone (Godolphin). Cathegus's reply, 11. 171-362, though nearly half the poem, provides no clear clues to his identity. He professes an "ancient Flame" for Sempronia, and with unconscious prophetic truth, he anticipates the banishing of Serena and Hortensio and other opponents of Sempronia. However he is compelled to accept the situation in which faction has embroiled the country. This is assuredly one of the most confused of satires, and its bearing on Marlborough is primarily in the portrayal of his Duchess as ambitious and intriguing.

443 An Argument against the Banishment or the Meeting of Disaffected Persons Abroad a Danger to a Government, with a Word or Two to the Present Residence of a Certain Person Abroad. London, J. Baker, 1713. Morgan P373. The "certain person" is of course Marlborough.

444 Steele, Sir Richard (1672-1729)

A Comparison between Cato and Caesar. 1713.
4to. Morgan P565. With observations on Addison's *Cato.* See No. 436.

445 Brodrick, Thomas, Gent.

A Compleat HISTORY of the *Late War.* In the *NETHERLANDS.* Together with an ABSTRACT Of the *Treaty* of *UTRECHT.* By *Tho. Brodrick,* Gent. The Whole Illustrated with 15 Curious Copper Plates; and the Coats of Arms of most of the Nobility, and several other Eminent Persons. *LONDON:* Printed by *William Pearson,* for *Thomas Ward,* in the *Inner-Temple Lane.* MDCCXIII.
    Royal 8vo: 2 vols. I, t.p., *bl., iii-iv* ded. to John Lord Bishop of London, *vii-x* The *Preface;* 1-23 List of 2339 Subscribers, *i-xvi* The Introduction, t.p., *bl.,* 3-218; II, half-t., *bl.,* 221-48, unmbd. 12 pp. The Abstract of the Treaty of Utrecht, 387-418. Morgan P100. Horn-Trevor copy used. Coats of arms surround three maps, and all are dedicated to noble personages. Aside from the handsome folding and two-page maps, the running titles, and marginal notes for each paragraph which supply the contents, the date of each year appears at the top of the broad marginal space on each page. Plainly this rather sumptuous work was issued for aristocratic readers. While it pays tribute to Marlborough, Blenheim, which is called Hochstet, is attributed to God's intervention as much as to the "sedateness" and courage of the two commanders. At Oudenarde Eugene and Marlborough, named in that order, resolve to attack. Ramillies is less grudgingly described, but many instances appear of slights and understatement.

It is not surprising that neither Marlborough's name,
nor any of the family, nor those of Addison, Steele,
Garth, nor Godolphin, Sunderland, Halifax and other Whig
leaders, appear in the list of subscribers. This is among
the earliest formal histories of Marlborough's military
career. Among the subscribers appear "Excell. Matthew
Prior, *Esq*;" and John Vanbrugh, *Esq*; but few others of
the panegyrists of the hero of the "Great War."

146 *The Duke of Marlborough* and the *Court's New Toast*.
1/2°: 1 side, 1 column, no pub., n.d. 30 lines,
couplets. Prob. 1713. Foxon-LSA. Not in Morgan. Opens:

A Health to *Great Britain* and long may she flourish
May she ne'er want a Protestant Prince for to nourish,
To save and protect both the *Church* and the *State*,
And *Jacobite* Fury and *Papists* defeat.

The poem invokes the axe for Jacobite traitors and their
parties.

47 *English Gratitude*: or the *Whig Miscellany*, Consisting of
the Following Poems: 1) On the Duke of Marlborough's Going into Germany; 2) The Oak and the Briar, a Tale; 3) An
Inscription on a Triumphal Arch Erected by the French
King; 4) The Same Revers'd; 5) On the Burning of the
Bishop of St. Asaph's Preface; 6) The Favourite, a Simile.
London, Printed by *A. Baldwin*, near the *Oxford-Arms* in
Warwick-Lane, 1713. (Price 6 *d*.)
8vo, Half-t., List of Books sold by Baldwin, *ii*, t.p.,
bl., 1-28. Separate drop-t. for each poem. To No. 5 is
added "On his Four Sermons." Morgan P220. Horn copy used.
The first two poems have Marlborough importance. The
first is treated under its first, separate printing, November 1, 1712, No. 378 (3) above. The second poem, *The Oak
and the Briar*, pp. 4-15, seems to have had no separate
printing. Written in 182 lines, rather stiff couplets,
it is a fable set at Woodstock. An aged Oak, losing its
branches and becoming bald and weak, is constantly taunted

by a pushing Briar. Eventually the Farmer comes, and listening to the latter's complaints, cuts down the great
tree. However, when winter comes, the Briar, now lacking
the protection of the tree, repents, but too late. It is
torn to shreds.

> So fare the Man, who fed with vain desires,
> By others Ruin, to be great aspires,
> And such the Fate of all Ambitious Briars!   } 180-2

Marlborough is the Oak, and the Briar could be Bolingbroke
or the Duke of Ormond. The other four poems have definite, though limited, bearing on Marlborough. The Inscription, pp. 16-19, supplies, in opposed Latin and English,
a picture of the pompous pretensions and claims of Louis
XIV. Its 24 lines are balanced by 26 in "The Same Revers'd," pp. 21-3. They present, also in Latin and English, the true picture of a bloody tyrant, suffering defeats and humiliations for defying God. His only gains
are won by bribery and perjury. The 24 lines On the Burning of the Bishop of St. Asaph's *Preface* reflect anti-Tory
bias, and in an allusion to Caesar and Cicero, suggest
concern with the wars of Marlborough. Finally, the 'Favourite, A Simile' in 31 lines of varying length, provides
a charming picture of a boy-tyrant at Eton. He asserts
himself, appoints officers, exacts tribute of salt, which
must be eaten, and then finally fades away.

> The New FAVOURITE in his Plumes,
> New *Manners* and New *Airs* assumes,   16-17

and begins to bully and bristle,

> Gives *Pensions*, *Places*, *Titles*, *Garters*;
> His Schemes, his Projects, all must be
> A Law to Bob, his *Grace*, and *Me*.   21-3

Bob would presumably be Harley, his Grace, Marlborough,
and the 'Me' the poet. In time the favorite falls, is
sent to the Tower, and finally returns to his Welsh farm.
    This little collection seems designed to play up
the poem on the Duke's going into exile.

448 *An Excellent New Song, On the Huffing, Heathen, Covetous, Quarrelsome, Uncivil, Hot-headed, Slovenly, Bold, Meddlesome, Heinous John Duke of M----.* To some Tune! London: Printed by Will Hart in Great Carter-Lane, 1713.
    1/2°: 17 4-line stanzas, plus refrain ending John Duke of M., 85 lines. TxU. Morgan 0426. Opens:

        At *Blenheim* so ill to treat Foes,
           To make poor Widows and Wives.

Same piece pr. Dublin: Printed by *Elizabeth Dickson* at the UNION on Cock-Hill, n.d. Cambridge U.
    The text is much the same as the *Excellent New Song* of the *Full Tryal* and *Condemnation*, which has Oudenard instead of Blenheim, but is n.d. Morgan suggests 1712.

449 The Flanders Ballad, or the Duke of Marlborough's Rare Show. No pub., n.d., 1713 ?
    1/2°: 1 side, 80 lines. Another version of No. 448, an Excellent New Song, etc. See also No. 376. Not in Morgan.

450 [Parnell, Dr. Thomas (1679-1718)] ?

The Horse and the Olive: Or, War and Peace. Printed for *John Morphew*, near *Stationers-Hall.*
    1/2°: 2 pp., 6 4-line stanzas, 48 lines. Foxon-LM gives as Parnell; MS 'Dr. Parnell' and '1713.' Morgan 0340 and P463. Clark copy used. Opens:

        With *Moral* Tale let Ancient *Wisdom* move.

    Minerva, aided by Apollo, and Neptune by Pluto, view the contest between the Horse (war) and the Olive (peace). Minerva wins as she gives Plenty, Safety, Science, Art, and Ease. Neptune gives only Victories. Queen Anne gives both the benefits of war and peace. No specific reference to Marlborough.

451   Wesley, Samuel, Sr. (1662-1735)

An Hymn to Peace. To the Prince of Peace. By Samuel
Wesley. Rector of Epworth. London, Printed by J. Leake
for Benjamin Parker and Charles King, 1713.
     [A²] B-C², [1-2], 3-12. MH, CtY, CSmH, TxU. Morgan
P564. Horn copy used.

452   A Letter from the Black Prince to his Grace the Duke of
Marlborough written in the Year 1713.
       16 pp. Morgan P348. "A political satire found in
Rawlinson [MS] D. 1298 f. 153-6."

453   [Oldmixon, John (1673-1742)]

The Life and History of Belisarius, who conquered Africa
and Italy, with an Account of his Disgrace, the Ingratitude of the Romans, and A Parallel between him and a
Modern Heroe. London, printed by A. Baldwin, 1713.
       8ᵛᵒ, viii, 63. Morgan P454 says also attributed
to George Paul; Wrenn Cat. assigns to Defoe. See No. 309.
       Belisarius, a great general under Justinian in the
6th century, was disgraced and imprisoned by a suspici-
ous sovereign in spite of his many victories, but finally
reinstated. His imperious, intriguing wife, Antonina,
was a favorite of Empress Theodora. These and other resemblances were not ignored by Marlborough's enemies.

454   Dunton, John (1659-1733)

Neck or Nothing: IN A LETTER TO THE RIGHT HONOURABLE THE
LORD ----- [Oxford] BEING A SUPPLEMENT To the SHORT History of Parliament. The NEW SCHEME (mention'd in the
foresaid History) which the English and Scotch Jacobites
have concerted for bringing the Pretender, Popery and
Slavery. With the True Character or Secret History of
the PRESENT MINISTRY. Written by his Grace JOHN Duke of
---- [Marlborough]. Aura pulsa fides, auro venalia jura
---- Prop. LONDON, Printed for T. Warner near Ludgate.

1713.
  A-G^8 H^4; t.p., bl., 3-60, 60 pp. Sgnd. p. 60
'JOHN DUKE OF ....' BM copy used. Morgan P212, who
also lists *Queen Robin*, or the Second Part, etc., 1713.
Says: "Marlborough of course was not the author," which
is evident from the content. Included here because of
the attribution. Marlborough is mentioned favorably
pp. 14 and 17; but the subject matter concerns the Treaty
of Utrecht, Dr. Sacheverell, and the Jacobite police in
general. The pamphlet is an assemblage of letters, references to the *Examiner*, *Guardian*, *Rehearsal*, and other
publications.
  The *Short History* referred to in the title is listed
by Morgan P644, where it is ascribed to Walpole. It deals
with his imprisonment in the Tower for opposing the Treaty
of Utrecht.

55 A NEW BALLAD: To the Tune of *Fair Rosamund*. (London?)
No pub., n.d.
  2°: 2 pp., 35 4-line stanzas, 140 lines. BM copy
used. Morgan O491. Rprtd. in *A Pill to Purge State Melancholy*, pp. 29-35, and *Political Merriment*, Pt. II,
74-81. Opens:

        Whenas Q--- A--- of great Renown
          Great Britain's Scepter sway'd,
        Besides the Church, she dearly lov'd
          A Dirty Chamber-Maid.

Allusion to Abigail Masham, who supplanted Marlborough's
Duchess in royal favor. Allusions to Marlborough, Dr.
Burgess.

56 A New Song. To the Tune of MARLBOROUGH *Push 'em Again*.
Printed in the Year, 1713.
  No pub. Does not deal with Marlborough. Not in
Morgan.

  Who mounts the loftiest Dignity Deals with *Millan*.

457 A PARAPHRASE ON THE XXIXth *PSALM*. Occasioned by the
PROSPECT *of* PEACE. INSCRIBED TO *JOSEPH ADDISON*, Esq;
O & Praesidium, & Dulce Decus meum. *LONDON*: Printed
for *Bernard Lintott*, at the *Cross-Keys* between the
Two Temple-Gates in *Fleetstreet*. 1713. Price Four
Pence.
    2°: A-B^2; t.p., *ii*, *iii-iv* Preface; [handsome orna-
ment] half-t., 1-3, *4* Adv. 14 books. Five 8-line stanzas,
40 lines. Horn copy used. Morgan P456 which cites Wrenn
Cat. attribution to Ned Ward.
    Preface says "inimitably fine in the Original."
David's design, and the author's, was to induce people to
gratitude, to God who has given success in war, and to
"that Illustrious Hero," who was his instrument. "If we
think the *French* will at last keep their Word with Us,
what Honours ought not to be pay'd to the Man who beat
them into Sincerity! . . . The Blessings which the Pro-
phetical Writer promises in the behalf of God to his
People, we may look upon to be the Reward of their military Toil, and the happy Consequence of such another Day
as that of *Hochstead* [*sic*] or *Rammily*." Opens:

> Arise O *Israel*, know the Lord,
> With flow'ry Garlands strew the Way.

However, the Preface clearly indicates the intention of
the poem to pay tribute to the great leader. Certainly
the poem is not by Ward.

458 PLOT upon PLOT: A Ballad. To the Tune of *Heigh Boys up
go we*.
    2°: 1 side, 2 columns, no pub., n.d. 9 8-line
stanzas, nmbd. in Roman. 72 lines, alternate rhyme.
BM copy used. Morgan P589. Opens:

> Oh, wicked Whigs! what can you mean?
> When will your Plotting cease?

Also printed in Two POEMS. *VIZ*. I. Plot upon Plot. II. To
the most illustrious Hero *GEORGE LEWIS*, Duke of *Brunswick*
and *Lunenberg*, &c. [ornament] *LONDON*: Printed for *R.
Janeway*, at the Corner of *Dogwell-Court* in *White-Friars*.

1713.   Rprtd. in *A Pill to Purge State melancholy*, pp.
110-13, and in *Political Merriment*, II, 82-5.
     2°:   no sigs., t.p. *bl.*, 3-6, 6 pp.   Drop-t. on p.3
for *Plot upon Plot*.   The poem is strongly partisan, ac-
cusing the Whigs of traitorously seeking the fall of St.
Paul's and bonfires on Good Queen Bess's Day.   More seriously, they are credited with sending the Mohocks abroad
with razors, knives, with filling the *Evening Post* with
explosive material, with sending bombs to the Treasurer.
That the ballad relates to Swift, who exposed the plot,
becomes apparent in the final stanza:

> Now God preserve our Gracious Queen:
> And for this Glorious Deed,
> May She the Doctor make a Dean
> With all convenient Speed:
>   What tho' the *Tub* hath *hinder'd* him,
>   As Common Story tells,
>   Yet surely now the *Ban box-whim*
>   Will *help* him down to *Wells*.   66-73

59   Reden-Voering Van den Hertog van MARLEBOURG Tot het Volk
van ALBION.   Over De VREDE met Vrankryk Gevolgt naar het
niews van Cartago enz. - - - *Ulla Putatis Dona Carere
dolis Danaum? sic notus Ulisses.*   No pub., n.d.   Probably
1712-13.
     8°:   no sigs.; t.p., *bl.*, 3-4 Den Batavieren En Lief
hebberen des VADERLANDS, 5-16, drop-t. on p. 5, 16 pp.
BM copy used, Den Batavieren, 42 lines, alternate rhyme;
text 322 lines, couplets, 464 lines in all.   Text opens:

Wek een verdwaasde drift heest u het hart verrukt
Ô Engelanders noyt van't oorlogs Lot verdrukt.

Seemingly an allegroical representation of Marlborough
addressing his country on the demands and consequences
of war.   Anticipates a glorious future.

460 Dive, Charles

The TREASURER, *and the* GENERAL: or, an *Historical Enquiry* into *Character* of STILICHO. [mottoes from Virgil and Juvenal] By Charles Dive, Gent. *London*: Printed for *A. Baldwin* in *Warwick-Lane*, 1713. (Price 4 *d.*)
   8vo: *i-ii*, *A* A^2-B^4-C^2; half-t., list of 10 books Just Publish'd, t.p., *iv*, 3-20. Morgan P205. Horn-Trevelyan copy used. Prose pamphlet, but with the lines "To his Grace the Duke of *Marlborough*, Upon his Going into GERMANY." The verses are in the 28-line form, and are unnoticed by Morgan *et al*. See No. 378 for other versions.
   Main interest in this poorly written production seems to lie in its being an apparent retort upon an earlier satire on Marlborough, the anonymous *Rufinus*, or an Historical Essay on the favourite ministry etc., no pub., 1712, which is No. 344 above. It opens:

> Upon Reading a late *Admired* Production called *Rufinus*, &c I could not help taking Notice of the Author's *Great* Candour, and *Ingenuous* Manner of Representing the Character of Stilicho.

The elaborate irony is designed to emphasize that Stilicho was almost opposite to the picture drawn, which the writer says would fit Cato the Younger. Since the earlier piece is plainly a satire on Marlborough, he is discernible in the *Treasurer and the General* by implication, and particularly in the added lines of verse. The writer rejects all the charges against his "Hero," i.e. Marlborough, and credits these to "the Mercenary FEW" (p. 17).

The eight years from Marlborough's triumphant return
from exile to the year preceding his death in 1722 were
distinguished by events reflective of a new era. Queen
Anne died August 1, 1714, and Marlborough, his ship having
been delayed by storm, arrived the day following. When he
stepped ashore at Dover, George I, with all the Hanoverian
power and policy, was now king. He was received with acclaim; but the disgruntled opposition put out satires asserting that the opposite was the case. On the King's
arrival, September 18, Marlborough was received cordially,
his honours and status restored, and for a brief period
he could feel himself in the old role as a national leader.
The rapid settling with the comic opera invasion by the
Pretender in 1715 brought a final stroke of his genius for
military strategy and political leadership. The death of
his life-long antagonist, Louis XIV, in September of the
same year seemed a signal that the curtain could now descend on the drama of his great career. In the following
year, 1716, the death of Anne, Countess of Sunderland,
Marlborough's favorite daughter, brought a cruel blow.
The Duke suffered a stroke, and Sarah sank into a gloom
that showed that they no longer had the resources of body
and mind with which they endured the loss of their son
early in his career. Even so, Marlborough recovered enough
to appear in Parliament, and the Duchess to launch into the
protracted quarreling with Vanbrugh over the completion of
Blenheim Palace. With what Churchill calls her "almost
repellent common sense," she maneuvered her husband out
of the market just before the collapse of the South Sea
Bubble in 1720, thus adding further to their already notorious welath. All of these events are reflected in the
mirror of panegyric and satire, even parody, though on a
scale of diminished quantity and passion.

461   January 12.

'Philo Strategos' [Steele, Richard, 1672-1719)] ?

Churchill's Annals: Being a *Compleat View* of the *Duke of Marlborough's* Life and, Glorious ACTIONS, Both In the *Field* and *Cabinet*. *Nil desperandum Teucro Duce & Auspice Teucro*. Virg. *LONDON*: Printed for *Sarah Popping* at the *Black Raven* in *Pater-Noster-Row*; and sold by the Booksellers of *London* and *Westminster*. 1714. (Price 6 *d.*)
    8vo, *A*, B-G⁴; t.p., *bl.*, Dedication to *The Englishman* sgnd. 'Philo Strategos,' *bl.*, Contents *v-viii*, 1-48, 56 pp. Morgan Q500. Morgan says "another ed. entitled Annals of *Churchill* and *Eugene*. Adv. in Steele's *Englishman*, Pt. I, No. 43, Jan. 12, 1714 as 'This day is publish'd.' *Ibid.*, No. 47, and Sec. ed. No. 51, Jan. 30. Horn copy of first ed. used. Prose pamphlet.
    Whoever compiled this work, it is largely just that, a compilation of extracts, in the latter portion reflecting the *Examiner's* attacks, and the response from *Medley* and the *Englishman*. The biographical portion is lifted, as usual without acknowledgement, from *The Lives of Two Illustrious Generals*, published less than a year previously, No. 434. Since this anonymous work had drawn largely on Hare's *Life and Glorious History*, of 1705, we again have the Duke's chaplain as the actual source. Both works include the verses on the *Duke's Going into Germany*, which became almost perennial, p. 40. See No. 378, by George Sewell. *Churchill's Annals* also reprints the verses *To the Duke . . . on Taking Bouchain*, pp. 35-6, No. 324.
    It is a temptation to suggest that Steele himself was 'Philo Strategos.' Certainly the author was one of the leading Whig apologists and propagandists. Heavy quotation from the *Englishman* makes Steele a contributor in fact at least. The work concludes with a Postscript, which is actually a four-page extract from *The Englishman*, No. 36 for December 26, 1713. Blanchard ed., pp. 144-8. This issue provides a vivid vignette of Swift and Steele engaged in a party skirmish, with pens rather than swords, but hardly less deadly. Marlborough's request to be made commander-in-chief for life and the power-politics of the two political parties are at the heart of the fracas.

Marlborough is represented as the champion of religion
and liberty in England. It may be observed that the poem
on his going into Germany, and exile, is the 25-line version which appears in the *Lives of Two Illustrious Generals*.

62 July 30.

A Change at COURT: Or, He's Out at Last.   OXFORD: Printed
in the YEAR, 1714. No pub. MH-Huth-Luttr. copy used; has
MS date '30 July 1714' and '1/2 d.'
       1/2°:   1 side, 1 column.   47 lines, couplets. Not in
Morgan. Opens:

> How often do's Dame Fortune Man beguile
> When she upon his Actions seems to Smile?
> From small Beginnings she doth many Raise.

Parallels to Marlborough's dismissal and exile are reviewed: Alexander's favorite Clytas slain, Belizarius
[*sic*] requited with rags and misery, Wolsey tumbled down
from his eminent position.

> See how a mighty P[rince] has lost his Place,
> Altho' he has not acted what is Base;
> But as good Deeds arn't [*sic*] minded which are past,
> Great Men Resign, or are Turn'd out at last.   44-7

The poem is more a 'casus virorum' homily on the
turns of Fate than the usual bitter attack on Marlborough.

3 August (?)

ADVICE TO A POET. Designing to write on the Duke of *Marlborough*'s Return to ENGLAND. In Imitation of *Waller*.
Printed for *C. Cross* near *Westminster*.
       1/4°, strip.   24 lines, couplets.   BM copy used. Not
in Morgan. Opens:

> First, let let thy Piece, address the mighty Man,
> And pay the Homage of His native Land.

447

Hastily printed, as the repetition of 'let' in the first
line and other errors show. Hence probably August, 1714,
as the Marlboroughs reached London August 4. The poem
urges the poet to praise Marlborough, then to describe
England's distress at his absence, and mainly it attacks
the betrayers of England who have become rich. It urges
joyous welcome quite vividly.

> Tet [*sic*] *Albion*'s Song the conq'ring Hero Meet,
> And Joy appear in ev'ry Peopled Street.
> Let Whispers glide thro' all th' attentive Croud,
> That *Marlborough's come*, and ecchoing cry aloud,
> *Heav'ns guard the Man, who* Gallia's *Pow'r o'ercame,*
> *Be* Marlborough's *Foe an execrable Name*!   15-20

The misspelling of "Tet" for "let" suggests hasty printing; the poem may well have appeared by August. The BM
has a variant copy, another evidence of hurried and spon-
taneous printing, as presumably added copies were in
demand. This is a kind of companion piece to George
Sewell's lines on the Duke's departure into "voluntary
exile," No. 378.

464 August

Dennis, John (1657-1734)

On the Accession of King GEORGE to the *British Throne*.
Pr. only in *Sel. Works*, I, 334-45, 1718. Western Reserve
U. copy used.
       Marlborough is introduced as anticipating King George
I's exploits in battle. Only lines 331-45 are in point.
The sound of cannons mingle with the hallelujahs sung by
Angels. The slain "In *Blenheim* and Ramillia's deathless
Fields" rejoice in Heaven. Praise of William and George's
heroic conduct at Audenard follow; but Marlborough, now
in exile, is slighted in favor of a royal hero.

65   October 8.

[Sewell, George (1690?-1726)]

A POEM UPON HIS MAJESTIES ACCESSION. Inscrib'd to His
Grace *JOHN* Duke of *Marlborough*. By the AUTHOR of the
VERSES upon His Grace's Retiring into *Germany*. [4 lines
Horace] London: Printed for *J. Roberts* in *Warwick-Lane*.
Price Six Pence.
      2°: A-C², *i-ii*, 3-11, *xii*, 12 pp. Drop-t., p. 3.
132 lines, couplets. InU-Luttr., CtY, "Mr. George
Sewell," TxU, "Sewell." TxU copy used. Morgan Q251 at-
tributes to Garth, Wrenn Cat. to John Hughes. Opens:

    What? Are at length the doubtful Nations freed?
    Does *Britain* smile again, and GEORGE Succeed?

Is there no new Spencer, Halifax, nor Congreve to sing?
After addressing his Muse, he urges Britannia to awaken.
Queen Anne is forgotten in allusions to England's fame
under William, and now a Brunswick, that is George 1.
Fame is already returning: "How chang'd the Scene! how
different is the View" (1. 61) as he looks back on the
England when "Envy prevail'd" and shortened Marlbro's
glories. He went into voluntary exile, leaving an ungrateful land and its feuds. But now, with the triumph
of the Protestant cause, Religion is freed from Super-
stition and new heroes rise.

    In the latter portion of the poem George is urged to
go forth and restore freedoms, heal discords, and in general to save England as he has twice saved his native
land. No more shall Britannia's scepter stand doubtful.

    While the Young Hero forms our Gen'rous Youth,
    To *British* Valour, and to *German* Truth.   131-2

See No. 378, November 1, 1712, for Sewell's Verses on
Marlborough's retiring into Germany.

66   October 16.

Eusden, Laurence (1688-1730)

A LETTER to Mr. Addison, on the KING's *Accession* to the
THRONE. By Mr. *EUSDEN*. Printed for *J. Tonson*, at *Shake-*

spear's Head, over-against *Catherine-street* in the *Strand*. 1714.

   2°: *A* B-D^2 (erroneous second B-sig., p. 3); t.p., *bl.*, 1-13, *bl.*, drop-t., p. 1. 16 pp. 292 lines, couplets. *P. Boy*, No. 3033, Thurs. Oct. 14 to Sat. Oct. 16. 'This Day is publish'd.' BM, Bod, CSmH, CtY, MH, TxU (2). Horn copy used. Morgan Q225. Opens:

   SIR,
      While to new Honours you, unenvy'd, soar,
      And too much Merit is a Crime no more.

Eusden congratulates Addison on his selection by unanimous choice, as Secretary of the Regency. Anne died August 1st, and this group took over the government till the King should arrive. The poem summarizes most of the Whig policies, a nation guarded by religion and laws, resisting faction and preserving freedom. The Hanoverian Line is of course particularly celebrated as having been designated by William III and sustained by Anne's action at the point of death. The Pretender, as "the shatter'd Youth," is urged not to attempt invasion, to remember the Boyne, and leave England to a pastoral peace, which is attractively depicted (ll. 38-61). A review of Whig champions, beginning with Halifax, is traced from Roman heroes down. Then King George is addressed, and his career summarized from infancy in extravagant terms. His participation in the Battle of Audenarde is noted (l. 217). Marlborough is the subject of a fervent passage.

      O *Marlb'rough*! how can I thy Fame survey,
      And to thy Praise not consecrate a Lay?
      Thou great *Camillus* of our Isle, return,
      Let Merit triumph, and pale Faction mourn.
      Nor think this grateful Theme I newly chose,
      Oft have I sung thee ev'n amidst they Foes,
      Amidst thy Country's Foes! for who could be
      A Friend to *Britain*, and a Foe to thee?   243-50

The poem closes with the assurance that King George will insure the reign of law and England's future security. The bearing on Marlborough is confined largely to the passage quoted, but his fortunes had now reached the turning point back to honor and complete vindication.

67   November 26.

VERSES Written to the DUKE of *MARLBOROUGH* Upon His Leaving
ENGLAND. Now first Printed, and recommended to Sir *Anthony*
Crabtree, who is best able to supply what's wanting in
them. [2 lines Virgil]   *LONDON*:   Printed for *R. Burleigh*
in *Amen-Corner*. 1715.
     2°: Half-t., *bl*., t.p., *bl*., *i-iv*, 1-2, 6 pp.,
drop-t. on p. 1. No sigs. *D. Cour.*, No. 4085, Nov. 26,
'This Day is publish'd.' 38 lines, couplets. MH, CtY,
OCU, NC Nov. 1714. MH copy used. Not in Morgan. Opens:

> Farewell, Great Man, th'ungrateful Land forgive,
> And, if thy Country can Thy Loss survive,
> Our Debt from our Posterity receive.

Marlborough's deeds shine as bright as the burning Sun,
making the shepherd and his flocks seek the shade. But
then the Viper and the Snake creep out, as do villains
who spit at Marlborough. Must he, like Sisyphus in Hell
roll the stone of his country's sins: "The Work of Years
in one short Moment lost?" (1. 24). Wondrous man, his
smallest triumphs have been those of war. As with Hanno
who thwarted conquering Hannibal, -

> War's dire Effects had ne'er been felt at Home,
> Nor his lov'd *Carthage* been a Slave to *Rome*.   37-8

Handsomely printed. Sir Anthony, who lived in Herefordshire, is the target of a bawdy, though hilarious
poem, *The Welsh Saint: or, a Full and True Account of the*
Burning of the defiled Bed at Sir Anthony Crabtree's House
in Herefordshire. Pr. in *Political Merriment*, Pt. II,
45-7, 1714. His servants John and Susan have put the bed
to lusty uses, which causes his lordship to burn it and
all about it in a mad fury as well as ill-concealed
chagrin. Crabtree's relation to the Verses on Marlborough seem a mystery. See Maynwaring's ed. of the *Poetic*
Works of Oldmixon for Hannibal and Hanno.

68   Turner, P., of Trinity-College, Cambridge (no dates)

AUGUSTUS A POEM ON THE ACCESSION Of His MAJESTY King GEORGE.
Humbly Dedicated to the Right Honourable CHARLES, Lord

Halifax, One of the Lords Justices appointed by His
MAJESTY. By P. *TURNER*   *Trinity College Cambridge.*
Deus nobis haec Otia fecit AUGUSTUS.   Virg.   *LONDON*:
Printed by W. *Wilkins*, at the Dolphin in *Little-Britain*;
and Sold by *Ferd. Burleigh*, in *Amen-Corner*.   1714.   Price
Six-pence.
     $2°$: A^2 B-C^2; t.p., *bl.*, 3-10, 10 pp.   Large orna-
ments before and after Ded., and top p. 3 above drop-t.
Ded. 16 lines, couplets.   *Poem* 175 lines, couplets,
total 191 lines.   Not in Morgan.   Williams Lib. copy
used.   Ded. opens:

> Great SIR,
>   *In that umbrag'ous Grott or op'ning Glade,*
>   *Where tuneful Love-sick *Pindar often play'd.*
>   *Cowley

In this pastoral setting Hallifax, like King David, combined harmonious singing and guardianship of his country.
He teaches by example more than by laws.   Concludes with
two lines from Horace.   The Poem opens:

> Close by where *Camus* moves his languid Streams,
> There stands a Hill, from which auspicious Themes
> Oft take their Flight.

Old poets tell that Apollo left Parnassus for this hill,
and here the shepherd, that is Turner, spends his days.
The pastoral opening includes the story of Daphne's trans-
formation into a tree and various allegorical figures,
quite possibly written without regard to the main theme.
At 1. 60 the historical subject matter is abruptly brought
in.   Lines 59-92 celebrate the achievements of Marlborough,
although only Blenheim is specified.   Emphasis is placed
on the acclaim with which the Duke was greeted on returning
from his victories, and then on the shameful treatment he
was subjected to, leading to exile.   Now he has returned,
like Aristides, and will be esteemed as long as Blenheim
Palace or the *Campaign* survive.

> While *Blenheim*-House or *Addison*'s *Campaign*,
> So long these Actions and your Fame remain.   79-80

The remainder of the poem, 11. 93-175, are devoted to
praising George I, with the usual predictions of good

fortune and deprecation of the poet's youth and lack of
singing strength. Since it came early in the new reign
and dynasty, it is impossible to do more than that. Thus
Marlborough and his achievements provide the link between
the Stuart and Hanoverian reigns, standing as the chief
evidence of English prowess and glory.

59 *Bridle for the Tories*:   or the Duke of *Marlborough*   *Public Entrance* no *Tumultuous Cavalcade*.   London, 1714.   8
pp. Morgan Q406 only ref. See *The Republican Procession*,
etc., 1714 below, No. 476.

70 Chapman, Richard (*fl*. 1698-1720) Vicar of Cheshunt
Britannia Rediviva: or, *Britain*   *Recovery*.   An·HEROICK
POEM Humbly Inscrib'd to the KING's *Most Excellent Majesty*.
By *R. CHAPMAN*, Vicar of *Cheshunt*, and Prebendary of *Chi-
chester*. [8 lines Horace] *LONDON*: Printed for BERNARD
LINTOTT at the Cross-Keys between the *Temple Gates* in
Fleet-street. 1714.
     2°: *A*² B-C², *1-4*, 5-10, 14 pp. BM, Clark, Half-t
on *i*; drop-t. p. 5, no wmk. 108 lines, couplets. Morgan
Q90, but without identification of the author, or full
title. Horn copy used. Opens:

> Tho' God in Wrath did first a King ordain
> For *Isra'l*, murm'ring at his milder Reign.

King George is lavishly saluted as bringer of William III's
preference in his choice to succeed Anne. This makes the
Revolution complete. Marlborough is briefly noticed as
having secured the way.

> Hail, Mighty Prince! from distant Regions come!   ⎫
> From *Thee*, abroad, Great Monarchs wait their Doom; ⎬
> From *Thee*, usurping Bigotries, at home.   ⎭
> *Marlbro'* by Triumphs *Brittish* Fame had rais'd,
> By Sov'raigns often, oft by Senates prais'd;
> When by Reverse of Fate, both sinking stood,
> Thou sav'st, by quelling the impetuous Flood.   28-34

Interest in the poem attaches primarily from its being
another expression of frothy flattery from the author of
the notorious *Le Feu de Joye*, November 30, 1704, No. 67
above. That Chapman had not outgrown his capacity to
rouse ridicule is apparent in the pseudonymous satire
Chapmanno-Whiskero: An Elegy on the Heroic Poem Lately
Published by the Vicar of Cheshunt, 1715, No. 482 below.

George I's coming is seen as an evidence of Providence, like life-giving showers to the scorched earth
(11. 43 f.), and, more to the point, he will revive dying
trade and subdue the hydras of faction and party fury.
Also in 1714 as *On Queen* ANNA's *Departure*, 1714. *By the
Rector of Cheshunt, and presented to the Lords of the
R*[egenc]*y*. In *Political Merriment*, Pt. II, 95, 14 lines.
Holds that Anne's death and Harley not misfortunes, since
she is too pliable, and he a double-dealer. Concludes:

> Our *George for England*, and a *Marlbro'* here,
> Great Things Presage to the Autumnal Year.

471   A DIALOGUE between my Lord *B----ke* and my Lord *W--on*;
Concerning the coming over of the Duke of *M----gh*.
Printed in the Year 1714. *Price* a Penny.

1/2°: 1 side, prose. Not in Morgan. BM copy used.
B[olingbro]*ke* sneers at Marlborough, but *W*[hart]*on* champions him and welcomes his return. He insists that the
Duke will be found to be a True Born Englishmen and that
he will win the victory as he has never yet yielded to any
man. Allusions to the *Flying-Post* and the *Lover* are the
only concrete details, except that B. holds that the Ministry "deigns nothing but Equity and Justice." W. maintains that they will try to stir up a second charge against
Marlborough. No conclusion of the argument is reached.

472   [Atterbury, Francis (1662-1732)?] Bishop of Rochester.

English Advice to the Freeholders of England. London,
1714.

4to, 31 pp. Morgan Q47. Also lists an ed. 32 pp.,
1714; pr. in *Somers Tracts*, IV, 1751, and XIII, 548-59,
Sec. Ed., 1809. Also assigned to C. Hornsby, and in the

Wrenn Cat. to Defoe. *Somers Coll.* accepts Atterbury and prints a tract to which this is a parody, *English Advice to the Freeholders of Britain, Ibid.*, 521-41. Only one reference to Marlborough, in retort on a defence of the Duke of Ormond's obeying orders not to fight the French (p. 546).

3   Johnson, Captain Thomas

An EPITAPH Upon His Grace *JOHN*, Duke of *Marlborough.* Who departed this Life July the 19th 1714, and lies now interr'd in the City of *Antwerp.* Written by a Monk of the Order of St. *Dominic.* And Translated into *English* by a Member of the *Marlborough-Club.* - *Extinctus amabitur idem.* LONDON: Printed, and Sold by *J. Roberts* in *Warwick-Lane.* 1714.   Price 3 *d.*

8vo: *A*4 B-C4; half-t., *bl.*, drop-t. on p. 5, 5-21, *bl.* 22, 24 pp. Horn copy used. Morgan Q354. 346 short lines, many one word, as an inscription. The prefatory statement, sgnd. "Tho. Johnson" asserts that the piece was translated from a Latin epitaph written by a monk at Antwerp at the request of the "Marlborough Clubb, held near Golden-Square." This and the Epitaph are complimentary to Marlborough, and no explanation is offered for the production. By a broad irony, the death of the banished hero is made to appear preposterous. His career is traced from its beginning through Blaregnies, his marches, sieges, and battles in which he overthrew the power of France and Popery. William III passes to Anne the injunction to recognize the Hanoverian line, and Marlborough is the agent in thus securing England's future. The need of an Iliad from such poets as Steele and Addison occupies the latter half of the piece. "The *Muse* must make *Him* live" (1. 173). Quite evidently the Dutch sovereign, William, is honored above Anne who had banished Marlborough, and Antwerp, the city that provided him a refuge, is also signalized. Toward the end, as he is breathing his last, he is represented,

> With earnest *Eyes*, and *Force* of Voice,
> Impressing *HANOVER*
> Upon his Royal Sister's Heart.   296-8

He reminds her of all that Churchill is to do to raise her high in glory, and urges that she let Churchill carry his sword in her behalf, and command her armies. The ironic point of the poem is emphasized in an added Latin distich, which is translated.

> Here *England*'s Glory, the Great CHURCHILL lies,
> Who, tho' he conquer'd here, here banished Dies.

Handsome ornamental bands and a decorative design at the end embellish the poem. Lediard printed the entire piece, III, 450-60, as a "very Curious Piece, which, I am inform'd, is not in many Hands," since it did not appear till presumably August, 1714. He describes it as a "Recapitulation of the Duke's whole *Life*" (p. 449).

474   The Memorable HISTORY of *JOHN* of *ANTWERP*. In a Brief Account of *JOHN*'s Pedigree, Birth, Rise, and glorious Achievements. With a Picture on a Copper Plate, displaying JOHN's Downfall; His Exile, and Return to his Native Country; and a proper Key to the Whole. From the ORIGINAL Done at *Antwerp*. Sold by *A. Dodd*, at the *Peacock* without *Temple-Bar*, and by the Book, and Printsellers of *London* and *Westminster*, and recommended to be Framed and hung up by all JOHN's Friends. Price 4 *d*.
      Atlas 1°: 1 side, 3 columns, 15-1/2" by 20", with the plate, which is 5-1/2" by 7" inserted in upper mid-col. Not in Morgan. Bodleian copy used. The point of view is established in the opening: "The JOHN of *ANTWERP* so called, from the Place of his Residence, during his Exile." Marlborough is seen as carrying on the policies of William III. A thinly veiled allegorical use of names is used in reviewing his career. England is Britomartia, Queen Anne is Feliciana, daughter of King Felix; Louis XIV is King Maximus, William III is King Henry; Marlborough is John and Sarah is Jennibella. The events outline Marlborough's career quite accurately. They are presented as occurring in the years of Redemption, beginning with 1703. The engraving is entirely allegorical, with an explanatory key at the bottom of the sheet. Envy, at the top, and her demons, have torn the laurels from Marlborough's head, and

he, seen against the background of a military camp, stands
with his retinue before Britomartia and the Genius of War.
The caption promises a similar engraving on John's return,
which will portray the Triumph of Honour and will "Contain
many Things very Curious."

75 D'Urfey, Thomas (1653-1723)

Political Merriment: Or TRUTHS told to some TUNE. Faithfully Translated from the Original *French* of R. G. S. H.
H. S. F. A. G. G. A. M. M. P. and Messieurs *Brinsden* and
Collier, the State Oculist, and Crooked Attorney, *Li Pro-
veditori delli curtisani*. By a LOVER of his Country.
LONDON: Printed for A BOULTER without *Temple-Bar*, and
sold by *S*. KEIMER at the *Printing-Press* in *Pater-Noster-
Row*, in the Glorious Year of our PRESERVATION, 1714.
    Hlf-t., *bl.*, t.p., *bl.*, To the Jacobitical Tories,
and Traiterous [*sic*] Rioters of Great Britain, *vi-x*, as
Dedication, sgnd. *Your Merry Physician* PHILOPAT. In three
parts, 376 pp. Numbering of Pt. II duplicates in a portion. Separate indexes, and titles. Morgan ascribes to
D'Urfey, Q209, and records an 8° 1714 ed. in one vol. Also
lists another 12° ed., which is used here, Horn copy.
    The collection is replete with allusions to Marlbor-
ough, most of them in ballads only partially concerned
with him. It anticipates *A Pill to Purge State-Melancholy*,
which is in 1715 along with Part III. A number of poems
appear in both collections. See No. 485. Separately
printed pieces, and a few more important items are listed
below:
    1. *A new Ballad*. To the Tune of *Fair Rosamund*, II,
74-81. See No. 455.
    2. *Plot upon Plot*, II, 82-5. See No. 458.
    3. *A Poem to the Earl of Godolphin* By Dr. G---th,
II, 94-5. See No. 306.
    4. *The Age of Wonders*, II, 103-8. See No. 308.
    5. *Britain Ungrateful*, II, 179-80. See No. 518.
    6. *A Prophecy*, II, 180, 169-70, 38 lines. Not sep-
arately pr. Lines 21-2 involve a pun on Churchill. This
and all others are identified by marginal note.

> A Church upon a hill shall cross the Main,
> New Conquests to attain and Trophies gain.

See No. 82

7. *GRENADEERS. A New Song by Mr.* Escourt, *upon the D---ke of* Marlborough's *being turn'd out*, III, 25, 4 4-line st. only. Also in *A Pill to Purge State-Melancholy*, pp. 141-3, in two parts, but as "Granadiers, now change your Song." Pt. II adds 3 st., 18 lines. On Ormond's failures, which remind the singer of Blenheim and Marlborough's fame.

476   [Ward, Edward (1667-1731)]

The *Republican Procession*; or, The *Tumultuous Cavalcade*. A Merry POEM. Printed in the Year MDCCXIV. Sec. ed. with addition of "The *Second* IMPRESSION, *with Additional CHARACTERS*."

8vo: A-E^4, F^2; t.p., *bl.*, *3*, 4-43, *bl.*, 44 pp. Drop-t on p. *3*. Morgan Q719. Horn copy of Second Impression used. 937 lines, hudibrastic couplets. Pp. 1-43 separately titled as *The Pompous Cavalcade*, 777 lines with an 8-line Moral attached at end. Rprtd. in *Merit and Gratitude conjoin'd*, No. 483. H. W. Troyer, *Ned Ward of Grubstreet*, 1946, supplies an excellent analysis, pp. 103-6 and 363. Opens:

> In Times of Libelling and Squabbling,
> When Fools in Politicks were dabbling.

A satire on Marlborough's return, showing how in these times of venality and faction a Queen, i. e. Anne, was beset by a "crafty crew of Great Pretenders" and "a noble *Fighting* Lord" (Marlborough) who had been raised to high fame and honor in spite of his misdeeds and self-interest. The old charges are revived, of defection from James II and gross materialism, and dark suspicions are aired.

> However, aiming to aspire
> As high as Monarchy, or higher,
> And fancy'ng he could rule the State,
> As well as *Noll* of ancient Date,

458

By *Zara's* Management he reckoned
To be an *Oliver* the Second,
Fore-knowing that his wise Directress
Would make an excellent Protectress,
Or prove a very useful Wife
To a Lord General for Life.   99-108

Most of the poem is devoted to a review of the "procession," various workers and tradesmen, raised to some eminence, and emphasis on such detested terms as Anabaptist,
fanatic, republican, and allusions to Cromwell. The return of Marlborough and his Duchess is treated as a
reception by a rabble of butcher's boys, clothiers, small-
coals dealers, brewers, and the like, a vulgar mob of
zealots.
    CBEL, II, 497, lists a 1727 ed. "to which is added
an answer by the same author, being a satyr against himself."

7 Newcomb, Thomas (1682?-1762)

To her Late Majesty, Queen Anne, upon the *Peace* of *Utrecht.*
London, n.d., *ca.* 1714.
    Morgan Q*460ª only ref. No copy known.

8 *The Welcome. Two Congratulatory Poems,* the first, humbly
inscrib'd to the most august Monarch GEORGE King of *Great
Britain, France and Ireland,* &c. On the prospect of his
happy arrival in these Kingdoms. The other to his GRACE
the *Duke* of MARLBOROUGH, on his return to *England. By
different HANDS. NOTTINGHAM:* Printed by J. COLLYER, and
sold by *HENRY ALLESTREE* Bookseller in *DERBY,* 1714. (Price
two Pence.)
    4ᵗᵒ: π, A, A3 on p. 5; t.p., *bl.,* 4-0, *bl.,* 12 pp.
Separate drop-titles, bands. 137 lines, couplets. BM
copy used. Not in Morgan.
    1) *The Welcome,* 16 lines, italics. Opens: "Pro-
pitious Auster, blow with gentle Gales, Keep smooth, the
Sea, yet fill great GEORGE's Sails." The shores of Albion

resound with shouts of welcome. Preceded by 7 lines Horace.

    2)   The poem to King George, 75 lines. Opens, "Great Sir, a Welcome, equal to our Joy / Must more than 20 Million Tongues imploy." George is hailed for his nobility and his prowess in battle. William and Anne have striven to allay strife at home, even though vic- torious in war abroad. Each glorious year Marlborough led Anne's forces to victory abroad; but now it will be for George to attain peace at home. Vicious and busy scribblers have done more harm to church and state than ever France achieved (11. 84-6). Now peace, love, and plenty will come with government and law under King George.

    3)   *A Poem, on the Duke of Marlborough*, 46 lines, 4 line Latin motto. Opens:

> We saw, great Sir, when every Year you wore,
> Lawrels that never *Briton* did before.

A conventional panegyric, but hails Marlborough's humil- ity and dauntless spirit, neither "by high Fortune rais'd, nor yet cast down by Low" (1. 19). He will now gain fresh glories, and continue to move, like the Sun, in higher orbs, heedless of "barking Curs" and night birds below.

> Your Name shall shine in Annals endless Date,
> And just Posterity shall call you Great.   45-6

The main interest in this production, which is rather dubious in grammatical detail and devoid of poetic value, is that it comes from outside London.

480. FOUR HUDIBRASTICK CANTO'S, BEING *Poems on Four of the greatest Heroes That liv'd in any Age since* Nero's, Don Juan Howlet, Hudibras, Dico-ba-nes *and* Bonniface. LONDON, Printed for *J. Roberts* in *Warwick-Lane.* 1715. Price 6 *d.* 4°: A-E⁴; t.p., *bl.*, *3*, 4-36, 36 pp. Ornament bot. p. 36. Drop-t. on *3*, and separate ornaments and "Arguments" and titles of "Canto I," etc., for each of the four parts. Total 477 lines, hudibrastics. Morgan R227, TxU copy used.

First Argument opens (in italics):

> SIR Hudibras in this first Canto
> Pretends to bring a *Quo Warranto.*

The relationships of this pretentious, but obscure, satire to Marlborough are exceedingly vague and ancillary. However, in view of the title, it seems necessary to include it. The First Canto opens:

> In *W------d* a while ago
> Was Rara S----t and Rara Show.

The satire is relieved by no important names or references, and is political throughout, definitely anti-Whiggish, but otherwise more inscrutable than a piece of such length warrants. If Marlborough is detectable it must be in Canto II, as Don Juan. It opens:

> This Scene presents unto your Sight
> A Squire that fain wou'd be a Knight.

Nature gives him an owl's intelligence, "and gently breathes it into *John*" (1. 20). He says:

> It was our Aim and Resolution
> At once to break the Constitution;
> T'unhinge the State, and in Conclusion
> To bring in Ruin and Confusion.   66 9

There is no need to challenge Richmond P. Bond's description of this piece as "worthless, unentertaining, almost unintelligible." *English Burlesque Poetry*, 278-9.

481   September 27.

VERSES To His *Grace* the *Duke* of *Marlborough*, Upon the
Present *Rebellion*. London: Printed for *J. Roberts*, near
the *Oxford-Arms* in *Warwick Lane*. MDCCXV.
      1/2°: 2 sides, 1 column, 38 lines, couplets. MH-
Luttr., '27 Sept. 1715 2 *d*.' MC Sept. 1715. Morgan R357.
Opens:

>   Once more, Great Prince, in shining Arms appear,
>   And draw that Sword which *Gallia* us'd to fear.

Marlborough's last great task is to free his own country
from the rebel Earl of Mar, who is identified in a footnote.

>   Go teach the Rebel who his SOVEREIGN Braves,
>   That thy Hand Punishes as well as Saves,

and that George, great and good, would free the slaves.
Justice will triumph and guilt fly away.

482   'Chapmanno-Wiskero,' pseud.

An Elegy On The *Heroic* POEM Lately Publish'd by the VICAR
of *Cheshunt*. By *CHAPMANNO*-WISKERO. [3 lines Horace]
LONDON, Printed and Sold by *J. Morphew* near *Stationers-
Hall* MDCCXV. (Price Six Pence)
      2°: A^2, B^2 C^1; t.p., *bl*., drop-t. on p. 3, 3-10, 12
pp., 150 lines, couplets. BM copy used. Morgan R106.
Opens:

>   God the first Poet was, and Poets made
>   Before the ALL was into Order laid.

In the original harmony Adam was the Orpheus, who named
the animals, and led in the line of poets and prophets.
But Chapman has reversed this. His lines "retain their
Earthy smell" (1. 48). Classical precedents for dull
versifying lead to this violation of the *Jus Divinum*,
and then to Dicky, i. e. Richard Chapman, and his Publisher Bernard Lintott. The interest in this satire lies
not only in Chapman's having published *Britannia Rediviva*

in the preceding year, No. 470, but more in his being
the author of the notorious *Le Feu de Joye*, No. 67,
1704, though dated 1705.

> May honest Bernard never want Pretence
> To vend thy Wares, and thou receive his Pence.
> May'st thou, O *Dicky*, still his Chap-man be,
> And never set his Purse or Presses free!
> May all succeeding *Grocers* never fail
> Of Spice and Sugar Caps from *Lintott*'s Stall.   35-40

Chapman's Sunday-lectures are good only because they are
short. He is hailed from Cadmus' "distant shore." Dryden
lately has won laurels. The satire wanders into uncertain
allusions, even Russian; then it alludes to the Whig satirists.

> Welcome, great *Bard*, as Christmas is to Priests,
> Like thee, who hate the Duty, love the Feasts.
> As after reading *Steele* and *Addison*,
> And other Wits, whose *brighter* Rays, have shone,
> I've often thrown thy Brother WESLEY by;
> May thy dull Ignorance to Hell return;
> 'Twas Fools that would be wise, who first did burn.
>   67-73

Later we learn that no scales in Button's shop can weigh
against him; he has the sole monopoly of German wit.
After satire on his prebendships and even his drooping
bay nag Jenny, the satire concludes:

> Dicky shall new-fledg'd *Owls* to Athens bring,
> And eke the Fame of *London-Prentice* sing,
> *Dicky* shall tell us in sweet Roundelay,
> How *George* of *England* did the *Dragon* slay.   147-50

83   [Ward, Edward (1667-1731)]

Merit and Gratitude Conjoin'd: OR, THE Duke of *Marlbor-
ough*'s ENTRY VINDICATED. Being a Short Answer to the
Republican Procession; OR, THE Tumultuous Cavalcade, &c.
Printed for *J. Johnson*, near *Charing-Cross*, and sold by

the Booksellers of *London* and *Westminster*, MDCCXV.
12mo: A-D^{12}; t.p., *bl.*, 3-46, 46 pp. NjP copy
used; only one known. Rptd. 1727 as The Republican Procession. . . To Which is added, An Answer By the Same
Author, Being a Satyr against Himself. 8vo, 48 pp. Not
in Morgan.

Merit and Gratitude Conjoin'd is a poem of 129 lines,
octosyllabic, or hudibrastic couplets, pp. 3-8. The remainder is as in the 1714 *Republican Procession*, with the
Moral, that is 937 lines, the total of both being 1066
lines, hudibrastics. See No. 476 above, 1714. Troyer
has the 1727 issue, but not *Merit and Gratitude Conjoin'd*.
Opens:

> As drowning Men a Straw will catch at,
> Or the least Thing whatever reach at.

So a falling political party desperately turns to lampoons
and libels. "Poor Scribling *Jack*" is asked what credit he
could think to get by writing such doggerel opposing the
"Revolution principle" on which England is founded. On
that King George makes his claim (1. 53), and quite obviously the Hanoverian succession induced Ward to satirize
his own poem. CBEL notices only the later printing, II,
597.

> But yet you'll see for all your spite,
> Your hated *Marlborough*, Favourite.
> Him, whom the Pen has been so rude   ⎫
> To brand with black Ingratitude,   ⎬
> For doing of his Country Good.   ⎭
> .   .   .   .   .
> Him, who by none but thee was reckoned,
> To aim at being *NOLL the Second*.   66-76 *passim*

Britain was happy when she recognized his merit, how many
battles he won; but her ingratitude led to insinuations
with the Queen, and his disgrace. But now he is welcomed
back again, and may Britain never more be ungrateful!

> With double Lustre may'st thou move
> At Court; possess'd of *GEORGE*'s Love,
> May he thy former Honours all restore,
> And make Thee greater now, than *Anne* before.   126-9

84 An ODE Humbly Inscrib'd to His GRACE The *Lord Archbishop of Canterbury*, On His *Majesty's Happy ACCESSION*. [3 lines Horace and passage from Cicero] *LONDON*: Printed for *Bernard Lintott*, at the *Cross-Keys*, between the *Two Temple Gates* in *Fleetstreet*. 1715. (Price 3 *d*.) 2°: *A* B²; t.p., *bl*., 3-6, 6 pp. Drop-t., p. 3, ornament bot. p. 6. Wmk. foolscap. 74 lines, couplets. Horn copy used. Morgan R576. Opens:

Thy long neglected Voice, sweet *Clio*, raise,
And tune once more thy sacred Harp to Praise.

The anonymous poet invokes Clio, i. e. history, to serve as muse to inspire him to such verse as sang William's "Godlike Actions," or the "Love of Liberty." The archbishop was Thomas Tenison.

Or, when thy glowing Breast, the HERO fir'd,
Thy MARLB'ROUGH was ador'd, Thy Song admir'd.   9-10

While this is the only naming of Marlborough, the poem praises King George and the Archbishop, who had from early in Anne's reign been receptive to Occasional or Nonconformity. Tenison is praised in his old age, for his care for his fold and charity, and the Jesuits are rejected. Bold, crude Georgian irreverence is shown in treating George as a "SECOND Saviour on the British Throne" (1. 48). Then, however, the muse is chided for such comparisons.

An allusion to Addison as "*Cato's* Great Author" who alone is capable of adequately praising George's reign, or rather its future triumphs wherein Law, Religion, Property will be made secure. His muse will

Show what TROPHIES are reserv'd to grace
The future Heroes of the *BRUNSWICK*-RACE.   69-70

85 *A Pill to Purge State-Melancholy*: OR, A COLLECTION OF Excellent New Ballads. [4 lines ballad from p. 127] [ornament] *LONDON*, Printed in the Year M.DCC.XV. 8°: A⁶ B-L⁸ M²; t.p., *bl*., Publisher's Preface *iii-viii*, Index *ix-xii*, 1-164, 174 pp. The Preface justifies ballads, since Homer and Horace were ballad-singers, and

Lillibulero affected the Revolution. Since most of the 63 ballads support Marlborough, or at least the government and policy which he himself upheld, the collection is an important contribution to Marlborough panegyric. It is impossible to deal with all. Those separately printed are described under their proper entries; a selection of the rest is listed here. Case 288 lists only BM, Bod, CtY. Not in Morgan. Horn copy used.

    1. *A Song in Praise of our Three Fam'd Generals. Tanslated from the French by Mr. Durfey.* 7 6-line stanzas, pp. 1-3. Marlborough, Eugene, and Auverquerque.

    2. *A New Health to the Duke of Marlborough.* Pp. 3-4. 4 10-line stanzas, 40 lines.

    3. *An Historical Account of the Battel of Audenarde.* Pp. 5-8. 14 6-line stanzas, 34 lines.

    4. *A New Song, the Words by Mr. Escourt.* Pp. 8-11. 13 4-line stanzas, with refrain, 65 lines.

    5. *A Song on the Victory gain'd over the* French *by the Duke of Marlborough and Prince Eugene, and also the Taking of Mons. The Words by Mr.* Durfey. 3 st., 46 lines, pp. 11-12. "Now Cannon-Smoke clouds all the Sky."

    6. *A Song occasion'd by the taking of* Lisle. *The Words by Mr.* Durfey. 4 16-line stanzas, 64 lines, pp. 13-15. "Grand *Lewis*, let Pride be abated."

    7. *A Song on the taking of* Doway *and Aire. The Words by Mr.* Durfey. 21 lines, pp. 15-16. "Once more the Great General home returns."

    8. *A Song on the ensuing campaign,* 1709. *Written by Mr.* Durfey. 3 8-line stanzas, 24 lines, pp. 16-17. "Now, now comes on the Glorious Year."

    9. *A New Ballad. To the Tune of* Fair Rosamond. 35 2-line stanzas, 140 lines, pp. 29-35. See No. 455.

    10. *A Ballad to the Tune of the* Dame of Honour, pp. 35-6. 5 8-line stanzas, 40 lines. Deals with Sarah, Duchess of Marlborough.

    11. *The Age of Wonders. To the Tune of* Chevy Chase. Pp. 51-6. See No. 307.

    12. *The Soldiers Lamentation for the Loss of their General.* Pp. 70-5. See No. 422.

    13. *On the Jewel in the Tower.* Pp. 95-7. See No. 403.

    14. *The Pedlar. To the Tune of*, The Abbot of *Canterbury.* 10 5-line stanzas, 50 lines. "Ye Lads, and ye

Lasses, that live in *Great Britain*." A French pedlar
brings elegant gew-gaws, snuff-boxes, tweezers, a fancy
sword, though *"Marlborough* taught 'em in nine dismal
Years," that English blades are much better. On the
peace offers. Pp. 120-2.
   15. "Great Marlborough's quite forgot, Sir." No
title, ballad in 4 6-line stanzas, 24 lines, pp. 140-1.
Anti-Sacheverell.
   16. "Grenadiers, now change your Song," in two
parts, *To the Tune of* Over the Hills and Far Away. 6
4-line stanzas, and 3 5-line, 39 lines, pp. 141-3. Allusion to Blenheim and in the second part to Ormond and
Oxford. See No. 475 (7).
   17. *An Excellent New Song, call'd* The Full Tryal
and Condemnation of John *Duke of* Marlborough. Pp. 161-4.
See No. 376.
   The remaining poems largely allude to Mrs. Masham,
Swift, the Tory triumph, and also to the South-Sea "whim"
and the peace and its makers, Prior, Oxford, etc. Since
all these have distinct bearing on Marlborough, the volume may be said to be primarily concerned with Whig pro-
tests in song against his downfall.

486   [Minshull, Edward]

To The E. of *O*[xfor]*d*; With The REPORT Of the COMMITTEE
OF SECRECY. [ornament] *LONDON*: Printed for *JOHN BAKER*,
at the *Black-Boy* in *Pater-Noster-Row*. 1715. (Price
Four-Pence.)
   2°: A^2 B^4; t.p., bl., 3-6, 6 pp. Drop-t. p. 3.
Contemporary MS on title-page of Horn copy, "By Edw.
Minshull Esq:" 58 lines, couplets. Wmk, Coat of arms
and 'I V.' Not in Morgan. Opens:

   O Thou great Patron of MYSTERIOUS FAME,
   A *Jew* in Learning, and a *Gaul* in Name.

A satire on Oxford, showing how his "Majestick Line must
end" (1. 6). Not born to honor nor bred to virtue, he is
credited with destroying "the long Labours of an Age,"
and he

467

Drove hovering Conquest from the Flandrian Plain,
Made *WILLIAM*'s Wounds and *MARLBRO*'s Triumphs vain.
                                                    21-2

The nation sits expectant for punishment of the traitor.
No Abigail, i. e. Mrs. Masham, can save him, "Nor some
new *G------g* a second Proxy die" (1. 28).
    The remainder of the poem invokes blessings on the
Patriots, who have striven for Honour, Liberty, and Laws.
Walpool [*sic*] first, "made Faction blush"; then Stanhope,
scholar, statesman, and Hero; Boscawen, Godolphin, Lech-
mere follow. All urge a proper destiny for Oxford, the
avenging of his insolence in power.

        So may thy Blood avert they Country's Shame,
        And wipe Reproach from fair *Britannia*'s Name. 57-8

    While only one allusion to Marlborough appears, the
satire is an invocation to the new Whig leaders to compen-
sate for the damage Oxford did to the policy of William
and Marlborough.
    Minshull was Steele's creditor in financial dealings.
These involved borrowings based on Steele's mortgaging his
share in Drury Lane theatre, 1715-16.

487 A SPEECH of his Grace the Duke of M[arlborough], which was
     verily and indeed spoken to the First Regiment of Foot-
     Guards, June 2, 1715.
         4to: bsd., no pub., n.d., 1 p., 75 lines, couplets.
     Foxon gives two versions, both 4to, at Clark and MH. Not
     in Morgan. Opens:

         Gentlemen,
             I am very concern'd to find,
             Your just complaints of any kind.
                 .   .   .   .   .   .
         When *Blenheim*'s Fate, the World's decided.

     Other lines defend charge of cheating troops against "de-
     faming Scribler's."

488   Croxall, Samuel (d. 1752)

THE VISION. A POEM. By Mr. *CROXALL*, Author of the Two
Original CANTOS of *SPENSER*.   [4 lines Horace] *LONDON*:
Printed for *J. Tonson*, at *Shakespear's-Head* over-against
Catherine-street in the *Strand*. 1715.
    2°: *A* B-F; t.p., *bl.*, *ii-iv* To the Right Honourable
the EARL of *HALIFAX* prose ded., 1-20, drop-t. on p. 1.
Wmk. TH. 24 pp., 446 lines, couplets. Dedication sgnd.
S. CROXALL. Morgan R139. Sutro Lib. Horn copy used.
    Dedication laments recent death of the great Earl of
Halifax, acknowledges his patronage, and an even more personal obligation. The writer sees his patron as now "foremost in the Rank of this *Visionary Assembly*" which, presumably, would be the Angelic gathering. With this clue
to its title, the poem opens:

    The Man, whose Life by *Virtue*'s Model fram'd
    Flows calmly on unspotted and unblam'd.

While there is only one reference to Marlborough, the over-
all tone of satisfaction in a Whig peace, and the praise
of Halifax in his scorn for "*Bourbon*'s Threats and Gold"
(1. 14) summarize the ideals and social state for which
the Duke had fought. In a loose way the poem follows the
pattern of *Cooper's Hill*, blending pastoral and natural
beauty and composure with historical allusions to the line
of kings. The poet falls asleep, dreams, and awakens to
relate his vision. This includes a pastoral landscape,
drenched in birdsong, a Pavilion to the House of Fame,
with twelve agate pillars, and five jasper thrones. The
growth of liberty as a national ideal is traced, from the
Barons who opposed King John, to Edward I and III, to Lisa,
William, and down to Anne and King George I. Edward III,
at Cressy and Poictiers, showed English power:

    Before great *Marlbrough* saw the living Light,
    Or Annals had recorded *Blenheim* Fight.   204-5

Queen Elizabeth and William III are shown as opponents of
Popery, and the general Georgian spirit of Protestant triumph pervades the poem. That Marlborough's role was considerable is evidenced by an allusion at the close:

> The *French*, as late on fam'd *Ramillia*'s Field,
>   Vanquish'd by *Protestant* Allies should yield.
> 431-2

The Plantagenet sovereigns bow to the Stuart Queen, and
the bards, Chaucer and Spenser, again acclaim the triumph
of England's freedom and her laws, which have enabled commerce to thrive and the land to be fruitful. Croxall's
two "original" cantos, added to the *Faerie Queene*, appeared 1713-14. See Morgan P166. They were written under
the pseud. "Nestor Ironside," a term taken from the
Guardian. This presumably led to their attribution to
Steele in the frequently erroneous *Wrenn Cat*.

489   [Swift, Jonathan (1667-1745)?]

Written in chalk on Bishop Burnet's Tomb; copies distributed. 16 lines, occasional rhymes. Opens:

> Here Sarum lyes, of late as wise,
>   As learned as your Aquinus,
> Yet to be sure he was no more
>   A Christian than Socinus.

He preached and prayed for gold, and betrayed his Mother
Church for Mammon. The lines end:

> If such a soul to heaven is stole,
>   And 'scaped old Satan's clutches,
> We may presume there will be room
>   For Marlborough and his Duchess.

Quoted in Mrs. Arthur Colville, *Duchess Sarah*, 1904, p.
260. Mrs. Colville relates that Swift, after hastily
scribbling the lines, took immense pains to conceal his
identity, but that the amused finder distributed copies.
Since Mrs. Colville was the daughter of the second son
of the Sixth Duke of Marlborough, Lord Alfred Spencer
Churchill, a certain credence can be given to this account.

490   Rowe, Nicholas (1674-1718)

ODE FOR THE *NEW YEAR* MDCCXVI. By *N. ROWE*, Esq; Servant
to His MAJESTY. [4 lines Horace] *LONDON*: Printed for
J. Tonson, at *Shakespear's-Head* over-against *Catherine-
street* in the Strand. 1716.
         2°: A^2 B-C^2; half-t., *bl.*, t.p., *bl.*, 1-7, [orna-
ment bot. p. 7], *8 bl.*, drop-t. on p. 1, 12 pp. Wmk.
T. H. 134 lines, 7 stanzas, ode style, varying line
length. Morgan S376. Opens:

>   Hail to thee Glorious rising Year,
> With what uncommon Grace thy Days appear!

Peace and prosperity are predicted for the future under
George I.

>   Faction, Fury, all are fled,
> And bold Rebellion hides her daring Head.   24-5

While Marlborough is not mentioned, George's presence at
Audenarde is brought in, lines 43-7. The poem is strictly
a panegyric to the King; but it provides an expression of
the Whig mood in the early years of the Hanoverian dynasty.
It finds evidences of plenty, wealth, connubial bliss, and
every other desideratum, and concludes:

>   Joy abounds in ev'ry Breast,
> For thy People all, for thee the Year is blest. 133-4

491   Chute, Mr. (no dates)

Beauty and Virtue: a *Poem Sacred* to the *Memory* of *Anne*,
Countess of *Sunderland*. London, Printed for *R. Burleigh*.
         8vo: 24 pp. Morgan S79. This elegy on Marlborough's
second, and favorite, daughter is the only other item of
specific Marlborough associations in 1716. Attention was
focused largely on the Jacobite rebellion, and hard upon
the death of Anne in April Marlborough was seized with a
violent illness. The paralytic stroke which ensued May

28th not only led to protracted incapacitation, but virtually marked the end of the Duke's public career even though
he lived on to 1722.

492 *An Elegy on his Grace the D. of* Marlborough, *occasion'd
by a Report of his Death a little before he came over.* In
MILITARY AND OTHER POEMS UPON Several Occasions, and to
SEVERAL PERSONS. *By an OFFICER of the Army. LONDON:*
Printed for the Author, and Sold by *J. Browne* at the *Black
Swan* without *Temple-bar.* 1716. Pp. 197-8. 20 lines,
couplets. BM, TxU copies used. Morgan S296. Opens:

> When Heroes die, the Poet's Task begins,
> And one Man weeps for a whole Nation's Sins.

The poet observes that Scipio and Belisarius suffered
exile and ingratitude. The latter has "not long since"
been the theme of "every Virgin's Song" (1. 12). Marlborough, not so fortunate, has been allowed to die abroad although he served his Queen and Country more than any General did before. By prudent foresight he has at least
fled "the too much obliging of a Throne" (1. 20). Also in
the same volume is: *On the late Ministry's admitting the
Jews for Witnesses against the Duke of* Marlborough. Pp.
40-1, 6 lines, couplets. Opens:

> In our Fore-fathers Days, when God was fear'd,
> A Jew against a Christian was not heard.

Beyond his Whig bias, nothing apparently suggests any
identity for the writer. Several poems to Lord Cutts,
suggesting association with his regiment, appear, as also
a Pindaric on the taking of Namur, and poems addressed to
Blackmore, and to Steel[e] appear. Morgan notes a five-
act tragedy *Socrates Triumphant*, as being included with
the volume. The poems were not separately printed. See
Captain Thomas Johnson, *An Epitaph upon...Marlborough*,
allegedly a translation, No. 473, 1714.

493   [Sewell, George (1690?-1726)] ?

An Appeal to the People of Great Britain, On The *Report* of
a *New Conspiracy*.   In Imitation of the Seventh *Epode* of
Horace.   *Quo, quo, Scelesti ruitis?*   *By the Author of the*
Verses to the DUKE OF MARLBOROUGH, *on his going to* Germany.
[colophon bot. p. 2]   Printed for *W. Mears* at the *Lamb*
without *Temple-Bar*:   And sold by *J. Roberts* near the
Oxford-Arms in *Warwick-Lane*, 1717.   Price 2 *d*.
        1/2°:   1 column, 2 sides.   34 lines, couplets.   Pp.
nmbd. 1 and 2.   Horn copy only one known; from Bicton
Library.   Not in Morgan.   Opens:

        Where, where, Degen'rate *Country-Men* — how high
        Will your fond Folly, and your Madness fly?

While the *Verses on Marlborough's Going to Germany* have
been attributed to Garth, a still later publication, subsequent to his death, is also attributed to the author of
these verses.   Hence Sewell seems a firmer choice for all
the poems.   The poem is concerned ostensibly with the
Jacobite-Scottish rebellions, and asks whether it is rashness or Despair that induces them to such wild actions.
They are assured that George's reign is secure.

        Hear then, you Sons of Blood, your destin'd Fate,
        Hear e're you *Sin too soon* — *Repent too late*.
        Madly you try to weaken *GEORGE's* Reign,
        And stem the Stream of Providence in vain.   25-8

The hand that gave the Right will preserve George's throne,

        For 'tis the Nature of that Sacred Line,
        To Conquer *Monsters*, and to grow *Divine*.   33-4

94   Jones, Richard (no dates)

Britannia Triumphans, a Poem, Humbly Inscrib'd to the Wor-
shipful Sir Richard Steel [*sic*].   *London*, Printed and Sold
by *J. Baker*, 1717.   (price 4 *d*.)
        4to: A-B⁴; *1-2*, 3-16, 16 pp.   MH only loc.   Not in
Morgan.

495   [Amhurst, Nicholas (1697-1742)] *pseud.*, Caleb d'Anvers

A Congratulatory Epistle to the Right Honorable *Joseph Addison* Esq. By a Student at Oxford, 1717. *London*, Printed for *E. Curll*. (Price Six Pence)
     8ᵛᵒ: T.p., *bl.*, drop-t. on 3, 3-15, 16 pp. 172 lines, couplets. MH copy used. The only one known. Not in Morgan. Opens:

> While Half the Globe is shook with Wars and Arms,
> And *Europe* labours with unripe Alarms.

Writing as a young student at Oxford, Amhurst largely praises Addison for his poetic career and his promise as a servant of the state. Five years later Amhurst wrote one of the elegies on Marlborough. Limited reference appears in this poem, *viz.*,

> When CHURCHILL, or NASSAU, inspire your Layes,
> Scarce can They Fight so well, as You can Praise.
>   57-8

Charles XII of Sweden is noticed for his impetuous actions in war. Using the pseudonym Caleb d'Anvers, Amhurst shared the editing of *The Craftsman* (1726-47) with Bolingbroke and others.

496   Huddesford, W., of All Souls Coll., Oxon. (no dates)

A Congratulatory Letter to Joseph Addison, upon his being Appointed one of his Majesty's Principal Secretaries of State. Oxford, 1717.
     Fol., 6 leaves. Dobell Cat. of 18th Century Verse, 708, only ref.

497   A VIEW OF THE Duke of MARLBOROUGH'*s* BATTLES, Painted by Mr. *Leguerre*, In His Grace's House at St. *James's*: IN-SCRIB'D To the Duke of MONTAGUE. [2 lines Virg.] *LONDON*: Printed for *E. CURLL* in *Fleet-street*. 1717.
     8°: t.p., *bl.*, text 5-16, 16 pp. TxU copy used.

Opens:

> While the Great-Vulgar shine with borrow'd Rays,
> By Help of Heraldry, or purchas'd Praise.

Montague is addressed as "The Soldier's Darling, and the
Muse's Friend" (1. 11) and Leguerre is urged to painting
scenes as famous as those Great Verrio drew. The poem
supplies one of the most complete summaries of the
battles, beginning with Blenheim, with scenes of the
Duke in combat. The verse, though formal, suggests the
fixed animation of battle painting.

> How gently fierce! how awfully serene!
> His Arm bears Thunder, and Command, his Mien.
> Now fixt th' Intrepid stands, now loose his Reign,
> His fiery Steed bounds o'er the gory Plain,
> While the great Leader animates the Fight,
> Here breaks the Foe, and there provokes the Flight.
> These to the *Danube*, those to *Blenheim* fly,
> Not from their Fate. -- The Victor still is nigh!
> 43-50

Ramellies, with the death of Bringfield, Oudenard, and
other scenes, down to the siege of Lisle, appear. The
poem concludes with the well-worn observation that Marlborough's actions surpass those of Caesar and Ammon, and
a tribute to Brunswick, that is King George.

    This advice-to-the-painter poem does not appear in
Dr. Mary Tom Osborn's catalog, cited above, pub. U. of
Texas, 1949.

The years between Marlborough's seizure, in 1716,
and his death in 1722, yielded almost no literary expressions beyond the few in 1717. The Duke's last years
were somewhat brightened by his visits to various resorts
and the satisfaction of living in the apartments at the
completed portion of Blenheim Palace, the performance of
a carefully expurgated version of Dryden's *All for Love*
performed largely by his grandchildren in Duchess Sarah's
bow-window in the East wing, and the satisfactions in
escaping the South Sea disaster. Sarah, with characteristic foresight, had withdrawn ₤100,000 not long before
the bubble burst in 1720. The Duke played cards, rode
and drove around Blenheim Park, and, as Churchill points
out, "realized some of the pleasures of home of which he
had dreamed throughout his campaigns" (IV, 643). Meanwhile, his Duchess who could predict the explosion of
the South Sea inflation, must equally well have anticipated the inevitable death of her beloved Duke. That
she did quarrel with her two surviving daughters, with
Vanbrugh, and almost everyone else, is too often interpreted as an expression of a vixen nature. Wasn't it
more the panic that seized her at this threat to her
happiness? It was at Windsor Lodge that Marlborough
suffered his first and only defeat. After a series of
paroxysms in face of which he still retained clearness
of mind, till the final coma, the First Duke of Marlborough died at dawn on June 16, 1722. The funeral and
interment in the Abbey took place August 9th.

98 *A Second Epistle* to Mr. *Tickell*. Author of the Incomparable Ode, call'd *A Voyage to France*, &c. *In tempere
veni*. . .Lilly's Grammar. London, Printed for J. Roberts,
in *Warwick-Lane*. (Price Two Pence.)
    1/2°: 2 sides, 40 lines, couplets, n.d. Crawford-
Foxon only loc. Foxon: "after Nov. 1717 and before 19
Dec., 1719." Opens:

    Of *Tickell*, greatly fated to inherit
    Thy Master *Joseph*'s Vertues with his Spirit!
    Thou Second-sighted Bard, who canst forebode
    Events of State in Epick or in Ode;
    Foretell us now when *Europe* shall be free
    From *Utrecht*'s Peace, so early sung by Thee.

This sceptical and ironic tone is maintained, with
Tickell challenged to make further prophecies, and to
adjust to political changes which may come. Addison, his
"pious Patron," might have brought from Hell the spell
which will bring release from the Treaty. Political allusions to France and Spain and the brokers of Change-
Alley are sufficiently enigmatic, but plainly the poem
is anti-Addison as it returns to speculations about his
occupation. No direct allusions to Marlborough, but a
definite concern with the embroilments of his final years.

99 Vanbrugh, Sir John (1664-1726) *et al*.

Sir *John Vanbrugh*'s Justification, Of what he depos'd in
the Duke of *Marlborough*'s late TRYAL.
    2°: 8 pp., no pub., n.d., prose. BM xerox used.
    An assemblage of letters and testimony defending Van-
brugh's claims for payment for his services in designing
Blenheim Palace, and for hiring workers. Letters of Godolphin and Duchess Sarah are included. Some excisions
suggest this may have been Vanbrugh's copy; certainly it
was done by him. Following Godolphin's authorization of
him as architect, June 9th, 1705, few specific dates appear, although reference to the new reign appears. Another warrant recognizes Bobart as comptroller, and of
the Tilleman brothers and Henry Joynes. The Duchess's

letters refer to financial arrangements, as well as the purchase of locks and hinges in London.

See No. 500, 1721, for continuation of the controversy.

500   Continuation of Vanbrugh's Justification, No. 499.

2°:   4 pp., prose. BM copy used. No title, but the explanation, printed in italics, supplies the equivalent, as follows:

Since I writ the precedent Paper, I heard there was a sort of Case handed privately about, relating to the Blenheim *Affair, in which my Name was pretty much us'd.*

I have at last got a sight of it, and find so much decent Language in it, fair stating of Facts, and right sound Reasoning from them, that one would almost swear it had been written by a Woman. Some Answer however it shall have.

The pamphlet consists of a warrant appointing Mr. Joynes and Vanbrugh's statement that he asked the Duke for authority as surveyor to have a part in employing workers. Four objections are answered. They deal with such matters as the Queen's intentions, her now employing Sir Christopher Wren for the building of Blenheim, and Vanbrugh's protest that he had received very little remuneration for his services.

501   The *Case* of the *Duke* of *Marlborough* versus Strong and Others: The Duke of Marlborough's Case and the Case of the Respondents.

2°, London, 1721. Concerning the building of Blenheim Palace. Morgan T719. BM.

502   A HYMN To the Victory in SCOTLAND. London, Printed by R. Thomas behind the Royal Exchange. N.d.

1/2°:   1 p., pr. in 2 cols. 45 lines, octosyllabic couplets. MH-Luttr. copy used. MS 'gratis. A banter upon ye victory show. 25. June. 1719'   Opens:

I sing the Praise of Heroes brave,
Whose *Warlike Merit* conquest gave,
And scorn'd to trample on a Foe
But beat them first, then let *them* go.

Ridicules both sides of the Battle of Glensheils, where
the Spaniards attempted an invasion in support of the
Scots. The fighting among rocks and fog seems to have
produced few casualties and fewer prisoners.

Such Mercy in this Fight was shown,
We sav'd Men's Lives and lost our own.
A Victory which no Age can show,
To let both Dead and Living go.   42-5

While the poem makes no allusions to Marlborough, it does
reflect the discontent with the Union and the uneasiness
of a period of Pretenders and threats of invasion. It
concludes with a glance at no Scots being slain or taken:

And, which our Reason has most shaken,
Not one poor single Rebel taken:
Three Hours beaten and none die,   }
Yet no Man knows the Reason why,   }
'Tis very strange 'tween You and *I*.   } 61-5

Of the twenty-five elegiac pieces on the death of Marlborough, seven are in broadsheet, and presumably the earliest. While these are listed alphabetically, by title, the first listed identifies no printer and is one of the crudest, both as verse and in printing. Actually the vast funeral procession and interment in the Abbey did not take place till seven weeks after the Duke expired. Though Lediard notes the date, August 9, and reviews the whole event, the precise date is not noted by Coxe, Reid, Churchill, and most biographers. A. L. Rowse, however, cites the Abbey register for the proper date and recital of Marlborough's titles. See *The Early Churchills*, p. 380.

03   Henley, John, "Orator" Henley (1692-1756)

APOTHEOSIS. A Funeral Oration. Sacred to the Memory
of the Most Noble JOHN Duke of Marlborough. As it was
spoken on the Day of his INTERRMENT [*sic*]. Form'd upon
the Manner of the Antients. By Mr. Henley. [motto from
Ovid] LONDON, Printed for Will. Mears at the Lamb, without Temple-Bar, MDCCXXII. (Price Sixpence)
         8VO with broad funerary band around t.p. Prose.
T.p., *bl.*, 3-35, *bl. 36*, 36 pp. Ornamental urn with
flowers bot. p. 35. BM copy used. Morgan T520.
         Pompous tone. "For indeed, never was Sorrow in
Greater Pomp . . [like] its Great Author, it CONQUERS ALL
MANKIND" (p. 4). Yet his Godlike spirit and fame afford
a "gleam of Pleasure."

> But since Fate has seiz'd the *Mighty Few*, that
> could have reach'd it; since the Powers of *Elys-
> ium* enjoy another Lucan, Ovid, Horace, and Vir-
> gil, in the Shape of a ROWE, a GARTH, a PRIOR,
> and an ADDISON: Let us, however, exert our
> Humble Care to rescue him from the Vulgar and
> Inferior Hand, and guard the PALMS that surround
> him. (pp. 6-7)

The attempt to do justice to Marlborough must surpass even
his victories. He is called "our *British* CAESAR," and in
succession his powers of mind, gifts of Nature, his valor,
his lineage and nuptials, his copiers even, Cadogan and
Eugene, all are cited. Above all he raised the despond-
ing Empire, and in Blenheim had his apotheosis.

> Let the Plains of BLENHEIM tell, How the Proud-
> est Force of *Gaul* was Humbled; and HER FLOWERS
> were blasted; Let the conscious DANUBE say, How
> the Tide was chang'd to Blood, and his *Naiads*
> were terrify'd . . . Wherever he pass'd, Tyranny,
> and Lawless Sway submitted to his Fetters. Fair
> LIBERTY surviv'd to bless the Clime, and the
> harsh accents of Slavery and Pain were banish'd
> by every Pleasing Sound of Publick Joy and Ac-
> clamation. (pp. 22-3)

The avowed oratorical intention of this tribute serves at
least to point up Blenheim as the key to Marlborough's

fame, as well as serving as a proclamation of Whig policy.
The work supplies a rare and interesting example of "Orator" Henley's style, nicely confirming his right to replace Eusden in *Dunciad*, II and III. His later association with Curll and his services to Walpole against *The
Craftsman* are consistent with *The Funeral*.

504 June, *ca.*

An Elegiac PASTORAL On the Death of the Duke of *MARLBOR-
OUGH*, Who Dy'd on SATURDAY, The 16th of *June*, 1722.
[Horace - Latin motto]
     1/2°: 2 pp., no pub., n.d. Foxon-MC only loc.
Over 32 lines, couplets. Not in Morgan. Opens:

     Sicilian Muse, exalt thy rural Strain,
     Begin a Song that shall amaze the Plain.

A heavenly bard chants the lament, as birds, flocks,
nymphs and swains from neighboring hamlets gather to
listen. The emotion, at best conventional, is hardly
surpassed by the stilted images and notions of the poem.
A sample will serve.

     At last he's gone, forc'd to resign his Breath;
     Who oft has been the Thunderbolt of Death.
     Speak, *Schellenberg*; speak, *Ramellies*, his Fame,
     Where deathless Trophies rose to his immortal Name.
                                                14-17

At the close the poet abandons the theme to an abler
"quill," since Marlborough's name and fame should sound
with that of Aeneas.

505 June, *ca.*

An ELEGY *Or a Poem upon the Death of his Grace John Duke
of Marlebourgh*.
     1/2°: 1 page, 2 columns, 105 lines, couplets. Bod-
ley copy used. Not in Morgan. The spelling *Marlebourgh*
suggests a French-speaking Dutchman or other foreign

source. Many misspellings and grammatical clinches indicate more of partisanship than poetry. Opens:

Who can Condole this Hero's Loss? who can?
Express the Merit of this marshal Man?

Posterity must call it a romance, since no human, nor
scarce celestial power could so overthrow France. His
opponents, Talard [*sic*], Vileroy, Vendom, and Vilars,
and his leading victories, Blenheim, Ramellies, Audenard,
and the sieges of Speers, Lisle, etc., are reviewed.

Let Envy spit her Venem [*sic*], burst her Gall,
And at this Hero knash her Teeth and Baul,
His Fame shall last to all Futurnity [*sic*],
His Courage, Canduor [*sic*], and Magninimity, [*sic*]
His Candor, Prowess, Vigilence [*sic*] and Skill,
Vast Volumes of Chronoligy [*sic*] shall fill.   66-71

The triumph over the French Monsieur and Envy set the tone
of the poem. There is no note of grief to justify the
title of elegy. The poem concludes with a warning to Envy
to burst her heart in vain. The stylistic and typograph-
ical blunders pervade the entire poem, as well as the passage quoted.

6   June, *ca.*

The SOLDIERS ELEGY On the Much lamented *Death* of *JOHN* Duke
of *MARLBOROUGH.* Who departed this Life on *Saturday* of this
Instant *June,* 1722, at *Windsor-Lodge,* in the 72d. Year of
his Age. Written and Printed for a Gentleman *Volunteir*
[*sic*] in the *Camp.*
        1/2°: 1 side, 2 columns, n.d., no pub., 55 lines,
with *Epitaph* in 10 lines, 65 lines, couplets, but the Epitaph in alternate rhyme. Bodley copy used. Not in Morgan.
        The most richly ornamented of all Marlborough poems.
Unusually enriched ornamental bands surround the whole
with symbols of death, skeletons and bones, muffled drums,
a casket with its shroud encrusted with shields, and the
inscription "Memento Mori," and the translation, "Remember
to Die" repeated on a scroll at the top, columns at the

sides. Opens:

> Amidst those Troops, who've put their stables
> [sables?] on
> My fainting Muse prepares a doleful Song.

Can Marlborough be dead? For ancient heroes earthquakes
and comets signalized their death. But for Marlborough
all is like that serenity in his breast, except for shrieks
and cries of grief.

> The Towns he won his Merit do proclaim,
> And lisping Babes henceforth shall sound his Fame.
>   29-30

The tottering Empire and reeling Dutch will honor him, and
the whole world can look on in wonder. The *Epitaph* opens:

> Under this tomb there lies interr'd
>   A Caesar, Scipio, Hannibal.

Pervasive crudities in spelling seem consistent with the
authorship by a soldier in camp.

507 July 11.

Gay, John (1685-1732)

AN *EPISTLE* TO HER GRACE HENRIETTA, Dutchess of *MARLBOROUGH*.
By Mr. *Gay*. Printed for JACOB TONSON, at *Shakespear*'s
Head, over-against *Katharine-street* in the *Strand*.
MDCCXXII.
  2°: A^2 B^2 C; *i-iv*, 1-5, *bl. 6*, 10 pp.   MH, ICN,
CSmH, CtY. 78 lines, couplets. Wmk. fleur de lys. Not
in Morgan. Opens:

> Excuse me, Madam, if amidst your Tears
> A Muse intrudes, a Muse who feels your cares.

How could he recite the dangers, the councils, sieges,
victorious fights. The father and the hero is no more.
Only Britain weeps. Holland fears for her safety. Germany remembers Hockstet. Apollo whispers to the poet to

be wise, and avoid the burden of praise. He cannot raise
up Homer or Virgil.

> But he requires not the strong glare of verse,
> Let punctual History his deeds rehearse.   43-4

But, he asks, how can such speculations bring comfort to
Henrietta? He but aggravates her woes.

> Would you the ruin'd merchant's soul appease,
> With talk of sands, and rocks, and stormy seas? 53-4

She is now urged to think on her father's lawrels, but
this too brings grief; still she will always hear Marlborough's name.

> Though in your life ten thousand summers roll,
> And though you compass earth from Pole to Pole,
> Where-e'er men talk of war and martial fame,
> They'll mention *Marlborough* and *Caesar*'s name.

Still there must be suffering, and the poem concludes with
the sad consolation the mind suffers from the loss of a
great man. "Virtue Virtue loves" (1. 78).

While this is neither a great poem, nor representa-
tive of Gay's best qualities, it is another example of the
wide range of authorship for Marlborough poems.

)8   August, *ca.*

S., R.

A POEM Occasioned by the FUNERAL of the Glorious and Invincible, *JOHN* Duke of *MARLBOROUGH*. *DUBLIN* Printed by
James Carson in *Coghills-Court* in *Dames Street*, opposite
the *Castle-Market*, MDCCXXII.
1/2°: 1 p., ornamental band at top, 94 lines, couplets in 2 cols. BM copy used. Repr. in Lediard, III,
421-32, with a few changes and corrections in wording,
and the signficant addition of four lines (91-4) painfully adulatory of "GEORGE. . .Greatest of KINGS; *Europe*'s
just Arbiter." The authenticity of the changes, and the

tone as being clearly that of a London poet, suggest that
there may well have been an original London edition. The
Bodley copy has 'By R. S.' at bottom.

> Whence this sad Pomp? the mighty Cause declare;
> Why mourn the brave intrepid Sons of War?

Now the trumpets and steeds of war must be subdued, while
Britannia mourns mighty Marlborough. The world has gained
by him; Belgia, Germany, and even France, who feared him
living, should admire and praise this man of such greatness and goodness. In camp and cabinet he was great. His
many victories are recalled. He has rivaled the heroes of
Greece and Rome, and David who fought the battles of the
Lord. He fought, not with thirst of glory, but for his
country's good. His acts could employ Homer's genius.

> What Bard will now the mighty Task explore,
> Great *Addison* began but ah! he's now no more
> Yet still behold his Immortal Lines,
> How Great, how Bright, the Godlike Heroe Shines;
> Blest Age, Blest Island, which alone could show,
> The chief of Heroes, and of Poets too.
> With like Applause thro' every Age shall reign
> Great *Virgil*'s *AEnead Addison*'s Camapain [*sic*]
> Poets unborn great Churchils Acts shall chuse.
> To add Sublimer Rapture to their Muse.   89-98

At the close comes the assurance that the future will
bring soldiers to take the hero's place: England will
"Not want a *Marlborough*, whilst she hath a George" (1.
94).

509   August 3.

Cooke, Thomas (1705-56)

MARLBOROUGH. A POEM, In Three CANTOS. Occasion'd by the
DEATH OF THE Late Duke of MARLBOROUGH. [3 lines Virg.]
LONDON: Printed for T. PAYNE at the *Crown* in *Pater-Noster-
Row*. 1722. (*Pr*. 6 *d*.) Morgan T527.
      4to: π^2 A^4 B-D^4; *i-vii, 1*, 2-24, 32 pp. Dedication
to the Honourable Brigadier HONYWOOD *iii-vi*; ornamental

band and drop-t. on *1*. Adv. in *Daily Journal*, ed. Aug.
1722, Canto I, 128 lines; II, 129; III, 90; 347 lines,
couplets, Latin mottoes for each Canto. 'Just publish'd.'
MH copy used, IU, U. of Hull. *Dedication* opens:

> Sir, Our Age abounding with so many mercenary
> Parasites, the Name of a Dedication is thought
> scandalous. To such a Height is the Boldness of
> our daring Sciblers [*sic*] arriv'd, that in defi-
> ance to the whole World, they will (or would)
> make the blackest Devil, vertuous; the meerest
> Ideot, a Solomon; and the most dastard Coward,
> a *Marlborough*: And he, poor Soul, with his
> borrow'd Dress, is very unwilling the World
> should not take the Picture for his own; tho'
> at the same time he blushes within himself, to
> think he has bought the Draught at so dear a
> Rate.

Most dedications are stuffed with encomiums, but this one
will depend only on the acts of its subject "an only hope
[without Despair thereof] to see you proceed a *Honywood*,
as you have begun." Signed "T. COOKE." The poem opens:

> Fair *Cytherea*, and her lovely Train,
> The am'rous Nymph, and the more am'rous Swain.

The poet turns from pastoral and love verse to "serious
Thoughts." Canto I reviews Marlborough's career from infancy at his mother's breast, through boyhood, with his
toys, to his service to James II, as a court favorite.
Primarily it defends the desertion of James for William.
Then Rome was the enemy: "Oft had we been damn'd, had
Rome the Pow'r" (1. 71). Not even Drake, in Eighty-Eight,
nor the Gunpowder Plot, "the dark Design" against James I,
could deter the Popish threat. Churchill foresaw, and
ponders his course of action. He leaves James II for Nassau. Alexander strove for empire over the world, but
Marlborough was "Preserver of our Liberty" (1. 108). A
paeon to liberty which is "Albion's Glory" concludes the
canto. The poet declines to follow Marlborough's career
under "glorious Whilliam" [*sic*].
   Canto II reviews Marlborough's victories under Anne,
particularly 1703-9. *Keyserswert*, *Landau*, *Venlo*, and *St.*

487

Michael, where Cutts won fame; *Liege*, *Stevenswert*, *Rure-mond*; and then the Blenheim year of 1704:

> Of Hochstet's Fight how shall I ought relate?
> With Gallia's big, and with *Bavaria*'s Fate.
> Where the fam'd *Danube* with his rapid Streams,
> (*Danube* the Rival of our glorious Thames!)
> His fertile Banks with swelling Waves o'erflow'd;
> Encreas'd with *Spanish*, and with *Gallick* Blood.   177-82

There Tallard was taken, though Dormer, Forbes, Cornwall, and Row fell. Cadogan wins glory, while next at Ramillies, the Belgian Auverquerque won fame. While ten thousand guardian angels protect Marlborough, Villeroy meets defeat. Then comes *Ghent*, *Dendermond*, *Ostend*, although in the next year, the French and Bavarians have a triumph, a loss which Marlborough "ransoms" at *Blaregnies* the next year, that is at Oudenard. Now the poet refuses to go farther. Such an account should require such "Strains as *Milton* wrote" (1. 237). The Canto ends with the picture of Envy, which re-sorts in palaces, puffed up with "putrid Gore," and with livid Eye-lids unclosed, seeking to tear down Marlborough's fame. But he is now beyond even Envy.

Canto III is elegiac, reflecting on death, which must overcome all heroes, as it has Marlborough. This man who has made so many thousands to flee, and "Who so encreas'd the Numbers of the Dead" (1. 263) can purchase no more of life. So it was with King Arthur, with Edward Harry, i.e. Henry V, and "imperious *Cromwell*," and "great *Nassau*." So it will be with the present king and his son George. So will it be with Cadogan.

> Nor you great *Honywood* must hope to shun
> Th' inevitable Race these Heroes run.   254-5

His patron may not have relished being assured that the Fair will no more love his "mould'ring Charms" nor the Foe dread his "tremendous Arms." A grim picture of the dying hero, "Who never from the Battle empty came" (1. 317), leads to the classical simile of a tall Oak falling in the forest from which is derived a moral on anticipating death.

> Ye Sons of Man, snatch a quick Thought sedate!
> And ponder well upon the Heroe's Fate!

See what had Wisdom, Conduct, Valour dead!
Nor could those Charmes prorogue the fatal Thread!
When the idea to your Eyes is shown,
Think MARLBRO's Fate must one Day be your own!   343-8

As with many Marlborough poems, this production
launched Cooke's career, as it appears to have been his
first published piece, in spite of his opening profession
of having turned from lighter subjects. Hence his quarrels with Pope, which won him a spot in both the *Dunciad*,
II, 130, and *The Epistle to Dr. Arbuthnot*, 1. 146. His
publication, in 1728, of a translation of Hesiod, won him
the sobriquet of 'Hesiod' Cooke, and this along with his
associations with Cibber and opposition to Pope and Swift
as a Whig apologist, all follow on his diploma piece, the
cantos on Marlborough. For a youth of 19 the verses are
not contemptible. He should not be confused with Ormond's
chaplain, of the same name.

0   August 9.

Amhurst, Nicholas (1697-1742)

THE BRITISH GENERAL; A POEM, Sacred to the MEMORY of his
Grace JOHN, Duke of MARLBOROUGH. Inscribed to the Right
Honourable *William*, Earl *Cadogan*. By N. AMHURST. [3
lines Virgil] *LONDON*: Printed for *R. Franklin*, 1722.
MH, Horn copy used; pub. and d. trimmed.
    8vo: A^8 B-E^8, half-t. Mr. *Amhurst*'s POEM on the
Death of his GRACE, Duke of MARLBOROUGH, *bl.*, t.p., *bl.*,
v-viii, drop-t. on p *1*, 2-31, *32 bl.*, 40 pp. Dedication,
34 lines; Poem, 405 lines, total 439 lines, couplets.
Large ornaments and decorations, wmk. fleur de lys. Lediard, III, 425-8, reprints 100 lines from the poem. He
also dates the poem: "On the Day, the late Duke of *Marlborough*'s Funeral was performed, an excellent Copy of
Verses, written by the ingenious Mr. *Amhurst*, was published as follows:"
    Dedication opens:

    DISDAIN not, mighty Chief, to whom descend
    The Virtues and Honours of your Friend.

489

Even though he is a "youthful" poet, he asks attention, and notices that Cadogan accompanied Marlborough on campaigns and sieges, learning from him the love of arms and conquest. He concludes "a new MARLBRO' in CADOGAN lives" (1. 34). The poem opens:

> CHURCHILL is dead! and in that Word is lost
> The bravest Leader of the bravest Host.

Marlborough achieved beyond ancient heroes, and for him Heaven

> . . rais'd for such a Chief an equal Bard;
> In ADDISON reviv'd the *Mantuan* strain,
> To sing the Triumphs of but one *Campaign.*   17-20

Prior also subdued the foe in verse, and Philips recited the great deeds in "Miltonian" verse. The plans for the campaign of 1703 are reviewed; Marlborough sails for Flanders, and addresses the Dutch Assembly, who approve his proposals. After victory he returns to England, and is awarded new titles by the Queen. Then his only son dies at Cambridge (139-50). "At length the great, important Year is come" (1. 197), and the march to Blenheim and the battle occupy most of the poem. First Schellenberg and then Blenheim, with the capture of Tallard and once more the squadrons of French plunging into "the Whirlpools of the *Danube*" (1. 258). The poet concludes the story lies beyond the range of poetry. The historian's work is demanded of Steele by Marlborough's progeny: Landau, Ramillia, Lisle, Audenard, Blarignia, and Bouchain would be vain to describe after Blenheim. For ten years Marlborough enjoyed success.

The remainder of the poem deplores the ungrateful treatment Marlborough received - "Never was such a Chief so ill repaid!" (1. 327), and the lament of the spectre of Louis XIV as he reviews the Duke's conquests. The poem is less an elegy than a recital of Marlborough's career, although the Funeral is noticed, "the last sad March" (11. 340-53).

11   August 11.

[Jacob, Giles (1686-1744)] ?   Sgnd. 'G. J.'

BRITAIN'S HERO: A POEM ON THE DEATH Of His GRACE *JOHN*,
Duke of *Marlborough*.   [4 lines from Addison's *Campaign*
beginning "*Marlborough*'s Exploits appear Divinely bright"]
LONDON: Printed for H. COLE, at *Rowe's-Head* without *Temple-
Bar*; and sold by J. PEELE, at *Locke's-Head in Paternoster-
Row*. M.DCC.XXII.   (Price Sixpence.)
        2°:   A-C^2; t.p., *bl*., Dedication "To Her Grace the
Dutchess Dowager of MARLBOROUGH," signed 'G. J.,' *bl*.,
5-12, 12 pp.   Ornamental band and drop-t., p. 5.   DLC,
only copy known, used.   Morgan T717 but without author.
Post Boy, 11 August, 'Just publish'd.'   121 lines, coup-
lets.   Opens:

        As when some Earthquake in a distant Land
        Shakes Kingdoms, Countries, all with Trembling stand.

It is striking to see the author of the *Historical Account
of Our Most Considerable English Poets* (1720), if Jacob is
the author, adding himself to the imposing list of Marlborough panegyrists.   His elegy does not offend by excess,
even though it evokes no deep feeling.   Jacob, fresh from
reviewing the work of the chief English poets, alludes to
none, and yet pilfers from none.   The shock of Marlborough's loss, "*Blenheim* and *Ramille*'s [*sic*] Towers," the
only battles mentioned, the cries of victory, a parallel
to Homer, Virgil, and Milton, a brief picture of the weeping widow and her "Lovely Daughters," and a glimpse of the
funeral procession, — all these are the components of a
poem that at least does not offend against good taste.
H. Cole, the publisher, gave the work a handsome format,
and may well have commissioned it as not wishing to be
behind his competitors in displaying a tribute to the
national hero.
        The poem upholds the now-accepted Whig policies.
"Churchill" has struck with terror kings and climes afar,

        And push'd Victorious Great *Europa*'s War;
        Who made Bavaria and Count Tallard fly,
        Whole Armies at his Feet expiring ly:

His Valiant Squadrons, fearless of all Harms,
Whilst He, their General, gave Laws to Arms.
As long as *Hockstet* and th'adjacent Plain,
Shall *Marlb'rough*'s Glory and his Fame remain.

                                                   14-20

   The poem moves with a rather swift, steady movement
even though its imagery of tribute is conventional. The
poet recognizes that not even the good and great can escape death, but observes that "Death has no Victory where
Fame survives" (1. 94), with an echo of Pope. He sees the
Duchess, then her lovely daughters, a crowd of nobles, and
even the domestic servants in tears. One passage appears
to confirm that it was written after the funeral on August
9, and thus it must have been hurried to press for its
publication on the 11th.

And last of all, methinks I view, in State,   ⎫
(Where Thousands on his sad Obsequies wait)   ⎬
The open Chariot and Procession great;   ⎭
Coaches and Horses in a num'rous Train,
Magnificent to sight, but nothing vain.   111-15

512   August 16.

M., S.

On seeing the Funeral of the Late Duke of MARLBOROUGH.
Inscribed to her Grace the Dutchess Dowager. Pr. in the
St. James's Journal, No. XVI, August 16, 1722. 9 4-line
stanzas, 36 lines with prefatory note:

SIR, If you please to print this little Tribute
to the Glorious Memory of the Great Duke of
Marlborough in your next Journal, you will
oblige 'Your Constant Reader,' S. M. [dated
Aug. 10, 1722]

Opens:
   The awful Hero's hallow'd Shrine,
      The solemn Process of the Day,
   The God of Parent Earth resign,
      When I had seen, his borrow'd Clay.

A Vision of the hero appears, circled in beams of
light. Jove bends his head and speaks, saying, "My
MARLBRO' Leaves the Earth," and urges publishing of his
praises. Marlborough enters heaven, Mars on his right,
Apollo on his left. Divine essences and songs of triumph surround him. No. XIX of *St. James's Journal* for
Aug. 2 has notice of plans for the funeral.

13   November.

A Gentleman of Cambridge.

VERSES TO THE LORD *CARTARET*, Occasioned by the PRESENT
CONSPIRACY. By a *Gentleman* of CAMBRIDGE. [3 lines Dryden
on "unmask'd Rebellion"] LONDON: Printed for Jacob TON-
SON, at *Shakespear's-Head*, over-against *Katherine-Street*
in the *Strand*. MDCCXXII.
        2°: A-C²; half-t., *bl.*, t.p. *iii*, *bl. iv*, 1-7,
bl. 8, 12 pp. No wmk. Rich ornamental band above drop-t.,
p. 1, ornamental letter and at end an ornament. 113 lines,
couplets. Horn Luttr. copy, '5 *d*. November.' Opens:

>   Since *Senates* safe in legal Rights rejoice,
>   And rescu'd Nations swell the Public Voice.

Following praise of Cartaret, successor of Dorset as poet,
the poet asks where sedition can spread her plagues.
Britain under George need not fear the altars and Romish
gloom of the past. King George is praised as giving security, so that the twin sisters, Freedom and Property,
can kiss in mutual bliss, and a realm where Mercy and
Equity can prevail over Rebellion and Faction. Only one
allusion to Marlborough appears, in a contrast between
his troops and those of George.

>   Not so, Great KING, thy military Band,
>   Brave Souls! as us'd to Conquest as Command,
>   Who o'er the *Flandrian* Fields their Trophies spread,
>   Where MARLBRÔ' pointed, or CADOGAN led.   79-82

George is urged to smile at what his worth inspires.

>   So may some future ADDISON arise,
>   Raise high your Fame, and mix it with the Skies.   91-2

Where now can Conspiracy hide; for the vigilance of
Townshend, Parker's legal skill, Walpole's spirit and
eloquence, and the virtues of Raymond and Harcourt all
are on guard? These and Providence will guard George
and Britain.

514 December.

Welsted, Leonard (1688-1747)

AN EPISTLE TO THE Late Dr. GARTH, Occasion'd by the DEATH
Of The DUKE Of *MARLBOROUGH*. By Mr. *WELSTED*. [ornament]
LONDON: Printed for J. PEELE, at *Locke's Head* in *Pater-
Noster-Row*. M. DCC. XXII.
    2°: A^2 B-C^2; *1-2*, 3-12, 12 pp. Elaborate ornament,
ornamental boxed initial, drop-t., p. 3. No wmk. Horn-
Luttr. copy used; '5 *d.*' twice at top; 'Decemb.' 218
lines, couplets. Morgan T1220. Opens:

> From the fair Banks of *Thame* this Verse I send,
> To those blest Realms, that late receiv'd my Friend.

Although Garth had died in 1718, Welsted pays him a warm
tribute as having been his "Prop and Sanction" in his own
youth, guiding him in his first efforts in poetry. He
urges Garth now to praïse Marlborough's glory in the
realms beyond, where both now dwell, since he is responsible for "no inglorious Part of CHURCHILL's Fame" (1. 20).

> For thy lov'd MARLBRO', yet thy Care employ,
> And point him out among the Lawns of Joy;
> Let every Warlike Shade the Leader view;
> A name so Glorious, and a Shade so New!
> Ev'n to the Ghosts, that purpled o're [*sic*] with Blood
> *Ramillia's* Fields, and swell'd the *Danube's* Flood;
> Ev'n to the *Gallic* Ghosts their Conqueror show;
> Alate how dreaded! now, no more their Foe!   23-30

The next twenty lines picture the shades gathering admir-
ingly around that of Marlborough, names from England's
proudest past, "For Prowess unexcell'd 'till *Anna's*
Reign!" (1. 42). Nassau welcomes him as "Mankind's

Deliverer" and as both subject and friend.
Then the poet is impelled to lament Garth's death
anew, since he is not here to celebrate Marlborough's
demise. He pictures the lavish funeral procession, the
banners, horse, battle-trophies, gleaming armor, and the
downcast march of the throng of soldiers. Then he reflects, in the manner of Montaigne, that happiness cannot
be ascribed to men till they die, and their story is complete. In this he finds consolation for the hero. He
then traces his career, from his youth to the glory of
his "riper Years," when "Glory clos'd the Scene, which
Love began" (1. 104). He was blessed with seventy win-
ters, the smiles of monarchs, and "The loveliest Offspring, and the fairest Wife" (1. 100). The elegies are
not replete with tributes to Marlborough's duchess.

A picture of Paradise that is primarily pastoral and
classical, with allusions to Ovid gives way to praise of
England's island security, where the forest-oak, proud
fleets, and a Godlike breed of hardy, wise, and bold men
sustain Liberty against tyrants.

> If this thy Theme; on CHURCHILL's every Deed
> Thy Tongue shall dwell and boast of *Europe* freed;
> Still in thy Thought his Battles shall prevail,
> And *Blenheim* never wander from the Tale.   149-52

Apologies for his inadequacy to Churchill's fame lead to
urging that Steele sustain Mindelheim (1. 165); Garth's
lays honoring Marlborough are praised as having often appeared. Belated erection of Dryden's tomb, with Garth
lying adjacent, brings a final picture of happy security
from the false values of this world, and there reside both
Garth and Marlborough among brave legions, pious priests
"that *Hoadley*'s doctrines taught," and they who inspired
bards and kings, like George. Considerable infusion of
pastoral imagery reflects further compliment to Garth.

15 An EPISTLE TO Mr. *POPE*, ON THE DEATH and ensuing FUNERAL
OF THE Duke of *Marlborough*. *Quae tantae tenuere Morae?*
[ornament] *LONDON*: Printed for F. CLAY, at the *Bible*
without *Temple-Bar*. M.DCC.XXII. (Price Six-Pence.)

2°: A^2 B-C^2; t.p., *bl.*, *3*, 4-12, 12 pp. Ornamental
band and drop-t. on *3*. 263 lines, couplets. BM copy
used. Not in Morgan. Opens:

> While *Britain* mourns, and pays her grateful Tears,
> While deep Distress in ev'ry Face appears.

The poet seeks someone to weep Marlborough's death; as
none but Homer could praise Achilles, so only Pope is
eligible.

> ADDISON could, but ADDISON is gone;
> CONGREVE is old; now You, Sir, stand alone.   8-9

While this long, beautifully printed poem may intend to
honor Pope, it assuredly does not do so, as prosody, unless a rich feast of bathos could be said to do so. The
next line amply illustrates this point: "The Joy, the
Darling you're of every Muse." While such sterile sinking
is exceptional, the whole piece abounds in conventionalisms
and redundancies that awkwardly link the deceased Hero and
his greatest poetic contemporary and the associate of his
Tory enemies. Over a month after the Duke's death Pope
was corresponding with Bishop Atterbury concerning the
funeral and character of Marlborough, but his letters show
no awareness of this anonymous poem. Pope's friendship
and correspondence with the Duchess of Marlborough falls
in their declining years, from 1740-44. Sherburn prints
some eighteen letters from Pope to the Duchess.

Marlborough is pictured as composed in battle, inspiring the troops by word and act, even though the anonymous poet admits to his own want of such elevation. He
falls, like Icarus, or a fluttering bird (11. 68-71).
Hence he urges Pope to praise Marlborough and paint his
image, with Titian's colors, Angelo's design, and Raphael's
grace and ease (11. 76-8); but then proceeds to make the
attempt himself. This is hardly successful, either in the
parade of emotions, "Wildness, Amazement, Horror, and Despair" (1. 121), or in the depiction of battle, "They
pant, they groan, and in their Groans expire" (1. 125).
After a final effort at heroic with the simile of a raging Lion who ravages a sheep-fold, a confusion of imagery
and point which justifies the cry:

O POPE! I faint, I sink beneath the Weight,
Too weak my Fancy, and the Task too great:
And can you, will you yet your Muse restrain?
Indulge her Wishes, give her Neck the Rein:
Then draw the Hero in another Light,
Draw him returning from the Glorious Fight.   128-33

Only the association with Pope's name, and the puffy excesses of Georgian baroque, justify quoting the poem. One
further passage will illustrate both:

But first observe how thro' the yielding Skies
His Arduous Soul like a bright Meteor flies:
The Angels throng their Brother to convey
To Light immortal, and eternal Day.
Glorious He triumphs as He flies along,
With Joy Seraphick, and Celestial Song.
There see — but no, there bound your searching Mind,
There only, POPE, Your Fancy is confin'd.   218-25

The long poem concludes with some description of Marlborough's funeral, which is in prospect, and Pope is urged
to let his muses consecrate the hearse as it moves along
with weeping soldiers and mothers attending.

O POPE, prepare your Heart, your Pen prepare,
The Sad, the Dismal, Mournful Day draws near;
His Praises sing, while the Harmonious Nine,
With solemn Numbers in the Chorus join.   270-3

Pope and his pen seem to have failed to heed this distress-
ful call.

16   A Funeral POEM, Sacred to the MEMORY of the Most Noble
     JOHN CHURCHILL, Duke and Earl of *Marlborough*, Marquess of
     Blandford, and Lord *Churchill of Sandridge* in the County
     of *Hertford*; Baron *Aymouth* in the County of *Berwick* in
     Scotland; Prince of the Holy *Roman* Empire; Captain Gen-
     eral, and General and Commander in Chief of His Majesty's
     Forces; Master General of the Ordnance; Colonel of the
     First Regiment of Guards; one of His Majesty's Most Hon-
     ourable Privy Council; and Knight of the Most Noble Order

of the Garter, &c. Who departed this Life at the *Lodge*
near *Windsor*, Saturday June 16, 1722.

Humbly presented to Sir *Hans Sloan*, Bart. *LONDON*,
Printed for the Author MDCCXXII.

8vo: A^8; half-t., *bl.*, *ii*, t.p., *bl. iv*, 5-14,
drop-t. on 5, 14 pp. 126 lines, couplets. Title framed
in black border, black lines frame running-t. BM copy
used; only one known. Morgan T22. Opens:

> DEATH, that the Fort of Life had long assail'd,
> Maugre all Aids of Physick, has prevail'd.

Marlborough's physicians, Doctors Friend and Gibson, are
named; at their failure to save him, all feared but Marlborough himself. His career is reviewed, skill and courage showing throughout: Turenne, who called him "His
handsome Englishman"; Charles II, who made him a Scottish
peer; James II, whom he deserted for religion and country;
William, who made him Commander in Chief, and entrusted
young Gloucester to his care; and Anne, for her first ten
years, a Harvest of Success. Yet, after Senates honored
him, the Queen was imposed upon by a bad peace, and "Ingratitude a base Return for Love," was his reward. But
now is the time for a "farewell to ev'ry earthly Claim"
(1. 103). The great victories are enumerated, except for
the sinister Blaregnies (Malplaquet), but in reverse order.

> For thee that gain'd the Fight at *Oudenard*,
> That triumph'd in *Ramellia*'s dusty Plain,
> Or trampled o'er thy Foes at *Blenheim* slain,
> That sav'd an Empire when at Ruin's Brink,
> And wou'dst not let the *German* Eagle sink.   108-12

Then, with a farewell to the trophies of Blaregnies and
Scellemberg [*sic*], the poem closes with a comment on retirement such as that of Rome's dictator after his conquests. This is distinctly an official poem, paying tribute, but achieving no poetic value nor original ideas.

517 Welsted, Leonard (1688-1747) wr. 1717

THE GENIUS, AN ODE, Written on Occasion of the Duke of
MARLBOROUGH's *First Apoplexy* AND Reserv'd not to be

publish'd till after his DEATH. WITH A PREFATORY EPISTLE
To Dr. Chamberlen. By Mr. *WELSTED*. *LONDON*: Printed for
BERNARD LINTOT, at the *Cross-Keys* between the *Temple-
Gates*, and sold by J. ROBERTS, at the *Oxford-Arms* in *Warwick-Lane*. 1722.
    2°: $A^2 B^1$; t.p., *bl. iii-iv* To Dr. Chamberlen prose,
1-2, 6 pp. Horn-Luttr. copy only one known. MS '2 *d.*
Novemb.' Two large allegorical decorative bands above
drop-titles, on pp. *iii* and *1*. 10 4-line stanzas, 40
lines. No wmk. J. Nichols, *Select Coll. of Poems*, VII,
1781, p. 222 finds "an evident allusion to the sixth
stanza of Welsted's elegant *Ode to the Duke of Marlborough*, 1717, intituled 'The Genius' in Bishop Hoadley's
A Hasty Prologue to *All for Love* acted at Blenheim House
in the Summer, 1718."
    Marlborough's first stroke came May 28, 1716, with
convalescence at Bath. Apparently it was anticipated that
his demise was near at hand; but a second stroke, on November 10th of the same year, followed by convalescence at
Tunbridge Wells, also failed to terminate the life of the
Duke. The final stage began with paroxysms early in June,
1722, and death ensued on the 16th of that month. No indication of specific connection between Dr. Chamberlen and
Marlborough appears in the Dedication. Welsted mentions
only the friendship between the doctor and himself, and
relates the occasion of the ode, the "Apoplexy and the
Fears that" Marlborough would not long survive. The Ode
opens:

      Awful Hero, MARLBOROUGH, rise:
      Sleepy Charms I come to break.

The Duke's Genius is summoned and instructed to survey his
career. This is done in very feeble verse. Stanza IV, on
Blenheim, illustrates:

      This is *Blenheim*'s crimson Field,
    Wet with Gore, with Slaughter stained!
    Here, retiring Squadrons yeild, [*sic*]
    And a blood-less Wreath is gained!

Marlborough is urged to rest here while life may last, and
then to join "Poets, Prophets, Hero's, Kings" (1. 29).
Foremost among these will be Godolphin his friend. Godolphin had died on September 15, 1712. The poem concludes

with a tribute to Marlborough as "Half an Angel; Man no
more." That Welsted should have thought it worth publishing the poem so long after writing it, can be seen
as evidence of this thinness of inspiration. Dr. Hugh
Chamberlen (1664-1728), Trinity College, Cambridge, wrote
a Latin epithalamium on the marriage of Princess Anne,
1683, attended Atterbury in the Tower, and appeared as
'Psylas' in Garth's *Dispensary*. While his father was
still living, it is presumably the son who is the recipi-
ent of the tribute. That it and the poem are little superior to the lavish tomb with his recumbent marble figure in Westminster Abbey, is only to recognize the ef-
fusiveness of baroque styles in flattery.

The poem was reprinted, with some slight variations
and only nine stanzas, in Theobald's *Miscellany of Poems*,
1732, pp. 67-70.

518 [Berkeley, George, Bishop of Cloyne (1685-1753)]

*BRITAIN Ungrateful. On the Duke of Marlborough's Leaving
England*. By the Author of *Advice to the Tories*. In coll.
Political Merriment: OR, TRUTHS Told to Some TUNE. Pt.
III, 1715, pp. 37-8. Also in Pt. II, 179-80. 32 lines,
couplets. See No. 475 (7) for full title. Morgan R44
gives Berkeley as author of *Advice to the Tories who have
taken the oath*, 1715. No separate pr. Not in Morgan.
Horn copy used. Opens:

>Ingratitude's the growth of *Britain*'s Isle,
>A Vice abhorr'd in every Foreign Soil.

Abroad heroes are honored, bells rung, poets declaim.

>But *here* illustrious Patriots are defam'd,
>And *Marlborough* by the worst of Monsters blam'd;
>Not that fam'd March describ'd in lofty Strains,
>Where *Addison* his noble Muse unreins;   11-14

nor Blenheim, Ramillies, nor all the victories "which made
Anna great" can save Marlborough from spite and wrongs.
He is honored in Belgium, and in Germany, by the Empire.
Even France's ruler loves the man though fearing the gen-
eral.

1722

Such diff'rent Treatment hath the Hero found,
At Home revil'd, abroad with Honours crown'd.

The 1714 version has "abroad WITH PRAISES CROWN'D."
Two poems "On Mr. Bedford's Sentence being Remitted,"
follow as 'By the Same,' that is Berkeley. See DNB on
this courageous, though unfortunate, nonjuror. At the
time of the poem Berkeley was in London, befriended by
Swift and the Tory wits.

19 "On the Duke of Marlborough's going from *England*." This
title in the Index of *Political Merriment* only. In the
text as *A New BALLAD*. To the Tune of the *Ordinance-Board*.
Another poem on Marlborough's exile, printed in *Political
Merriment*, Pt. I, 20-1. (See preceding entry.) 5 8-line
stanzas, 40 lines, ballad. Not in Morgan. Opens:

> Since *Marlborough's* gone,
> Our Joys are all flown.

The Doctor (Sacheverell) has undone us with his physic,
trade has fallen off, the French king is dancing.
Strictly economic with no allusions to Marlborough. The
South-Sea whim has deluded Britons, and Bob (Harley) has
started a debt that will reduce us more than war.

20 [Sewell, George (1690?-1726)]

Verses Written on the MORNING of the Duke of MARLBOROUGH's
FUNERAL. By the Author of those on his GRACE's *Going* into
Germany. Printed for *John Pemberton*, at the *Golden Buck*
in *Fleetstreet*. 1722.
1/2°: 1 c 1, 2 sides, 2 pp., 22 lines, couplets. BM
copy used. Only one known. Not in Morgan. Opens:

> The Sun appears to take a Farewell View
> Of the best Warriour that his Beams e'er knew.

As with Sewell's other poems, a brief poem built
around a single, integrating idea. On page 2, still addressing the Sun, he says:

501

"Gaze on, great Eye. . .survey his Trophies. . .the Blood-dy'd Standard from *Bavaria* torn." Tallard's sword is another trophy. The closing sentiment is that if Marlborough could renew his light as the Sun can "there's not a Region where Tyranny insults" but that would be rescued by Marlborough and that would be "as Britain Free."

Ornamental initials and an Urn filled with fruit decorate the elegy.

521 S., P. M.

LUCTUS Aulae *Westmonasteriensis* in OBITUM Invictissimi *HEROIS* JOHANNIS Ducis *Marlburiensis*, &c. Cui Adjicitur EPITAPHIUM [2 lines Horace] *LONDINI*: Typis *PEARSONI-ANIS*. MDCCXXII.

2°: *A* B^1 B^2; t.p., 1-4, 5 pp. head-titles; drop-t. p. 1, 'Ad Regem.' Sgnd. 'P. M. S.' at end. 91 lines, Latin elegy. Bod. copy used; only one known. Opens:

> Vestros ante pedes, Làcrymarum flumine largo,
> Impareat Officio, se sistit, Maxime *CAESAR*,
> Cansidicum pullata Cohors.

Grief at Westminster Hall, William III, and tributes to Marlborough's courage and great public services occupy most of the poem. Who does not know of his fame? The epitaph promised in the title appears to be missing, but the poem is signed, bottom of page 4, and no catchword appears to indicate any further text. The foundation of Westminster Hall as center for the legal profession might give a clue to the identity of the author. Morgan T725.

522 *On the Death of his Grace*, JOHN, Duke of MARLBOROUGH. Printed in Lediard, III, 410-11. 40 lines, couplets. While Lediard's *Life* did not appear till 1736, it seems appropriate to list this item with the body of the elegies. Opens:

> At Length! GREAT LEADER! does th'indulgent Grave,
> As Generous as the Realms you fought to save,

Finish thy Labours, and Recess afford
To the long Toils of thy PROTECTING SWORD.

Fate and his Genius urge the hero to realize that he has
reached the end of his "Race of Glory" (1. 11). Search
history for comparable heroes, Caesar, and the heroes of
France and Spain, and none surpassing Marlborough can be
found. He is not merely Britain's hero, but all Europe's
as well. What land does not know of *Hochstadt*'s [*sic*]
Plain? The poem concludes with the Picture of his Muse
dropping tears on the dead body.

23   Marriott, Thomas (no dates)

Ode on the *Death* of the *Duke* of [Marlborough]
        Adv. in Percy Dobell Cat. 145, No. 375.   Only ref.
Not in Morgan.

24   THE ORDER OF THE PROCESSION AT THE FUNERAL of His *GRACE*
John Duke of *Marlborough*.   WITH AN Exact LIST of the NAMES
OF All who are to assist at that CEREMONY.   [ornament]
LONDON: Printed for J. ROBERTS at the *Oxford-Arms* in
Warwick-Lane.   n.d.
        2°:   no sigs.; t.p., *bl. iii*, funerary ornament and
drop-t. on *iii*, text *iii*-5, *bl. 6*, 6 pp., prose.
        Divides the procession into twelve units.   A spare
account, naming important persons and units, but giving
none of the color and sad pomp of the actual procession.
Not in Morgan.

25   An Exact REPRESENTATION of the Solemn and Magnificant
Funeral PROCESSION of His Grace *JOHN* late Duke of MARL-
BOROUGH, as it was perform'd on *Thursday* the 9th of Aug-
ust, 1722, with proper References, &c. explaining every
Part of that Pompous *Solemnity*.
        An engraving, reproduced in reduced size, appears
in the ed. of John Gay's *TRIVIA*, p. 6, by W. A. Williams,
London, 1922.   No original has been located of this beau-
tiful depiction, with state coaches in the foreground,

and the hearse in the center; twelve lines of marchers and
riders are shown, going in alternate directions, and in
receding perspective. The depiction of plumes, costumes,
even excited dogs, and the stately horses, all combine to
produce a striking portrayal. Of course *Trivia* preceded
Marlborough's death by six years, but Gay supplies a funerary passage, III, 125-36.

It should be noted that Lediard in his *Life of Marlborough*, 1736, supplies the most detailed and authentic
account of the funeral and interment. First describing
the lying in state at Marlborough House, III, 411-13, he
then proceeds to give in rich detail the costuming and
deployment of all the participants, and their actions,
en route, and at the Chapel of Henry VII, where the Duke
was interred. It has all the authenticity and precision
of an eyewitness account.

526 Harris, Timothy (no dates)

THE POMP of DEATH. A Panegyrical ELEGY On the Illustrious
JOHN DUKE of Marlborough, Prince of the Sacred *Roman* Empire,
&c. [Latin prose motto from Cambden de Phil. Syd.] *LONDON*:
Printed for the Author. MDCXXII.
A^1, B-D^2; t.p., *bl.*, Dedication 'To the Right Honourable, FRANCIS Earl of GODOLPHIN,' sgnd. Timothy Harris,
drop-t. and wood engraving pp. 1, 3, The INTRODUCTION *1-2*,
the ELEGY, pp. *3*-12, 16 pp. Introduction 37 lines; Elegy
272 lines, total 309 lines. Copy at National Library of
Wales used. Only one known. Not in Morgan. Introduction
opens:

> Where is the tuneful Tribe that sang so well
> The Glorious MARLB'ROUGH's Acts before he fell?

The "Sons of Harmony" who were fed by Marlborough's hand
should praise him now he is dead, as they did while he was
living. Harris names no poets, and does not give specific
clues to himself. The poem opens:

> When Fate some mighty Genius has design'd,
> For the Relief and Wonder of Mankind.

Nature devotes herself to creating such a man as Marlbor-

ough. Now he is gone, and Art is too lacking in hearti-
ness to do justice to his memory. Rather "manly sorrow"
must be called upon for sincere accents. Even his political enemies revere his memory; all the world mourns. The
Belgick Lion, the Imperial Eagle join in. He fought for
Europe's freedom, humbling tyrants and unfettering slaves.
"Majestick, Prudent, Gracious, and Refin'd" (1. 102) he
was equally versed in the arts of war and peace. The entire poem is expressed in such general terms, deliverer of
mankind, the "Ornament and Terror of the Age" (1. 98), and
the like. What words can paint him adequately?

> Oh! MARLB'ROUGH! I am raised! I'm all on Fire!
> And if my Strength cou'd answer my Desire,
> In speaking Paint, thy Figure shou'd be seen,
> Like *Jove* thy Grandeur, and like *Mars* thy Mien, }
> And Gods descending shou'd adorn the Scene.   150-4 }

The poet now proceeds to depict Marlborough on the
Danube, at Blenheim, but no new nor authentic details.
Marlborough addresses his forces in words that might well
have made the deceased general shudder.

> Come, Fellow Soldiers, follow me once more,
> And fix the fate of Europe on that Shoar:
> Your Courage only waits from me, the Word,
> And Britain's Glory now commands each Sword.   169-72

We are told that the soldiers are inspired, and like a
swelling ocean bursting its bounds, rush on in an irresistible deluge. This verse is a virtual travesty of heroic
poetry.

> Who now shall Head our Armies in the Field?
> Who wave the Sword? and who shall bear the Shield?
> Who shall our Troops with generous Courage fire,
> And all around him, Martial Rage inspire?   201-4

Marlborough's soul has flown to Heaven, and there armies
of cherubs have welcomed him, while troops of Saints line
the shining way. There he has joyously greeted his children, Bridgwater, Sunderland, his daughters, and Blandford, his son, "first made happy there!" (1. 246). From
Heaven he will reign till the "reviving Day."
The poem concludes with a hope that Brunswick, that

is George I, will be inspired by Marlborough's soul to
lead the British to victories, bringing "Fame and Glory
Home" (1. 270).

This is assuredly a vanity piece, whoever Harris may
be. "Printed for the author," the verse does little credit
to Marlborough or the poet, and the dedication to the only
son of Godolphin is ostensibly only an added bid for notice.

527 Swift, Jonathan (1667-1745)

A SATIRICAL ELEGY On the Death of a late FAMOUS GENERAL.
First pr. in *The Gentleman's Magazine*, xxix, p. 244, May,
1764. Next in Deane Swift ed. of *Works*, VIII, p. 205,
1765, and in Faulkner ed. XIII, p. 333, 1765. 32 lines,
octosyllabic couplets. With notes, Harold Williams, *Poems*,
I, 296-7. Teerink No. 820A. Not in Morgan. Opens:

> His Grace! impossible! what dead!
> Of old age too, and in his bed!

The verses add a final fillip to Swift's campaign of detraction against Marlborough. That England's greatest
satirist, at least in prose, should pursue her greatest
commander even beyond the grave may perhaps be taken as
evidence of the uncompromising qualities of both satire
and Swift. The lack of feeling gives what feeling there
is. Marlborough attained to the age of 70.

> Threescore, I think, is pretty high;
> 'Twas time in conscience he should die.   11-12

That the poem was written following the funeral is apparent:

> Behold his funeral appears,
> Nor widow's sighs, nor orphan's tears,
> Wont at such times each heart to pierce,
> Attend the progress of his herse [*sic*].   17-20

Swift's irony, so powerfully directed against the Great
Man phenomenon, does elevate the lines momentarily toward
the close:

Come hither, all ye empty things,
Ye bubbles rais'd by breath of Kings;
Who float upon the tide of state,
Come hither and behold your fate.
Let pride be taught by this rebuke,
How very mean a thing's a Duke;   25-30

However, the final couplet reduces this expression to
egregious insult.

From all his ill-got honours flung,
Turn'd to that dirt from whence he sprung. 31-2

28   Settle, Elkanah (1648-1724)

THRENODIA BRITANNICA.   A Funeral Oblation TO THE MEMORY
OF THE Most Noble Prince JOHN DUKE OF MARLBOROUGH.   [2
lines Juvenal] By *E. SETTLE*.   *LONDON*: Printed by S.
GILBERT, in *Tart's* Court, *West-Smithfield*, for the AUTHOR,
1722. T.p. framed in black borders and rules; drop-t. on
p. 3; head titles, *THRENODIA BRITANNICUS*, on each page.
    2°: *A*² B-D²; t.p., *bl.*, 3-16, 16 pp. CSmH copy used.
Foxon reports Guildhall copy with 'To the Reader' criti-
cising funeral pieces, and referring to 'Presentation
Books.' A copy at Blenheim Palace. 331 lines, couplets.
Morgan T1027. Opens:

    AS the Great DEAD, by lawful Tenure, claim
    Their Sacred Right to *never-dying* FAME.

    Unlike *Eusebia Triumphans*, 1705, and other earlier
poems, no parallel Latin version appears. The poem alludes to Marlborough's funeral and interment briefly, but
is mainly concerned with his career. Since it is a Settle
production little is to be expected in the way of poetry
or ideas. The copy at Blenheim Palace is bound in black
leather and the armorial decorations, such as Settle used
for presentation copies.
    As the Sacred Nine hymned ancient heroes, so did the
Bards since Edward Third and Henry the Fifth. However,
Marlborough surpasses both in deeds, if not in blood. Alexander and Caesar were ancient heroes, but these men shed
blood, whereas Marlborough serves liberty and frees the

oppressed. Significantly, the march to the Danube and
Blenheim represent the only battles specified.

> Thus in thy *Service* whilst his Sword he drew,
> Say, *ALBION*, with what Wings thy *MARLBRO'* flew:
> Whether thro' Hundred travel'd Leagues marcht o'er,
> A Stride ev'n strecht to the *Danubian Shore*. 44-7

For this he won a coat of arms and Mindelheim. No expressions of grief or loss appear; rather Marlborough's appointment by William III, i.e. Nassau, as champion against
Rome and the Catholic Church, made him comparable to Hannibal (1. 107). His sword surpassed even "the whole
EXCLUSION-BILL." He uplifted the Empire. The poet determines to sing the "Fount" from which his long line of victories sprang, since "Those by more Celebrated *Bards* are
long sung" (1. 93). This leads to a Whiggish praise of
Albion, the Revolution of 1688, and finally of George I;
but with less assured praise for the House of Hanover than
marked the poem of 1705.

The oblation concludes with deploring Marlborough's
being thrown aside, while Envy grins and Malice rails (1.
256). His conquests are prized very cheaply as Honour is
attacked, even though with his last breath William had appointed him as his successor in arms (1. 285). Janus
closes his Temple, and Marlborough's labours cease. Marlborough, no more the invincible, is finally conquered by
death and is laid to rest in the Abbey, Henry VII's "dome."
There he rests amidst the dust of Royalty.

> Lo! Where this Venerable Pile invites
> His *Great* REMAINS to their last Fun'ral Rites:
> Here *MARLBOROUGH* to his long *Requiem* led,
> To Royal Dust his Neigh'bring Pillow spread.
> 198-201

While Settle admits inability to do justice to the
theme of Marlborough's death, it was somewhat superfluous
for him to call attention to that fact.

29   Newcomb, Thomas, A. M. (1682?-1762)

Verses to the Right Honourable the Earl of *CADOGAN*, Occasion'd by the Late FUNERAL OF THE Duke of *Marlborough*.
By THOMAS NEWCOMB, A. M.   Chaplain to his Grace the Duke
of *Richmond*. *Non de ficit Alter*. Virg. LONDON: Printed
for *J. Roberts*, in *Warwick-Lane*. M DCC XXII.
     8vo: A^4 B-D^8 E^4; half-t., *bl.*, t.p., Errata on *iv*,
1-28, 32 pp., ornamental band and drop-t. on p. 1.   495
lines, couplets. Horn copy used. Not in Foxon or Morgan,
and possibly a unique copy. Six errata are listed, but at
least 18 more appear, of which 10 are marked in contemporary brown ink. These are possibly inserted by the author,
or from his manuscript, as they include insertion of the
word 'Sages,' p. 27. Opens:

    Ye living Heroes, who with Grief o'erspread,
    Weep o'er the Relicks of the mighty Dead.

William Cadogan (1675-1726), who had first won Marlborough's notice at Cork and Kinsale, had increasingly won
his confidence, at Blenheim, Ramellies, and particularly
at Oudenard, is here the main theme. His ultimate succession to Marlborough's command, and his intimate knowledge
of the Duke's career, provide the main subject matter.
After lamenting Marlborough's death, Newcomb observes that
"the brave good Man shall meet his rest in Death" (1. 57),
beyond the reach of "Publick Scorn." He notices the sad
pomp of the funeral; he reviews the long succession of
Marlborough's triumphs over death and the Gallic foe,
"Tho' now beneath the Grave's Embraces cold" (1. 168).
Then a succession of heroes welcome Marlborough's ghost
to the "Realms of Death below," — Alexander, the Scipios
and Caesar, Henry V, who is pleased to see how Marlborough
bore French standards from *"Mon's [sic]* Field, and *Hochstet's* bloody Plain" (1. 272). The picture of "the widow'd Fair," Duchess Sarah, forsaken by her dead husband,
turning from grief to exulting in his triumphs finally
leads to the questions as to Marlborough's successor.
That King George has decreed that his sword shall pass to
Earl Cadogan, brings assurance to weeping Britannia that
the future will be secure. The verse of this over-extended
poem is conventional, although in the long course of Marlborough panegyric it provides an interesting comment on

his successor.

> By turns each Hero's Acts delight, and shine,
> Now fir'd with *Marlbro*'s Deeds, and now with thine.
>
> . . . .
>
> While thus by thee led on to such Renown,
> To merit Fame, and guard Britannia's Crown,
> New Heroes rise, instructed how to wield,
> Their dreadful Arms along each hostile Field;
> Our Tears, the Emblems of our kindest Woe,
> Less frequent round thy *Churchil*'s [*sic*] Grave
> shall flow:
> While Heaven's impartial Ways no more we blame,
> His Fate forgot in thy surviving Fame.   478-9;
>   488-95

530 Boyer, Abel (1667-1729)

The HISTORY of *Queen* ANNE. Wherein All the *Civil* and Military Transactions of that MEMORABLE REIGN Are Faithfully *Compiled* from the *Best* AUTHORITIES, and *Impartially Related*. The Whole Intermixed With several Authentic and Remarkable Papers; together with all the *Important Debates* in Parliament; A Compleat List of the most *Eminent Persons* who died in the Course of this Reign; with *Proper Characters* of those who render'd themselves most conspicuous in *Church* and *State*. Illustrated with A Regular Series of all the *Medals* that were struck to commemorate the *Great Events* of this Reign; with a Variety of other *Useful* and *Ornamental Plates*. *By Mr*. A. BOYER. *LONDON*: Printed and Sold by *T. Woodward* at the *Half Moon* between the Two *Temple* Gates, *Fleet-street*; and *C. Davis*, the Corner of *Pater-noster-Row*. MDCCXXXV. (First ed. 1722)
     Large fol.: engraving of Anne; t.p., *bl. i*-xii The *Preface*; 1-722, Main Text; 1-65 The *Appendix*; 15 pp., unmbd., 872 pp. Morgan T136.
     Horn copy used. This handsomely decorated and illustrated work adds to Boyer's *History of King William* III, 3 vols., 1702-3, his *History* of the *Reign* of *Queen Anne* Digested into *Annals*, 11 vols., 1703-13, and The *Political State* of *Great Britain*, 60 vols., 1711-40, for which Boyer

is responsible for 1711-29.

While Boyer was a Huguenot who encountered the contempt of Swift, he became a productive and not unimportant Whig pamphleteer and journalist, especially in Anne's final years and those of Marlborough's decline in favor.

531 May.

An EPISTLE FROM A Half-Pay OFFICER In the *Country*, to his
Friend in *Town*. Occasion'd by the late CONSPIRACY, AND
THE BIRTH of the Young *PRINCESS*. *Summum crede nefas,
Animum praeferre Pudori*. Juv.---*Redeunt Saturnia Regna*.
Virg. [Ornament] *LONDON*: Printed for J. PEELE, at
Locke's *Head* in *Pater-Noster-Row*. M.DCC.XXIII.
     2°: A^2 B-C^2; t.p., *bl*., ornamental band and drop-t.
on *3*, 4-12, 12 pp., 219 lines, couplets. Horn-Luttr. copy
used. MS '5 *d*. May.' Not in Morgan. Opens:

> From Woods and Lawns, serene and hush'd Retreats,
> Inglorious, now disbanded, Warriors Seats,
> In Love unfeign'd, this artless Verse I send,
> To smoky Walls that still detain my Friend.

The poet reluctantly sings, since he is used to pastoral
poetry, of fields and woods, and "smiling Meads and Silver
streaming Floods." But now he is forced to "rough Satire's
Sting" and bolder verse (1. 33). Actually the poem hardly
goes beyond the plaintive note, and in the main follows
pastoral conventions. After a tribute to those who fought
for William "on the fam'd Banks of *Boyne*," he comes to
Marlborough's men who sacrificed their blood "near foaming
Danube's rapid Flood" (1. 61). Then the theme of the Conspiracy is brought in, primarily as something Marlborough's
ghost should be spared hearing,

> With gentlest Art and softning Accents bear
> The hateful, odious Sounds to MARLBRO's Ear.
> O spare his Ghost! Much has the Hero bore
> Of Faction's Spite, whilst on this earthly Shore,
> Let not fresh Tydings, of her Rage, invade
> The peaceful Realms, that claim his mighty Shade;
> Too much 'twould grieve the gen'rous Chief to hear
> His once-own'd Friends, Companions of the War,
> So lost to Honour, and so sunk in Shame,
> As to espouse a vile Pretender's Claim,
> And setting Oaths and sacred Vows aside,
> The Laws of Heav'n and Man alike deride.   70-81

While this is all that relates directly to Marlborough, it
is interesting to see that it is now only his shade and

the fiery loyalty of his widow that provide themes. The
Jesuits, with their craft and venality, are condemned,
and then the poem returns to the quieter rural note.
Blessings for England and the Brunswick line and George's
reign are invoked. Steele is called upon to sing the
King's fame: "How great in War! how mild and good in
Peace!" (1. 209).

> My Soul's on Flames, transported at the Name!
> Where shall I find a Bard to sing his Fame?
> Begin, O STEELE, and strike the tuneful Shell,
> On thy lov'd Monarch's Praise for Ages dwell.   203-6

2   Knapp, Francis (no dates)

Gloria Birtannorum or the *British Worthies*: A Poem. Being an Essay on the Characters of the most Illustrious
Persons in Camp or Cabinet since the Glorious Revolution
to this Present Time. More particularly of this present
Ministry under our own renowned Sovereign King George.
To which is added an Ode on his Majesty's Coronation and
an Elegy on the Death of the Late Glorious Duke of Marlborough. By a Lover of the Present Constitution. London,
Printed by J. Franklin for W. Buttolph, 1723.
    Morgan T623 only ref.

3   Sherburn, William (no dates)

On His Grace the Duke of Marlborough.
One of several poems appended to The Fourth Book of Virgil's Aeneid. Being the entire Episode of the Loves of
Dido and Aeneas. Translated into English Verse. Printed
for J. Pemberton, 1723. Listed in Peter Murray Hill Cat.
34, April 1950, No. 327. Not in Morgan.

534   Smedley, Dean Jonathan (1671-1729?)

An ODE to the *Earl* of *CADOGAN*. By D--n Sm---y.
Pr. in *Misc. Poems, Original and Translated*, By Several
Hands.   Pubd. by Mr. Concanen, London: Pr. for J. Peele,
at Locke's-Head in Pater-Noster-Row, 1724, pp. 164-9.   11
7-line stanzas, 77 lines.   Horn copy used.   Opens:

> Hero! sprung from ancient Blood;
> *Cadogan*, valiant, wise, and good.

Who can sing his praises?   Only Welsted, who is soft as
Ovid and strong as Flaccus, i.e. Horace.   Such virtues as
Cadogan's demand a master.   Marlborough occupies Stanza
III.

> Whether thy Deeds he backward trace,
> With Achievements past to grace
> The num'rous *Ode*, and bring anew
> Fields, with Slaughter stain'd, to view:
>   Part in *Marlbro'* shalt thou claim,
>   Next to *Marlbro'* rise in Fame;
> The Strain resounds with each immortal Name. } 15-21

The lines return to Welsted, urging him to sing Cadogan's
actions and bright future, even at the "Helm of State."
While neither the *Ode* nor the retort upon it seems to have
been printed separately, together they provide an interesting glimpse into the uncertain atmosphere in Marlborough's last years.   While both were printed in 1724, an
allusion at the end of the second poem indicates that
death has not yet found the Duke.   The second poem is
anonymous, witty, and rich in allusions to Swift.   It
is: A LETTER to the AUTHOR; Occasion'd by the foregoing
ODE.   It is printed by Concanen, pp. 170-81, and its 190
lines, octosyllabic couplets, are over twice the length
of the Smedley piece.   It opens:

> Well, *Sm--y*, since thou wilt expose
> Thy self in Verse as well as Prose,   }
> And sieze [*sic*] thy Friends as well as Foes. }

Smedley is urged to use his "gingling, empty, doggerel
Rhyme" on telling what Swift, his fellow dean, is doing,
since he's "always Odd and always New." The satire is
sprightly enough for Swift at his best, as it pictures
him "at Ombre or at Tea," writing pamphlets or plays, riding in the Strand for air, or writing "The nastiest Thing
in cleanest Verse." Smedley is not without justice urged
to abandon heroic verse, and turn to satire.

> Describe thy Bishop, Learn'd and Wise,
> Lab'ring at senseless Niceties,
> Inventing Sins, creating Evil,
> And making new Work for the Devil.   80-3

To Welsted, blooming and young, belong the Barrier and
the Dutch, and praise of Cadogan. Quoting Smedley's *Ode*,
the anonymous poet urges that Welsted, who was therein
urged to sing Cadogan, continue to be the chief panegyrist:

> And, in short, when *Marlbro'* dies,
> And Fate has clos'd those glorious Eyes,
> There's no one Subject in this Land
> Fit the Army to Command,
> But *C*[adoga]*n*, — and for Rhyme.
> Good b'ye smart Poet till next Time.   185-90

It should be noted that Smedley, apparently accepting the
advice, returned to the light Horatian style, and hudibrastic form, in A *Familiar* EPISTLE to the *Earl* of SUNDER-
LAND, which appears next in the Concanen anthology, pp.
182-90, and it too has its *Familiar Answer*, pp. 191-7.
Allusions to Addison, Garth, Philips, Tickell, and Welsted
turn these poems as much to the question of style as to
political issues.

Not in Morgan.

535   d'Anvers, Arthur (no dates)

The FUNERAL, A Poem in Memory of the Late Duke of Marlborough.   By *Arthur d'Anvers*, L.L.B., Chaplain to His
Excellency the Lord *Cartaret*, Lord Lieutenant of *Ireland*.   [8 lines Virgil] *Dublin*: Printed by *Thomas Hume*
at the *Custom-house-Printing-house* in *Essex-street*, 1725.
    2°: A-B^2 C-D^2; t.p., *Preface iii-iv*, 1-12, 16 pp.
523 lines, couplets.   BM copy used.   Not in Morgan.
        Though not remarkable as a poem, this production
does remarkably cap and also appraise the course of Marlborough panegyric, from Blenheim to his death, of course
from the Whig point of view.   Marlborough, the nation's
hero, is remembered not alone for his ten years of unbroken victories, but also as the champion of English
freedom and the freedom of Europe and humanity as well.
His career, launched by William III, is closely identified with the entire Whig program and policy, and Anne's
rejection of him was a disgraceful surrender to French
power.   The Hanoverian cause is strongly supported, with
Steele as one of its leading defenders.   The betrayal of
the loyal and brave Catalans reminds of the Treaty of
Utrecht, and Dunkirk of subsequent issues.   The theme of
Female Reign also casts back on numerous panegyrics and
the attitude toward Queen Anne.   However, the core of
the poem is the relationship between Marlborough's career and Addison as his greatest panegyrist.   No other
tributes are mentioned; the *Campaign* stands as the supreme
tribute, comparable to Homer and Virgil.   Because of these
features it will be useful to quote both Preface and poem
rather extensively.
        In The Preface, after pointing to Bishop Smalridge
as a precedent for writing verse, d'Anvers points out
that he wrote the poem over two years previous, to

> . . . the Memory of the most consummate General,
> any Age has produced: whose Heroick Exploits,
> and uninterrupted Successes abroad, for many
> Years together, not only preserved the Balance
> of *Europe*, but made *Great Britain* the Praise
> and Envy of all Nations.

He also wishes to stir loyalty to King George. Then he
defends the large amount of "Room in the Poem" which he
has given to Addison: "but, as in the Contraste [*sic*]
between him and the Duke of *Marlbro*, the Poet and the
Hero serve actually as Foils, to set off each other," he
insists that the unity of action was maintained.
The poem opens:

> Not Rival Chiefs engag'd in bloody Strife,
> But for the Love of Glory spilling Life.

Not these, nor marches over the Alps, "Not Rivers well'd
with Blood and choak'd with Slain," nor kings and cities
conquered are the subject of his song, but rather the sad
theme of a hero in his hearse. The Man who fought the
Campaigns has died in bed. The most detailed of all descriptions of Marlborough's splendid funeral procession
follows. Mourning drums and trumpets, his war horse, not
wearing rich trappings but arrayed in sober weeds which
sweep the ground; chiefs and soldiers with their arms inverted; too many coaches to relate, and mourners bearing
the pall; these are the subject.

> At length the Corpse with slow Procession's brought,
> In *Henry*'s Chapel to the Royal vau't.
> Lo! here the Hero in his Grave is laid;
> And all his Titles by the Herauld read;
> And the last Honour to his Merit paid.
> And lo! the doleful Herauld breaks his Rod,
> While on the Tomb fresh flowers are strow'd.
> Thus *Marlbro*'s left among the Kings to sleep,
> (Who rather chose to have a crown, than keep).   37-45

1727

56   Cobham, Lord (no dates)

Blenheim, A Poem, written at the University of Oxford in
1727. In *A Collection of Poems by Several Hands*. II, 26.
Harrach, *John Philips*, p. 20. This is Lyttelton's *Bleinheim*. See No. 540. Not in Morgan.

537   Somerville, William (1675-1742)

AN ODE. Humbly Inscrib'd to the Duke of Marlborough, Upon
his Removal from all his Places. Pub. in *Occasional Poems,
Translations, Fables, Tales* &c.·, 1727. Text from Chalmers' *English Poets*, XI, 183-4. Not sep. pr.. 175 lines,
varying rhyme and length. 4 lines Horace. Opens:

> When, in meridian glory bright,
> You shine with more illustrious rays.

In spite of Dr. Johnson's admission that there are some
"beautiful lines" in the poem, it seems strangely lacking
in poetic quality. It suggests at best the scattered frag-
ments of columns and pavements of a classic ruin. Appealing to Pindar, he says that the Theban swan soars on high,
but simple bathos is more apparent. Allusions to Blenheim,
Schellenberg, and Ramillies do not add much toward lifting
the poem. Marlborough is urged to retire to the "gilded
globes and pointed spires" of Blenheim Palace to enjoy security from envy and factious rage. Somerville was a Whig.
The poem might have been written about 1712, as seems true
of the second ode to Marlborough.   Not in Morgan.

538   ODE, Occasion'd by the Duke of Marlborough's Embarking for
Ostend, An. 1712. 2 lines Horace, 158 lines, predominantly couplets, but uneven in length and pattern. Johnson,
again, makes the proper observations. He notes that "in
the second ode, he shows that he knew little of his hero,
when he talks of his private virtues." Chalmers XI, 389-
90. Not in Morgan. The ode opens:

> Ye powers who rule the boundless deep,
> Whose dread commands the winds obey.

After urging winds and waters to become calm as they transport their hero, the poet seeks a parallel. To whom shall
he compare the "mighty wrong" which has led to exile?
Themistocles, or a Roman victim of injustice, might serve.
Even as Marlborough departs in exile, he labors to preserve his country, spurning the "vile, degenerate race."
"How Marlborough fought, how gasping tyrants fell" may be

the theme, but the poet succumbs to the challenge of the vast events. Somerville has presented us with panegyrics without ideas or inspiration, as Johnson remarks.

1728

39 Whaley, John (1710-1745)

Bleinheim A Poem. 1728.
CBEL, II, 332. In *A Collection of Poems*, 1732; *A Collection of Original Poems and Translations*, 1745.
This is Lyttelton's *Bleinheim*. See No. 540.
Not in Morgan.

40 [Lyttelton, George, First Baron Lyttelton (1709-1773)]

BLEINHEIM. [ornamental basket of fruit] *LONDON*: Printed for J. ROBERTS, near the *Oxford-Arms* in *Warwick-Lane*. MDCCXXVIII.
    2°: A^2 B^2 C^1; t.p., *bl. iii-iv* To the Lady *DIANA SPENSER*. In large type with wide ornamental band and initial letter. "Dedication" top p. *iv*; 1-6, 10 pp. Ornamental band and drop-t., p. 1 and ornamental band at end. A handsomely printed, showy production. 167 lines, blank verse. Horn copy used. BM, MH, CtY, *et al*. Morgan T693. Dedication opens:

> *MADAM*, This Paper of Verses is printed by the Commands of an indulgent Governor, whose Partiality to me, may have made him think better of them, than perhaps they deserve.

The author hopes they had same effect on the Duchess of Marlborough and Lady Diana; but whatever the motive her approbation will be of great advantage to her "humble servant." No name is given. The poem opens:

> Parent of Arts, whose skilful Hand first taught
> The tow-ring Pile to rise, and form'd the Plan.

519

The young poet addresses Minerva, whose shield guarded
the hero to whom "*BLEINHEMIA*, Monument to British Fame,"
is raised, and whose wisdom "steered" him. Thalia, Muse
of sylvan, or pastoral poetry, is also called upon, for
she loves "Woodstock's happy Grove," and the rural pipe
and dryads. Although some physical features of the palace are noted, this is not an architectural so much as a
political poem.

> A Trophy of SUCCESS; with Spoils adorn'd
> Of conquer'd Towns, and glorying in the Name
> Of that auspicious Field, where CHURCHILL's Sword
> Vanquish'd the Might of *Gallia*, and chastis'd
> Rebel BAVAR. —— Majestick in its Strength
> Stands the proud Dome, and speaks its great Design.
>
> 23-8

That a grateful nation presented the building in Marlborough's honor, is Whig retort on charges relating to payments and motive. The Empire as Germans (Caesar) is commanded to blush at its ingratitude, since Britain and
Marlborough saved the throne (11. 36-45).
  The muse now roves through the "Palace," as it is
now called. The rich tapestries attract and remind of
the Ister and Granick rivers and the battles fought on
their banks. Marlborough and Alexander, in arms, vie for
fame. Ostensibly Lyttelton did not visit the private
apartments, and absence of reference to the Long Library
or the lofty entrance hall suggests a limited visit, or
that these rooms were yet unfinished or unfurnished. He
passes through "the stately Portals" to the woodlands and
the "Mazy Gloom of this Romantick Wilderness," where the
bower of Rosamonda once stood. This portion is particularly interesting as evidence of the taste of the period,
and Lyttelton's development of Hagley Park, his own estate.
Following an allusion to Spenser, he comes to the great
bridge of Vanbrugh, and the lake.

> But see where flowing with a nobler Stream,
> A limpid Lake of purest Waters rolls
> Beneath the wide-stretch'd Arch, stupendous Work,
> Through which the *Danube* might collected pour
> His spacious Urn! Silent a while, and smooth.
> The current glides, till with an headlong Force,

Broke and disorder'd down the Steep it falls,
In loud Cascades.   74-81

In this restatement of the tradition of the *locus
amoenis*, of the garden of peace, Churchill finds repose
from the "Toils of War and State" (l. 84), while Bleinheim's Dome reminds him of his triumphs. Such repose was
enjoyed by Lucullus, after successful war against Asia,
and Mithridates, who returned to Rome "in magnificent Retirement" to spend the evening of his life. But Marlborough also has a companion, that is his Duchess. In mutual
fineness, they shone like two stars, till "the Cloud of
Night" obscured one. Churchill went first, and a tall
column honors his memory.

          Lo! where tow'ring on the Heighth
     Of yon Aerial Pillar proudly stands
     Thy Image, like a Guardian God, Sublime,
     And awes the Subject Plain.   117-20

His bearing is that which frightened the French at Blenheim. Lyttelton recalls a meaner trophy once erected on
Hochstet's plain, but now, by the rage of malice, leveled
to the ground. But this monument will stand, raised by
the constant love of "her who rais'd this Monument," a
reference certainly more appropriate to the Duchess than
to Queen Anne.

          That shall be the Theme
     Of future Bards in Ages yet unborn,
     Inspir'd with CHAUCER's Fire, who in these Groves
     First tun'd the *British* Harp, and little deem'd
     His humble Dwelling should the Neighbour be
     Of BLEINHEIM, House Superb; to which the Throng
     Of Travellers approaching, shall not pass
     His roof unnoted.   137-44

The poem concludes on the political note, with the hope
that the Palace may escape both Time's destruction and
"factious Envy's more relentless Rage" (l. 155). For
long ages British youth will find inspiration here, "When
Honour calls them to the Field of War." Europe's Freedom
and England's fame will here be supported:

                till other Battels won,
      And Nations sav'd, new Monuments require,
      And other *BLEINHEIMS* shall adorn the Land.   165-7

The Palace housed recruits training for World War II, and
wounded from the precise defence of Europe's freedom that
Lyttelton prophesied. That it also was to be the birth-
place of Marlborough's greatest descendant and biographer,
Sir Winston Churchill, adds depth to a not unworthy poem.
As with many others, Lyttelton, at 19, made his first
poetic effort with the theme of Blenheim. Poetry and
history are fused into a nearly final tribute to the
great Duke who had little respect for poets.
     Reprinted in Dodsley's *Collection*, Vol. II, and in
other collections. Mistakenly attributed to Cobham, John
Whaley, and others.

1729

541   Ralph, James (1705?-1762)

On Blenheim-House.

      Here, glorious *Marlborough*, for thy Wars receive,
      Not as they me it, but as Love can give.

542   Evans, Dr. Abel

On BLENHEIM HOUSE. In J. W. Nichols, *Sel. Coll. of Poems*,
III, 1780, 161. The poem is erroneously ascribed to Pope
by the editor of the Additions to Pope's Works. 16 lines,
couplets. Opens:

      See Sir, here's the grand approach,
      This way is for his Grace's Coach.

A manuscript version, in 18 lines, is reproduced in David
Green's splended *Blenheim Palace*, Country Life Press, 1951,

p. 112. The Index correctly ascribes the lines to Dr.
Evans. This version was transcribed by Thornhill on the
back of one of his sketches at Blenheim. The poem calls
attention to the Bridge, the Clock, the Chimneys and other
features. David Green deplores that Blenheim Palace is
remembered for Evans' epigram on Vanbrugh, and for the
Duchess's quarrels with him as architect, *Blenheim Palace*, 92-112. The concluding lines of the poem might well
be included.

> Thanks friend cry'd I; 'tis very fine,
> But where d'ye sleep! or where d'ye dine!
> I find by all you have been telling
> That 'tis a House, but not a dwelling.

1731

43 Chapman, Richard (*fl.* 1698-1720) Vicar of Cheshunt

New-Year's GIFT: Being *A Seasonable Call to Repentance*,
As Well Upon the Account of some Threat'ning Vices of the
present Age; and as preluding to th'approaching Holy Season. In a POEM, Moral *and* Divine, By *RICHARD CHAPMAN*,
Vicar of *Cheshunt* in *Herefordshire*, and Prebendary of
Chichester. [Isaiah xxvi, 9; Horace, 1 line Latin]
Printed in the Year 1731.
    2°: A²-C, t.p., *bl.*, Preface, *iii-iv*, 1-8, 12 pp.
Drop-t. p. 1. 235 lines, couplets, nmbd. in twenties.
BM copy used. Not in Morgan.
    The Preface refers to the poet's "rural muse" although he has been encouraged to publish. A witty dialogue with a religious cynic leads to the theme of the
poem which is the bringing of the sinner to repentance.
The verse opens:

> Such Desperadoes sure were never known,
> In any Age or Country, as our own.

Although Britannia is blest with the best laws, religion,
and government, Mohocks and lawbreakers abound. This

leads to an account of David's stoic courage and faith in
the face of defeat, and his final overcoming of the Philis-
tines. The importance of the piece lies almost exclusively
in its showing how Chapman has abandoned heroic themes,
except as they provide moral lessons. Perhaps one can
detect personal disappointment at neglect of his tributes
to Marlborough in *Le Feu de Joye* and later. Scriptural
authority is frequently footnoted.

> A *MARLBRO'* or *EUGENE* may hence be taught,
> Under whose Conduct they so bravely fought:
> Not then t'ascribe to their own Force and Skill,
> Th'Events of War, whether they're good or ill;
> But to look upwards, whence all Aids descend,
> Which can to Wars give a successful End.   135-40

This is the only reference to modern heroes.

544   [Bolingbroke, Henry St. John, Viscount (1673-1751)]

The MONUMENTAL INSCRIPTION ON THE COLUMN at *BLENHEIM-HOUSE*
Erected to the IMMORTAL MEMORY Of the late DUKE of MARLBOR-
OUGH.
>   *His noble Name, his Country's Honour grown,*
>   *Was venerably round the Nations known,*
>   *And* BRITAIN's *fairest Light and brightest Glory shone.*
>   ROWE's *Lucan*, Book ix.
LONDON: Printed for W. HINCHLIFFE, at *Dryden's Head*,
under the *Royal-Exchange*. 1731. [Price 6 *d.*]
     2°: *A*² B²; t.p., *bl.*, *3*-8, 8 pp. Drop-t. on p. *3*.
Black band around t.p., and top of *3*; ornament with hive
of bees at end. Wmk. I and star. Prose. Reprinted in
Lediard III, 438-45. Opens:
>   The Castle of BLENHEIM was founded by Queen ANNE,
>   In the Fourth Year of her Reign,
>   In the Year of the Christian *Æra* 1705,
> A Monument design'd to perpetuate the Memory of the
>   signal Victory
>   Obtain'd over the FRENCH and BAVARIANS,
>   Near the Village of BLENHEIM,
>   On the Banks of the DANUBE,
>   By JOHN Duke of MARLBOROUGH.

1731
1732

The total inscription summarizes Marlborough's career,
following his appointment by William to lead the armies of
the Allies against the forces of France and Spain, through
the reign of Queen Anne. The main campaigns and victories
are included, the dates of Blenheim and Ramillies and
Tournay being given in New Style. The style is terse and
matter of fact, viz., "The Battle was bloody: The Event
decisive. The Woods were pierced: The Fortifications
trampled down. The Enemy fled. The Town was taken" (p. 7).
The Inscription concludes:

The ACTS of PARLIAMENT inscribed on this Pillar
Shall stand, as long as the BRITISH Name and Language last,
Illustrious Monuments
Of MARLBOROUGH's Glory
And
Of Britain's Gratitude.

1732

5   *Upon the Duke of Marlborough*;   Occasion'd by seeing his
Picture at Blenheim.
    In a *Miscellany* of Poems Collected and Published by
Mr. Theobald. London,   W. Mears, 1732.

1733

6   [Manning, Francis (*fl.* 1695)]

THE BRITISH HERO; OR THE VISION. A POEM. Sacred to the
Immortal Memory of *JOHN* late Duke of *MARLBOROUGH*, Prince
of the ROMAN EMPIRE &c. He was a Man, take him for all in
all, I ne'er shall look upon his like again. Hamlet.
[ornament] *LONDON*: Printed for FRAN. CLAY at the *Bible*
without *Temple-Bar*; And Sold by J. ROBERTS at the *Oxford-
Arms* in *Warwick-Lane*. MDCCXXXIII.

525

2°: $a-b^2$ A-L^2, t.p., $bl.$, Dedicated to HENRIETTA,
Dutchess of *Marlborough*, Princess of the Sacred *Roman
Empire*, &c. *iii-iv, v-viii* [wide ornamental band] *1*-44,
52 pp. Wide ornamental band with vignette of seated man
writing, ornamental initial, and drop-t. on *1*. 1130 lines
in 6-line stanzas, rhymed aabcbc. Folger copy used.
CSmH, ICN. Morgan T718.
   Dedication opens:

> Madam, The following Stanzas, which were once
> under the Disadvantage of appearing before Your
> Grace in their original Undress for Your private
> Perusal, now beg leave to wait upon You in a
> Form more suitable to the publick Manner. .

The author has had leisure to revise, and it is "almost
a new Structure. . .a Man of War rebuilt." He begs her
Grace's acceptance, in extra large type, and signed elab-
orately, ending in "humble Servant," but with no name.
The Preface, printed entirely in italics, opens: "Any
Attempt to revive the Memory of the Greatest Captain, that
ever *Britain* produced, can surely need no Apology with
Britons." Nothing of "any consequence, at least in the
Poetical Way, has been attempted since his Decease. . ."
Where are such divine artists as perpetuated Alexander
and Jove to be found for Marlborough and Eugene? Must
William IIId, "the Founder of our present happy Establishment," be remembered only in reports of fathers to children? The writer does not doubt that Britain has historians and poets as "bright and transcendant" as did Alexander and Julius Caesar. He is conscious of having little
to boast of in his performance, beyond sketching out some
of the Hero's surprising exploits and interlacing them
with such reflections and characters as seem appropriate
to the purpose. Originally the piece was intended only
for his own amusement, and in making it public his purpose
was to animate "some more elevated Genius."
   Commenting on the stanza, he justified it by the
precedent of "Spencer" and also of Ariosto, Tasso, and
Camoens. He believes there is no fixed rule as to the
number of lines and the rhyme pattern, except that the
stanzas should be uniform throughout. The concluding
paragraph is weighted with an elaborate self-justification

for writing at all, as a harmless expression of his "great
Leisure," which at least is devoid of vice. He reminds
the reader of the Scriptural answer given to those who
accused the woman taken in adultery as "worthy of Remark
and Imitation."
The poem opens:

> What *Europe* owes to *Marlborough*'s Martial Flame,
> His matchless Victories, and immortal Name,
> First of the sacred Maids is Thine to tell.

Again, with the revival theme, we are reminded of the
third Edward and the fifth Henry. Also the theme of party
faction appears, in the second stanza, with the question
as to how gloom could succeed light: "What but a rooted
Hate of *Britain*'s Cause, And Party-Schemes," could explain?
It is thus apparent that political satire as well as panegyric intentions motivate this long poem. As printing,
it is a fine terminal monument. As poetry, it is negli-
gible without being entirely absurd, replete with the kind
of ecclesiastical dullness that resulted from the authorship of so many poetic gestures.
The Muse flies to Blenheim Palace, which Anne had
commanded.

> Was it a Gift, or Debt to Valour due?
> Where modern Hands so well our Eyes beguile,
> We fancy 'tis throughout some *Roman* Pile,
> Or that the *British Jones* the Model drew.   27-30

Something of the appeal of Blenheim is suggested, though
with too much dependence on mere itemizing of features,
"Lawns, Woods, Waters, Glades." With unconscious prophetic
irony, the poem anticipates a time when thousands would
troop through the palace and grounds, forming impressions
of monumental grandeur and privileged wealth, rather than
reading the historical accounts for the indefatigigable
services and patriotic ardor of the Duke in whose honor
the assemblage was created. His column, as "Blenheim's
Pillar, tow'ring to the Sky" (1. 65), is noticed, but not
Vanbrugh's sensational Bridge.
Henrietta died October 24, 1733; hence the poem must
have been published prior to that date. The death of William Godolphin, Second Marquess of Blandford, in 1731,

introduces a sad note; but this is relieved by an extensive recital of Marlborough's career. This begins with
"Shellenberg," then Blenheim.

> Thou *Hochstet*, follow'st close, whose louder Fame
> Bears to remotest Ages *Churchill*'s Name.   151-2

The capture of Tallard and the inevitable Danube drowning
are noticed.

> What Verse, immortal *Addison*, could trace
> Like thine, th'impetuous Ardours of the Chase,
> When his unnumbered Foes the Hero press'd?
> How seiz'd with wild Amaze, and panick Dread,
> When to the *Danube*'s Arm for help they fled,
> Th'inhospitable Flood o'erwhelmed each sinking Guest!
>   163-8

Austria is saved, and Eugenius is described for exploits
in Italy and in securing Germany against the Mahometans.
Marlborough of course dominates the poem, being presented
through the reflections of the foe, i.e. Louis XIV. In
turn he recalls Ramillies, Oudenard, and Malplaquet, and
also Webb's triumph at Winendal. His dreams "of boundless
Rule" have been disturbed, and even the "buskin'd Troop"
in opera no longer honors him; and strangers cautiously
look up at his painted representations by Le Brun, where
in the person of Jove he thunders at whole nations. When
young Despreaux, i.e. Boileau, Corneille and Racine lifted
him to great heights, but now he is fallen, like Phaeton.
His discourse occupies lines 260-430, whereupon a rather
vague "gifted Matron" recites the remainder of the poem,
both consoling and warning the defeated king. She tells
him that Paris was about to be taken, but fortunately was
saved by Faction in England.

A succession of statesmen are noted: Temple, Townshend, Somers, and especially "great Godolphin" consummate
Statesman "steady, faithful, wise" (1. 529). But both he
and Marlborough fell victim to malice, party-broils, and
headlong Faction. Though presented through the eyes of
the enemy, the picture of the Duke is fair and generous.
England is condemned for its treatment of him.

> Fairest of Isles, for Liberty renown'd,
> But changeful as the Waves that gird thee round,

Whom Deeps unfathom'd from the World divide:
What Frenzy prompts thee to transfer thy Trust
From him whose Valour laid thy Foes in Dust.   605-9

Although unnamed, the Duke of Ormond, as "succeeding
Chief" (1. 611), is given limited recognition, but without partisan rancor.

While *Marlborough* o'er her conquering Arms presides,
And wise *Godolphin* all her Councils guides,
No Queen in Story was like *Anna* bright.   629-31

Yet, by feuds at home, Gaul gains abroad. Albion should
blush for "letting brutal Force decide their Fate" (1.
700). The deceived, yet brave Catalans, treacherously
betrayed at Utrecht, are noticed, 11. 707-12. But one
bar to French ambition remains, since "*Sophia*'s son to
Anna's Throne succeeds" (1. 727). Pacific George begins
a reign of distinction, and a new race of kings, the
Hanoverian, points to a brighter future; and Marlborough,
restored to his command, is back. He directs the subduing of the Scots clans, whose leaders "scow'r away" (1.
746). Again leaders receive notice, Halifax, Stanhope,
but they and Marlborough too, have been lost by death.
That Marlborough was appointed by William, emphasizes the
Whig-Protestant note, and France and party enemies are
warned:

Nor think, tho' *Marlborough*, late of *Gaul* the Dread,
Be number'd now among the peaceful Dead,
That HOPE revives, or Danger threats no more. 1109-11

Cobham, formerly Sir Richard Temple, Wade, Argyle and
"Martial George" would conquer as Marlborough did before.
At this observation the light-circled form of the Muse
ascends to the realms of light, and the long poem ends.
The only distinction that could be claimed for this
rather prodigious tribute is its date, as virtually terminating the long line of panegyrics, and its position in
the body of partisan writing in support of the Hanoverian
line and policy. Very little appeared between 1733 and
Sarah's death in 1744, and most of the pieces, before and
after that event, belong to satire. *The British Hero*, for
all its deficiencies as poetry, does summarize Marlborough's career in its relationship to national welfare and

principles of English sponsorship of liberty and freedom.
Furthermore, it establishes the permanent position of the
Battle of Blenheim in that career, the preeminence of Addison as its poet, and Blenheim Palace as the nation's
monument to England's greatest soldier.

547   An ESSAY on FACTION.   [4 lines Rowe's *Ambitious Stepmother*;
8 lines Amhurst's *Conspiracy*]   *LONDON*, Printed for J.
PEELE at *Locke's-Head* in *Amen-Corner* MDCCXXXIII.   (Price
One Shilling.)   No wmk.
      2°: A^2 B-D^2; t.p., *bl.*, 3-16, drop-t. on p. 3, 16
pp. Handsome ornamental band and initial letter, p. 3.
454 lines, couplets. Horn copy used. Not in Morgan. Opens:

> Shall baleful Hate unwearied Vigour use;
> And black Sedition prostitute the Muse:

Though political throughout, this poem makes no very strong
statement.   It supports George II and the House of Brunswick.   Faction is condemned, while religion and Liberty
are upheld, with Justice and Wisdom sustaining them.   Among
names, Walpole's is most prominent.

> Still, *Walpole*, live Superior to thy Foes,
> Still, fly thy own, and seek the World's Repose.
>   212-13

Peace, and the security of Civil Right are Walpole's
chief concern.   Utters an ironic tribute to "glorious
Discord," Faction appearing as a winged monster.   Fog and
mud are hurled at Nassau's statue, but patriot visions see
Tory and Whig in Harmony.   The poem ends with an invocation
to the Brunswick line to preserve freedom to the "Verge of
Time" (1. 453).
      Only one allusion to Marlborough appears, wherein Fac-
tion is told that *"Marlbro*'s Lawrels but increas'd thy
Rage" (1. 146).   Even so, it is clear that in 1733 Marlborough's name and contribution to British peace and the
preservation of freedom are recognized.

48   Chapman, Richard, Vicar of Cheshunt (*fl.* 1695-1720)

An ESSAY on the JUDGMENT of *PARIS*. Most Humbly Inscrib'd
to *His Highness the Prince of Orange*, &c. And Occasion'd
by His Intended Marriage with her Royal Highness the
PRINCESS ROYAL. By the Reverend Mr. R. CHAPMAN, Vicar of
Cheshunt in *Hertfordshire*, and Prebendary of *Chichester*.
[4 lines Horace; 5 lines Eng. verse] *LONDON*: Printed in
the YEAR MCDDXXXIII.
        2°: A only; t.p., *bl.*, *3*-4 An *Essay*; 5-8 The Fable
moraliz'd, and, with the utmost Deference and Submission,
address'd to their ROYAL HIGHNESSES. The Princess Royal,
Princess Amelia, Princess Caroline. 106 lines, couplets,
the Essay 30; the Fable 76. Clark copy used. Opens:

            Once, on a Time, Queen *Hecub*'s [*sic*] Boy
            (Which was the Cause of burning *Troy*).

Paris confronted with Beauty, Wealth, and Wit provides a
flattering parallel to the English princesses. No reference to Marlborough, but the poem since it is by the author
of *Le Feu de Joye*, and a persistent panegyrist of the Duke,
is at least of associative interest. One section, addressed
to the Prince of Orange, welcomes him to England, which was
once "saved by an Orange" (l. 33) harks back to William
IIId, and of course reflects Whig partisanship/

9   Millner, Serjeant John (no dates)

A Compendious JOURNAL of all the MARCHES, Famous BATTLES,
SIEGES, And other most note-worthy, heroical, and ever
memorable ACTIONS of Triumphant ARMIES, Of the ever-
glorious *Confederate High Allies*, In their Late and victorious WAR Against the Powerful Armies of proud and lofty *FRANCE* In and on the *Confines* of *HOLLAND, GERMANY
FLANDERS*, So far as our successful BRITISH TROOPS extended
Conjunction therein. Digested into *Twelve Campaigns*, begun A. D. 1701, and ended 1712. All, but the first and
last, the *Grand Confederate Armies* were under the Conduct
and Command of our Honourable and much Honour-worthy,
ever-renown'd, graceful, and excellent war-like HERO JOHN
DUKE of *MARLBOROUGH*, Prince of the HOLY EMPIRE, &c.

Truly and punctually collected, form'd, compos'd, and written in the Time of said WAR, By *JOHN MILLNER*, Serjeant in the Honourable Royal Regiment of Foot in *Ireland*; Having been therewith during the War an Eyewitness of the most of the following Marches and Actions of the said War, Compleated at *Ghent* on the 31st Day of *December* 1712. LONDON, Printed in the Year MDCCXXXIII.

8VO: A-Z⁸, A⁸; t.p., *bl.*, *iii-iv Preface, v-xiv, Introduction*, 1-364; 8 pp., Subscribers unmbd. Horn-Bridgewater Library copy used. Morgan U353.

550 *The Satirists, a Satire.* Humbly Inscrib'd to his Grace the Duke of *Marlborough*. LONDON, Printed for C. Corbett, at *Addison's Head* over-against St. *Dunstan's Church, Fleetstreet*, and Sold by the Pamphlet-sellers of *Loudon* [*sic*] and *Westminster*. (Price One Shilling.) [Prose motto from Shaftesbury's *Characteristicks*]

2°: A² B-D²; t.p., *ii-iii*, 4-16, 16 pp. Morgan M414 gives 1710?. MH, Folg., TxU, IU. Horn copy used. Foxon: "It was probably written about 1713." The date of actual publication appears to be around 1733. Charles Corbett, the publisher, succeeded his father Thomas Corbett. Even though the father held the business from 1732-52, the son's name appears here. The 1732 date establishes that the poem was not printed prior to that date; but, more important, a 1733 poem of Pope is quoted, 1. 40.

> Shou'd I *P*---'s self here venture to accuse;
> Shou'd I this gross, this shocking Line repeat,
> "Pox'd by her Love and Libel'd by her hate"; 38-40

The line is from *The Imitations of Horace*, Sat II, 84, pub. 1733. 'And' is substituted for 'or' in "or Libel'd for her hate."

A note is prefixed to the poem, p. *ii*: "*N.B.* This Poem was intended to have made it's [*sic*] Appearance much sooner; but through unaccountable unforeseen Accidents the Publication has been retarded." Opens:

> A While to Satire we have seen a Truce---
> The Town now fills, and now expect Abuse.

The poem seems to be dedicated, not to the first Duke of Marlborough, but to one of his successors. Nothing in it suggests either the first Duke, nor his times and career. Pope is again named in 1. 151,

> Nor print more Satires tho' a *Pope* advise;
> Satires that are rank Libels in Disguise.

This is the only naming of a poet, though many appear inscrutably with a single initial. In content the poem is relatively scabrous, and its loose style hardly establishes the author as a fair censor of morals or the purposes of satire. He does consistently insist that abuse is not true satire.

> Ingenious general Satire, I can love,
> While all that's Personal I disapprove.
> The delicate Reproof I blushing feel,
> Mend at each Touch of finely pointed Steel;
> But mangled, grow not Juster or more Wise--
> Inur'd to Censure we at last despise.   229-34

1735

51   Kane, Colonel Richard (1661-1736)

Campaigns of King William and the Duke of Marlborough
Sec. ed., iv, 140, 1747.
Third ed., 1757, with additions as follows:
A SYSTEM OF CAMP-DISCIPLINE, Military Honors, Garrison-Duty, And other REGULATIONS for the LAND FORCES.   Collected by a *Gentleman* of the *Army*, In which are included, Kane's Discipline for a *Battalion* in Action.   With a MAP of the Seat of the War, Lines and Plans of Battles, and above Sixty Military Schemes, finely engraved from the Originals of the most eminent Generals, &c.   To which is added, General *KANE*'s CAMPAIGN of King *WILLIAM* and the DUKE of *MARLBOROUGH*, Improved from the late Earl of *Crauford*'s and Colonel *Dunbar*'s Copies, taken from Gen. Kane's own Writing.   With His Remarks on the several Stratagems

by which every Battle was won or lost, from 1689 to 1712.
The Second Edition. Continued from the Restoration, where
our Standing Army commences, in a Series of Historical
and Chronological Facts of the Military and Naval Transactions of Great Britain; being a concise History (to supply the Scenes of Action in which the General was not engaged) to 1757. By an IMPARTIAL HAND. *LONDON*: Printed
for J. MILLAN, opposite the Admiralty Office. 1757.
(Price Seven Shillings and Six Pence.) *Where may be had*,
MULLER's Mathematicks, Fortification, and Artillery, six
Volumes, Price 1 *l.* 16, vi, 146. Complete System *1*-83.
In this ed. General Kane's *Campaigns* of King William, pp.
20-38 and Marlborough's *Campaigns*, 38-94. Deals principally with Blenheim, Ramellies, and the Siege of Tournay.
A fresh account, with some personal touches, as with Tal-
lard's flight at Blenheim and ". . .I rode thro' them the
next Morning as they lay dead in Rank and File" (p. 61).
　　　Horn copy used. BM, Oregon (second ed.). Morgan T604.

552　*The Grand Accuser the Greatest of all CRIMINALS*. Part I.
LONDON: Printed for *J. Roberts* at the *Oxford Arms* in *Warwick-Lane*, 1735. Price 1 *s.*
　　　8vo: *A*^{8} A2-K; t.p., *bl.*, *3*-80, 80 pp. Drop-t. on *3*
Morgan T721. Apparently Part I all pr. Horn copy used.
　　　The writer professes to have come across a 3 vol.
edition of the *Examiner* at a friend's house in the country.
The pamphlet is devoted to exposing and refuting the attacks of that paper and the *Craftsman* on Marlborough and
Godolphin, Queen Anne's two chief ministers till she turned
against them. Bishop Burnet's *History of his Own Times* is
quoted for an account of the two ministers and their displacement (pp. 7-10). The old charges against Marlborough
are reviewed, with frequent quoting from the *Examiners*.
The *Medley* is cited in opposition to the calumny and what
is later referred to as the "brutal Propensity to Defama-
tion" and the "ungovernable fell Malignity of Temper" of
the *Examiner*. The Sacheverell case is brought in, along
with other events, for its relation to political controversies and their impact on Marlborough's career. The
"Grand Accuser" of the title is the Director of the *Examiner*, as he is called. Identification of Bolingbroke as

this personage, and also as author of the *Conduct of the Allies* and the *Remarks on the Barrier Treaty*, may reflect an unawareness of the large role of Swift in tearing down Marlborough and the Whigs.

1736

553 Lediard, Thomas (1685-1743)

The LIFE of JOHN, *Duke of Marlborough*, Prince of the *Roman* Empire; Illustrated with Maps, Plans of *Battles*, *Sieges*, and *Medals*, And a great Number of *Original Letters* and *Papers* Never before Published. By THOMAS LEDIARD, Gent. [4 lines Addison's *Campaign*] *LONDON*: Printed for *J. Wilcox*, against the New Church in the *Strand*; and *T. Osborne* in Gray's Inn. MDCCXXXVI. 3 vols., 8vo. I, xxx, 1-529; II, 1-574; III, 1-464, Index i-ii. Engraving of Marlborough in periwig and plate armor as frontispiece to Vol. I. Numerous maps and plans of battles, and an Appendix, III, 435-64, which contains several poems and inscriptions, added to similar and related material in the text. In addition to the *Ode* on Marlborough's final sickness, pp. 408-9, and the verses *On the Death*, etc., pp. 410-11, the detailed description of the Funeral pro- cession is followed by three further pieces. These in- clude Amhurst's "Churchill is dead," pp. 435-8, an anony- mous *Poem Occasioned by the Funeral*, pp. 429-33, and a Latin *Epitaphium* by a Gentleman of Perth. The Appendix includes "On Her Majesty's Grant of Woodstock Park," pp. 436-7; Lines on the Gate, 437-8; and on pp. 438-45 the long "Monumental Inscription for the Pillar at Blenheim," No. 544, and, as an acknowledged curiosity, the *Epitaph* by Captain Thomas Johnson on Marlborough's reported death at Antwerp, July 19, 1714, 450-60, No. 473. These re- printings of verse tributes, in addition to the generous extracts from The *Campaign*, I, 335-6 and 435-7 and 10 lines of the anonymous "The Conquering Genius of the Isle Returns," I, 430, are particularly interesting since they are selected by a man who knew Marlborough, who shared in

some of the campaigns, and who wrote the first extended,
full biography. That he was generous in his inclusions,
but still gave only a limited suggestion of the total
output of panegyric is in itself significant. Morgan T656.

554 *On the Duke of* MARLBOROUGH*'s* Sickness. *An* ODE. Printed
as conclusion to Paul Chamberlen's translation of Dumont-
Roussot *Military History of Eugene and Marlborough*, Lon-
don, 1736, p. 620. 9 4-line stanzas, 36 lines. No separate printing known. Also printed in Lediard's *History*,
1736, III, 408-9. Opens:

> Awful HERO: MARLBRO', rise,
> Sleepy Charms I come to break;
> Hither turn thy languid Eyes,
> Lo! thy GENIUS calls, awake!

"*Blenheim*'s Crimson Field" is particularly noticed, the
only action to be named. Patriots, captains, heroes, and
kings welcome Marlborough, and Godolphin stands foremost.
With ravished thoughts, as they are panting for his flight,
"Half an ANGEL, Man no more" (1. 36).

555 Dumont, Baron of Carlescroon, and Mr. Rousset, transl. by
556 Paul Chamberlen.

W
The MILITARY HISTORY Of His Serene Highness Prince *EUGENE*
of *Savoy*, Now Generalissimo of the *Imperial* Army. As also
of His *Grace* the late *Duke* of *MARLBOROUGH*, Prince of the
Roman Empire, And of His *Serene Highness* the Prince of
ORANGE. . . .Written in *French* by M. *Dumont* Baron of *Carlescroon*, and Historiographer to the present *Emperor*, and
Mr. *Rousset*; and now faithfully translated into *English*
by *PAUL CHAMBERLEN*, The Whole embellished. . .all the
Battles and *Sieges*. . . *LONDON* Printed by *W. Rayner*,
and sold by the Booksellers in Town and Country. MDCCXXXVI.
    Large fol.: handsomely ornamented engraving of Eu-
gene, t.p., *bl*., *iii-iv* The *Preface*; Life of Prince Eugene,
1-134; Life of Marlborough, 1-620, Index 22 pp. unmbd.,

that your review must be available to the public by now.

I am doing pretty well, and I have one cat here at the apartment for company - with warm wishes,

Very sincerely,

Eric Hass

1080 Patterson #608
Eugene, Oregon 97401
October sixth.

Dear Henry,

I want to tell you how much I appreciate the good review you wrote on Bob's Marlborough volume. You gave a thorough and fine state-ment of its value to present day scholars, and to scholars of the future. It is my hope that many have already turned to it for all the information that it contains.

It was thoughtful to send this to me &
it appeared in th
Eighteenth C

780 pp.   Horn-Royal Military College copy used.   Prints
On the Duke of Marlborough's Sickness, an Ode, see preceding line.   Morgan T201-202.

Chamberlen makes frequent allusions to Dumont, and
occasionally corrects his figures.   The importance of
this history is considerably in its use of John Campbell's *History*, which is largely a translation of Dumont
and Rousset.   See next item.

557   [Campbell, John (1708-1775)]

The MILITARY HISTORY Of the Late *Prince EUGENE* of *SAVOY*
And of the Late *John* Duke of *MARLBOROUGH*. . .To which is
Added a SUPPLEMENT. . .The Whole illustrated with a Vari-
ety of Copper Plates of *Battles, Sieges, Plans*, &c. care-
fully engraven by CLAUDE DU BOSC. *LONDON*:   Printed by
James Bettenham, for *Claude Du Bosc*, Engraver at the
Golden Head in *Charles-Street, Covent-Garden*.   MDCCXXXVI,
for Vol. I; Vol. II, 1737.

Half-t., engraved portraits, embellished, t.p., *bl.*,
i-viii Prefaces, 1-391; 402 pp., Vol. II, half-t., *bl.*,
t.p., *bl.*, 1-360, 364 pp.   Morgan T180.

Since the title indicates that Du Bosc was main producer, the unnamed John Campbell, as translator, takes
second place.   Certainly it is the splendid engravings
that signalize this work.   The Preface accounts for these:
"as to the Plates, we shall make bold to remind the Reader
that there are eighteen Battle-pieces, all new Designs;
twelve Sieges; and about sixty Plans of various kinds, together with correct Maps of the various Countries, drawn
on the Spot by Able Designers. . ." (p. *iii*).

Horn copy used.   The undeniable splendor of this
work, particularly in the numerous engravings, establishes
it as a monument comparable to the finest panegyrics and,
in its scale, to Blenheim Palace itself.   The folio pages
measure 10 by 16 inches, and the two volumes weigh 15
pounds.   While it is not usual to measure literary, nor
even historical works, by size and weight, this is a convenient and positive way to indicate the massiveness of
this pair of volumes, which are physically comparable to
the famous folio edition of the *Poetical Work of Matthew*

Prior of 1718.

In 1747 the *Military History* was advertised on the final page of the *Memoirs* of Captain Robert Parker, No. 574, where it is described as "A Work proper to be consulted by all Military Persons, especially at this Juncture." However, a note indicates that this is for "but the few remaining Copies," and that the original price was three guineas, in sheets, and that now they are only two guineas, with 12 shillings more bound. A few copies on fine large paper are 2l. 12s 6d in sheets, or 3l. 3s. bound and lettered.

1738

558   Johnson, Dr. Samuel (1709-1784)

LONDON: A Poem, In *Imitation* of the Third SATIRE of *JUVENAL*.   [2 lines Juvenal]   *LONDON*:   Printed for *R. Dodsley*, at *Tully*'s Head in *Pall-Mall*.   MDCCXXXVIII.
    Fol., actually Dodsley pub. 4 folios in 1738, and Falkner an octavo in Dublin.   The poem is included here for two lines:

But thou, should tempting villainy present
All Marlb'rough hoarded, or all Villiers spent.
85-6

The lines do link Dryden's Zimri, the second Duke of Buckingham, and Marlborough, thus emphasizing the latter's role in associating persons and events of the Restoration and age of Queen Anne.   Such linkage is even more apparent in the famous lines of the *Vanity of Human Wishes*, 1749, *q. v.*, where Johnson's attitude toward Marlborough is summarized.   Full bibliographical details are given in the edition of Johnson's *Poems*, ed D. N. Smith and E. L. McAdams, Oxford Pr., 141, pp. 1-23.   Not in Morgan.

1739

559 ESSAY. I. *On NOBILITY. To His Grace the* Duke of SOMER-
SET. II. *On the* ANTIENT *and Modern* STATE of BRITAIN,
and on the present Posture of Affirs in EUROPE. *To his
Grace the* DUKE *of* MARLBOROUGH. [ornament] LONDON:
Printed for T. Cooper, at the *Globe, Pater-noster-row.*
MDCCXXXIX. (Price One Shilling.)
2°: A^2 B-C, D^1; t.p., *bl.*, *7-13*, *bl.*, 16 pp. *Essay
on Nobility,* 72 lines, couplets, drop-t. on *1; Essay on
Britain,* 144 lines, couplets. Drop-t. on *7* has added
phrase, "*and on the* POSTURE *of* AFFAIRS in EUROPE *in the
Years* 1734, *and* 1735." No wmk. Rich ornamental bands
and drop-titles and initial letters. Horn copy used. Not
in Morgan.
Essay on Nobility opens:

Glory by few is rightly understood,
What's truly glorious must be greatly good.

Praises just titles and rewards for noble actions, such
as the Seymours, the Somerset family name. Somerset
(1662-1748) enjoyed both long life and high place at court
till his retirement. At the time of the poem he was living on memories, among them his education at Trinity College, Cambridge. This association is the occasion for
allusions to Spenser, Milton, and Dryden, See, and, of interest for Marlborough panegyric, Charles Johnson, who
there "first indulged his comic vein." Barrow, Sir Isaac
Newton, Tillotson and Clarke are also mentioned, since
Somerset was known as a patron of arts and sciences.
The second poem opens:

Shall *France* triumphant over *Europe* ride,
And spread her Arms extensive as her Pride.

Shall war again be heard,

And *Britain* offer Terms of Peace in vain,
And not a patriot Muse with *Marlb'rough's* Name
Rouse up her Country to assert her Fame?   4-6

The poem, being dedicated to Marlborough's grandson, the
Third Duke, is throughout a tribute to the first duke,
who, in contrast to Alexander, "pull'd a Tyrant down"

539

instead of being one. His championship of Liberty, his
hardihood and courage in campaigning, the association of
increased trade with conquests, and the theme of female
reign in urging the powers to "Learn from a Woman to be
brave and just" (1. 134), all these are restatements of
Whig doctrines. Since Charles Johnson lived till 1748,
it may well be that this is another expression of his
panegyric pen. That Marlborough sustained the Whig policy and military resistance to France is the culminating
theme.

> What was deny'd t'encrease great *William*'s praise
> Was kep'd [*sic*] for *Marlb'rough*'s Arms and *Anna*'s Days.
> 99-100

When, forgetting Agincourt and Cressy, the French monarch
pursued the Austrian Eagle, Marlborough stepped forth to
scourge him with Anna's Thunder. Following this, and the
ensuing peace, France is now raging abroad once more;
Austria again trembles, even though Russia, under a woman
ruler, is advancing against Poland. England and all good
powers are urged to join in the resistance to tyranny.

1740

560   [Newcomb, Thomas (1682?-1762)]

A MISCELLANEOUS COLLECTION OF ORIGINAL POEMS, Consisting
of *Odes*, *Epistles*, *Translations*, &c. Written Chiefly on
Political and *Moral* Subjects. To which are added, Occasional LETTERS and ESSAYS, formerly published in *Defence*
of the present *Government* and *Administration*. *LONDON*,
Printed by J. WILSON, at the *Turk's Head* in *Grecechurch-
street*. MDCCXL. i-vi, 1-388. Verse Dedication to Mr.
*** indicates Whig associations. See 277, though not in
the *Coll*. Not in CBEL. U. Oregon copy used. Not in Morgan.
     The volume contains seven short pieces, from four to
twenty-two lines, all undistinguished but showing the persistence of Marlborough as a theme. Some suggest a date

of writing much earlier, but all are listed here, as
follows:
    1. Written on the morning of the Duke of Marlbor-
ough's funeral, 22 lines.
    2. On the enterment of the Duke of Marlborough
in Westminster-Abbey, 4 lines.
    3. On the Battle of Hockstet. 12 lines.
    4. On the Duke of Marlborough, 6 lines.
    5. On a learned device over the gate at *Blenheim*
-- a lion tearing a cock in pieces. 8 lines.
    6. On the *Salique* law. Written after the battle
of *Hocksted*. 8 lines.
    7. On the statue of the *Duke* of *Marlborough*. 4 lines.

Newcomb fails to attain more than a small measure of
the epigramatic smartness and finish of the type of poem
he attempts here. Perhaps quoting of one will suffice.

> *On the Duke of Marlborough*
>
> When *Marlb'rough* to his Queen each wonder sent
> His sword had wrought upon the *Continent*,
> Where *Gallia*'s legions to his troops gave way,
> Armies, and realms, the triumphs of a day;
> She never ask'd, for vain had been the thought,
> If he still conquer'd --- only, if he fought?

1741

51   November 4

The Year FORTY-ONE. *Carmen Seculare.* [3 lines Cicero]
LONDON: Printed for *J. Robinson* , 1741. (Price One
Shilling).

Ibid. The Second Edition. *LONDON*: Printed for J. HUG-
GONSON, in *Sword-and-Buckler-Court*, on *Ludgate-Hill.*
M.DCC.XLI. (Price One Shilling.)
    2°: A^2-E^2; t.p., (advs. of 8 pieces, all This Day
is published, the last being Fielding's *Apology for the
Life of Mrs. Shamela Andrews*), pub. Nov 4, *ii*, *iii-iv* To

Her GRACE the Dutchess Dowager of MARLBOROUGH, 1-16, 20
pp. Drop-t. p. 1. Rich ornamental and pictorial bands.
No wmk; horizontal chain lines. 300 lines, couplets.
Morgan T734. Horn copy of Sec. Ed. used.

The Dedication associates "immortal *Marlborough*" with
Horace's Carmen Seculare [*sic*], and deplores the current
sad times.

> But alas the times of *Reversing* are come;
> all the Honour which was then won to the *British*
> Arms by that victorious Prince, has since been
> meanly negotiated away; and that State of Inde-
> pendency both at home and abroad, for which the
> generous Labours of his Life were exerted, been
> barter'd for a State of ---- a very different
> Nature.

Marlborough's Duchess is appealed to, to contribute to
resisting haughty France and remedying public mischiefs
in the land. Opens:

> It's finished ---- lo the long PREDICTED Year!
> Lo FORTY ONE's black *Cycle* reappear!

A corrupt world is depicted in which every vice is
rampant, in which private faith is a public jest, and foreign influence empty, while religion is a "mock *Fast-day*"
(1. 10). While only two references to Marlborough appear,
his memory is associated with justice in a law-abiding
society, and a passage on the soldier is pertinent to him.

> The *Soldier* who of old to Toils inur'd,
> Was only in the Field of War endur'd;
> Now, for a very diff'rent End obtain'd,
> In Sloth and Riot is at *Home* maintain'd;
> Dress, Dancing, Drinking, Gaming his Delight,
> His *Conquest* in *Elections* not in *Fight*   35-40

The fine arts, painting, music, sculpture, and architecture, are called in, with logic, as supported against
tyranny. Through wise public rule the public good will
be served:

> Till other *Locks* and *Newtons* shall arise,
> Another *Marlbro'* other *Gauls* chastise.   161-2

542

One line with a reference to a third return of St. John
is extended to fourteen syllables. A Fieldingesque footnote states: "The Reader will pardon the *wonderful* length
of this Line, on account of the *wonderful Intelligence* it
contains." The poem, mildly ironic throughout, concludes
with a vision in which the writer sees a weeping, defeated
Britannia bewailing her fate to Neptune; but a cry for
Liberty is heard and the poet awakes to cry Amen!

62 [Banks, John (1709-1741)]

The HISTORY of *FRANCIS-EUGENE* Prince of *SAVOY*. Knight of
the Golden Fleece, Privy-Counsellor and Prime Minister to
his Imperial Majesty, President of the Aulic Council of
War, Field-Marshall-General and Commander in Chief of all
the Forces of the Emperor, Empire, &c. &c. Containing,
The Military Transactions of above Thirty Campaigns, made
by his *Serene Highness* in *Hungary*, *Italy*, *Germany*, and
the *Low-Countries*. And Interspersed with Memorable *Events*,
during a Course of more than Fifty-Years. The Whole compiled from the best *Authorities*, Printed and Manuscript.
By an ENGLISH OFFICER, Who served under his Highness in
the last War with *France*. [6 lines Addison's *Campaign*]
LONDON: Printed for *James Hodges*, at the *Looking-Glass*
on *London-Bridge*. MDCCXLI.
  12mo: portrait of Eugene, t.p., verso two advs., "In
the Press, and speedily will be Publish'd," The *History of
Marlborough*, and "largely Publish'd," The *History of Czar
Peter the Great*; folding map; 1 2-252, 10 pp. Index,
unmbd., 366 pp. Horn copy used. Not in Morgan.
  The author remains anonymous, but professes to have
been an officer and specifies the use of Rousset's *History*,
among other sources. Prince Eugene lived 1663-1735. In a
note on p. 164, the author indicates the use of a 5 volume
History of Eugene in French, and promises to insert another
account of Blenheim in his history of Marlborough.

563   [Banks, John (1709-1741)]

ℕ   The HISTORY of *JOHN Duke* of MARLBOROUGH. Prince of *Min-delheim*, Captain-General and Commander in Chief of the
Armies of Her *Britannick* Majesty and the States of the
United Provinces, Knight of the Most Noble Order of the
Garter, Master of the Ordnance, &c, *Including* A more ex-
act, impartial, and mathodical [*sic*] Narrative of the late
War upon the *Danube*, the *Rhine*, and in the *Netherlands*,
than as [*sic*] ever yet appeared. Compiled from Authentick
Journals, without Regard to any Former Attempt of the same
Nature. By the Author of *the Hist. of Prince Eugene*. [5
lines of Dryden's King Arthur] *LONDON*: Printed for *James
Hodges*, at the *Looking-Glass* over-against *St. Magnus*
Church, *London-Bridge*. M.DCC.XLI.
    12mo: engraved portrait of Marlborough, *bl. i-ii*,
t.p., *bl. iv, v-vi* Ded. To His Grace the Duke of *Marlborough 1* 2-347, 9 pp. Index unmbd., 362 pp. Horn copy
used, "The Third Edition, Corrected," 1755. Sec. ed.,
both 8vo, Morgan T722.
    Loyal to Marlborough but adds little to Lediard
(1736). Banks rejects Mrs. Manley and the *New Atlantis*,
without identifying her as author, as having been written
"under the Direction of a Party in Opposition to the Duke
of *Marlborough*, at a Time when no Artifices were neglected
to blacken his *moral*, as well at [*sic*] his *martial* and
political character" (p. 3).

1742

564   Marlborough, Sarah, Duchess Dowager (1660-1744)

ℕ   [Hooke, Nathaniel, the Younger (d. 1763) as compiler]

An ACCOUNT of the CONDUCT of the Dowager Duchess of MARL-
BOROUGH, From her first coming to Court, To the Year 1710.
In a LETTER from Herself to MY LORD —— *LONDON*: Printed
by James Bettenham, For GEORGE HAWKINS, at *Milton*'s *Head*,
between the two *Temple-Gates*. MDCCXLII.

8vo: t.p., *bl.*, 3-316, 316 pp. Morgan T547. Horn copy used.

Although published only two years prior to her death, the *Conduct* is largely based on writings and letters in the Duchess's possession. While she can be roused to characteristic fire and spirit at times, for example at thoughts of the attacks of Swift and Prior in dragging down her heroic Duke, the account is a genuinely valuable historical summary, with much color and authenticity to recommend it. Sarah mentions two earlier efforts, an unpublished account of her treatment by Queen Anne in her dismissal from office. This she was persuaded by a person "whom I thought my friend," not to publish. The second was an appraisal of the artifices of Oxford and Mrs. Masham. In this, which was not intended to be published till after her death, she acknolwedges the assistance of a friend. Now that, as she writes, "I am nearing my end. . .I am desirous, under the little capacity which age and infirmities have left me. ." to leave the name which she bears secure against the folly and injustice of false interpretation.

The *Conduct* is reprinted, edited and with an introduction by William King, London, George Routledge, 1930. Included in the volume are *The Opinions of Sarah Duchess-Dowager of Marlborough*, first printed in 1838, pp. 227-69, and another section of Opinions, originally set down in 1737.

65 THE SARAH-AD: OR, A FLIGHT for FAME. A BURLESQUE POEM IN Three *CANTO*'s, IN HUDIBRASTIC VERSE. FOUNDED ON *An Account* of the *Conduct* of the Dowager Du---ss of *M----gh*, from her first coming to Court, to the Year 1710. In a Letter from herself to my Lord -----. Proper to be bound up therewith [6 lines Butler, 'Two Trumpets she does sound at once,' etc.] *LONDON*: Printed for T. COOPER, at the *Globe* in *Pater-Noster-Row*. 1742. [Price Six-pence]

8°: A-D^8; t.p., *bl.*, *3*, 4-32, 32 pp. 566 lines, hudibrastics. Ornamental band and drop-t. for Canto I. MH copy used. Opens:

Stiff as I am, worn out with Age,
With Gaming, Politicks and Rage.

The poem is adequately treated in Richmond P. Bond, *English Burlesque Poetry*, 1700-1750, Harvard Pr., 1932, No. 177, pp. 411-12. It lacks distinction, as Bond emphasizes; but the emphasis is less satire on the Marlboroughs than on Duchess Sarah's eagerness to seek fame by writing the work on which it is based, that is her *Account of the Conduct*, etc., No. 564 above. The three cantos correspond to the three parts of *The Conduct*. In both she addresses an anonymous "My Lord ---," and also speaks of her aged condition. Canto I covers the period from her first friendship with Princess Anne to the death of William III. Canto II, which Bond correctly describes as being the cleverest part, describes the court as the Crown Inn. Here Anne is at the Bar, while Sarah conducts the operation of the household. As she says, "No Ostler, Porter, Groom, or Chambermaid" could come or go without her authority. Two Clubs, Whig and Tory, contend for preference in the dining-room above. Bishop *Sh*[ar]*p* appears, he having preached at Queen Anne's coronation. The Tories cry up the Church, to win Anne's support, while Sarah responds. The names of Morley and Freeman enter as evidence of close friendship; but this is soon marred by a quarrel, particularly over Mash (Abigail Masham) whom Sarah herself introduced at court. Canto III shows Mash and Harley conspiring against Sarah. Lying papers are spread widely against her. Particular episodes appear such as Anne's offer of a gift to Henrietta, which Sarah cuts in half, and the allegations of her selling places, which of course she denies. With this and a reiteration of the "Flight for Fame" the poem closes, though with an ending no more abrupt than that of *The Conduct*.

While it was no particular distinction to be the subject of a poem analogous to *The Dunciad*, it is interesting that here again the Marlborough do find a position in every mode and facet of satire. Here also is one of the few poems to have received more than passing attention.

566 Aquila pseud.

The Old Wife's Tale: or, *E-----d's* Wish. A Satire. Humbly Inscrib'd to her Grace the Duchess Dowager of M----. By Aquila. *London*, Printed for *T. Cooper*, 1742.
    2°: 8 pp. Maggs Cat. 536 (1930).

567 Her Grace of *MARLBOROUGH*'s *Party-Gibberish Explained*, and
the *True Sons* of the *Church Vindicated*. - By an *Honourable Hand*. - *LONDON*:   Printed for *T. Cooper* at the *Globe*
in Pater-noster Row, MDCCXLII
        8vo: A^8 B-D, E^4; t.p., *bl*., 5-36. Drop-t. on p. 5.
Prose attack.   Horn copy used.   Morgan T429.
        Aside from opening sneer and one other interpolated
reference, less concerned with the Duchess than with Tory
attitudes on non-resistance and passive obedience.   In
view of the fact that 34 of the total 36 pages are quoted
from Roger North, younger brother of the Lord-Keeper, in
his *Examen* of Dr. White Kennet's complete history, the
pamphlet might be assigned to his authorship.   The extract
deals with the reign of Charles II.   The pamphlet opens:

> It could indeed be reasonably expected,
> that a fine Lady who owns her *having never read
> nor employed her time in any thing but playing at
> cards*, in the early part of her life, should throw
> away any of that precious time afterwards. . .on
> the meaning of *Party-Gibberish*.

568 April

Fielding, Henry (1707-1754)

A Full VINDICATION of the Dutchess Dowager of MARLBOROUGH:
both with Regard to the Account lately Published by HER
GRACE, and to Her Character in general; Against the *base*
and *malicious* Invectives contained in a late *scurrilous*
Pamphlet, entitled REMARKS on the Account, &c. ──── In a
Letter to the Noble AUTHOR of those *Remarks*.   ── *LONDON*:
Printed for J. ROBERTS, in *Warwick-Lane*.   M.DCC.XLII.
        Half-t., *bl*., t.p., *bl*., 40 pp.   Prose.   Morgan T420.
        Though first published as by Fielding in *Works*, Hen-
ley ed., N. Y., 1903, XV, 5-34, this piece is now fully
accepted as his.   Aside from other interest, it is striking as associating three of the Eighteenth Century's
greatest men, Marlborough, Fielding, and Dr. Johnson, for
Fielding is replying to an anonymous writer, who was actually Johnson.   Writing for Cave's *Gentleman's Magazine*,

Johnson published in four issues, from March to June,
1742, his longest piece relative to the Marlboroughs.
While his authorship of all but the first number has
been challenged, certainly the doctrine of scepticism
about greatness and urging of caution in writing history
and biography is Johnson's. Actually Fielding, in the
Champion, 1739-41, and in the short piece "Of True Greatness," 1741, was not far from the scepticism of Swift and
Johnson, not to speak of *Shamela*, 1741, and *Joseph Andrews*,
which preceded the *Vindication* by only a month. In all
these Fielding anticipates Johnson's most memorable comment in the *Vanity of Human Wishes*, *q.v.*, 1749, No. 576.

The Duchess as a champion of English liberties is
strongly represented. That she is rich he cannot deny;
but

> the influence of power, which her grace from her
> great fortune enjoys, hath been constantly ex-
> erted in defence of the liberties of her country
> against the highest, most powerful, and most in-
> solent invaders of it.

569 [Ralph, James (1705?-1762)]

THE *Other Side of the* QUESTION: OR, AN ATTEMPT To Rescue
the CHARACTERS Of the Two Royal Sisters Q. *Mary* and Q.
Anne, Out of the Hands of the D - - - s D - - - - of
- - - - - - - IN WHICH All the REMARKABLES in her Grace's late
Account are stated in their full Strength, and as fully
answer'd; the Conduct of Several Noble Persons justify'd;
and all the necessary Lights are thrown on our COURT-
HISTORY from the Revolution, to the Change in the Ministry
in 1710. In a LETTER to her GRACE. By a WOMAN of QUALITY.
LONDON: Printed for T. COOPER, at the *Globe* in *Pater-
Noster-Row*. 1742
    8°: *iv* 467. Morgan T951. Horn copy used.
    Commonly regarded as one of the most severe attacks
on the Duchess's book, No. 564, this ambitious work leaves
open the question as to why this obscure hack, who came to
England with Benjamin Franklin, turned to Tory political
writing. Presumably he was no more than one of the hired
scribblers, so often denounced. He simply follows through

the Sarah-Hooke account, often quoting strings of letters
entire as well as long extracts. Beyond asserting out of
hand that the Marlborough family were guilty of intrigues
and ambition, Ralph has no original material. That he may
have come under Swift's malign influence may be suggested.
At the close he quotes entire Swift's *Bill of Roman Gratitude*, No. 307, of November 1710, ascribing it "to one of
the greatest Wits that ever did Honour to Human Nature."
Ralph employs much irony, though hardly with Swiftian edge.

<u>1743</u>

70   [Hill, Aaron (1685-1750)]

THE FANCIAD. AN HEROIC POEM. In SIX CANTOS. To His
GRACE the Duke of *MARLBOROUGH* ON THE TURN OF His GENIUS
to ARMS. *Up, Sword: and know thou a more proper Time.*
HAMLET. *LONDON*: Printed for J. OSBORN, at the *Golden-
Ball* in *Pater-noster Row*. M.DCC.XLIII.
     8vo; A^8 B-E^8; t.p., *bl.*, *i-viii* The *Preface*; 6 pp.
unmbd. Contents of each Canto; 1-54, *2 bl.*, 72 pp. Running titles for Preface and text. Cantos numbered separately; total 891 lines, couplets. Lines are numbered.
Horn copy used, sewn. Note to Canto I in Blenheim Library
suggests the Dedication to Charles Spencer, born 1706, as
son of Anne Churchill and the Earl of Sunderland, a compliment to the Sunderland Library, which was one of the
glories of Blenheim Palace. This *-iad* poem is not listed
by R. P. Bond in his article "-IAD: Progeny of the
Dunciad," PMLA, XLIV (1929) 100-5, nor in his fine *English
Burlesque Poetry* 1700-1750. Since it is very turgid stuff,
as blank verse and in its content, aside from its pretentious printing with handsome ornamental bands for each canto,
the *Fanciad*'s claim to notice is primarily negative. It
is a masterpiece of bathos, and it shows the persistence
of languidly loyal interest in Marlborough in the year
prior to the demise of his duchess, and it shows a poetic
decline in the work of a friend of Samuel Richardson, the
novelist who showed how sentiment could be turned to the

purposes of true genius.

The Preface tells of encounter with a person who had been misled into the notion that Marlborough did not win his battles, but delegated leadership to others! Soon after, in 1735, the poet conferred with a great general, presumably Cadogan, and fully confirmed Marlborough's genius as a commander.

Canto I, the most concrete, has an interesting passage on the Third Duke of Marlborough, on his Library, and tributes to its greatness. While he hardly establishes the genre of "library" poem, he calls it a "learn'd Collection," and he pictures Marlborough in the candlelit room examining ponderous volumes:

> While, here and there, he stopp'd; as Doubts engage:
> Eas'd a try'd Shelf; and turn'd th'examined Page.
> Bent on a Theme that all his Ardour claim'd,
> His Grandsire's Glory, and his Country fam'd!
> While suppliant *France* he view'd, and victim *Spain*,
> Prostrate adorners of a female Reign.   57-62

His father appears in a vision, and urges him to leave his books and create new Blenheims. None of the books identified.

After this beginning the poem subsides into pallid allegory. Fury, the Force of Faction, and Calumny appear, with the yowling of dogs and demons in a "War of Tongues." In Canto III the Chariot of Fancy, drawn by incredible horses whose very breath is a perfume, arrives to contemplate the emergence of England's Genius, a Spectre, from beneath the sea. She has slept there, but now rises, and with her shadow which reaches across the Atlantic to America, calms the Fury. All this is a recognition of England's need of sea power. In Canto IV is shown how commerce is related to war as the Genius affirms the superior virtues of soldiery of the past, not mercenaries, but fiery Britishers eager to fight for liberty and England's fame. But now it is different, as luxury has weakened resolve, and in Canto V the Genius sighs in fearful anticipation of such doom as destroyed Greece, Carthage, and Rome. France is now strong again. Not gold, nor Trade, a "Fair Dalilah" can save England. Rather Trade, War, Power, and Liberty in a balance will save England, centering on "A *Skill'd Militia*! and a *Guardian Fleet*!" The Genius wipes three

tears and sinks into clouds and sea, as, with a truly
Dunciadic note:

Happy *Content* saw Fame's close Curtain drawn:
And Three stretch'd Nations shar'd one pangless Yawn.
V, 143-4

The last Canto VI shows the disappearance of Fancy,
and presents the Third Duke of Marlborough, cut off from
glory for the time being since he was born an "Age too
late." He is urged to suspend military warmth, and the
embroilments of faction in a "lamented Nation" are again
depicted. The poem concludes with a picture of Marlborough's Duchess Dowager sustaining his fame and memory, in
brass and marble:

Hers, to whose Choice his Love-drawn Heart inclin'd:
The soft, *sole* CONQU'ROR, He was born to find!
VI, 131-2

She is urged to seek out some poet, whose lines will out-
last monumental tributes. "But *Who*? -- What Strength such
Atlas Weight can bear?" (VI, 145). He can only hope her
happy judgment may find such a man.
Not in Morgan.

1744

71 Marlborough, Sarah, Dowager Duchess (1660-1744)

A TRUE COPY of the *LAST WILL* and TESTAMENT Of Her Grace
SARAH, late Duchess Dowager of MARLBOROUGH: With the
CODICIL Thereto Annexed. *LONDON*: Printed for M. COOPER,
at the *Globe* in *Pater-noster-Row*. 1744. (Price 1 *s* 6 *d*.)
8vo: T.p., *bl. 1*, drop-t. 2-94, 94 pp. Not in Morgan.
Duchess Sarah died at Marlborough House, on October
19th, 1744. No elegies appeared to acknowledge the event.
The opening sentence of the will is dated August 11, 1744.
Her request that she and her husband be buried together
at Blenheim was complied with shortly after her decease.
The only passage of literary interest is that in the

Codicil directing the two executors to permit Richard
Glover and David Mallet to have access to all her letters
and papers toward their project of writing a two-volume
life of Marlborough. She stipulated that the Earl of Ches-
terfield should direct the work and approve of it prior to
its being printed. Most significant, perhaps, for this
volume, is the statement: "And I desire that no part of
the said History may be in Verse, and that it may not begin
in the usual form of writing Histories, but only from the
Revolution." She doubtless remembered the Duke's irrita-
tion at satires and his indifference to panegyrics.

The will was proved on November 2d, 1744, with the
two original executors signing, that is, Hugh Earl of
Marchmont and Beversham Filmer, along with Thomas Lord
Bishop of Oxford and James Stephens.

572   Bishop, Matthew (*fl.* 1701-11)

The *Life* and *Adventures* of *MATTHEW BISHOP* of DEDDINGTON
in *Oxford-shire*. Containing an ACCOUNT of several Actions
by Sea, Battles and Sieges by Land, in which he was present
from 1701 to 1711, interspersed with many curious Incidents,
entertaining Conversations and judicious Reflections.
Written by *Himself*. LONDON: Printed for *J. Brindley* in
New Bond-street; *G. Hawkins* in *Fleet-Street*; *R. Dodsley* in
Pall-Mall; and *J. Millan* opposite to the *Admiralty-Office*.
1744.

8vo: T.p., *bl.*, *iii* Ded. to Earl of Stair, *bl.*, *v-
viii* The Publisher to the Reader; 1-284, Errata p. 284,
296 pp. Contents bd. between 278-9. Horn copy used.

One of the liveliest accounts, written by an uncom-
plicated man who sought adventures through love of Queen
and country. By enlisting in the Navy, he was present at
the breaking of the boom at Vigo and the capture of Gibraltar, in the squadron of Sir Cloudsley Shovel. He exhibits great courage in battle, but ample details are
given to make the account convincing. Being of "a roving
nature" and having heard of Marlborough's action on the
Danube, "I promised to myself, in God's Name, that if nothing prevented I would go and assist the Duke" (p. 80). He
leaves the sea service, marries a good wife, visits his

mother and home, and then enlists in the army, under Sir
Richard Temple. The picaresque character of the age is
reflected in his being taken prisoner by the French, making his escape, and falling in with the command of General Webb. Although he missed participation in the Battle
of Ramillies, this being 1706, he still was present at
Oudenard and Malplaquet. The account never wants for excitement and spirit, not excluding 22 lines of couplet
verse to his wife on leaving her for military services:

> My Dear! it grieves my Soul to part from you,
> Though this in Honour I'm compelled to do. p. 119

Service at the sieges of Ghent and Lisle, and with Webb at
Winendale bring the account up to 1711 when, feeling that
"the Neck of the War was broke" Bishop pays a fine tribute
to Marlborough's leadership, but decides, on learning of
the Duke's resigning his commands, to leave the service
and enlist for an expedition to Canada. Following observations and adventure in New England, he returns with his
regiment only to find his wife married to another man,
and about to bear a child. The shock of his return and
the protracted pangs of childbirth bring on her death,
not to speak of a verse epitaph in Bishop's rather spare
style.

Sir Winston Churchill cites Bishop no less than nine
times, and remarks that "his moving story is too little
known," IV, 117. Actually much of the racy detail of the
campaigns comes from Bishop and he is quoted, along with
General Kane and others on the consternation among military men at Marlborough's dismissal. Churchill quotes
four of the twelve lines of verse which Bishop wrote on
the breaking up of his regiment in 1713. Certainly they
should have a place in a bibliography which includes Marlborough panegyrics, as well as along with all verse concerned with the soldier and the poet and scholar. As with
Bishop's other verses, they have no title, and though
Churchill says they are "often quoted" they seem not to
have been published elsewhere.

> God and a Soldier Men alike adore,
> When at the Brink of Danger, not before;
> The Danger past, alike are both required,
> God is forgot, and the brave Soldier slighted. 1-4

Bishop points out that learning and arts gain honor "the older grown," but soldiers are slighted after the conquests are forgotten.

> Because grown old, must Valour be neglected,
> And all past Services be quite rejected?   9-10

The editors of Bishop's *Life and Adventures* call attention to his simple honesty and devotion to the truth, and ask allowances for his "Want of Method or Diction," but modern readers will find him worthy of comparison to Defoe. Since his writing has the artless air of truth that makes it worthy of comparison to Defoe, it is perhaps fortunate that the creator of Robinson Crusoe was safely in his grave in Bunhill Fields, or one more work might have been ascribed to that worthy author of fictitious narratives.
Morgan U38.

1746

573   Pope, Alexander (1688-1744)

Verses upon the (Duchess of Marlborough) 1746. Fol. Also Verses upon the Late D---ss of M----- By Mr. P---, 1746.
8vo, 36 lines, couplets. Opens:

> But what are these to great Atossa's mind?
> Scarce once herself, by turns all Womankind!

The passage, which was finally inserted in the *Moral Essays,* II, 115-50, did not appear in the 1735 edition, but Pope had inserted it in an edition prepared and published just prior to his death. Also they appear, anonymously, in the *Harleian Miscellany*, ed. William Oldys, Vols. I-II, 1744. Much has been written, particularly showing what is evident, that the lines do not fit Sarah. That they were written on the Duchess of Buckingham was asserted by Bishop Warburton, while Walpole reversed the roles of the two ladies in his version. The rather lively correspondence, exchange of gifts and visits, and other contacts

between the great poet and the eminent widow of Marlborough is to be found recorded in the edition of Pope's
Letters, Vol. IV, ed. by George Sherburn.

Bateson's summary of the whole matter appears in the
Twickenham ed. III, Pr. 2, App. A. He concludes that at
about 1733 Pope wrote two verse characters, the 'Orsini'
and the 'Atossa.' The first satirized the Duchess of
Marlborough and the second the Duchess of Buckinghamshire.
On becoming friendly with the Duchess of Marlborough in
1739, he scrapped the Orsini character, keeping only a few
lines for the portrait of Atossa. Nevertheless, this portrait was persistently associated with Sarah in the gos-
sip of the century and persisted down to modern scholarship. V. A. Dearing gives at least four versions of the
finding of the verses in a copy of Pope's works given to
the Prince of Wales in 1738. *Harv. Lib. Bull.*, IV, 1950,
320-36.

The whole story involves the alleged acceptance by
Pope of £1000 from the Duchess to withhold the satirical
portrait. This gift was more probably to avoid his publishing the defamatory picture of Marlborough which appears in the *Essay on Man*, 291-308. See *Twick. Ed.*, *Minor
Poems*, VI, 358-9, ed. Norman Ault and John Butt.

Since most of the published matter in the Pope-Marl-
borough relationship is posthumous, it seems desirable to
review the whole matter at this one point. That the
Atossa portrait, though not designed for Sarah, is a
brilliant example of Popean satire, cannot be denied. On
the other hand, the suppressed lines which appear to be on
the Duke seem hardly to justify his statement to Spence,
that the character was "one of the best I had ever written."
See Spence, *Anecdotes*, p. 43. They do reflect the, not always admirable, attitude of Pope and Swift toward greatness,
particularly military achievement, but they embody scandalous implications - "some Vices were too high and none too
low" - and a personal allusion to "an offspring lost,"
which are dubious as satire. The evidences of Marlborough's wealth, particularly "the trophy'd Arches," which
suggest Blenheim Palace, and the ironic comments on the
blending of guilt and greatness, and of glory and shame,
do at least suggest the aged, ailing commander as seen
through malignant eyes. One passage seems leveled less
at the dead Marlborough than at his still living Duchess:

> Go then indulge thy age in Wealth and ease
> Stretch'd on the spoils of plunder'd palaces
> Alas what *wealth*, which no one act of fame
> E'er taught to shine, or sanctified from shame
> Alas what *ease* those furies of the life
> Ambition Av'rice and th'imperious Wife.   11-16

This passage, and the total character, are generalized in the *Essay on Man*. A scattering of passing allusions to the Marlboroughs appear in various squibs throughout Pope's latter career. These are indexed, and only those in the *Verses* on Blackmore, as "England's Arch-Poet," have much pertinence, and these in view of Blackmore's assumed role as one of the Whig champions of the Duke. See *Minor Poems*, *op. cit.*, 290-1.

1747

574   Parker, Captain Robert (*fl.* 1683-1718)

MEMOIRS Of the most *Remarkable Military Transactions* From the Year 1683, to 1718. Containing A More PARTICULAR AC-COUNT, than any ever yet published, of the several BATTLES, SIEGES, &c. In *Ireland* and *Flanders*, During the REIGNS of K. WILLIAM and Q. ANNE. By Captain ROBERT PARKER, late of the *Royal Regiment* of Foot in *Ireland*, who was an Eye-witness to most of them. Published by his SON. *LONDON*: Printed for *S. Austen*, in *Newgate-Street*; and *W. Frederick*, Bookseller in *Bath*, M.DCC.XLVII.

   Tall 8VO: t.p., *bl.*, *iii-iv*, The Publisher's PREFACE, *1* 2-275, 3 advs. on *276* including the Campbell-Du Bosc, *Military History of the Wars in Flanders* (1736-7). Actually the remaining sheets were being sold.

   Horn copy used of 1747 ed. Churchill gives a 1746 date and differing pagination, the Dublin ed. pub. by G. and E. Ewing, 215 pp. 8VO. Morgan T853.

   While Parker's account does have resemblances to Col. Kane's of the year previous, 1745, it shows more of the intimate details of campaigning and battle. Both report

Blenheim well, and both tell of riding over the field of
battle and collecting observations from participants the
next morning. Both use Old Style dating, and both cover
the entire military career of Marlborough, although with
less of the picaresque tone of adventure and the personal
touch of Matthew Bishop. All three constantly express a
loyalty to Marlborough and an admiration for his bearing,
his courage and temper of mind in battle, that should
fully discredit his detractors. After stating that he
had no obligations to the Duke, and in fact had once suffered the injustice of having a Captain "put over his
head," Parker says,

> My zeal for the man is founded on his merit and
> his service, and I do him no more than bare jus-
> tice. I had been an eye-witness to all his
> great actions.   p. 202

Parker resigned his commission in 1718, and returned
to Ireland for a well-deserved retirement. However, both
he and Kane supply brief, though highly depreciatory accounts of Marlborough's successor, the Duke of Ormonde,
and the shameful decline in British command and prestige.
Two further personal accounts of the campaigns were
published so considerably later as to warrant their inclusion at this point. Both cover Marlborough's career
and extend considerably beyond. They are the *Life* of Lt.
Col. Blackader and the *Memoirs* of Captain Peter Drake.

75 Blackader, Lt. Col. John (1664-1729)

The *Life* and *Diary* of Lieut. Col. J. *Blackader*, Of the
Cameronian Regiment, and Deputy Governor of Stirling
Castle; Who served with Distinguished Honour in the Wars
under KING WILLIAM and the DUKE of MARLBOROUGH and after-
wards In the *Rebellion* of 1715 in *Scotland*. By ANDREW
CRICHTON, Author of the Memoirs of Rev. John Blackader.
EDINBURGH: 15, Union Place, and 17, Picardy Place. *W.
Baynes & Son, London*. M.DCCC.XXIV.
12mo: portraits, t.p., *bl.*, *v-viii* PREFACE, *ix-xii*
Contents, *13* 14-578, 578 pp. Horn copy used. Morgan U110.

Two features, aside from the authority of his account, distinguish the Blackader narrative; his Scottish derivation, where most of the others are Irish, and his consuming piety, which appears throughout. He also uses Old Style dating, and the mixture of Crichton's expository comment and direct extracts from the diary produces a much less arresting account than those of Bishop and Parker. Thus Blenheim for him is marked more by his personal sense of Providence than by details of the conflict. He uses Old Style dating.

> *August* 2. Many deliverances I have met with, but this day I had the greatest ever I experienced. We fought a bloody battle, and, by the mercy of God, have obtained one of the greatest and completest victories the age can boast of. In the morning, while marching towards the enemy, I was enabled to exercise a lively faith, relying and encouraging myself in God, whereupon I was easy, sedate, and cheerful. I believed firmly that his angels had me in charge, and that not a bone should be broken.

That Blackader did survive amidst the heavy casualties of the Cameronians, in spite of a wound, he could readily ascribe to a kind Providence. Certainly the book is a rich and authoritative document in Calvinistic sensibility and language. His religious interpretation of events includes his promotion to a lieutenant-colonelcy for his services at Malplaquet. His compassion for the wounded and suffering brings passages of great poignancy. Perhaps the most valuable contribution to Marlborough studies is his treatment of the Duke's participation in putting down the Jacobite Rebellion of 1715, his final act of military service.

576   January 9.

Johnson, Dr. Samuel (1709-1784)

The VANITY of HUMAN WISHES. The Tenth Satire of *Juvenal*.
Imitated By *SAMUEL JOHNSON* [ornament] LONDON: Printed
for R. DODSLEY at *Tully's Head* in *Pall-Mall*, and Sold by
M COOPER in *Pater-Noster Row*.   1749.
    Large 4to: A^4 B-C^4 D^2; t.p., *bl*., drop-t. on *3*, 4-
28, 28 pp. Only one ed. pubd., sec. ed. revised for Dodsley's Coll., 1755, IV, 156. Full bibliographical details
are supplied in D. N. Smith's excellent ed. of Johnson's
Poems, ed. David Nichol Smith and Edward L. McAdam, Oxford Press, 1941, pp. 25-48. Unquestionably the sad couplet linking Marlborough and Swift constitutes a fascinating commentary:

        From Marlb'rough's Eyes the Streams of Dotage flow,
        And *Swift* expires a Driv'ler and a Show.   317-18

However, no discussions of the poem seem to have shown its
preoccupation with military matters. Not in Morgan.

577   Jeffries, George (1678-1755)

Anticipatory notice, No. 195, has been taken of two short
poems, presumably written as early as 1706, and not separately published. These are: *On Blenheim House* and *An Ode
on the Battle of Ramillies*, which appear in *Miscellanies
in Prose and Verse*. Published by the Author, 4to. Dobell
Cat. of 18th Century Verse, No. 734.

578   Drake, Captain Peter (1671-1753)

The MEMOIRS of Capt. *PETER DRAKE*. CONTAINING an ACCOUNT
of many Strange and Surprising EVENTS, which happened to
HIM through a Series of Sixty Years, and upwards; and
several material Anecdotes, regarding King WILLIAM and
Queen ANNE's Wars with LEWIS XIV. of France.   [ornament]

DUBLIN: Printed and Sold by S. POWELL in Crane-Lane,
for the AUTHOR. MDCCLV.
8ᵛᵒ: 2 vols. bd. as one. I, xvi, 196, II, pp. 281.
Description taken from ed. titled *Amiable Renegade*, ed.
Paul Jordan-Smith with an Introd. by S. A. Burrell, Stan-
ford Univ. Press, 1950.
This is the only example of an eyewitness account of
the campaigns with modern editing and textual study. Only
eight copies were located, rather remarkable for such a
work, though not for Marlborough panegyrics and satires in
general. The reprint makes available a narrative of distinctly picaresque appeal. Drake served in the French
army, at both Ramillies and Malplaquet, and with the English at lesser engagements; was imprisoned, was tried for
treason, pardoned, fought duels, engaged in various adventures.

579 A Letter from the Duchess of M---r----gh, in the SHADES,
to the Great Man. London, Printed for *H. Hooper*, 1759.
8°, 82 pp. Prose pamphlet. Only vaguely anti-
Marlborough, but has allusions to his avarice. Not in
Morgan.

580 MALBROUGH S'EN VA-T-EN GUERRE.
First printed in England in 1775, and again in 1785,
this famous song was certainly not written about Marlborough, for all its becoming associated with him. French
troops, as early as 1705, are alleged to have hurled it
at him. Sometimes it is attributed to 1709, the year of
Malplaquet. However, the events are certainly medieval,
dating back to a Crusader named Malbron. The French pro-
nunciation of the Duke's name as 'Malbrouk' easily suggested application of the poem to Marlborough. Only the
title, however, has any pertinence, as the events deal
with the death of the hero and a page bringing word of
his funeral. He tells how, after the burial, men planted
rosemary about his tomb, and a nightingale's song could
be heard as his soul soared away among the lawrels. At

least in the surviving version, no allusions to Marlborough appear.
The vigorous tune - "For he's a jolly good fellow" -
more than the words gave the piece its wide popularity.
Napoleon did sing it and Goethe expressed extreme distaste for it, while Beaumarchais introduced it into "Marriage de Figaro," but Marlborough knew nothing of it. If
French nurses used it to subdue their charges with proper
fear, it was not until a century after "Malbrouk's" time.
Morgan T726.

81 ODE Presented TO *THE KING*, AT BLENHEIM, BY HIS GRACE The
DUKE of *MARLBOROUGH*. WITH CONSIDERABLE VARIATIONS BY THE
AUTHOR, AND NOTES BY FARMER *GEORGE*. LONDON: Printed, by
the Author's Permission, for M. SMITH only; and sold at
No. 46 Fleet-street. MDCCLXXXVI.
2°: *A*, B-E²; t.p., *bl.*, *v-vi*, *1*, 2-28, 34 pp.
Half-t. and *bl.* presumably missing. Advertisement sgnd.
M-----h, pp. *iv-v* states: "An incorrect Edition of the
following admirable Work having made its appearance, the
Author, And the Noble Duke by whom it was presented, have
thought it necessary, that one more correct should be
given to the Public." It is also noted that since lyric
poetry is of necessity obscure, notes have been added "by
an eminent Personage." Drop-t. "ODE, &C." p. *1*. The poem
is 138 lines, Strophe, Antistrophe, and Epode. At the
bottom of most pages appear stanzas labeled "Original
Copy," which are considerably different, and these total
56 lines. The grand total is then 194 lines in ode form.
Horn copy used.
Marlborough is the Fourth Duke, George Spencer, famous for his devotion to astronomy and the fine family
portrait with his Duchess and six children painted by Sir
Joshua Reynolds, which hangs at Blenheim Palace. Since
he lived there as Duke for 60 years, 1758-1817, he left
many changes in the palace. Dramatic and musical enter-
tainments were presented there; and this ode, read to King
George III, marks a date, however little it could do to
enliven his visit, August 14, 1786.
Opens:

> DREAD SOVEREIGN, Hail! an humble Bard
> *Disinterested* homage pays.

As poetry, the lines are no more than conventional and meager in allusions to Blenheim or the Marlborough line. Farmer George's notes, thirteen in all, suggest that he may have been the author. Of the verses which deal with Edward III and Cressy, he notes:

> I observed, that whilst I was reading them,
> Marlborough was contemplating the pictures
> of the Duke his ancestor, and Queen Anne, which
> are placed opposite each other, in gilt frames.
> What could he have meant by that?

Still, that the whole work was intended, as satire is quite possible. Farmer George may well be King George, as a note on p. 7 refers to his gratifying welcome at Woodstock, marred only by the obstinate refusal of the cook to have his head shaved, and another alludes to the diminished pleasure he would have felt had "*all* my family been there," which is one of several obvious references to the Prince of Wales. Some allusions to Thomas Warton add interest. He is referred to as Tommy, and is pictured as "eternally reckoning with his fingers under the table" (note, p.3). References to William Whitehead, and to his attacks on Pitt also appear in notes to the poem.

The Fourth Duke of Marlborough had carried the scepter and cross at the coronation of King George. Aside from its linking the First Duke, Blenheim, Woodstock and even the Beef-Eaters with the "happy, happy days" of a relatively unworthy sovereign, the poem has little more than its title to link it with the Marlborough tradition. Still, as David Green observes, George III remarked on the occasion of his brief visit: "We have nothing equal to this." (*Blenheim*, p. 189, 1951)

582   Mavor, Dr. William Fordyce, L.L.D., Rector of Bladon (1758-1837)

A New Description of BLENHEIM *THE SEAT OF HIS GRACE* The DUKE of MARLBOROUGH: Containing a full and accurate Account of the PAINTINGS, TAPESTRY, AND FURNITURE; A PIC-

TURESQUE TOUR OF THE *GARDENS & PARK*: AND A GENERAL DESCRIP-
TION OF THE CHINA GALLERY, &c. Oxford, Printed and Sold by
J. Munday, Herald Office. First ed., 1787; 8th ed. Horn
copy used. As David Green points out, it is a guide book
which ran into thirteen editions, and no visitor to Blenheim felt complete without it. Green states that Mavor became the self-appointed Laureate of the Palace, writing
odes on every possible occasion -- "On Converting the
Green-House into a Private Theatre; On Launching the Sovereign, a Magnificent Pleasure-Boat on the Lake at Blenheim, July 27, 1787. . .On Seeing Some Hundred Additional
Acres in Blenheim Park Converted into Tillage, 1795."
Mavor also contributed an ode on King George's visit.
Blenheim, 188-9, 12 lines, couplets. Morgan X1315. Opens:

Immortal Chief! of Albion's isle the pride,
By martial deeds to greatest names ally'd.

Conclusion

No absolute terminal date for a work on Marlborough
is possible. As with all great leaders, his name and fame
will live forever. Inevitably his reputation fluctuates
with the repute of international warfare. The current
reaction against the war in southeast Asia has led to a
discrediting of the military on a national scale. The
well-deserved honoring of gallantry in military service
survives; but the lavish praises of Eighteenth Century
panegyric does not. Today's poets fancy themselves as
satirists of combat. Patriotic fervor, self-sacrifice,
even courage are not in their vocabulary. This sentiment
can be seen in Robert Southey's *The Battle of Blenheim* in
1798, a poem which might have been used to conclude this
survey. While old Kaspar could not recall the name of
the battle, nearly a century had elapsed. Still the implied slight on Marlborough's fame has served to make the
poem synonymous with the anti-war sentiment described above.
That this attitude was not absent during Marlborough's
times may be seen in a poem which, while surviving in manuscript, did not appear in print till 1901, with its publication in the *Papers Illustrating the History of the Scots*

583 *Brigade*, Vol. 38, pp. 307-577, *Scottish History Society Publications*. This work is called *The Remembrance*, and in it the author, John Scot, a private soldier, records eyewitness impressions of battles, sieges, and encampments. Though a portion is missing, this huge work reaches over 12,000 lines. The verse is crude, in alternating long and short lines, with varying infusions of rhyme. Scot's deficiencies as a poet actually add to the tone of authenticity as he follows the course of Marlborough's armies. Since he was serving on the Dutch border during Blenheim, he does not describe that battle, but all the other great battles, and many sieges are given brilliantly detailed accounts. Professor Trevelyan quotes him, particularly on Ramillies. Morgan T1009.

That Scot, while a veteran of the entire war, was also a humanitarian and strongly hostile to the grim aspects of war, is apparent in many passages. This quality, as well as his rough and ready spelling and grammar, are evident in the following account of the desolation in Lille during the siege of 1708.

> The signs of hunger with dismale collour,
>   Is painted in mens face.
> The hunger and cold nipeth very sore,
>   And likewayes the dearth of the meall,
> Which maketh us cry on curssing the day,
>   That ever we came into Leille.
> Since I of war have writen so far,
>   With al its willful projects.
> I beg your pardon although I set doun,
>   Some pairt of its woeful effects.
> As the dearth of meal in the toun of Leile,
>   Which every day we do see.
> The great desolation and cruel devastation,
>   Of wind milles once standing hie.   p. 458

The shattered cottages of the villagers, soldiers running through the streets seeking bread, masses of the dead, and these being eaten by masterless dogs which go mad -- these and many other sights build up a strong Breughel-like picture of the bitter side of war. Scot, in his native accent and Covenanter's idiom, interprets all this as the "Judgment of God for the sheeding [*sic*] of blood." He heartily wishes for peace. What he, at the lowest of military ranks, sought for was also the objective of the commander at the top.

Marlborough constantly envisions and invokes a "just and lasting peace." That this is the almost universally professed goal in all modern wars is a sad reminder of the futility of human conflict.

584   Robert Southey's Old Kaspar, in *The Battle of Blenheim* (1798), searches the battlefield and his tired old brain for an answer for which the contemporary world still seeks in vain. It is ironic that the glories of Blenheim should dim out in this final poem bearing its name. As an expression of Southey's anti-war sentiments it has some merit, even though in its shallowness it is dangerously near the flatulence of some of his lesser labors. Nevertheless, Kaspar's refrain, "In truth 'twas a famous victory," has lasted as a summary of Blenheim's role in history.

It has been the intention of the writer to maintain an impartial attitude toward the Duke and his Duchess. While the abundance of panegyric may seem to build up a mountain of adulation that is far from detached, it is amply balanced by the mass of satire and vituperation. Though he was compared to heroes, saints, and even angels, Marlborough was a man, not an angel. Still Addison's simile has endured. Criticism of Marlborough has persistently been quite as political and tendentious as it was in his own day. It seems appropriate to close with the concluding remarks of his greatest descendant. In their fair-minded restraint, they exhibit admirable poise in summarizing a long and heroic career to which Sir Winston's has many parallels. After noting that Marlborough's career began in the service of France and Louis XIV, Sir Winston Churchill says:

> He had consolidated all that England gained by the Revolution of 1688 and the achievements of William III. By his invincible genius in war and his scarcely less admirable qualities of wisdom and management he had completed that glorious process that carried England from her dependency upon France under Charles II to ten years' leadership of Europe. Although this proud task was for a space cast aside by faction, the union and the

565

greatness of Britain and her claims to empire were established upon foundations that have lasted to this day. He had proved himself the "good Englishman" he aspired to be, and History may declare that if he had had more power his country would have had more strength and happiness, and Europe a surer progress.   (IV, 652)

INDEX OF AUTHORS

INDEX OF TITLES

573

Numbers refer to entries only. Apparent misspellings are not indicated by the *sic* in the Indexes, as in
Nos. 405, 316, and 273. Corrections are given in the
text because of the numerous variant spellings in the
period.